The Second **Signs** *Reader*

The Second *Signs* Reader

Feminist Scholarship, 1983-1996

Editors

RUTH-ELLEN B. JOERES

BARBARA LASLETT

THE UNIVERSITY OF CHICAGO PRESS
Chicago & London

The essays in this volume originally appeared in various issues of SIGNS: JOURNAL OF WOMEN IN CULTURE AND SOCIETY. Acknowledgment of the original publication data can be found in the first page of each essay.

The University of Chicago Press, Chicago 60637
The University of Chicago Press, Ltd., London
© 1996 by the University of Chicago
All rights reserved. Published 1996
Printed in the United States of America
00 99 98 97 96   5 4 3 2 1

Library of Congress Cataloging-in-Publication Data

The Second Signs reader : feminist scholarship, 1983–1996 / edited by
Ruth-Ellen B. Joeres and Barbara Laslett.
    p.   cm.
    Includes bibliographical references and index.
    ISBN 0-226-40060-3 (cloth : alk paper). — ISBN 0-226-40061-1
(pbk.)
    1. Women's studies. 2. Feminist theory. 3. Sex role. I. Joeres,
Ruth-Ellen B., 1939– II. Laslett, Barbara. III. Signs.
HQ1180.S43   1996   96-31516
305.4'07—dc20   CIP

CONTENTS

Acknowledgments

We are grateful for the able assistance of Andrea Sachs, a *Signs* graduate intern, and of Jeanne Barker-Nunn, the *Signs* managing editor, in the preparation and production of this volume.

Introduction

Barbara Laslett and

Ruth-Ellen Boetcher Joeres

OON AFTER *SIGNS* came to the University of Minnesota
for the five-year term from 1990 to 1995, we began to think
about compiling a second *Signs Reader* to build on the impulses
represented by the articles contained in the first *Reader* published
in 1983.[1] In the intervening decade-plus, many new, fascinating, and
wonderfully diverse discussions have appeared in the pages of the jour-
nal. Feminist scholarship has, in fact, undergone considerable revision.
The scope and variety of the issues discussed, the increasingly multidisci-
plinary and international directions in U.S. feminist scholarship, and the
continuing attempts to confront concerns and problems of interdisciplin-
arity are vividly reflected in the articles that have been published in *Signs*
since 1983 and certainly in those we have selected for this second *Signs
Reader.*

Since the appearance of the first *Reader*, there has indeed been an
explosion in the varieties of feminist scholarship. Whereas the editors of
that volume celebrated a new tradition of scholarly work that today
could appear openly under the label of "feminist," as opposed to the
less specifically defined category of "women" who were the designated
subjects of study during the very early *Signs* years, we can now look
back on more than twenty years of feminist scholarly work in *Signs* that
has delved into ever wider and more complex issues of gender and other
analytical categories that inevitably interact and are interdependent with
it. Like that first *Reader*, this one offers work by historians, psycholo-
gists, literary scholars, philosophers, sociologists, and political scientists,
but the disciplinary boundaries between them continue to be questioned,
revised, and expanded. New areas of interest are also apparent: cultural
studies, for example, is interpreted from feminist positions in the articles
of Ann duCille and Susan Stanford Friedman, and sports and the com-
plexities of feminist political and philosophical theory are interwoven in

---

[1] Elizabeth Abel and Emily K. Abel, eds., *The Signs Reader: Women, Gender and
Scholarship* (Chicago: University of Chicago Press, 1983).

the piece by Lisa Disch and Mary Jo Kane. Nancy Chodorow in her article and Maureen Mahoney and Barbara Yngvesson in theirs offer interdisciplinary approaches to feminist discussions of psychology; Marilyn Frye and María Lugones respond as feminist philosophers to current social and cultural developments; and Iris Marion Young offers an innovative way to think about the social collectivity known as "women."

No single selection in this *Reader* could be said to represent a unitary or unified discipline. All of the pieces consciously examine their subject matter through broad interdisciplinary lenses; all of them also illustrate the inherent benefits and difficulties of such work. Evelyn Brooks Higginbotham, a historian, places African-American women's history in the larger analytical framework of race; Gayle Greene, a literary scholar, uses the psychology of memory to interpret feminist fictional writings of the 1970s; Trisha Franzen, a historian, probes the nature of a lesbian community through lenses of race, ethnicity, sexuality, and culture as well as of gender. Wendy Luttrell, a sociologist and cultural anthropologist, complicates her ethnographic study of women reflecting on their school years by applying theories of knowledge and knowing to her racially and socially diverse informants; Evelyn Nakano Glenn, a sociologist working in ethnic studies, deals with the racial, gendered, and class-based oppression of women. The work of all these scholars is complex, detailed, and rich in its presentation of the factors that both divide and unite women.

We offer this second *Signs Reader* as a marker in the development of American feminist scholarship in the 1990s, as evidence of the exciting new directions the field continues to take. If feminist scholarship "challenges and stimulates the larger enterprise of scholarship itself," as Elizabeth Abel and Emily Abel, the editors of the first *Reader,* claim, then in the years between these collections such scholarship has also begun to stimulate its own practitioners into thinking in increasingly subtle and differentiating fashion.[2] We look forward to the innovations that will emerge during the next decade of feminist inquiry in the pages of *Signs*.

[2] Ibid., 10.

African-American Women's History
and the Metalanguage of Race

Evelyn Brooks Higginbotham

THEORETICAL DISCUSSION in African-American wom-
en's history begs for greater voice. I say this as a black woman
who is cognizant of the strengths and limitations of current
feminist theory. Feminist scholars have moved rapidly forward
in addressing theories of subjectivity, questions of difference, the con-
struction of social relations as relations of power, the conceptual impli-
cations of binary oppositions such as male versus female or equality
versus difference—all issues defined with relevance to gender and with
potential for intellectual and social transformations.[1] Notwithstanding a
few notable exceptions, this new wave of feminist theorists finds little to
say about race. The general trend has been to mention black and Third
World feminists who first called attention to the glaring fallacies in es-
sentialist analysis and to claims of a homogeneous "womanhood,"
"woman's culture," and "patriarchal oppression of women."[2] Beyond
this recognition, however, white feminist scholars pay hardly more than

A number of people read earlier versions of this article. I am especially grateful to
the insights, suggestions, and probing questions of Sharon Harley, Paul Hanson, Darlene
Clark-Hine, and Carroll Smith-Rosenberg.

[1] See, e.g., Teresa de Lauretis, *Alice Doesn't: Feminism, Semiotics, Cinema* (Bloom-
ington: Indiana University Press, 1984), and Teresa de Lauretis, ed., *Feminist Studies,
Feminist Criticism* (Bloomington: Indiana University Press, 1986); Toril Moi, *Sexual/
Textual Politics* (New York: Routledge, 1985); Joan W. Scott, *Gender and the Politics of
History* (New York: Columbia University Press, 1988); Judith Butler, *Gender Trouble:
Feminism and the Subversion of Identity* (New York: Routledge, 1990).

[2] By the early 1980s women of color from various disciplines had challenged the no-
tion of a homogeneous womanhood. A few include: Sharon Harley and Rosalyn
Terborg-Penn, eds., *The Afro-American Woman: Struggles and Images* (Port Washing-
ton, N.Y.: Kennikat, 1978); Gloria T. Hull, Patricia Bell Scott, and Barbara Smith, eds.,
But Some of Us Are Brave (Old Westbury, N.Y.: Feminist Press, 1982); Barbara Smith,
ed., *Home Girls: A Black Feminist Anthology* (New York: Kitchen Table: Women of
Color Press, 1983); Cherrie Moraga and Gloria Anzaldua, eds., *This Bridge Called My
Back: Writings by Radical Women of Color* (New York: Kitchen Table: Women of
Color Press, 1983); Bonnie Thornton Dill, "Race, Class, and Gender: Prospects for an
All-Inclusive Sisterhood," *Feminist Studies* 9 (Spring 1983): 131–50.

[*Signs: Journal of Women in Culture and Society* 1992, vol. 17, no. 2]

lip service to race as they continue to analyze their own experience in ever more sophisticated forms.

This narrowness of vision is particularly ironic in that these very issues of equality and difference, the constructive strategies of power, and subjectivity and consciousness have stood at the core of black scholarship for some half-century or more. Historian W. E. B. Du Bois, sociologist Oliver Cox, and scientist Charles R. Drew are only some of the more significant pre-1950s contributors to the discussion of race as a social category and to the refutation of essentialist biological and genetic explanations.[3] These issues continue to be salient in our own time, when racism in America grows with both verve and subtlety and when "enlightened" women's historians witness, as has been the case in recent years, recurrent racial tensions at our own professional and scholarly gatherings.

Feminist scholars, especially those of African-American women's history, must accept the challenge to bring race more prominently into their analyses of power. The explication of race entails three interrelated strategies, separated here merely for the sake of analysis. First of all, we must define the construction and "technologies" of race as well as those of gender and sexuality.[4] Second, we must expose the role of race as a metalanguage by calling attention to its powerful, all-encompassing effect on the construction and representation of other social and power relations, namely, gender, class, and sexuality. Third, we must recognize race as providing sites of dialogic exchange and contestation, since race has constituted a discursive tool for both oppression and liberation. As Michael Omi and Howard Winant argue, "the effort must be made to understand race as an unstable and 'decentered' complex of social meanings constantly being transformed by political struggle."[5] Such a three-

[3] Charles Drew, in developing a method of blood preservation and organizing blood banks, contributed to the explosion of the myth that blacks were physiologically different from whites. See Charles E. Wynes, *Charles Richard Drew: The Man and the Myth* (Urbana: University of Illinois Press, 1988), 65–71; and C. R. Drew and J. Scudder, "Studies in Blood Preservation: Fate of Cellular Elements and Prothrombin in Citrated Blood," *Journal of Laboratory and Clinical Medicine* 26 (June 1941): 1473–78. Also see W. E. B. Du Bois, "Races," *Crisis* (August 1911), 157–58, and *Dusk of Dawn: An Essay toward an Autobiography of a Race Concept* (New York: Harcourt Brace, 1940), 116–17, 137; Oliver C. Cox, *Caste, Class and Race* (1948; reprint, New York: Monthly Review Press, 1970), 317–20.
[4] Michel Foucault, *History of Sexuality*, vol. 1, *An Introduction*, trans. Robert Hurley (New York: Vintage, 1980), 127, 146. Teresa De Lauretis criticizes Foucault for presenting a male-centered class analysis that disregards gender (see *Technologies of Gender* [Bloomington: Indiana University Press, 1987], 3–30). In both cases "technology" is used to signify the elaboration and implementation of discourses (classificatory and evaluative) in order to maintain the survival and hegemony of one group over another. These discourses are implemented through pedagogy, medicine, mass media, etc.
[5] For discussion of race and signification, see Robert Miles, *Racism* (New York: Routledge, 1989), 69–98; also, Michael Omi and Howard Winant, *Racial Formation in*

pronged approach to the history of African-American women will require borrowing and blending work by black intellectuals, white feminist scholars, and other theorists such as white male philosophers and linguists. Indeed, the very process of borrowing and blending speaks to the tradition of syncretism that has characterized the Afro-American experience.

Defining race

When the U.S. Supreme Court had before it the task of defining obscenity, Justice Potter Stewart claimed that, while he could not intelligibly define it, "I know it when I see it."[6] When we talk about the concept of race, most people believe that they know it when they see it but arrive at nothing short of confusion when pressed to define it. Chromosome research reveals the fallacy of race as an accurate measure of genotypic or phenotypic difference between human beings. Cross-cultural and historical studies of miscegenation law reveal shifting, arbitrary, and contradictory definitions of race. Literary critics, as in the collection of essays *"Race," Writing, and Difference*, edited by Henry Louis Gates, compellingly present race as the "ultimate trope of difference"—as artificially and arbitrarily contrived to produce and maintain relations of power and subordination. Likewise, historian Barbara Fields argues that race is neither natural nor transhistorical, but must rather be analyzed with an eye to its functioning and maintenance within specific contexts.[7]

Like gender and class, then, race must be seen as a social construction predicated upon the recognition of difference and signifying the simultaneous distinguishing and positioning of groups vis-à-vis one another. More than this, race is a highly contested representation of relations of power between social categories by which individuals are identified and identify themselves. The recognition of racial distinctions emanates from and adapts to multiple uses of power in society. Perceived as "natural" and "appropriate," such racial categories are strategically necessary for the functioning of power in countless institutional and ideological forms,

the United States from the 1960s to the 1980s (New York: Routledge & Kegan Paul, 1986), 68.

[6] Jacobellis v. State of Ohio, 378 U.S. 184, 197 (1964).

[7] Although Fields does not use the term "trope," her discussion of race parallels that of Gates. Henry Louis Gates, Jr., ed., *"Race," Writing, and Difference* (Chicago: University of Chicago Press, 1986), esp. articles by Gates, Jr., "Introduction: Writing 'Race' and the Difference It Makes," 1–20; Anthony Appiah, "The Uncompleted Argument: Du Bois and the Illusion of Race," 21–37; and Tzvetan Todorov, " 'Race,' Writing, and Culture," 370–80. See also Barbara J. Fields, "Ideology and Race in American History," in *Region, Race, and Reconstruction: Essays in Honor of C. Vann Woodward*, ed. J. Morgan Kousser and James M. McPherson (New York: Oxford University Press, 1982), 143–47.

both explicit and subtle. As Michel Foucault has written, societies engage in "a perpetual process of strategic elaboration" or a constant shifting and reforming of the apparatus of power in response to their particular cultural or economic needs.[8]

Furthermore, in societies where racial demarcation is endemic to their sociocultural fabric and heritage—to their laws and economy, to their institutionalized structures and discourses, and to their epistemologies and everyday customs—gender identity is inextricably linked to and even determined by racial identity. In the Jim Crow South prior to the 1960s and in South Africa until very recently, for instance, little black girls learned at an early age to place themselves in the bathroom for "black women," not in that for "white ladies." As such a distinction suggests, in these societies the representation of both gender and class is colored by race. Their social construction becomes racialized as their concrete implications and normative meanings are continuously shaped by what Louis Althusser terms "ideological state apparatuses"—the school, family, welfare agency, hospital, television and cinema, the press.[9]

For example, the metaphoric and metonymic identification of welfare with the black population by the American public has resulted in tremendous generalization about the supposed unwillingness of many blacks to work. Welfare immediately conjures up images of black female-headed families, despite the fact that the aggregate number of poor persons who receive benefits in the form of aid to dependent children or medicare is predominantly white. Likewise, the drug problem too often is depicted in the mass media as a pathology of black lower-class life set in motion by drug dealers, youthful drug runners, and addicted victims of the ghetto. The drug problem is less often portrayed as an underground economy that mirrors and reproduces the exploitative relations of the dominant economy. The "supply-side" executives who make the "big" money are neither black nor residents of urban ghettos.

Race might also be viewed as myth, "not at all an abstract, purified essence" (to cite Roland Barthes on myth) but, rather, "a formless, unstable, nebulous condensation, whose unity and coherence are above all

---

[8] Michel Foucault describes the strategic function of the apparatus of power as a system of relations between diverse elements (e.g., discourses, laws, architecture, moral values, institutions) that are supported by types of knowledge: "I understand by the 'term' apparatus a sort of . . . formation which has its major function at a given historical moment that of responding to an *urgent need.* . . . This may have been, for example, the assimilation of a floating population found to be burdensome for an essentially mercantilist economy" (*Power/Knowledge: Selected Interviews and Other Writings, 1972– 1977*, ed. Colin Gordon [New York: Pantheon, 1980], 194–95).

[9] Louis Althusser, "Ideology and Ideological State Apparatuses (Notes toward an Investigation)," in his *Lenin and Philosophy, and Other Essays*, trans. Ben Brewster (New York: Monthly Review Press, 1972), 165.

due to its function."[10] As a fluid set of overlapping discourses, race is perceived as arbitrary and illusionary, on the one hand, while natural and fixed on the other. To argue that race is myth and that it is an ideological rather than a biological fact does not deny that ideology has real effects on people's lives. Race serves as a "global sign," a "metalanguage," since it speaks about and lends meaning to a host of terms and expressions, to myriad aspects of life that would otherwise fall outside the referential domain of race.[11] By continually expressing overt and covert analogic relationships, race impregnates the simplest meanings we take for granted. It makes hair "good" or "bad," speech patterns "correct" or "incorrect." It is, in fact, the apparent overdeterminancy of race in Western culture, and particularly in the United States, that has permitted it to function as a metalanguage in its discursive representation and construction of social relations. Race not only tends to subsume other sets of social relations, namely, gender and class, but it blurs and disguises, suppresses and negates its own complex interplay with the very social relations it envelops. It precludes unity within the same gender group but often appears to solidify people of opposing economic classes. Whether race is textually omitted or textually privileged, its totalizing effect in obscuring class and gender remains.

This may well explain why women's studies for so long rested upon the unstated premise of racial (i.e., white) homogeneity and with this presumption proceeded to universalize "woman's" culture and oppression, while failing to see white women's own investment and complicity in the oppression of other groups of men and women. Elizabeth Spelman takes to task this idea of "homogeneous womanhood" in her exploration of race and gender in *Inessential Woman*. Examining thinkers such as Aristotle, Simone de Beauvoir, and Nancy Chodorow, among others, Spelman observes a double standard on the part of many feminists who fail to separate their whiteness from their womanness. White feminists, she argues, typically discern two separate identities for black women, the racial and the gender, and conclude that the gender identity of black women is the same as their own: "In other words, the womanness underneath the black woman's skin is a white woman's and deep down inside the Latina woman is an Anglo woman waiting to burst through."[12]

Afro-American history, on the other hand, has accentuated race by calling explicit attention to the cultural as well as socioeconomic implications of American racism but has failed to examine the differential class

---

[10] Roland Barthes, *Mythologies*, trans. Annette Lavers (New York: Hill & Wang, 1972), 118, 120.
[11] Ibid., 114–15.
[12] Elizabeth V. Spelman, *Inessential Woman: Problems of Exclusion in Feminist Thought* (Boston: Beacon, 1988), 13, 80–113.

and gender positions men and women occupy in black communities—
thus uncritically rendering a monolithic "black community," "black ex-
perience," and "voice of the Negro." Notwithstanding that this discursive
monolith most often resonates with a male voice and as the experience of
men, such a rendering precludes gender subordination by black men by
virtue of their own blackness and social subordination. Even black wo-
men's history, which has consciously sought to identify the importance of
gender relations and the interworkings of race, class, and gender, none-
theless reflects the totalizing impulse of race in such concepts as "black
womanhood" or the "black woman cross-culturally"—concepts that
mask real differences of class, status and color, regional culture, and a
host of other configurations of difference.

Racial constructions of gender

To understand race as a metalanguage, we must recognize its historical
and material grounding—what Russian linguist and critic M. M. Bakhtin
referred to as "the power of the word to mean."[13] This power evolves
from concrete situational and ideological contexts, that is, from a posi-
tion of enunciation that reflects not only time and place but values as
well. The concept of race, in its verbal and extraverbal dimension, and
even more specifically, in its role in the representation as well as self-
representation of individuals in American society (what psychoanalytic
theorists call "subjectification"), is constituted in language in which (as
Bakhtin points out) there have never been " 'neutral' words and forms—
words and forms that can belong to 'no one'; language has been com-
pletely taken over, shot through with intentions and accents."[14]

The social context for the construction of race as a tool for black
oppression is historically rooted in the context of slavery. Barbara Fields
reminds us: "The idea one people has of another, even when the differ-
ence between them is embodied in the most striking physical character-
istics, is always mediated by the social context within which the two
come in contact."[15] Race came to life primarily as the signifier of the
master/slave relation and thus emerged superimposed upon class and

[13] M. M. Bakhtin, *The Dialogic Imagination: Four Essays*, ed. Michael Holquist,
trans. Caryl Emerson and Michael Holquist (Austin: University of Texas Press, 1981),
352.

[14] Bakhtin argues: "Language is not an abstract system of normative forms but
rather a concrete heteroglot conception of the world." For my purposes of discussion,
"race," therefore, would convey multiple, even conflicting meanings (heteroglossia) when
expressed by different groups—the multiplicity of meanings and intentions not simply
rendered between blacks and whites, but within each of these two groups. See Bakhtin
on "heteroglossia" (293, 352).

[15] Fields, "Race and Ideology in American History," 148–49.

property relations. Defined by law as "animate chattel," slaves constituted property as well as a social class and were exploited under a system that sanctioned white ownership of black bodies and black labor.[16] Studies of black women in slavery, however, make poignantly clear the role of race not only in shaping the class relations of the South's "peculiar institution," but also in constructing gender's "power to mean." Sojourner Truth's famous and haunting question, "Ar'n't I a Woman?" laid bare the racialized configuration of gender under a system of class rule that compelled and expropriated women's physical labor and denied them legal right to their own bodies and sexuality, much less to the bodies to which they gave birth. While law and public opinion idealized motherhood and enforced the protection of white women's bodies, the opposite held true for black women's. Sojourner Truth's personal testimony demonstrated gender's racial meaning. She had "ploughed, and planted, and gathered into barns," and no male slave had outdone her. She had given birth to thirteen children, all of whom were sold away from her. When she cried out in grief from the depths of her motherhood, "none but Jesus heard."[17]

Wasn't Sojourner Truth a woman? The courts answered this question for slavewomen by ruling them outside the statutory rubric "woman."[18] In discussing the case of *State of Missouri v. Celia,* A. Leon Higginbotham, Jr., elucidates the racial signification of gender. Celia was fourteen years old when purchased by a successful farmer, Robert Newsome. During the five years of his ownership, Newsome habitually forced her into sexual intercourse. At age nineteen she had borne a child by him and was expecting another. In June 1855, while pregnant and ill, Celia defended herself against attempted rape by her master. Her testimony reveals that she warned him she would hurt him if he continued to abuse her while sick. When her threats would not deter his advances, she hit him over the head with a stick, immediately killing him. In an act presaging Richard Wright's *Native Son,* she then burned his body in the fireplace and the next morning spread his ashes on the pathway. Celia was apprehended and tried for first-degree murder. Her counsel sought to lower the charge of first degree to murder in self-defense, arguing that

[16] Eugene D. Genovese, *Roll Jordan Roll: The World the Slaves Made* (New York: Pantheon, 1974), 3–7, 28.

[17] Sojourner Truth's speech appears in Bert James Loewenberg and Ruth Bogin, *Black Women in Nineteenth Century American Life* (University Park: Pennsylvania State University Press, 1976), 235. For works on slave women, see Deborah Gray White, *Ar'n't I a Woman: Female Slaves in the Plantation South* (New York: Norton, 1985); Elizabeth Fox-Genovese, *Within the Plantation Household: Black and White Women of the Old South* (Chapel Hill: University of North Carolina Press, 1988), esp. chaps. 3 and 6.

[18] Fox-Genovese, 326.

Celia had a right to resist her master's sexual advances, especially because of the imminent danger to her health. A slave master's economic and property rights, the defense contended, did not include rape. The defense rested its case on Missouri statutes that protected women from attempts to ravish, rape, or defile. The language of these particular statutes explicitly used the term "any woman," while other unrelated Missouri statutes explicitly used terms such as "white female" and "slave" or "negro" in their criminal codes. The question centered on her womanhood. The court found Celia guilty: "If Newsome was in the habit of having intercourse with the defendant who was his slave, . . . it is murder in the first degree." Celia was sentenced to death, having been denied an appeal, and was hanged in December 1855 after the birth of her child.[19]

Since racially based justifications of slavery stood at the core of Southern law, race relations, and social etiquette in general, then proof of "womanhood" did not rest on a common female essence, shared culture, or mere physical appearance. (Sojourner Truth, on one occasion, was forced to bare her breasts to a doubting audience in order to vindicate her womanhood.) This is not to deny gender's role within the social and power relations of race. Black women experienced the vicissitudes of slavery through gendered lives and thus differently from slave men. They bore and nursed children and performed domestic duties—all on top of doing fieldwork. Unlike slave men, slave women fell victim to rape precisely because of their gender. Yet gender itself was both constructed and fragmented by race. Gender, so colored by race, remained from birth until death inextricably linked to one's personal identity and social status. For black and white women, gendered identity was reconstructed and represented in very different, indeed antagonistic, racialized contexts.

Racial constructions of class

Henry Louis Gates argues that "race has become a trope of ultimate, irreducible difference between cultures, linguistic groups, or adherents of specific belief systems which—more often than not—also have fundamentally opposed economic interest."[20] It is interesting that the power of race as a metalanguage that transcends and masks real differences lies in

[19] A. Leon Higginbotham, Jr., notes: "One of the ironies is that the master's estate was denied a profit from Celia's rape. Despite the court's 'mercy' in delaying execution until the birth of the child, the record reflects that a Doctor Carter delivered Celia's child, who was born dead" ("Race, Sex, Education and Missouri Jurisprudence: Shelley v. Kraemer in a Historical Perspective," *Washington University Law Quarterly* 67 [1989]: 684–85).

[20] Gates, Jr., "Introduction: Writing 'Race' and the Difference It Makes" (n. 7 above), 5.

the remarkable and longstanding success with which it unites whites of disparate economic positions against blacks. Until the Civil Rights era of the 1960s, race effectively served as a metaphor for class, albeit a metaphor rife with complications. For example, not all Southern whites were slave owners. Nor did they share the same economic and political interests. Upcountry yeomen protested the predominance of planters' interests over their own in state legislatures, and white artisans decried competition from the use of slave labor.[21] Yet, while Southern whites hardly constituted a homogeneous class, they united for radically different reasons around the banner of white supremacy, waged civil war, and for generations bemoaned the Lost Cause.

The metalanguage of race also transcended the voices of class and ethnic conflict among Northern whites in the great upheavals of labor during the late nineteenth and early twentieth centuries. Amid their opposition, capital and labor agreed sufficiently to exclude blacks from union membership and from more than a marginal place within the emerging industrial work force.[22] Job ceilings and hiring practices limited the overwhelming majority of black men and women to dead-end, low-paying employment—employment whites disdained or were in the process of abandoning.[23] The actual class positions of blacks did not matter, nor did the acknowledgment of differential statuses (such as by income, type of employment, morals and manners, education, or color) by blacks themselves. An entire system of cultural preconceptions disregarded these complexities and tensions by grouping all blacks into a normative well of inferiority and subserviency.[24]

The interplay of the race-class conflation with gender evoked very different social perceptions of black and white women's work roles. This is exhibited by the concern about "female loaferism," which arose in the

[21] Fields, "Ideology and Race in American History" (n. 7 above), 156.

[22] Abram Harris and Sterling Spero, *The Black Worker: A Study of the Negro in the Labor Movement* (1931; reprint, New York: Atheneum, 1968), 158–61, 167–81; Joe William Trotter, *Black Milwaukee: The Making of an Industrial Proletariat, 1915–45* (Urbana: University of Illinois Press, 1985), 13–14, 18, 39–79; Dolores Janiewski, *Sisterhood Denied: Race, Gender, and Class in a New South Community* (Philadelphia: Temple University Press, 1985), 152–78; Jacqueline Jones, *Labor of Love: Labor of Sorrow* (New York: Basic, 1985), 148, 168, 177–79.

[23] See Sharon Harley, "For the Good of Family and Race," *Signs: Journal of Women in Culture and Society* 15, no. 2 (Winter 1990): 340–41.

[24] Patricia Hill Collins argues persuasively for the continued role of race in explaining social class position in her analysis of studies of contemporary black low-income, female-headed families. In her critique of the Moynihan report and the televised Bill Moyers documentary on the "vanishing black family," Collins argues that social class is conceptualized in both these studies as "an outcome variable" of race and gender rather than the product of such structural factors as industrial flight, mechanization, inadequate schools, etc. ("A Comparison of Two Works on Black Family Life," *Signs* 14, no. 4 [Summer 1989]: 876–77, 882–84).

years immediately following Emancipation. Jacqueline Jones vividly exposes the ridicule and hostility meted out to black families who attempted to remove their wives and mothers from the work force to attend to their own households. In contrast to the domestic ideal for white women of all classes, the larger society deemed it "unnatural," in fact an "evil," for black married women "to play the lady" while their husbands supported them. In the immediate postwar South, the role of menial worker outside their homes was demanded of black women, even at the cost of physical coercion.[25]

Dolores Janiewski calls attention to the racialized meaning of class in her study of women's employment in a North Carolina tobacco factory during the twentieth century. She shows that race fractured the division of labor by gender. Southern etiquette demanded protection of white women's "racial honor" and required that they work under conditions described as "suitable for ladies" in contradistinction to the drudgery and dirty working conditions considered acceptable for black women. Janiewski notes that at least one employer felt no inhibition against publicly admitting his "brute treatment" of black female employees.[26]

The most effective tool in the discursive welding of race and class proved to be segregation in its myriad institutional and customary forms. Jim Crow railroad cars, for instance, became strategic sites of contestation over the conflated meaning of class and race: blacks who could afford "first class" accommodations vehemently protested the racial basis for being denied access to them. This is dramatically evident in the case of Arthur Mitchell, Democratic congressman to the U.S. House of Representatives from Illinois during the 1930s. Mitchell was evicted from first-class railroad accommodations while traveling through Hot Springs, Arkansas. Despite his protests, he was forced to join his social "inferiors" in a Jim Crow coach with no flush toilet, washbasin, running water, or soap. The transcript of the trial reveals the following testimony:

> When I offered my ticket, the train conductor took my ticket and tore off a piece of it, but told me at that time that I couldn't ride in that car. We had quite a little controversy about it, and when he said I couldn't ride there I thought it might do some good for me to tell him who I was. I said . . . : "I am Mr. Mitchell, serving in the Congress of the United States." He said it didn't make a damn bit

---

[25] For discussion of "female loaferism," see Jacqueline Jones, 45, 58–60.

[26] Dolores Janiewski, "Seeking 'a New Day and a New Way': Black Women and Unions in the Southern Tobacco Industry," in *"To Toil the Livelong Day": America's Women at Work, 1780–1980*, ed. Carol Groneman and Mary Beth Norton (Ithaca, N.Y.: Cornell University Press, 1987), 163.

of difference who I was, that as long as I was a nigger I couldn't ride in that car.[27]

Neither the imprimatur of the U.S. House of Representatives nor the ability to purchase a first-class ticket afforded Mitchell the more privileged accommodations. The collective image of race represented Mitchell, the individual, just as he singularly represented the entire black race. Despite the complicating factor of his representing the federal government itself, Mitchell, like his socially constructed race, was unambiguously assigned to the second-class car, ergo lower-class space.

A long tradition of black protest focused on such treatment of women. During the late nineteenth century, segregated railroad trains were emblematic of racial configurations of both class and gender; the first-class railroad car also was called the "ladies car." Indeed, segregation's meaning for gender was exemplified in the trope of "lady." Ladies were not merely women; they represented a class, a differentiated status within the generic category of "women." Nor did society confer such status on all white women. White prostitutes, along with many working-class white women, fell outside its rubric. But no black woman, regardless of income, education, refinement, or character, enjoyed the status of lady. John R. Lynch, black congressman from Mississippi during Reconstruction, denounced the practice of forcing black women of means and refinement out of first-class accommodations and into smoking cars. He characterized the latter accommodations as "filthy . . . with drunkards, gamblers, and criminals." Arguing in support of the Civil Rights Bill of 1875, Lynch used the trope of "lady" in calling attention to race's inscription upon class distinctions:

Under our present system of race distinctions a *white woman* of a questionable social standing, yea, I may say, of an admitted immoral character, can go to any public place or upon any public conveyance and be the recipient of the same treatment, the same courtesy, and the same respect that is usually accorded to the most refined and virtuous; but let an intelligent, modest, refined *colored lady* present herself and ask that the same privileges be accorded to her that have just been accorded to her social inferior of the white race, and in nine cases out of ten, except in certain portions of the country, she will not only be refused, but insulted for making the request. [Emphasis added][28]

[27] Mitchell v. United States, 313 U.S. 80 (1941), app.; also see Catherine A. Barnes, *Journey from Jim Crow: The Desegregation of Southern Transit* (New York: Columbia University Press, 1983), 1–2.

[28] See John R. Lynch's speech on the Civil Rights Bill of 1875 in U.S. Congress, *Congressional Record* (February 3, 1875), 944–45.

Early court cases involving discrimination in public transportation reveal that railroad companies seldom if ever looked upon black women as "ladies." The case of Catherine Brown, a black woman, was the first racial public transportation case to come before the U.S. Supreme Court. In February 1868, Brown was denied passage in the "ladies car" on a train traveling from Alexandria, Virginia, to Washington, D.C. Brown disregarded the demand that she sit in the "colored car" instead. Her persistence in entering the ladies car was met with violence and verbal insults.[29] The resultant court case, decided in her favor in 1873, indicated not an end to such practices but merely the federal government's short-lived support of black civil rights during the era of radical Reconstruction. The outcome of Brown's case proved to be an exception to those that would follow.

Within a decade, Ida B. Wells sued the Chesapeake, Ohio, and Southwestern Railroad for physically ejecting her out of the "ladies" car. When the conductor grabbed her arm, she bit him and held firmly to her seat. It took two men finally to dislodge her. They dragged her into the smoking car and (as she recalled in her autobiography) "the white ladies and gentlemen in the car even stood on the seats so that they could get a good view and continued applauding the conductor for his brave stand." Although her lawsuit was successful at the lower court level, the state Supreme Court of Tennessee reversed the earlier decision, sustaining both the discrimination and the bodily harm against her.[30] The racist decision, like others of the courts, led to *Plessy v. Ferguson* in 1896 and the euphemistic doctrine of "separate but equal."

Racial constructions of sexuality

The exclusion of black women from the dominant society's definition of "lady" said as much about sexuality as it did about class. The metalanguage of race signifies, too, the imbrication of race within the representation of sexuality. Historians of women and of science, largely influenced by Michel Foucault, now attest to the variable quality of changing conceptions of sexuality over time—conceptions informed as much by

[29] Railroad Co. v. Brown, 84 U.S. 445 (Wall) 445 (1873).
[30] See Ida B. Wells-Barnett, *Crusade for Justice: The Autobiography of Ida B. Wells,* ed. Alfreda M. Duster (Chicago: University of Chicago Press, 1970), 18–20; for full discussion of this case and those of other black women on buses and streetcars, see Willie Mae Coleman, "Black Women and Segregated Public Transportation: Ninety Years of Resistance," *Truth: Newsletter of the Association of Black Women Historians* (1986), reprinted in Darlene Clark Hine, ed., *Black Women in United States History* (Brooklyn: Carlson, 1990), 5:296–98.

race and class as by gender.[31] Sexuality has come to be defined not in terms of biological essentials or as a universal truth detached and transcendent from other aspects of human life and society. Rather, it is an evolving conception applied to the body but given meaning and identity by economic, cultural, and historical context.[32]

In the centuries between the Renaissance and the Victorian era, Western culture constructed and represented changing and conflicting images of woman's sexuality, which shifted diametrically from images of lasciviousness to moral purity. Yet Western conceptions of black women's sexuality resisted change during this same time.[33] Winthrop Jordan's now classic study of racial attitudes toward blacks between the sixteenth and nineteenth centuries argues that black women's bodies epitomized centuries-long European perceptions of Africans as primitive, animal-like, and savage. In America, no less distinguished and learned a figure than Thomas Jefferson conjectured that black women mated with orangutans.[34] While such thinking rationalized slavery and the sexual exploitation of slave women by white masters, it also perpetuated an enormous division between black people and white people on the "scale of humanity": carnality as opposed to intellect and/or spirit; savagery as opposed to civilization; deviance as opposed to normality; promiscuity as opposed to purity; passion as opposed to passionlessness. The black woman came to symbolize, according to Sander Gilman, an "icon for black sexuality in general."[35] This discursive gap between the races was if anything greater between white and black women than between white and black men.

Violence figured preeminently in racialized constructions of sexuality. From the days of slavery, the social construction and representation of black sexuality reinforced violence, rhetorical and real, against black

[31] For work by historians on sexuality's relation to class and race, see the essays in Kathy Peiss and Christina Simmons, with Robert Padgug, eds., *Passion and Power: Sexuality in History* (Philadelphia: Temple University Press, 1989).

[32] Foucault, *History of Sexuality*, 1:14, 140, 143, 145–146, and *Power/Knowledge* (n. 8 above), 210–11.

[33] Nancy Cott calls attention to the role of evangelical Protestantism and, later, science in contributing to the image of "passionlessness" for American northern women ("Passionlessness: An Interpretation of Victorian Sexual Ideology, 1790–1850," *Signs* 4, no. 2 (Winter 1978): 219–36); for changing Western representations, see Thomas Laqueur, *Making Sex: Body and Gender from the Greeks to Freud* (Cambridge, Mass.: Harvard University Press, 1990).

[34] See discussion of Jefferson and larger discussion of Western views toward blacks in Winthrop D. Jordan, *White over Black: American Attitudes toward the Negro, 1550–1812* (New York: Norton, 1977), 24–40, 151, 154–59, 458–59.

[35] See Sander L. Gilman, "Black Bodies, White Bodies: Toward an Iconography of Female Sexuality in Late Nineteenth-Century Art, Medicine, and Literature," in Gates, ed. (n. 7 above), 223–40.

women and men.[36] That the rape of black women could continue to go on with impunity long after slavery's demise underscores the pervasive belief in black female promiscuity. This belief found expression in the statement of one Southern white woman in 1904: "I cannot imagine such a creation as a virtuous black woman."[37]

The lynching of black men, with its often attendant castration, reeked of sexualized representations of race.[38] The work of black feminists of the late nineteenth century makes clear that lynching, while often rationalized by whites as a punishment for the rape of white women, more often was perpetrated to maintain racial etiquette and the socioeconomic and political hegemony of whites. Ida Wells-Barnett, Anna J. Cooper, Mary Church Terrell, and Pauline Hopkins exposed and contrasted the specter of the white woman's rape in the case of lynching and the sanctioned rape of black women by white men. Hazel Carby, in discussing these black feminist writers, established their understanding of the intersection of strategies of power with lynching and rape:

> Their legacy to us is theories that expose the colonization of the black female body by white male power and the destruction of black males who attempted to exercise any oppositional patriarchal control. When accused of threatening the white female body, the repository of heirs to property and power, the black male, and his economic, political, and social advancement, is lynched out of existence. Cooper, Wells, and Hopkins assert the necessity of seeing the relation between histories: the rape of black women in the

[36] Jacquelyn Dowd Hall, *Revolt against Chivalry: Jessie Daniel Ames and the Women's Campaign against Lynching* (New York: Columbia University Press, 1979), 129–57, 220; Ida Wells-Barnett, *On Lynching*, reprint ed. (New York: Arno Press, 1969); Joel Williamson, *A Rage for Order* (New York: Oxford University Press, 1986), 117–51; Howard Smead, *Blood Justice: The Lynching of Mack Charles Parker* (New York: Oxford University Press, 1986).

[37] "Experiences of the Race Problem: By a Southern White Woman," *Independent*, vol. 56 (March 17, 1904), as quoted in Anne Firor Scott, "Most Invisible of All: Black Women's Voluntary Associations," *Journal of Southern History* 56 (February 1990): 10. Neil R. McMillen observes for the early twentieth century that courts did not usually convict white men for the rape of black women, "because whites generally agreed that no black female above the age of puberty was chaste" (*Dark Journey: Black Mississippians in the Age of Jim Crow* [Urbana: University of Illinois Press, 1989], 205–6).

[38] A number of writers have dealt with the issue of castration. For historical studies of the early slave era, see Jordan, 154–58, 463, 473; also discussing castration statutes as part of the slave codes in colonial Virginia, South Carolina, and Pennsylvania is A. Leon Higginbotham, Jr., *In the Matter of Color: Race and the American Legal Process* (New York: Oxford University Press, 1978), 58, 168, 177, 282, 413, n. 107. For discussion of castration during the twentieth century, see Richard Wright, "The Ethics of Living Jim Crow: An Autobiographical Sketch," in his *Uncle Tom's Children* (1938; reprint, New York: Harper & Row, 1965); and Trudier Harris, *Exorcising Blackness: Historical and Literary Lynching and Burning Rituals* (Bloomington: Indiana University Press, 1984), 29–68.

nineties is directly linked to the rape of the female slave. Their analyses are dynamic and not limited to a parochial understanding of "women's issues"; they have firmly established the dialectical relation between economic/political power and economic/sexual power in the battle for control of women's bodies.[39]

Through a variety of mediums—theater, art, the press, and literature—discourses of racism developed and reified stereotypes of sexuality. Such representations grew out of and facilitated the larger subjugation and control of the black population. The categorization of class and racial groups according to culturally constituted sexual identities facilitated blacks' subordination within a stratified society and rendered them powerless against the intrusion of the state into their innermost private lives. This intrusion went hand in hand with the role of the state in legislating and enforcing racial segregation, disfranchisement, and economic discrimination.

James Jones's *Bad Blood: The Tuskegee Syphilis Experiment* provides us with a profoundly disturbing example of such intrusion into blacks' private lives. Jones recounts how a federal agency, the Public Health Service, embarked in 1932 upon decades of tests on black men with syphilis, denying them access to its cure in order to assess the disease's debilitating effects on the body.[40] The federal agency felt at liberty to make the study because of its unquestioning acceptance of stereotypes that conflated race, gender, and class. By defining this health problem in racial terms, "objective scientific researchers" could be absolved of all responsibility. Some even posited that blacks had "earned their illness as just recompense for wicked life-styles."[41]

The Public Health Service's willingness to prolong syphilis despite the discovery of penicillin discloses not only the federal government's lack of concern for the health of the men in its study, but its even lesser concern for black women in relationships with these men. Black women failed to receive so much as a pretense of protection, so widely accepted was the belief that the spread of the disease was inevitable because black women were promiscuous by nature. This emphasis on black immorality pre-

[39] Bettina Aptheker, *Woman's Legacy: Essays on Race, Sex and Class in American History* (Amherst: University of Massachusetts Press, 1982), 53–77; Hazel V. Carby, " 'On the Threshold of Woman's Era': Lynching, Empire, and Sexuality in Black Feminist Theory," in Gates, ed., 314–15.

[40] James H. Jones, *Bad Blood: The Tuskegee Syphilis Experiment* (New York: Free Press, 1981), 11–29.

[41] Ibid., 22. Elizabeth Fee argues that in the 1920s and 1930s, before a cure was found for syphilis, physicians did not speak in the dispassionate tone of germ theory but, rather, reinforced the image of syphilis as a "black problem" (see her study of Baltimore, "Venereal Disease: The Wages of Sin?" in Peiss and Simmons, eds. [n. 31 above], 182–84).

cluded any sensitivity to congenital syphilis; thus innocent black babies born with the disease went unnoticed and equally unprotected. Certainly the officials of the Public Health Service realized that blacks lived amid staggering poverty, amid a socioeconomic environment conducive to disease. Yet these public servants encoded hegemonic articulations of race into the language of medicine and scientific theory. Their perceptions of sexually transmitted disease, like those of the larger society, were affected by race.[42] Jones concludes:

> The effect of these views was to isolate blacks even further within American society—to remove them from the world of health and to lock them within a prison of sickness. Whether by accident or design, physicians had come dangerously close to depicting the syphilitic black as the representative black. As sickness replaced health as the normal condition of the race, something was lost from the sense of horror and urgency with which physicians had defined disease. The result was a powerful rationale for inactivity in the face of disease, which by their own estimates, physicians believed to be epidemic.[43]

In response to assaults upon black sexuality, according to Darlene Clark Hine, there arose among black women a politics of silence, a "culture of dissemblance." In order to "protect the sanctity of inner aspects of their lives," black women, especially those of the middle class, reconstructed and represented their sexuality through its absence—through silence, secrecy, and invisibility. In so doing, they sought to combat the pervasive negative images and stereotypes. Black clubwomen's adherence to Victorian ideology, as well as their self-representation as "super moral," according to Hine, was perceived as crucial not only to the protection and upward mobility of black women but also to the attainment of respect, justice, and opportunity for all black Americans.[44]

Race as a double-voiced discourse

As this culture of dissemblance illustrates, black people endeavored not only to silence and conceal but also to dismantle and deconstruct the

[42] For a study of the social construction of venereal disease, from the late nineteenth century through the AIDS crisis of our own time, see Allan M. Brandt, *No Magic Bullet: A Social History of Venereal Disease in the United States since 1880* (New York: Oxford University Press, 1987); also see Doris Y. Wilkinson and Gary King, "Conceptual and Methodological Issues in the Use of Race as a Variable: Policy Implications," *Milbank Quarterly* 65 (1987): 68.

[43] James H. Jones, 25, 28.

[44] Darlene Clark Hine, "Rape and the Inner Lives of Black Women in the Middle West: Preliminary Thoughts on the Culture of Dissemblance," *Signs* 14, no. 4 (Summer 1989): 915.

dominant society's deployment of race. Racial meanings were never internalized by blacks and whites in an identical way. The language of race has historically been what Bakhtin calls a double-voiced discourse — serving the voice of black oppression and the voice of black liberation. Bakhtin observes: "The word in language is half someone else's. It becomes 'one's own' only when the speaker populates it with his [or her] own intention, his [or her] own accent, when he [or she] appropriates the word, adapting it to his [or her] own semantic and expressive intention."[45] Blacks took "race" and empowered its language with their own meaning and intent, just as the slaves and freedpeople had appropriated white surnames, even those of their masters, and made them their own.[46]

For African-Americans, race signified a cultural identity that defined and connected them as a people, even as a nation. To be called a "race leader," "race man," or "race woman" by the black community was not a sign of insult or disapproval, nor did such titles refer to any and every black person. Quite to the contrary, they were conferred on Carter G. Woodson, W. E. B. Du Bois, Ida Wells-Barnett, Mary McLeod Bethune, and the other men and women who devoted their lives to the advancement of their people. When the National Association of Colored Women referred to its activities as "race work," it expressed both allegiance and commitment to the concerns of black people. Through a range of shifting, even contradictory meanings and accentuations expressed at the level of individual and group consciousness, blacks fashioned race into a cultural identity that resisted white hegemonic discourses.

The "two-ness" of being both American and Negro, which Du Bois so eloquently captured in 1903, resonates across time. If blacks as individuals referred to a divided subjectivity — "two warring ideals in one dark body" — they also spoke of a collective identity in the colonial terms of a "nation within a nation."[47] The many and varied voices of black nationalism have resounded again and again from the earliest days of the American republic. Black nationalism found advocates in Paul Cuffee, John Russwurm, and Martin Delany in the nineteenth century, and Marcus

[45] Bakhtin (n. 13 above), 293, 324.

[46] On slave surnames, see Herbert G. Gutman, *The Black Family in Slavery and Freedom, 1750–1925* (New York: Pantheon, 1976), 230–56; also George P. Cunningham, " 'Called into Existence': Desire, Gender, and Voice in Frederick Douglass's Narrative of 1845," *Differences* 1, no. 3 (1989): 112–13, 117, 129–31.

[47] Martin Robison Delany wrote in the 1850s of blacks in the United States: "We are a nation within a nation; — as the Poles in Russia, the Hungarians in Austria, the Welsh, Irish, and Scotch in the British Dominions" (see his *The Condition, Elevation, Emigration and Destiny of the Colored People of the United States*, reprint ed. [New York: Arno, 1969], 209; also W. E. Burghardt Du Bois, *The Souls of Black Folks* [New York: Washington Square Press, 1970], 3).

Garvey, Malcolm X, and Stokely Carmichael in the twentieth.[48] We know far too little about women's perceptions of nationalism, but Pauline Hopkins's serialized novel *Of One Blood* (1903) counterposes black and Anglo-Saxon races: "The dawn of the Twentieth century finds the Black race fighting for existence in every quarter of the globe. From over the sea Africa stretches her hands to the American Negro and cries aloud for sympathy in her hour of trial. . . . In America, caste prejudice has received fresh impetus as the 'Southern brother' of the Anglo-Saxon family has arisen from the ashes of secession, and like the prodigal of old, has been gorged with fatted calf and 'fixin's.' "[49]

Likewise Hannah Nelson, an elementary school graduate employed most of her life in domestic service, told anthropologist John Langston Gwaltney in the 1970s: "We are a nation. The best of us have said it and everybody feels it. I know that will probably bother your white readers, but it is nonetheless true that black people think of themselves as an entity."[50] Thus, when historian Barbara Fields observes that "Afro-Americans invented themselves, not as a race, but as a nation," she alludes to race as a double-voiced discourse.[51] For blacks, race signified cultural identity and heritage, not biological inferiority. However, Fields's discussion understates the power of race to mean nation—specifically, race as the sign of perceived kinship ties between blacks in Africa and throughout the diaspora. In the crucible of the Middle Passage and American slavery, the multiple linguistic, tribal, and ethnic divisions among Africans came to be forged into a single, common ancestry. While not

---

[48] See, devoted to the subject of nationalism, John H. Bracey, Jr., August Meier, and Elliott Rudwick, eds., *Black Nationalism in America* (New York: Bobbs-Merrill, 1970); Sterling Stuckey, *Slave Culture: Nationalist Theory and the Foundations of Black America* (New York: Oxford University Press, 1987), and *The Ideological Origins of Black Nationalism* (Boston: Beacon, 1972); Wilson Jeremiah Moses, *The Golden Age of Black Nationalism, 1850–1925* (Hamden, Conn.: Archon, 1978).

[49] Pauline Hopkins, "Heroes and Heroines in Black," *Colored American Magazine* 6 (January 1903): 211. The original publication of *Of One Blood* was serialized in issues of the *Colored American Magazine* between November 1902 and November 1903. See the novel in its entirety, along with Hazel Carby's introduction to the Oxford edition, in Pauline Hopkins, *Magazine Novels of Pauline Hopkins* (New York: Oxford University Press, 1988); also Hazel V. Carby, *Reconstructing Womanhood: The Emergence of the Afro-American Woman Novelist* (New York: Oxford University Press, 1987), 155–62.

[50] See John Langston Gwaltney, "A Nation within a Nation," in *Drylongso: A Self-Portrait of Black America*, ed. John Langston Gwaltney (New York: Random House, 1980), 3–23; and Patricia Hill Collins, "The Social Construction of Black Feminist Thought," *Signs* 14, no. 4 (Summer 1989): 765–70. For a critique of race and essentialism, see Diana Fuss, *Essentially Speaking: Feminism, Nature, and Difference* (New York: Routledge, 1989), 73–96.

[51] Robert Miles (n. 5 above) argues that both race and nation are "supra-class and supra-gender forms of categorisation with considerable potential for articulation" (89–90). Also, see Barbara Jeanne Fields, "Slavery, Race, and Ideology in the United States of America," *New Left Review*, no. 181 (May/June 1990), 115.

adhering to "scientific" explanations of superior and inferior races, African-Americans inscribed the black nation with racially laden meanings of blood ties that bespoke a lineage and culture more imagined than real.

Such imaginings were not unique to African-Americans.[52] As nation states emerged in Europe during the fifteenth and sixteenth centuries, the concept of "race" came increasingly to articulate a nationalist ideology. Racial representations of nation included, on the one hand, "cosmopolitan" views that characterized each national grouping as contributing its own "special gift" to the complementarity of humankind, and, on the other hand, views of hierarchical difference that justified the existence of nation states and the historical dominance of certain groupings over others. Hence, Thomas Arnold could speak of the Anglo-Saxon's lineage in an 1841 lecture at Oxford: "Our English race is the German race; for though our Norman forefathers had learnt to speak a stranger's language, yet in blood, as we know, they were the Saxons' brethren: both alike belonged to the Teutonic or German stock."[53] Such cultural conceptions surely informed nineteenth-century African-American perceptions of the black nation as a site of group uniqueness.

Throughout the nineteenth century, blacks and whites alike subscribed to what George Fredrickson terms "romantic racialism."[54] Blacks constructed and valorized a self-representation essentially antithetical to that of whites. In his article "The Conservation of Races," published in 1897, Harvard-trained W. E. B. Du Bois disclosed his admiration for what he believed to be the "spiritual, psychical" uniqueness of his people—their "special gift" to humanity.[55] Twentieth-century essentialist concepts

---

[52] See Benedict R. Anderson's discussion of nation as "imagined" in the sense of its being limited (not inclusive of all mankind), sovereign, and a community, in his *Imagined Communities: Reflections on the Origin and Spread of Nationalism* (New York and London: Verso, 1983), 14–16.

[53] Arthur Penryhn Stanley, *The Life and Correspondence of Thomas Arnold, D.D.*, 12th ed. (London 1881), 2:324, quoted and cited in Reginald Horsman, *Race and Manifest Destiny: The Origins of American Racial Anglo-Saxonism* (Cambridge, Mass.: Harvard University Press, 1981), 66.

[54] George Fredrickson discusses "romantic racialism" within the context of "benign" views of black distinctiveness. This view was upheld by romanticism, abolitionism, and evangelical religion and should be distinguished from "scientific" explanations or cultural interpretations that vilified blacks as beasts and unworthy of human dignity (*The Black Image in the White Mind* [New York: Harper & Row, 1972], 97–99, 101–15, 125–26).

[55] W. E. B. Du Bois stated: "But while race differences have followed mainly physical race lines, yet no mere physical distinctions would really define or explain the deeper differences—the cohesiveness and continuity of these groups. The deeper differences are spiritual, psychical, differences—undoubtedly based on the physical but infinitely transcending them" ("The Conservation of Races," in *W. E. B. Du Bois Speaks: Speeches*

such as "negritude," "soul," and most recently "Afrocentricity" express in new and altered form the continued desire to capture transcendent threads of racial "oneness." Frantz Fanon described the quest for cultural identity and self-recovery as "the whole body of efforts made by a people in the sphere of thought to describe, justify and praise action through which that people has created itself and keeps itself in existence."[56] These efforts seek to negate white stereotypes of blacks and in their place insert a black worldview or standpoint. Of critical importance here are the dialogic racial representations effected by blacks themselves against negative representations—or more precisely, blacks' appropriation of the productive power of language for the purpose of resistance.[57]

Such a discursive rendering of race counters images of physical and psychical rupture with images of wholeness. Yet once again, race serves as myth and as a global sign, for it superimposes a "natural" unity over a plethora of historical, socioeconomic, and ideological differences among blacks themselves. This is not to understate the critical liberating intention implicit in blacks' own usage of the term "the race," when referring to themselves as a group. But the characterization obscures rather than mirrors the reality of black heterogeneity. In fact, essentialist or other racialized conceptions of national culture hardly reflect paradigmatic consistency. Black nationalism itself has been a heteroglot conception, categorized variously as revolutionary, bourgeois reformist, cultural, religious, economic, or emigrationist.[58] Race as the sign of cultural identity has been neither a coherent nor static concept among African-Americans. Its perpetuation and resilience have reflected shifting, often monolithic and essentialist assumptions on the part of thinkers attempting to identify and define a black peoplehood or nation.

Acceptance of a nation-based, racialized perspective even appears in the work of black women scholars, who seek to ground a black feminist standpoint in the concrete experience of race and gender oppression. Notwithstanding the critical importance of this work in contesting racism and sexism in the academy and larger society, its focus does not permit sufficient exploration of ideological spaces of difference among

---

and Addresses, 1890–1919, ed. Philip S. Foner [New York: Pathfinder, 1970], 77–79, 84); see also Appiah's critique of Du Bois (n. 7 above), 23–29.

[56] Frantz Fanon offers this definition of national culture in contradistinction to one based on "an abstract populism that believes it can discover the people's true nature" (*The Wretched of the Earth* [New York: Grove, 1968], 233).

[57] Raymond Williams asserts: "Language has then to be seen as a persistent kind of creation and re-creation: a dynamic presence and a constant regenerative process" (*Marxism and Literature* [New York: Oxford University Press, 1977], 31).

[58] See Bracey, Meier, and Rudwick, eds. (n. 48 above), xxvi–xxx; Winant and Omi (n. 5 above), 38–51.

black women themselves. For example, sociologist Patricia Hill Collins identifies an ethic of caring and an ethic of personal accountability at the root of Afrocentric values and particularly of Afrocentric feminist epistemology, yet she does not investigate how such values and epistemology are affected by differing class positions.[59] In short, she posits but does not account for the *singularity* of an Afro-American women's standpoint amid diverse and conflicting positions of enunciation.

The rallying notion of "racial uplift" among black Americans during the late nineteenth and early twentieth centuries illustrates the problematic aspects of identifying a standpoint that encompasses all black women. Racial uplift was celebrated in the motto of the National Association of Colored Women—"lifting as we climb." The motto itself expressed a paradox: belief in black womanhood's common cause and recognition of differential values and socioeconomic positions. Racial uplift, while invoking a discursive ground on which to explode negative stereotypes of black women, remained locked within hegemonic articulations of gender, class, and sexuality. Black women teachers, missionaries, and club members zealously promoted values of temperance, sexual repression, and polite manners among the poor.

"Race work" or "racial uplift" equated normality with conformity to white middle-class models of gender roles and sexuality. Given the extremely limited educational and income opportunities during the late nineteenth–early twentieth centuries, many black women linked mainstream domestic duties, codes of dress, sexual conduct, and public etiquette with both individual success and group progress.[60] Black leaders argued that "proper" and "respectable" behavior proved blacks worthy of equal civil and political rights. Conversely, nonconformity was equated with deviance and pathology and was often cited as a cause of racial inequality and injustice. S. W. Layten, founder of the National League for the Protection of Colored Women and leader of one million black Baptist women, typified this attitude in her statement of 1904: "Unfortunately the minority or bad Negroes have given the race a ques-

---

[59] E. Frances White's perceptive analysis of African-Americans' contestation of the discursive representation of Africa calls attention to the conservative implications of Afrocentric feminism. See E. Frances White, "Africa on My Mind: Gender, Counter Discourse and African-American Nationalism," *Journal of Women's History* 2 (Spring 1990): 90–94; Patricia Hill Collins, "The Social Construction of Black Feminist Thought" (n. 50 above), 765–70, and *Black Feminist Thought: Knowledge, Consciousness, and the Politics of Empowerment* (Boston: Unwin Hyman, 1990), 10–11, 15. Also for a good critique, see bell hooks, *Yearning: Race, Gender, and Cultural Politics* (Boston: South End Press, 1990).

[60] Evelyn Brooks Higginbotham, "Beyond the Sound of Silence: Afro-American Women in History," *Gender and History* 1 (Spring 1989): 58–59.

tionable reputation; these degenerates are responsible for every discrimination we suffer."[61]

On a host of levels, racial uplift stood at odds with the daily practices and aesthetic tastes of many poor, uneducated, and "unassimilated" black men and women dispersed throughout the rural South or newly huddled in urban centers.[62] The politics of "respectability" disavowed, in often repressive ways, much of the expressive culture of the "folk," for example, sexual behavior, dress style, leisure activity, music, speech patterns, and religious worship patterns. Similar class and sexual tensions between the discourse of the intelligentsia (the "New Negro") and that of the "people" (the "folk" turned proletariat in the northern urban context) appear in Hazel Carby's discussion of black women novelists of the Harlem Renaissance during the 1920s.[63]

Today, the metalanguage of race continues to bequeath its problematic legacy. While its discursive construction of reality into two opposing camps—blacks versus whites or Afrocentric versus Eurocentric standpoints—provides the basis for resistance against external forces of black subordination, it tends to forestall resolution of problems of gender, class, and sexual orientation internal to black communities. The resolution of such differences is also requisite to the liberation and well-being of "the race." Worse yet, problems deemed too far astray of respectability are subsumed within a culture of dissemblance. The AIDS crisis serves as a case in point, with AIDS usually contextualized within a Manichean opposition of good versus evil that translates into heterosexuality versus homosexuality or wholesome living versus intravenous drug use. At a time when AIDS is a leading killer of black women and their children in impoverished inner-city neighborhoods, educational and support strate-

[61] National Baptist Convention, *Journal of the Twenty-fourth Annual Session of the National Baptist Convention and the Fifth Annual Session of the Woman's Convention, Held in Austin, Texas, September 14–19, 1904* (Nashville: National Baptist Publishing Board, 1904), 324; also, I discuss the politics of respectability as both subversive and conservative in Evelyn Brooks Higginbotham, *Righteous Discontent: The Women's Movement in the Black Baptist Church, 1880–1920* (Cambridge, Mass.: Harvard University Press, 1992), in press, chap. 7.

[62] Houston A. Baker, Jr., in his discussion of the black vernacular, characterizes the "quotidian sounds of black every day life" as both a defiant and entrancing voice (*Afro-American Poetics: Revisions of Harlem and the Black Aesthetic* [Madison: University of Wisconsin Press, 1988], 95–107); see also Houston A. Baker, Jr., *Blues, Ideology and Afro-American Literature: A Vernacular Theory* (Chicago: University of Chicago Press, 1984), 11–13. Similarly, John Langston Gwaltney calls the "folk" culture of today's cities a "core black culture," which is "more than ad hoc synchronic adaptive survival." Gwaltney links its values and epistemology to a long peasant tradition. See Gwaltney, ed. (n. 50 above), xv–xvii.

[63] Carby, *Reconstructing Womanhood* (n. 49 above), 163–75; also Henry Louis Gates, Jr., "The Trope of a New Negro and the Reconstruction of the Image of the Black," *Representations* 24 (Fall 1988): 129–55.

gies lag far behind those of white gay communities.[64] Black women's groups and community organizations fail to tackle the problem with the priority it merits. They shy away from public discussion in large measure because of the historic association of disease and racial/sexual stereotyping.

Conclusion

By analyzing white America's deployment of race in the construction of power relations, perhaps we can better understand why black women historians have largely refrained from an analysis of gender along the lines of the male/female dichotomy so prevalent among white feminists. Indeed, some black women scholars adopt the term *womanist* instead of *feminist* in rejection of gender-based dichotomies that lead to a false homogenizing of women. By so doing they follow in the spirit of black scholar and educator Anna J. Cooper, who in *A Voice from the South* (1892) inextricably linked her racial identity to the "quiet, undisputed dignity" of her womanhood.[65] At the threshold of the twenty-first century, black women scholars continue to emphasize the inseparable unity of race and gender in their thought. They dismiss efforts to bifurcate the identity of black women (and indeed of all women) into discrete categories—as if culture, consciousness, and lived experience could at times constitute "woman" isolated from the contexts of race, class, and sexuality that give form and content to the particular women we are.[66]

On the other hand, we should challenge both the overdeterminancy of race vis-à-vis social relations among blacks themselves and conceptions of the black community as harmonious and monolithic. The historic reality of racial conflict in America has tended to devalue and discourage attention to gender conflict within black communities and to tensions of class or sexuality among black women. The totalizing tendency of race

[64] See Bruce Lambert, "AIDS in Black Women Seen as Leading Killer," *New York Times* (July 11, 1990); Ernest Quimby and Samuel R. Friedman, "Dynamics of Black Mobilization against AIDS in New York City," *Social Problems* 36 (October 1989): 407–13; Evelynn Hammonds, "Race, Sex, Aids: The Construction of 'Other,'" *Radical America* 29 (November–December 1987): 28–36; also Brandt (n. 42 above), 186–92.

[65] Anna Julia Cooper stated: "When and where I enter in the quiet, undisputed dignity of my womanhood without violence and without suing or special patronage, then and there the whole Negro race enters with me" (*A Voice from the South,* reprint of the 1892 ed. [New York: Negro Universities Press, 1969], 31).

[66] Alice Walker, *In Search of Our Mothers' Gardens: Womanist Prose* (New York: Harcourt, Brace, Jovanovich, 1983), xi–xii; also see, e.g., Elsa Barkley Brown's introductory pages and historical treatment of Maggie Lena Walker, black Richmond banker in the early twentieth century, which reflect this perspective ("Womanist Consciousness: Maggie Lena Walker and the Independent Order of Saint Luke," *Signs* 14, no. 3 [Spring 1989]: 610–15, 630–33).

precludes recognition and acknowledgment of intragroup social relations as relations of power. With its implicit understandings, shared cultural codes, and inchoate sense of a common heritage and destiny, the meta-language of race resounds over and above a plethora of conflicting voices. But it cannot silence them.

Black women of different economic and regional backgrounds, of different skin tones and sexual orientations, have found themselves in conflict over interpretation of symbols and norms, public behavior, coping strategies, and a variety of micropolitical acts of resistance to structures of domination.[67] Although racialized cultural identity has clearly served blacks in the struggle against discrimination, it has not sufficiently addressed the empirical reality of gender conflict within the black community or class differences among black women themselves. Historian E. Frances White makes this point brilliantly when she asserts that "the site of counter-discourse is itself contested terrain."[68] By fully recognizing race as an unstable, shifting, and strategic reconstruction, feminist scholars must take up new challenges to inform and confound many of the assumptions currently underlying Afro-American history and women's history. We must problematize much more of what we take for granted. We must bring to light and to coherence the one and the many that we always were in history and still actually are today.

Department of History
University of Pennsylvania

---

[67] I am using "micropolitics" synonymously with James C. Scott's term "infrapolitics." According to Scott, the infrapolitics of subordinate groups not only constitute the everyday, prosaic, "unobtrusive" level of political struggle in contradistinction to overt protests but also constitute the "cultural and structural underpinning" of more visible discontent (*Domination and the Arts of Resistance: Hidden Transcripts* [New Haven, Conn.: Yale University Press, 1990], 183–92).

[68] White (n. 59 above), 82.

From Servitude to Service Work: Historical Continuities in the Racial Division of Paid Reproductive Labor

Evelyn Nakano Glenn

RECENT SCHOLARSHIP on African American, Latina, Asian American, and Native American women reveals the complex interaction of race and gender oppression in their lives. These studies expose the inadequacy of additive models that treat gender and race as separate and discrete systems of hierarchy (Collins 1986; King 1988; Brown 1989). In an additive model, white women are viewed solely in terms of gender, while women of color are thought to be "doubly" subordinated by the cumulative effects of gender plus race. Yet achieving a more adequate framework, one that captures the interlocking, interactive nature of these systems, has been extraordinarily difficult. Historically, race and gender have developed as separate topics of inquiry, each with its own literature and concepts. Thus features of social life considered central in understanding one system have been overlooked in analyses of the other.

One domain that has been explored extensively in analyses of gender but ignored in studies of race is social reproduction. The term *social reproduction* is used by feminist scholars to refer to the array of activities and relationships involved in maintaining people both on a daily basis and intergenerationally. Reproductive labor includes activities such as purchasing household goods, preparing and serving food, laundering and repairing clothing, maintaining furnishings and appliances, socializing children, providing care and emotional support for adults, and maintaining kin and community ties.

Work on this project was made possible by a Title F leave from the State University of New York at Binghamton and a visiting scholar appointment at the Murray Research Center at Radcliffe College. Discussions with Elsa Barkley Brown, Gary Glenn, Carole Turbin, and Barrie Thorne contributed immeasurably to the ideas developed here. My thanks to Joyce Chinen for directing me to archival materials in Hawaii. I am also grateful to members of the Women and Work Group and to Norma Alarcon, Gary Dymski, Antonia Glenn, Margaret Guilette, Terence Hopkins, Eileen McDonagh, JoAnne Preston, Mary Ryan, and four anonymous *Signs* reviewers for their suggestions.

[*Signs: Journal of Women in Culture and Society* 1992, vol. 18, no. 1]

Marxist feminists place the gendered construction of reproductive labor at the center of women's oppression. They point out that this labor is performed disproportionately by women and is essential to the industrial economy. Yet because it takes place mostly outside the market, it is invisible, not recognized as real work. Men benefit directly and indirectly from this arrangement—directly in that they contribute less labor in the home while enjoying the services women provide as wives and mothers and indirectly in that, freed of domestic labor, they can concentrate their efforts in paid employment and attain primacy in that area. Thus the sexual division of reproductive labor in the home interacts with and reinforces sexual division in the labor market.[1] These analyses draw attention to the dialectics of production and reproduction and male privilege in both realms. When they represent gender as the sole basis for assigning reproductive labor, however, they imply that all women have the same relationship to it and that it is therefore a universal female experience.[2]

In the meantime, theories of racial hierarchy do not include any analysis of reproductive labor. Perhaps because, consciously or unconsciously, they are male centered, they focus exclusively on the paid labor market and especially on male-dominated areas of production.[3] In the 1970s several writers seeking to explain the historic subordination of peoples of color pointed to dualism in the labor market—its division into distinct markets for white workers and for racial-ethnic workers—as a major vehicle for maintaining white domination (Blauner 1972; Barrera 1979).[4] According to these formulations, the labor system has been organized to ensure that racial-ethnic workers are relegated to a lower tier of low-wage, dead-end, marginal jobs; institutional barriers, including restrictions on legal and political rights, prevent their moving out of that tier and competing with Euro-American workers for better jobs. These theories draw attention to the material advantages whites gain from the racial division of labor. How-

---

[1] For various formulations, see Benston (1969), Secombe (1974), Barrett (1980), Fox (1980), and Sokoloff (1980).

[2] Recently, white feminists have begun to pay attention to scholarship by and about racial-ethnic women and to recognize racial stratification in the labor market and other public arenas. My point here is that they still assume that women's relationship to domestic labor is universal; thus they have not been concerned with explicating differences across race, ethnic, and class groups in women's relationship to that labor.

[3] See, e.g., Reisler (1976), which, despite its title, is exclusively about male Mexican labor.

[4] I use the term *racial-ethnic* to refer collectively to groups that have been socially constructed and constituted as racially as well as culturally distinct from European Americans and placed in separate legal statuses from "free whites" (c.f. Omi and Winant 1986). Historically, African Americans, Latinos, Asian Americans, and Native Americans were so constructed. Similarly, I have capitalized the word *Black* throughout this article to signify the racial-ethnic construction of that category.

ever, they either take for granted or ignore women's unpaid household labor and fail to consider whether this work might also be "racially divided."

In short, the racial division of reproductive labor has been a missing piece of the picture in both literatures. This piece, I would contend, is key to the distinct exploitation of women of color and is a source of both hierarchy and interdependence among white women and women of color. It is thus essential to the development of an integrated model of race and gender, one that treats them as interlocking, rather than additive, systems.

In this article I present a historical analysis of the simultaneous race and gender construction of reproductive labor in the United States, based on comparative study of women's work in the South, the Southwest, and the Far West. I argue that reproductive labor has divided along racial as well as gender lines and that the specific characteristics of the division have varied regionally and changed over time as capitalism has reorganized reproductive labor, shifting parts of it from the household to the market. In the first half of the century racial-ethnic women were employed as servants to perform reproductive labor in white households, relieving white middle-class women of onerous aspects of that work; in the second half of the century, with the expansion of commodified services (services turned into commercial products or activities), racial-ethnic women are disproportionately employed as service workers in institutional settings to carry out lower-level "public" reproductive labor, while cleaner white collar supervisory and lower professional positions are filled by white women.

I will examine the ways race and gender were constructed around the division of labor by sketching changes in the organization of reproductive labor since the early nineteenth century, presenting a case study of domestic service among African American women in the South, Mexican American women in the Southwest, and Japanese American women in California and Hawaii, and finally examining the shift to institutional service work, focusing on race and gender stratification in health care and the racial division of labor within the nursing labor force. Race and gender emerge as socially constructed, interlocking systems that shape the material conditions, identities, and consciousnesses of all women.

Historical changes in the organization of reproduction

The concept of reproductive labor originated in Karl Marx's remark that every system of production involves both the production of the necessities of life and the reproduction of the tools and labor power

necessary for production (Marx and Engels 1969, 31). Recent elabora-
tions of the concept grow out of Engels's dictum that the "determining
force in history is, in the last resort, the production and reproduction of
immediate life." This has, he noted, "a two-fold character, on the one
hand the production of subsistence and on the other the production of
human beings themselves" (Engels 1972, 71). Although often equated
with domestic labor or defined narrowly as referring to the renewal of
labor power, the term *social reproduction* has come to be more broadly
conceived, particularly by social historians, to refer to the creation and
recreation of people as cultural and social, as well as physical, beings
(Ryan 1981, 15). Thus, it involves mental, emotional, and manual labor
(Brenner and Laslett 1986, 117). This labor can be organized in myriad
ways—in and out of the household, as paid or unpaid work, creating
exchange value or only use value—and these ways are not mutually
exclusive. An example is the preparation of food, which can be done by
a family member as unwaged work in the household, by a servant as
waged work in the household, or by a short-order cook in a fast-food
restaurant as waged work that generates profit for the employer. These
forms exist contemporaneously.

Prior to industrialization, however, both production and reproduction
were organized almost exclusively at the household level. Women were
responsible for most of what might be designated as reproduction, but
they were simultaneously engaged in the production of foodstuffs, cloth-
ing, shoes, candles, soap, and other goods consumed by the household.
With industrialization, production of these basic goods gradually was
taken over by capitalist industry. Reproduction, however, remained
largely the responsibility of individual households. The ideological sep-
aration between men's "productive" labor and women's non-market-
based activity that had evolved at the end of the eighteenth century was
elaborated in the early decades of the nineteenth. An idealized division of
labor arose in which men's work was to follow production outside the
home, while women's work was to remain centered in the household
(Boydston 1990, esp. 46–48). Household work continued to include the
production of many goods consumed by members (Smuts 1959, 11–13;
Kessler-Harris 1981), but as an expanding range of outside-manufactured
goods became available, household work became increasingly focused on
reproduction.[5] This idealized division of labor was largely illusory for
working-class households, including immigrant and racial-ethnic families,
in which men seldom earned a family wage; in these households women

---

[5] Capitalism, however, changed the nature of reproductive labor, which became more
and more devoted to consumption activities, i.e., using wages to acquire necessities in
the market and then processing these commodities to make them usable (see Weinbaum
and Bridges 1976; and Luxton 1980).

and children were forced into income-earning activities in and out of the home (Kessler-Harris 1982).

In the second half of the twentieth century, with goods production almost completely incorporated into the market, reproduction has become the next major target for commodification. Aside from the tendency of capital to expand into new areas for profit making, the very conditions of life brought about by large-scale commodity production have increased the need for commercial services. As household members spend more of their waking hours employed outside the home, they have less time and inclination to provide for one another's social and emotional needs. With the growth of a more geographically mobile and urbanized society, individuals and households have become increasingly cut off from larger kinship circles, neighbors, and traditional communities. Thus, as Harry Braverman notes, "The population no longer relies upon social organization in the form of family, friends, neighbors, community, elders, children, but with few exceptions must go to the market and only to the market, not only for food, clothing, and shelter, but also for recreation, amusement, security, for the care of the young, the old, the sick, the handicapped. In time not only the material and service needs but even the emotional patterns of life are channeled through the market" (Braverman 1974, 276). Conditions of capitalist urbanism also have enlarged the population of those requiring daily care and support: elderly and very young people, mentally and physically disabled people, criminals, and other people incapable of fending for themselves. Because the care of such dependents becomes difficult for the "stripped-down" nuclear family or the atomized community to bear, more of it becomes relegated to institutions outside the family.[6]

The final phase in this process is what Braverman calls the "product cycle," which "invents new products and services, some of which become indispensable as the conditions of modern life change and destroy alternatives" (Braverman 1974, 281). In many areas (e.g., health care), we no longer have choices outside the market. New services and products also alter the definition of an acceptable standard of living. Dependence on the market is further reinforced by what happened earlier with goods production, namely, an "atrophy of competence," so that individuals no longer know how to do what they formerly did for themselves.

As a result of these tendencies, an increasing range of services has been removed wholly or partially from the household and converted into paid services yielding profits. Today, activities such as preparing and serving food (in restaurants and fast-food establishments), caring for handi-

---

[6] This is not to deny that family members, especially women, still provide the bulk of care of dependents, but to point out that there has been a marked increase in institutionalized care in the second half of the twentieth century.

capped and elderly people (in nursing homes), caring for children (in child-care centers), and providing emotional support, amusement, and companionship (in counseling offices, recreation centers, and health clubs) have become part of the cash nexus. In addition, whether impelled by a need to maintain social control or in response to pressure exerted by worker and community organizations, the state has stepped in to assume minimal responsibility for some reproductive tasks, such as child protection and welfare programs.[7] Whether supplied by corporations or the state, these services are labor-intensive. Thus, a large army of low-wage workers, mostly women and disproportionately women of color, must be recruited to supply the labor.

Still, despite vastly expanded commodification and institutionalization, much reproduction remains organized at the household level. Sometimes an activity is too labor-intensive to be very profitable. Sometimes households or individuals in them have resisted commodification. The limited commodification of child care, for example, involves both elements. The extent of commercialization in different areas of life is uneven, and the variation in its extent is the outcome of political and economic struggles (Brenner and Laslett 1986, 121; Laslett and Brenner 1989, 384). What is consistent across forms, whether commodified or not, is that reproductive labor is constructed as "female." The gendered organization of reproduction is widely recognized. Less obvious, but equally characteristic, is its racial construction: historically, racial-ethnic women have been assigned a distinct place in the organization of reproductive labor.

Elsewhere I have talked about the reproductive labor racial-ethnic women have carried out for their own families; this labor was intensified as the women struggled to maintain family life and indigenous cultures in the face of cultural assaults, ghettoization, and a labor system that relegated men and women to low-wage, seasonal, and hazardous employment (Glenn 1985; 1986, 86–108; Dill 1988). Here I want to talk about two forms of waged reproductive work that racial-ethnic women have performed disproportionately: domestic service in private households and institutional service work.

Domestic service as the racial division of reproductive labor

Both the demand for household help and the number of women employed as servants expanded rapidly in the latter half of the nineteenth

---

[7] For a discussion of varying views on the relative importance of control versus agency in shaping state welfare policy, see Gordon (1990). Piven and Cloward note that programs have been created only when poor people have mobilized and are intended to defuse pressure for more radical change (1971, 66). In their *Poor People's Movements* (Piven and Cloward 1979), they document the role of working-class struggles to win concessions from the state. For a feminist social control perspective, see Abramovitz (1988).

century (Chaplin 1978). This expansion paralleled the rise of industrial capital and the elaboration of middle-class women's reproductive responsibilities. Rising standards of cleanliness, larger and more ornately furnished homes, the sentimentalization of the home as a "haven in a heartless world" (Lasch 1977), and the new emphasis on childhood and the mother's role in nurturing children all served to enlarge middle-class women's responsibilities for reproduction at a time when technology had done little to reduce the sheer physical drudgery of housework.[8]

By all accounts middle-class women did not challenge the gender-based division of labor or the enlargement of their reproductive responsibilities. Indeed, middle-class women—as readers and writers of literature; as members and leaders of clubs, charitable organizations, associations, reform movements, and religious revivals; and as supporters of the cause of abolition—helped to elaborate the domestic code (Brenner and Laslett 1986).[9] Feminists seeking an expanded public role for women argued that the same nurturant and moral qualities that made women centers of the home should be brought to bear in public service. In the domestic sphere, instead of questioning the inequitable gender division of labor, they sought to slough off the more burdensome tasks onto more oppressed groups of women.[10]

Phyllis Palmer observes that at least through the first half of the twentieth century, "most white middle class women could hire another woman—a recent immigrant, a working class woman, a woman of color, or all three—to perform much of the hard labor of household tasks" (Palmer 1987, 182–83). Domestics were employed to clean house, launder and iron clothes, scrub floors, and care for infants and children. They relieved their mistresses of the heavier and dirtier domestic chores.[11] White middle-class women were thereby freed for supervisory tasks and for cultural, leisure, and volunteer activity or, more rarely during this period, for a career.[12]

---

[8] These developments are discussed in Degler (1980), Strasser (1982), Cowan (1983), and Dudden (1983, esp. 240–42).

[9] See also Blair (1980); Epstein (1981); Ryan (1981); Dudden (1983); and Brenner and Laslett (1986).

[10] See, e.g., Kaplan (1987).

[11] Phyllis Palmer, in her *Domesticity and Dirt*, found evidence that mistresses and servants agreed on what were the least desirable tasks—washing clothes, washing dishes, and taking care of children on evenings and weekends—and that domestics were more likely to perform the least desirable tasks (1990, 70).

[12] It may be worth mentioning the importance of unpaid cultural and charitable activities in perpetuating middle-class privilege and power. Middle-class reformers often aimed to mold the poor in ways that mirrored middle-class values but without actually altering their subordinate position. See, e.g., Sanchez (1990) for discussion of efforts of Anglo reformers to train Chicanas in domestic skills.

Palmer suggests that the use of domestic servants also helped resolve certain contradictions created by the domestic code. She notes that the early twentieth-century housewife confronted inconsistent expectations of middle-class womanhood: domesticity and "feminine virtue." Domesticity—defined as creating a warm, clean, and attractive home for husband and children—required hard physical labor and meant contending with dirt. The virtuous woman, however, was defined in terms of spirituality, refinement, and the denial of the physical body. Additionally, in the 1920s and 1930s there emerged a new ideal of the modern wife as an intelligent and attractive companion. If the heavy parts of household work could be transferred to paid help, the middle-class housewife could fulfill her domestic duties, yet distance herself from the physical labor and dirt and also have time for personal development (Palmer 1990, 127–51).

Who was to perform the "dirty work" varied by region. In the Northeast, European immigrant women, particularly those who were Irish and German, constituted the majority of domestic servants from the mid-nineteenth century to World War I (Katzman 1978, 65–70). In regions where there was a large concentration of people of color, subordinate-race women formed a more or less permanent servant stratum. Despite differences in the composition of the populations and the mix of industries in the regions, there were important similarities in the situation of Mexicans in the Southwest, African Americans in the South, and Japanese people in northern California and Hawaii. Each of these groups was placed in a separate legal category from whites, excluded from rights and protections accorded full citizens. This severely limited their ability to organize, compete for jobs, and acquire capital (Glenn 1985). The racial division of private reproductive work mirrored this racial dualism in the legal, political, and economic systems.

In the South, African American women constituted the main and almost exclusive servant caste. Except in times of extreme economic crisis, whites and Blacks did not compete for domestic jobs. Until the First World War 90 percent of all nonagriculturally employed Black women in the South were employed as domestics. Even at the national level, servants and laundresses accounted for close to half (48.4 percent) of non-agriculturally employed Black women in 1930.[13]

In the Southwest, especially in the states with the highest proprotions of Mexicans in the population—Texas, Colorado, and New Mexico—Chicanas were disproportionately concentrated in domestic service.[14] In El Paso nearly half of all Chicanas in the labor market were

[13] U.S. Bureau of the Census 1933, chap. 3, "Color and Nativity of Gainful Workers," tables 2, 4, 6. For discussion of the concentration of African American women in domestic service, see Glenn (1985).
[14] I use the terms *Chicano, Chicana,* and *Mexican American* to refer to both native-born and immigrant Mexican people/women in the United States.

employed as servants or laundresses in the early decades of the century (Garcia 1981, 76). In Denver, according to Sarah Deutsch, perhaps half of all households had at least one female member employed as a domestic at some time, and if a woman became a widow, she was almost certain to take in laundry (Deutsch 1987a, 147). Nationally, 39.1 percent of nonagriculturally employed Chicanas were servants or laundresses in 1930.[15]

In the Far West—especially in California and Hawaii, with their large populations of Asian immigrants—an unfavorable sex ratio made female labor scarce in the late nineteenth and early twentieth centuries. In contrast to the rest of the nation, the majority of domestic servants in California and Hawaii were men: in California until 1880 (Katzman 1978, 55) and in Hawaii as late as 1920 (Lind 1951, table 1). The men were Asian—Chinese and later Japanese. Chinese houseboys and cooks were familiar figures in late nineteenth-century San Francisco; so too were Japanese male retainers in early twentieth-century Honolulu. After 1907 Japanese women began to immigrate in substantial numbers, and they inherited the mantle of service in both California and Hawaii. In the pre–World War II years, close to half of all immigrant and native-born Japanese American women in the San Francisco Bay area and in Honolulu were employed as servants or laundresses (U.S. Bureau of the Census 1932, table 8; Glenn 1986, 76–79). Nationally, excluding Hawaii, 25.4 percent of nonagricultural Japanese American women workers were listed as servants in 1930.[16]

In areas where racial dualism prevailed, being served by members of the subordinate group was a perquisite of membership in the dominant group. According to Elizabeth Rae Tyson, an Anglo woman who grew up in El Paso in the early years of the century, "almost every Anglo-American family had at least one, sometimes two or three servants: a maid and laundress, and perhaps a nursemaid or yardman. The maid came in after breakfast and cleaned up the breakfast dishes, and very likely last night's supper dishes as well; did the routine cleaning, washing and ironing, and after the family dinner in the middle of the day, washed dishes again, and then went home to perform similar services in her own home" (Garcia 1980, 327). In southwest cities, Mexican American girls were trained at an early age to do domestic work and girls as young as nine or ten were hired to clean house.[17]

In Hawaii, where the major social division was between the haole (Caucasian) planter class and the largely Asian plantation worker class,

[15] U.S. Bureau of the Census 1933.
[16] Ibid.
[17] For personal accounts of Chicano children being inducted into domestic service, see Ruíz (1987a) and interview of Josephine Turietta in Elsasser, MacKenzie, and Tixier y Vigil (1980, 28–35).

haole residents were required to employ one or more Chinese or Japanese servants to demonstrate their status and their social distance from those less privileged. Andrew Lind notes that "the literature on Hawaii, especially during the second half of the nineteenth century, is full of references to the open-handed hospitality of Island residents, dispensed by the ever-present maids and houseboys" (Lind 1951, 73). A public school teacher who arrived in Honolulu in 1925 was placed in a teacher's cottage with four other mainland teachers. She discovered a maid had already been hired by the principal: "A maid! None of us had ever had a maid. We were all used to doing our own work. Furthermore, we were all in debt and did not feel that we wanted to spend even four dollars a month on a maid. Our principal was quite insistent. Everyone on the plantation had a maid. It was, therefore, the thing to do" (Lind 1951, 76).

In the South, virtually every middle-class housewife employed at least one African American woman to do cleaning and child care in her home. Southern household workers told one writer that in the old days, "if you worked for a family, your daughter was expected to, too" (Tucker 1988, 98). Daughters of Black domestics were sometimes inducted as children into service to baby-sit, wash diapers, and help clean (Clark-Lewis 1987, 200–201).[18] White-skin privilege transcended class lines, and it was not uncommon for working-class whites to hire Black women for housework (Anderson and Bowman 1953). In the 1930s white women tobacco workers in Durham, North Carolina, could mitigate the effects of the "double day"—household labor on top of paid labor—by employing Black women to work in their homes for about one-third of their own wages (Janiewski 1983, 93). Black women tobacco workers were too poorly paid to have this option and had to rely on the help of overworked husbands, older children, Black women too old to be employed, neighbors, or kin.

Where more than one group was available for service, a differentiated hierarchy of race, color, and culture emerged. White and racial-ethnic domestics were hired for different tasks. In her study of women workers in Atlanta, New Orleans, and San Antonio during the 1920s and 1930s, Julia Kirk Blackwelder reported that "anglo women in the employ of private households were nearly always reported as housekeepers, while Blacks and Chicanas were reported as laundresses, cooks or servants" (Blackwelder 1978, 349).[19]

---

[18] See also life history accounts of Black domestics, such as that of Bolden (1976) and of Anna Mae Dickson by Wendy Watriss (Watriss 1984).

[19] Blackwelder also found that domestics themselves were attuned to the racial-ethnic hierarchy among them. When advertising for jobs, women who did not identify themselves as Black overwhelmingly requested "housekeeping" or "governess" positions, whereas Blacks advertised for "cooking," "laundering," or just plain "domestic work."

In the Southwest, where Anglos considered Mexican or "Spanish" culture inferior, Anglos displayed considerable ambivalence about employing Mexicans for child care. Although a modern-day example, this statement by an El Paso businessman illustrates the contradictions in Anglo attitudes. The man told an interviewer that he and his wife were putting off parenthood because "the major dilemma would be what to do with the child. We don't really like the idea of leaving the baby at home with a maid . . . for the simple reason if the maid is Mexican, the child may assume that the other person is its mother. Nothing wrong with Mexicans, they'd just assume that this other person is its mother. There have been all sorts of cases where the infants learned Spanish before they learned English. There've been incidents of the Mexican maid stealing the child and taking it over to Mexico and selling it" (Ruíz 1987b, 71).

In border towns, the Mexican group was further stratified by English-speaking ability, place of nativity, and immigrant status, with non-English-speaking women residing south of the border occupying the lowest rung. In Laredo and El Paso, Mexican American factory operatives often employed Mexican women who crossed the border daily or weekly to do domestic work for a fraction of a U.S. operative's wages (Hield 1984, 95; Ruíz 1987a, 64).

The race and gender construction of domestic service

Despite their preference for European immigrant domestics, employers could not easily retain their services. Most European immigrant women left service upon marriage, and their daughters moved into the expanding manufacturing, clerical, and sales occupations during the 1910s and twenties.[20] With the flow of immigration slowed to a trickle during World War I, there were few new recruits from Europe. In the 1920s, domestic service became increasingly the specialty of minority-race women (Palmer 1990, 12). Women of color were advantageous employees in one respect: they could be compelled more easily to remain in service. There is considerable evidence that middle-class whites acted to ensure the domestic labor supply by tracking racial-ethnic women into domestic service and blocking their entry into other fields. Urban school systems in the Southwest tracked Chicana students into homemaking courses designed to prepare them for domestic service. The El Paso school board established a segregated school system in the 1880s that remained in place for the next thirty years; education for Mexican chil-

---

[20] This is not to say that daughters of European immigrants experienced great social mobility and soon attained affluence. The nondomestic jobs they took were usually low paying and the conditions of work often deplorable. Nonetheless, white native-born and immigrant women clearly preferred the relative freedom of industrial, office, or shop employment to the constraints of domestic service (see Katzman 1978, 71–72).

dren emphasized manual and domestic skills that would prepare them to work at an early age. In 1909 the Women's Civic Improvement League, an Anglo organization, advocated domestic training for older Mexican girls. Their rationale is explained by Mario Garcia: "According to the league the housegirls for the entire city came from the Mexican settlement and if they could be taught housekeeping, cooking and sewing, every American family would benefit. The Mexican girls would likewise profit since their services would improve and hence be in greater demand" (Garcia 1981, 113).

The education of Chicanas in the Denver school system was similarly directed toward preparing students for domestic service and handicrafts. Sarah Deutsch found that Anglo women there persisted in viewing Chicanas and other "inferior-race" women as dependent, slovenly, and ignorant. Thus, they argued, training Mexican girls for domestic service not only would solve "one phase of women's work we seem to be incapable of handling" but it would simultaneously help raise the (Mexican) community by improving women's standard of living, elevating their morals, and facilitating Americanization (Deutsch 1987b, 736). One Anglo writer, in an article published in 1917 titled "Problems and Progress among Mexicans in Our Own Southwest," claimed, "When trained there is no better servant than the gentle, quiet Mexicana girl" (Romero 1988a, 16).

In Hawaii, with its plantation economy, Japanese and Chinese women were coerced into service for their husbands' or fathers' employers. According to Lind, prior to World War II:

> It has been a usual practice for a department head or a member of the managerial staff of the plantation to indicate to members of his work group that his household is in need of domestic help and to expect them to provide a wife or daughter to fill the need. Under the conditions which have prevailed in the past, the worker has felt obligated to make a member of his own family available for such service, if required, since his own position and advancement depend upon keeping the goodwill of his boss. Not infrequently, girls have been prevented from pursuing a high school or college education because someone on the supervisory staff has needed a servant and it has seemed inadvisable for the family to disregard the claim. [Lind 1951, 77]

Economic coercion also could take bureaucratic forms, especially for women in desperate straits. During the Depression, local officials of the federal Works Project Administration (WPA) and the National Youth Administration (NYA), programs set up by the Roosevelt administration to help the unemployed find work, tried to direct Chicanas and Blacks to domestic service jobs exclusively (Blackwelder 1984, 120–22; Deutsch 1987a, 182–83). In Colorado, local officials of the WPA and NYA advocated household training projects for Chicanas. George Bickel, assistant state director of the WPA for Colorado, wrote: "The average Spanish-American girl on the NYA program looks forward to little save a life devoted to motherhood often under the most miserable circumstances" (Deutsch 1987a, 183). Given such an outlook, it made sense to provide training in domestic skills.

Young Chicanas disliked domestic service so much that slots in the programs went begging. Older women, especially single mothers struggling to support their families, could not afford to refuse what was offered. The cruel dilemma that such women faced was poignantly expressed in one woman's letter to President Roosevelt:

> My name is Lula Gordon. I am a Negro woman. I am on the relief. I have three children. I have no husband and no job. I have worked hard ever since I was old enough. I am willing to do any kind of work because I have to support myself and my children. I was under the impression that the government or the W.P.A. would give the Physical [sic] fit relief clients work. I have been praying for that time to come. A lady, Elizabeth Ramsie, almost in my condition, told me she was going to try to get some work. I went with her. We went to the Court House here in San Antonio, we talked to a Mrs. Beckmon. Mrs. Beckmon told me to phone a Mrs. Coyle because she wanted some one to clean house and cook for ($5) five dollars a week. Mrs. Beckmon said if I did not take the job in the Private home I would be cut off from everything all together. I told her I was afraid to accept the job in the private home because I have registered for a government job and when it opens up I want to take it. She said that she was taking people off of the relief and I have to take the job in the private home or none. . . . I need work and I will do anything the government gives me to do. . . . Will you please give me some work. [Blackwelder 1984, 68–69]

Japanese American women were similarly compelled to accept domestic service jobs when they left the internment camps in which they were imprisoned during World War II. To leave the camps they had to have a job and a residence, and many women were forced to take positions as live-in servants in various parts of the country. When women from the San Francisco Bay area returned there after the camps were closed, agencies set up to assist the returnees directed them to domestic service jobs. Because they had lost their homes and possessions and had no savings, returnees had to take whatever jobs were offered them. Some became live-in servants to secure housing, which was in short supply after the war. In many cases domestic employment became a lifelong career (Glenn 1986).

In Hawaii the Japanese were not interned, but there nonetheless developed a "maid shortage" as war-related employment expanded. Accustomed to cheap and abundant household help, haole employers became increasingly agitated about being deprived of the services of their "mamasans." The suspicion that many able-bodied former maids were staying at home idle because their husbands or fathers had lucrative defense jobs was taken seriously enough to prompt an investigation by a university researcher.[21]

Housewives told their nisei maids it was the maids' patriotic duty to remain on the job. A student working as a live-in domestic during the war was dumbfounded by her mistress's response when she notified her she was leaving to take a room in the dormitory at the university. Her cultured and educated mistress, whom the student had heretofore admired, exclaimed with annoyance: "'I think especially in war time, the University should close down the dormitory.' Although she didn't say it in words, I sensed the implication that she believed all the (Japanese) girls should be placed in different homes, making it easier for the haole woman."[22] The student noted with some bitterness that although her employer told her that working as a maid was the way for her to do "your bit for the war effort," she and other haole women did not, in turn, consider giving up the "conveniences and luxuries of pre-war Hawaii" as their bit for the war.[23]

The dominant group ideology in all these cases was that women of color—African American women, Chicanas, and Japanese American women—were particularly suited for service. These racial justifications ranged from the argument that Black and Mexican women were incapable of governing their own lives and thus were dependent on whites—making white employment of them an act of benevolence—to the argument that Asian servants were naturally quiet, subordinate, and accustomed to a lower standard of living. Whatever the specific content of the racial characterizations, it defined the proper place of these groups as in service: they belonged there, just as it was the dominant group's place to be served.

David Katzman notes that "ethnic stereotyping was the stock in trade of all employers of servants, and it is difficult at times to figure out

---

[21] Document Ma 24, Romanzo Adams Social Research Laboratory papers. I used these records when they were lodged in the sociology department; they are currently being cataloged by the university archives and a finding aid is in process.

[22] Ibid., document Ma 15, 5.

[23] Ibid.

whether blacks and immigrants were held in contempt because they were servants or whether urban servants were denigrated because most of the servants were blacks and immigrants" (Katzman 1978, 221). Even though racial stereotypes undoubtedly preceded their entry into domestic work, it is also the case that domestics were forced to enact the role of the inferior. Judith Rollins and Mary Romero describe a variety of rituals that affirmed the subordination and dependence of the domestic; for example, employers addressed household workers by their first names and required them to enter by the back door, eat in the kitchen, and wear uniforms. Domestics understood they were not to initiate conversation but were to remain standing or visibly engaged in work whenever the employer was in the room. They also had to accept with gratitude "gifts" of discarded clothing and leftover food (Rollins 1985, chap. 5; Romero 1987).

For their part, racial-ethnic women were acutely aware that they were trapped in domestic service by racism and not by lack of skills or intelligence. In their study of Black life in prewar Chicago, St. Clair Drake and Horace Cayton found that education did not provide African Americans with an entree into white collar work. They noted, "Colored girls are often bitter in their comments about a society which condemns them to the 'white folks' kitchen'" (Drake and Cayton 1962, 246). Thirty-five years later, Anna May Madison minced no words when she declared to anthropologist John Gwaltney: "Now, I don't do nothing for white women or men that they couldn't do for themselves. They don't do anything I couldn't learn to do every bit as well as they do it. But, you see, that goes right back to the life that you have to live. If that was the life I had been raised up in, I could be President or any other thing I got a chance to be" (Gwaltney 1980, 173).

Chicana domestics interviewed by Mary Romero in Colorado seemed at one level to accept the dominant culture's evaluation of their capabilities. Several said their options were limited by lack of education and training. However, they also realized they were restricted just because they were Mexican. Sixty-eight-year-old Mrs. Portillo told Romero: "There was a lot of discrimination, and Spanish people got just regular housework or laundry work. There was so much discrimination that Spanish people couldn't get jobs outside of washing dishes—things like that" (Romero 1988b, 86).

Similarly, many Japanese domestics reported that their choices were constrained because of language difficulties and lack of education, but they, too, recognized that color was decisive. Some nisei domestics had taken typing and business courses and some had college degrees, yet they had to settle for "school girl" jobs after completing their schooling. Mrs. Morita, who grew up in San Francisco and was graduated from high school in the 1930s, bluntly summarized her options: "In those days there was no two ways about it. If you were Japanese, you either worked in an art store ('oriental curios' shop) where they sell those little junks, or you worked as a domestic. . . . There was no Japanese girl working in an American firm" (Glenn 1986, 122).

Hanna Nelson, another of Gwaltney's informants, took the analysis one step further; she recognized the coercion that kept African American women in domestic service. She saw this arrangement as one that allowed white women to exploit Black women economically and emotionally and exposed Black women to sexual assaults by white men, often with white women's complicity. She says, "I am a woman sixty-one years old and I was born into this world with some talent. But I have done the work that my grandmother's mother did. It is not through any failing of mine that this is so. The whites took my mother's milk by force, and I have lived to hear a human creature of my sex try to force me by threat of hunger to give my milk to an able man. I have grown to womanhood in a world where the saner you are, the madder you are made to appear" (Gwaltney 1980, 7).

Race and gender consciousness

Hanna Nelson displays a consciousness of the politics of race and gender not found among white employers. Employers' and employees' fundamentally different positions within the division of reproductive labor gave them different interests and perspectives. Phyllis Palmer describes the problems the YWCA and other reform groups encountered when they attempted to establish voluntary standards and working hours for live-in domestics in the 1930s. White housewives invariably argued against any "rigid" limitation of hours; they insisted on provisions for emergencies that would override any hour limits. Housewives saw their own responsibilities as limitless, and apparently felt there was no justification for boundaries on domestics' responsibilities. They did not acknowledge the fundamental difference in their positions: they themselves gained status and privileges from their relationships with their husbands—relationships that depended on the performance of wifely duties. They expected domestics to devote long hours and hard work to help them succeed as wives, without, however, commensurate privileges and status. To challenge the inequitable gender division of labor was too difficult and threatening, so white housewives pushed the dilemma onto other women, holding them to the same high standards by which they themselves were imprisoned (Kaplan 1987; Palmer 1990).

Some domestic workers were highly conscious of their mistresses' subordination to their husbands and condemned their unwillingness to challenge their husbands' authority. Mabel Johns, a sixty-four-year-old widow, told Gwaltney:

> I work for a woman who has a good husband; the devil is good to her, anyway. Now that woman could be a good person if she didn't think she could just do everything and have everything. In this world whatsoever you get you will pay for. Now she is a grown woman, but she won't know that simple thing. I don't think there's anything wrong with her mind, but she is greedy and she don't believe in admitting that she is greedy. Now you may say what you willormay [sic] about people being good to you, but there just ain' a living soul in this world that thinks more of you than you do of yourself. . . . She's a grown woman, but she have to keep accounts and her husband tells her whether or not he will let her do thus-and-so or buy this or that. [Gwaltney 1980, 167]

Black domestics are also conscious that a white woman's status comes from her relationship to a white man, that she gains privileges from the relationship that blinds her to her own oppression, and that she therefore willingly participates in and gains advantages from the oppression of racial-ethnic women. Nancy White puts the matter powerfully when she says,

> My mother used to say that the black woman is the white man's mule and the white woman is his dog. Now, she said that to say this: we do the heavy work and get beat whether we do it well or not. But the white woman is closer to the master and he pats them on the head and lets them sleep in the house, but he ain' gon' treat neither one like he was dealing with a person. Now, if I was to tell a white woman that, the first thing she would do is to call you a nigger and then she'd be real nice to her husband so he would come out here and beat you for telling his wife the truth. [Gwaltney 1980, 148]

Rather than challenge the inequity in the relationship with their husbands, white women pushed the burden onto women with even less power. They could justify this only by denying the domestic worker's womanhood, by ignoring the employee's family ties and responsibilities. Susan Tucker found that southern white women talked about their servants with affection and expressed gratitude that they shared work with the servant that they would otherwise have to do alone. Yet the sense of commonality based on gender that the women expressed turned out to be one-way. Domestic workers knew that employers did not want to know much about their home situations (Kaplan 1987, 96; Tucker 1988). Mostly, the employers did not want domestics' personal needs to interfere with serving them. One domestic wrote that her employer berated her when she asked for a few hours off to pay her bills and take care of pressing business (Palmer 1990, 74). Of relations between white mistresses and Black domestics in the period from 1870 to 1920, Katzman says that in extreme cases "even the shared roles of motherhood could be denied." A Black child nurse reported in 1912 that she worked fourteen to sixteen hours a day caring for her mistress's four children. Describing her exist-ence as a "treadmill life," she reported that she was allowed to go home "only once in every two weeks, every other Sunday afternoon—even then I'm not permitted to stay all night. I see my own children only when they happen to see me on the streets when I am out with the children [of her mistress], or when my children come to the yard to see me, which isn't often, because my white folks don't like to see their servants' children hanging around their premises."[24]

While this case may be extreme, Tucker reports, on the basis of ex-tensive interviews with southern African American domestics, that even among live-out workers in the 1960s,

> White women were also not noted for asking about childcare ar-rangements. All whites, said one black woman, "assume you have a mother, or an older daughter to keep your child, so it's all right to leave your kids." Stories of white employers not believing the children of domestics were sick, but hearing this as an excuse not to work, were also common. Stories, too, of white women who did not inquire of a domestic's family—even when that domestic went on extended trips with the family—were not uncommon. And work on Christmas morning and other holidays for black mothers was not considered by white employers as unfair. Indeed, work on these days was seen as particularly important to the job. [Tucker 1988, 99]

The irony is, of course, that domestics saw their responsibilities as mothers as the central core of their identity. The Japanese American women I interviewed, the Chicana day workers Romero interviewed, and the African American domestics Bonnie Thornton Dill interviewed all emphasized the primacy of their role as mothers (Dill 1980; Glenn 1986; Romero 1988b). As a Japanese immigrant single parent expressed it, "My children come first. I'm working to upgrade my children." Another domestic, Mrs. Hiraoka, confided she hated household work but would

---

[24] "More Slavery at the South: A Negro Nurse," from the *Independent* (1912), in Katzman and Tuttle (1982, 176–85, 179).

keep working until her daughter graduated from optometry school.[25] Romero's day workers arranged their work hours to fit around their children's school hours so that they could be there when needed. For domestics, then, working had meaning precisely because it enabled them to provide for their children.

Perhaps the most universal theme in domestic workers' statements is that they are working so their own daughters will not have to go into domestic service and confront the same dilemmas of leaving their babies to work. A Japanese American domestic noted, "I tell my daughters all the time, 'As long as you get a steady job, stay in school. I want you to get a good job, not like me.' That's what I always tell my daughters: make sure you're not stuck."[26]

In a similar vein, Pearl Runner told Dill, "My main goal was I didn't want them to follow in my footsteps as far as working" (Dill 1980, 109). Domestic workers wanted to protect their daughters from both the hardships and the dangers that working in white homes posed. A Black domestic told Drake and Cayton of her hopes for her daughters: "I hope they may be able to escape a life as a domestic worker, for I know too well the things that make a girl desperate on these jobs" (Drake and Cayton 1962, 246).

When they succeed in helping their children do better than they themselves did, domestics may consider that the hardships were worthwhile. Looking back, Mrs. Runner is able to say, "I really feel that with all the struggling that I went through, I feel happy and proud that I was able to keep helping my children, that they listened and that they all went to high school. So when I look back, I really feel proud, even though at times the work was very hard and I came home very tired. But now, I feel proud about it. They all got their education" (Dill 1980, 113). Domestics thus have to grapple with yet another contradiction. They must confront, acknowledge, and convey the undesirable nature of the work they do to their children, as an object lesson and an admonition, and at the same time maintain their children's respect and their own sense of personal worth and dignity (Dill 1980, 110). When they successfully manage that contradiction, they refute their white employers' belief that "you are your work" (Gwaltney 1980, 174).

The racial division of public reproductive labor

As noted earlier, the increasing commodification of social reproduction since World War II has led to a dramatic growth in employment by

---

[25] From an interview conducted by the author in the San Francisco Bay area in 1977.

[26] Ibid.

women in such areas as food preparation and service, health care services, child care, and recreational services. The division of labor in public settings mirrors the division of labor in the household. Racial-ethnic women are employed to do the heavy, dirty, "back-room" chores of cooking and serving food in restaurants and cafeterias, cleaning rooms in hotels and office buildings, and caring for the elderly and ill in hospitals and nursing homes, including cleaning rooms, making beds, changing bed pans, and preparing food. In these same settings white women are disproportionately employed as lower-level professionals (e.g., nurses and social workers), technicians, and administrative support workers to carry out the more skilled and supervisory tasks.

The U.S. Census category of "service occupations except private household and protective services" roughly approximates what I mean by "institutional service work." It includes food preparation and service, health care service, cleaning and building services, and personal services.[27] In the United States as a whole, Black and Spanish-origin women are overrepresented in this set of occupations; in 1980 they made up 13.7 percent of all workers in the field, nearly double their proportion (7.0 percent) in the work force. White women (some of whom were of Spanish origin) were also overrepresented, but not to the same extent, making up 50.1 percent of all "service" workers, compared with their 36 percent share in the overall work force. (Black and Spanish-origin men made up 9.6 percent, and white men, who were 50 percent of the work force, made up the remaining 27.5 percent.)[28]

Because white women constitute the majority, institutional service work may not at first glance appear to be racialized. However, if we look more closely at the composition of specific jobs within the larger category, we find clear patterns of racial specialization. White women are preferred in positions requiring physical and social contact with the public, that is, waiters/waitresses, transportation attendants, hairdressers/cosmetologists, and dental assistants, while racial-ethnic women are preferred in dirty back-room jobs as maids, janitors/cleaners, kitchen workers, and nurse's aides.[29]

---

[27] The U.S. Labor Department and the U.S. Bureau of the Census divide service occupations into three major categories: "private household," "protective service," and "service occupations except private household and protective services." In this discussion, "service work" refers only to the latter. I omit private household workers, who have been discussed previously, and protective service workers, who include firefighters and police: these jobs, in addition to being male dominated and relatively well paid, carry some degree of authority, including the right to use force.

[28] Computed from U.S. Bureau of the Census (1984), chap. D, "Detailed Population Characteristics," pt. 1; "United States Summary," table 278: "Detailed Occupation of Employed Persons by Sex, Race and Spanish Origin, 1980.28."

[29] Ibid.

As in the case of domestic service, who does what varies regionally, following racial-ethnic caste lines in local economies. Racialization is clearest in local economies where a subordinate race/ethnic group is sizable enough to fill a substantial portion of jobs. In southern cities, Black women are twice as likely to be employed in service occupations as white women. For example, in Atlanta in 1980, 20.8 percent of African American women were so employed, compared with 10.4 percent of white women. While they were less than one-quarter (23.9 percent) of all women workers, they were nearly two-fifths (38.3 percent) of women service workers. In Memphis, 25.9 percent of African American women compared with 10.2 percent of white women were in services; though they made up only a third (34.5 percent) of the female work force, African American women were nearly three-fifths (57.2 percent) of women employed in this field. In southwestern cities Spanish-origin women specialize in service work. In San Antonio, 21.9 percent of Spanish-origin women were so employed, compared with 11.6 percent of non-Spanish-origin white women; in that city half (49.8 percent) of all women service workers were Spanish-origin, while Anglos, who made up two-thirds (64.0 percent) of the female work force, were a little over a third (36.4 percent) of those in the service category. In El Paso, 16.9 percent of Spanish-origin women were service workers compared with 10.8 percent of Anglo women, and they made up two-thirds (66.1 percent) of those in service. Finally, in Honolulu, Asian and Pacific Islanders constituted 68.6 percent of the female work force, but 74.8 percent of those were in service jobs. Overall, these jobs employed 21.6 percent of all Asian and Pacific Islander women, compared with 13.7 percent of white non-Spanish-origin women.[30]

[30] Figures computed from table 279 in each of the state chapters of the following: U.S. Bureau of the Census (1984), chap. D, "Detailed Population Characteristics," pt. 6: "California"; pt. 12: "Georgia"; pt. 13: "Hawaii"; pt. 15: "Illinois"; pt. 44: "Tennessee"; and pt. 45: "Texas." The figures for Anglos in the Southwest are estimates, based on the assumption that most "Spanish-origin" people are Mexican, and that Mexicans, when given a racial designation, are counted as whites. Specifically, the excess left after the "total" is subtracted from the "sum" of white, Black, American Indian/Eskimo-/Aleut, Asian and Pacific Islander, and "Spanish-origin" is subtracted from the white figure. The remainder is counted as "Anglo." Because of the way "Spanish-origin" cross-cuts race (Spanish-origin individuals can be counted as white, Black, or any other race), I did not attempt to compute figures for Latinos or Anglos in cities where Spanish-origin individuals are likely to be more distributed in some unknown proportion between Black and white. This would be the case, e.g., with the large Puerto Rican population in New York City. Thus I have not attempted to compute Latino versus Anglo data for New York and Chicago. Note also that the meaning of *white* differs by locale and that the local terms *Anglo* and *haole* are not synonymous with *white*. The "white" category in Hawaii includes Portuguese, who, because of their history as plantation labor, are distinguished from haoles in the local ethnic ranking system. The U.S. Census category system does not capture the local construction of race/ethnicity.

Particularly striking is the case of cleaning and building services. This category—which includes maids, housemen, janitors, and cleaners—is prototypically "dirty work." In Memphis, one out of every twelve Black women (8.2 percent) was in cleaning and building services, and Blacks were 88.1 percent of the women in this occupation. In contrast, only one out of every 200 white women (0.5 percent) was so employed. In Atlanta, 6.6 percent of Black women were in this field—constituting 74.6 percent of the women in these jobs—compared with only 0.7 percent of white women. Similarly, in El Paso, 4.2 percent of Spanish-origin women (versus 0.6 percent of Anglo women) were in cleaning and building services—making up 90.0 percent of the women in this field. And in San Antonio the Spanish and Anglo percentages were 5.3 percent versus 1.1 percent, respectively, with Spanish-origin women 73.5 percent of women in these occupations. Finally, in Honolulu, 4.7 percent of Asian and Pacific Islander women were in these occupations, making up 86.6 percent of the total. Only 1.3 percent of white women were so employed.[31]

From personal to structural hierarchy

Does a shift from domestic service to low-level service occupations represent progress for racial-ethnic women? At first glance it appears not to bring much improvement. After domestic service, these are the lowest paid of all occupational groupings. In 1986 service workers were nearly two-thirds (62 percent) of workers in the United States earning at or below minimum wage.[32] As in domestic service, the jobs are often part-time and seasonal, offer few or no medical and other benefits, have low rates of unionization, and subject workers to arbitrary supervision. The service worker also often performs in a public setting the same sorts of tasks that servants did in a private setting. Furthermore, established patterns of race/gender domination-subordination are often incorporated into the authority structure of organizations. Traditional gender-race etiquette shapes face-to-face interaction in the workplace. Duke University Hospital in North Carolina from its founding in 1929 adopted paternalistic policies toward its Black employees. Black workers were highly conscious of this, as evidenced by their references to "the plantation system" at Duke (Sacks 1988, 46).[33]

Still, service workers, especially those who have worked as domestics, are convinced that "public jobs" are preferable to domestic service. They appreciate not being personally subordinate to an individual employer

---

[31] Computed from tables specified in ibid.

[32] The federal minimum wage was $3.35 in 1986. Over a quarter (26.0 percent) of all workers in these service occupations worked at or below this wage. See Mellor (1987, esp. 37).

[33] Paternalism is not limited to southern hospitals; similar policies were in place at Montefiore Hospital in New York City. See Fink and Greenberg (1979).

and not having to do "their" dirty work on "their" property. Relations with supervisors and clients are hierarchical, but they are embedded in an impersonal structure governed by more explicit contractual obligations and limits. Also important is the presence of a work group for sociability and support. Workplace culture offers an alternative system of values from that imposed by managers (Benson 1986).[34] Experienced workers socialize newcomers, teaching them how to respond to pressures to speed up work, to negotiate work loads, and to demand respect from superiors. While the isolated domestic finds it difficult to resist demeaning treatment, the peer group in public settings provides backing for individuals to stand up to the boss.

That subordination is usually not as direct and personal in public settings as in the private household does not mean, however, that race and gender hierarchy is diminished in importance. Rather, it changes form, becoming institutionalized within organizational structures. Hierarchy is elaborated through a detailed division of labor that separates conception from execution and allows those at the top to control the work process. Ranking is based ostensibly on expertise, education, and formal credentials.

The elaboration is especially marked in technologically oriented organizations that employ large numbers of professionals, as is the case with health care institutions. Visual observation of any hospital reveals the hierarchical race and gender division of labor: at the top are the physicians, setting policy and initiating work for others; they are disproportionately white and male. Directly below, performing medical tasks and patient care as delegated by physicians and enforcing hospital rules, are the registered nurses (RNs), who are overwhelmingly female and disproportionately white. Under the registered nurses and often supervised by them are the licensed practical nurses (LPNs), also female but disproportionately women of color. At about the same level are the technologists and technicians who carry out various tests and procedures and the "administrative service" staff in the offices; these categories tend to be female and white. Finally, at the bottom of the pyramid are the nurse's aides, predominantly women of color; housekeepers and kitchen workers, overwhelmingly women of color; and orderlies and cleaners, primarily men of color. They constitute the "hands" that perform routine work directed by others.

The racial division of labor in nursing

A study of stratification in the nursing labor force illustrates the race and gender construction of public reproductive labor. At the top in terms

---

[34] See also many examples of workplace cultures supporting resistance in Sacks and Remy (1984) and Lamphere (1987).

of status, authority, and pay are the RNs, graduates of two-, three-, or four-year hospital or college-based programs. Unlike the lower ranks, registered nursing offers a career ladder. Starting as a staff nurse, a hospital RN can rise to head nurse, nursing supervisor, and finally, director of nursing. In 1980 whites were 86.7 percent of RNs even though they were only 76.7 percent of the population. The LPNs, who make up the second grade of nursing, generally have had twelve months' training in a technical institute or community college. The LPNs are supervised by RNs and may oversee the work of aides. Racial-ethnic workers constituted 23.4 percent of LPNs, with Blacks, who were 11.7 percent of the population, making up fully 17.9 percent. Below the LPNs in the hierarchy are the nurse's aides (NAs), who typically have on-the-job training of four to six weeks. Orderlies, attendants, home health aides, and patient care assistants also fall into this category. These workers perform housekeeping and routine caregiving tasks "delegated by an RN and performed under the direction of an RN or LPN." Among nurse's aides, 34.6 percent were minorities, with Blacks making up 27.0 percent of all aides.[35]

Nationally, Latinas were underrepresented in health care services but were found in nurse's aide positions in proportion to their numbers—making up 5.2 percent of the total. The lower two grades of nursing labor thus appear to be Black specialties. However, in some localities other women of color are concentrated in these jobs. In San Antonio, 48 percent of aides were Spanish-origin, while only 15.1 percent of the RNs were. Similarly, in El Paso, 61.5 percent of aides were Spanish-origin, compared with 22.8 percent of RNs. In Honolulu, Asian and Pacific Islanders who were 68.6 percent of the female labor force made up 72.3 percent of the NAs but only 45.7 percent of the RNs.[36]

Familial symbolism and the race and gender construction of nursing. How did the present ranking system and sorting by race/ethnic category in nursing come about? How did the activities of white nurses contribute to the structuring? And how did racial-ethnic women respond to constraints?

[35] American Nurses' Association 1965, 6. Reflecting differences in status and authority, RNs earn 20–40 percent more than LPNs and 60–150 percent more than NAs (U.S. Department of Labor 1987a, 1987b).

[36] For the national level, see U.S. Bureau of the Census (1984), chap. D, "Detailed Population Characteristics," pt. 1: "United States Summary," table 278. For statistics on RNs and aides in San Antonio, El Paso, and Honolulu, see U.S. Bureau of the Census (1984), chap. D, "Detailed Population Characteristics," pt. 13: "Hawaii"; and pt. 45: "Texas," table 279.

The stratification of nursing labor can be traced to the beginnings of organized nursing in the 1870s. However, until the 1930s grading was loose. A broad distinction was made between so-called trained nurses, who were graduates of hospital schools or collegiate programs, and untrained nurses, referred to—often interchangeably—as "practical nurses," "hospital helpers," "nursing assistants," "nursing aides," or simply as "aides" (Cannings and Lazonik 1975; Reverby 1987).

During this period health work in hospitals was divided between male physicians (patient diagnosis and curing) and female nursing staff (patient care) in a fashion analogous to the separate spheres prescribed for middle-class households. Nurses and physicians each had primary responsibility for and authority within their own spheres, but nurses were subject to the ultimate authority of physicians. The separation gave women power in a way that did not challenge male domination. Eva Gamarinikow likens the position of the British nursing matron to that of an upper-class woman in a Victorian household who supervised a large household staff but was subordinate to her husband (Gamarinikow 1978). Taking the analogy a step further, Ann Game and Rosemary Pringle describe the pre–World War II hospital as operating under a system of controls based on familial symbolism. Physicians were the authoritative father figures, while trained nurses were the mothers overseeing the care of patients, who were viewed as dependent children. Student nurses and practical nurses were, in this scheme, in the position of servants, expected to follow orders and subject to strict discipline (Game and Pringle 1983, 99–100).

Like the middle-class white housewives who accepted the domestic ideology, white nursing leaders rarely challenged the familial symbolism supporting the gender division of labor in health care. The boldest advocated at most a dual-headed family (Reverby 1987, 71–75). They acceded to the racial implications of the family metaphor as well. If nurses were mothers in a family headed by white men, they had to be white. And, indeed, trained nursing was an almost exclusively white preserve. As Susan Reverby notes, "In 1910 and 1920, for example, less than 3% of the trained nurses in the United States were black, whereas black women made up 17.6% and 24.0% respectively of the female working population" (Reverby 1987, 71–75).

The scarcity of Black women is hardly surprising. Nursing schools in the South excluded Blacks altogether, while northern schools maintained strict quotas. Typical was the policy of the New England Hospital for Women and Children, which by charter could only admit "one Negro and one Jewish student" a year (Hine 1989, 6). Black women who managed to become trained nurses did so through separate Black training schools and were usually restricted to serving Black patients, whether in "integrated" hospitals in the North or segregated Black hospitals in the South.[37]

White nursing leaders and administrators justified exclusion by appeals to racist ideology. Anne Bess Feeback, the superintendent of nurses for Henry Grady Hospital in Atlanta, declared that Negro women under her supervision had no morals: "They are such liars. . . . They shift responsibility whenever they can. . . . They quarrel constantly among themselves and will cut up each other's clothes for spite. . . . Unless they are constantly watched, they will steal anything in sight" (Hine 1985, 101). Perhaps the most consistent refrain was that Black women were deficient in the qualities needed to be good nurses: they lacked executive skills, intelligence, strength of character, and the ability to withstand pressure. Thus Margaret Butler, chief nurse in the Chicago City Health Department, contended that Black nurses' techniques were "inferior to that of the white nurses, they are not punctual, and are incapable of analyzing a social situation." Apparently Black nurses did not accept white notions of racial inferiority, for Butler also complains about their tendency "to organize against authority" and "to engage in political intrigue" (Hine 1989, 99). Another white nursing educator, Margaret Bruesche, suggested that although Black women lacked the ability to become trained nurses, they "could fill a great need in the South as a trained attendant, who would work for a lower wage than a fully trained woman" (Hine 1989, 101). Even those white nursing leaders sympathetic to Black aspirations agreed that Black nurses should not be put in supervisory positions because white nurses would never submit to their authority.

Similar ideas about the proper place of "Orientals" in nursing were held by haole nursing leaders in pre–World War II Hawaii. White-run hospitals and clinics recruited haoles from the mainland, especially for senior nurse positions, rather than hiring or promoting locally trained Asian American nurses. This pattern was well known enough for a University of Hawaii researcher to ask a haole health administrator whether it was true that "oriental nurses do not reach the higher positions of the profession?" Mr. "C" confirmed this: "Well, there again it is a matter of qualification. There is a limit to the number of nurses we can produce

---

[37] For accounts of Black women in nursing, see also Hine (1985) and Carnegie (1986). Hine (1989, chap. 7) makes it clear that Black nurses served Black patients not just because they were restricted but because they wanted to meet Black health care needs. Blacks were excluded from membership in two of the main national organizations for nurses, the National League of Nursing Education and the American Nurses' Association. And although they formed their own organizations such as the National Association of Colored Graduate Nurses and enjoyed the respect of the Black community, Black nurses remained subordinated within the white-dominated nursing profession.

here. For that reason we have to hire from the mainland. Local girls cannot compete with the experience of mainland haole girls. In order to induce haole nurses here we could not possibly put them under an oriental nurse because that would make them race conscious right at the start. And as I said before, Japanese don't make good executives."[38] Because of the racial caste system in Hawaii, Japanese American women who managed to get into nursing were not seen as qualified or competent to do professional work. The chairman of the Territorial Nurses Association noted that "before the war (started), our local nurses were looked down (upon) because they were mostly Japanese. . . . The Japanese nurses feel they can get along better with Mainland nurses than local haole nurses. That is true even outside of the profession. I remember hearing a Hawaiian born haole dentist say, 'I was never so shocked as when I saw a white man shine shoes when I first went to the Mainland.' Haoles here feel only orientals and other non-haoles should do menial work."[39]

The systematic grading of nursing labor into three ranks was accomplished in the 1930s and forties as physician-controlled hospital administrations moved to establish "sound business" practices to contain costs and consolidate physician control of health care.[40] High-tech medical and diagnostic procedures provided an impetus for ever-greater specialization. Hospitals adopted Taylorist principles of "scientific management," separating planning and technical tasks from execution and manual labor. They began to hire thousands of subsidiary workers and created the licensed practical nurse, a position for a graduate of a one-year technical program, to perform routine housekeeping and patient care. With fewer discriminatory barriers and shorter training requirements, LPN positions were accessible to women of color who wanted to become nurses.

The lowest level of nursing workers, nurse's aides, also was defined in the 1930s, when the American Red Cross started offering ten-week courses to train aides for hospitals. This category expanded rapidly in the 1940s, doubling from 102,000 workers in 1940 to 212,000 in 1950 (Cannings and Lazonik 1975, 200–201). This occupation seems to have been designed deliberately to make use of African American labor in the

[38] Document Nu21-I, p. 2, Romanzo Adams Research Laboratory papers, A1989-006, box 17, folder 1.
[39] Document Nu10-I, p. 3, Romanzo Adams Research Laboratory papers, A1989-006, box 17, folder 4.
[40] This was one outcome of the protracted and eventually successful struggle waged by physicians to gain control over all health care. For an account of how physicians established hospitals as the main site for medical treatment and gained authority over "subsidiary" health occupations, see Starr (1982). For accounts of nurses' struggle for autonomy and their incorporation into hospitals, see Reverby (1987) and also Wagner (1980).

wake of labor shortages during and after World War II. A 1948 report on nursing told the story of how nurse's aides replaced the heretofore volunteer corps of ward attendants: "In response to this request for persons designated as nursing aides, the hospital discovered among the large Negro community a hitherto untapped reservoir of personnel, well above the ward attendant group in intelligence and personality" (Cannings and Lazonik 1975, 201).

One reason for their superiority can be deduced: they often were overqualified. Barred from entry into better occupations, capable, well-educated Black women turned to nurse's aide work as an alternative to domestic service.

In the meantime RNs continued their struggle to achieve professional status by claiming exclusive rights over "skilled" nursing work. Some nurses, especially rank-and-file general duty nurses, called for an outright ban on employing untrained nurses. Many leaders of nursing organizations, however, favored accepting subsidiary workers to perform housekeeping and other routine chores so that graduate nurses would be free for more professional work. Hospital administrators assured RNs that aides would be paid less and assigned non-nursing functions and that only trained nurses would be allowed supervisory roles. One administrator claimed that aide trainees were told repeatedly that "they are not and will not be nurses" (Reverby 1987, 194).

In the end, the leaders of organized nursing accepted the formal stratification of nursing and turned their attention to circumscribing the education and duties of the lower grades to ensure their differentiation from "professional" nurses. Indeed, an RN arguing for the need to train and license practical nurses and laying out a model curriculum for LPNs warned: "Overtraining can be a serious danger. The practical nurse who has a course of over fifteen months (theory and practice) gets a false impression of her abilities and builds up the unwarranted belief that she can practice as a professional nurse" (Deming 1947, 26). Hospital administrators took advantage of race and class divisions and RNs' anxieties about their status to further their own agenda. Their strategy of co-opting part of the work force (RNs) and restricting the mobility and wages of another part (LPNs and NAs) undermined solidarity among groups that might otherwise have united around common interests.

Nursing aides: Consciousness of race and gender.   The hierarchy in health care has come to be justified less in terms of family symbolism and more in terms of bureaucratic efficiency. Within the new bureaucratic structures, race and gender ordering is inherent in the job definitions. The nurse's aide job is defined as unskilled and menial; hence, the women who do it are, too. Nurse's aides frequently confront a discrepancy, however, between how their jobs are defined (unskilled and subordinate) and what they actually are allowed or expected to do (exercise skill and judgment). Lillian Roberts's experiences illustrate the disjunction. Assigned to the nursery, she was fortunate to work with a white southern RN who was willing to teach her. "I would ask her about all kinds of deformities that we would see in the nursery, the color of a baby, and why this was happening and why the other was happening. And then I explored with her using my own analysis of things. Sometimes I'd be right just in observing and putting some common sense into it. Before long, when the interns would come in to examine the babies, I could tell them what was wrong with every baby. I'd have them lined up for them" (Reverby 1979, 297–98).

The expertise Roberts developed through observation, questioning, and deduction was not recognized, however. Thirty years later Roberts still smarts from the injustice of not being allowed to sit in on the shift reports: "They never dignify you with that. Even though it would help you give better care. There were limitations on what I could do" (Reverby 1979, 298–99).

She had to assume a deferential manner when dealing with white medical students and personnel, even those who had much less experience than she had. Sometimes she would be left in charge of the nursery and "I'd get a whole mess of new students in there who didn't know what to do. I would very diplomatically have to direct them, although they resented to hell that I was both black and a nurse's aide. But I had to do it in such a way that they didn't feel I was claiming to know more than they did" (Reverby 1979, 298). One of her biggest frustrations was not being allowed to get on-the-job training to advance. Roberts describes the "box" she was in: "I couldn't have afforded to go to nursing school. I needed the income, and you can't just quit a job and go to school. I was caught in a box, and the salary wasn't big enough to save to go to school. And getting into the nursing schools was a real racist problem as well. So there was a combination of many things. And I used to say, '"Why does this country have to go elsewhere and get people when people like myself want to do something?"'" (Reverby 1979, 299). When she became a union organizer, her proudest accomplishment was to set up a program in New York that allowed aides to be trained on the job to become LPNs.

While Roberts's experience working in a hospital was typical in the 1940s and 1950s, today the typical aide is employed in a nursing home, in a convalescent home, or in home health care. In these settings, aides are the primary caregivers.[41] The demand for their services continues to

[41] For example, it has been estimated that 80 percent of all patient care in nursing homes is provided by nurse's aides (see Coleman 1989, 5). In 1988, 1,559,000 persons

grow as treatment increasingly shifts out of hospitals and into such set-
tings. Thus, even though aides have lost ground to RNs in hospitals,
which have reorganized nursing services to recreate RNs as generalists,
aides are expected to remain among the fastest-growing occupations
through the end of the century (Sekcenski 1981, 10–16).[42]

Whatever the setting, aide work continues to be a specialty of racial-
ethnic women. The work is seen as unskilled and subordinate and thus
appropriate to their qualifications and status. This point was brought
home to Timothy Diamond during the training course he attended as the
sole white male in a mostly Black female group of trainees: "We learned
elementary biology and how we were never to do health care without first
consulting someone in authority; and we learned not to ask questions but
to do as we were told. As one of the students, a black woman from
Jamaica used to joke, 'I can't figure out whether they're trying to teach us
to be nurses' aides or black women' " (Diamond 1988, 40).

What exactly is the nature of the reproductive labor that these largely
minority and supposedly unskilled aides and assistants perform? They do
most of the day-to-day, face-to-face work of caring for the ill and dis-
abled: helping patients dress or change gowns, taking vital signs (tem-
perature, blood pressure, pulse), assisting patients to shower or giving
bed baths, emptying bedpans or assisting patients to toilet, changing
sheets and keeping the area tidy, and feeding patients who cannot feed
themselves. There is much "dirty" work, such as cleaning up incontinent
patients. Yet there is another, unacknowledged, mental and emotional
dimension to the work: listening to the reminiscences of elderly patients
to help them hold on to their memory, comforting frightened patients
about to undergo surgery, and providing the only human contact some
patients get. This caring work is largely invisible, and the skills required
to do it are not recognized as real skills.[43]

That these nurse's aides are performing reproductive labor on behalf
of other women (and ultimately for the benefit of households, industry,
and the state) becomes clear when one considers who would do it if paid
workers did not. Indeed, we confront that situation frequently today, as
hospitals reduce the length of patient stays to cut costs. Patients are
released "quicker and sicker" (Sacks 1988, 165). This policy makes sense

---

were employed as RNs, 423,00 as LPNs, 1,404,00 as nurse's aides, orderlies, and atten-
dants, and 407,000 as health aides (U.S. Department of Labor 1989, table 22). Nurse's
aides and home health care aides are expected to be the fastest-growing occupations
through the 1990s, according to Silvestri and Lukasiewicz (1987, 59).

[42] For a description of trends and projections to the year 2000, see Silvestri and
Lukasiewicz (1987).

[43] Feminists have pointed to the undervaluing of female-typed skills, especially those
involved in "caring" work (see Rose 1986).

only if it is assumed that patients have someone to provide interim care, administer medication, prepare meals, and clean for them until they can care for themselves. If such a person exists, most likely it is a woman—a daughter, wife, mother, or sister. She may have to take time off from her job or quit. Her unpaid labor takes the place of the paid work of a nurse's aide or assistant and saves the hospital labor costs. Her labor is thereby appropriated to ensure profit (Glazer 1988). Thus, the situation of women as unpaid reproductive workers at home is inextricably bound to that of women as paid reproductive workers.

Conclusions and implications

This article began with the observation that the racial division of reproductive labor has been overlooked in the separate literatures on race and gender. The distinct exploitation of women of color and an important source of difference among women have thereby been ignored. How, though, does a historical analysis of the racial division of reproductive labor illuminate the lives of women of color and white women? What are its implications for concerted political action? In order to tackle these questions, we need to address a broader question, namely, how does the analysis advance our understanding of race and gender? Does it take us beyond the additive models I have criticized?

The social construction of race and gender

Tracing how race and gender have been fashioned in one area of women's work helps us understand them as socially constructed systems of relationships—including symbols, normative beliefs, and practices—organized around perceived differences. This understanding is an important counter to the universalizing tendencies in feminist thought. When feminists perceive reproductive labor only as gendered, they imply that domestic labor is identical for all women and that it therefore can be the basis of a common identity of womanhood. By not recognizing the different relationships women have had to such supposedly universal female experiences as motherhood and domesticity, they risk essentializing gender—treating it as static, fixed, eternal, and natural. They fail to take seriously a basic premise of feminist thought, that gender is a social construct.

If race and gender are socially constructed systems, then they must arise at specific moments in particular circumstances and change as these circumstances change. We can study their appearance, variation, and modification over time. I have suggested that one vantage point for looking at their development in the United States is in the changing division of labor in local economies. A key site for the emergence of concepts of gendered and racialized labor has been in regions characterized by dual labor systems.

As subordinate-race women within dual labor systems, African American, Mexican American, and Japanese American women were drawn into domestic service by a combination of economic need, restricted opportunities, and educational and employment tracking mechanisms. Once they were in service, their association with "degraded" labor affirmed their supposed natural inferiority. Although ideologies of "race" and "racial difference" justifying the dual labor system already were in place, specific ideas about racial-ethnic womanhood were invented and enacted in everyday interactions between mistresses and workers. Thus ideologies of race and gender were created and verified in daily life (Fields 1982).

Two fundamental elements in the construction of racial-ethnic womanhood were the notion of inherent traits that suited the women for service and the denial of the women's identities as wives and mothers in their own right. Employers accepted a cult of domesticity that purported to elevate the status of women as mothers and homemakers, yet they made demands on domestics that hampered them from carrying out these responsibilities in their own households. How could employers maintain such seemingly inconsistent orientations? Racial ideology was critical in resolving the contradiction: it explained why women of color were suited for degrading work. Racial characterizations effectively neutralized the racial-ethnic woman's womanhood, allowing the mistress to be "unaware" of the domestic's relationship to her own children and household. The exploitation of racial-ethnic women's physical, emotional, and mental work for the benefit of white households thus could be rendered invisible in consciousness if not in reality.

With the shift of reproductive labor from household to market, face-to-face hierarchy has been replaced by structural hierarchy. In institutional settings, stratification is built into organizational structures, including lines of authority, job descriptions, rules, and spatial and temporal segregation. Distance between higher and lower orders is ensured by structural segregation. Indeed, much routine service work is organized to be out of sight: it takes place behind institutional walls where outsiders rarely penetrate (e.g., nursing homes, chronic care facilities), in back rooms (e.g., restaurant kitchens), or at night or other times when occupants are gone (e.g., in office buildings and hotels). Workers may appreciate this time and space segregation because it allows them some autonomy and freedom from demeaning interactions. It also makes them and their work invisible, however. In this situation, more privileged women do not have to acknowledge the workers or to confront the contradiction between shared womanhood and inequality by race and class. Racial ideology is not necessary to explain or justify exploitation, not for lack of racism, but because the justification for inequality does not have to be elaborated in specifically racial terms: instead it can be cast in terms of differences in training, skill, or education.[44]

Because they are socially constructed, race and gender systems are subject to contestation and struggle. Racial-ethnic women continually have challenged the devaluation of their womanhood. Domestics often did so covertly. They learned to dissemble, consciously "putting on an act" while inwardly rejecting their employers' premises and maintaining a separate identity rooted in their families and communities. As noted earlier, institutional service workers can resist demeaning treatment more openly because they have the support of peers. Minority-race women hospital workers have been in the forefront of labor militancy, staging walkouts and strikes and organizing workplaces. In both domestic service and institutional service work, women have transcended the limitations of their work by focusing on longer-term goals, such as their children's future.

Beyond additive models: Race and gender as interlocking systems

As the foregoing examples show, race and gender constructs are inextricably intertwined. Each develops in the context of the other; they cannot be separated. This is important because when we see reproductive labor only as gendered, we extract gender from its context, which includes other interacting systems of power. If we begin with gender separated out, then we have to put race and class back in when we consider women of color and working-class women. We thus end up with an additive model in which white women have only gender and women of color have gender plus race.

The interlock is evident in the case studies of domestic workers and nurse's aides. In the traditional middle-class household, the availability of cheap female domestic labor buttressed white male privilege by perpetuating the concept of reproductive labor as women's work, sustaining the illusion of a protected private sphere for women and displacing conflict away from husband and wife to struggles between housewife and domestic.

The racial division of labor also bolstered the gender division of labor indirectly by offering white women a slightly more privileged position in exchange for accepting domesticity. Expanding on Judith Rollins's notion that white housewives gained an elevated self-identity by casting Black domestics as inferior contrast figures, Phyllis Palmer suggests the dependent position of the middle-class housewife made a contrasting

---

[44] That is, the concentration of minority workers in lower-level jobs can be attributed to their lack of "human capital"—qualifications—needed for certain jobs.

figure necessary. A dualistic conception of women as "good" and "bad," long a part of western cultural tradition, provided ready-made categories for casting white and racial-ethnic women as oppositional figures (Davidoff 1979; Palmer 1990, 11, 137–39). The racial division of reproductive labor served to channel and recast these dualistic conceptions into racialized gender constructs. By providing them an acceptable self-image, racial constructs gave white housewives a stake in a system that ultimately oppressed them.

The racial division of labor similarly protects white male privilege in institutional settings. White men, after all, still dominate in professional and higher management positions where they benefit from the paid and unpaid services of women. And as in domestic service, conflict between men and women is redirected into clashes among women. This displacement is evident in health care organizations. Because physicians and administrators control the work of other health workers, we would expect the main conflict to be between doctors and nurses over work load, allocation of tasks, wages, and working conditions. The racial division of nursing labor allows some of the tension to be redirected so that friction arises between registered nurses and aides over work assignments and supervision.

In both household and institutional settings, white professional and managerial men are the group most insulated from dirty work and contact with those who do it. White women are frequently the mediators who have to negotiate between white male superiors and racial-ethnic subordinates. Thus race and gender dynamics are played out in a three-way relationship involving white men, white women, and women of color.

Beyond difference: Race and gender as relational constructs

Focusing on the racial division of reproductive labor also uncovers the relational nature of race and gender. By "relational" I mean that each is made up of categories (e.g., male/female, Anglo/Latino) that are positioned, and therefore gain meaning, in relation to each other (Barrett 1987). Power, status, and privilege are axes along which categories are positioned. Thus, to represent race and gender as relationally constructed is to assert that the experiences of white women and women of color are not just different but connected in systematic ways.

The interdependence is easier to see in the domestic work setting because the two groups of women confront one another face-to-face. That the higher standard of living of one woman is made possible by, and also helps to perpetuate, the other's lower standard of living is clearly evident. In institutional service work the relationship between those who do the dirty work and those who benefit from it is mediated and buffered by institutional structures, so the dependence of one group on the other for its standard of living is not apparent. Nonetheless, interdependence exists, even if white women do not come into actual contact with women of color.[45]

The notion of relationality also recognizes that white and racial-ethnic women have different standpoints by virtue of their divergent positions. This is an important corrective to feminist theories of gendered thought that posit universal female modes of thinking growing out of common experiences such as domesticity and motherhood. When they portray reproductive labor only as gendered, they assume there is only one standpoint—that of white women. Hence, the activities and experiences of middle-class women become generic "female" experiences and activities, and those of other groups become variant, deviant, or specialized.

In line with recent works on African American, Asian American, and Latina feminist thought, we see that taking the standpoint of women of color gives us a different and more critical perspective on race and gender systems (Garcia 1989; Anzaldúa 1990; Collins 1990.) Domestic workers in particular—because they directly confront the contradictions in their lives and those of their mistresses—develop an acute consciousness of the interlocking nature of race and gender oppression.

Perhaps a less obvious point is that understanding race and gender as relational systems also illuminates the lives of white American women. White womanhood has been constructed not in isolation but in relation to that of women of color. Therefore, race is integral to white women's gender identities. In addition, seeing variation in racial division of labor across time in different regions gives us a more variegated picture of white middle-class womanhood. White women's lives have been lived in many circumstances; their "gender" has been constructed in relation to varying others, not just to Black women. Conceptualizing white womanhood as monolithically defined in opposition to men or to Black women ignores complexity and variation in the experiences of white women.

Implications for feminist politics

Understanding race and gender as relational, interlocking, socially constructed systems affects how we strategize for change. If race and gender are socially constructed rather than being "real" referents in the material world, then they can be deconstructed and challenged. Feminists have made considerable strides in deconstructing gender; we now need to focus on deconstructing gender and race simultaneously. An initial step in this process is to expose the structures that support the present division of labor and the constructions of race and gender around it.

---

[45] Elsa Barkley Brown pointed this out to me in a personal communication.

Seeing race and gender as interlocking systems, however, alerts us to sources of inertia and resistance to change. The discussion of how the racial division of labor reinforced the gender division of labor makes clear that tackling gender hierarchy requires simultaneously addressing race hierarchy. As long as the gender division of labor remains intact, it will be in the short-term interest of white women to support or at least overlook the racial division of labor because it ensures that the very worst labor is performed by someone else. Yet, as long as white women support the racial division of labor, they will have less impetus to struggle to change the gender division of labor. This quandary is apparent in cities such as Los Angeles, which have witnessed a large influx of immigrant women fleeing violence and poverty in Latin America, Southeast Asia, and the Caribbean. These women form a large reserve army of low-wage labor for both domestic service and institutional service work. Anglo women who ordinarily would not be able to afford servants are employing illegal immigrants as maids at below-minimum wages (McConoway 1987). Not only does this practice diffuse pressure for a more equitable sharing of household work but it also recreates race and gender ideologies that justify the subordination of women of color. Having a Latino or Black maid picking up and cleaning after them teaches Anglo children that some people exist primarily to do work that Anglos do not want to do for themselves.

Acknowledging the relational nature of race and gender and therefore the interdependence between groups means that we recognize conflicting interests among women. Two examples illustrate the divergence. With the move into the labor force of all races and classes of women, it is tempting to think that we can find unity around the common problems of "working women." With that in mind, feminist policymakers have called for expanding services to assist employed mothers in such areas as child care and elderly care. We need to ask, Who is going to do the work? Who will benefit from increased services? The historical record suggests that it will be women of color, many of them new immigrants, who will do the work and that it will be middle-class women who will receive the services. Not so coincidentally, public officials seeking to reduce welfare costs are promulgating regulations requiring women on public assistance to work. The needs of employed middle-class women and women on welfare might thus be thought to coincide: the needs of the former for services might be met by employing the latter to provide the services. The divergence in interest becomes apparent, however, when we consider that employment in service jobs at current wage levels guarantees that their occupants will remain poor. However, raising their wages so that they can actually support themselves and their children at a decent level would mean many middle-class women could not afford these services.

A second example of an issue that at first blush appears to bridge race and ethnic lines is the continuing earnings disparity between men and women. Because occupational segregation, the concentration of women in low-paying, female-dominated occupations, stands as the major obstacle to wage equity, some feminist policymakers have embraced the concept of comparable worth (Hartmann 1985; Acker 1989). This strategy calls for equalizing pay for "male" and "female" jobs requiring similar levels of skill and responsibility, even if differing in content. Comparable worth accepts the validity of a job hierarchy and differential pay based on "real" differences in skills and responsibility. Thus, for example, it attacks the differential between nurses and pharmacists but leaves intact the differential between nurses and nurse's aides. Yet the division between "skilled" and "unskilled" jobs is exactly where the racial division typically falls. To address the problems of women of color service workers would require a fundamental attack on the concept of a hierarchy of worth; it would call for flattening the wage differentials between highest- and lowest-paid ranks. A claim would have to be made for the right of all workers to a living wage, regardless of skill or responsibility.

These examples suggest that forging a political agenda that addresses the universal needs of women is highly problematic not just because women's priorities differ but because gains for some groups may require a corresponding loss of advantage and privilege for others. As the history of the racial division of reproductive labor reveals, conflict and contestation among women over definitions of womanhood, over work, and over the conditions of family life are part of our legacy as well as the current reality. This does not mean we give up the goal of concerted struggle. It means we give up trying falsely to harmonize women's interests. Appreciating the ways race and gender division of labor creates both hierarchy and interdependence may be a better way to reach an understanding of the interconnectedness of women's lives.

Departments of Ethnic Studies and Women's Studies
University of California, Berkeley

References

Abramovitz, Mimi. 1988. *Regulating the Lives of Women: Social Welfare Policy from Colonial Times to the Present.* Boston: South End Press.

Acker, Joan. 1989. *Doing Comparable Worth: Gender, Class, and Pay Equity.* Philadelphia: Temple University Press.

Adams, Romanzo. Social Research Laboratory papers. University of Hawaii Archives, Manoa.

American Nurses' Association. 1965. *Health Occupations Supportive to Nursing.* New York: American Nurses' Association.

Anderson, C. Arnold, and Mary Jean Bowman. 1953. "The Vanishing Servant and the Contemporary Status System of the American South." *American Journal of Sociology* 59:215–30.

Anzaldúa, Gloria. 1990. *Making Face, Making Soul—Haciendo Caras: Creative Critical Perspectives by Women of Color.* San Francisco: Aunt Lute Foundation.

Barrera, Mario. 1979. *Race and Class in the Southwest: A Theory of Racial Inequality.* Notre Dame, Ind., and London: University of Notre Dame Press.

Barrett, Michèle. 1980. *Women's Oppression Today: Problems in Marxist Feminist Analysis.* London: Verso.

————. 1987. "The Concept of 'Difference.'" *Feminist Review* 26(July):29–41.

Benson, Susan Porter. 1986. *Counter Cultures: Saleswomen, Customers, and Managers in American Department Stores, 1890–1940.* Urbana and Chicago: University of Illinois Press.

Benston, Margaret. 1969. "The Political Economy of Women's Liberation." *Monthly Review* 21(September):13–27.

Blackwelder, Julia Kirk. 1978. "Women in the Work Force: Atlanta, New Orleans, and San Antonio, 1930 to 1940." *Journal of Urban History* 4(3):331–58, 349.

————. 1984. *Women of the Depression: Caste and Culture in San Antonio, 1929–1939.* College Station: Texas A&M University Press.

Blair, Karen. 1980. *The Clubwoman as Feminist: True Womanhood Redefined, 1868–1914.* New York: Holmes & Meier.

Blauner, Robert. 1972. *Racial Oppression in America.* Berkeley: University of California Press.

Bolden, Dorothy. 1976. "Forty-two Years a Maid: Starting at Nine in Atlanta." In *Nobody Speaks for Me! Self-Portraits of American Working Class Women,* ed. Nancy Seifer. New York: Simon & Schuster.

Boydston, Jeanne. 1990. *Home and Work: Housework, Wages, and the Ideology of Labor in the Early Republic.* New York: Oxford University Press.

Braverman, Harry. 1974. *Labor and Monopoly Capital: The Degradation of Labor in the Twentieth Century.* New York and London: Monthly Review Press.

Brenner, Johanna, and Barbara Laslett. 1986. "Social Reproduction and the Family." In *Sociology, from Crisis to Science?* Vol. 2, *The Social Reproduction of Organization and Culture,* ed. Ulf Himmelstrand, 116–31. London: Sage.

Brown, Elsa Barkley. 1989. "Womanist Consciousness: Maggie Lena Walker and the Independent Order of Saint Luke." *Signs: Journal of Women in Culture and Society* 14(3):610–33.

Cannings, Kathleen, and William Lazonik. 1975. "The Development of the Nursing Labor Force in the United States: A Basic Analysis." *International Journal of Health Sciences* 5(2):185–216.

Carnegie, Mary Elizabeth. 1986. *The Path We Tread: Blacks in Nursing, 1854–1954.* Philadelphia: Lippincott.

Chaplin, David. 1978. "Domestic Service and Industrialization." *Comparative Studies in Sociology* 1:97–127.

Clark-Lewis, Elizabeth. 1987. "This Work Had an End: African American Domestic Workers in Washington, D.C., 1910–1940." In *"To Toil the Livelong Day": America's Women at Work, 1780–1980*, ed. Carole Groneman and Mary Beth Norton. Ithaca, N.Y.: Cornell University Press.

Coleman, Barbara. 1989. "States Grapple with New Law." *AARP News Bulletin*, 30(2):4–5.

Collins, Patricia Hill. 1986. "Learning from the Outsider Within: The Sociological Significance of Black Feminist Thought." *Social Problems* 33(6):14–32.

_____ . 1990. *Black Feminist Thought: Knowledge, Consciousness, and the Politics of Empowerment*. New York: Allen & Unwin.

Cowan, Ruth Schwartz. 1983. *More Work for Mother: The Ironies of Household Technology from the Open Hearth to the Microwave*. New York: Basic.

Davidoff, Lenore. 1979. "Class and Gender in Victorian England: The Diaries of Arthur J. Munby and Hannah Cullwick." *Feminist Studies* 5(Spring): 86–114.

Degler, Carl N. 1980. *At Odds: Women and the Family in America from the Revolution to the Present*. New York: Oxford University Press.

Deming, Dorothy. 1947. *The Practical Nurse*. New York: Commonwealth Fund.

Deutsch, Sarah. 1987a. *No Separate Refuge: Culture, Class, and Gender on an Anglo-Hispanic Frontier in the American Southwest, 1880–1940*. New York: Oxford University Press.

_____ . 1987b. "Women and Intercultural Relations: The Case of Hispanic New Mexico and Colorado." *Signs* 12(4):719–39.

Diamond, Timothy. 1988. "Social Policy and Everyday Life in Nursing Homes: A Critical Ethnography." In *The Worth of Women's Work: A Qualitative Synthesis*, ed. Anne Statham, Eleanor M. Miller, and Hans O. Mauksch. Albany, N.Y.: SUNY Press.

Dill, Bonnie Thornton. 1980. "The Means to Put My Children Through: Childrearing Goals and Strategies among Black Female Domestic Servants." In *The Black Woman*, ed. La Frances Rodgers-Rose. Beverly Hills and London: Sage.

_____ . 1988. "Our Mothers' Grief: Racial Ethnic Women and the Maintenance of Families." *Journal of Family History* 12(4):415–31.

Drake, St. Clair, and Horace Cayton. (1945) 1962. *Black Metropolis: A Study of Negro Life in a Northern City*, vol. 1. New York: Harper Torchbook.

Dudden, Faye E. 1983. *Serving Women: Household Service in Nineteenth Century America*. Middletown, Conn.: Wesleyan University Press.

Elsasser, Nan, Kyle MacKenzie, and Yvonne Tixier y Vigil. 1980. *Las Mujeres: Conversations from a Hispanic Community*. Old Westbury, N.Y.: Feminist Press.

Engels, Friedrich. 1972. *The Origins of the Family, Private Property and the State*. New York: International Publishers.

Epstein, Barbara. 1981. *The Politics of Domesticity: Women, Evangelism, and Temperance in Nineteenth Century America*. Middletown, Conn.: Wesleyan University Press.

Fields, Barbara. 1982. "Ideology and Race in American History." In *Region, Race, and Reconstruction: Essays in Honor of C. Vann Woodward*, ed. J. Morgan Kousser and James M. McPherson. New York: Oxford University Press.

Fink, Leon, and Brian Greenberg. 1979. "Organizing Montefiore: Labor Militancy Meets a Progressive Health Care Empire." In *Health Care in America: Essays in Social History*, ed. Susan Reverby and David Rosner. Philadelphia: Temple University Press.

Fox, Bonnie, ed. 1980. *Hidden in the Household: Women's Domestic Labour under Capitalism*. Toronto: Women's Press.

Gamarinikow, Eva. 1978. "Sexual Division of Labour: The Case of Nursing." In *Feminism and Materialism: Women and Modes of Production*, ed. Annette Kuhn and Ann-Marie Wolpe, 96–123. London: Routledge & Kegan Paul.

Game, Ann, and Rosemary Pringle. 1983. *Gender at Work*. Sydney: Allen & Unwin.

Garcia, Alma. 1989. "The Development of Chicana Feminist Discourse, 1970–1980." *Gender and Society* 3(2):217–38.

Garcia, Mario T. 1980. "The Chicana in American History: The Mexican Women of El Paso, 1880–1920: A Case Study." *Pacific Historical Review* 49(2):315–39.

———. 1981. *Desert Immigrants: The Mexicans of El Paso, 1880–1920*. New Haven, Conn.: Yale University Press.

Glazer, Nona. 1988. "Overlooked, Overworked: Women's Unpaid and Paid Work in the Health Services' 'Cost Crisis,'" *International Journal of Health Services* 18(2):119–37.

Glenn, Evelyn Nakano. 1985. "Racial Ethnic Women's Labor: The Intersection of Race, Gender and Class Oppression." *Review of Radical Political Economy* 17(3):86–108.

———. 1986. *Issei, Nisei, Warbride: Three Generations of Japanese American Women in Domestic Service*. Philadelphia: Temple University Press.

Gordon, Linda. 1990. "The New Feminist Scholarship on the Welfare State." In *Women, the State, and Welfare*, ed. Linda Gordon, 9–35. Madison: University of Wisconsin Press.

Gwaltney, John, ed. 1980. *Drylongso: A Self-Portrait of Black America*. New York: Random House.

Hartmann, Heidi I., ed. 1985. *Comparable Worth: New Directions for Research*. Washington, D.C.: National Academy Press.

Hield, Melissa. 1984. "Women in the Texas ILGWU, 1933–50." In *Speaking for Ourselves: Women of the South*, ed. Maxine Alexander, 87–97. New York, Pantheon.

Hine, Darlene Clark, ed. 1985. *Black Women in the Nursing Profession: A Documentary History*. New York: Pathfinder.

———. 1989. *Black Women in White: Racial Conflict and Cooperation in the Nursing Profession, 1890–1950*. Bloomington: Indiana University Press.

Janiewski, Delores. 1983. "Flawed Victories: The Experiences of Black and White Women Workers in Durham during the 1930s." In *Decades of Discontent: The Women's Movement, 1920–1940*, ed. Lois Scharf and Joan M. Jensen, 85–112. Westport, Conn., and London: Greenwood.

Kaplan, Elaine Bell. 1987. "'I Don't Do No Windows': Competition between the Domestic Worker and the Housewife." In *Competition: A Feminist Taboo?"* ed. Valerie Miner and Helen E. Longino. New York: Feminist Press at CUNY.

Katzman, David M. 1978. *Seven Days a Week: Women and Domestic Service in Industrializing America.* New York: Oxford University Press.

Katzman, David M., and William M. Tuttle, Jr., eds. 1982. *Plain Folk: The Life Stories of Undistinguished Americans.* Urbana and Chicago: University of Illinois Press.

Kessler-Harris, Alice. 1981. *Women Have Always Worked: A Historical Overview.* Old Westbury, N.Y.: Feminist Press.

———. 1982. *Out to Work: A History of Wage-earning Women in the United States.* New York: Oxford University Press.

King, Deborah K. 1988. "Multiple Jeopardy, Multiple Consciousness: The Context of a Black Feminist Ideology." *Signs* 14(1):42–72.

Lamphere, Louise. 1987. *From Working Daughters to Working Mothers: Immigrant Women in a New England Industrial Community.* Ithaca, N.Y.: Cornell University Press.

Lasch, Christopher. 1977. *Haven in a Heartless World: The Family Besieged.* New York: Basic.

Laslett, Barbara, and Johanna Brenner. 1989. "Gender and Social Reproduction: Historical Perspectives." *Annual Review of Sociology* 15:381–404.

Lind, Andrew. 1951. "The Changing Position of Domestic Service in Hawaii." *Social Process in Hawaii* 15:71–87.

Luxton, Meg. 1980. *More than a Labour of Love: Three Generations of Women's Work in the Home.* Toronto: Women's Press.

McConoway, Mary Jo. 1987. "The Intimate Experiment." *Los Angeles Times Magazine,* February 19, 18–23, 37–38.

Marx, Karl, and Friedrich Engels. 1969. *Selected Works,* vol. 1. Moscow: Progress.

Mellor, Earl F. 1987. "Workers at the Minimum Wage or Less: Who They Are and the Jobs They Hold." *Monthly Labor Review,* July, 34–38.

Omi, Michael, and Howard Winant. 1986. *Racial Formation in the United States.* New York: Routledge.

Palmer, Phyllis. 1987. "Housewife and Household Worker: Employer-Employee Relations in the Home, 1928–1941." In *"To Toil the Livelong Day": America's Women at Work, 1780–1980,* ed. Carole Groneman and Mary Beth Norton, 179–95. Ithaca, N.Y.: Cornell University Press.

———. 1990. *Domesticity and Dirt: Housewives and Domestic Servants in the United States, 1920–1945.* Philadelphia: Temple University Press.

Piven, Frances Fox, and Richard A. Cloward. 1971. *Regulating the Poor: The Functions of Public Welfare.* New York: Pantheon.

———. 1979. *Poor People's Movements: Why They Succeed, How They Fail.* New York: Pantheon.

Reisler, Mark. 1976. *By the Sweat of Their Brow: Mexican Immigrant Labor in the United States, 1900–1940.* Westport, Conn.: Greenwood.

Reverby, Susan M. 1979. "From Aide to Organizer: The Oral History of Lillian Roberts." In *Women of America: A History,* ed. Carol Ruth Berkin and Mary Beth Norton. Boston: Houghton Mifflin.

———. 1987. *Ordered to Care: The Dilemma of American Nursing, 1850–1945.* Cambridge: Cambridge University Press.

Rollins, Judith. 1985. *Between Women: Domestics and Their Employers*. Philadelphia: Temple University Press.

Romero, Mary. 1987. "Chicanas Modernize Domestic Service." Unpublished manuscript.

————. 1988a. "Day Work in the Suburbs: The Work Experience of Chicana Private Housekeepers." In *The Worth of Women's Work: A Qualitative Synthesis*, ed. Anne Statham, Eleanor M. Miller, and Hans O. Mauksch, 77–92. Albany: SUNY Press.

————. 1988b. "Renegotiating Race, Class and Gender Hierarchies in the Everyday Interactions between Chicana Private Household Workers and Employers." Paper presented at the 1988 meetings of the Society for the Study of Social Problems, Atlanta.

Rose, Hilary. 1986. "Women's Work: Women's Knowledge." In *What Is Feminism?* ed. Juliet Mitchell and Ann Oakley, 161–83. Oxford: Basil Blackwell.

Ruíz, Vicki L. 1987a. "By the Day or the Week: Mexicana Domestic Workers in El Paso." In *Women on the U.S.-Mexico Border: Responses to Change*, ed. Vicki L. Ruíz and Susan Tiano, 61–76. Boston: Allen & Unwin.

————. 1987b. "Oral History and La Mujer: The Rosa Guerrero Story." In *Women on the U.S.-Mexico Border: Responses to Change*, ed. Vicki L. Ruíz and Susan Tiano, 219–32. Boston: Allen & Unwin.

Ryan, Mary P. 1981. *Cradle of the Middle Class: The Family in Oneida County, New York, 1790–1865*. Cambridge: Cambridge University Press.

Sacks, Karen Brodkin. 1988. *Caring by the Hour: Women, Work, and Organizing at Duke Medical Center*. Urbana and Chicago: University of Illinois Press.

Sacks, Karen Brodkin, and Dorothy Remy, eds. 1984. *My Troubles Are Going to Have Trouble with Me: Everyday Trials and Triumphs of Women Workers*. New Brunswick, N.J.: Rutgers University Press.

Sanchez, George J. 1990. " 'Go after the Women': Americanization and the Mexican Immigrant Woman, 1915–1929." In *Unequal Sisters: A Multicultural Reader in Women's History*, ed. Ellen Carol DuBois and Vicki L. Ruiz, 250–63. New York: Routledge.

Secombe, Wally. 1974. "The Housewife and Her Labour under Capitalism." *New Left Review* 83(January–February):3–24.

Sekcenski, Edward S. 1981. "The Health Services Industry: A Decade of Expansion." *Monthly Labor Review* (May):10–16.

Silvestri, George T., and John M. Lukasiewicz. 1987. "A Look at Occupational Employment Trends to the Year 2000." *Monthly Labor Review* (September): 46–63.

Smuts, Robert W. 1959. *Women and Work in America*. New York: Schocken.

Sokoloff, Natalie J. 1980. *Between Money and Love: The Dialectics of Women's Home and Market Work*. New York: Praeger.

Starr, Paul. 1982. *The Social Transformation of American Medicine*. New York: Basic.

Strasser, Susan. 1982. *Never Done: A History of American Housework*. New York: Pantheon.

Tucker, Susan. 1988. "The Black Domestic in the South: Her Legacy as Mother and Mother Surrogate." In *Southern Women*, ed. Carolyn Matheny Dillman, 93–102. New York: Hemisphere.

U.S. Bureau of the Census. 1932. *Fifteenth Census of the United States: 1930, Outlying Territories and Possessions.* Washington, D.C.: Government Printing Office.

————. 1933. *Fifteenth Census of the United States: 1930, Population.* Vol. 5, *General Report on Occupations.* Washington, D.C.: Government Printing Office.

————. 1984. *Census of the Population, 1980.* Vol. 1, *Characteristics of the Population.* Washington, D.C.: Government Printing Office.

U.S. Department of Labor. 1987a. *Industry Wage Survey: Hospitals, August 1985.* Bureau of Labor Statistics Bulletin 2273. Washington, D.C.: Government Printing Office.

————. 1987b. *Industry Wage Survey: Nursing and Personal Care Facilities, September 1985.* Bureau of Labor Statistics Bulletin 2275. Washington, D.C.: Government Printing Office.

————. 1989. *Employment and Earnings, January 1989.* Bureau of Labor Statistics Bulletin. Washington, D.C.: Government Printing Office.

Wagner, David. 1980. "The Proletarianization of Nursing in the United States, 1932–1945." *International Journal of Health Services* 10(2):271–89.

Watriss, Wendy. 1984. "It's Something Inside You." In *Speaking for Ourselves: Women of the South,* ed. Maxine Alexander. New York: Pantheon.

Weinbaum, Batya, and Amy Bridges. 1976. "The Other Side of the Paycheck." *Monthly Review* 28:88–103.

The Occult of True Black Womanhood: Critical Demeanor and Black Feminist Studies

Ann duCille

> *The Black Woman; The Black Woman: An Anthology; The Black Woman in America; The Black Woman in American Society; The Black Woman Cross-Culturally; Black Women in America; Black Women in White America; Black Women in the Nineteenth Century; Black Women in Nineteenth-Century American Life; Black Women Writers; Black Women Writers at Work; Black Women Writing Autobiography; Black Women Writing the American Experience; Black Women Novelists; Black Women Novelists in the Wake of the Civil Rights Movement; Black Women, Fiction, and Literary Tradition; The Sexual Mountain and Black Women Writers; Ain't I a Woman?; Arn't I a Woman?*

F OR REASONS that may already be obvious, the books named above and numerous others like them have led me to think of myself as a kind of sacred text. Not me personally, of course, but me black woman object, Other. Within and around the modern academy, racial and gender alterity has become a hot commodity that has claimed black women as its principal signifier. I am alternately pleased, puzzled, and perturbed—bewitched, bothered, and bewildered—by this, by the alterity that is perpetually thrust upon African American women, by the production of black women as infinitely deconstructable "othered" matter. Why are black women always

I wish to thank the many friends, colleagues, and readers whose insights and critiques helped shape this essay, including Elizabeth Weed, Laura Kipnis, and *Signs*'s anonymous reviewers. I am particularly indebted to Indira Karamcheti, Laura Santigian, and Sharon Holland for their wisdom and their willingness to talk me through the many lives (and deaths) of what was for me a very difficult article to write and what will be for some, I am sure, a very difficult article to read.

[*Signs: Journal of Women in Culture and Society* 1994, vol. 19, no. 3]

already Other? I wonder. To myself, of course, I am not Other; to me it is the white women and men so intent on theorizing my difference who are the Other. Why are they so interested in me and people who look like me (metaphorically speaking)? Why have we—black women—become the subjected subjects of so much contemporary scholarly investigation, the peasants under glass of intellectual inquiry in the 1990s?

The attention is not altogether unpleasant, especially after generations of neglect, but I am hardly alone in suspecting that the overwhelming interest in black women may have at least as much to do with the pluralism and perhaps even the primitivism of this particular postmodern moment as with the stunning quality of black women's accomplishments and the breadth of their contributions to American civilization. It is not news that by virtue of our race and gender, black women are not only the "second sex"—*the Other,* in postmodern parlance—but we are also the last race, the most oppressed, the most marginalized, the most deviant, the quintessential site of difference. And through the inversionary properties of deconstruction, feminism, cultural studies, multiculturalism, and contemporary commodity culture, the last shall be first. Perhaps.

I say *perhaps* because we have experienced the problematic of such inversions before: the preoccupation with black women, with the blues, the black folk, the authentic, the real colored thing in the 1920s, for example, a preoccupation fueled at least in part by the primitivist proclivities of the historical moment. In the twenties, the fascination with the black female body, in particular, and the primitive sexual anatomy and appetite attributed to the African woman increased the degree to which the black female functioned as an erotic icon in the racial and sexual ideology of Western civilization.

Black feminist theorist bell hooks calls the contemporary version of this preoccupation with alterity "the commodification of Otherness" or "eating the Other." "Within commodity culture," she writes in *Black Looks,* "ethnicity becomes spice, seasoning that can liven up the dull dish that is mainstream white culture." Mass culture, then, in hooks's view, perpetuates the primitivistic notion "that there is pleasure to be found in the acknowledgment and enjoyment of racial difference" (1992, 21).

Where gender and racial difference meet in the bodies of black women, the result is the invention of an other Otherness, a hyperstatic alterity. Mass culture, as hooks argues, produces, promotes, and perpetuates the commodification of Otherness through the exploitation of the black female body. In the 1990s, however, the principal sites of exploitation are not simply the cabaret, the speakeasy, the music video, the glamour magazine; they are also the academy, the publishing industry, the intellectual community. In the words of black male theorist Houston Baker, who is among those who have recently taken up African American women (and taken on black feminist critics): "Afro-American women's expressivity and the analyses that it has promoted during the past two decades represent the most dramatically charged field for the convergence of matters of race, class, and gender today" (1991, 1–2). Of course, one of the dangers of standing at an intersection—particularly at such a suddenly busy, three-way intersection—is the likelihood of being run over by oncoming traffic.

Michele Wallace likens the traffic jam that has built up around Zora Neale Hurston, in particular, to a "rainbow coalition" of critics, who, "like groupies descending on Elvis Presley's estate," are engaged in "a mostly ill-mannered stampede to have some memento of the black woman" (1990, 174), who is, at least to some degree, a figment of their individual and collective critical imaginations.

Precisely the question I want to explore in this essay is what it means for black women academics to stand in the midst of the "dramatically charged field"—the traffic jam—that black feminist studies has become. Are we in the way of the critical stampede that accompanies what I am calling here "the occult of true black womanhood"? Are we in danger of being trampled by the "rainbow coalition" of critics—"black, white, male, female, artists and academics, historicists and deconstructionists"— that our own once isolated and isolating intellectual labors have attracted to the magnetic field of black feminist studies?

"Hurstonism" and the black feminist phenomenon

In her foreword to the 1978 University of Illinois Press reprint of *Their Eyes Were Watching God,* black poet, novelist, and critic Sherley Anne Williams tells of first encountering Zora Neale Hurston and *Their Eyes* while a graduate student enrolled in a two-semester survey of black poetry and prose. "Afro-American literature was still an exotic subject then," Williams writes, "rarely taught on any regular basis" (1978, vi). She goes on to describe how she and her classmates fought over the pitifully few copies of African American texts, long out of print, that they were able to beg, borrow, and otherwise procure from musty basements, rare book collections, and reserved reading rooms. When it finally became her turn to read *Their Eyes Were Watching God,* Williams says she found in the speech of Hurston's characters her own country self and, like Alice Walker and numerous others, became Zora Neale's for life.

For many of us who came of intellectual age in the late sixties and early seventies, Sherley Anne Williams's "discovery" of Zora is an almost painfully familiar textual encounter of the first kind. While Hurston was not the first black woman writer I encountered or claimed as my own (that was Ann Petry), it was during this same period—1971, in fact—

that I, too, discovered Zora. I was introduced to her and to her work by my friend and fellow graduate student, another gifted black woman writer, Gayl Jones. When I began my teaching career a few years later at a college in upstate New York, Gayl was again generous enough to lend me her well-worn, oft-read copy of *Their Eyes*. Only a lingering fear of being prosecuted for copyright infringement prevents me from detailing how I went about sharing among the dozen or so students in my seminar, none of whom had heard of Hurston, the fruits that bloomed within the single, precious, tattered copy of *Their Eyes Were Watching God*.

Twenty years later, African American studies courses and black women writers such as Hurston are once again exotic subjects. They are exotic this time out, however, not because they are rarely taught or seldom read, but because in the midst of the present, multicultural moment, they have become politically correct, intellectually popular, and commercially precious sites of literary and historical inquiry. Long either altogether ignored as historical and literary subjects or badly misfigured as magnanimous mammies, man-eating matriarchs, or immoral Jezebels, black women—that is, certain black women—and their texts have been taken up by and reconfigured within the academy, elevated and invoked by the intellectual elite as well as the scholarly marginal. Currently in print in several editions, *Their Eyes Were Watching God* has become quasi-canonical, holding a place of honor on syllabi of mainstream history, social science, literature, and American studies courses, as well as of perhaps more marginalized disciplines such as African American studies and women's studies. Much the same holds true for Alice Walker's *The Color Purple* and Toni Morrison's *Beloved*, each of which has been awarded the Pulitzer Prize for fiction.

It is important to note that black women critics and scholars have played a crucial role in bringing to the academic fore the works of "lost" writers such as Hurston and Nella Larsen and in opening up spaces within the academy both for the fiction of contemporary African American women writers and for the study of black and other women of color more generally. While I am usually suspicious of efforts to define benchmarks and signposts, there are nevertheless a number of important essays, anthologies, and monographs that I think can be rightly claimed as the founding texts of contemporary black feminist studies. Toni Cade Bambara's anthology *The Black Woman* (1970), for example—which showcased the prose and poetry of writers such as Nikki Giovanni, Audre Lorde, Paule Marshall, Alice Walker, and Sherley Anne Williams—stands as a pivotal text along with critical essays and literary, historical, and sociological studies by Barbara Smith, Barbara Christian, Frances Beal, Joyce Ladner, Jeanne Noble, Darlene Clark Hine, Angela Davis,

Frances Foster, Filomina Chioma Steady, Sharon Harley and Rosalyn Terborg-Penn, and Mary Helen Washington.[1]

While keepers of (dominant) culture have given the lion's share of credit for the development of black literary and cultural studies to male scholars such as Houston Baker, Henry Louis Gates, and Cornel West, Mary Helen Washington nevertheless has been a key player in efforts to define and institutionalize the fields of African American literature and black feminist studies for more than twenty years.[2] Among my most precious personal possessions is a tattered copy of the August 1974 issue of *Black World,* which contains an article by Washington entitled "Their Fiction Becomes Our Reality: Black Women Image Makers." In this article, one of the first pieces of black feminist criticism I "discovered" and learned from (and in others that began appearing in *Black World* in 1972), Washington read, reviewed, and critiqued the works of black women writers such as Gwendolyn Brooks, Maya Angelou, Ann Petry, and Toni Cade Bambara, as well as Walker, Marshall, and Morrison.

Much the same can and must be said of Barbara Christian and Barbara Smith, whose essays on African American women writers began appearing in print in the mid and latter 1970s. Christian's first book, *Black Women Novelists: The Development of a Tradition, 1892–1976* (1980), which brilliantly analyzed the work of black women writers from Frances Harper to Marshall, Morrison, and Walker, remains a foundational text—"the Bible in the field of black feminist criticism," according to Michele Wallace (1990, 184). Nor have the more than fifteen years since its publication dulled the impact and significance of Barbara Smith's pivotal essay "Toward a Black Feminist Criticism" ([1977] 1985), a widely reprinted, often anthologized black lesbian feminist critical declaration that, as Cheryl Wall points out, gave name,

---

[1] See, among many others, Bambara 1970; Beal 1970; Davis 1971, 1981; Ladner 1972; Washington 1972, 1974, 1975, 1980; Foster 1973; Skeeter 1973; Christian (1975) 1985, 1980, 1985; Smith (1977) 1985, 1979; Harley and Terborg-Penn 1978; Noble 1978; Bell, Parker, and Guy-Shaftall 1979; Dill 1979a, 1979b, 1983; Hine and Wittenstein 1979; Hine 1980, 1981; hooks 1981; Steady 1981; Hull, Scott, and Smith 1982.

[2] For whatever it may suggest about the crisis and the production of the black intellectual, it is interesting to note that the intellectual labors of Baker, Gates, and West have been chronicled and lauded in cover stories and feature articles in such publications as the *New York Times,* the *Boston Globe, Newsweek,* the *Washington Post,* and *Time* magazine. I recall seeing only one article on Mary Helen Washington, in the "Learning" section of the Sunday *Globe* (although, of course, there may have been others). The article was dominated by a stunning picture of Washington, accompanied by a caption describing her as a scholar-teacher who "helps restore sight to the 'darkened eye' of American literary tradition." Despite this very fitting and promising caption, the article went on to say remarkably little about Washington's actual scholarship and its impact on American literary studies (see Weld 1988).

definition, and political persuasion to the perspective from which Bambara, Washington, and others had been writing (Wall 1989, 45). Smith's work in literary criticism and that of her sister Beverly Smith in the area of black women's health have played crucial roles in developing the fields of black feminist and black lesbian feminist studies.

Within the realm of literary studies alone, the names making up even a partial list of pioneering black feminist scholars are, as Houston Baker has said, "legion" (1991, 10): Deborah McDowell, Nellie McKay, Hortense Spillers, Gloria Hull, Patr_.a Bell Scott, Cheryl Wall, Valerie Smith, Mae Henderson, Gloria Wade-Gayles, Thadious Davis, Trudier Harris, Frances Smith Foster, Hazel Carby, Joyce Joyce, and Claudia Tate, as well as Christian, Washington, Smith, and many many others.[3] Both as an inspiration to aspiring young black women writers and as an editor at Random House in the 1970s, Toni Morrison, too, has played a particularly dramatic role in opening up spaces for and directing critical attention toward African American women.

While I, as a beneficiary of their research and writing, am anxious to give credit where credit is long overdue, this essay is not intended as a praisesong for black women scholars, critics, and artists, or even as a review of the literature they have generated.[4] Rather, I would like to examine critically some of the implications and consequences of the current explosion of interest in black women as literary and historical subjects. Among the issues I hope to explore are the ways in which this interest—which seems to me to have reached occult status—increasingly marginalizes both the black women critics and scholars who excavated the fields in question and their black feminist "daughters" who would further develop those fields.

What does it mean, for example, that many prestigious university presses and influential literary publications such as the *New York Times Book Review* regularly rely not on these seasoned black women scholars but on male intellectuals—black and white—to read, evaluate, and review the book manuscripts of young black women just entering the profession? What does it mean for the black female professoriate that departments often ask powerful senior black male scholars to referee the

---

[3] Most of the black feminist critics Baker lists have produced essays, articles, and books too numerous to name. In addition to a wealth of critical essays, Thadious Davis, Trudier Harris, and Deborah McDowell, e.g., have made tremendous contributions to the fields of African American and black feminist literary studies through their editorial work on a number of important projects, including vol. 51 of the Dictionary of Literary Biography series (Harris 1986) and Beacon Press's Black Women Writers Series (McDowell). See among many other pivotal essays, introductions, and books, McDowell (1980) 1985; Tate 1981; Hull, Scott, and Smith 1982; Wall 1982; McKay 1984; Wade-Gayles 1984; Carby 1986, 1987; Joyce 1987; Smith 1987; Spillers 1987.

[4] For such a review of the critical literature, see Carby 1987 and Wall 1989.

tenure and promotion cases of the same black women scholars who have challenged or affronted these men in some way? What does it mean for the field in general and for junior African Americanists in particular that senior scholars, who are not trained in African American studies and whose career-building work often has excluded (or at least not included) black women, are now teaching courses in and publishing texts about African American literature and generating supposedly "new scholar- ship" on black women writers? What does it mean for the future of black feminist studies that a large portion of the growing body of scholarship on black women is now being written by white feminists and by men whose work frequently achieves greater critical and commercial success than that of the black female scholars who carved out a field in which few "others" were then interested?

My questions are by no means new; nor do I claim to have any particularly insightful answers. I only know that as an African Ameri- canist who has been studying the literature and history of black women for almost thirty years and teaching it for more than twenty, I have a burning need to try to work through on paper my own ambivalence, antipathy, and, at times, animosity over the new-found enthusiasm for these fields that I readily—perhaps too readily—think of as my own hard-won territory. I feel a little like the parent who tells the child she is about to reprimand that "this hurts me more than it hurts you." But lest anyone think that this is an easily authored Portnoy's complaint in blackface—yet another black womanist indictment of white feminists who can do no right and men who can do only wrong—I want to make explicit my own dis-ease with the antagonism to which I have admitted and by which I am myself somewhat baffled.

Elsewhere I have argued against territoriality, against racial, cultural, and gender essentialism, against treating African American studies as the private property of what Gayatri Spivak calls "black blacks" (Spivak 1989).[5] Yet questions of turf and territoriality, appropriation and co- optation persist within my own black feminist consciousness, despite my best efforts to intellectualize them away. Again, this is not a new di- lemma. The modern, academic version of the ageless argument over who owns the sacred text of me and mine is at least as old as the work of white anthropologists Melville and Frances Herskovits dating back to the 1920s and reaching a controversial peak in 1941 with the publication of *The Myth of the Negro Past,* a study of African cultural retensions scorned by many black intellectuals (Herskovits [1928] 1985, 1938, 1941; Herskovits and Herskovits 1936). It was in the fifties, however, that

---

[5] See, e.g., the introduction and conclusion to my study *The Coupling Convention: Sex, Text, and Tradition in Black Women's Fiction* (1993).

white scholars began to loom large in the realm of black historiography and literary criticism, often receiving within the academy a kind of attention and credibility that the pioneering work of many black historians and literary critics had not enjoyed. Black historian Darlene Clark Hine noted in 1980 that "most of the highly-acclaimed historical works were, with few exceptions, written by white scholars." In fact, in her estimation, the legitimization of black history as a field proved a "bonanza for the [white] professional historians already in positions [as university professors and/or recognized scholars] to capitalize from the movement" (Hine 1980, 115, as quoted in Meier and Rudwick 1986, 294).

One hundred thirty years ago, former slave Harriet Jacobs was able to publish her life's story only with the authenticating stamp of the well-known white abolitionist Lydia Maria Child as editor and copyright holder. "I have signed and sealed the contract with Thayer & Eldridge, in my name, and told them to take out the copyright in my name," Child wrote in a letter to Jacobs in 1860. "Under the circumstances *your* name could not be used, you know" (Jacobs [1861] 1987, 246). The circumstances to which Child alluded (but did not name) were of course the conditions of slavery under which Jacobs had lived for most of her life and from which she had not completely escaped. Now, as then, it often seems to take the interest and intervention of white scholars to legitimize and institutionalize African American history and literature or such "minority discourses" as postcoloniality and multiculturalism. Let me offer two examples: Gerda Lerner's *Black Women in White America* (1972) and Shelley Fisher Fishkin's *Was Huck Black?* (1993).

Black feminist critic Gloria Wade-Gayles has identified Toni Cade Bambara's *The Black Woman* (1970) as "the first book that pulled together black women's views on black womanhood" and Jeanne Noble's *Beautiful, Also, Are the Souls of My Black Sisters* (1978) as the "first history of black women in America written by a black woman" (Wade-Gayles 1984, 41–2). Yet, despite the recovery and reconnaissance missions of Bambara, Noble, Joyce Ladner, and other black women intellectuals who did groundbreaking work in the seventies, it is white feminist historian Gerda Lerner whom the academy recognizes as the pioneer in reconstructing the history of African American women.

With the 1972 publication of her documentary anthology *Black Women in White America,* Lerner became by many reckonings the first historian to produce a book-length study devoted to African American women. Her goal, as she outlined in her preface, was to call attention to such "unused sources" as black women's own records of their experiences and "to bring another forgotten aspect of the black past to life" (xviii). In drawing on such first-person accounts as diaries, narratives, testimonies, and organizational records and reports, Lerner endeavored in her volume, she says, "to let black women speak for themselves" (xx).

While the notion of letting someone speak for herself is surely problematic, I want to note as well that Lerner was by no means the first to draw on what she implies were unexamined resources. Black artists, activists, and intellectuals had made use of these kinds of resources since the nineteenth century. Former slave William Wells Brown (1853), for one, drew on such sources in the many novels, narratives, and histories he published between 1847 and his death in 1884. Although written in a vein admittedly different from Lerner's work, Mrs. N. F. Mossell's *The Work of the Afro-American Woman*, first published in 1894, represents an early effort on the part of an African American woman to acknowledge the accomplishments and contributions of her black sisters ([1894] 1988). Black activist, educator, and "race woman" Anna Julia Cooper wrote of the "long dull pain" of the "open-eyed but hitherto voiceless Black Women of America" in *A Voice from the South*, published in 1892. In fact, the longevity of the insider/outsider debate is reflected in Cooper's one-hundred-year-old pronouncement: "Only the BLACK WOMAN can say 'when and where I enter, in the quiet, undisputed dignity of my womanhood, without violence and without suing or special patronage, then and there the whole *Negro race enters with me*' " ([1892] 1988, 31). Their own travails, joys, sorrows, and the testimonies and plaintive cries of other African American women, poor women, working women were the imperatives that propelled much of the political activism among black clubwomen at the turn of the century.

Nor should we ignore the intellectual labors of black literary scholar Charles Nichols, whose masterwork *Many Thousand Gone: The Ex-Slaves' Account of Their Bondage and Freedom* (1963) has directed two generations of researchers interested in slavery to a significant source: the "forgotten testimony of its victims" (ix).[6] In fact, the methodology Lerner employed in *Black Women in White America* is one perfected by Nichols.

To take up a more contemporary example, I might point out that for decades black writers, critics, and scholars have attempted to delineate the tremendous impact African American culture has had on the mainstream American literary tradition. Their efforts, however, have received little attention from the academy. But when a white scholar recently asked, "Was Huckleberry Finn Black?" the academy, the publishing industry, and the media sat up and took notice. I am referring, of course,

---

[6] Lerner does mention Nichols briefly in the bibliographical essay at the end of *Black Women in White America*. Nichols's book, she writes, "offers an excellent synthesis of the literature of slave narratives and evaluates their authenticity" (1972, 620).

to the hoopla over Shelley Fisher Fishkin's book *Was Huck Black?* (1993). As much as a year before it appeared in bookstores, Fishkin's study was lauded in such influential publications as the *New York Times, Newsweek,* and the *Chronicle of Higher Education.* In fact, according to the London *Times,* more than fifty news items on the book appeared across the country, sporting such headlines as: "Scholar Concludes That Young Black Was Model for Huck Finn's Voice; Huck Finn Speaks 'Black,' Scholar Says; and Theory Might Warm Foes to Twain's Novel" (Fender 1993, 27). I quote from one such article that appeared in the *Chronicle:* "Ms. Fishkin's book, *Was Huck Black?: Mark Twain and African-American Voices,* is likely to have a major impact, not just on the way scholars interpret a mainstay of the American literary canon, but also on the way scholars define that canon. By calling attention to the way multicultural voices have influenced mainstream literature, it suggests that traditional views of the dichotomy between majority and minority cultures may be flawed. In so doing, the book gives the term multiculturalism a new meaning" (Winkler 1992, A6).

I do not mean to make little or light of Shelley Fishkin's research and conclusions: hers is important and provocative work. What I am intrigued by, however, is the response from the white intellectual establishment. Why is the conclusion that "we need to pay more attention to African-American culture, even when we study the canon" suddenly being greeted as news? Haven't black scholars long argued the reflexive nature of cultural appropriation and the interrelatedness of so-called minor and major traditions? Speaking at a socialist conference in 1917, James Weldon Johnson, whom David Levering Lewis calls the "dean of Afro-American letters," reportedly shocked his audience by declaring that " 'the only things artistic in America that have sprung from American soil, permeated American life, and been universally acknowledged as distinctively American' were the creations of the Afro-American" (Lewis 1984). No African Americanist I know has been surprised at being told at this late date what many of us have argued for a long time: that Twain, like many major white American writers, drew canon fodder from "the black experiences" that are a fundamental, if often unacknowledged, part of American culture.

These and numerous other examples suggest to me a kind of color line and intellectual passing within and around the academy: black culture is more easily intellectualized (and canonized) when transferred from the danger of lived black experience to the safety of white metaphor, when you can have that "signifying black difference" without the difference of significant blackness. Fishkin's work, like Lerner's, is undeniably important, but it does not stand alone as revolutionary. "Sociable Jimmy," the young black boy on whose vernacular speech Twain may have based

Huck's colorful language, may never have gotten to speak for himself in print, but black women had been speaking for themselves and on behalf of each other long before Gerda Lerner endeavored "to let" them do so.

As I have suggested, the question of who speaks for me, who can write my sacred text, is as emotionally and politically charged as it is enduring and controversial. Asked about the explosion of interest in the lives and literature of black women among male scholars and white feminists, Barbara Christian responded in part: "It is galling to me that after black women critics of the 1970s plowed the neglected field of Afro-American women's literature when such an act was academically dangerous, that some male and white feminist scholars now seem to be reaping the harvest and are major commentators on this literature in influential, though not necessarily feminist journals such as *The New York Review of Books*. Historical amnesia seems to be as much a feature of intellectual life as other aspects of American society" (Christian et al. 1990, 61).

Historical amnesia may displace her at any time, but for this moment anyway, the black woman writer has become a bonanza. Her near phenomenal popularity as subject matter has spawned a wealth of critical scholarship and has spontaneously generated scores of scholars determined to claim her material and cultural production—what Houston Baker calls "Afro-American women's expressivity"—as their intellectual discourse. But as Barbara Christian's remarks imply, black women's expressivity is not merely discourse; it has become lucre in the intellectual marketplace, cultural commerce. What for many began as a search for our mothers' gardens, to appropriate Alice Walker's metaphor (1974), has become for some a Random House harvest worth millions in book sales and prestigious university professorships. Sensitive as the issue is, it must be said at some point and even at the risk of hurt feelings that the explosion of interest in the black female subject is at least in some measure about economics—about jobs. White feminist scholar Elizabeth Abel has acknowledged as much. "This new attentiveness [to texts by women of color] has been overdetermined," she argues, "by the sheer brilliance and power of this writing and its escalating status in the literary marketplace and, consequently, the academy; [and] by white feminist restlessness with an already well-mined white female literary tradition" (1993, 478). For many scholars trained in these well-mined fields, the shift to African American studies has yielded more prominent positions at more prestigious institutions.

But is this, as it seems to be for Barbara Christian, necessarily a bitter harvest? We—"we" being here African American women scholars—have complained long and loud about exclusion, about the degree to which white feminists and male critics have ignored the work of black women. Can we now legitimately complain that they are taking up (and taking over?) this important work? And what do such complaints tell us about ourselves and our relationship to what many of us continue to speak of as *our* literature?[7]

While, as I have acknowledged, I, too, am troubled, even galled by what at times feels like the appropriation and co-optation of black women by white feminists and by men, what I ultimately want to get at in this article is not simply about property rights, about racial or gender territoriality. It is by no means my intention to claim Hurston, Morrison, Walker, et al. as the private property of black women readers who, like Sherley Anne Williams, see themselves in their characters. In fact, I have argued elsewhere that rather than liberating and valorizing black female voices, the celebration of African American women's literature and history as the discursively familiar, as a "truth" to which black women scholars have privileged access rooted in common experience, both delimits and demeans those discourses. For, however inadvertently, it restricts this work to a narrow orbit in which it can be readily validated only by those black and female for whom it reproduces what they already know.[8]

Undeniably critical contributions to the study of black women and their literature and history have been made by scholars who are neither black nor female. The name of William L. Andrews comes to mind immediately, as does that of Robert Hemenway (Hemenway 1977; Andrews 1986). That we have increased access to the autobiographical writings of nineteenth-century African American women is due in part to Andrews's effort. That Hurston's work is now so readily accessible is due in no small measure not only to the efforts of black feminist writer Alice Walker, but also to those of white male scholar Robert Hemenway. Through the research and publishing efforts of white feminist scholar Jean Fagan Yellin and black male theorist Henry Louis Gates, to cite two other examples, we now have authentification of and access to two fundamental texts from the nineteenth century: Harriet Jacobs's *Incidents in the Life of a Slave Girl, Written by Herself* ([1861] 1987) and Harriet Wilson's *Our Nig* ([1859] 1983). Moreover, since 1988 the Schomburg

---

[7] White deconstructivist Barbara Johnson has called Henry Louis Gates on his repeated use of the term "our own." Johnson notes that in a single discussion "Gates uses the expression 'our own' no fewer than nineteen times." She goes on to query the meaning behind his ambiguous phrase: "Does Gates mean all black people (whatever that might mean)? All Afro-Americans? All scholars of Afro-American literature? All black men? All scholars trained in literary theory who are now interested in the black vernacular?" See Gates 1989 and Johnson 1989.

[8] For those of us tempted to make common (black female) experience the essence of critical interpretation or to view black women's fiction as expressive realism, Belsey's words may be prohibitively instructive: "The claim that a literary form reflects the world is simply tautological," she writes. "What is intelligible as realism is the conventional and therefore familiar. . . . It is intelligible as 'realistic' precisely because it reproduces what we already seem to know" (1980, 47).

Library of Nineteenth-Century Black Women Writers, of which Gates is general editor, has made available to critics and scholars dozens of previously lost texts. The recent work of white feminist scholar Elizabeth Ammons also represents a positive turn in literary studies. In its intercultural readings of works by African, Asian, Native, Jewish, and white American women, her book *Conflicting Stories: American Women Writers at the Turn into the Twentieth Century* (1992) represents a model we all would do well to follow.

Surely this is great work and good news. Why, then, am I and so many other black feminist scholars left wrestling with such enduring questions about co-optation and exploitation? Why are we haunted by a growing sense that we are witnessing (and perhaps even have inspired in some way) the commodification of the same black womanhood we have championed? It is a mistake, I think, to define this persistent (but perhaps inherently unresolvable) debate over who can read black female texts as strictly or even perhaps primarily racial or cultural or gendered: black/white, male/female, insider/outsider, our literature/your theory, my familiar/their foreign. The most important questions, I have begun to suspect, may not be about the essentialism and territoriality, the biology, sociology, or even the ideology about which we hear so much but, rather, about professionalism and disciplinarity; about cultural literacy and intellectual competence; about taking ourselves seriously and insisting that we be taken seriously not as objectified subjects in someone else's histories—as native informants—but as critics and as scholars reading and writing our own literature and history.

Disciplinary matters: When demeanor demeans

So I have arrived at what for me is at the heart of what's the matter. Much of the newfound interest in African American women that seems to honor the field of black feminist studies actually demeans it by treating it not like a discipline with a history and a body of rigorous scholarship and distinguished scholars underpinning it, but like an anybody-can-play pick-up game performed on a wide-open, untrammeled field. Often the object of the game seems to be to reinvent the intellectual wheel: to boldly go where in fact others have gone before, to flood the field with supposedly new "new scholarship" that evinces little or no sense of the discipline's genealogy. Moreover, many of the rules that the academy generally invokes in doing its institutional business—in making appointments, assigning courses, and advancing faculty—are suddenly suspended when what is at stake is not the valorized, traditional disciplines of Western civilization but the more marginal, if extremely popular, fields within African American studies.

Among those elements considered when English departments hire Medievalists, Victorianists, Americanists, and so on, at least in my experience in the academy, are school(s) attended, the nature of one's graduate training, the subject of one's dissertation, and not only what one has published but where one has published as well. Were the articles refereed? Were they published in reputable academic journals? Are the journals discipline-specific, edited and juried by experts in the candidate's field, scholars who know whereof they read? I have seen these valorized criteria relaxed time and time again, however, when these same traditionally trained, nonblack scholars are being hired not in the fields in which they were educated but in African American studies. Interestingly enough, the same loosening of standards does not readily occur when black scholars— particularly young black scholars—apply for positions as generalists in American or world literature. The fact that the educational system is such that it is still largely impossible to specialize in African American literature without first being trained in the European and Anglo-American canons does not keep the powers that be from questioning the preparedness of blacks who apply for jobs as generalists. A dissertation on Toni Morrison or C. L. R. James or W. E. B. Du Bois does not necessarily qualify one as an Americanist, but a thesis on Chaucer or the Brontës or Byron is not an impediment to an appointment as an African Americanist.

Indeed, the question of who is authorized to teach African American discourse is riddled with ironies, paradoxes, and contradictions. Black scholars duly and properly trained and credentialed in traditional fields— medieval studies, for example—are often assumed or expected to be ready, willing, and able to teach black studies courses. African American studies programs and department are not supposed to be intellectual ghettos populated exclusively by black scholars, particularly when white scholars want to enter such programs, but the field of African American studies often is treated like a black ghetto—like the one right and proper place for black intellectuals—when black scholars dare to step out of it, dare to be Medievalists or classicists or British Victorianists.

Moreover, while many of our white colleagues and administrators may theorize African American and black feminist studies as open fields, as acquirable tastes ("You don't have to be one to teach one," as someone put it), this intellectual position often is not lived up to in institutional practice. For when these same individuals want someone to provide a black reading of their work or black representation on a committee or black resources for their students or information about a particular black author or details about an event in black history, more times than not it is to black faculty that they turn, and not to the white Victorianists they have hired as African Americanists and have authorized to teach courses in black literature and history.

So here we have another paradox of critical demeanor: the difference between authority and authenticity. Black scholars on predominantly or overwhelmingly white campuses are rarely authorized simply as scholars. Rather, our racial difference is an authenticating stamp that, as Indira Karamcheti has argued, often casts us in the role of Caliban in the classroom and on the campus. Speaking of minority scholars in general, Karamcheti writes:

> We are sometimes seen, it seems to me, as traveling icons of culture, both traditional (as long as we're over there) and nontraditional (when we're right here), unbearably ancient in our folk wisdom and childlike in our infantile need for the sophistication of the West. We are flesh and blood information retrieval systems, native informants who demonstrate and act out difference, often with an imperfectly concealed political agenda. We are the local and the regional opposed to the universality of the West, nature to its culture, instinct to its intellect, body to its brain. We are, in fact, encased in the personal and visible facts of our visible selves, walking exemplars of ethnicity and of race. [1994]

Walking exemplars of ethnicity and race. It seems to me that this is particularly true for black women scholars on white college campuses where they experience both a hypervisibility and a superisolation by virtue of their racial and gender difference. Unfortunately, icons are not granted tenure automatically; when their canonical year rolls around, all too often these same black women faculty members who have been drawn on as exemplars and used up as icons will find themselves chewed up and spit out because they did not publish. (Consider the startling number of brilliant black women scholars who have produced only one book or no book.) Sympathetic white colleagues lament their black colleagues' departures from the university: "Why didn't she just say 'no'?" they ask each other, rarely remembering the many times they implored her to just say "yes," the numerous occasions on which they sent her students with questions only she could answer or problems only she could solve, or the many instances in which they treated her not like a colleague but like their personal research assistant or native informant.

Given the occult of true black womanhood, to be (not so) young, female, and black on today's college campuses is difficult, to be sure. But more troubling still is the fact that commodified, Calibanized black women intellectuals, whose authority as academicians often has been questioned at every turn in their careers, are not supposed to resent, or even to notice, the double standard that propels others forward even as it keeps them back. For the most part, however, black women in the academy not only have noticed, we have refused to suffer in silence; our complaints are by now old news. Many ears, once sympathetic to "the black woman's plight," her "double jeopardy," her "exceptional burdens," have been frozen by the many winters of our discontent. Our grievances have begun to be heard only as "anti-intellectual identity politics" and "proprietary claims." What Houston Baker describes as our "black feminist manifestos"—our "admonitions, injunctions, and cautions to those who wish to share the open road" (1991, 11)—reveal us to be, even to our most supportive colleagues, small-minded, mean-spirited, and downright petty.

Of course, my point is that for many of us, for many black women scholars, questioning the race, ethnicity, culture, and credentials of those the academy authorizes to write *our* histories and to teach and interpret *our* literature is anything but petty. Rather, it is a concern that rises from the deepest recesses of who we are in relation to where we live and work. Black women have pioneered a field that even after more than twenty years remains marginalized within the university, regardless of how popular both the field and its black women practitioners are with students. Our at once precarious and overdetermined positions in the academy and our intimate knowledge of social, intellectual, and academic history prompt us not simply to guard our turf, as often accused, but also to discipline *our* field, to preserve its integrity and our own.

I have emphasized the pronoun *our* in order to problematize the admitted possessiveness of our disciplinary concerns. For no matter how compelling—no matter how historically resonant—the sense of personal stake that permeates the scholarship by black women about black women just may be an aspect of the insider/outsider problematic for which African American women academics have to take responsibility. It may be time for us to interrogate in new and increasingly clinical ways our proprietary relationship to the field many of us continue to think of as *our own*.

Such internal review presents its own problematic, however. To claim privileged access to the lives and literature of African American women through what we hold to be the shared experiences of our black female bodies is to cooperate with our own commodification, to buy from and sell back to the dominant culture its constitution of our always already essentialized identity. On the other hand, to relinquish claim to the experiences of the black body and to confirm and affirm its study purely as discourse, simply as a field of inquiry equally open to all, is to collaborate with our own objectification. We become objects of study where we are authorized to be the story but have no special claim to decoding that story. We can be, but someone else gets to tell us what we mean.

This conundrum operates, of course, in realms beyond the either/or options I have established here. But how to find the middle ground, that happier medium? How do we negotiate an intellectually charged space for experience in a way that is not totalizing and essentializing—a space that acknowledges the constructedness of and the differences within our lived experiences while at the same time attending to the inclining, rather than the declining, significance of race, class, culture, and gender?

I once was blind, but now I see—you

By and large, it is only those who enjoy the privileges of white skin who can hold matters of race at arm's length. White feminist theorist Jane Gallop, for instance, can say that "race only posed itself as an urgent issue to me in the last couple of years" (Gallop, Hirsch, and Miller 1990, 363), but race always has been an urgent issue for Mary Helen Washington, Barbara Christian, and Barbara Smith—indeed for most, if not all, black feminist critics. Gallop can say that she did not feel the need to discuss race until the focus of her work shifted from French poststructuralist theory to American feminist literary criticism. But Gayatri Spivak and other Third World women know only too well the fallacies and consequences of treating race as something only *other* (nonwhite) people own and racism as a problem particular to the United States. As Spivak writes in *In Other Worlds:* "In the matter of race-sensitive analysis, the chief problem of American feminist criticism is its identification of racism as such with the constitution of racism in America. Thus, today I see the object of investigation to be not only the history of 'Third World Women' or their testimony but also the production, through the great European theories, often by way of literature, of the colonial object" (1988, 81).

The colonial object is furthered not only by the canonical literature of the West, as Spivak suggests, but also by a would-be oppositional feminist criticism whose practitioners continue to see whiteness as so natural, normative, and unproblematic that racial identity is a property only of the nonwhite. Unless the object of study happens to be the Other, race is placed under erasure as something outside immediate consideration, at once extratextual and extraterrestrial. Despite decades of painful debate, denial, defensiveness, and color-consciousness-raising, "as a woman" in mainstream feminist discourse all too often continues to mean "as a white woman." White feminist philosopher Elizabeth Spelman calls this enduring, thoroughly internalized myopia the "Trojan horse of feminist ethnocentrism" (1988, 13).[9] Indeed, for women of color who are often

[9] Echoing the complaint that women of color have leveled for some time (at least since Sojourner Truth's public query, "Ain't I a woman," first asked more than 140 years ago), Spelman argues that holding their own experiences to be normative, many white feminists historically have given little more than lip service to the significance of race and class in the lives of women.

asked to prove their feminism by placing their gender before their race, the exclusionary ethnocentrism of seemingly innocent constructions such as "women and minorities" is at once as hollow and as loaded as the Greeks' wooden horse.

But there is a larger and somewhat more convoluted point I want to get at here, and maybe I can use Jane Gallop's words to make it for me. In the same conversation referred to above, Gallop confesses that African American women have become for her what French men used to be: the people she feels inadequate in relation to and tries hardest to please in her writing. This fear of black feminists "is not just idiosyncratic," Gallop believes—not just hers alone—but a shared anxiety among white women academics. She traces her own awareness of this anxiety to what she calls a "non-encounter" with black feminist critic Deborah McDowell, who teaches at the University of Virginia where Gallop once gave a talk. "I had hoped Deborah McDowell would come to my talk," she says; "she was there, she was the one person in the audience that I was really hoping to please" (Gallop, Hirsch, and Miller 1990, 363–64). Gallop goes on to explain that as part of her lecture she read from the manuscript that became *Around 1981: Academic Feminist Literary Theory* (1992), after which someone in the audience asked if she was including any black feminist critical anthologies in her study. "I answered no and tried to justify it, but my justifications rang false in my ears," she admits. She continues:

> Some weeks later a friend of mine showed me a letter from Mc-Dowell which mentioned my talk and said that I was just doing the same old thing, citing that I was not talking about any books edited by black women. I obsessed over McDowell's comment until I decided to add a chapter on Pryse and Spillers's *Conjuring*. I had already vowed not to add any more chapters out of fear that I would never finish the book. As powerful as my fear of not finishing is, it was not as strong as my wish for McDowell's approval. For McDowell, whom I do not know, read black feminist critic. [Gallop, Hirsch, and Miller 1990, 363]

Gallop ends her commentary on what might be called "the influence of anxiety" by noting that McDowell ("read black feminist critic") has come to occupy the place of Lacan in her psyche in much the same way that "emphasis on race has replaced for [her] something like French vs. American feminism" (364).

It is interesting to me that while she clearly desired McDowell's approval, like the white child who insults its mammy one moment and demands a hug from her the next, Gallop seemed to expect that approval without having to do the thing most likely to win it: include McDowell and other black women scholars in the category of feminist theorists or treat black feminist critics as colleagues to be respected for the quality of their scholarship rather than as monsters to be feared for the quantity of their difference.

Gallop's confessional narrative—and McDowell's nonspeaking part in it—is problematic on so many levels that it is difficult to unpack and isolate its multiple fractures. Among other things, her remarks seem to me to exoticize, eroticize, anomalize, and masculinize (if not demonize) Deborah McDowell and the whole category of "black feminist critic" for which she is made to stand. Just what are the implications of conflating white French men and black American women as thorns in the side of white feminists, as Father Law? Gallop's transference is all the more vexed because she and her collaborators define "the men"—"them"—as "the enemy" throughout their conversation. In fact, as Nancy K. Miller puts it at one point, where feminist critique and French male theorists meet, the result is a "David and Goliath thing, with little Jane Gallop from Duluth taking out her slingshot to use on the great man" (Gallop, Hirsch, and Miller 1990, 358).

Not-so-little (academically speaking) Jane Gallop wields words like a slingshot; but McDowell, daunting as her scholarly accomplishments are, is no Goliath. There is a very different power relation in play. McDowell, whom I believe Gallop means in some way to honor, is actually demeaned by a narrative that casts her (and, by virtue of Gallop's own symbolic action, "the black feminist critic") somewhere between monster and mammy: demanding, demeaning, impossible to please, but at the same time possessing irresistible custodial power and erotic allure as the larger than life (racialized) Other.

I must rush to insert that mammy is my metaphor, not Gallop's. In fact there is nothing in Gallop's commentary that defines McDowell as anything other than "black feminist critic"—nothing that describes her work or that explains why she looms so large in Gallop's psyche while writ so small in her text. McDowell, the black feminist critic, is never anything other than *the Other* in "Criticizing Feminist Criticism." Race enters the conversation between these three white feminists only through the referenced bodies of objectified black women and only in those moments when the speakers tally their own and each other's sins of omission against women of color and their irritation at being chastised or, as they say, "trashed" for those exclusions.

Spurred by McDowell's criticism, Jane Gallop did indeed go on to add the Pryse and Spillers anthology *Conjuring* (1985) to her study of academic feminist theory, with quite interesting results. Provocative if tentative, Gallop's critique is at its most incisive where it attends to the tensions between the different organizing principles set out in the coeditors' individually authored introduction and afterword. Her critique is, for me anyway, most engaging where it claims and attempts to explain that *Conjuring* comes with its own deconstruction.

As Gallop reads it, Marjorie Pryse's introduction argues for a continuum of black women writers—a single, unified tradition rooted in and passing on what Pryse describes as the magic, folk wisdom, and "ancient power" of black women. Hortense Spillers's afterword, on the other hand, foregrounds cross-currents and discontinuities—differences within a tradition that is itself always in flux. Gallop concludes that Pryse frames and Spillers reframes. While Spillers's reframing turns the reader's expectations inside out, Pryse's introductory framing, according to Gallop, "corresponds to and evokes in the reader, at least in the white female academic, a fantasy which orients our reading of black women. I want the conjure woman; I want some ancient power that stands beyond the reaches of white male culture. I want black women as the idealized and exoticized alternative to European high culture. I want some pure outside and am fool enough to think I might find it in a volume published by Indiana University Press, with full scholarly apparatus" (1992, 169). Again, a difficult passage to unpack, made even more so by the author's subsequent admission that she was disappointed that the book was "so 'academic' " and that she attributed its particularly erudite essays, with their classical allusions, to critics she imagined to be white. Surely Gallop does not mean what she seems to me to say here. Is she really admitting in print that she expected a critical anthology subtitled *Black Women, Fiction, and Literary Tradition*—a book edited by two university professors, one of whom has long been regarded as one of the deans of black feminist criticism—to be other than scholarly, literate, and intellectually sophisticated?

To be fair, I think Gallop's tone is meant to be ironic, to point out—and perhaps even to poke fun at—the essentializing fantasies of "the white female academic" reader who desires the Other to be *other,* who brings to the text of the Other a different set of assumptions, who in effect expects to leave high theory behind when she goes slumming in low culture. Hers is a dangerous strategy, but one that seems to be popular among white readers of "black texts," who feel compelled to supplement their critiques with exposés of their former racism (and/or sexism) in a kind of I-once-was-blind-but-now-I-see way. (It worked for the composer of "Amazing Grace," a reformed slave trader.) I will have more to say about this strategy in a moment, but for now I want to linger over what is for me as much a critique of "the white female academic" reader as of *Conjuring.*

Gallop in terms perhaps a bit too subtle for the subject is telling us that she, as a white woman reader, wanted to find in this black book the exotic black female Other, the "new delight," the "spice," to liven up the dull dish of Western culture she as an academic usually consumes. "Since I am a white academic," she writes, "what sort of fantasy not only renders those attributes contemptible but, from an imagined identification with some righteous outside, allows me to cast them as aspersions on others?" (1992, 169). In this instance, anyway, Gallop's anomalizing and exoticizing movements are not entirely unself-conscious, as they seemed to be in "Criticizing Feminist Criticism." As her self-reflective question suggests, her essay is underpinned by an implicit critique of the primitivistic assumptions and expectations that "the white female academic" (I would be more generous and say *some* white female academics) brings to the reading of texts by and/or about black women.

Even more interesting, however, is Gallop's contention that Pryse's introduction invokes and evokes such desires in the reader, especially the white reader. She says that reading *Conjuring* for a second time, even knowing that Spillers's corrective essay lay ahead, she still nearly gave herself over to the introduction's romantic vision of the black female folk. "In this chapter I wanted to transmit this illusory take on the anthology," Gallop writes, "because I consider this illusion central to *our* reading of black women. *We* must confront *our* wish to find this ancient power, this pure outside of academic culture, before *we* deconstruct or correct *our* illusion" (170; my emphasis). In other words, the reader needs to absorb Pryse's framing before Spillers's reframing can take effect.

I am not quite sure how this follows: Why we need this critical *felix culpa*, this happy fall into what Gallop describes as the folk fantasies of Pryse before *we* can be rescued by the refined vision of Spillers? But perhaps my failure to follow Gallop's logic fully here stems from the fact that her "we" and "our" are at least as problematic as the ones I used earlier. I am not a part of her "we," and she is not a part of mine. Pryse's introduction did not evoke in *me* as a reader the kind of desires Gallop evidently assumes it evokes in her universal "we." While I cannot appropriate her "we," her larger point about the opposing strategies of Pryse's introduction and Spillers's afterword is one I want to take up and to politicize.

What happens if we add to Gallop's notion of the framing/reframing, idealizing/realizing, "good cop/bad cop" routine of the coeditors the fact that Marjorie Pryse is white and Hortense Spillers black? What does it mean, then, that Spillers both brings up the rear and has the last word and, according to Gallop, "deconstructs or corrects" not only Pryse's romantic vision of a black female folk but the primitivistic expectations of the "white female academic"? Can one correct where there has been no error? Perhaps because she does not quite dare to play critical hardball with those whom she seems to take to be two black feminist critics, Gallop bends over backward to soft-pedal away the very ideological disjuncture she has so astutely identified. If the coeditors are simply playing out a well-rehearsed, mutually agreed upon routine, as Gallop ultimately concludes, why has Pryse positioned herself as the essentializing, idealizing white woman academic and left the real, corrective black feminist criticism to Spillers?

Gallop's reading of editorial matters in *Conjuring* unwittingly plays into my hand and punctuates my principal point about the dangers of a critical demeanor that demeans its subject in the very act of analyzing it. It is, of course, no better for me to use Gallop (or Pryse) as a metonym for white feminist critics than it is for Gallop to so use Deborah Mc-Dowell. Yet the wide-eyed wonderful illusions Gallop attributes to Pryse's introduction and the closed-eyed myopia of her own remarks in "Criticizing Feminist Criticism" demonstrate precisely why it remains so difficult for some black feminist scholars to entrust the texts of our familiar to the critical caretaking of white women (and men) for whom black women are newly discovered foreign bodies, always already Other.

Critical apologia: The *Driving Miss Daisy* crazy syndrome

Yet. Still. And but. If a Ph.D. in British literature is not a title deed to the African American text, neither is black skin. Romantic fantasies of an authentic, cohesive, magical, ancient, all-knowing black female folk are certainly not unique to white academics who would read black women. Some might argue that what is at issue is not simply the color or culture of the scholar but the kind, quality, and cultural competence of the scholarship. Black historian Carter Woodson reportedly welcomed the contributions of white scholars, "so long as they were the products of rigorous scholarship and were not contaminated by the venom of racial [and, I would add, gender] bias" (quoted by Meier and Rudwick 1986, 289). Unfortunately, however, such biases are ideologically inscribed and institutionally reproduced and as such are not easily elided—not even by the most liberal, the most sensitive, the most well-intentioned among us. I think, for example, of Adrienne Rich.

I had long been a fan of Rich's poetry, but I was rather late in coming to her prose. *Of Woman Born: Motherhood as Experience and Institution* (1986), originally published in 1976, was more than a dozen years old before I gave myself the pleasure of reading it. For once, however, my timing could not have been better, for I "discovered" this essential book at a critical moment in my life and in the development of my feminism:

on the eve of my fortieth birthday, as I wrestled with the likelihood of never having a child. Rich's brilliant analysis of motherhood as an instrument of patriarchy helped me come to terms with the constructedness of what I had been reared to believe were natural maternal instincts without which I was no woman. But for all that Rich's book gave me, it also took something away; and what it snatched from me, ironically and perhaps a little unfairly, has come to mean almost as much to me as what it gave.

For a moment in the penultimate chapter of this passionate and painful critique of motherhood, Rich turns her remarks toward the black woman who helped raise her. To this woman, who remains nameless, Rich assigns the designation "my Black mother." "My Black mother was 'mine,' " she writes, "only for four years, during which she fed me, dressed me, played with me, watched over me, sang to me, cared for me tenderly and intimately" ([1976] 1986, 254). Rich goes on to describe poetically the physical presence of her Black mother, from whom she "learned—*nonverbally*—a great deal about the possibilities of dignity in a degrading situation" (254; my emphasis). Unaware of the degrading situation she creates with her words, she continues: "When I began writing this chapter I began to remember my Black mother again: her calm, realistic vision of things, her physical grace and pride, her beautiful soft voice. For years, she had drifted out of reach, in my searches backward through time, exactly as the double silence of sexism and racism intended her to do. She was meant to be utterly annihilated" (254–55).

To the double silences of sexism and racism Rich adds a third: the silence (and the blindness) of feminism. Like Jane Gallop, who I am sure meant to praise Deborah McDowell, Adrienne Rich no doubt means to honor the woman who cared for her as a child. But the poetry of her prose should not disguise the paternal arrogance of her words or mask the annihilating effect of her claim on the being she resurrects and re-creates as "my Black mother." Silent and nameless in Rich's book, "my Black mother" has no identity of her own and, in fact, does not exist beyond the care and nurture she gave exclusively to the young Adrienne.

" 'Childless' herself, she *was* a mother," Rich writes of her objectified subject. Her claim to "my Black mother" and her attempt to thrust motherhood upon a childless black woman domestic worker are all the more ironic because of what she claims for all women in the introduction to the anniversary edition of *Of Woman Born:* "The claim to personhood; the claim to share justly in the products of our labor, not to be used merely as an instrument, a role, a womb, a pair of hands or a back or a set of fingers; to participate fully in the decisions of our workplace, our community; to speak for ourselves, in our own right" (xxviii). Even in the midst of her own extended critique of the mystification of motherhood and the objectification of women as mothers, Rich has both mystified and objectified someone she can see only in the possessive case as "my Black mother." "My Black mother" is a role, a pair of hands; her function is to instruct the white child "nonverbally" in the ways of the world, even as she cannot speak "in [her] own right."[10]

The kind of transformative move Rich makes in invoking the silent racial, maternalized Other is in no way unique to her prose. The child may be father of the man in poetry, but frequently when white scholars reminisce about blacks from their past it is black mammy (metaphorically speaking, even where the mammy figure is a man) who mothers the ignorant white infant into enlightenment. Often as the youthful, sometimes guilty witness to or cause of the silent martyrdom of the older Other, the privileged white person inherits a wisdom, an agelessness, perhaps even a racelessness that entitles him or her to the raw materials of another's life and culture but, of course, not to the Other's condition.

Such transformative moves often occur in the forewords, afterwords, rationales, even apologias white scholars affix to their would-be scholarly readings of the black Other—discussions that methinks just may protest too much, perhaps suggesting a somewhat uneasy relationship between author and objectified subject. These prefaces acknowledge the "outsider" status of the authors—their privileged positions as white women or as men—even as they insist on the rightness of their entry into and the significance of their impact on the fields of black literature and history.

Gerda Lerner offers such a rationale in her preface to *Black Women in White America:* "Black people at this moment in history need above all to define themselves autonomously and to interpret their past, their present and their future" (1972, xviii). Having called upon the black "physician" to heal her/himself, Lerner then goes on to explain her presence in the operating room: "Certainly, historians who are members of the culture, or subculture, about which they write will bring a special quality to their material. Their understanding and interpretation is apt to be different from that of the outsider. On the other hand, scholars from outside a culture have frequently had a *more challenging vision* than those closely involved in and bound by their own culture. Both angles of vision are complementary in arriving at the truth about the past and in finding out 'what actually happened' " (xix; my emphasis). A more chal-

---

[10] In the tenth anniversary rev. ed. of *Of Woman Born*, a wiser, reflective Adrienne Rich attempts to expand and adjust her vision in light of 1980s concerns and considerations. To her discussion of "my Black mother" she appends a footnote that reads in part: "The above passage overpersonalizes and does not, it seems to me now, give enough concrete sense of the actual position of the Black domestic worker caring for white children" (255). Even ten years later, Rich has failed to recognize that she is talking about another woman—another woman who is not her black mother but a laborer whose role as mammy is also socially, politically, and economically constructed.

lenging vision? Why does the perspective of the white scholar reading "the black experience" represent a more challenging vision?

Lerner is not alone in prefacing her work with such a self-serving claim. For reasons that I hope will become clear, I am reminded of "Who You For?"—the opening chapter of John Callahan's study *In the African-American Grain: Call-and-Response in Twentieth-Century Black Fiction* (1989). In this chapter, Callahan takes us on a sentimental journey through his Irish-American youth, which was *colored* not only by his being likened to niggers—(" 'Do you know the definition of an Irishman?' " the eight-year-old Callahan was asked by a much bigger Italian boy. " 'A Nigger turned inside-out' " [5])—but also by the black male guardians and protectors who "taught [him] a great deal about the hard work of becoming a man" (9). The teaching tools used by one of these guardians—Bill Jackson, the chauffeur for the insurance company for which Callahan worked while in college—include a "prolonged *silent* challenge" after Callahan called him a black bastard (9; my emphasis) and his "trickster's way" of teaching Callahan certain lessons.

Like Adrienne Rich, Callahan describes his black guide as "silent," even as he credits the chauffeur with teaching him many things "essential to [his] own evolving voice and story" (10). Indeed Bill Jackson, the stereotypical black trickster, remains silent as he is employed by Callahan to claim not only Callahan's own Irish-American voice but also entitlement to African-American fictions of voice, fictions that in the author's words "connect and reconnect generations of Americans—African-American, yes and preeminently, but all others too, Irish-Americans like me, for instance—with those past and present oral traditions behind our evolving spoken and written voices" (21).

Here again a critical posturing that means to celebrate a literature to my mind actually demeans it by leveling and universalizing it. Callahan's introduction suggests that we are all brothers not only under the skin but under the book jacket as well. The white scholar understands "the African American experience" not in its own right, not on its own terms, but because he can make it like his own. With his voice, he can translate another's silence into his speech. He speaks through and for the Other. Bill Jackson's silence is telling in this translative move, but so too is his profession. It is altogether fitting and proper that Jackson is a chauffeur, for indeed Callahan's introduction and Jackson's role in it invoke for me what I call the *Driving Miss Daisy* syndrome: an intellectual slight of hand that transforms power and race relations to make best friends out of driver and driven, master and slave, boss and servant, white boy and black man.

When Callahan overhears the company vice-president lumping together Irish and African Americans as "contemptible, expendable lower caste," he wishes for the craft, strength, skill, and smarts of a black football player he admires from a distance to help him speak up for himself (though apparently not for the niggers with whom he is compared). "My fate linked to African-Americans by that Yankee bank officer," Callahan writes, "I became more alert and sympathetic to black Americans my own age and younger who, though cursed, spat upon, and beaten, put their lives and voices on the line to uphold the law of the land and integrate public schools in the South" (8).

I feel as if I am supposed to applaud this declaration of allegiance, empathy, and understanding, but instead the claim of fellow feeling and universality—of linked fates and shared voice—makes me profoundly angry and mars my reading of what is actually a very fine book. Ultimately, Callahan's personal narrative, like Rich's, takes symbolic wealth from the martyred, romanticized black body but retains the luxury of refusing, erasing, or ignoring its material poverty. Twenty-five years later, John Callahan is a well-respected university professor while, as he tells us in his introduction, Roy Fitch—the protective black mailroom manager under whom he once worked—"looks after" a building near the "plebeian end" of the city green (xi). Intent as he is on using Fitch to tell his story, Callahan does not comment on or I suspect even see the historical irony of their relative positions. Nor does he grasp the ironic implications of his own storytelling. "Don't climb no mountain on my back," he recalls Fitch saying to him years before in response to his awkward attempt to apologize for yet another racial slur. Had Callahan understood the signifying significance of Fitch's word—were he as good at interpreting speech as silence—he could not possibly have written the introduction he did.

However troubling Rich's and Callahan's apologias may be to me as a black woman reader, white British Victorianist Missy Dehn Kubitschek acknowledges an indebtedness to the latter for the inspiration behind the personal commentary that opens her own study of black women writers. "My admiration for 'Who You For?' " she writes in the preface to *Claiming the Heritage: African-American Women Novelists and History,* "led me to consider voicing my own simultaneously social and psychic travels as a prelude to this study of African-American women's novels" (1991, xii).

Following Callahan's lead, Kubitschek opens her study with what she calls "A Personal Preface," in which she offers a first-hand account (complete with family history) of how she as a white woman British Victorianist came to write a book about African American women novelists. Hers is a long story, but, briefly told, one of the principal players in her disciplinary conversion was her grandmother, a long-time armchair racist, who "changed her mind about race" after watching a television program about the "dangerous urban black ghetto" of East St. Louis. Mediated through the medium of television, urban blacks became objects of pity for Mrs. Dehn rather than fear. The possibilities of Grandmother Dehn's "impossible" change of heart at such an advanced age were "seismic" for Kubitschek, who was a graduate student at the time and who found in her grandmother's conversion the seeds of her own (xviii).

But other transformative encounters lay ahead for Kubitschek in her graduate student years—experiences that not only helped her get over her family's racism but over her own as well. Arriving early and alone for work one morning in the basement office of the English department building, Kubitschek was terrified first by a male voice and then by the sudden appearance of a black man. Reading her horror writ large across her face, the man, a construction worker apparently also early on site for the task of renovating the building, "quickly" and "quietly" explained that he just wanted to use the phone. "Of course, I had been afraid before I had seen that he was black," Kubitschek writes. "Rape is always a threat to women, always a possibility" (xxi). But seeing his black skin heightened her fear, she admits, and revealed her racism. Because she had recently read Richard Wright's "Big Boy Leaves Home," she knew, she says, the historical implications of her reaction. " 'Race' ceased to be something that had constructed other people, especially blacks," as she began to understand herself as a racial as well as gendered being.

Rape *is* always a threat to women, particularly to a woman alone with a man. Black man, white man, green man from Mars, I darn well would have been afraid in Kubitschek's shoes, too. Her fear feels far more legitimate to me than the white liberal guilt that I suspect leads her to call that fear racism and to apologize for it in her preface to a book that is supposed to be about African American women writers. Through yet another troubling slight of text, Kubitschek's articulated awareness of her former racism becomes the authorizing agent behind her strange metamorphosis from British Victorianist to African Americanist.

I know I am misbehaving. I know I should be more patient, more sisterly, more respectful of other people's discoveries. I know my bad attitude comes from what in this instance might be called the arrogance of "black privilege": after all, I—whose earliest childhood memories include finding a snake in our mailbox shortly after we moved into an all-white neighborhood and being called "nigger" on my first day at an all-white elementary school—did not learn my racial consciousness from reading Richard Wright's "Big Boy Leaves Home" as an adult. But I mean my criticism as a kindness. Perhaps if I can approximate in words—however haltingly—what is so inexplicably problematic and profoundly offensive about these *Driving-Miss-Daisy*/some-of-my-best-friends-are-black/I-once-was-a-racist confessionals, I will do the field and all those who want to work in it a genuine favor. Perhaps if I can begin to delineate the difference between critical analysis that honors the field and guilty conscience rhetoric that demeans it, I can contribute something positive to the future production of scholarship on African American women. Unfortunately, the words do not come easily and the heart of what's the matter is a difficult place to get to. How do you tell people who do not get it in the first instance that it is only out of the arrogance of white privilege and/or male prerogative that they assume that it is an honor for a black woman to be proclaimed their black mother or their black friend or their black guardian or their black conscience?

It would be a mistake, however, for me to imply that these demeaning gestures are solely the product of white privilege and racial difference. For my money, the occult of true black womanhood has generated few more offensive renderings of African American women writers and critics than that offered by black literary theorist Houston Baker in *Workings of the Spirit: The Poetics of Afro-American Women's Writing* (1991). Having largely ignored black women as cultural producers throughout his long and distinguished career, Baker suddenly takes them up in *Workings*. And like Missy Dehn Kubitschek, for whom the writing of African American women is a kind of survival kit,[11] Baker tells us in his conclusion that the shared horror of a friend's rape led him to seek solace in the "expressive resistances of Afro-American women's talking books." The writings of black women authors like Hurston, Morrison, and Shange helped teach him and his friend to move beyond being victim to being survivor. "The texts of Afro-American women writers," Baker says, "became mine and my friend's harrowing but sustaining path to a new, common, and, we thought, empowering discourse and commitment. To 'victim,' in my friend's semantics, was added the title and entitlement 'survivor.' Are we not all only that? Victim/Survivors?" (208–9).

Both Kubitschek and Baker seem unaware of the ways in which their survival kit claims to the black texts they critique potentially reinscribe African American women writers and their characters as magnanimous mammies who not only endure like Faulkner's Dilsey but whose primary function is to teach others to do the same as well. While Baker is certainly entitled to tell his story, using his friend's rape to claim en-

---

[11] In the final moments of her personal preface, we learn that the lessons of Grandma Dehn and the black construction worker notwithstanding, it was actually the survival strategies embedded in black literature that ultimately led Kubitschek to the work of African American women writers. "The stories that constitute African-American literature say that oppression kills and that people survive oppression," she tells us. "Wanting to know more about survival brought me here" (1991, xxiii).

titlement to the texts of black women writers—to authorize his entry into a field he has virtually ignored—makes for a story that I, for one, resent being asked to read as part of his critical discourse. For me, this maneuver compromises the integrity of his intellectual project; it makes the feminist concept that the personal is political a kind of bad joke. Like the some-of-my-best-friends-are-black tone of Kubitschek's preface, Callahan's introduction, and Rich's chapter, Baker's conclusion makes me distrust not his cultural competence, perhaps, but his gender sensibility—his ability to handle with care the sacred text of me and mine.

But I was made suspicious of *Workings of the Spirit* long before I got to its conclusion. For, like Lerner, Kubitschek, and Callahan, Baker also has included an introduction that calls attention to himself as outsider. He begins his study by acknowledging the prior claim and what he calls the justifiably "cautious anxieties" of black feminist critics such as Barbara Smith, Barbara Christian, and Mary Helen Washington, who long ago mined the "provinces of Afro-American women's expressivity" that he is just now entering. A "blackmale" scholar "will find cause to mind his steps in a demanding territory," he asserts, seemingly unaware of the step he misses with his province/metropole metaphor. Baker's language here works linguistically to confirm him in the very role he wants most to avoid—that of colonizing, come-lately "blackmale" critic. His diction is a small example of what I found to be a big problem with *Workings of the Spirit:* the hierarchical relation between what he inevitably treats as master (male) and minor (female) narrative traditions, even in this book dedicated to exploring black female expressivity. Rather than building on the work of black women scholars who excavated the field he is just now entering, Baker, for the most part, either ignores or dismisses what he implies is their primarily historical (as opposed to theoretical) feminist criticism in favor of his own masculinist theorizing and the black male writers and white male theorists he champions.

In *Workings of the Spirit,* our mothers' gardens are populated by what Baker terms *phenomenological* white men such as Gaston Bachelard along with the phenomenal black women—Hurston, Morrison, and Shange—who are the book's announced subjects. Indeed, Baker's study of black women writers marginalizes its female objectified subjects as male writers, critics, theorists, and male experience prevail as the text's principal referents. In *Workings*'s third chapter, for example, to even get to Baker's reading of Toni Morrison's *Sula,* one must first wade through thirty pages on Richard Wright. The attention to Wright (and other male artists and intellectuals) is justified, Baker argues, because "classic Afro-American male texts" provide a touchstone from which "to proceed by distinctions" in exploring the provinces of black female expressivity.

Baker's posterior positioning of Morrison within a chapter supposedly devoted to her work intersects the problematic I have been working with in this article. Like much of the new "new scholarship" that has come out of the occult of true black womanhood, Baker's book fails to live up to its own postmodern, deconstructive principles. It achieves neither inversion nor subversion; black women writers and the black feminist critics who read them remain fetishized bodies juxtaposed against analytical white or superior male minds. As objects of investigation in studies like Baker's, black women are constructed in terms of their difference from or (in the name of sisterhood) similarity to the spectator, whether the spectator is a black male theorist or a white feminist critic. In other words, the black female Other is made only more Other by the male theorist or by the "white female academic" (to use Jane Gallop's phrase) who views the objectified subject from a position of unrelinquished authority.

This failure of inversion is particularly alarming in Baker's case because of the enormous power he wields in the academy and the publishing industry. That *Workings of the Spirit* was published as part of a series Baker edits under the University of Chicago imprint suggests just how absolutely absolute power authorizes and reproduces itself. For black feminist studies, the ramifications of this power dynamic are potentially devasting: black feminist critics can be de-authorized with a roll of the presses, even as black women are deployed in a decidedly masculinist project that claims to "enter into dialogue" with them.

Baker is, of course, free to disagree with black women scholars (as we frequently do with each other), but his failure to take seriously their critical insights ultimately undermines his effort to enter into what he acknowledges is an already established dialogue. His privileging of male subjects in this book supposedly about black women writers becomes an act of silencing and makes his text the victim of its own intentional phallacy. By "intentional phallacy," I mean the gap between Baker's stated wish to avoid appropriating and objectifying the work and images of African American women through a "blackmale" gaze and the degree to which his text fosters rather than avoids such appropriations.

His essential and, I think, essentializing metaphors—black women as "departed daughters" and "spirit workers"—taken together with the uncontextualized photographs of black women interspersed throughout his book, raise questions about the gaze, about specularization and objectification, that Baker, despite his desire not to "colonize" the female subject, does not address or, I suspect, even see. This is both ironic and unfortunate, since Mae Henderson—one of the black feminist critics Baker faintly praises for her "fine theorizing"—called his attention to the problematic of the gaze generated by his work in a critique of an earlier essay of his that was the prototype for *Workings of the Spirit.* The danger, she warned, "is not only that of essentializing but of reinforcing the most conventional constructs of (black) femininity." Henderson was troubled in particular by the "*specularity* of [Baker's] rather spectacular theory" of black female spirituality. She cautioned him to rethink his treatment of black women in terms that would not objectify and idealize them (1989, 159).

While the words of praise from Henderson excerpted on *Workings's* back cover imply her endorsement of Baker's finished project, she in fact has offered the author both an elegantly incisive critique and an eloquently pointed admonition. Her cautionary tale has been little heeded, however; *Workings of the Spirit,* I would argue, continues the idealization and specularization of black women that its prototypical essay began. The book's complementary phototext seems to me, in fact, to evoke precisely what Henderson identified as "the male activity of scopophilia." Largely unremarked except for occasional captioned quotations from Baker's written word, the images of black women interspersed throughout the text objectify graphically those whom the book objectifies linguistically. But in another example of Baker's strategic deployment of women, this objectification is made *okay* by the author's claim that the phototext is the handiwork not of senior "blackmale" theorist Houston Baker but of junior female scholars Elizabeth Alexander and Patricia Redmond. This, in fact, is Baker's final point, his "last word":

> The phototext is the artistry of two young scholars. Their complementary text is a rich enhancement of the present work, and I cannot thank Elizabeth Alexander and Patricia Redmond enough for their collaboration. It seems to me that the intertextuality represented by their effort makes the present work more engaging than it would otherwise have been. My initial idea was that such a text would comprise a type of countercurrent of signification, soliciting always my own words, qualifying their "maleness." What emerged from the labors of Redmond and Alexander, however, is a visualization of an Afro-American women's poetics. Eyes and events engage the reader/viewer in a solicitous order of discourse that asks: "Who reads here?" [212]

If these photos indeed could ask such a question, I suspect that their answer would be, "A man." Baker means for the photographs to speak for themselves of "the space, place, and time of Afro-American women" (213), but it is unclear how they are to do so placed unproblematically in the midst of what is—despite his claims about the collaborative efforts of

Alexander and Redmond—*his* project. Whose project the phototext is becomes even clearer when we know that at the time the book was compiled Alexander and Redmond were graduate students to whom Baker assigned the task of assembling a complementary photo essay. The image that Alexander and Redmond presented to Baker as the "parting shot" of his book is of a young black woman, her mouth open wide as if in a scream. I wonder what it means that the black woman depicted in midscream is literally, physically, clinically mute.

Toward a conclusion

I am not quite certain what to make of the ground I have covered in this article or where to go from here. More bewitched, bothered, and bewildered than ever by my own problematic, I find myself oddly drawn to (gulp) William Faulkner. The griefs of great literature, Faulkner suggested in his Nobel Prize acceptance speech, must grieve on universal bones. I realize that I have heard this before—and not just from Faulkner. The Self recognition spontaneously generated by the literature of the ennobled Other is the essence of Callahan's professed link to African American "fictions of voice" and the medium of Baker's and Kubitschek's claimed connection to the texts of black women. And they are not alone in this kind of association with the ennobled Other. In the words of three white feminist academics who claim to identify closely with the explicit depiction of physical and psychic abuse in the fiction of black women writers such as Toni Morrison, Alice Walker, and Gayl Jones: "We, as white feminists, are drawn to black women's visions because they concretize and make vivid a system of oppression." Indeed, they continue, "it has not been unusual for white women writers to seek to understand their oppression through reference to the atrocities experienced by other groups" (Sharpe, Mascia-Lees, and Cohen 1990, 146). For these feminists, as for Baker and Kubitschek, the lure of black women's fiction is, at least in part, its capacity to teach others how to endure and prevail, how to understand and rise above not necessarily the pain of black women but their own.

Is this usage of black women's texts a bad thing? If Faulkner is right—if it is the writer's duty to help humankind endure by reminding us of our capacity for courage and honor and hope and pride and compassion and pity and sacrifice and survival—black women writers have done the job particularly well. The griefs of African American women indeed seem to grieve on universal bones—"to concretize and make vivid a system of oppression." But it also seems (and herein lies the rub) that in order to grieve "universally," to be "concrete," to have "larger meaning," the flesh on these bones ultimately always must be white or male.

This, then, is the final paradox and the ultimate failure of the evidence of experience: to be valid—to be true—black womanhood must be legible as white or male; the texts of black women must be readable as maps, indexes to someone else's experience, subject to a seemingly endless process of translation and transference. Under the cult of true black womanhood, the colored body, as Cherríe Moraga has argued, is "thrown over a river of tormented history to bridge the gap" (1981, xv), to make connections—connections that in this instance enable scholars working in exhausted fields to cross over into the promised land of the academy.

Both black women writers and the black feminist critics who have brought them from the depths of obscurity into the ranks of the academy have been such bridges. The trouble is that, as Moraga points out, bridges get walked on over and over and over again. This sense of being a bridge—of being walked on and passed over, of being used up and burnt out, of having to "publish while perishing," as some have described their situations—seems to be a part of the human condition of many black women scholars. While neither the academy nor mainstream feminism has paid much attention to the crisis of black female intellectuals, the issue is much on the minds of black feminist scholars, particularly in the wake of the Thomas/Hill hearings, the critique of professional women and family values, and the loss of Audre Lorde and Sylvia Boone in a single year. So serious are these issues that the state and fate of black women in and around the university were the subjects of a national conference held at the Massachusetts Institute of Technology in January 1994. Entitled "Black Women in the Academy: Defending Our Name, 1894–1994," this conference, the first of its kind, drew together nearly two thousand black women from institutions across the country. The conference organizers have said that they were overwhelmed by the response to their call for papers: they were instantly bombarded by hundreds of abstracts, letters, faxes, and phone calls from black women describing the hypervisibility, superisolation, emotional quarantine, and psychic violence of their precarious positions in academia.

I do not mean to imply that all black women scholars see themselves as what Hurston called "tragically colored," but I think that it is safe to say that these testimonies from across the country represent a plaintive cry from black women academics who see themselves and their sisters consumed by exhaustion, depression, loneliness, and a higher incidence of such killing diseases as hypertension, lupus, cancer, diabetes, and obesity. But it also seems to me that Jane Gallop's anxieties about African American women, Nancy K. Miller's fear that there is no position from which a middle-class white woman can speak about race without being offensive, and Houston Baker's desire for dialogue with black women scholars also represent plaintive cries. Clearly both white women and women and men of color experience the pain and disappointment of failed community.

As much as I would like to end on a positive note, I have little faith that our generation of scholars—black and nonblack, male and female—will succeed in solving the problems I have taken up in this article. We are too set in our ways, too alternately defensive and offensive, too much the products of the white patriarchal society that has reared us and the white Eurocentric educational system that has trained us. If ever there comes a day when white scholars are forced by the systems that educate them to know as much about "the Other" as scholars of color are required to know about so-called dominant cultures, perhaps black women will no longer be treated as consumable commodities.

Until that day, I see a glimmer of hope shining in the bright eyes of my students who seem to me better equipped than we to explore the intersection of racial and gender difference. I was impressed by the way young women—black and white—and one lone white man in a seminar I offered on black feminist critical theory were able to grapple less with each other and more with issues, to disagree without being disagreeable, and to learn from and with each other. I wonder if there is a lesson for us older (but not necessarily wiser) academics in their interaction. I wonder what it would mean for feminist scholarship in general if "woman" were truly an all-inclusive category, if "as a woman" ceased to mean "as a white woman." I wonder what it would mean for women's studies, for black studies, for American studies, if women of color, white women, and men were truly able to work together to produce the best of all possible scholarship.

While the editorial scheme of *Conjuring* may employ different, even contradictory notions of text and tradition, as Jane Gallop suggests, perhaps the strategy of black and white women working together on intellectual projects is one we should embrace. I do not mean to suggest that we can or should police each other, but I wonder about the possibilities of what my colleague Sharon Holland calls "complementary theorizing."[12] I wonder what shape Gallop's conversation with Nancy K. Miller and Marianne Hirsch might have taken were women of color talked with rather than about. I wonder what kind of book *Workings of the Spirit* might have been were it truly a collaborative effort with black women or even with one black woman—perhaps the woman with whom Baker says he first discovered the healing powers of African American women's fiction. I have never met Adrienne Rich, but if we had been friends or colleagues, if I had had the honor of reading *Of Woman Born* in manuscript, perhaps I could have given back to her some of what her

---

[12] Sharon Holland, personal communication, September 1993.

book gave me by pointing out to *her* (rather than to the readers of *Signs*) the problems of "my Black mother." However idle they may appear, for me these speculations about what might have been offer a measure of hope about what yet might be.

English and African American Studies
Wesleyan University

References

Abel, Elizabeth. 1993. "Black Writing, White Reading: Race and the Politics of Feminist Interpretation." *Critical Inquiry* 19 (Spring): 470–98.
Ammons, Elizabeth. 1992. *Conflicting Stories: American Women Writers at the Turn into the Twentieth Century.* New York: Oxford University Press.
Andrews, William L., ed. 1986. *Sisters of the Spirit: Three Black Women's Autobiographies of the Nineteenth Century.* Bloomington: Indiana University Press.
Baker, Houston, Jr. 1991. *Workings of the Spirit: The Poetics of Afro-American Women's Writing.* Chicago: University of Chicago Press.
Bambara, Toni Cade. 1970. *The Black Woman.* New York: New American Library.
Beal, Frances. 1970. "Double Jeopardy: To Be Black and Female." In *Sisterhood Is Powerful,* ed. Robin Morgan, 340–52. New York: Random House.
Bell, Roseanne P., Bettye J. Parker, and Beverly Guy-Sheftall, eds. 1979. *Sturdy Black Bridges: Visions of Black Women in Literature.* Garden City, N.Y.: Anchor.
Belsey, Catherine. 1980. *Critical Practices.* New York: Routledge.
Brown, William Wells. (1853) 1989. *Clotel; or, The President's Daughter: A Narrative of Slave Life in the United States,* with an introduction by William Farrison. London: Patridge & Oakey; New York: Carol Publishing.
Callahan, John F. 1989. *In the African-American Grain: Call-and-Response in Twentieth-Century Black Fiction.* 2d ed. Middletown, Conn.: Wesleyan University Press.
Carby, Hazel. 1986. "It Jus' Be's Dat Way Sometime: The Sexual Politics of Women's Blues." *Radical America* 20(4):9–22.
———. 1987. *Reconstructing Womanhood: The Emergence of the Afro-American Woman Novelist.* New York: Oxford University Press.
Christian, Barbara. (1975) 1985. "Images of Black Women in Afro-American Literature: From Stereotype to Character." In her *Black Feminist Criticism: Perspectives on Black Women Writers,* 1–30. New York: Pergamon.
———. 1980. *Black Women Novelists: The Development of a Tradition, 1892–1976.* Westport, Conn.: Greenwood.
Christian, Barbara, Ann duCille, Sharon Marcus, Elaine Marks, Nancy K. Miller, Sylvia Schafer, and Joan W. Scott. 1990. "Conference Call." *differences* 2 (Fall): 52–108.
Cooper, Anna Julia. (1892) 1988. *A Voice from the South,* with an introduction by Mary Helen Washington. Xenia, Ohio: Aldine Printing House; reprint, New York: Oxford University Press.

Davis, Angela. 1971. "Reflections on the Black Woman's Role in the Community of Slaves." *Black Scholar* 3 (December): 3–15.

———. 1981. *Women, Race and Class*. New York: Random House.

Dill, Bonnie Thornton. 1979a. "Across the Barriers of Race and Class: An Exploration of the Relationship between Female Domestic Servants." Ph.D. dissertation, New York University.

———. 1979b. "The Dialectics of Black Womanhood." *Signs* 4 (Spring): 543–55.

———. 1983. "Race, Class, and Gender: Prospects for an All-inclusive Sisterhood." *Feminist Studies* 9 (Spring): 131–50.

duCille, Ann. 1993. *The Coupling Convention: Sex, Text, and Tradition in Black Women's Fiction*. New York: Oxford University Press.

Fender, Stephen. 1993. "African Accents, Tall Tales," review of *Was Huck Black? Mark Twain and African-American Voices*, by Shelley Fisher Fishkin, and *Mark Twain and the Art of the Tall Tale*, by Henry B. Wonham. *Times Literary Supplement* (July 16), 27.

Fishkin, Shelley Fisher. 1993. *Was Huck Black? Mark Twain and African American Voices*. New York: Oxford University Press.

Foster, Frances. 1973. "Changing Concept of the Black Woman." *Journal of Black Studies* (June), 433–52.

Gallop, Jane. 1992. *Around 1981: Accademic Feminist Literary Theory*. New York: Routledge.

Gallop, Jane, Marianne Hirsch, and Nancy K. Miller. 1990. "Criticizing Feminist Criticism." In *Conflicts in Feminism,* ed. Marianne Hirsch and Evelyn Fox Keller, 349–69. New York: Routledge.

Gates, Henry Louis, Jr. 1989. "Canon-Formation and the Afro-American Tradition." In *Afro-American Literary Studies in the 1990s,* ed. Houston Baker, Jr., and Patricia Redmond, 13–49. Chicago: University of Chicago Press.

Harley, Sharon, and Rosalyn Terborg-Penn, eds. 1978. *The Afro-American Woman: Struggles and Images*. New York: Kennikat.

Harris, Trudier, ed. 1986. *Afro-American Writers from the Harlem Renaissance to 1940*. Dictionary of Literary Biography, vol. 51. Detroit: Gale Research.

Hemenway, Robert. 1977. *Zora Neale Hurston: A Literary Biography*. Urbana: University of Illinois Press.

Henderson, Mae. 1989. "Commentary on 'There Is No More Beautiful Way: Theory and the Poetics of Afro-American Women's Writing,' by Houston Baker." In *Afro-American Literary Studies in the 1990s,* ed. Houston A. Baker, Jr., and Patricia Redmond. Chicago: University of Chicago Press.

Herskovits, Melville J. (1928) 1985. *The American Negro: A Study in Racial Crossing*. Westport, Conn.: Greenwood.

———. 1938. *Dahomey*. New York: Augustin.

———. 1941. *The Myth of the Negro Past*. Boston: Beacon.

Herskovits, Melville J., and Frances Herskovits. 1936. *Suriname Folklore*. New York: Columbia University Press.

Hine, Darlene Clark. 1980. "The Four Black History Movements: A Case for the Teaching of Black History." *Teaching History: A Journal of Methods* 5 (Fall): 115. Quoted in Meier and Rudwick 1986.

————. 1981. *When the Truth Is Told: A History of Black Women's Culture and Community in Indiana, 1875–1950*. Indianapolis: National Council of Negro Women.

Hine, Darlene Clark, and Kate Wittenstein. 1979. "Female Slave Resistance: The Economics of Sex." *Western Journal of Black Studies* 3(2):123–27.

Hirsch, Marianne, and Evelyn Fox Keller. 1990. *Conflicts in Feminism*. New York: Routledge.

hooks, bell. 1981. *Ain't I a Woman?* Boston: South End.

————. 1992. *Black Looks: Race and Representation*. Boston: South End.

Hull, Gloria, Patricia Bell Scott, and Barbara Smith, eds. 1982. *All the Women Are White, All the Blacks Are Men, but Some of Us Are Brave*. Old Westbury, N.Y.: Feminist Press.

Jacobs, Harriet. (1861) 1987. *Incidents in the Life of a Slave Girl, Written by Herself*, ed. Jean Fagan Yellin. Cambridge, Mass.: Harvard University Press.

Johnson, Barbara. 1989. Response to Gates. In *Afro-American Literary Studies in the 1990s*, ed. Houston Baker, Jr., and Patricia Redmond, 39–44. Chicago: University of Chicago Press.

Joyce, Joyce A. 1987. "The Black Canon: Reconstructing Black American Literary Criticism." *New Literary History* 18 (Winter): 335–44.

Karamcheti, Indira. 1993. "Caliban in the Classroom." *Radical Teacher* 44 (Winter): 13–17.

Kubitschek, Missy Dehn. 1991. *Claiming the Heritage: African-American Women Novelists and History*. Jackson: University Press of Mississippi.

Ladner, Joyce. 1972. *Tomorrow's Tomorrow: The Black Woman*. New York: Doubleday.

Lerner, Gerda. 1972. *Black Women in White America: A Documentary History*. New York: Random House.

Lewis, David Levering. 1984. "Parallels and Divergences: Assimilationist Strategies of Afro-American and Jewish Elites from 1910 to the Early 1930s." *Journal of American History* 71 (December): 543–64.

McDowell, Deborah. (1980) 1985. "New Directions for Black Feminist Criticism." In *The New Feminist Criticism: Essays on Women, Literature, and Theory*, ed. Elaine Showalter. New York: Pantheon.

McKay, Nellie. 1984. *Jean Toomer, Artist: A Study of His Literary Life and Work, 1894–1936*. Chapel Hill: University of North Carolina Press.

Meier, August, and Elliot Rudwick. 1986. *Black History and the Historical Profession, 1915–1980*. Urbana: University of Illinois Press.

Moraga, Cherríe. 1981. "Preface." In *This Bridge Called My Back: Writings by Radical Women of Color*, ed. Cherríe Moraga and Gloria Anzaldúa, xiii–xix. New York: Kitchen Table: Women of Color Press.

Mossell, Mrs. N. F. (1894) 1988. *The Work of the Afro-American Woman*, with an introduction by Joanne Braxton. New York: Oxford University Press.

Nichols, Charles. 1963. *Many Thousand Gone: The Ex-Slaves' Account of Their Bondage and Freedom*. Bloomington: Indiana University Press.

Noble, Jeanne. 1978. *Beautiful, Also, Are the Souls of My Black Sisters*. Englewood Cliffs, N.J.: Prentice-Hall.

Pryse, Marjorie, and Hortense Spillers, eds. 1985. *Conjuring: Black Women, Fiction, and Literary Tradition*. Bloomington: Indiana University Press.

Rich, Adrienne. (1976) 1986. *Of Woman Born*. Tenth anniversary ed. New York: Norton.

Sharpe, Patricia, F. E. Mascia-Lee, and C. B. Cohen. 1990. "White Women and Black Men: Different Responses to Reading Black Women's Texts." *College English* 52 (February): 142–53.

Skeeter, Sharon J. 1973. "Black Women Writers: Levels of Identity." *Essence* 4 (May): 3–10.

Smith, Barbara. (1977) 1985. "Toward a Black Feminist Criticism." In *The New Feminist Criticism: Essays on Women, Literature, and Theory*, ed. Elaine Showalter. New York: Pantheon.

——— . 1979. "Notes for Yet Another Paper on Black Feminism, or Will the Real Enemy Please Stand Up?" *Conditions: Five*, 123–27.

Smith, Valerie. 1987. *Self-Discovery and Authority in Afro-American Narrative*. Cambridge, Mass.: Harvard University Press.

Spelman, Elizabeth. 1988. *Inessential Woman: Problems of Exclusion in Feminist Thought*. Boston: Beacon.

Spillers, Hortense. 1987. "Mama's Baby, Papa's Maybe: An American Grammar Book." *Diacritics* 17 (Summer): 65–81.

Spivack, Gayatri Chakravorty. 1988. *In Other Worlds: Essays in Cultural Politics*. New York: Routledge.

——— . 1989. "In Praise of *Sammy and Rosie Get Laid*." *Critical Quarterly* 31(2):80–88.

Steady, Filomina Chioma, ed. 1981. *The Black Woman Cross-Culturally*. Cambridge, Mass.: Schenkman.

Tate, Claudia. 1981. *Interviews with Black Women Writers*. New York: Continuum.

Wade-Gayles, Gloria. 1984. *No Crystal Stair: Visions of Race and Sex in Black Women's Fiction*. New York: Pilgrim Press.

Walker, Alice. 1974. "In Search of Our Mothers' Gardens." *Ms.* 2 (May): 64–70, 105.

Wall, Cheryl A. 1982. "Poets and Versifiers, Singers and Signifiers: Women Writers of the Harlem Renaissance." In *Women, the Arts, and the 1920s in Paris and New York*, ed. Kenneth W. Wheeler and Virginia Lee Lussier, 74–98. New Brunswick, N.J.: Transaction.

——— , ed. 1989. "Taking Positions and Changing Words." In her *Changing Our Own Words: Essays on Criticism, Theory, and Writing by Black Women*, 1–15. New Brunswick, N.J.: Rutgers University Press.

Wallace, Michele. 1990. "Who Owns Zora Neale Hurston? Critics Carve Up the Legend." In her *Invisibility Blues*, 172–86. New York: Verso.

Washington, Mary Helen. 1972. "Zora Neale Hurston: The Black Woman's Search for Identity." *Black World* (August): 68–75.

——— . 1974. "Their Fiction Becomes Our Reality: Black Women Image Makers." *Black World* (August), 10–18.

——— . 1975. "Introduction." In *Black-Eyed Susans: Classic Stories by and about Black Women*, ed. Mary Helen Washington, ix–xxxii. Garden City, N.Y.: Anchor.

————. 1980. "In Pursuit of Our Own History." In *Midnight Birds: Stories of Contemporary Black Women Writers*, ed. Mary Helen Washington, xiii–xxv. Garden City, N.Y.: Anchor.

Weld, Elizabeth New. 1988. "The Voice of Black Women." *Boston Globe* (February 14), 98, 100.

Williams, Sherley Anne. 1978. "Foreword." In Zora Neale Hurston, *Their Eyes Were Watching God*. Urbana: University of Illinois Press.

Wilson, Harriet. (1859) 1983. *Our Nig; or, Sketches from the Life of a Free Black*. New York: Vintage.

Winkler, Karen J. 1992. "A Scholar's Provocative Query: Was Huckleberry Finn Black?" *Chronicle of Higher Education* (July 8), A6–A8.

Beyond White and Other: Relationality and Narratives of Race in Feminist Discourse

Susan   Stanford   Friedman

T HE BEATING OF Rodney King by four police officers and
the violent aftermath of their acquittal in Los Angeles in April
of 1992 underlines the explosive status of race and ethnicity in
the United States in the 1990s. The videotape of the beating—
played and replayed on TV screens for months—captures the "black and
white" of the beating in a double sense. It images metonymically the
whiteness of the police and the blackness of Rodney King, the brutality
of power and the powerlessness of victimization, and the binary of
white/black as it has materialized in the history of European American
racism toward African Americans in the United States. But the violent
upheaval after the trial—also imprinted repeatedly on the national con-
sciousness by the media—tells other stories, ones that supplement rather
than replace the story of white and black in America.

These narratives pit not just black against white but African Ameri-
cans, Latinos, and Asian Americans (especially Korean Americans)
against each other. Reginald Denny was not the only man to be pulled
from his truck. Guatemalan immigrant Fidel Lopez, for instance, was
seized, beaten, doused with gasoline, and nearly torched by an angry mob
that included the same African American men accused of attacking
Denny—Damian Williams and Henry Watson. Like Denny, Lopez was
saved by courageous African Americans (Gross 1993). In spite of the
media's tendency to emphasize African American violence, the rage and

Earlier versions of this article were delivered at the Carolyn G. Heilbrun conference,
New York, October 1992; the International Conference on Narrative, Troy, N.Y. 1993;
the Modern Language Association convention, Toronto, December 1993; and the Wom-
en's Studies Research Center at University of Wisconsin—Madison. For their challenges
and encouragement, I am indebted to these audiences, to the many who read earlier
drafts (especially Joseph Boone, Edward Friedman, Linda Gordon, Amy Ling, Nellie
McKay and the Faculty Draft Group of the University of Wisconsin—Madison English
department), and to my toughest critics, the anonymous readers for *Signs*.

[*Signs: Journal of Women in Culture and Society* 1995, vol. 21, no. 1]

looting were not restricted to a single cultural group. Unlike the Watts uprising of 1965, Asian American, African American, Latino, and Euro-American shopkeepers faced rainbow mobs of people joined in anger, resentment, and desire overdetermined by the politics of race, ethnicity, class, gender, and immigration. Blacks and Latinos in particular attacked Korean American shop owners and targeted Koreatown, scapegoating the group that the media has made into "the model minority," the new American Dream story, whose very "success" covertly blames those who remain poor for their "failure" to succeed. Moreover, fault lines erupted between members of related racial or ethnic groups, often exacerbated by differences of class and immigration status—particularly, Mexican Americans versus Central Americans and Korean Americans versus other Asian Americans. What essayist and PBS commentator Richard Rodriguez calls the dualistic "black and white checkerboard" of race that has long dominated the American consciousness of racism has been reconfigured in multiracial, multicultural terms by the aftermath of the white police officers' acquittal for beating Rodney King (Rodriguez 1993, 14).[1]

These narratives of multiethnic, multiracial, and multicultural conflict do not, of course, render irrelevant the systemic forms of white racism against people of color in the United States. As both Elaine Kim (1993) and David Polumbo-Liu (1994) demonstrate in their analyses of media representations of Korean Americans during the Los Angeles events, the institutional and attitudinal manifestations of white racism played a significant role in the media portrayal of besieged Korean Americans both as near-white, model Americans defending their property against barbaric African Americans and Latinos and as ruthless shopkeepers at blame for the economic deprivations of other Americans. The media focus on the interracial, interethnic, and intraethnic dimensions of the uprising performs in part the cultural work of suppressing awareness of the way the structures of white racism intensify conflict between racial and ethnic others. The worsening socioeconomic profile for inner cities all across the United States in which white racism plays a large part functions as a crucial context in which immigrant groups are set up to scramble with impoverished African Americans for less and less in an increasingly polarized and transnational economy.

At the same time, however, these events urgently testify to another reading that exists as a supplement to, not a displacement of, the effects of white racism. This reading of multiethnic, multiracial, and multicul-

---

[1] See esp. Robert Gooding-Williams's invaluable collection, *Reading Rodney King/Reading Urban Uprising* (1993) for information about and different interpretations of the Los Angeles events, some of which attest to the continued relevance of the white/black binary, others of which place the events within larger socioeconomic contexts, and others of which reflect upon the multiracial aspect of the events.

tural conflict and connection focuses on the significance of the changing demographics in the United States as we move into the twenty-first century in an increasingly globalized, mobile, and cyberspatial world. (I do not mean *multiethnic, multiracial,* and *multicultural* to refer only to people of color, a usage that reinforces the racist notion that whiteness or Euro-Americanness is a "natural" identity, not a social construct.)[2] For many, Los Angeles represents the avant-garde of the "browning of America," a phrase that ambiguously invokes the rise of nonblack racial minorities, the enormous influx of nonwhite immigrants into the United States, the proportional decrease of Euro-Americans, the widespread phenomenon of racial and ethnic mixing, the growing heterogeneity or syncretism of all cultural groups (and individuals within those groups), and even the dissolution of fixed boundaries in the "conventional black and white dialectic" (Rodriguez 1993, 14). As parable, the events in Los Angeles suggest that binary categories of race should be supplemented with a more complicated discourse, one that acknowledges the ongoing impact of white racism but also goes beyond an analysis of white strategies that divide and conquer people of color. We need a language beyond fixed categories of good and evil, of victims and victimizers, a discourse beyond the binary of black and white, a language that could explain the statement by Lopez's daughter, who said she did not hate her father's attackers because "I understood why they were so mad" (Gross 1993).[3]

Feminists have much to learn from the demographic landscape and tumult of Los Angeles as race and ethnicity become ever more central concerns in our classrooms, organizations, conferences, and writing.[4]

[2] Racist ideologies often assume that "race" is a property only of the racial other. For analysis of the construction of whiteness as a racial identity, see, e.g., Frye (1981) 1983, 1992; Pratt 1984; Nielson 1988; Frankenberg 1993; and duCille's critique of "a would-be oppositional feminist criticism whose practitioners continue to see whiteness as so natural, normative, and unproblematic that racial identity is a property only of the nonwhite" (1994, 607).

[3] For explicit critiques of the white/black binary, see esp. Spillers 1989; Lorne 1991; Cho 1993; Omi and Winant 1993; and Oliver et al. 1993. For analysis of the rise of multiracialism in the context of census data collection and affirmative action in the United States, see Wright 1994. For an anthropological perspective on increasing mobility, the "global ethnoscape," and identity, see Appadurai 1991.

[4] Throughout, I refer to race and ethnicity as related but not identical categories, both of which reflect the propensity of human beings to organize themselves into groups defined in opposition to others. I assume both *race* and *ethnicity* to be cultural constructs, with *race* usually connoting biological and *ethnicity* suggesting cultural difference, although this distinction repeatedly breaks down in actual usage (see, e.g., Michaels 1992, and Rensberger 1993, who reports on a multimillion dollar research project aimed at analyzing DNA samples from four hundred ethnic groups worldwide). For overviews of social science treatments of these terms, see Stocking 1968; Fortney 1977; Peterson, Novak, and Gleason 1980; Stepan 1982; Omi and Winant 1986; Banton 1987; and Thompson 1989. For anaysis of racial discourse, see Fields 1982; Gates 1986a; Goldberg 1990; Dikötter 1992; and Higginbotham 1992. For a sampling of those who regard "race" as a false, dangerous construct, see Appiah 1986; Gates 1986b;

Since the 1970s, feminism in the United States has increasingly had to come to grips with issues of racism: with race as a central constituent of identity and as the basis of both domination and resistance. The feminist analysis of gender and race (along with other components of identity) as interactive systems of stratification has developed extensively, alongside the rapid expansion of knowledge about the varied specificities of women's cultural histories. American feminists have had more difficulty confronting the issue of racism and engaging in meaningful cross-racial interaction, however. The shattering of binary thinking represented in the Los Angeles events holds out creative possibilities for feminists to think about, talk about, and act upon this difficult dimension of race in a more fruitful way.

"The very act of writing or speaking about race," Dominick LaCapra writes in his introduction to *The Bounds of Race,* "is fraught with difficulty even when one attempts to go about it in a critical and self-critical manner," especially for "those who are not 'people of color' " (1991, 2). As a Euro-American woman who inevitably benefits from the system of racial stratification in the United States, I am particularly aware of how difficult it is for me to address these questions, affected as the process is by my own and my readers' different positions within a society in which "racism is the clearest way Americans have of understanding social division" (Rodriguez 1993, 14). This problem is all the more pressing in the context of the academy's current "race for race," especially for white academics to teach and write about race.[5] As Ann duCille points out in reference to black women, this desire on the part of white academics to write about black women all too often includes a failure to include real black women in the discussion or to understand black women as cultural producers rather than simply as objects of the racial gaze (1994). Nonetheless, I cannot accept the notion that the racial privilege of my whiteness should enforce my silence about race and ethnicity, issues of vital ethical and political importance not only in the United States but also in a global context. The land mines are everywhere—my own ignorances based on racial privilege and the rush of others to dismiss, censor, not hear, condemn, withdraw. Yet I ask that you hear me out. I offer these reflections in the spirit of dialogue, of what Sharon Holland calls

---

Radhakrishnan 1991; Appiah and Gates 1992a, 625–29; and Higginbotham 1992. For those who advocate continued use of racial categories because of their ideological force and material consequences, see, e.g., Baker 1986 and West 1988. For examples of the conflation of race and ethnicity, see Sollors 1986, 1989; and Boelhower 1987; for examples of insistence on their distinction, see Omi and Winant 1986; and Wald 1987.

    [5] I here adapt Barbara Christian's title, "The Race for Theory" (1988) to suggest that similar power dynamics are at work in discussions of race in the 1990s as in those she critiqued in the academy's "race for theory" in the 1980s. See also n. 14.

"complementary theorizing" among people of different perspectives and racial identities (duCille 1994, 624)—a precondition, I believe, for growth and change in the academy and feminist movement.

In my view, feminist discourses about race and ethnicity are too often caught up in repetitive cultural narratives structured around the white/other binary: victims and victimizers, colonized and colonizers, slaves and masters, dominated and dominators, "us and them," the "good guys against the bad guys." As a result, discussions about race and racism often collapse in frustration, anger, hurt, yelling, silence, withdrawal, and profound belief that different "sides" are unable to listen and learn from the other. This all-too-familiar dead end, what Mary Louise Fellows and Sherene Razack have called "the difference impasse" (1994, 1051), often occurs in spite of the best intentions and efforts of many feminists to move beyond such repetitive patterns. Overdetermined by the different locations feminists occupy in racial hierarchies, these discussions often recapitulate instead of moving through and beyond the ignorance, anger, guilt, and silences about race and racism that are the products of power relations in the larger society.[6]

More hopeful, attempts by women of color to build bridges across their own differences with other women of color have usefully initiated the dissolution of the white/other and white/black binaries by looking at relations between two or more marginalized groups and by insisting that racial issues in the United States need to be more broadly understood than as the power relations between European Americans and African Americans. But because these coalitions are based on a shared difference from white women, they often end up reconfiguring binary thinking in the form of white women/women of color or First World/Third World binaries. Vast differences in culture and history among nonwhite women of different racial and ethnic backgrounds and even among women of the same racial or ethnic backgrounds have made alliances difficult, often conflict-ridden and ephemeral.[7]

[6] For some accounts of such stalled discussions, see Frye (1981) 1983; Huntado 1989; Anzaldúa 1990c, xix–xxi; Pheterson 1990; and Fellows and Razack 1994. Conferences of the National Women's Studies Association (NWSA) have included many partially fruitful but also often nonproductive discussions. See, e.g., Sandoval's 1990 report on the 1981 NWSA conference; Albrecht and Brewer's collection about the 1988 NWSA conference focused on coalitional politics (1990); and the accounts of the walkout of women of color from the 1990 NWSA conference and the consequent near demise of NWSA in Longnecker 1990; Musil 1990; NWSA Women of Color Caucus 1990; Osborne 1990; Ruby and Douglas 1990; Sales 1990; and Schweickart 1990. For more hopeful accounts in the classroom, see Romero 1991; and Thompson and Disch 1992.

[7] For the white/color binary as the basis for alliance among women of color, see, e.g., Moraga and Anzalda 1981; Anzalda 1990c; Longnecker 1990; Musil 1990; NWSA Women of Color Caucus 1990; Osborne 1990; Ruby 1990; Sales 1990; Sandoval 1990; and Schweickart 1990. For discussion of the difficulties of alliance among different

Such tentative progress around issues of race among different groups of feminists is still matched by the anger, failures of dialogue, and withdrawal that can suddenly explode or slowly sour the dynamics of feminist classrooms, conferences, and organizations. The existence of racism within the larger society has surely undermined many efforts of feminists to move the dialogue forward. But the cultural narratives in which we think about race and ethnicity not only reflect but also shape the material realities of racism. The binary structures of thought that generally serve to shape these narratives may well develop out of what Jean-François Lyotard regards as the very nature of language and narrative, which he views as agonistic, or based in conflicting oppositions revolving around a struggle.[8] Historically produced discursive formations about race often take narrative forms that circulate overtly and covertly throughout both ideological and oppositional values, texts, and cultural artifacts of all kinds. These cultural narratives about race thus both reflect and shape racial politics. Like David Theo Goldberg, editor of *Anatomy of Racism*, I do not see racial thinking as fixed, "singular and monolithic, simply the same attitude complex manifested in varying circumstances" (1990, xii). Rather, I see it as an unfixed set of linguistic and narrative formations that emerge from, respond to, and help construct changing historical conditions. Consequently, a great deal is at stake in understanding the narratives that underlie our racial discourse. To move forward, the feminist agenda against racism requires not only an examination of power and privilege; it also requires interrogation of the cultural narratives about race that affect what we see, say, write, and do. As Masao Miyoshi writes, "Discourse and practice are interdependent. Practice follows discourse, while discourse is generated by practice" (1993, 726). Just as the material effects of racism affect patterns of thought about race, so the language of race matters and has material consequences.

Binary modes of thinking about race often have explanatory power, especially for identifying certain systems of domination. Witness the "black and white" of Rodney King's beating or of Harriet Jacobs's *Incidents in the Life of a Slave Girl* ([1861]1973); the "brown and white" of Gloria Anzaldúa's *Borderlands/La Frontera* (1987); the "red and white" of Leslie Marmon Silko's *Storyteller* (1981); the "yellow and white" of Joy Kogawa's *Obasan* (1981). I want neither to deconstruct nor to displace this binary thinking. But I do believe that by themselves such bi-

---

groups, see esp. Chai 1985; Anzaldúa 1990a; Harris and Ordoña 1990; Lorde 1990a; Sandoval 1990; and Uttal 1990. For alliance building among women of color that includes white women, see Molina 1990.

[8] See Lyotard 1979, esp. 10–11, 16. While agonistic narrative may well be universal, narrative is not exclusively agonistic; see, e.g., Allen 1986. For other discussions of cultural narratives, see Jameson 1981; DuPlessis 1985; and Heilbrun 1988.

naries create dead ends. They must be supplemented by what I call re-lational narratives in which the agonistic struggle between victim and victimizer is significantly complicated, as it is in the Los Angeles events. The legitimate insight of binary narratives is blind to many other stories that cannot be fully contained within them. Most especially, binary nar-ratives are too blunt an instrument to capture the liminality of contra-dictory subject positions or the fluid, nomadic, and migratory subjectivi-ties of what I have elsewhere called the "new geography of identity."[9] A feminist analysis of identity as it is constituted at the crossroads of dif-ferent systems of stratification requires acknowledging how privilege and oppression are often not absolute categories but, rather, shift in relation to different axes of power and powerlessness.

To explore ways in which feminist discourse might move beyond bi-nary thinking, I will identify four cultural narratives about race and ethnicity that have circulated since the late 1960s in the often highly charged and overdetermined arenas of North American feminist confer-ences, classrooms, manifestos, collectives, coalitions, rallies, marches, meetings, essays, collections, and books. The first three scripts—which I call narratives of denial, accusation, and confession—have operated within the agonistic white/other binary. While they have all contributed important narratives to the formation of a multicultural feminism, they also represent stories that are caught in a cul-de-sac, in a round of rep-etition. By themselves, they cannot lead beyond the boundaries and into the fertile borderlands. The fourth script—the narrative of relational positionality—moves beyond binary thinking. It has begun to emerge more recently, at first considerably muted in the 1980s by the first three scripts, but gaining visibility and frequency in the 1990s.

What I intend to do here is to call greater attention to the script of relational positionality as a supplement to, not a replacement for, the scripts of denial, accusation, and confession. I do so in an effort to jump-start a stalled dialogue about racism and racial interaction. To encourage self-reflection and conversation across racial boundaries, I suggest that feminists can also look outside the academy for cultural narratives about race and ethnicity that forge a discourse beyond the white/other binary—not only in the multilayered parable of the Los Angeles upheavals but also in representations of race and ethnicity in the news media and in popular cultural texts like film. Cultural praxis sometimes outpaces feminist theory, as I will attempt to show with a

---

[9] In Friedman 1994, I note the omnipresence of spatial figurations of identity (e.g., positionality, location, borderland, terrain, migratory, nomadic, traveling, wandering, network, intersection, axial, circuits, etc.) that have supplanted organic metaphors (e.g., wholeness, centers, cores) rooted in romanticism. See also Hicks 1991; Lowe 1991; Pérez-Torres 1993–94; and Davies 1994.

discussion of globalized accounts of race and ethnicity in the news media and in the fictionalized explorations of relational identities in two contemporary films, Mira Nair's *Mississippi Masala* (1991) and Neil Jordan's *The Crying Game* (1992). In spite of the mediated nature of news and film as commodified and ideological institutions of mass culture, both at times break out of the white/other binary; both perform important cultural work around issues of race from which feminists can learn a great deal.

Cultural narratives of denial, accusation, and confession

These three feminist scripts about race—denial, accusation, and confession—are, on the one hand, diachronic cultural formations that reflect the epistemological positionalities of the feminists who produced them and the historical conditions out of which they arose. They are, in other words, what Donna Haraway (1988) calls "situated knowledges," located at the intersection of different systems of alterity.[10] On the other hand, they can also function synchronically as theoretical formulations about race that stake out different political stances. A "thick description" of these scripts (to echo Clifford Geertz [1973]) would detail their deployment in space and time as reflections of different locations on the terrain of racial stratification. My purpose here, however, is to evoke these narratives in starkly structural terms. I use them not as a fixed taxonomy but, rather, as a strategic schematization designed to address the theoretical gridlock that characterizes much current feminist discourse about race, racism, and ethnicity.

Scripts of denial, produced largely by white women for whom race has not been a source of oppression, cover a range of stories affirming female and feminist sisterhood that, in their exclusive focus on gender, covertly refuse the significance of race. Such texts as *Sisterhood Is Powerful* (Morgan 1970) and *Woman in Sexist Society* (Gornick and Moran 1971) represented an exhilarating assertion of the category *woman* as a central prism through which to perceive human experience. Women's lives, these scripts held, had been ignored, trivialized, or distorted in the structures and repositories of human knowledge—in what has come to be called the symbolic order. Feminism would create, so the story went, an alliance of women everywhere based in the commonality of women and

[10] Haraway considers only gender, but for other articulations of locational politics and epistemology that include other constituents of subjectivity, see esp. DuPlessis (1979) 1985; Dill 1983; Hartsock 1983; Pratt 1984; Rich (1984) 1986; Martin and Mohanty 1986; Spivak 1987a; Alcoff 1988; King 1988; Hurtado 1989; de Lauretis 1990; Mohanty 1991a; Russo 1991; Smiley 1992; Friedman 1993, 1994; Harding 1993; Laslett 1993; duCille 1994; and Fellows and Razack 1994.

in opposition to the patriarchal societies within which women live. This insight—and I stress the importance of its initial and continuing contribution as a foundational premise of women's studies—represents a blindness to categories of race and ethnicity as coordinates of identity. In defining the otherness of woman, it denies the structural process of "othering" by a host of other factors such as race, ethnicity, class, sexuality, religion, national origin, and age.

Scripts of denial implicit in such a framework reflect an epistemological standpoint of racial privilege from which they are largely spoken. They take many forms, but some of the underlying narrative fragments can be provisionally reconstituted as follows: "I'm not a racist." "I'm a feminist, so how could I be a racist?" "I'm oppressed, so how could I be an oppressor?" "My experience is just like your experience." "We are all sisters." "Tell me all about yourself; I'm sure I can understand." "Are you a woman or are you black (Jewish, Chicana, etc.)?" "Which have you suffered from more, being a woman or being a minority?" "We are all oppressed as women," with its unsaid corollary, that other oppressions are not relevant to feminism.[11] And so forth.

Scripts of accusation, produced largely by feminist (or womanist, as some prefer to be called) women of color who were marginalized by racism both in and beyond the feminist movement, sprung up dialectically in response to the scripts of denial in the 1970s and 1980s. Denying the universality of *woman,* these scripts accused white feminists of ignoring, trivializing, or distorting the lives of women who were "different" through other forms of othering. As an advance in feminist theory pioneered especially by women of color, lesbian women, and Jewish women, these accusations led to important reconceptualizations of feminist theory in relation to other systems of oppression. In structural terms, they paralleled those that all feminists had been making against men—but with a difference. Many feminists who engaged in scripts of accusation felt themselves to be in a liminal position—linked to the men of their cultural group by race and ethnicity but separated from them by gender and, conversely, linked to other feminists by reason of gender but separated by reasons of race and ethnicity. In academic feminism specifically, essays like Alice Walker's "In Search of Our Mothers' Gardens" ([1974] 1983a) and "One Child of One's Own" ([1979] 1983b), Barbara Smith's "Toward a Black Feminist Criticism" ([1977] 1985), and Audre Lorde's

---

[11] Mary Daly's notorious response (1979) to a question about race at the 1979 Simone de Beauvoir conference—words to the effect that race did not interest her—epitomizes these scripts of denial. Daly's appropriation of Indian, Chinese, and African women's experience to a gender analysis isolated from an analysis of race, class, and colonialism in *Gyn/Ecology* (1978) led to the question. See Lorde's critique of Daly's *Gyn/Ecology* in "An Open Letter to Mary Daly" ([1979] 1984).

essays from the 1970s and early 1980s collected in *Sister Outsider* (1984) led to a groundswell of (still) necessary attack on white feminists for suppressing the differences among women, to the formation of distinct feminisms based on racial and ethnic identities, and to the creation of coalitions among women of color and Third World feminists. Scripts of accusation resulted in the important formation of the categories women of color and Third World women, and of discourses that have fostered analysis of the common ground shared by nonwhite women of different racial and ethnic groups.

Scripts of accusation, reflecting the material and psychological effects of racism, often contain core messages that can be synopsized as follows: "You are a racist." "I am not like you." "You haven't confronted your racial privilege." "I am both a woman and black (Jewish, Chicana, Native American, etc.), and I can't sort out the oppressions of race and gender." "Gender can't be separated from race and class." "You can never understand my experience or perspective." "You are oppressing me and you don't even know it." "You have left out women of color and assumed that your own experience is like all other women's." "You shouldn't write (teach, talk, etc.) about women of color because we women of color must speak for ourselves." "You must include women of color in your classes (books, articles, etc.)." "You have to take the responsibility for learning about us on your own; we should not have to take the responsibility (time, energy, etc.) to educate you." "I don't want to waste my time trying to talk with you; I'm going to devote all my energy to my sisters of color." And so forth.

Scripts of confession, produced overwhelmingly by white women for whom their own racial privilege had recently become visible or denaturalized, mushroomed in response to scripts of accusation in the 1980s and 1990s. Agreeing with the attacks, many white feminists rushed to turn the accusations upon themselves—as individuals and collectively as white, ethnocentric feminists.[12] Not all accusation was met with confession; some women responded by reconstituting scripts of denial. But white feminist stories of guilt proliferated from the late 1970s on, taking a number of forms, some more constructive than others. At its best, this confessional script led to significant reformulations of feminism that acknowledged some women's complicity in other systems of oppression and called for social change that addressed all forms of alterity.[13] But at

[12] For discussion of the rhetoric of feminist confession, see Bernstein 1992. Confessional scripts focus mainly on race in the United States, not, e.g., on anti-Semitism or heterosexism. For feminist discussions of Christian ethnocentrism and Jewish identity, see e.g., Bulkin, Pratt, and Smith 1984; Bourne 1987; and Pheterson 1990.

[13] See, e.g, Adrienne Rich's examination of her two "mothers," white and black (1976, 253–55), and her subsequent attempts to construct a global feminist theory based in her lesbian/feminism in "Disloyal to Civilization" ([1978] 1979).

times, this gaze at the Medusa of white feminist racism has led to paralysis, frozen guilt, perpetual mea culpas, chest beating, hand-wringing, race to confession—in short, to a performance of guilt whose very display tends to displace and thereby reconstitute the other as other. At still other times, this guilt has resulted in an embrace of "other" women—which in academic feminism has meant a rush to include, focus entirely on, or even become the other, as Biddy Martin and Chandra Talpade Mohanty point out (1986, 207). At its most extreme, this embrace tends toward a fetishization of women of color that once again reconstitutes them as other caught in the gaze of white feminist desire.[14] Called into being by scripts of accusation, scripts of confession nonetheless have contributed importantly to feminist theory by making white women in particular turn the lens of critique upon themselves, upon the web of racial and ethnic privilege that had remained invisible to them.

Scripts of confession, reflecting the racial privilege of those who attempt (with questionable success) to disavow that historically given power, circulate among such familiar lines as these: "I am a racist." "I am guilty." "I'm so guilty that I can't do anything but think about how guilty I am." "Feminism is a white middle class movement." "Western culture is totally oppressive." "There must be something bad in being white." "I want to help women of color." "I must listen to women of color and not answer back."[15] "White women (always) leave out women of color." "I am not going to leave out women of color any more." "I want women of color to like me, approve of me, be my friend." "Women of color are more authentic than me, more oppressed than me, better than me, and always right." And so forth.

These three cultural narratives of denial, accusation, and confession—emerging as they do from different locations in the societal distribution of power along racial lines—can be interpreted provisionally as parts of a single story about race and ethnicity in the feminist movement,

---

[14] See, e.g., Jane Gallop's assertion that black women now occupy the position of authority for her that she once gave to Jacques Lacan and other French theorists (Gallop et al. 1990, 363–64). See also Smith 1989; Abel 1993; duCille 1994; and Homans 1994, who variously critique the white feminist tendency to place women of color in the position of ultimate authority and authenticity as a fetishized object of desire or as a form of embodiment for theory; Martin and Mohanty's view that the "assignment of fixed positions—the educator/critic (woman of color) and the guilty and silent listener (white woman)" prevents a "working through [of] the complex historical relations between and among structures of domination and oppression" (1986, 199); and Suleri's criticism of women of color who use "strategies designed to induce a racial discomfort" and accord an "iconic status" for themselves and postcolonial feminism in relation to white women (1992, 764, 759).

[15] One structured format for promoting antiracism used at some women's studies conferences and programs involves women of color speaking about racism to white women, who must remain silent for a predetermined amount of time, after which they may speak, but only about their own racism.

a metanarrative that can be reconstructed in its simplest structural form as follows: "I'm not a racist, we are all women," says a white feminist. "You are a racist, you are different from me," says a woman-of-color feminist. "You are right, I am a racist," says a white woman. I do not propose this metanarrative as a fixed structure that drives all feminist discourses on race. To do so would be reductionistic, blind to the nuanced heterogeneity of many manifestations of these cultural narratives. Moreover, each script has made and continues to make important contributions to feminist discourse. But what this strategically constituted metanarrative discloses is the underlying binary of white/other that operates within a victim paradigm of race relations. This is, I want to suggest, a story we have heard repeatedly. By itself, it represents a dead end. It is hindering the development of a more broadly defined multicultural feminism whose agenda centrally includes the eradication of racism and the globalization of feminist theory and praxis.

Both the metanarrative and the dead end are starkly present in Gloria Anzaldúa's description of a course on U.S. women of color that she taught at the University of California, Santa Cruz. I quote at length to give full play to the "soundings" of denial, accusation, and confession that reverberate throughout her account:[16]

> At first, what erupted in class was anger—anger from *mujeres*-of-color, anger and guilt from whites, anger, frustration and mixed feelings by Jewishwomen who were caught in the middle. . . , and anger and frustration on my part from having to mediate between all these groups [note the scripts of denial and accusation]. Soon my body became a vessel for all the tensions and anger, and I dreaded going to class. Some of my students dreaded going to class. But gradually the *mujeres*-of-color became more assertive in confronting and holding whites accountable for their unaware, "blocked" and chronically oppressive ways [accusation]. . . . When whitewomen or Jewishwomen attempted to subvert the focus from women-of-color's feelings to their own feelings of confusion, helplessness, anger, guilt, fear of change and other insecurities [confession], the women-of-color again and again redirected the focus back to *mujeres-de-color* [accusation]. When several whitewomen stood up in class and either asked politely, pleaded or passionately demanded (one had tears streaming down her face) that women-of-color teach them, when whitewomen wanted to engage women-of-color in time-consuming dialogues [confession], *las mujeres-de-*

---

[16] I am borrowing Houston Baker's metaphor of soundings for the different racial narratives that underlie African American modernity (1987).

color expressed their hundred years weariness of trying to teach whites about Racism. They were eloquent in expressing their skepticism about making alliances with whites when most whitewomen . . . needed reassurance, acceptance and validation from *mujeres-de-color* [accusation]. . . . The problem was that whitewomen and white Jewishwomen, while seeming to listen, were not really "hearing" women-of-color and could not get it into their heads that this was a space and class on and about women-of-color [denial and accusation]. As one student-of-color wrote: "I think the hardest thing for me was having to understand that the white students in class . . . [could not] understand the experiences we have lived" [accusation]. Though there were important lessons learned, the inability to listen and hear, along with the confusion, anger and doubts about ever being able to work together almost tore our class apart [dead end]. (1990c, xx)

Anzaldúa is to be commended for her honesty in exposing the difficult racial dynamics in her class. The pedagogical processes of frustration, anger, guilt, and miscommunication produced by these interwoven scripts of denial, accusation, and confession no doubt raised consciousness about racial and ethnic chasms. But I think that, as educational and inevitable as these scripts are because of the different racial and ethnic positionalities represented in the class, they contribute greatly to the "difference impasse," the blocked movement, and the dead-endedness of many feminist discussions about race and racism—for several reasons.

First, these cultural narratives foster the continued production of scripts in which white remains the center, the defining core, in opposition to the other, which remains at the margins. As a result these cultural narratives end up reinscribing the very pattern they set out to replace. Second, they require the construction of white (or Western) as a monolithic, unchanging category that even in racial and ethnic terms erases vast differences of culture and history punctuated by violence—witness the conflict between the English and the Irish; the Germans and the French; the Bosnians, Serbs, and Croats; the Europeans and the Jews or the Gypsies, both of whom in the European context have been treated as scapegoat races (not ethnicities). Along with the Holocaust and decades of twentieth-century ethnic violence in Europe (both of which have been fueled by racial concepts of national identity), World War I and II ought to be sufficient in themselves in calling into question the concepts of white and Western as unitary categories.[17]

[17] See Stocking 1968; Poliakov 1971; Stepan 1982; and Banton 1987 for discussions of European racialism, which included not only identification of major racial groups but

Third, the binary of white/other embedded in these scripts is itself ethnocentric, not sufficiently global in perspective. It does not acknowledge how the processes of racial and ethnic othering are a worldwide phenomenon, not the exclusive product of Caucasians or the West in dealings with people of color. (More on this later.) Fourth, these scripts inhibit the development of scripts about the relation of one kind of other to (an)other—a Korean to a Japanese woman, an African American to an Asian American woman, a Cuban American to an African American woman, a Hindu to a Muslim woman in India, a Hutu to a Tutsi woman in Rwanda, for example. Not all boundaries between nonwhite or non-Western women can be explained in terms of white or Western racism. Too often, the word *racism* implies the assumed modifier *white*. This construction of *racism* as always already *white* reflects the hegemony of white racism in the United States. But it also rests on biologism and operates to make invisible the existence of other racisms (whether in the United States or elsewhere in the world).

Fifth, these cultural narratives are often founded on a misleading notion of racial and ethnic purity that denies the worldwide phenomenon of constantly produced biological and cultural syncretism. People and cultures are not so easily put into fixed categories based on race and ethnicity; claims for such purity are often based on the binary opposition of pure/impure in which mixing constitutes a form of pollution. As Anzaldúa writes, "Racial purity, like language purity, is a fallacy" (1990b, 146). She attacks specifically the Chicana/o "denial of our sisters who for one reason or another cannot 'pass' as 100% ethnic—as if such a thing exists" (1990b, 146). It is a cornerstone of racist thinking that people and cultures do, and must be made to, occupy spaces of racial or ethnic purity. In her visionary call for "the new *mestiza* consciousness," Anzaldúa configures the liminal space she occupies as a frightening, disorienting, but ultimately fertile borderland beyond the stagnations of purist identity politics (1987, esp. 77–98).[18]

Sixth, these cultural narratives that proscribe the white/other binary implicitly privilege race and ethnicity as the primary category of oppression to which all other systems of alterity must be subsumed, thus reproducing, with all its limitations, the categorical hegemony attempted by certain Marxists with class and radical feminists with gender. Consequently, for all their explanatory power in some contexts, these three scripts actually hinder the analysis of how different systems of stratifi-

also the division of Europeans into many different races. See Kamm 1993 on the current status of the Roma (Gypsies) in Europe.

[18] For discussions of syncretism and hybridization, see, e.g., Kaplan 1990; Appadurai 1991; Hicks 1991; Lowe 1991; Pratt 1991; Davies 1994; Friedman 1994; Pérez-Torres 1993–94; and Wright 1994.

cation intersect in the construction of identity and the experience of oppression. In particular, they suppress an understanding of contradictory subject positions.[19] Nor can they explain the interplay of privilege and alterity in a woman who is part of both a dominant culture and a marginalized one—such as a relatively dark-skinned Brahmin woman who moves back and forth between London and Calcutta. As a Brahmin she is privileged by caste; as a woman, she is oppressed. As a frequent traveler, she is well-off in class terms, but called black by the British and subject to the disorientations of a bicontinental postcolonial identity. As a dark-skinned woman, she is differently disadvantaged within the Indian context of colorism and the British context of racism. The categories "woman of color" and "Third World woman" are insufficient to explain her position at the crossroads of different formations of power relations.

Finally, these binary scripts dim to near invisibility any common ground that might exist between women who occupy the opposing sites of "white" and "color." At times, exclusive emphasis on the differences among women threatens the category of feminism itself, eliminating not only the concept of worldwide efforts to better women's status but also the very possibility of multiple feminisms. Even in the plural, feminism depends upon the premise that gender, in combination with other categories, is a constituent element of hierarchical social organization. I am not for a moment suggesting an abandonment of the recognition and celebration of differences as a necessity and source of strength in feminism. But the identification of differences among women needs to be complemented by a search for common ground, however differently that commonality is materially manifested. For example, a white woman raped by a black man and a black woman raped by a white man in the United States share the experience of rape and have much to learn from each other about its psychological, sexual, familial, and legal consequences. But the different histories of interracial rape between whites and blacks with the legacy of slavery color what these women share, inflecting their commonality with difference. Understanding this difference depends upon first identifying rape as a shared issue based on gender.[20]

"The shared ground [between Us and Them]," writes S. P. Mohanty in his critique of cultural relativism, "helps us situate and specify difference, understand where its deepest resonances might originate" (1989, 21). In his view, "a simple recognition of *differences* across cultures" leads only "to a sentimental charity, for there is nothing in its logic that necessitates

[19] Fellows and Razack report on this phenomenon in the roundtable discussions they led among a group of women in which, "with respect of one another, every participant was simultaneously a member of a subordinate as well as a dominant group" (1994, 1051).

[20] See Cole 1986 and Gordon 1991 for discussions of the importance of feminist identification of commonality among women as well as differences. See also Crossette's report on this issue at the 1994 U.N. conference on population in Cairo (1994).

our attention to the other" (23). The primary shared ground between Us and Them, he argues, begins with the assumption of the other's agency, which he defines as "the capacity that all human 'persons' and 'cultures' in principle possess to understand their actions and evaluate them in terms of their (social and historical) significance for them" (23). The white/other binary discourages the location of such shared ground and tends to deny the agency and subjectivity of the other.

"Women all over the world have a lot of things in common," said Wang Jiaxiang, a women's studies activist and teacher from Beijing and an exhilarated delegate at the United Nations Conference on Population and Development in Cairo (Crossette 1994). Given the multiple systems of domination that separate women, the search for common ground often seems utopian. This longing for alliance represents a desire for pleasure in and connection across difference, not a pleasure that oppresses but one that flourishes in the intimate spaces that confound the pathologies of otherness.[21] Such desire underlies the kind of agency that exists as a form of healing in Anzaldúa's *Borderlands/La Frontera:* "But it is not enough to stand on the opposite bank, shouting questions, challenging patriarchal, white conventions. A counterstance locks one into a duel of oppressor and oppressed; locked in mortal combat, like the cop and the criminal, both are reduced to a common denominator of violence. The counterstance . . . is a step toward liberation from cultural domination. But it's not a way of life. At some point, on our way to a new consciousness, we will have to leave the opposite bank, the split between the two mortal combatants somehow healed so that we are on both shores at once" (1987, 78).[22]

Cultural narratives of relational positionality

What I call (for want of a better term) scripts of relational positionality began to emerge during the 1980s in feminist theoretical discourse

---

[21] See Ruth Bloch's critique of what she sees as feminist theory's exclusive emphasis on models of domination, exploitation, and power, which she believes omit aspects of gender that cannot be explained entirely within a victim paradigm (1993). While criticizing parts of Bloch's call for a "culturalist feminist theory," Barbara Laslett argues for the need to understand feminist pleasure in terms that exceed models of domination (1993). See also Harding's response (1993).

[22] Anzaldúa's vision of healing here refers specifically to the syncretism of Anglo, Mexican, and Indian (Aztec) within herself, not to alliances among different groups of women. In *Borderlands/La Frontera* (1987), however, Anzaldúa suggests the possibility of broader alliance through her dedications of poems to Judy Grahn, Vita Sackville-West, and Irena Klepfisz. In "Bridge, Drawbridge, Sandbar or Island," she also acknowledges the role of "love and friendship" and ritual behaviors such as breaking bread together as a "good basis" for alliance work, as long as it does not render differences of power invisible (1990a, 229–30).

out of the accusatory and confessional stories about race, ethnicity, and racism. Produced by women and men of different racial and ethnic standpoints, these scripts regard identity as situationally constructed and defined and at the crossroads of different systems of alterity and stratification. They rest upon significant advances in feminist discourse initiated by narratives of accusation and confession, namely, the analysis of multiple oppressions and interlocking systems of oppression that has been pioneered especially by women of color and the new discourses of location, positionality, and standpoint. It is also rooted in feminist object relations theory, which in its feminist revision of psychoanalysis has emphasized how the formation of identity, particularly women's identity, unfolds in relation to desire for and separation from others. Moreover, it shows the influence of poststructuralist and postcolonial critiques of identity and formulations of subjectivity, which stress the nonunitary, indeterminate, nomadic, and hybrid nature of a linguistically constructed identity.[23]

But cultural narratives of relational positionality go beyond these foundations by resisting and dissolving the fixities of the white/other binary. They deconstruct what Homi Bhabha describes as "an important feature of colonial discourse": "its dependence on the concept of 'fixity' in the ideological construction of otherness" (1983, 18). Within a relational framework, identities shift with a changing context, dependent always upon the point of reference. Not essences or absolutes, identities are fluid sites that can be understood differently depending on the vantage point of their formation and function. For example, in relation to white people, Leslie Marmon Silko and Paula Gunn Allen are women of color, Native American, and partially white. In relation to women of color, they are Native American. In relation to Native Americans, they are members of the Laguna Pueblo. In relation to each other, they are individual women who characterize the Laguna Pueblo culture in startlingly different ways. Scripts of relational positionality construct a multiplicity of fluid identities defined and acting situationally. They also go

---

[23] For earlier formulations of what I am calling relational positionality, see Friedman 1993, 1994. Throughout his essays, Radhakrishnan uses the terms *relational* and *relationality* in similar ways; see also Chandra Mohanty's somewhat different use of *relationality* (1991a, 12–13). For examples of integrated analysis of multiple oppressions, see esp. Walker (1974) 1983a, (1979) 1983b; Smith (1977) 1985; Lorde (1979) 1984; Moraga and Anzaldúa 1981; Dill 1983; Chai 1985; Anzaldúa 1987, 1990c; King 1988; hooks 1989; Mohanty 1991a, 1991b; and Higginbotham 1992. For rhetoric of *standpoint, location,* and *positionality,* see references in n. 10. For object relations theory, see, e.g., Chodorow 1978; Gardiner 1981; and Benjamin 1988. For a sampling of the vast literature on subjectivity influenced by poststructuralism and postcolonial studies, see Belsey 1980; Bhabha 1983; de Lauretis 1986, 1987, 1990; Radhakrishnan 1987, 1989a, 1993; Spivak 1987b, 1988; Miller 1988; Smith 1988; Smith 1989; Hicks 1991; Lowe 1991; Appiah and Gates 1992b; Pérez-Torres 1993–94; and Davies 1994.

beyond feminist discourses of static positionality, which are often (re)appropriated for scripts of accusation and confession.

The fluidity of situational identity suggests as well a concept of permeable boundaries, a notion that adapts object relations theory to the theorization of cultural syncretism. Such mixtures of cultural strands are especially (but not exclusively) evident in the United States, a nation that has drawn immigrants from all over the world. "Hyphenation," however denied, is built into American identity formation, even for members of American Indian nations. Moreover, different hyphenated Americans continually affect other hyphenated Americans. Scripts of relational positionality are more suited to dealing with the permeable boundaries between races and ethnicities. Such scripts also move beyond the essentialism of fundamentalist identity politics without denying the material realities of identity, as poststructuralist deconstructions and performance theory tend to do.[24] Stressing that individuals are constituted through many group identities and cannot be reduced to any one collectivity, they are able to be flexible in dealing with global variation in forms of otherness and contradictory subject positions.

The concept of relational positionality should not be confused with pluralism, which always runs the risk, as Chandra Talpade Mohanty points out, of suppressing the analysis of structural power relations and systems of domination. American celebrations of diversity, she rightly argues, all too often domesticate difference and descend into an empty "discourse of civility" by presenting it in individualistic, personal terms (1989–90, 203). I do not mean to suggest that all positions are unique and "equal" within a menu of differences. Scripts of relational positionality foster neither pluralism nor identity politics based on a single collectivity. Rather, they acknowledge that the flow of power in multiple systems of domination is not always unidirectional. Victims can also be victimizers; agents of change can also be complicitous, depending on the particular axis of power one considers. This complicates analysis of power relations by insisting on identification of what R. Radhakrishnan calls a "totality" of the different constituent elements of identity (1992, 81). It complicates as well organizational strategies: around which collectivities can one organize political entities if everyone belongs to multiple groups? Nonetheless, scripts of relational positionality still open the door for dialogue, affiliations, alliances, and coalitions across racial and ethnic boundaries.

---

[24] I distinguish here *fundamentalist* identity politics from other kinds of identity politics, particularly what I might call a syncretist identity politics based in a notion of identity as culturally constructed, historically specific, and open to change and interweaving with other identities. As I have written elsewhere, I do not believe that feminists and other marginalized groups can afford to give up the concept of identity and political organizing based on various group identities in favor of poststructuralist notions of identity as sheer play and performance (Friedman 1991).

June Jordan's autobiographical essay "Report from the Bahamas" (1985) lends concreteness to my attempts to theorize scripts of relational positionality. As a deliberately self-reflexive and pedagogical narrative, the essay takes us through Jordan's discovery of how to read the complexities of relational identity in which no single system of domination determines the totality of experience. Jordan tells the story of how she, an African American of West Indian descent, harried by the demands of teaching at a New York public university, settles wearily into the Sheraton British Colonial Hotel in the Bahamas for a relaxing vacation. Instead, the hotel greets her with markers of colonial, racial, and class history within which she—as black, West Indian, college professor, single mother, tourist—occupies contradictory subject positions. What does she share and not share with Olive, the maid who cleans her room, she wonders? In relation to race, they are connected; in relation to class, they are disconnected. She reflects, "Even though both 'Olive' and 'I' live inside a conflict neither one of us created, and even though both of us therefore hurt inside that conflict, I may be one of the monsters she needs to eliminate from her universe and, in a sense, she may be one of the monsters in mine" (47).

Both the bond and the gulf between Jordan and Olive trigger reflections about fluid identities based in race, class, and gender. She recollects the bond she shared with a Jewish student who brought her Anzia Yezierska's *The Bread Givers,* a novel about a Jewish woman's immigration that resonated with her own experience. His love of Yiddish matched her own love of West Indian language. But the racial gulf opened suddenly when he said he did not care about the cutbacks in aid to college students, a policy that directly affected her son and many other African Americans. Jordan's experience of her own otherness in the white student's indifference interweaves with the otherness of Olive, from whom she is separated by geography and class in spite of their shared race and ethnicity.

Such shifting positionalities form the basis, Jordan reflects, for lifesaving connections made out of need and partial commonalities. She recalls such a connection she helped make between a white Irish American woman (Cathy), who had had an alcoholic, abusive father, and a black South African woman (Sokutu), whose alcoholic husband, Jordan's friend in the antiapartheid movement, was beating her to death. Power and powerlessness, privilege and oppression, move fluidly through the axes of race, ethnicity, gender, class, and national origin. In relation to race, Jordan and Sokutu were connected not only because of Jordan's activism in the antiapartheid movement but also because she "grew up terrorized by Irish kids who introduced me to the word 'nigga' " (1985, 48). But in relation to gender, the Irish and South African women had more in common than either had with Jordan. Shy because of their racial difference, Cathy reaches out to Sokutu to provide the help that Jordan cannot give her. "I walked behind them," Jordan remembers during her trip home from the Bahamas, "the young Irish woman and the young South African, and I saw them walking as sisters walk, hugging each other, and whispering and sure of each other and I felt how it was not who they were but what they both know and what they were both preparing to do about what they know that was going to make them both free at last" (49).

Like feminists before her, Jordan in "Report from the Bahamas" insists that we understand race, class, and gender as multiple and interlocking systems of oppression. But she writes against the grain of fundamentalist identity politics as she questions the use of race, class, and gender "as automatic concepts of connection" (1985, 46). "The ultimate connection" between people, she writes, "cannot be the enemy. . . . It is not only who you are, in other words, but what we can do for each other that will determine the connection" (47). She breaks through to a new story—a new multicultural feminist discourse—in proposing fluid identities that shift in focus depending upon situation and reference point and in mapping connections forged by different peoples struggling against complex oppressions. Her approach suggests the possibility of opening up the kind of impasse that tore apart Anzaldúa's class and that stymies so many feminist attempts to cross racial and ethnic boundaries.

June Jordan is not alone in contemporary feminist discourse in promoting and performing relational thinking about identity. Others, here and there, speak in similar terms. Scripts of relational positionality are variously present in the work of such people as Gayatri Chakravorty Spivak, Sara Suleri, William Boelhower, R. Radhakrishnan, Papusa Molina, Jenny Bourne, Mary Louise Fellows, Sherene Razack, Arjun Appadurai, Aída Hurtado, Carole Boyce Davies, Minnie Bruce Pratt, Patricia Williams, Biddy Martin, and Chandra Talpade Mohanty—to name a sampling. Martin and Mohanty's "Feminist Politics: What's Home Got to Do with It?" (1986), for example, uses Minnie Bruce Pratt's autobiographical reflections in "Identity: Skin Blood Heart" (1984) to theorize "the fundamentally relational nature of identity" (1986, 196). As a white, lesbian Southerner whose father and grandfather were town patriarchs, Pratt lives in a predominantly black community in Washington, D.C., where she realizes that every exchange with her African American neighbors is overdetermined by the politics of racial location. But her status as a lesbian—ever an outsider in her father's world—holds out some hope for the remapping of "community." Concerned that "white" or "Western" feminism tends to "leave the terms of West/East, white/nonwhite polarities intact," Martin and Mohanty find in Pratt's essay resistance to "the feigned homogeneity of the West and what seems to be a discursive and political stability of the hierarchical West/East divide" (193). Although not theorized as such, some feminist theorists and teachers have begun to posit relational positionalities in which power circulates in multifaceted ways instead of flowing unidirectionally according to a white/other binary.

Beyond white/other in contemporary news media

In spite of the scattered existence of relational narratives in contemporary feminist discourse, the scripts of denial, accusation, and confession tend to dominate feminist classrooms, conferences, organizations, and research. This state of affairs is due partly, I believe, to the rise of racial polarization and nationalist/separatist sentiment in the United States, developments that reflect the worsening socioeconomic health of inner cities and the growing racially inflected backlash against immigrants, the poor, and affirmative action—all symptomatically evident in the overwhelming, multiracial support for California's Proposition 187, aimed at eliminating aid for illegal immigrants, in the 1994 election.

But I also believe that the repetitive round of denial, accusation, and confession among feminists is also partly the result of a degree of hermeticism in feminist theory itself, especially in the academy. I refer to the tendency of academic feminism to feed off itself, in spite of our interdisciplinarity—an insularity that is endemic to the development of intellectual fields of discourse. This aspect of the culture of the academy accounts for much of its insight, but also for some of its blindness to cultural praxis. In the United States, demographic and societal changes have converged to produce in the mass media an increasing number of relational scripts—far more than occur within feminist discourse. The mass media bombard us daily with varied cultural narratives about race, ethnicity, and racism—some structured by the white/other binary, but many constituted outside it. I suggest that we feminists, whatever our racial and ethnic standpoints, step outside our academic frameworks for a moment to see what surrounds us, to seek what might release us from the broken record of so many of our exchanges about race, ethnicity, and racism. In some ways a powerful avant-garde, we are in other ways behind the times.

Television, newspapers, magazines, and movies abound in narratives about racial/ethnic conflict and bridge building that exist outside the white/other binary. This is not to say that the white/other binary and narratives of denial, accusation, and confession do not exist pervasively in popular culture. They certainly do. (The campaign ads using Willie Horton in 1988 and promoting Proposition 187 in 1994 testify to that.) Even the celebrations of "diversity" encased in the metaphors of American pluralism—American culture as a gorgeous mosaic, tossed salad, stir-fry, stew, orchestra, patchwork quilt, symphony, or rainbow, for instance—contribute to the essentialism toward which some identity politics tends. Such metaphors depend heavily on the senses—above all, sight—that figure prominently in racialism in all its forms. Like a mosaic itself, they tend to fix everyone's difference in stone, safely bordered within impenetrable boundaries. Even the widely used term *multicultural* in its most common meanings operates as a code signifying nonwhite races and ethnicities, thus covertly reinstating the white/other binary.[25]

Nonetheless, the mass media also produce, reflect, and report narratives that refuse fixity, exhibit relational thinking, and operate beyond the white/other binary—narratives to which we academic feminists would do well to pay attention. I urge this immersion in mass and popular culture with some trepidation. First, feminist theorists seldom look to such sources for theoretical insight; rather, such cultural formations are more often a site for critique. Second, these cultural texts are highly mediated, subject to the demands of an increasingly globalized market, and prone to package "facts" and stories as commodities aimed at gaining the greatest possible market share. As is evident in the accounts of the Los Angeles upheavals, the news media often sensationalize stories, playing the "race card" for all it is (financially) worth. As Jimmie Reeves and Richard Campbell write in *Cracked Coverage*, the news media do not objectively report facts, but function "as a vital social force in the construction of reality, . . . the enforcement of norms, and the production of deviancy" (1994, 7). And in the Hollywood entertainment industry, the wider the audience, the more likely white perspectives define issues of race and ethnicity and the less likely people of color (especially women of color) shape the production of their own social realities.[26] Such mediations, particularly the economically driven ones, appear to make mass culture a poor source for theoretical insight.

Some cultural studies approaches to mass culture, however, refuse a reductionistic equation of media with ideology as a hegemonic force

[25] The multicultural mosaic appears quite frequently in ethnic studies as a replacement for the assimilationist image of the "melting pot" without sufficient attention to its potential reinforcement of fundamentalist identity politics. See Peterson, Novak, and Gleason 1980; and Chametzky 1989–90. The term *multicultural* is highly problematic, without consistent meanings in its many usages and easily open to co-optation into celebrations of pluralist diversity that obscure underlying power relations. In its North American context *multicultural* most often means nonwhite racial groups considered together, but it also sometimes refers to cultural diversity of all kinds (including white and Western), to a group that is itself multicultural (e.g., African Americans or Asian Americans), and even to individuals of mixed heritage (e.g., Louise Erdrich or Leslie Marmon Silko). See Jameson 1991; Miyoski 1993; Pérez-Torres 1993–94; and Gutmann 1994.

[26] For discussions of minority filmmakers and the entertainment industry, see e.g., Parkerson 1990; Dash 1992; and Fregoso 1993. For discussion of the increasingly globalized economy of mass media, see Jameson 1991; and Miyoshi 1993.

allied with power.[27] Instead, many critics insist that mass media texts can be read as sites of contested meaning in which producers, consumers, and various constituencies interpret events and stories in accord with different agendas and political standpoints. In writing of television representations of race, for example, television critic Herman Gray delineates "possible strategies of counter hegemonic readings, locations, and interruptions of television's domesticating power" (1993, 194) and asserts that the meanings of such representations as *The Cosby Show* "are not given; rather, viewers define and use the representations differently and for different reasons" (1989, 376). Although I acknowledge mass and popular culture as mediated articulations, I treat them as locations for wresting meanings about race and ethnicity beyond the white/other binary, meanings that feminists can use for progressive political and theoretical purposes.

Take, for example, newspaper accounts of events about race and ethnicity (sometimes inseparable from religion) for which the white/other binary offers only partial or no explanatory power. A brief catalog of stories (however mediated) that I have clipped from national and local newspapers since the events in Los Angeles forcefully suggests that we should broaden our understanding of racial and ethnic division.[28] These stories can potentially internationalize our understanding of othering as a global phenomenon that includes but cannot be reduced to white racism against nonwhite people. Some events reflect binary thinking in which neither side is "white"; others reflect racial or ethnic othering with more than two groups. All demonstrate how conflict over resources and power tends to be racially or ethnically inflected, whether racism/ethnocentrism is the cause or the effect of such conflict. I list these reports provisionally, not to argue for a transhistorical and universal racism but in full recognition that each instance is historically specific, multilayered, and overdetermined. I do so strategically, in catalog form, to let the sheer weight of global events force us out of an exclusive focus on white/other in the context of the United States.

—The forty-eight ethnic wars being fought in Europe, Asia, Africa, South America, and the Middle East during 1993 (Binder 1993).

—The Serbian use of systematic rape, concentration camps, and merciless shelling of besieged civilians as part of its "ethnic cleansing" of the Bosnian Muslims—this, in the context of a three-way ethnic/religious war rooted in centuries of conflict, evident not so long ago in the Croat and Bosnian Muslim genocidal extermination of hundreds of thousands of Serbs during World War II.

[27] See, e.g., Fiske 1987; Gray 1989, 1993; and D'Acci 1994.
[28] These examples have been taken mostly from the *New York Times*, the *Wisconsin State Journal*, and the *Washington Post National Weekly Edition* since July of 1992.

—Clan warfare in Somalia that led to millions of deaths by starvation.

—The longstanding conflict between the majority Hutus and minority (but traditionally dominant) Tutsis in Rwanda that flared up into the killing of some half-million people in April and May of 1994, this on top of the murder of some one hundred thousand Tutsis and Hutus in Burundi in 1993.

—Fundamentalist Hindu destruction of a sixteenth-century mosque at Ayodhya (supposedly the site of a Hindu temple destroyed with the Muslim conquest of India) that led to thousands of deaths, especially in pogroms against Muslims in Bombay.

—The Israeli-Palestinian conflict in which the victims of anti-Semitism become victimizers of cousin Semites, in which each victim group lashes out against the other for who they are, in which attempts at peace are regularly subverted by violence on both sides.

—The racial/ethnic/political cauldron in South Africa among Zulu, Hxosa, South Asian, "coloreds," Afrikaaners, Jews, and other whites of British or European descent.

—The seventy-six areas of ethnic strife emerging after the breakup of the Soviet Union, including the Armenian and Azerbaijani hostilities.

—The Protestant/Catholic violence in Northern Ireland, rooted in a centuries-old English racial and ethnic prejudice against the Irish.

—Kuwaiti abuse of Asian women who enter the country as domestic workers.

—Conflict between the Buddhist Tamils and Hindu Sinhalese in Sri Lanka.

—Long-standing racism of the Japanese against the Koreans, evident most vividly in the recent exposure of the Japanese use of Korean women as "comfort women" held captive in camps for sexual exploitation by Japanese soldiers during World War II.

—Resurgence of anti-Gypsy, anti-Jewish, and anti-"foreign" feelings in Germany and Eastern Europe.

—Ethnic strife between the Katangans and the Kasai in Zaire.

—Clan conflict in China, as well as Chinese racism against its African students and the Chinese policy of wiping out Tibetan culture in its occupation of Tibet.

—Divisions between the Spanish-Indian Mestizos and the British-Indian-African Creoles of Belize.

—The uprising in Chiapas, Mexico, heavily inflected with conflict between indigenous Indians and the dominant *mestizos,* of mixed Spanish and Indian descent.

—The complicated multiethnic, decades-old war in Myanmar (formerly Burma) among the ethnic Burmese, Kachin, Wa, Kikang, Palaung, Shan, and other groups.

—Three-way divisions threatening national unity among the First Nation peoples, the Euro-Canadians of British descent, and the Québécois in Canada, increasingly complicated by extensive immigration from East Asia, South Asia, and the Caribbean.

—Conflicts between African Americans and Korean Americans in Los Angeles and Brooklyn, between African Americans and Latinos in Los Angeles, between Latinos and Asian Americans in Los Angeles, between African Americans and Cuban Americans in Miami, and between African Americans and Jewish Americans in Crown Heights. This, in the context not only of the structural foundations of white racism in the United States, but also of a 1994 survey showing that "minorities held more negative views of other minorities than do whites" (Holmes 1994).[29]

The point of this catalog is not to fetishize racial and ethnic conflict. The news media tend to report, even sensationalize, racial and ethnic violence and to ignore efforts at building bridges across cultural divides. Douglas Martin's New York Times (1993) story of the Korean-American Grocers Association of New York, which now sponsors scholarships for African American students, is a rare exception to the focus on violence. So also are such examples as the plea for "rooting out the unfortunate link between ethnicity and the bogeymen" by Sri Lankan poet Indran Amirthanayagam in the New York Times (1993); a PBS documentary on Malaysia, which includes a segment on not only the 1969 race riots but also a joint business school effort by a few Chinese and Malays to move beyond the racial hatred and distrust that divides their society; and a CNN feature on the village in Northern Ireland, home of an Irish Republican Army terrorist whose bomb killed a little boy, that produced a Christmas play in the boy's hometown as a peace offering. The U.S. news media's focus on ethnic violence around the world may well function as a commodified displacement of violence at home, mostly perpetrated by the institutions of white racism. The covert effect of such mediated reporting might feed white paranoia about racial others and ease white guilt about racism in the United States.

But as sites of contested meaning, these news reports can also be read as forceful disruptions of the white/other binary. Thick descriptions of some of the events behind these reports reveal some continuing effects of white and Western racism. As colonial rulers, for example, the Belgians issued ethnic identity cards in the 1930s to the majority Hutus and minority Tutsis, groups between whom the physical differences were so

---

[29] If accurate, this Louis Harris survey, called "Taking America's Pulse," may reflect the success of scripts of accusation resulting in white self-censorship of continued stereotypical thinking, as well as the permission victimization often brings to think stereotypically of all others. Two other polls had similar results.

insignificant that "ownership of cattle became the basis for ethnic classification—an owner of 10 or more cattle became a Tutsi," whom the Belgians made their middlemen (Bonner 1994). But the slaughter in Rwanda cannot be explained solely in terms of Belgian colonialism since the notion of biological difference between Hutus and Tutsis has explanatory power for many Rwandans today, indeed, enough cogency to justify murder. As one woman told a reporter, "They said, 'You are Tutsi, therefore we have to kill you' " (Bonner 1994). When power is at stake, as it is in Rwanda, people often resort to ethnic and racial othering to explain and justify conflict. Whether as cause or effect of conflict, racial and ethnic division is a global phenomenon where people compete for resources. Such global instances of othering shatter the fixity of the white/other binary as exclusive explanation for all racial and ethnic conflict.

Some theorists and critics regard race and ethnicity as constructions of Western culture, particularly post-Renaissance conquest and post-Enlightenment imperialism. I share their constructivist view of racial and ethnic classifications as products of culture, not absolutes of nature. I acknowledge as well that Western science, especially in the nineteenth century, systematized racial and ethnic classifications to an extraordinary, indeed, obsessive, degree, a development that provided ideological rationales for imperialism, slavery, various legal apartheids, anti-immigration laws, and other forms of racial and ethnic stratification. But the notion that the West invented racial and ethnic classifications and their institutionalization or has been the only culture to engage in such otherings is highly ethnocentric, itself an embodiment of the white/other binary.[30] To cite some counterexamples, the Chinese, according to Frank Dikötter, had a fully developed concept of racial difference and hierarchy before contact with the West (1992). Many people believe that the caste system in India originated in hierarchical divisions based on color variations produced in the wake of the Aryan invasion of the Dravidian people on the Indian subcontinent, a view supported by the Hindu word for caste, *varna,* that also means *color* (Dumont [1966] 1970).[31] A Somali saying reported in relation to clan conflict applies more generally to the shifting collectivities of human society: "My clan against the enemy, my family against the clan, my brother and I against my family, me against my brother" (Ozanne 1992).

I am not proposing a homogenized, universal, static, transhistorical, primal, or biologically deterministic view of conflict based in ethnocen-

---

[30] See, e.g., West 1982; and Sollors 1989, ix–xx. The belief that racism and ethnocentrism are European and Euro-American inventions widely underwrites cultural narratives of accusation.

[31] My thanks to Edward Friedman and Sivagami Subbaraman for directing my attention to the forms of colorism in China and India.

trism. Each form of "centrism" clearly takes on historically specific forms and can be understood only through a synchronic and diachronic thick description of any given society. But the capacity of human societies to engage in a kind of us-against-them thinking is global—not, in my view, because of some genetic feature of the human species but because of the competition for resources, power, and position as a central ingredient in the production of racial and ethnic othering.[32] The white/other binary has a powerful explanatory power in some contexts, but it does not encompass countless narratives about race and ethnicity worldwide that appear daily in our newspapers and on our television screens. Internationalizing our thinking on these issues can contribute to breaking the logjam in our discourses about race and ethnicity in the United States.

Relationality in popular cinema

Contemporary popular film, like newspapers, is an arena of representation in which the white/other binary of race relations is often shattered. Like many other mass culture artifacts, films package, commodify, market, and disseminate "race" and "ethnicity" as social constructs. As a site of contradiction (like fictional narrative), film potentially subverts and reinscribes racism—simultaneously working through and containing widespread anxieties about difference. It both allows and co-opts expression of taboo anger. It both imagines utopian desire for connection and underlines its impossibilities. Rather than seek a single meaning—particularly the meaning—of a given film, I see a film text as a site for negotiating meanings that might well function both regressively and progressively, depending on who is doing the reading and for what purpose. I want to discuss two such films, both of which show limited insight about gender (feminist theory is certainly more advanced in this regard) but provide fascinating explorations of relational identity from which feminists can learn a great deal. Mira Nair's realist romance *Mississippi Masala* (1991) and Neil Jordan's postmodern *The Crying Game* (1992) were produced outside the mainstream Hollywood film industry but nevertheless "caught on" to achieve popularity and success far beyond initial expectations.[33] This success—like that of such other recent films as *The Wedding Banquet; Farewell, My Concubine;* and *Fried Green Tomatoes*—may reflect the way that race and ethnicity titillate and "sell" in today's

---

[32] For critique of primordialist views of ethnic conflict, see Thompson 1989. For discussions of othering applicable globally (even if not discussed as such), see, e.g., Gates 1986a; Appiah 1989; and Radhakrishnan 1991.

[33] For some of Jordan's other films, see *A Neil Jordan Reader* (1993). Nair, educated in sociology at Delhi University and documentary film at Harvard University, is known for her award-winning documentaries like *India Cabaret* (1985) and *Salaam Bombay!* (1989). See Nair and Taraporevala 1989; Appadurai 1991.

market. But it may also reflect how the relational narratives and utopian desire for cross-racial connection in both films tap into a longing for new ways to think about race beyond the white/other binary.

In providing relational readings of the films' transgressive border crossings, it is not my intent to present here a full analysis of the richly layered cultural narratives in these films, to produce a cultural studies analysis of the production and consumption of these representations, to offer a feminist reading of their gender politics, or to hold each film up as a perfect example of relational thinking. I offer instead a reading that intends to make more visible to feminists the potentialities of relational thinking about race and ethnicity, with full awareness that the gender and racial politics of both films are nonetheless open to critique.[34]

Mississippi Masala centers around a love story between an Indian American woman and an African American man living in Greenwood, Mississippi, in 1990—a new take, with a happy ending, on the old plot of *Romeo and Juliet* and its more recent avatar in *West Side Story*. Mina, an obedient young woman of twenty-four, lives and works in a motel with her parents, pressured by her mother to marry and by her father to go to college; Demetrius passed up college after his mother's death, runs his small carpet-cleaning business out of a truck, and takes care of his father, Willie Ben, and his brother, Dexter. Living in the United States, both Mina and Demetrius are figures of diaspora: she has never been to India and he has never been to Africa.

The film cuts back and forth between the sharply etched worlds of Mina and Demetrius, reproducing for a popular audience the ethnographic, documentary style of Nair's earlier films.[35] Mina belongs to the tight-knit community of Indian refugees who were forced to flee from Uganda when Idi Amin's black nationalist dictatorship outlawed the Indian immigrant class, which was as a whole much better off economically

---

[34] For a critical reading of *Mississippi Masala*, see hooks and Dingwaney, who retain the white/other binary in their condemnation of the film as antinationalist and colonialist and as "another shallow comment on interracial, inter-ethnic, transnational 'lust' " (1992, 41). My thanks to Meryl Schwartz for sending me this review. Hooks also objects to the racial politics of *The Crying Game*, which she interprets as an appropriative film that commodifies race while denying its significance, "cannibalizes" the other, and perpetuates "white cultural imperialism" (1994, 53–62). While hooks and Dingwaney are usefully alert to the political limitations of popular film, their readings of the filmic texts are often one-dimensional, ignoring important iconographic and narrative nuances and demonstrating the Procrustean dangers of interpreting texts entirely through the lens of culture as a system of (white/Western) domination.

[35] Although hooks and Dingwaney (1992) complain that the film's seeming realism obscures its stereotypical mockery of Indian culture, I think they miss the self-mocking but also celebratory humor characteristic of many "ethnic" films produced by members of the ethnic group they portray, films such as *The Wedding Banquet, The Joy Luck Club, Dim Sum, The Great Wall, Brighton Beach Memoirs, Stardust Memories,* and *Moonstruck.* Such humor has often been a central survival strategy.

than most black Ugandans. Trying to hold on to their religious and cultural traditions, experiencing the intergenerational conflict common to many American immigrants, they pursue the American dream of material success by living frugally and helping each other get started in businesses such as motels and liquor stores. Demetrius's world is the family-centered Southern black community, where each of the African American characters images the considerable generational, gendered, and individual variation in black response to centuries of racism. In his community, the white/other binary is fully in play. The racist paternalism of the white restaurant owner and banker constitute a backdrop of threat and humiliation countered by the strength of the black family, the hard work of people like Demetrius and Willie Ben, and the richness of black culture, clearly rooted in but distinct from African traditions.

The film undermines the white/other binary by exploding the unitary nature of the category of other while leaving the white power structure monolithically in place. The racism of white America is assumed, evoked with the occasional presence of synecdochal figures who function as reminders of a fixed, hostile, and racist power structure built on economic and political dominance over all people of color. But this power structure is not the narrative center of the film, which focuses on the racism, distrust, and longing for love that can exist between two different racial/ethnic groups. As lovers, Mina and Demetrius constitute a Mississippi masala—a mixture of spices—that is violently ruptured by the anger of the Indian community for whom intermarriage in America, as in Africa, constitutes a disgrace to family honor. Both the Indian and black communities come down hard against the lovers—the Indians against Mina for shaming her family by having sex with a black man, the African Americans against Demetrius for a variety of reasons, including what they see as his rejection of black women, his desire for a light-skinned woman like Lisa Bonet (the actress who plays Denise on *The Cosby Show*), his foolishness for getting involved with a foreigner, or his ambition in owning his own business. The Indian community, which has more collective economic power than the black community, retaliates by canceling all its orders for Demetrius to clean motel rugs; this in turn leads the banker to cancel his loan, to which Demetrius responds by filing a suit against one of the Indian motel owners.

The unity of "people of color" against white racism that another Indian had touted to Demetrius earlier in the film disintegrates into a bitter confrontation between Asian Americans and African Americans. "United we stand, divided we fall," sarcastically snorts Demetrius's friend Tyrone, who leaves in disgust for Los Angeles. The film's relational approach to race and ethnicity exposes the racism endemic in Indian culture, prejudice directed not only at African Americans but also at the darker-skinned people like Mina within their own cultural group. This conflict between two groups constituted as other by white society reveals the process of othering with which each of these groups regards the other. This represents a partial displacement of the white/other binary: the category of other explodes into its heterogeneous parts, while the category of whiteness remains fixed and monolithic.

The film's relational approach complicates the story of Indian racism, however. The film opens in Uganda with the terror and pain caused by Amin's decision in 1972 to "cleanse" the country of its Asian Ugandans. Mina's grandfather had immigrated to Uganda to work on the railroad; her father, Jay, was born there and achieves considerable affluence as a lawyer—living out an African version of the American dream held by many immigrants, progress that leaves many black Ugandans disadvantaged (just as the success of immigrants from other groups to the United States has often been instrumental in keeping African Americans as a group from substantial advancement). What hurts the most is the loss of her father's closest friend, his black "brother," Okelo, who tells Jay that he must leave, that "Africa is for Africans, black Africans." Mina and her mother weep at the parting from Okelo while Jay refuses to say goodbye, hurt far more by Okelo's rejection and the loss of his homeland than the theft of his material goods and position.

As the love story unfolds, both Mina and her father are haunted by images of Uganda, flashbacks that underline how what happened in 1972 shapes the events in 1990. Mina's attraction to Demetrius begins at the Leopard Lounge, a black dance club whose sights and sounds echo—with a difference—some of the film's Ugandan scenes. Mina's love for Demetrius triggers memories of Okelo. As they make love on her birthday in Biloxi, Ugandan music plays on the sound track, and Mina remembers an earlier birthday in Uganda when her father's preoccupation with Ugandan politics makes him forget to sing "Happy Birthday." As Demetrius sings "Happy Birthday," longing for her father, Okelo, and Uganda merge, only to be brought up short by her nightmarish memory of finding the dead body of a black Ugandan covered by flies. Demetrius comforts her, but she cannot tell him about Uganda, just as she remained silent when his family asked why she left. She can only explain herself to him as "mixed masala": born in Africa of Indian descent, refugee in London for fifteen years, resident of Greenwood for three.

Mina's father is similarly unable to explain to Demetrius what he means by saying that he has forbidden the relationship to "spare her the struggle." Unaware of the family's experiences in Africa, where Jay had been known for his criticism of Indian racism and his advocacy on behalf of black Ugandans, Demetrius accuses him of trying to act white. Ignorant of the long-standing racialism in Indian culture that predates (and has been intensified by) British colonialism, Demetrius does not understand that in blocking the relationship, Jay is "acting Indian," that is, aligning himself with racist elements within his own tradition. But speaking out of his own racial location in the United States (a positionality that Jay likewise does not understand), Demetrius reflects the anger of African Americans who have been embittered by the Americanization of successive immigrant groups, a process that Toni Morrison describes as learning to say "nigger"—learning, in other words, to raise their own status by seeing African Americans at the bottom of a system of racial stratification.[36] Demetrius taunts Jay with the color of his own skin, only a shade lighter than his own, and angrily denounces the Indian community's destruction of everything for which he has worked so hard. Within an American context, as a member of a preferred minority (even a "model minority"), Jay has the license to "act white." Like Mina before him, Jay cannot speak to Demetrius about the events in Uganda that at least partially govern his actions. Instead, memories of Uganda flood the silent Jay, especially Okelo's rejection, repeated in expanded form for the second time in the film: "'Go to London, Bombay.' 'Uganda is my home.' 'Not any more. Africa is for Africans, black Africans.' "

Jay tries to explain to Mina what he could not say to Demetrius: "After thirty-four years, what it came down to was the color of my skin. People stick to their own kind. I am only trying to spare you this pain." Mina responds by reminding him that Okelo risked his life to get Jay out of jail after he rashly spoke against Amin on the BBC. This act of love across racial barriers in Uganda validates her attempt to do likewise with Demetrius and foreshadows her decision to leave her family to be with him. Jay's subsequent return to Uganda to get back his home from a new regime sustains Mina's interpretation of Okelo's brotherhood. Jay learns that Okelo's help of his Indian "brother" cost him his life in 1972. The film ends with Jay holding a black Ugandan child who has reached out to touch his face as they watch a woman joyously dancing for a circle of admiring Ugandans. This utopic moment of racial and cultural communion fades out to the film's credits, which are twice interrupted by the brilliantly lit embrace of Mina and Demetrius—she in sparkling Indian dress, he in an African hat and shirt, both in a seemingly timeless space beyond racial division. Like all utopic moments, it leaves us with a lingering question about how long it can last in the "real" world of racial separateness, stratification, miscommunication, and silence. The very power of the film's depiction of conflict based in cultural and historical difference calls into question the happy ending of the lovers' future.

In *Mississippi Masala* cultural identity, privilege, and oppression remain fluidly open to redefinition in changing contexts. Although power

---

[36] Morrison made this point at a lecture at the University of Wisconsin—Madison in October 1990; see also Morrison 1992, 47.

based in white hegemony remains fixed, other power structures do not flow unidirectionally but, rather, circulate among the two racially other groups. In relation to most black Ugandans, the Indian Ugandans are both economically advantaged and politically vulnerable. In Uganda, the Indians refuse intermarriage, a point Nair emphasizes by having Amin's television diatribe against the racism of the Asians drone on in the background of Mina's birthday party. And as Jay himself points out moments before his arrest, the Ugandan Asians have focused entirely on acquiring wealth for their "own kind." "Amin is a monster of our own making," he tells his Asian friends. Yet expelled from their homeland, they too are victims of racism, as the black Ugandan soldier's brutal treatment of Mina's mother demonstrates. As immigrants in the United States, they are recipients of racist and culturally insensitive remarks, from black as well as white communities. But like other immigrant groups, their economic situation in relation to African Americans improves more rapidly. The Indian community uses its economic power to destroy Demetrius's business, but Demetrius's ignorance about the history of South Asians in Uganda leads him to misread the complexities of Jay's opposition to his relationship with Mina.

Calling into question the whole concept of race, the film probes the irony that Jay is more African than Demetrius, although Demetrius is the same "race" as the black Ugandans who expelled Jay from Africa. Conversely, the film through its structural parallels between Uganda and Greenwood highlights how Jay repeats with Demetrius the racism of which he himself was a victim in Uganda. And as a woman, Mina exists in a racially liminal position: as darker than her parents, Mina requires a higher dowry to get a good husband in the Indian community; in the black community, her lighter skin and long, straight hair make her ambivalently desirable, akin to light-skinned women with straight hair like Lisa Bonet. In relation to white society, both the Indian and African American communities experience racism as "people of color." But in relation to each other, the conditions of their privilege and alterity continually shift, dependent upon ever-changing reference points for judgment.

The Crying Game goes even farther than *Mississippi Masala* to explode the fixity of the white/other binary. Where *Mississippi Masala* focuses on the (dis)connections between two groups that exist as other in relation to a fixed white society, *The Crying Game* calls into question the unitary concept of white (and its corollaries, European and Western), as the film proliferates a dizzying array of shifting alterities. Gender and sexuality supplement race, ethnicity, and nationality as components of fluid identities. Set first in Northern Ireland and then London, the film narrates the Irish Republican Army's (IRA) kidnapping of a black British soldier (Jody), the relationship he forms with one of his IRA captors

(Fergus), and the aftermath of Jody's death. Seduced into capture by a white woman (Jude) in the IRA, Jody weans Fergus from his fixed notions of good and evil through a human fellowship that Fergus cannot resist. Their friendship across racial, cultural, and political boundaries begins when Fergus has to remove the tied-up soldier's penis from his pants to help him urinate. The bond is cemented when Jody gives Fergus a picture of himself in cricket clothes with his beautiful lover, Dil, and extracts a promise that Fergus would find Dil if he dies. It culminates in Fergus's inability to shoot Jody at his commander's order. Jody dies in an attempted escape under the wheels of the British convoy—in part saved, in part killed by Fergus.

In fulfilling his promise, Fergus increasingly comes to occupy the position of the black soldier in London. His attempt to protect Dil becomes love, in part a displaced love for the man he could not protect or love openly. This love mutates first into revulsion when he discovers that Dil is a transvestite who is gendered female, bodied male, and then into an ambivalent continuation of desire and protectiveness. In the place of Jody, he plays "the gentleman" to Dil and eventually goes to jail in Dil's place for the murder of Jude, who tries to kill Fergus for failing to perform an IRA execution. The film concludes with Fergus telling Dil during jail visiting hours the story about a frog and a scorpion that Jody had told him. The colonial subject becomes the captor, then the captured; the woman becomes a man, then a woman again. The heterosexual turns into the homosexual, then back into (at least the appearance of) the heterosexual. No identity is a fixed essence; no hierarchy is unchanging; every positionality is open to change in the processes of historical deconstruction and becoming.

The film's radical relationality shows how the position of otherness shifts according to one's comparative reference point. On the issues of race, ethnicity, and nationality, for example, Jody and Fergus are each—but differently—"(ambiguously) non-hegemonic," to echo Rachel Blau DuPlessis's resonant phrase for contradictory subject positions ([1979] 1985). Fergus is a colonial subject but also a white man; Jody is a black man but also a member of an imperial army. As a member of the Catholic minority in Northern Ireland, Fergus belongs to the group economically and politically dominated by the Protestant majority that Jody defends. But Jody tells Fergus that "he has been sent to the only place in the world where they call you nigger to your face" and tell you to "go back to your banana tree, nigger" (Jordan 1993, 191).[37] From the point of view of the IRA, Jody is a member of an occupying army, but from Jody's perspective

---

[37] Repressed within the cultural unconscious of the film, as well as in June Jordan's "Report from the Bahamas," is the history of nineteenth-century English racist designations of the Irish as "white monkeys," a "simian race" closely linked to Africa. See Michie 1992; and Cheng 1995.

he is a victim of Irish racism and the IRA. Jody signed up for the army because he needed a job in racist England, yet Fergus gets a job immediately in London as a construction worker on an all-white crew. In relational terms, each occupies the position of racial/ethnic victim and victimizer in terms of the other.

Jody's association with cricket encapsulates these contradictions. Photos and surreal images of Jody in cricket whites flash repetitively on the screen, clashing his very dark skin against the very white uniform. As tropes, these cricket images juxtapose the aristocratic sport of the colonialists with the colonized's embrace of that sport as their own. Jody's love of cricket comes from his father, who taught him the game in Antigua, where "cricket's the black man's game" (191). But in Tottenham, to which the family came from Antigua, the game is played by whites. Preferring the Irish game of furling, Fergus associates cricket with the colonizers, a point visually made as he watches English schoolboys play cricket from the scaffolding at his construction job.[38] Similarly, Fergus's gun functions as a trope that emphasizes the relational duality of his position. As colonial subject and IRA soldier, Fergus is relatively powerless to remove the British from Northern Ireland. But his gun brings him enormous power of life and death over individuals selected for leverage and execution. It is this power that his relationships with Jody and Dil convince him to renounce; and it is this power for which he atones when he accepts responsibility for Dil's crime of murdering Jude with the very gun he had used to terrorize Jody.

Gender and sexuality complicate the shifting power relations of race, ethnicity, and nationality in *The Crying Game*. Fergus thinks of himself as a heterosexual. Misled by Jody's clear references to Dil as a woman and deaf to his coded allusion to her ambiguous status, Fergus is repulsed by homosexuality, bisexuality, and transvestism. Occupying the position of heterosexual privilege, he wants fixed and clearly delineated categories: male/female, heterosexual/homosexual. But just as his essentialist notions of Irish victim and British oppressor break down in his relation with Jody, so he must face, in the form of Dil, the displacement of gender, sex, and sexuality binaries.

As a liminal figure of racial and sexual ambiguity, Dil exists between fixed categories of white and black, male and female, and functions in the film as a disruption of all rigid definitions. As such, she functions much

---

[38] Despite its historical association with the former colonialists, cricket has become a passionately nationalist sport in South Asia and the British West Indies and is often the site of relational politics. When India, Pakistan, and Sri Lanka jointly hosted the 1993 World Cup in cricket, e.g., the president of the Bombay Cricket Association, who is also a leader of the militant Hindu party, threatened to refuse to allow the Pakistanis to play in Bombay. Yet when India played England in Bombay, Muslim and Hindi fans flocked to the stadium to support the Indian cricket team (Wagstyl 1993).

like the figure of the modern "tragic mulatta" that, as Hortense Spillers notes, carries the potential for "neither/nor" (1989). Gendered feminine, Dil is Jody's "girl" and then Fergus's. The revelation of Dil's male body shocks Fergus, not only because of his homophobia but also because of his belief in absolute sexual difference. Try as he might, he cannot quite stop loving Dil-as-woman and must forcibly remind himself that "she" is also "he." His demand that Dil cut her long hair, remove her makeup, and dress in the soldier's cricket whites is a ruse designed to protect Dil from the IRA, but it also represents his attempt to force Dil out of a feminine identification, as if the clothes and appearance could construct a masculine gender to go along with Dil's male body. This violation of Dil's gender, however motivated by protectiveness, recapitulates Fergus's earlier violence against Jody, whose clothes Dil now wears. On a covert level, dressing Dil in Jody's clothes may also act out what Fergus has been unable to admit: his own homoerotic attraction to Jody.[39] The film's final scene cuts sharply from the murder of Jude, performed by Dil in bobbed hair and Jody's cricket suit, to the jail's visiting room, where wives visit their incarcerated husbands. Dil's reasserted feminine gender as she occupies the position of wife in relation to Fergus gives the appearance of heterosexuality to their relationship. Dil's third transformation calls into question once again binary notions of fixed identities of gender, sex, and sexuality.

Yet the very conventionality of their positions in the visiting room, which maintains an unspeakable love within the closet of disguise, suggests as well a melancholy return to fixed identities and roles, underlined by the film's fade-out to the song "Stand by Your Man." Fergus's retelling of Jody's story of the frog and the scorpion breaks down the binaries of white/other and English/Irish, but it can also be read as a sign of the film's covert return to essentialist fixities. This story, that Neil Jordan adapts from Orson Welles's film *Mr. Akadin* (1955), tells how the scorpion begs a fearful frog to carry it across the river and then stings it anyway. To the frog's query as to why the scorpion stung him when it meant their death, the scorpion can only answer, "I can't help it, it's in my nature" (Jordan 1993, 196). The fable's use of the term *nature* (changed from Welles's use of the term *character*) appears to contradict the film's performance of identity as cultural construction.[40] Its invocation of the nature/culture binary in the film's final speech appears to halt the narrative's relational

[39] My thanks to Linda Rugg for this insight. At another level, Dil's donning of Jody's clothes prefigures her refusal of the position of victim, for in this garb she ties up Fergus, takes his gun, and shoots Jude. (In using female pronouns for Dil, I follow the screenplay.)

[40] My thanks to Morris Beja for pointing this out; see also Beja 1979, 126. I am indebted as well to James Phelan and Jacques Lezra for suggestions on the multilayered interpretations of this fable.

deconstruction of fixed identities and agonistic narrative at a moment of proverbial conventionality. On the other hand, the fable can be read as an insistence on keeping both poles of the nature/culture binary forever in play. However conventional they appear at the end, Fergus and Dil are not what they seem, subtly emphasized by the fact that "Stand by Your Man" is sung by Boy George. Moreover, Jody originally recites the fable to suggest that connection across difference is possible. As a speech act in a murderous context, Jody's telling begs Fergus to act according to his "nature," which Jody intuitively knows is not that of a killer but of a man capable of love across conventional racial and sexual boundaries.

The film's deconstruction of gender and sexual binaries can also be read as nonetheless caught up within a gynophobic economy of desire. Jude is the film's only significant biologically female character. Her position initially shifts between the white woman used as a sexual object to seduce a black man for political ends to the white woman who enjoys power over others, evident when she smashes Jody's face with Fergus's gun. Jody's response to Fergus—"Women are trouble" (Jordan 1993, 199)—sharply evokes a fixed cultural narrative of evil female sexuality. Jude's transformation from a blond in a traditional Irish sweater into a brunette sophisticate can be viewed as a trope for the disguise and performance constituent of all identities in the film. But it also functions as a revelation of her fixed malevolence. For the rest of the film, Jude remains singularly evil. Like Eve, Pandora, and Mata Hari, this dragon-lady-as-IRA-terrorist uses her sexuality and gender to seduce men into death. Just as *Mississippi Masala* retains the category of white as fixed and monolithic, *The Crying Game* covertly leaves the binary of male subject/female other in place. We are left with the message that the only good woman is a dead one. Dil as transvestite fills the position of "woman" whose exchange between men (first as photo, then in the flesh) cements their relationship, a homoerotic twist to the exchange of women identified as central to male bonding by Eve Kosofsky Sedgwick in *Between Men* (1985).[41]

However partial the film's deconstruction of fixed binaries, *The Crying Game,* like *Mississippi Masala,* promotes an existential leap of love across the bridge of difference. Although *The Crying Game* ends on a less

[41] The multiple resonances of the film certainly support other readings of Jude, as well as the other androgynous names in the film, Dil and Jody. As an echo of Jody, the name Jude undermines absolute gender difference as do its associations with the biblical figures of Judith, who decapitated Holifernes, and Judas, who betrayed Jesus. Eric Rothstein suggested to me that Dil's name may be a shortened form of "daffodil," slang since about 1945 for an effeminate youth; that Maguire, the ruthless IRA commander, may invoke the nineteenth-century secret society called the Molly Maguires, known for their transvestite disguises; and that Jude's masculinist behavior could be read as a critique of, rather than a reflection of, patriarchy. Helen Cooper also noted to me that Jude's power can be read as a revision of feminine passivity and her death as yet another transformation from victimizer to victim.

euphoric note than *Mississippi Masala,* its appeal to cross-cultural bonding is nonetheless visionary and utopic. Allusions to the Christian mythos of love and sacrifice abound in the film, countering the forces of division. When Jody asks Fergus to tell him a story to ease the tension of his captivity, an ambivalent Fergus responds by citing a part of Paul's famous letter about love in 1 Cor. 13:11: "When I was a child . . . I thought as a child. But when I became a man I put away childish things" (Jordan 1993, 202). Fergus misappropriates the context of the quotation—Paul's advocacy of love—to suggest that as an IRA soldier he can no longer afford such "childish things" as love, although the irony is that his love for Jody makes him unable to shoot on command. As figures of suffering, sacrifice, and revelation, Jody and Dil echo the story of Christ to become the means through which Fergus recovers Paul's vision about the necessity of love expressed in the opening of 1 Cor. 12:1, the verse that Fergus does not directly quote: "Though I speak with the tongues of men and of angels, and have not love, I am become as sounding brass, or a tinkling cymbal." Fergus, in turn, occupies the position of symbolic sacrifice for Jody and Dil as he fulfills his promise to the doomed Jody and goes to jail in Dil's place.[42]

Their race (black or white) and their national identity (British or Irish) alternately construct Jody, Fergus, and Dil as privileged, on the one hand, and as marginalized, on the other. Their capacity to love across these racial and national boundaries signifies their ability to occupy a liminal borderland between fixed identities of black/white, British/Irish, homosexual/heterosexual. Dil, as the androgynous figure moving between all these binaries, functions as the mark and agency of this love. Like the romantic narrative of love in *Mississippi Masala,* the religious narrative of love in *The Crying Game* (which also screens a homoerotic one) can be interpreted as a retreat from political critique. But it can also be read as a narrative of a desire for connection that counters the urge to separate along racial and ethnic lines.

Conclusion

For feminists seeking to move beyond the repetitive rounds of denial, accusation, and confession in our discourses about race and ethnicity, the

---

[42] My thanks to Rebecca Saunders for pointing out to me the importance of these religious allusions. Jordan's use of African British homosexual figures as symbolic occasions for the *bildung* of a white, heterosexual man undermines the film's relational narrative, an element that Sharon Capel finds all too common in the film industry. "Unrealistic and degrading images of black people" often serve, she writes, as "mule" to a "message" directed at a "specific audience: a white one." "What relevance," she asks, "did interracial relations have to the story line other than expediency? And would the film have worked with an all-white cast?" (1993). Within relational terms, however, interracial connections are central to the story, and Dil and Jody are not one-dimensional figures; both have nuanced subjectivities.

specifically romantic and religious forms of utopianism in *Mississippi Masala* and *The Crying Game* are not in themselves compelling. Both films, however, present the desire, however utopian, to make connection across racial and ethnic division as a fertile and vital part of human existence. They also provide us with the narrativization of a theory of subjectivity based in relational positionalities in which power circulates in complicated ways rather than unidirectionally, in which contradictory subject positions allow for the possibility of connection across racial and ethnic boundaries. I believe that our growth as a movement academically and organizationally depends in part on the continued search for such relational scripts and for a common ground that acknowledges but is not erased by difference.

Scripts of relational positionality cannot, I hasten to say, provide a simple cure for the politics of race within and beyond the feminist movement. Categories of thinking do not by themselves erase the materialities of racism and ethnocentrism. My own brand of feminism is too materialist and historicist for me to believe that a revolution in the linguistic/symbolic order can, by itself, transform the world. But discourses do have power, even material consequences. Cultural narratives do help construct as well as reflect power relations within and beyond the academy. The categories in which we think do perform cultural work within a larger dialectical context in which language and material reality interpenetrate.

The agency necessary for ethical and political change begins in what S. P. Mohanty describes as the human capacity to reflect upon the meaning of our actions in relation to larger systems of the social order. To cross the divide between Us and Them, he insists, involves being able to imagine the agency of those other from ourselves, to assume their capacity, like our own, to reflect upon and negotiate the shifting confinements and privileges of their multiply constituted positions (1989, 19–21). And for this task we need flexible and nuanced categories of positionality that do not assume an always already constituted status of fixed power and powerlessness. Exclusive reliance on binary models of domination—however much explanatory power they have in certain circumstances—may well retard instead of hasten cultural and political transformation.

There are dangers for feminists in using scripts of relational positionality. Like discourses of "multiculturalism" and "diversity," emphasis on contradictory subject positions can all too easily collapse into the pluralism against which S. P. Mohanty and Chandra Talpade Mohanty both warn us, a pluralism that obscures the inequalities of power for different groups in the social order (Mohanty 1989, 25–26; Mohanty 1989–90, 203). Moreover, stressing the endless play of contradiction runs the risk, as Radhakrishnan points out, of making relationality "a pure concept, an end in itself" (1992, 81). Such Derridean deferral (*différance*) can inhibit concrete political action, which requires some patch of terra firma from which to advocate change and exercise agency. Fluidity displaces fixity, but as the frog/scorpion parable in *The Crying Game* demonstrates, fluidity can also bring drowning and flooding. Furthermore, the discourse of relationality borders at times on the rhetoric of a complexity and cultural relativism that can obscure important power differentials between individuals and peoples. The politics of endless deferral and deconstruction is not inherently progressive and can function regressively depending upon the use to which it is put and the point at which the deconstructor stops the chain of deferrals.[43]

Finally, the insight that relational narrative brings to the discourse of race and ethnicity potentially carries within itself a blindness of its own. An exclusive focus on relational positionality runs the risk of obscuring the continuing necessity for the scripts of denial, accusation, and confession. The historical conditions that led to these three cultural narratives continue to exist and thus to compel their ongoing circulation. Just as the white/other binary has continued cogency in the beating of Rodney King and its aftermath, just as the white/people of color binary has important explanatory power in the Los Angeles upheavals and reports of them, so the binary of white women/women of color continues to have relevance in some contexts. Moreover, discourses of relational positionality should not deflect attention and resources from the critically important archaeological and theoretical work being done to recover, reflect upon, and transmit the often lost or repressed narratives of peoples whose history and culture have been marginalized by the dominant culture.[44] Commitment to multiculturalism in the academy involves ongoing efforts in what Anthony Appiah and Henry Louis Gates call the essential task of producing the "local histories" of different racial and ethnic groups (1992a, 625).

In spite of these potential difficulties, however, I strongly believe that narratives of relational positionality can play a vitally important role in feminist discourse in the 1990s and on into the twenty-first century. Relationality does not have to be a pure concept existing as an end in itself but can be a conceptual cornerstone of a political teleology and practice. It can help to break the logjam of belligerence and apology that paralyzes so many of our classrooms, organizations, and conferences and that appears formulaically in so many of our writings. To move beyond the repetitive tropes of denial, accusation, and confession, we need a

---

[43] My thanks to Jacques Lezra for the insight about fluidity in *The Crying Game* and its relation to the work of Jacques Derrida and Luce Irigaray; also to Hortense Spillers for her warning about the politics of deconstruction.

[44] My thanks to Amy Ling for this observation.

discourse about race and ethnicity that can acknowledge the differences and locate the connections in a complexly constituted global multiculturalism that avoids ethnocentrism of any kind. We need a discourse that does not (re)construct a multicultural other with a covert equation of the term *multicultural* with nonwhite. We need a narrative that does not reinstate white as center and multicultural as margin.

Relational narratives can form the basis for what Radhakrishnan calls a new kind of "coalitional politics" based on "relationality as a field-in-process" (1989b, 311). They make possible the route to a genuine connection between different kinds of people that June Jordan identifies as essential for real change. As she argues, this kind of connection emerges neither out of appeals to universality (scripts of denial), refusals of similarity (scripts of accusation), nor out of expressions of guilt (scripts of confession) but, rather, out of unions based on common experience and need: "The ultimate connection must be the need that we find between us. It is not only who you are, in other words, but what we can do for each other that will determine the connection" (1985, 47). The kind of coalitions that Radhakrishnan and Jordan call for, that movies like *Mississippi Masala* and *The Crying Game* reach for, are based on relational narratives. They are not bridges made between fixed differences. Rather, they go beyond absolute categories of pure/impure and oppressor/oppressed to work instead with the location of shifting positions of privilege and exclusion in global perspective. As Gates writes: "The challenge is to move from a politics of identity to a politics of identification. . . . A politics of identification doesn't enjoin us to ignore or devalue our collective identities. For it's only by exploring the multiplicity of human life in culture that we can come to terms with the commonalities that cement communitas. . . . We may be anti-utopian, but we have dreams, too" (1994, 17). The epigraph from Proverbs that opens Lisa Albrecht and Rose Brewer's hopeful collection, *Bridges of Power: Women's Multicultural Alliances,* articulates the vital necessity of such dreams: "When there is no vision, the people perish" (1990, vi).

A feminist multiculturalism that is global in its reach and configuration needs scripts of relational positionality that can supplement and be enriched by thick descriptions and local histories of racial and ethnic difference. Without these relational scripts, feminist classrooms, conferences, organizations, and writing run the politically dangerous risk of promoting a fundamentalist identity politics that can easily regress into binaries mirroring hegemonic racism: pure/impure, us/them, self/other. We cannot afford to give up the utopian dream of coalition and connection. As the globe shrinks, as racially and ethnically inflected confrontations increase worldwide, as weapons become ever more deadly and available, as transnational economies further polarize wealth and poverty, as U.S. demographics (like those of many other countries) move toward an even more multiracial and multicultural society, our survival as a species depends on our ability to recognize the borders between difference as fertile spaces of desire and fluid sites of syncretism, interaction, and mutual change. As June Jordan reflects during her flight home from the Bahamas: "I look about the cabin at the hundred strangers drinking as they fly and I think even here and even now I must make the connection real between me and these strangers everywhere before those other clouds unify this ragged bunch of us, too late" (1985, 49).

Department of English
University of Wisconsin—Madison

References

Abel, Elizabeth. 1993. "Black Writing, White Reading: Race and the Politics of Feminist Interpretation." *Critical Inquiry* 19 (Spring): 470–98.

Albrecht, Lisa, and Rose M. Brewer, eds. 1990. *Bridges of Power: Women's Multicultural Alliances.* Philadelphia: New Society.

Alcoff, Linda. 1988. "Cultural Feminism versus Poststructuralism: The Identity Crisis in Feminist Theory." *Signs: Journal of Women in Culture and Society* 13 (Spring): 405–36.

Allen, Paula Gunn. 1986. "Kochinnenako in Academe: Three Approaches to Interpreting a Keres Indian Tale." In her *The Sacred Hoop: Recovering the Feminine in American Indian Traditions,* 222–44. Boston: Beacon.

Amirthanayagam, Indran. 1993. "Rogue Elephants, Deadly Tigers." *New York Times,* May 19.

Anzaldúa, Gloria. 1987. *Borderlands/La Frontera.* San Francisco: Spinsters/Aunt Lute.

———. 1990a. "Bridge, Drawbridge, Sandbar or Island: Lesbians of Color Hacienda Alianzas." In Albrecht and Brewer, 216–31.

———. 1990b. "En rapport, In Opposition: Cobrando cuentas a las nuestras." In her *Making Face,* 142–50.

———, ed. 1990c. *Making Face/Making Soul—Haciendo Caras: Creative and Critical Perspectives by Women of Color.* San Francisco: Aunt Lute.

Appadurai, Arjun. 1991. "Global Ethnoscapes: Notes and Queries for a Transnational Anthropology." In *Recapturing Anthropology: Working in the Present,* ed. Richard G. Fox, 191–210. Sante Fe, N. Mex.: School of American Research Press.

Appiah, Anthony. 1986. "The Uncompleted Argument: Du Bois and the Illusion of Race." In Gates 1986a, 21–37.

———. 1989. "The Conversation of 'Race.'" *Black American Literary Forum* 23 (Spring): 37–60.

Appiah, Kwame Anthony, and Henry Louis Gates Jr., eds. 1992a. "Editors' Introduction: Multiplying Identities." In Appiah and Gates 1992b, 625–29.

————. 1992b. "Identities," special issue of *Critical Inquiry,* vol. 18 (Summer).

Baker, Houston, Jr. 1986. "Caliban's Triple Play." In Gates 1986a, 381–95.

————. 1987. *Modernism and the Harlem Renaissance.* Chicago: University of Chicago Press.

Banton, Michael P. 1987. *Racial Theories.* Cambridge: Cambridge University Press.

Beja, Morris. 1979. *Film and Literature.* New York: Longman.

Belsey, Catherine. 1980. *Critical Practice.* London: Methuen.

Benjamin, Jessica. 1988. *The Bonds of Love: Psychoanalysis, Feminism, and the Problem of Domination.* New York: Pantheon.

Bernstein, Susan. 1992. "Confessing Feminist Theory: What's 'I' Got to Do with It?" *Hypatia* 7 (Spring): 120–47.

Bhabha, Homi K. 1983. "The Other Question . . . " *Screen* 24 (November/December): 18–36.

Binder, David, with Barbara Crossette. 1993. "As Ethnic Wars Multiply, U.S. Strives for a Policy." *New York Times,* February 7.

Bloch, Ruth H. 1993. "A Culturalist Critique of Trends in Feminist Theory." *Contention* 2 (Spring): 79–106.

Boelhower, William. 1987. *Through a Glass Darkly: Ethnic Semiosis in American Literature.* Oxford: Oxford University Press.

Bonner, Raymond. 1994. "A Once-Peaceful Village Shows the Roots of Rwanda's Violence." *New York Times,* July 11.

Bourne, Jenny. 1987. "Homelands of the Mind: Jewish Feminism and Identity Politics." *Race and Class* 29(1):1–24.

Bulkin, Elly, Minnie Bruce Pratt, and Barbara Smith. 1984. *Yours in Struggle: Three Feminist Perspectives on Anti-Semitism and Racism.* Brooklyn, N.Y.: Long Haul.

Capel, Sharon. 1993. Letter to *New York Times,* March 7.

Chai, Alice Yun. 1985. "Toward a Holistic Paradigm for Asian American Women's Studies: A Synthesis of Feminist Scholarship and Women of Color's Feminist Politics." *Women's Studies International Forum* 8(1):59–66.

Chametzky, Jules. 1989–90. "Beyond Melting Pots, Cultural Pluralism, Ethnicity—or, *Deja Vu* All Over Again." *Melus* 16 (Winter): 3–17.

Cheng, Vincent J. 1995. *Joyce, Race, and Empire.* Cambridge: Cambridge University Press.

Cho, Sumi K. 1993. "Korean Americans vs. African Americans: Conflict and Construction." In Gooding-Williams 1993, 196–211.

Chodorow, Nancy. 1978. *The Reproduction of Mothering: Psychoanalysis and the Sociology of Gender.* Berkeley: University of California Press.

Christian, Barbara. 1988. "The Race for Theory." *Feminist Studies* 14 (Spring): 67–80.

Cole, Johnnetta B., ed. 1986. "Commonalities and Differences." In her *All American Women: Lines That Divide, Ties That Bind,* 1–30. New York: Free Press.

Crossette, Barbara. 1994. "Women's Advocates Flocking to Cairo, Eager for Gains." *New York Times,* September 2.

D'Acci, Julie. 1994. *Defining Women: The Case of Cagney and Lacy.* Durham, N.C.: Duke University Press.

Daly, Mary. 1978. *Gyn/Ecology: The Metaethics of Radical Feminism*. Boston: Beacon.

———. 1979. "Response." Session titled "Developing Feminist Theory" at "The Second Sex—Thirty Years Later: A Commemorative Conference on Feminist Theory," September 28, New York City.

Dash, Julie. 1992. *Daughters of the Dust: The Making of an African American Woman's Film*. New York: New Press.

Davies, Carole Boyce. 1994. *Black Women, Writing and Identity: Migrations of the Subject*. London: Routledge.

de Lauretis, Teresa. 1986. "Feminist Studies/Critical Studies: Issues, Terms, and Contexts." In her *Feminist Studies/Critical Studies*, 1–19. Bloomington: Indiana University Press.

———. 1987. *Technologies of Gender: Essays on Theory, Film, and Fiction*. Bloomington: Indiana University Press.

———. 1990. "Eccentric Subjects: Feminist Theory and Historical Consciousness." *Feminist Studies* 16 (Spring): 115–50.

Dikötter, Frank. 1992. *The Discourse of Race in Modern China*. Stanford, Calif.: Stanford University Press.

Dill, Bonnie Thornton. 1983. "Race, Class, and Gender: Prospects for an All-Inclusive Sisterhood." *Feminist Studies* 9 (Spring): 129–50.

duCille, Ann. 1994. "The Occult of True Black Womanhood: Critical Demeanor and Black Feminist Studies." *Signs* 19 (Spring): 591–629.

Dumont, Louis. (1966) 1970. *Homo Hierarchicus: An Essay on the Caste System*, trans. Mark Sainsbury. Chicago: University of Chicago Press.

DuPlessis, Rachel Blau. (1979) 1985. "For the Etruscans." In *The New Feminist Criticism*, ed. Elaine Showalter, 271–91. New York: Pantheon.

———. 1985. *Writing beyond the Ending: Narrative Strategies of Twentieth-Century Women Writers*. Bloomington: Indiana University Press.

Fellows, Mary Louise, and Sherene Razack. 1994. "Seeking Relations: Law and Feminism Roundtables." *Signs* 19 (Summer): 1048–83.

Ferguson, James, and Akhil Grupta, eds. 1992. "Space, Place, and Identity," special issue of *Current Anthropology*, vol. 7 (February).

Fields, Barbara. 1982. "Ideology and Race in American History." In *Region, Race, and Reconstruction*, ed. J. Morgan Kinsser and James M. McPherson, 143–77. New York: Oxford University Press.

Fiske, John. 1987. *Television Culture*. London: Methuen.

Fortney, Nancy D. 1977. "The Anthropological Concept of Race." *Journal of Black Studies* 8 (September): 35–54.

Frankenberg, Ruth. 1993. *White Women, Race Matters: The Social Construction of Whiteness*. Minneapolis: University of Minnesota Press.

Fregoso, Rosa Linda. 1993. *The Bronze Screen: Chicana and Chicano Film Culture*. Minneapolis: University of Minnesota Press.

Friedman, Susan Stanford. 1991. "Post/Poststructuralist Feminist Criticism: The Politics of Recuperation and Negotiation." *New Literary History* 22 (Spring): 465–90.

———. 1993. "Relational Epistemology and the Question of Anglo-American Feminist Criticism." *Tulsa Studies in Women's Literature* 12 (Fall): 247–63.

152   *Friedman*

———. 1994. "Beyond Gynocriticism and Gynesis: The New Geography of Identity and Narrative Studies in the 1990s." Paper presented at the Modern Language Association convention, December, San Diego.

Frye, Marilyn. (1981) 1983. "On Being White: Thinking toward a Feminist Understanding of Race and Race Supremacy." In her *The Politics of Reality: Essays in Feminist Theory,* 110–27. Trumansburg, N.Y.: Crossing Press.

———. 1992. "White Woman Feminist." In her *Willful Virgin: Essays in Feminism,* 147–69. Trumansburg, N.Y.: Crossing Press.

Gallop, Jane, et al. 1990. "Criticizing Feminist Criticism." In *Conflicts in Feminism,* ed. Marianne Hirsch and Evelyn Fox Keller, 349–69. New York: Routledge.

Gardiner, Judith Kegan. 1981. "On Female Identity and Writing by Women." *Critical Inquiry* 8 (Winter): 347–61.

Gates, Henry Louis, Jr., ed. 1986a. *"Race," Writing, and Difference.* Chicago: University of Chicago Press.

———. 1986b. "Introduction." In Gates 1986a, 1–20.

———. 1994. "A Liberalism of Heart and Spine." *New York Times,* March 27.

Geertz, Clifford. 1973. *The Interpretation of Cultures: Selected Essays.* New York: Basic.

Goldberg, David Theo, ed. 1990. *Anatomy of Racism.* Minneapolis: University of Minnesota Press.

Gooding-Williams, Robert, ed. 1993. *Reading Rodney King/Reading Urban Uprising.* London: Routledge.

Gordon, Linda. 1991. "On 'Difference.' " *Genders,* no. 10 (Spring), 91–111.

Gornick, Vivian, and Barbara K. Moran, eds. 1971. *Woman in Sexist Society: Studies in Power and Powerlessness.* New York: Basic.

Gray, Herman. 1989. "Television, Black Americans, and the American Dream." *Critical Studies in Mass Communication* 6 (December): 376–86.

———. 1993. "The Endless Slide of Difference: Critical Television Studies, Television and the Question of Race." *Critical Studies in Mass Communication* 10 (June): 190–97.

Gross, Jane. 1993. "Body and Victim Trampled, a Riot Victim Fights On." *New York Times,* October 22.

Gutmann, Amy, ed. 1994. *Multiculturalism: Examining the Politics of Recognition.* Princeton, N.J.: Princeton University Press.

Haraway, Donna. 1988. "Situated Knowledges: The Science Question in Feminism and the Privilege of Partial Perspective." *Feminist Studies* 14 (Fall): 575–99.

Harding, Sarah. 1993. "Culture as an Object of Knowledge." *Contention* 2 (Spring): 121–26.

Harris, Virginia R., and Trinity A. Ordoña. 1990. "Developing Unity among Women of Color: Crossing the Barriers of Internalized Racism and Cross-Racial Hostility." In Anzaldúa 1990c, 304–16.

Hartsock, Nancy C. M. 1983. "The Feminist Standpoint: Developing the Ground for a Specifically Feminist Historical Materialism." In *Discovering Reality: Feminist Perspectives on Epistemology, Metaphysics, Methodology, and Philosophy of Science,* ed. Sandra Harding and Merrill B. Hintikka, 283–310. Boston: Reidel.

Heilbrun, Carolyn G. 1988. *Writing a Woman's Life*. New York: Norton.

Hicks, D. Emily. 1991. *Border Writing: The Multidimensional Text*. Minneapolis: University of Minnesota Press.

Higginbotham, Evelyn Brooks. 1992. "African-American Women's History and the Metalanguage of Race." *Signs* 17 (Winter): 251–74.

Holmes, Steven A. 1994. "Study Finds Minorities Resent One Another Almost as Much as They Do Whites." *New York Times*, March 3.

Homans, Margaret. 1994. "'Women of Color' Writers and Feminist Theory." *New Literary History* 25 (Winter): 73–94.

hooks, bell. 1989. "Feminism: A Transformational Politic." In her *Talking Back*, 19–27. Philadelphia: South End Press.

———. 1994. "Seduction and Betrayal: *The Crying Game* Meets *The Bodyguard*." In her *Outlaw Culture: Resisting Representations*, 53–62. London: Routledge.

hooks, bell, and Anuradha Dingwaney. 1992. "Mississippi Masala." *Z Magazine* 5 (July/August): 41–43.

Hurtado, Aída. 1989. "Relating to Privilege: Seduction and Rejection in the Subordination of White Women and Women of Color." *Signs* 14(4):833–55.

Jacobs, Harriet A. (1861) 1973. *Incidents in the Life of a Slave Girl*. New York: Harcourt Brace Jovanovich.

Jameson, Fredric. 1981. *The Political Unconscious: Narrative as a Socially Symbolic Act*. Ithaca, N.Y.: Cornell University Press.

———. 1991. *Postmodernism, or, The Cultural Logic of Late Capitalism*. Durham, N.C.: Duke University Press.

Jordan, June. 1985. "Report from the Bahamas." In her *On Call: Political Essays*, 39–54. Boston: South End Press.

Jordan, Neil. 1992. *The Crying Game*, film written and directed by Jordan.

———. 1993a. *The Crying Game*. In Jordan 1993b, 177–267.

———. 1993b. *A Neil Jordan Reader*. New York: Vintage.

Kamm, Henry. 1993. "In New Eastern Europe, an Old Anti-Gypsy Bias." *New York Times*, November 17.

Kaplan, Caren. 1990. "Deterritorializations: The Rewriting of Home and Exile in Western Feminist Discourse." In *The Nature and Context of Minority Discourse*, ed. Abdul R. JanMohamed and David Lloyd, 357–68. Oxford: Oxford University Press.

Kim, Elaine H. 1993. "Home Is Where the *Han* Is: A Korean-American Perspective on the Los Angeles Upheavals." In Gooding-Williams 1993, 215–35.

King, Deborah K. 1988. "Multiple Jeopardy, Multiple Consciousness: The Context of Black Feminist Ideology." *Signs* 14 (Autumn): 42–72.

Kogawa, Joy. 1981. *Obasan*. Boston: Godine.

LaCapra, Dominick, ed. 1991. *The Bounds of Race: Perspectives on Hegemony and Resistance*. Ithaca, N.Y.: Cornell University Press.

Laslett, Barbara. 1993. "Gender Analysis and Social Theory: Building on Ruth Bloch's Proposals." *Contention* 2 (Spring): 107–20.

Longnecker, Marlene. 1990. "Marlene Longnecker Responds." *off our backs* 20 (October): 24.

Lorde, Audre. (1979) 1984. "An Open Letter to Mary Daly." In Lorde 1984, 66–71.

————. 1984. *Sister Outsider: Essays and Speeches.* Trumansburg, N.Y.: Crossing Press.

————. 1990. "I Am Your Sister: Black Women Organizing across Sexualities." In Anzaldúa 1990c, 321–25.

Lowe, Lisa. 1991. "Heterogeneity, Hybridity, Multiplicity: Marking Asian American Differences." *Diaspora* 1 (Spring): 24–44.

Lyotard, Jean-François. (1979) 1984. *The Postmodern Condition: A Report on Knowledge,* trans. Geoff Bennington and Brian Massumi. Minneapolis: University of Minnesota Press.

Martin, Biddy, and Chandra Talpade Mohanty. 1986. "Feminist Politics: What's Home Got to Do with It?" In de Lauretis 1986, 191–212.

Martin, Douglas. 1993. "Korean Store Owners Join Forces, Seeking Ties, Opportunity and Clout." *New York Times,* March 22.

Michaels, Walter Benn. 1992. "Race into Culture: A Critical Genealogy of Cultural Identity." *Critical Inquiry* 18 (Summer): 655–85.

Michie, Elsie. 1992. "Race, Empire, and the Brontës." *Novel* 25 (Winter): 125–40.

Miller, Nancy K. 1988. *Subject to Change: Reading Feminist Writing.* New York: Columbia University Press.

Miyoshi, Masao. 1993. "A Borderless World? From Colonialism to Transnationalism and the Decline of the Nation-State." *Critical Inquiry* 19 (Summer): 726–51.

Mohanty, Chandra Talpade. 1989–90. "On Race and Voice: Challenges for Liberal Education for the 1990s." *Cultural Critique* 14 (Winter): 179–208.

————. 1991a. "Cartographies of Struggle: Third World Women and the Politics of Feminism." In *Third World Women and the Politics of Feminism,* ed. Chandra Talpade Mohanty, Ann Russo, and Lourdes Torres, 1–50. Bloomington: Indiana University Press.

————. 1991b. "Under Western Eyes: Feminist Scholarship and Colonial Discourses." In *Third World Feminisms and the Politics of Feminism,* ed. Chandra Talpade Mohanty, Ann Russo, and Lourdes Torres, 51–80. Bloomington: Indiana University Press.

Mohanty, S. P. 1989. "Us and Them: On the Philosophical Bases of Political Criticism." *Yale Journal of Criticism* 2(2):1–31.

Molina, Papusa. 1990. "Recognizing, Accepting and Celebrating Our Differences." In Anzaldúa 1990c, 326–35.

Moraga, Cherríe, and Gloria Anzaldúa, eds. 1981. *This Bridge Called My Back: Writings by Radical Women of Color.* Watertown, Mass.: Persephone.

Morgan, Robin, ed. 1970. *Sisterhood Is Powerful: An Anthology of Writings from the Women's Liberation Movement.* New York: Vintage.

Morrison, Toni. 1992. *Playing in the Dark: Whiteness and the Literary Imagination.* Cambridge, Mass.: Harvard University Press.

Musil, Caryn McTighe. 1990. " 'Rivers, Swamps, and Vanishing Ponds.' " *NWS-Action* 3 (Winter): 2–4, 22.

Nair, Mira. 1991. *Mississippi Masala,* film written by Sooni Taraporevala and directed by Mira Nair. Mirabai Films.

Nair, Mira, and Sooni Taraporevala. 1989. *Salaam Bombay!* New York: Penguin.

Nielsen, Aldon Lynn. 1988. *Reading Race: White American Poets and the Racial Discourse in the Twentieth Century.* Athens: University of Georgia Press.

NWSA Women of Color Caucus. 1990. "Institutionalized Racism and the National Women's Studies Association." *Sojourner: The Women's Forum* (August), 8–9.

Oliver, Melvin L., James H. Johnson Jr., and Walter C. Farrell Jr. 1993. "Anatomy of a Rebellion: A Political-Economic Analysis." In Gooding-Williams 1993, 117–41.

Omi, Michael, and Howard Winant. 1986. *Racial Formation in the United States: From the 1960s to the 1980s.* London: Routledge.

———. 1993. "The Los Angeles 'Race Riot' and Contemporary U.S. Politics." In Gooding-Williams 1993, 97–16.

Osborne, Nancy Seale. 1990. "Caryn McTighe Musil Resigns after Six Years as Director." *NWSAction* 3 (Winter): 1–2.

Ozanne, Julian. 1992. "Old Clan Rivalries Fuel Bloodshed in Somalia." *Financial Times of London,* August 8–9.

Parkerson, Michelle. 1990. "Did You Say the Mirror Talks?" In Albrecht and Brewer 1990, 108–17.

Pérez-Torres, Rafael. 1993–94. "Nomads and Migrants: Negotiating a Multicultural Modernism." *Cultural Critique* 26 (Winter): 161–89.

Peterson, William, Michael Novak, and Philip Gleason. 1980. *Concepts of Ethnicity.* Cambridge, Mass.: Harvard University Press.

Pheterson, Gail. 1990. "Alliances between Women: Overcoming Internalized Oppression and Internalized Domination." In Albrecht and Brewer 1990, 34–48.

Poliakov, Leon. 1971. *The Ayran Myth: A History of Racist and Nationalist Ideas in Europe,* trans. Edmund Howard. New York: Basic.

Polumbo-Liu, David. 1994. "Los Angeles, Asians, and Perverse Ventriloquisms: On the Functions of Asian America in the Recent American Imaginary." *Public Culture* 6(2):365–81.

Pratt, Mary Louise. 1991. "Arts of the Contact Zone." In *Profession 91,* 33–40. New York: Modern Language Association.

Pratt, Minnie Bruce. 1984. "Identity: Skin Blood Heart." In Bulkin, Pratt, and Smith 1984, 9–64.

Radhakrishnan, R. 1987. "Culture as Common Ground: Ethnicity and Beyond." *Melus* 14 (Summer): 5–19.

———. 1989a. "Negotiating Subject Positions in an Uneven World." In *Feminism and Institutions,* ed. Linda Kaufman, 276–90. Oxford: Basil Blackwell.

———. 1989b. "Post-Structuralist Politics: Toward a Theory of Coalition." In *Jameson/Postmodernism/Critique,* ed. Douglas Kellner, 276–90. Washington, D.C.: Maisonneuve.

———. 1991. "Ethnicity in an Age of Diaspora." *Transition* 54 (November): 104–15.

———. 1992. "Nationalism, Gender, and the Narrative of Identity." In *Nationalism and Sexualities,* ed. Andrew Parker, et al., 77–95. London: Routledge.

———. 1993. "Cultural Theory and the Politics of Location." In *Views beyond the Border Country: Raymond Williams and Cultural Politics,* ed. Leslie G. Roman and Dennis Dworkin, 275–93. London: Routledge.

Reeves, Jimmie L., and Richard Campbell. 1994. *Cracked Coverage: Television News, the Anti-Cocaine Crusade, and the Reagan Legacy.* Durham, N.C.: Duke University Press.

Rensberger, Boyce. 1993. "The Melting Pot under a Microscope." *Washington Post National Weekly Edition* (March 15–21), 38.

Rich, Adrienne. 1976. *Of Woman Born: Motherhood as Experience and Institution.* New York: Norton.

——— . (1978) 1979. "Disloyal to Civilization: Feminism, Racism, Gynophobia." In her *On Lies, Secrets, and Silence: Selected Prose, 1966–1978,* 275–310. New York: Norton.

——— . (1984) 1986. "Notes toward a Politics of Location." In her *Blood, Bread, and Poetry: Selected Prose, 1979–1985,* 210–32. New York: Norton.

Rodriguez, Richard. 1993. "Changing Faces." Transcript of *MacNeil/Lehrer Newshour,* show 4756, 13–14. September 16.

Romero, Gloria J. 1991. " 'Nose raje, chicanita': Some Thoughts on Race, Class and Gender in the Classroom." *Aztlan* 29 (Spring/Fall): 203–18.

Ruby, Jennie, and Carol Anne Douglas. 1990. "NWSA: Troubles Surface at Conference." *off our backs* 20 (August/September): 1, 10–16.

Russo, Ann. 1991. " 'We Cannot Live without Our Lives': White Women, Antiracism, and Feminism." In *Third World Women and the Politics of Feminism,* ed. Chandra Talpade Mohanty, Ann Russo, and Lourdes Torres, 288–96. Bloomington: Indiana University Press.

Sales, Ruby. 1990. "Letter from Ruby Sales." *off our backs* 20 (August/September): 25.

Sandoval, Chela. 1990. "Feminism and Racism: A Report on the 1981 National Women's Studies Association Conference." In Anzaldúa 1990c, 55–74.

Schweikart, Patsy. 1990. "Reflections on NWSA 190." *NWSAction* 3 (Fall): 3–4, 9–10.

Sedgwick, Eve Kosofsky. 1985. *Between Men: English Literature and Male Homosocial Desire.* New York: Columbia University Press.

Silko, Leslie Marmon. 1981. *The Storyteller.* New York: Little, Brown.

Smiley, Marion. 1992. "Feminist Theory and the Question of Identity." *Women and Politics* 13(2):91–122.

Smith, Barbara. (1977) 1985. "Toward a Black Feminist Criticism." In *The New Feminist Criticism,* ed. Elaine Showalter, 168–85. New York: Pantheon.

Smith, Paul. 1988. *Discerning the Subject.* Minneapolis: University of Minnesota Press.

Smith, Valerie. 1989. "Black Feminist Theory and the Representation of the 'Other.' " In *Changing Our Own Words: Essays on Criticism, Theory, and Writing by Black Women,* ed. Cheryl A. Wall, 38–57. New Brunswick, N.J.: Rutgers University Press.

Sollors, Werner. 1986. *Beyond Ethnicity: Consent and Descent in American Culture.* New York: Oxford University Press.

——— , ed. 1989. *The Invention of Ethnicity.* Oxford: Oxford University Press.

Spillers, Hortense. 1989. "Notes on an Alternative Model—Neither/Nor." In *The Difference Within: Feminism and Critical Theory,* ed. Elizabeth Meese and Alice Parker, 165–87. Philadelphia: John Benjamins.

Spivak, Gayatri Chakravorty. 1987a. "French Feminism in an International Frame." In Spivak 1987b, 134–53.

———. 1987b. *In Other Worlds: Essays in Cultural Politics.* New York: Methuen.

———. 1988. "Can the Subaltern Speak?" In *Marxism and the Interpretation of Culture,* ed. Cary Nelson and Lawrence Grossberg, 271–313. Urbana: University of Illinois Press.

Stepan, Nancy. 1982. *The Idea of Race in Science: Great Britain, 1800–1960.* New York: Archon.

Stocking, George W., Jr. 1968. *Race, Culture, and Evolution: Essays in the History of Anthropology.* New York: Free Press.

Suleri, Sara. 1992. "Woman Skin Deep: Feminism and the Postcolonial Condition." *Critical Inquiry* 18 (Summer): 756–69.

Thompson, Becky, and Estelle Disch. 1992. "Feminist, Anti-Racist, Anti-Oppresion Teaching: Two White Women's Experience." *Radical Teacher,* no. 41 (Spring), 4–10.

Thompson, Richard H. 1989. *Theories of Ethnicity: A Critical Appraisal.* New York: Greenwood.

Uttal, Lynet. 1990. "Nods That Silence." In Anzaldúa 1990c, 317–20.

Wagstyl, Stefan. 1993. "Inter-religious Forgiveness Is Just Not Cricket." *Financial Times of London,* February 22.

Wald, Alan. 1987. "Theorizing Cultural Difference: A Critique of the Ethnicity School." *Melus* 14 (Summer): 21–33.

Walker, Alice. (1974) 1983a. "In Search of Our Mothers' Gardens." In her *In Search of Our Mothers' Gardens.* 231–43. New York: Harcourt Brace Jovanovich.

———. (1979) 1983b. "One Child of One's Own." In her *In Search of Our Mothers' Gardens,* 361–83. New York: Harcourt Brace Jovanovich.

West, Cornel. 1982. "A Genealogy of Modern Racism." In his *Prophesy Deliverance! An Afro-American Revolutionary Christianity,* 47–68. Philadelphia: Westminster.

———. 1988. "Marxist Theory and the Specificity of Afro-American Oppression." In *Marxism and the Interpretation of Culture,* ed. Cary Nelson and Lawrence Grossberg, 17–34. Urbana: University of Illinois Press.

Williams, Patricia J. 1989. "The Obliging Shell." In her *The Alchemy of Race and Rights: Diary of a Law Professor,* 98–132. Cambridge, Mass.: Harvard University Press.

Wright, Lawrence. 1994. "One Drop of Blood." *New Yorker* 70 (July 25): 46–55.

Gender as Seriality: Thinking about Women as a Social Collective

Iris Marion Young

I N THE SUMMER of 1989 I worked in Shirley Wright's cam-
paign for a seat on the Worcester School Committee. Shirley is
African American in a city where about 5–7 percent of the popula-
tion are African American, and 7–10 percent are Hispanic. As in
many other cities, however, more than 35 percent of the children in the
public schools are black, Hispanic, or Asian, and the proportion of chil-
dren of color is growing rapidly. For more than ten years all six of the
school committee seats have been held by white people, and only one
woman has served, for about two years. In her announcement speech
Shirley Wright pledged to represent all the people of Worcester. But she
noted the particular need to represent minorities, and she also empha-
sized the importance of having a woman's voice on the committee.

A few weeks later a friend and I distributed Shirley Wright flyers
outside a grocery store. The flyers displayed a photo of Shirley and some
basics about her qualifications and issues. In the course of the morning at
least two women, both white, exclaimed to me, "I'm so glad to see a
woman running for school committee!" This African American woman
claimed to speak for women in Worcester, and some white women no-
ticed and felt affinity with her as a woman.

This seemed to me at the time an unremarkable, easily understandable
affinity. Recent discussions among feminists about the difficulties and
dangers of talking about women as a single group, however, make such
incidents appear at least puzzling. These discussions have cast doubt on
the project of conceptualizing women as a group, arguing that the search
for the common characteristics of women or of women's oppression
leads to normalizations and exclusions. While I agree with such cri-
tiques, I also agree with those who argue that there are pragmatic

I am grateful to Linda Alcoff, David Alexander, Sandra Bartky, Sonia Kruks, Lynda
Lange, Bill McBride, Uma Narayan, Linda Nicholson, Vicki Spelman, and anonymous
reviewers for *Signs* for comments on earlier versions of this article.

[*Signs: Journal of Women in Culture and Society* 1994, vol. 19, no. 3]

political reasons for insisting on the possibility of thinking about women as some kind of group.

Clearly, these two positions pose a dilemma for feminist theory. On the one hand, without some sense in which "woman" is the name of a social collective, there is nothing specific to feminist politics. On the other hand, any effort to identify the attributes of that collective appears to undermine feminist politics by leaving out some women whom feminists ought to include. To solve this dilemma I argue for reconceptualizing social collectivity or the meaning of social groups as what Sartre describes as a phenomenon of serial collectivity in his *Critique of Dialectical Reason* (1976). Such a way of thinking about women, I will argue, allows us to see women as a collective without identifying common attributes that all women have or implying that all women have a common identity.

I

Doubts about the possibility of saying that women can be thought of as one social collective arose from challenges to a generalized conception of gender and women's oppression by women of color, in both the northern and southern hemispheres, and by lesbians. Black, Latina, Asian, and indigenous women demonstrated that white feminist theory and rhetoric tended to be ethnocentric in its analysis of gender experience and oppression. Lesbians, furthermore, persistently argued that much of this analysis relied on the experience of heterosexual women. The influence of philosophical deconstruction completed the suspension of the category of "women" begun by this process of political differentiation. Exciting theorizing has shown (not for the first time) the logical problems in efforts to define clear, essential categories of being. Let me review some of the most articulate recent statements of the claim that feminists should abandon or be very suspicious of a general category of woman or female gender.

Elizabeth Spelman (1988) shows definitively the mistake in any attempt to isolate gender from identities such as race, class, age, sexuality, and ethnicity to uncover the attributes, experiences, or oppressions that women have in common. To be sure, we have no trouble identifying ourselves as women, white, middle class, Jewish, American, and so on. But knowing the "right" labels to call ourselves and others does not imply the existence of any checklist of attributes that all those with the same label have in common. The absurdity of trying to isolate gender identity from race or class identity becomes apparent if you ask of any individual woman whether she can distinguish the "woman part" of herself from the "white part" or the "Jewish part." Feminist theorists nevertheless have often assumed that the distinctive and specific attributes of gender can be identified by holding race and class constant or by examining the lives of women who suffer only sexist oppression and not also oppressions of race, class, age, or sexuality.

The categories according to which people are identified as the same or different, Spelman suggests, are social constructs that reflect no natures or essences. They carry and express relations of privilege and subordination, the power of some to determine for others how they will be named, what differences are important for what purposes. Because it has assumed that women form a single group with common experiences, attributes, or oppressions, much feminist theorizing has exhibited privileged points of view by unwittingly taking the experience of white middle-class heterosexual women as representative for all women. Even when feminists attempt to take account of differences among women, moreover, they often manifest such biases because they fail to notice the race or class specificity of white middle-class women and how these also modify our gender. Much feminist talk about paying attention to differences among women, Spelman points out, tends to label only women of color or old women or disabled women as "different."

Chandra Mohanty believes that the "assumption of women as an already constituted, coherent group with identical interests and desires, regardless of class, ethnic or racial location, or contradictions, implies a notion of gender or sexual difference or even patriarchy which can be applied universally or even cross-culturally" (1991, 55). She believes that this category of "woman" as designating a single, coherent, already constituted group influences feminists to regard all women as equally powerless and oppressed victims. Rather than developing questions about how and whether women in a particular time and place suffer discrimination and limitation on their action and desires, questions that can then be empirically investigated, the assumption of universal gender categories bypasses such empirical investigation by finding oppression a priori. This tendency is especially damaging in the way European and American feminists think and write about women in the southern and eastern hemispheres. Assumptions about a homogeneous category of women helps create a homogeneous category of Third World women who stand as the Other to western feminists, who define Third World women as powerless victims of patriarchy.

Judith Butler draws more explicitly on postmodern theories to argue against the viability of the category of "woman" and of gender (1990). In a Foucauldian mode, Butler argues that the idea of gender identity and the attempt to describe it has a normalizing power. The very act of defining a gender identity excludes or devalues some bodies, practices, and discourses at the same time that it obscures the constructed, and thus contestable, character of that gender identity.

Feminism has assumed that it can be neither theoretical nor political without a subject. Female gender identity and experience delineate that subject. Feminist politics, it is assumed, speaks for or in the name of someone, the group women, who are defined by this female gender identity.

The category of gender was promoted by feminism precisely to criticize and reject traditional efforts to define women's nature through "biological" sex. In its own way, however, according to Butler, gender discourse tends to reify the fluid and shifting social processes in which people relate, communicate, play, work, and struggle with one another over the means of production and interpretation. The insistence on a subject for feminism obscures the social and discursive production of identities.

In one of the most important arguments of her book, Butler shows that the feminist effort to distinguish sex and gender itself contributes to such obscuring by ignoring the centrality of enforced heterosexuality in the social construction of gender. However variable its content is understood to be, the form of gender differentiation is always a binary opposition between the masculine and the feminine. Inasmuch as sexual difference is classified only as man and woman, then, gender always mirrors sex. The binary complementarity of this sex/gender system is required and makes sense, however, only with the assumption of heterosexual complementarity. Gender identification thus turns out not to be a culturally variable overlay on a given biological sex; rather, the categories of gender construct sexual difference itself. "Gender can delineate a *unity* of experience, of sex, gender and desire, only when sex can be understood in some sense to necessitate gender. The internal coherence or unity of either gender, man or woman, thereby requires both a stable and oppositional heterosexuality. Thus we see the political reasons for substantializing gender" (Butler 1990, 23).

This mutual reinforcement of (hetero)sex and gender as fixed categories suppresses any ambiguities and incoherences among heterosexual, homosexual, and bisexual practices. This unity of sex and gender organizes the variability of desiring practices along a single scale of normal and deviant behavior. Butler concludes that feminism's attempt to construct or speak for a subject, to forge the unity of coalition from the diversities of history and practice, will always lead to such ossifications. The primary task for feminist theory and politics is critical: to formulate genealogies that show how a given category of practice is socially constructed. Feminist discourse and practice should become and remain open, its totality permanently deferred, accepting and affirming the flows and shifts in the contingent relations of social practices and institutions.

These analyses are powerful and accurate. They identify ways that essentializing assumptions and the point of view of privileged women dominate much feminist discourse, even when it tries to avoid such hegemonic moves. They draw important lessons for any future feminist theorizing that wishes to avoid excluding some women from its theories or freezing contingent social relations into a false necessity. But I find the exclusively critical orientation of such arguments rather paralyzing. Do these arguments imply that it makes no sense and is morally wrong ever to talk about women as a group or, in fact, to talk about social groups at all? It is not clear that these writers claim this. If not, then what can it mean to use the term *woman?* More important, in the light of these critiques, what sort of positive claims can feminists make about the way social life is and ought to be? I find questions like these unaddressed by these critiques of feminist essentialism.

II

What is the genealogy of the essentializing discourse that established a normative feminist subject, woman, that excluded, devalued, or found deviant the lives and practices of many women? Like most discursive constructs, this one is overdetermined. But I suggest that one important source of the oppressive and paradoxical consequences of conceptualizing women as a group is the adoption of a *theoretical* stance. In large part feminist discourse about gender was motivated by the desire to establish a countertheory to Marxism, to develop a feminist theory that would conceive sex or gender as a category with as much theoretical weight as class. This desire employs a totalizing impulse. What *is* a woman? What *is* woman's social position such that it is not reducible to class? Are all societies structured by male domination, and of the same form or of variable forms? What are the origins and causes of this male domination?

These are all general and rather abstract theoretical questions. By "theory" I mean a kind of discourse that aims to be comprehensive, to give a systematic account and explanation of social relations as a whole. A theory tries to tell the way things are in some universal sense. From it one can derive particular instances or at least one can apply the theoretical propositions to particular facts that the theory's generalities are supposed to cover. A social theory is self-enclosed, in the sense that it offers no particular purpose other than to understand, to reveal the way things are.

Despite much work in the last twenty years to make such theories, feminists do not need and should not want theory in this sense. Instead, we should take a more pragmatic orientation to our intellectual discourse. By being pragmatic I mean categorizing, explaining, developing accounts and arguments that are tied to specific practical and political problems, where the purpose of this theoretical activity is clearly related to those problems (see, e.g., Bordo 1989). Pragmatic theorizing in this sense is not necessarily any less complex or sophisticated than totalizing theory, but rather it is driven by some problem that has ultimate practical importance and is not concerned to give an account of a whole. In this article I take the pragmatic problem to be a political dilemma generated by feminist critiques of the concept of "woman," and I aim to solve it by articulating some concepts without claiming to provide an entire social theory.

From this pragmatic point of view, I wish to ask, why does it matter whether we even consider conceptualizing women as a group? One reason to conceptualize women as a collective, I think, is to maintain a point of view outside of liberal individualism. The discourse of liberal individualism denies the reality of groups. According to liberal individualism, categorizing people in groups by race, gender, religion, and sexuality and acting as though these ascriptions say something significant about the person, his or her experience, capacities and possibilities, is invidious and oppressive. The only liberatory approach is to think of and treat people as individuals, variable and unique. This individualist ideology, however, in fact obscures oppression. Without conceptualizing women as a group in some sense, it is not possible to conceptualize oppression as a systematic, structured, institutional process. If we obey the injunction to think of people only as individuals, then the disadvantages and exclusions we call oppressions reduce to individuals in one of two ways. Either we blame the victims and say that disadvantaged people's choices and capacities render them less competitive, or we attribute their disadvantage to the attitudes of other individuals, who for whatever reason don't "like" the disadvantaged ones. In either case structural and political ways to address and rectify the disadvantage are written out of the discourse, leaving individuals to wrestle with their bootstraps. The importance of being able to talk about disadvantage and oppression in terms of groups exists just as much for those oppressed through race, class, sexuality, ethnicity, and the like as through gender (cf. Young 1990, chap. 2).

The naming of women as a specific and distinct social collective, moreover, is a difficult achievement and one that gives feminism its specificity as a political movement. The possibility of conceptualizing ethnic, religious, cultural, or national groups, for example, rarely comes into question because their social existence itself usually involves some common traditions—language, or rituals, or songs and stories, or dwelling place. Women, however, are dispersed among all these groups. The operations of most marriage and kinship forms bring women under the identity of men in each and all of these groups, in the privacy of household and bed. The exclusions, oppressions, and disadvantages that women often suffer can hardly be thought of at all without a structural conception of women as a collective social position. The first step in feminist resistance to such oppressions is the affirmation of women as a group, so that women can cease to be divided and to believe that their sufferings are natural or merely personal. Denial of the reality of a social collective termed *women* reinforces the privilege of those who benefit from keeping women divided (Lange 1991).

Feminist politics evaporates, that is, without some conception of women as a social collective. Radical politics may remain as a commitment to social justice for all people, among them those called women. Yet the claim that feminism expresses a distinct politics allied with anti-imperialism, antiracism, and gay liberation but asking a unique set of enlightening questions about a distinct axis of social oppression cannot be sustained without some means of conceptualizing women and gender as social structures.

The logical and political difficulties inherent in the attempt to conceptualize women as a single group with a set of common attributes and shared identity appear to be insurmountable. Yet if we cannot conceptualize women as a group, feminist politics appears to lose any meaning. Is there a way out of this dilemma? Recent feminist discussions of this problem have presented two strategies for solving it: the attempt to theorize gender identity as multiple rather than binary and the argument that women constitute a group only in the politicized context of feminist struggle. I shall argue now that both of these strategies fail.

Spelman herself explores the strategy of multiple genders. She does not dispense with the category of gender but, instead, suggests that a women's gender identity and gender attributes are different according to what race, class, religion, and the like she belongs to. Gender, she argues, is a relational concept, not the naming of an essence. One finds the specific characteristics and attributes of the gender identity of women by comparing their situation with that of men. But if one wishes to locate the gender-based oppression of women, it is wrong to compare all women with all men. For some women are definitely privileged when compared to some men. To find the gender-specific attributes of a woman's experience, Spelman suggests, one must restrict the comparison to men and women of the same race or class or nationality. Women of different races or classes, moreover, often have opposing gender attributes. In this reasoning, women as such cannot be said to be a group. Properly designated groups are "white women," "black women," "Jewish women," "working-class women," "Brazilian woman," each with specific gender characteristics (Spelman 1988, 170–78).

In a recent paper Ann Ferguson proposes a similar solution to the contradictions and quandaries that arise when feminists assume that all women share a common identity and set of gendered attributes. "Instead of a concept of sisterhood based on a shared gender identity," she suggests, "it may be more helpful to posit different racial gender positions, and possibly different class gender positions. Processes of racialization in U.S. history have created at least ten gender identities informed with racial difference if we consider the various subordinate races: black, Latino, Native American, and Asian, as well as the dominant white race" (1991, 114–15).

There is much to recommend this concept of multiple genders as a way of describing the differentiations and contradictions in the social experience of gender. The idea of multiple genders highlights the fact that not all men are equally privileged by gender. It also makes clear that some women are privileged in relation to some men, a privilege that derives partly from their gender. It allows the theorist to look for race or class in specific gender interactions and expectations without essentializing them. Multiple gender conceptualization may also address the problems of binarism and heterosexism that Butler finds in gender theory. According to a concept of multiple genders, the gender identity of lesbians, for example, can be conceptualized as different from that of straight women.

Despite its promising virtues, the strategy of multiplying gender also has some dangers. First, it is just not true, as Spelman suggests, that gender relations are structured primarily within a class, race, nationality, and so on. A working-class woman's gendered experience and oppression is not properly identified only by comparing her situation to working-class men. Much of her gendered experience is conditioned by her relation to middle-class or ruling-class men. If she experiences sexual harassment at work, for example, her harasser is at least as likely to be a middle-class professional man as a working-class assembler or delivery man. Examples of such cross-class or cross-race relations between men and women can be multiplied. In such relations it would be false to say that the class or race difference is not as important as the gender difference, but it would be equally false to say that the cross-class or cross-race relations between men and women are not gendered relations. But if we conceive of an African American feminine gender, for example, as having one set of attributes in relation to African American men and another in relation to white men, one of two things results: either we need to multiply genders further or we need to draw back and ask what makes both of these genders womanly.

Second, the idea of multiple genders presumes a stability and unity to the categories of race, class, religion, and ethnicity that divide women. To conceptualize "American Indian woman" as a single identity different from "white woman," we must implicitly assume "American Indian" or "white" as stable categories. As Susan Bordo points out, feminist arguments against conceptualizing women as a single group often privilege categories of race or class, failing to challenge the appropriateness of these group categories (Bordo 1989). But the same arguments against considering these categories as unities can be used as the arguments against thinking about women as a unity. American Indians are divided by class, region, religion, sexuality, and ethnicity as well as by gender. Working-class people are divided by race, ethnicity, region, religion, and sexuality as well as by gender. The idea of multiple genders can solve the problems and paradoxes involved in conceptualizing women as a group only by presuming categorical unities to class and race.

This last point leads to my final objection to the idea of multiple genders. This strategy can generate an infinite regress that dissolves groups into individuals. Any category can be considered an arbitrary unity. Why claim that Black women, for example, have a distinct and unified gender identity? Black women are American, Haitian, Jamaican, African, Northern, Southern, poor, working class, lesbian, or old. Each of these divisions may be important to a particular woman's gender identity. But then we are back to the question of what it means to call her a woman. The strategy of multiple genders, then, while useful in directing attention to the social specificities of gender differentiation and gender interaction, does not resolve the dilemma I have posed. Instead, it seems to swing back and forth between the two poles of that dilemma.

Some feminist theorists propose "identity politics" as a different answer to the criticism of essentializing gender while retaining a conception of women as a group. According to this view, an identity *woman* that unites subjects into a group is not a natural or social given but rather the fluid construct of a political movement, feminism. Thus Diana Fuss agrees that *woman* cannot name a set of attributes that a group of individuals has in common, that there is not a single female gender identity that defines the social experience of womanhood. Instead, she holds, feminist politics itself creates an identity *woman* out of a coalition of diverse female persons dispersed across the world. "Coalition politics precedes class and determines its limits and boundaries; we cannot identify a group of women until various social, historical, political conditions construct the conditions and possibilities for membership. Many anti-essentialists fear that positing a political coalition of *women* risks presuming that there must first be a natural class of women; but this belief only makes the fact that it is coalition politics which constructs the category of women (and men) in the first place" (Fuss 1989, 36).

Interpreting the theoretical writings of several Black feminist writers, Nancie Caraway proposes a similar understanding of women as a group. She argues that unity and solidarity among women is a product of political discussion and struggle among people of diverse backgrounds, experiences, and interests who are differently situated in matrices of power and privilege. The process of discussion and disagreement among feminists forges a common commitment to a politics against oppression that produces the identity "woman" as a coalition. Thus, says Caraway, "identity politics advances a space for political action, praxis, justified by the critical *positioning* of the marginalized subjects against hierarchies of power—the Enlightenment promise of transcendence. . . . These emerging theories are codes about the fluid construction of identity. They are not racially specific; they speak to both white and Black feminists about the shared and differentiated faces of female oppression" (1989, 9).

The identity politics position has some important virtues. It rightly recognizes that the perception of a common identity among persons must be the product of social or political process that brings them together around a purpose. It retains a conception of women as a group that it believes feminist politics needs, at the same time clearly rejecting an essentialist or substantive conception of gender identity. There are, however, at least two problems with identity politics as a way to get out of the dilemma I have articulated.

Judith Butler points out the first. Even though identity politics' coalition politics and deconstructive discourse avoids the substantialization of gender, the dangers of normalization are not thereby also avoided.' The feminist politics that produces a coalition of mutually identifying women nevertheless privileges some norms or experiences over others. Thus Butler suggests that feminist politics should be suspicious of settling into a unified coalition. The question of solidarity should never be settled, and identities should shift and be deconstructed in a play of possibilities that exclude no one.

My second objection to the idea that women are a group only as the construction of feminist politics is that it seems to make feminist politics arbitrary. Some women choose to come together in a political movement, to form themselves as a group of mutually identifying agents. But on the basis of what do they come together? What are the social conditions that have motivated the politics? Perhaps even more important, do feminist politics leave out women who do not identify as feminists? These questions all point to the need for some conception of women as a group prior to the formation of self-conscious feminist politics, as designating a certain set of relations or positions that motivate the particular politics of feminism.

III

Stories like Shirley Wright's race for school committee remind us that everyday language seems to be able to talk about women as a collective in some sense, even though women's experiences vary considerably by class, race, sexuality, age, or society. But Spelman, Mohanty, Butler, and others are right to criticize the exclusionary and normalizing implications of most attempts to theorize this everyday experience. We want and need to describe women as a group, yet it appears that we cannot do so without being normalizing and essentialist.

I propose a way out of this dilemma through a use of the concept of seriality that Sartre develops in his *Critique of Dialectical Reason.* I propose that we understand gender as referring to a social series, a specific kind of social collectivity that Sartre distinguishes from groups. Understanding gender as seriality, I suggest, has several virtues. It provides a way of thinking about women as a social collective without requiring that all women have common attributes or a common situation. Gender as seriality, moreover, does not rely on identity or self-identity for understanding the social production and meaning of membership in collectives.

One might well question any project that appropriates Sartrian philosophy positively for feminist theory (see Murphy 1989). Much of Sartre's writing is hopelessly sexist and male biased. This is certainly manifest in his theorization and functionalization of heterosexual relations. Perhaps more fundamentally, Sartre's early existentialist ontology presumes human relations as oppositional, egoistical, and basically violent. While his later philosophy on which I will draw is less individualistic than his early philosophy, the later thinking retains the assumption of human relations as latently violent. In it, boxing is a paradigm of the relation of self and other as mediated by a third.

Although Sartre's writing is sexist and his ontological assumptions about human relations tend to derive from masculine experience, I nevertheless have found the idea of seriality in particular, and its distinction from other kinds of social collective, of use in thinking about women as a collective. Linda Singer has talked about the feminist philosopher as a "Bandita," an intellectual outlaw who raids the texts of male philosophers and steals from them what she finds pretty or useful, leaving the rest behind (1992). I aim to approach Sartre's texts with the spirit of this Bandita, taking and rearticulating for my purposes the concepts I think will help resolve the dilemma I have posed. In doing so I need not drag all of Sartre with me, and I may be "disloyal" to him.

In the *Critique of Dialectical Reason,* Sartre distinguishes several levels of social collectivity by their order of internal complexity and reflexivity. For the purposes of addressing the problem of thinking about women as a social collective, the important distinction is between a group and a series. A group is a collection of persons who recognize themselves and one another as in a unified relation with one another. Members of the group mutually acknowledge that together they undertake a common project. Members of the group, that is, are united by action that they undertake together. In acknowledging oneself as a member of the group, an individual acknowledges oneself as oriented toward the same goals as the others; each individual thereby assumes the common project as a project for his or her individual action. What makes the project shared, however, is the mutual acknowledgment among the members of the group that they are engaged in the project together; this acknowledgment usually becomes explicit at some point in a pledge, contract, constitution, set of by-laws, or statement of purpose. The project of the group is a collective project, moreover, insofar as the members of the group mutually acknowledge that it can only be or is best undertaken by a group— storming the Bastille, staging an international women's conference, achieving women's suffrage, building an amphitheater (Sartre 1976, bk. 2, secs. 1, 2, and 3).[1]

So far in this article I have used the term *group* loosely, as does ordinary language, to designate any collection of people. Since my theorizing about women depends on Sartre's distinction between group and series, however, from now on in this article I shall reserve the term *group* for the self-consciously, mutually acknowledging collective with a self-conscious purpose. Much of an individual's life and action takes place in and is structured by a multitude of groups in this sense. Not all structured social action occurs in groups, however. As Sartre explains it, groups arise from and often fall back into a less organized and unself-conscious collective unity, which he calls a series.

Within Sartre's conception of human freedom, all social relations must be understood as the production of action. Unlike a group, which forms around actively shared objectives, a series is a social collective whose members are unified passively by the objects around which their actions are oriented or by the objectified results of the material effects of the actions of the others. In everyday life we often experience ourselves and others impersonally, as participating in amorphous collectives defined by routine practices and habits. The unity of the series derives from the way that individuals pursue their own individual ends with respect to the same objects conditioned by a continuous material environment, in response to structures that have been created by the unintended collective result of past actions.

Sartre describes people waiting for a bus as such a series. They are a collective insofar as they minimally relate to one another and follow the

---

[1] Sartre in fact distinguishes several levels of group: the group in fusion, the statutory group, the organization, and the institution. Each is less spontaneous, more organized and rule bound, and more materialized than the last. All come under the more general definition I am offering here, which is all that is necessary to develop my argument. Although my summaries of Sartre throughout this article leave out a great deal of detail, I believe they are nevertheless adequate to the text and sufficient for developing my argument.

rules of bus waiting. As a collective they are brought together by their relation to a material object, the bus, and the social practices of public transportation. Their actions and goals may be different, and they have nothing necessarily in common in their histories, experiences, or identity. They are united only by their desire to ride on that route. Though they are in this way a social collective, they do not identify with one another, do not affirm themselves as engaged in a shared enterprise, or identify themselves with common experiences. The latent potential of this series to organize itself as a group will become manifest, however, if the bus fails to come; they will complain to one another about the lousy bus service, share horror stories of lateness and breakdowns, perhaps assign one of their number to go call the company, or discuss sharing a taxi.

Such serial collectivity, according to Sartre, is precisely the obverse of the mutual identification typical of the group. Each goes about his or her own business. But each is also aware of the serialized context of that activity in a social collective whose structure constitutes them within certain limits and constraints. In seriality, a person not only experiences others but also himself or herself as an Other, that is, as an anonymous someone: "Everyone is the same as the other insofar as he is Other than himself" (p. 260). Individuals in the series are interchangeable; while not identical, from the point of view of the social practices and objects that generate the series, the individuals could be in one another's place. It is contingent that I am third in line for the bus today. Thus in the series individuals are isolated but not alone. They understand themselves as constituted as a collective, as serialized, by the objects and practices through which they aim to accomplish their individual purposes. Often their actions take into account their expectations of the behavior of others in the series whom they nevertheless do not encounter. For example, I ask for a later schedule at work so that I will miss the crowd of bus riders at the rush hour.

Sartre uses the example of radio listening to illustrate some of the characteristics of seriality. The collective of radio listeners is constituted by their individual orientation toward objects, in this case radios and their material possibilities of sound transmission. As listeners they are isolated, but nevertheless they are aware of being part of a series of radio listeners, of others listening simultaneously linked to them indirectly through broadcasting. One's experience of radio listening is partly conditioned by the awareness of being linked to others from whom one is separated and of serving as Other for them. Frequently the radio announcer explicitly refers to the serialized being of the listeners.

Sartre calls the series a practico-inert reality. The series is structured by actions linked to practico-inert objects. Social objects and their effects are the results of human action; they are practical. But as material they also constitute constraints on and resistances to action that make them experienced as inert. The built environment is a practico-inert reality. The products of human decision and action daily used by and dwelt in by people, the streets and buildings, are inert. Their material qualities enable and constrain many aspects of action.

Sartre calls the system of practico-inert objects and the material results of actions in relation to them that generate and are reproduced by serial collectives the milieu of action. The milieu is the already-there set of material things and collectivized habits against the background of which any particular action occurs. Thus for the series, commuters, for example, the milieu is the totality of the structured relations of the physical space of streets and rail lines, together with the predictable traffic patterns that emerge from the confluence of individual actions, together with the rules, habits, and cultural idiosyncracies of driving, riding, and walking.

Serialized action within the milieu results in *counterfinalities:* the confluence of individual intentional actions to produce a result that is counter to some purposes and that no one intended. Within a certain kind of milieu the series commuters will produce a gridlock; each individual driver pursues his or her own individual ends under material conditions that eventually makes a large cluster of them unable to move.

The collective otherness of serialized existence is thus often experienced as constraint, as felt necessities that often are experienced as given or natural. Members of the series experience themselves as powerless to alter this material milieu, and they understand that the others in the series are equally constrained. "A series reveals itself to everyone when they perceive in themselves and Others their common inability to eliminate their material differences" (277). At the same time, the material milieu and objects are conditions of enablement for action. Objectives can be realized only through the mediation of already there things, practices, and structures. A market is paradigmatic of such structured relations of alienation and anonymity that are felt as constraints on everyone. I take my corn to market in hopes of getting a good price, knowing that some people are trading on its price in a futures market and that other farmers bring their corn as well. We know that by bringing our large quantity of corn that we contribute to a fall in its price, and we might each play the futures market ourselves. But we are all equally as individuals unable to alter the collective results of these individual choices, choices that themselves have been made partly because of our expectations of what is happening to market prices.

Membership in serial collectives define an individual's being, in a sense—one "is" a farmer, or a commuter, or a radio listener, and so on, together in series with others similarly positioned. But the definition is anonymous, and the unity of the series is amorphous, without determinate limits, attributes, or intentions. Sartre calls it a unity "in flight," a collective gathering that slips away at the edges, whose qualities and characteristics are impossible to pin down because they are an inert result of the confluence of actions. There is no concept of the series, no specific set of attributes that form the sufficient conditions for membership in it. Who belongs to the series of bus riders? Only those riding today? Those who regularly ride? Occasionally? Who may ride buses and know the social practices of bus riding? While serial membership delimits and constrains an individual's possible actions, it does not define the person's identity in the sense of forming his or her individual purposes, projects, and sense of self in relation to others.

Thus far the examples of seriality have been rather simple and one-dimensional. Sartre's theoretical purpose in developing the concept, however, is to describe the meaning of social class. Most of the time what it means to be a member of the working class or the capitalist class is to live in series with others in that class through a complex interlocking set of objects, structures, and practices in relation to work, exchange, and consumption.

Class being does not define a person's identity, however, because one is a class member in a mode of otherness, otherness to oneself in one's subjectivity. If one says, "I am a worker," in naming serialized class being, this does not designate for one a felt and internalized identity but a social facticity about the material conditions of one's life. (To be sure, one can and many do say, "I am a worker," as a badge of pride and identity. But when this happens the class being is not experienced in seriality; rather, one has formed a *group* with other workers with whom one has established self-conscious bonds of solidarity.) As serialized, class lies as a historical and materialized background to individual lives. A person is born into a class in the sense that a history of class relations precedes one, and the characteristics of the work that one will do or not do are already inscribed in machines, the physical structure of factories and offices, the geographic relations of city and suburb. An individual encounters other members of the class as alienated others, separated from one through the materiality of the things that define and delimit his or her class being— the factory with its machines, the physical movements and demands of the production process, the residential districts, buses, and highways that bring the workers into contact. As class members the individuals are relatively interchangeable, and nothing defines them as workers but the practico-inert constraints on their actions that they find themselves powerless to change. "If you want to eat, then you have to get a job," expresses the anonymous constraints on anyone who lacks independent means of support.

Let me now summarize the major elements in the concept of seriality. A series is a collective whose members are unified passively by the relation their actions have to material objects and practico-inert histories. The practico-inert milieu, within which and by means of whose structures individuals realize their aims, is experienced as constraints on the mode and limits of action. To be said to be part of the same series it is not necessary to identify a set of common attributes that every member has, because their membership is defined not by something they are but rather by the fact that in their diverse existences and actions they are oriented around the same objects or practico-inert structures. Membership in the series does not define one's identity. Each member of the series is isolated, Other to the Others, and as a member of the series Other than themselves. Finally, there is no concept of the series within attributes that clearly demarcate what about individuals makes them belong. The series is a blurry, shifting unity, an amorphous collective.

Seriality designates a level of social life and action, the level of habit and the unreflective reproduction of ongoing historical social structures. Self-conscious groups arise from and on the basis of serialized existence, as a reaction to it and an active reversal of its anonymous and isolating conditions. Next I shall examine how gender is seriality and then explain the relationship between groups of women and the series, women.

IV

Applying the concept of seriality to gender, I suggest, makes theoretical sense out of saying that "women" is a reasonable social category expressing a certain kind of social unity. At the same time, conceptualizing gender as a serial collectivity avoids the problems that emerge from saying that women are a single group.

As I explained earlier, seriality designates a certain *level* of social existence and relations with others, the level of routine, habitual action, which is rule-bound and socially structured but serves as a prereflective background to action. Seriality is lived as medium or as milieu, where action is directed at particular ends that presuppose the series without taking them up self-consciously.

Thus, as a series *woman* is the name of a structural relation to material objects as they have been produced and organized by a prior history. But the series *women* is not as simple and one-dimensional as bus riders or radio listeners. Gender, like class, is a vast, multifaceted, layered, complex, and overlapping set of structures and objects. *Women* are the individuals who are positioned as feminine by the activities surrounding those structures and objects.

The loose unity of the series, I have said, derives from the fact that individuals' actions are oriented toward the same or similarly structured objects. What are the practico-inert realities that construct gender?

Clearly female bodies have something to do with the constitution of the series *women,* but it is not merely the physical facts of these female bodies themselves—attributes of breasts, vaginas, clitoris, and so on—that constructs female gender. Social objects are not merely physical but also inscribed by and the products of past practices. The female body as a practico-inert object toward which action is oriented is a rule-bound body, a body with understood meanings and possibilities. Menstruation, for example, is a regular biological event occurring in most female bodies within a certain age range. It is not this biological process alone, however, that locates individuals in the series of women. Rather, the social rules of menstruation, along with the material objects associated with menstrual practices, constitute the activity within which the women live as serialized. One can say the same about biological events like pregnancy, childbirth, and lactation.

The structure of the social body defining these bodily practices, however, is enforced heterosexuality. The meanings, rules, practices, and assumptions of institutionalized heterosexuality constitute the series, women, as in a relation of potential appropriation by men. Likewise the series *men* appears in the structures of enforced heterosexuality. The assumptions and practices of heterosexuality define the meaning of bodies—vaginas, clitorises, penises—not as mere physical objects but as practico-inert.

Even one so anti-essentialist as Gayatri Spivak locates heterosexuality as a set of material-ideological facts that constitute women crossculturally. The material practices of enforced heterosexuality serialize women as objects of exchange and appropriation by men, with a consequent repression of autonomous active female desire. In Spivak's terms, "In legally defining woman as object of exchange, passage, or possession in terms of reproduction, it is not only the womb that is literally 'appropriated'; it is the clitoris and signifier of the sexed object that is effaced. All historical theoretical investigation into the definition of women as legal object—in or out of marriage; or as politico-economic passageway for property and legitimacy would fall within the investigation of the varieties of the effacement of the clitoris" (1987, 151).

Bodies, however, are only one of the practico-inert objects that position individuals in the gender series. A vast complex of other objects and materialized historical products condition women's lives as gendered. Pronouns locate individual people, along with animals and other objects, in a gender system. Verbal and visual representations more generally create and reproduce gender meanings that condition a person's action and her interpretation of the actions of others. A multitude of artifacts and social spaces in which people act are flooded with gender codes. Clothes are the primary example, but there are also cosmetics, tools, even in some cases furniture and spaces that materially inscribe the norms of gender. I may discover myself "as a woman" by being on the "wrong" dorm floor.

What usually structures the gendered relation of these practico-inert objects is a sexual division of labor. Though their content varies with each social system, a division of at least some tasks and activities by sex appears as a felt necessity. The division between caring for babies and bodies, and not doing so, is the most common sexual division of labor, over which many other labor divisions are layered in social specific ways. Other sexual divisions of tasks and activities are more arbitrary but, in practice, also felt as natural. (Think, e.g., about the genderization of football and field hockey in most American colleges.) The context of the sexual division of labor varies enormously across history, culture, and institutions. Where the division appears, however, it usually produces a multitude of practico-inert objects that constitute the gendered series. The offices, workstations, locker rooms, uniforms, and instruments of a particular activity presuppose a certain sex. The language, gestures, and rituals of exclusion or inclusion of persons in activities reproduce the divisions by attracting people to or repelling people from those activities.

In short, then, bodies and objects constitute the gendered series women through structures like enforced heterosexuality and the sexual division of labor. As I have interpreted Sartre's concept, being positioned by these structures in the series women does not itself designate attributes that attach to the person in the series, nor does it define her identity. Individuals move and act in relation to practico-inert objects that position them as women. The practico-inert structures that generate the milieu of gendered serialized existence both enable and constrain action, but they do not determine or define it. The individuals pursue their own ends; they get a living for themselves in order to have some pleasures of eating and relaxation. The sexual division of labor both enables them to gain that living and constrains their manner of doing so by ruling out or making difficult some possibilities of action. The bathroom enables me to relieve myself, and its gender-marked door constrains the space in which I do it and next to whom.

The practico-inert structures of the gender series are abstract in relation to individuals and to groups of individuals. They are possibilities and orientations for concrete actions that give them content.[2] The gender structures are not defining attributes of individuals but are material social

<hr />

[2] In terms of Sartre's early work, I am here interpreting seriality as a condition of facticity that helps constitute a situation but in no way determines action. Action, the having of projects and goals, the realizing of ends, is what constitutes the identities and experiences of persons. Action is situated against a background of serialized existence, which means that it is constrained but neither general nor determined.

facts that each individual must relate to and deal with. The subjective experiential relation that each person has, and sometimes groups have, to the gender structure, are infinitely variable. In a heterosexist society, for example, everyone must deal with and act in relation to structures of enforced heterosexuality. But there are many attitudes a particular individual can take toward that necessity: she can internalize norms of feminine masochism, she can try to avoid sexual interaction, she can affirmatively take up her sexual role as a tool for her own ends, she can reject heterosexual requirements and love other women, to name just a few.

In seriality, I have said above, the individual experiences herself as anonymous, as Other to herself and Other to the others, contingently interchangeable with them. Sometimes when I become aware of myself "as a woman" I experience this serial anonymous facticity. The serialized experience of being gendered is precisely the obverse of mutual recognition and positive identification of oneself as in a group. "I am a woman" at this level is an anonymous fact that does not define me in my active individuality. It means that I check one box rather than another on my driver's license application, that I use maxipads, wear pumps, and sometimes find myself in situations in which I anticipate deprecation or humiliation from a man. As I utter the phrase, I experience a serial interchangeability between myself and others. In the newspaper I read about a woman who was raped, and I empathize with her because I recognize that in my serialized existence I am rapeable, the potential object of male appropriation. But this awareness depersonalizes me, constructs me as Other to her and Other to myself in a serial interchangeability rather than defining my sense of identity. I do not here mean to deny that many women have a sense of identity as women, an issue I will discuss in the next section. Here I only claim that the level of gender as series is a background to rather than constitutive of personal or group identity.

Sartre's main purpose in developing the concept of seriality is to describe unorganized class existence, the positioning of individuals in relations of production and consumption. Race or nationality can also be fruitfully conceptualized as seriality.[3] At the level of seriality racial position is constructed by a relation of persons to a materialized racist history that has constructed

[3] While Sartre does not thematize race as such, I think he provides grounds for understanding race positioning as seriality. He describes being Jewish as initially belonging to a series. As a social fact or social label, being Jewish in a society that marks or devalues Jews does not name some concept, a set of specific attributes a person must be identified as having in order to be classed as Jewish. In the social relation of being Jewish, there is no separate substance that Jews have in common that makes them Jews. The group label is never real, specific limited, here; it always names an alien otherness coming from elsewhere, from the facticity of "them," the anonymous others who say things about the Jews, who "know" what the Jews are: "In fact, the being-Jewish of every Jew in a hostile society, which persecutes and insults them, and opens itself to them only to

racially separated spaces, a racial division of labor, racist language and discourse, and so on. A person can and often does construct a positive racial identity along with others from out of these serialized positionings. But such racial identification is an active taking up of a serialized situation. Which, if any, of a person's serial memberships become salient or meaningful at any time is a variable matter.

Like gender structures, class or race structures do not primarily name attributes of individuals or aspects of their identity but practico-inert necessities that condition their lives and with which they must deal. Individuals may take up varying attitudes toward these structures, including forming a sense of class or racial identity and forming groups with others they identify with.

Thus the concept of seriality provides a useful way of thinking about the relationship of race, class, gender, and other collective structures, to the individual person. If these are each forms of seriality, then they do not necessarily define the identity of individuals and do not necessarily name attributes they share with others. They are material structures arising from people's historically congealed institutionalized actions and expectations that position and limit individuals in determinate ways that they must deal with. An individual's position in each of the series means that they have differing experiences and perceptions from those differently

---

reject them again, cannot be the only relation between the individual Jew and the anti-semitic, racist society which surrounds him; it is this relation insofar as it is lived by every Jew in his direct or indirect relations with all the other Jews, and in so far as it constitutes him, through them all, an Other and threatens him in and through the Others. To the extent that, for the conscious, lived Jews, being-Jewish (which is his status to *non-Jews*) is interiorized as his responsibility in relation to all other Jews and his being-in-danger, out there, owing to some possible carelessness caused by Others who mean nothing to him, over whom he has no power and every one of whom is himself like Others (in so far as he makes them exist as such in spite of himself,) the *Jew*, far from being *the type* common to each separate instance, represents *on the contrary* the perpetual being *outside-themselves-in-the-other* of members of this practico-inert grouping" (268). Sartre also discusses colonialism as a serial social relation, mediated by an anonymous public opinion that constitutes racist discourse. He says that the most important thing about racist ideas and utterances is that they are not *thoughts*. Racism as operative in everyday life and as a medium of works and beliefs for reproducing practically congealed social relations of oppression and privilege is not a *system* of beliefs, thought through and deliberated. On the contrary, the racist language is unconsidered, uttered as the obvious, and spoken and heard always as the words of an Other. Everyday repeated stereotypes such as that Blacks are lazy or more prone to be aggressive, or that they prefer to stay with their own kind, "have never been anything more than this system itself producing itself as a determination of the language of the colonists in the milieu of alterity. And, for this point of view, they must be seen as material exigencies of language (the *verbal milieu* of all practico-inert apparatuses) addressed to colonialists both in their eyes and in those of others, in the unity of a gathering. . . . The sentence which is uttered, as a reference to the common interest, is not presented as the determination of language by the individual himself, but as his *other* opinion, that is to say, the claims to get it from and give it to others, insofar as their unity is based purely on alternity" (301).

situated. But individuals can relate to these social positionings in different ways; the same person may relate to them in different ways in different social contexts or at different times in their lives.

A person can choose to make none of her serial memberships important for her sense of identity. Or she can find that her family, neighborhood, and church network makes the serial facts of race, for example, important for her identity and development of a group solidarity. Or she can develop a sense of herself and membership in group affiliations that makes different serial structures important to her in different respects or salient in different kinds of circumstances.

V

The purpose of saying that *women* names a series thus resolves the dilemma that has developed in feminist theory: that we must be able to describe women as a social collective yet apparently cannot do so without falling into a false essentialism. An essentialist approach to conceiving women as a social collective treats women as a substance, as a kind of entity in which some specific attributes inhere. One classifies a person as a woman according to whether that person has the essential attributes of womanness, characteristics all women share: something about their bodies, their behavior or dispositions as persons, or their experience of oppression. The problem with this approach to conceptualizing women as a collective is that any effort to locate those essential attributes has one of two consequences. Either it empties the category *woman* of social meaning by reducing it to the attributes of biological female, or in the effort to locate essential social attributes it founders on the variability and diversity of women's actual lives. Thus, the effort to locate particular social attributes that all women share is likely to leave out some persons called women or to distort their lives to fit the categories.

Conceptualizing gender as seriality avoids this problem because it does not claim to identify specific attributes that all women have. There is a unity to the series of women, but it is a passive unity, one that does not arise from the individuals called women but rather positions them through the material organization of social relations as enabled and constrained by the structural relations of enforced heterosexuality and the sexual division of labor. The content of these structures varies enormously from one social context to the next. Saying that a person is a woman may predict something about the general constraints and expectations she must deal with. But it predicts nothing in particular about who she is, what she does, how she takes up her social positioning.

Thinking of gender as seriality also avoids the problem of identity. At least since Nancy Chodorow developed her theory of the psychodynamics of mother-infant relations, gender has been understood as a mode of personal identity (1978). By identity, I mean one of two conceptions, which sometimes appear together. First, identity designates something about who persons are in a deep psychological sense. This is the primary meaning of identity in Chodorow's theory of gender identity. She argues that feminine gender identity gives women more permeable ego boundaries than men, thus making relations with other persons important for their self-conception. Many recent moral and epistemological theories have been influenced by this notion of gender identity and suggest that theories, modes of reasoning, and ways of acting tend to be structured by those feminine and masculine identities.

Second, identity can mean self-ascription as belonging to a group with others who similarly identify themselves, who affirm or are committed together to a set of values, practices, and meanings. This is the sense of identity expressed by theorists of identity politics. Identity here means a self-consciously shared set of meanings interpreting conditions and commitments of being a woman.

Criticisms of gender as identity in either of these senses are similar to criticisms of gender essentialism. This approach either leaves out or distorts the experience of some individuals who call themselves or are called women. Many women regard their womanness as an accidental or contingent aspect of their lives and conceive other social group relations—ethnic or national relations, for example—as more important in defining their identity. Many women resist efforts to theorize shared values and experiences specific to a feminine gender identity—in a caring orientation to relationships, for example—claiming that such theories privilege the identities of particular classes of women in particular social contexts. Even among women who do take their womanhood as an important aspect of their identity, the meaning of that identity will vary a great deal (cf. Ferguson 1991).

Thinking about gender as seriality disconnects gender from identity. On the one hand, as Elizabeth Spelman argues, at the level of individual personal identity there is no way to distinguish the "gender part" of the person from her "race part" or "class part." It may be appropriate, as Butler argues, to think of subjects or personal identities as constituted rather than as some transcendental origin of consciousness or action. It nevertheless would be misleading to think of individual persons as mixtures of gender, race, class, and national attributes. Each person's identity is unique—the history and meaning she makes and develops from her dealings with other people, her communicative interactions through media, and her manner of taking up the particular serialized structures whose prior history position her. No individual woman's identity, then, will escape the markings of gender, but how gender marks her life is her own.

Conceptions of gender as an identity, however, more often seek to name women as a group—that is, a self-conscious social collective with common experiences, perspectives, or values—than to describe individual identity. Conceiving gender as seriality becomes especially important for addressing this mistake. In Sartre's conceptualization, a group is a collection of persons who do mutually identify, who recognize one another as belonging to the group with a common project that defines their collective action. A series, on the other hand, is not a mutually acknowledging identity with any common project or shared experience. Women need have nothing in common in their individual lives to be serialized as women.

A relationship between series and groups does exist, however. As self-conscious collectives of persons with a common objective that they pursue together, groups arise on the basis of and in response to a serialized condition. The group in fusion is a spontaneous group formation out of seriality. When those who have waited for the bus too long begin complaining to each other and discussing possible courses of action, they are a group in fusion. Once groups form and take action, they either institutionalize themselves by establishing meetings, leaders, decision-making structures, methods of acquiring and expending resources, and so on, or they disperse back into seriality. Social life consists of constant ebbs and flows of groupings out of series; some groups remain and grow into institutions that produce new serialities, others disperse soon after they are born.

At its most unreflective and universal level, being a women is a serial fact. But women often do form groups, that is, self-conscious collectives that mutually acknowledge one another as having common purposes or shared experiences. Let me give an example of a movement from women as a serial collective to a group of women. In her novel, *Rivington Street,* Meredith Tax vividly portrays the lives of Russian Jewish immigrant women in the Lower East Side of Manhattan at the turn of the century (1982). In one episode of the novel, some women in the neighborhood discover that a local merchant has manipulated the chicken market in order to make more profits. They talk with one another with anger and then go about their business. One of them, however, thinks a bit more in her anger and decides to act. She calls her three or four women friends together and tells them that they should boycott the butcher. The women organize a boycott by going from apartment to apartment talking to women. Gradually these neighborhood women, formerly serialized only as shoppers, come to understand themselves as a group, with some shared experiences and the power of collective action. When the boycott succeeds, they hold a street celebration and honor their leader, but then they quickly disperse back into the passive unity of the series.

The gendered being of women's groups arises from the serial being of women, as taking up actively and reconstituting the gendered structures that have passively unified them. The chicken boycott arises from the serialized condition of these women defined by the sexual division of labor as purchasers and preparers of food. While the gendered series *women* refers to the structured social relations positioning all biologically sexed females, groups of women are always partial in relation to the series—they bring together only some women for some purposes involving their gender serialized experience. Groups of women are usually more socially, historically, and culturally specified than simply women—they are from the same neighborhood or university, they have the same religion or occupation. Groups of women, that is, will likely, though not necessarily, emerge from the serialities of race and class as well as gender. The chicken boycotters live in the same neighborhood, speak the same Russian-Yiddish, and are passively united in a marginal working-class series in the class structure of Manhattan. All of these serialized facts are relevant to their story and partially explain their grouping.

The chicken boycott example shows a case of women grouping self-consciously as women and on the basis of their gendered condition, but the boycott is not feminist. There can be many groupings of women as women that are not feminist, and indeed some are explicitly antifeminist. Feminism is a particularly reflexive impulse of women grouping, women grouping as women in order to change or eliminate the structures that serialize them as women.

In order to clarify and elaborate the relation of series and group in understanding women as a collective, let me return to my story of Shirley Wright. In her announcement of her candidacy for school committee, when Shirley Wright says that she intends to represent women, she is referring to a gender series defined primarily by the sexual division of labor. *Women* names a position in the division of labor that tends to be specifically related to schools, the primary parent to deal with schools, at the same time that it names a position outside authority structures. In that speech Wright is not claiming a group solidarity among the women of Worcester, either around her candidacy or in any other respect, but is referring to, gesturing toward, a serial structure that conditions her own position and that she aims to politicize. To the degree that Shirley Wright aims to politicize gender structures in her campaign and on the school committee, she invites or invokes the positive grouping of women out of the gender series, but her candidacy speech neither names a group nor generates it. Her claiming to represent "minorities" is also a reference to a serial structure of race and racism that she claims conditions her position and that she aims to politicize.

The women who responded to my handing them a flyer with satisfaction at seeing a woman running are also serialized, as women, as voters. Their identification with Shirley Wright as a woman, however, makes for a proto-group. If some women are motivated to come together to form a "Women for Shirley Wright" committee, they have constituted an active grouping. In relation to the series women, or even to the series "the women of Worcester," the group is necessarily partial—it will probably attract only certain kinds of women, with only some kinds of experiences, and it will focus only on some issues.

In summary, then, I propose that using the concept of seriality and its distinction from the concept of a group can help solve the conundrums about talking about women as a group in which feminist theory has recently found itself. *Woman* is a serial collective defined neither by any common identity nor by a common set of attributes that all the individuals in the series share, but, rather, it names a set of structural constraints and relations to practio-inert objects that condition action and its meaning. I am inclined to say that the series includes all female human beings in the world, and others of the past, but how and where we draw the historical lines is an open question. We can also claim that there are also social and historical subseries. Since the series is not a concept but a more practical-material mode of the social construction of individuals, one need not think of it in terms of genus and species, but as vectors of action and meaning.

Unlike most groups of women, feminist groups take something about women's condition as the explicit aim of their action, and thus feminist groups at least implicitly refer to the series of women that lies beyond the group. Feminist politics and theory refers to or gestures toward this serial reality. Feminist reflection and explicit theorizing draw on the experience of serialized gender, which has multiple layers and aspects. Feminism itself is not a grouping of women; rather, there are many feminisms, many groupings of women whose purpose is to politicize gender and change the power relations between women and men in some respect. When women group, their womanliness will not be the only thing that brings them together; there are other concrete details of their lives that give them affinity, such as their class or race position, their nationality, their neighborhood, their religious affiliation, or their role as teachers of philosophy. For this reason groupings of women will always be partial in relation to the series. Women's groups will be partial in relation to the series also because a group will have particular objectives or purposes that cannot encompass or even refer to the totality of the condition of women as a series. This is why feminist politics must be coalition politics. Feminist organizing and theorizing always refers beyond itself to conditions and experiences that have not been reflected on, and to women whose lives are conditioned by enforced heterosexuality and a sexual division of labor who are not feminist and are not part of feminist groups. We should maintain our humility by recognizing that partiality and by remaining open to inquiring about the facts of the series beyond us.

Graduate School of Public and International Affairs
University of Pittsburgh

References

Allen, Jeffner, and Iris Marion Young, eds. 1989. *Thinking Muse: Feminism and Modern French Philosophy.* Bloomington: Indiana University Press.

Bordo, Susan. 1989. "Feminism, Postmodernism, and Gender-Scepticism." In *Feminism/Postmodernism,* ed. Linda Nicholson. New York: Routledge.

Butler, Judith. 1990. *Gender Trouble.* New York: Routledge.

Caraway, Nancy. 1989. "Identity Politics and Shifting Selves: Black Feminist Coalition Theory." Paper presented at American Political Science Association.

Chodorow, Nancy. 1978. *Reproduction of Mothering: Psychoanalysis and the Sociology of Gender.* Berkeley: University of California Press.

Ferguson, Ann. 1991. "Is There a Lesbian Culture?" In *Lesbian Philosophies and Cultures,* ed. Jeffner Allen, 63–88. Albany: State University of New York Press.

Fuss, Diana. 1989. *Essentially Speaking.* New York: Routledge.

Lange, Lynda. 1991. "Arguing for Democratic Feminism: Postmodern Doubts and Political Amnesia." Paper presented to the meeting of the American Philosophical Association, Midwest Division, Chicago.

Mohanty, Chandra Talpade. 1991. "Under Western Eyes: Feminist Scholarship and Colonial Discourses." In *Third World Women and the Politics of Feminism,* ed. Chandra Talpade Mohanty, Ann Russo, and Lourdes Torres, 51–80. Bloomington: Indiana University Press.

Murphy, Julien. 1989. "The Look in Sartre and Rich." In Allen and Young 1989.

Sartre, Jean-Paul. 1976. *Critique of Dialectical Reason,* trans. Alan Sheridan Smith, ed. Jonathan Ree. London: New Left Books.

Singer, Linda. 1992. *Erotic Welfare.* New York: Routledge.

Spelman, Elizabeth. 1988. *Inessential Woman.* Boston: Beacon.

Spivak, Gayatri Chakravorty. 1987. "French Feminism in an International Frame." In *In Other Worlds: Essays in Cultural Politics.* New York: Methuen.

Tax, Meredith. 1982. *Rivington Street.* New York: Morrow.

Young, Iris Marion. 1990. *Justice and the Politics of Difference.* Princeton, N.J.: Princeton University Press.

Feminist Fiction and the Uses of Memory

Gayle Greene

The gap between the known potential—who you once were and wanted to be—and what your housewife role has turned you into, is enormous and, in most cases, unbridgable. The hordes of happy housewives that every man testifies to when the role of women is being discussed are simply those women who have successfully forgotten who they might have been. The act of forgetting is their only contribution to the world. [Lee Sanders Comer, *Women's Liberation Review,* 1972][1]

He has stolen your wisdom from you, he has closed your memory to what you were, he has made of you that which is not which does not speak which does not possess which does not write. . . . He has invented your history. . . . But remember. Make an effort to remember. Or, failing that, invent. [Monique Wittig, *Les guerilleres,* 1969][2]

With thanks to the Scripps Humanities Institute and especially to Michael S. Roth, Elizabeth Minnich, and Jean Wyatt. The section on *Beloved* was enriched by conversations with Toni Morrison, Sue Houchins, Toni Clark, and Cris Miller. Parts of this article were read at Scripps College and at "The Poetics and Politics of Women's Writing," Dubrovnik, Yugoslavia, May 1988.

[1] Lee Sanders Comer, *Women's Liberation Review* (1972), as quoted in *Rewriting English: Cultural Politics of Gender and Class,* ed. Janet Batsleer, Tony Davies, Rebecca O'Rourke, and Chris Weedon (New York: Methuen, 1985), 139.

[2] Monique Wittig, *Les guerilleres* (Boston: Beacon, 1985), 110–11, 89.

[*Signs: Journal of Women in Culture and Society* 1991, vol. 16, no. 2]

All writers are concerned with memory, since all writing is a remembrance of things past; all writers draw on the past, mine it as a quarry. Memory is especially important to anyone who cares about change, for forgetting dooms us to repetition; and it is of particular importance to feminists. This essay concerns feminist fiction by Doris Lessing, Margaret Drabble, Margaret Atwood, Margaret Laurence, and Toni Morrison that addresses memory as a means to liberation and explores this at the level of narrative form.[3]

Feminist fiction is not the same as "women's fiction" or fiction by women. Not all women writers are women's writers and not all women's writers are feminist writers, since to write about "women's issues" is not necessarily to address them from a feminist perspective. Nor are feminist writers necessarily so all the time— Lessing is feminist in *The Golden Notebook* (1962) and is not in *The Diaries of Jane Somers* (1984); nor do they necessarily identify themselves as feminists. Yet whatever a writer's relation to the women's movement, a novel may be termed "feminist" for its analysis of gender as socially constructed and capable of being reconstructed and for its enlistment of narrative in the process of change.

In a sense, all narrative is concerned with change: there is something in the impulse to narrative that is related to the impulse to liberation. Narrative re-collects, re-members, repeats—as Peter Brooks and others have said—in order for there to be an escape from repetition, in order for there to be change or progress; like psychotherapy, it aspires to "a narrative redescription of reality," to a "new

---

[3] All of Doris Lessing's major works are concerned with change: Martha Quest, overwhelmed by her sense of "the nightmare *repetition*," wearied that "*It had all been done and said already*" (*A Proper Marriage*, 77, 95, 34 [hereafter cited as *PM*]), determines "to move onto something new" (*Martha Quest*, 8–9 [hereafter cited as *MQ*]). The term "something new" recurs in *The Golden Notebook* (New York: Bantam, 1973), 61, 353, 472–73, 479 (hereafter cited as *GN*), in *Martha Quest*, 53, 141, 216, *Landlocked*, 117, and *The Four-Gated City*, 69, 176 (hereafter cited as *FGC*). (References to *Children of Violence* are to the New American Library editions; *A Ripple from the Storm* is referred to as *RS*.) Margaret Drabble describes women's writing as providing "patterns . . . for a possible future," "actively engaged in creating a new pattern, a new blueprint" ("A Woman Writer," in *On Gender and Writing*, ed. Michelene Wandor [London: Pandora, 1983], 156–59, esp. 159). Margaret Laurence also describes her work as "an attempt at something new" ("Gadgetry or Growing: Form and Voice in the Novel," *Journal of Canadian Fiction* ["The Work of Margaret Laurence," ed. John R. Sorfleet] 27 [1980]: 54–62). Toni Morrison describes her desire to "make you feel something profoundly . . . to change and to modify" (Mari Evans, "Rootedness: The Ancestor as Foundation," in *Black Women Writers [1950–1980]: A Critical Evaluation*, ed. Mari Evans [Garden City, N.Y.: Doubleday, 1984], 339–45, esp. 341).

story."[4] Not surprisingly, this function is foregrounded in fiction that is most explicitly concerned with change. The feminist fiction that flourished in the late sixties and early seventies came out of a liberation movement, the so-called second wave of feminism in this century, and focused on women's efforts to liberate themselves from the structures of the past. As a literary movement it had certain similarities with Modernism: originating in a sense of the unprecedentedness of contemporary experience, it developed new fictional forms to express the "newness" of now; but it differed from Modernism in being part of a collective effort at social change and in viewing the past not (as some Modernists did) as a repository of lost value but as the source of—in Lessing's term—"something new." Though there are nostalgic tendencies in some feminist efforts to reclaim the past—in the search for women's cultures and communities, for lost matriarchies and goddesses—the novelists I am interested in critique nostalgia and disallow complacency about the past.

Feminist fiction is inherently unsettling, for by suggesting that a category as seemingly "natural" as gender is conventional and subject to change, it challenges established assumptions. Yet—as Rosalind Coward suggests—in order to distinguish between texts that have "a surface commitment to feminism" and those that have a deeper commitment, we must ask how "they achieve their versions of reality," "*how* representations work . . . how the text is constructed by writing practices and what ideologies are involved in it."[5] The most revolutionary feminist fiction is so by virtue of textual practice as well as content, and is unsettling not only formally and structurally but in unsettling our relation to the past, in revealing the past as changing in response to the present and as capable of transforming present and future as well.

"What is it for, the past, one's own or the world's? To what end question it so closely?" asks the protagonist of Margaret Drabble's *The Realms of Gold*.[6] In exploring memory in seventies feminist fiction, I will inquire why memory assumes particular importance

[4] Peter Brooks, *Reading for the Plot: Design and Intention in Narrative* (New York: Vintage, 1985), 98, 235, 285. Roy Schafer, "Narration in the Psychoanalytic Dialogue," in *On Narrative*, ed. W. J. T. Mitchell (Chicago: University of Chicago Press, 1981), 25–49, refers to the goal of "narrative redescription" (44, 46). Michael S. Roth, *Psychoanalysis as History: Negation and Freedom in Freud* (Ithaca, N.Y.: Cornell University Press, 1987), 124, also describes the transference process in these terms.

[5] Rosalind Coward, "Are Women's Novels Feminist Novels?" in *The New Feminist Criticism: Essays on Women, Literature, Theory*, ed. Elaine Showalter (New York: Pantheon, 1985), 225–39, esp. 228–29.

[6] Margaret Drabble, *The Realms of Gold* (New York: Knopf, 1975), 121.

at particular cultural moments and suggest distinctions between memory and nostalgia. I am especially interested in works that thematize memory and reflect this concern narratively, metafictions that relate memory and liberation to questions of narrative (Doris Lessing's *The Summer before the Dark* [1973], Margaret Drabble's *The Middle Ground* [1980], Toni Morrison's *Beloved* [1987]) and *Kunstlerromane* that envision writing as the means of revising the past (Doris Lessing's *The Golden Notebook*, Margaret Laurence's *The Diviners* [1974], Margaret Atwood's *Lady Oracle* [1976]). Though metafiction, fiction that includes within itself commentary on its own narrative identity (as Linda Hutcheon defines it), is more often associated with postmodern (i.e., male) writers than with feminist writers, it is a powerful tool of feminist critique, for to draw attention to the structures of fiction is also to draw attention to the conventionality of the codes that govern human behavior—to reveal (as Patricia Waugh says) "how the meanings and values of [the] world have been constructed and how, therefore, they can be challenged or changed."[7] Metafiction is "a process-oriented mode" (as Hutcheon suggests); it is also a transgressive mode (as Wallace Martin suggests), for when a writer talks about narrative within narrative, she unsettles traditional distinctions between reality and fiction and exposes the arbitrary nature of boundaries.[8] Like the "women's writing" described by Mary Jacobus, feminist metafiction is "a process" played out across literary and ideological boundaries, a "transgression of literary boundaries" "that exposes those very boundaries for what they are—the product of phallocentric discourse,"[9] though what Jacobus describes theoretically, I demonstrate as an actual practice in feminist metafiction.

* * *

Memory is our means of connecting past and present and constructing a self and versions of experience we can live with. To doubt it is to doubt ourselves, to lose it is to lose ourselves; yet doubt it we must, for it is treacherous. All Margaret Laurence's protagonists contend with it: in *The Diviners*, "memory-bank movies" play themselves through Morag's head; Stacey of *The*

[7] Linda Hutcheon, *Narcissistic Narrative: The Metafictional Paradox* (New York: Methuen, 1984), 1, 6–7; Patricia Waugh, *Metafiction: The Theory and Practice of Self-conscious Fiction* (London: Methuen, 1984), 2, 34.

[8] Hutcheon, 6–7; Wallace Martin, *Recent Theories of Narrative* (Ithaca, N.Y.: Cornell University Press, 1986), 181.

[9] Mary Jacobus, "The Difference of View," in *Women Writing and Writing about Women*, ed. Mary Jacobus (New York: Barnes & Noble, 1979), 12, 17.

Fire-Dwellers (1969) is "conned into memory"; ninety-two-year-old Hagar of *The Stone Angel* (1964) is "rampant with memory."[10] Sethe of Morrison's *Beloved* deplores her "devious" brain for "remembering the . . . trees rather than the boys [hanging from them]. . . . She could not forgive her memory for that."[11] A character in Fay Weldon's *Praxis* (1978) reflects that "memory is a chancy thing, experience experienced, filtered coarse or fine according to the mood of the day, the pattern of the times, the company we happened to be keeping."[12] Memory revises, reorders, refigures, resignifies; it includes or omits, embellishes or represses, decorates or drops, according to imperatives of its own. Far from being a trustworthy transcriber of "reality," it is a shaper and shape shifter that takes liberties with the past as artful and lying as any taken by the creative writer.

In fact, memory is a creative writer, Mother of the Muses (Mnemosyne in Greek mythology), maker of stories—the stories by which we construct meaning through temporality and assure ourselves that time past is not time lost. By means of enabling fictions we make sense of our lives, and even "disabling" fictions, dysfunctional versions of the past that lock us into repetition of the past, make a kind of sense. When a disjunction occurs between our present reality and the stories we have created to explain how we got here—when our fictions lose explanatory force—we call this "crisis." Kate Armstrong of Margaret Drabble's *The Middle Ground* expresses midlife crisis in these terms: "I no longer trust my own memories. . . . I thought they made sense, that there was a clear pattern, but maybe I've got it all wrong, maybe there's some other darker pattern, entirely different"; "the past no longer seems to make sense, for if it did, how would it have left her here, in this peculiar draughty open space?"[13] To lose the connection between past and present, as Kate has, is also to lose the narrative thread that supports her identity and reality: thus Drabble suggests parallels between Kate's crisis and problems of narrative construction. Kate will need to remember her past, or re-remember it ("rememory" it, in Morrison's coinage from *Beloved*)[14] in order to come up with a new story.

[10] Margaret Laurence, *The Diviners* (New York: Bantam, 1975), *The Fire-Dwellers* (Toronto: McClelland & Stewart-Bantam, 1969), 66, and *The Stone Angel* (New York: Bantam, 1981), 3.

[11] Toni Morrison, *Beloved* (New York: Random House, 1987), 6 (hereafter cited as B). For a discussion of memory and revision, see David Lowenthal, *The Past Is a Foreign Country* (Cambridge: Cambridge University Press, 1985), 206–10.

[12] Fay Weldon, *Praxis* (New York: Simon & Schuster, 1978), 78.

[13] Margaret Drabble, *The Middle Ground* (New York: Bantam, 1980), 121, 10 (hereafter cited as *MG*).

[14] Morrison, 36, 95, 99, 160, 189, 201.

The concern with memory surfaced in the early years of this century, with Modernist writers, and it emerged in response to crisis: with cultures, as with individuals, memory becomes problematic when continuity with the past is threatened. Early twentieth-century writers experienced their age as a time when the systems of the past—social, ethical, religious—lost explanatory force, and they expressed their sense of difference from the past in an intense interest in the past, an effort to understand the world that had been lost—to remember. Proust was obsessed with "time regained"; Woolf and Joyce were obsessed with time and memory, and so too were Eliot, Ford, and Faulkner, who tended to romanticize the past as a better place.[15] In the decades subsequent to Modernism, British fiction was steeped in nostalgia: always the good days were the bygone days, first in a time before World War I, and then in a time before World War II.[16] American literature also has its own intense, obsessive longings for a lost childhood innocence—for a lost southern past, for a frontier where men were men and women were women.[17] Alicia Ostriker differentiates the poetry written by women in this century from that written by men: "It contains no trace of nostalgia, no faith that the past is a repository of truth, goodness, or desirable social organization. While the myth of a golden age has exerted incalculable pressure in the shaping of Western literature and its attitude toward history, the revisionist woman poet does not care if the hills of Arcady are dead. Or rather, she does not believe they are dead."[18]

Nostalgia is a powerful impulse that is by no means gender specific. Everyone has longings to return home, which is what the word means: *nostos*, the return home. Even when the past is as horrendous as that described in Morrison's *Beloved*, the characters think back to "Sweet Home," the plantation they escaped from—"It

---

[15] See Shari Benstock, *Women of the Left Bank: Paris, 1900–1940* (Austin: University of Texas Press, 1986), 24–36, for a discussion of nostalgic tendencies in Modernism; and Sandra M. Gilbert and Susan Gubar, *No Man's Land: The Place of the Woman Writer in the Twentieth Century,* vol. 1, *The War of the Words* (New Haven, Conn.: Yale University Press, 1988), 155–56, for nostalgia in Eliot.

[16] See chaps. 2 and 3 in Randall Stevenson, *The British Novel since the Thirties: An Introduction* (Athens: University of Georgia Press, 1986); and chap. 6 in Bernard Bergonzi, *The Situation of the Novel* (Pittsburgh: University of Pittsburgh Press, 1970), for discussions of nostalgia in postwar British fiction.

[17] R. W. B. Lewis, *The American Adam: Innocence, Tragedy, and Tradition in the Nineteenth Century* (Chicago: University of Chicago Press, 1955); and Leslie A. Fiedler, *An End to Innocence: Essays on Culture and Politics* (Boston: Beacon, 1948) discuss this aspect of American fiction.

[18] Alicia Ostriker, "The Thieves of Language: Women Poets and Revisionist Mythmaking," in Showalter, ed. (n. 5 above), 314–38, esp. 330.

wasn't sweet and it sure wasn't home." "But it's where we were . . . all together. Comes back whether we want it to or not."[19] But nostalgia has different meanings for men and women. Though from one perspective, women might seem to have more incentives than men to be nostalgic—deprived of outlets in the present, they live more in the past, which is why they are the keepers of diaries, journals, family records, and photograph albums—from another perspective, women have little to be nostalgic about, for the good old days when the grass was greener and young people knew their place was also the time when women knew their place, and it is not a place to which most women want to return.[20] As Ostriker suggests, "Prufrock may yearn to be Hamlet, but what woman would want to be Ophelia?"[21] Nostalgia is not only a longing to return home; it is also a longing to return to the state of things in which woman keeps the home and in which she awaits, like Penelope, the return of her wandering Odysseus. But if going back is advantageous to those who have enjoyed power, it is dangerous to those who have not. Thus Janice Doane and Devon Hodges describe nostalgia as "a frightening antifeminist impulse": "the nostalgia that permeates American politics and mass culture" is a desire for an imagined past that "authenticates woman's traditional place" when "men were men, women were women, and reality was real."[22]

Besides, whatever nostalgic fantasies women have are less likely to be indulged than men's: quite simply, women are less likely to get to go home. At the end of John Fowles's *Daniel Martin*, Daniel steps back into a relationship left behind half a lifetime ago; at the end of William Kennedy's *Ironweed* the protagonist returns to "a nice little room" his wife has kept for twenty years; and at the end of Pat Conroy's *The Prince of Tides* the hero returns to a wife who has been patiently awaiting him. But such homecomings are rarely options for the woman, whose role is, rather, to wait and to keep the room waiting. Women's fiction often expresses a longing for a reconciliation with the mother (e.g., Woolf's *To The Light-*

[19] Morrison, 14–15.

[20] Rosalind Coward describes the way women function as "guardians of the unwritten history of the family," "attempting to record and capture transcient moments, to fix them and ensure their permanence," to "re-create an undamaged world . . . where we have not encountered the pain of separation and loss" ("The Mirror with a Memory," in her *Female Desires: How They Are Sought, Bought and Packaged* [New York: Grove, 1985], 49–54, esp. 49–50, 53–54).

[21] Ostriker, 330.

[22] Janice Doane and Devon Hodges, *Nostalgia and Sexual Difference: The Resistance to Contemporary Feminism* (New York: Methuen, 1987), xiii.

house, Lessing's *The Diaries of Jane Somers*), but this is not quite the same as the longing to return home.[23]

A character in Drabble's *The Middle Ground* recalls a sunny summer Sunday spent among friends ten years earlier in a time before their lives flew apart: "If we could have known. . . . Well, would we have savoured it more? And were we really happy? Were we not, rather, half bored, and surreptitiously tormented by infidelities, unfulfilled ambitions, fatigue, financial anxieties. . . . Our minds more than half elsewhere. . . . No doubt all of us were suffering from sleepless nights and coughing children with earaches. If questioned, would we not then have looked back to the carefree days of youth, to . . . Cambridge . . . to love . . . ? Yet, nevertheless, one can look back to such afternoons as though they possessed a true tranquility. In ten years will I look back upon myself sitting at this table and think, Ah, I was happy then?"[24] The answer is Yes, you will look back and think "I was happy then," because there is something about memory that edits unpleasant details—the anxiety, irritation, fatigue, boredom, impatience, and pain of daily existence—in favor of the big picture, which is always done over with a flattering brush. Nostalgia is an uncritical acceptance of this rewriting, a view of the past as a foreign country where "they do things differently," in the celebrated opening line of L. P. Hartley's *The Go-between*—one of those nostalgic postwar British novels that laments a lost prewar innocence.[25]

It is not always easy to differentiate nostalgia from more productive forms of memory. But the roots of the words suggest different impulses: whereas "nostalgia" is the desire to return home, "to remember" is "to bring to mind" or "think of again," "to be mindful of," "to recollect." Both "re-membering" and "re-collecting" suggest a connecting, assembling, a bringing together of things in relation to one another—which is why Woolf calls memory a "seamstress" who "run[s] her needle in and out, up and down,

[23] Few female protagonists return home, though the protagonist of Rita Mae Brown's *Ruby Fruit Jungle* is a notable exception. As Hélène Cixous says, "A boy's journey is the return to the native land, the *Heimweh* Freud speaks of, the nostalgia that makes man a being who tends to come back to the point of departure. . . . A girl's journey is farther—to the unknown" (Hélène Cixous and Catherine Clement, *The Newly Born Woman* [Minneapolis: University of Minnesota Press, 1986], 93). For a fascinating discussion of the loss of Eden in women's fiction as a loss of the mother, see Madelon Sprengnether, "(M)other Eve: Some Revisions of the Fall in Fiction," in *Feminism and Psychoanalysis*, ed. Richard Feldstein and Judith Roof (Ithaca, N.Y.: Cornell University Press, 1989), 298–322.

[24] Drabble, *The Middle Ground* (n. 13 above), 155.

[25] L. P. Hartley, *The Go-between* (London: Hamish Hamilton, 1953), 1.

hither and thither."[26] In fact, nostalgia and remembering are in some sense antithetical, since nostalgia is a forgetting, merely regressive, whereas memory may look back in order to move forward and transform disabling fictions to enabling fictions, altering our relation to the present and future.

* * *

Women especially need to remember because forgetting is a major obstacle to change. One of the most painful facts about the struggle for emancipation is that we have to keep starting it over again. This may be true of any effort at social change: each generation seems to need to make its own errors, and a kind of collective amnesia wipes out all memory of the struggles of the past. But anyone who teaches feminism today is struck by how quickly the struggle for women's rights has been forgotten: women's rights to vote, to hold property, to engage in certain types of work are taken for granted as God-given rights, with no sense of how recently they have been won, how much they cost. Nancy Cott refers to the "disremembering process" by which "feminism is aborted and repressed";[27] Adrienne Rich refers to "the erasure of women's political and historic past" wherein the "history of women's struggle for self-determination has been muffled in silence over and over";[28] Elaine Showalter notes that "each generation of women writers has found itself . . . without a history, forced to rediscover the past anew, forging again and again the consciousness of their sex."[29] The protagonist of Alix Kates Shulman's *Burning Questions* (1978) finds it "chilling . . . that in only a few brief decades so much had been forgotten . . . it seemed that almost every idea we were now exploring . . . had been delved by our predecessors. Delved, some even embraced by millions—and then somehow murdered and forgotten. How had it happened? We would have to find out . . . so it couldn't happen again." She consoles herself that "even if the backlash were to eclipse us as it

[26] Virginia Woolf, *Orlando* (New York: Harcourt Brace & Co., 1956), 78.

[27] Nancy F. Cott, *The Grounding of Modern Feminism* (New Haven, Conn.: Yale University Press, 1987), 274.

[28] Adrienne Rich, "Foreword: On History, Illiteracy, Passivity, Violence, and Women's Culture," in her *On Lies, Secrets, and Silence: Selected Prose, 1966–1978* (New York: Norton, 1979), 9–18, esp. 11.

[29] Elaine Showalter, *A Literature of Their Own: British Women Novelists from Brontë to Lessing* (London: Virago, 1978), 11–12. See also Dale Spender, *For the Record: The Making and Meaning of Feminist Knowledge* (London: Women's Press, 1985), 2: "Unless we keep reminding each other of our heritage we endanger it, we risk losing it as we contribute to our own amnesia."

had eclipsed all the earlier waves of feminism . . . when the next wave came (and they would keep coming, as they always had . . .) they'd find us there in the microfilm records . . . on library shelves, in feminist archives, a testament to our spirit."[30]

We are now living through the second backlash against feminism in this century. The similarities between the first reaction—which occurred immediately after women won the vote in the second decade—and the backlash today are indeed chilling. Once again women are sure that women's rights are all won; once again women yield to more urgent concerns—in the thirties, it was the Depression and preparations for a second world war; today it is the threat of the destruction of the planet that makes "the aims of Women's Liberation . . . look very small and quaint," as Lessing, our foremost and most infuriating feminist writer, puts it (GN, ix). In fact the word "postfeminist," which sprang brilliantly to the pages of the New York Times in October 1982 and spoke so directly to a new generation of young women who imagined themselves beyond all that,[31] was actually first used in 1919, when (as Nancy Cott tells us) "a group of female literary radicals in Greenwich Village" founded a new journal declaring an interest "in people . . . not in men and women"; they called their stance "post-feminist."[32] Moving forward into the past, women forget; and worse than forgetting, they make "feminism" a dirty word, a "term of opprobrium," as Dorothy Dunbar Bromley said in 1927.[33] By the 1950s there were fewer women in higher education—fewer Ph.D.s, fewer women on faculties—than there had been in any decade since 1900;[34] and as Shulamith Firestone says, "all authentic knowledge of the old feminist movement by this time had been buried."[35] After the war, women were urged back into the home with the massive propaganda of the "feminine mystique," the results of which we know: the new cult of womanhood produced the malaise Betty Friedan named "the problem that has no name" and became the impetus for the resurgence of feminism.[36]

[30] Alix Kates Shulman, *Burning Questions* (New York: Bantam, 1979), 270–71.

[31] Susan Bolotin, "Voices from the Post-Feminist Generation," *New York Times Magazine* (October 17, 1982).

[32] See *Judy*, vol. 1, no. 1 (June 1919), and *Judy*, vol. 2, no. 3 (1919) at the Arthur and Elizabeth Schlesinger Library on the History of Women in America, Radcliffe College, Cambridge, Mass. (quoted in Cott, 282, 365, n. 23).

[33] Quoted in William H. Chafe, *The American Woman: Her Changing Social, Economic, and Political Roles, 1920–1970* (London: Oxford University Press, 1972), 92.

[34] Cott, 218.

[35] Shulamith Firestone, *The Dialectic of Sex: The Case for Feminist Revolution* (New York: Bantam, 1972), 27.

[36] Betty Friedan, *The Feminine Mystique* (1962; reprint, New York: Dell, 1983).

So each time we take up the struggle for women's rights we have to begin anew. Maybe if the work is there "in the microfilm records," as Shulman says, some progress has been made, for in 1929 when Woolf wrote *A Room of One's Own,* the books she sought on the library shelves had not yet been written.[37] Since then many have been written but many also have been lost, fallen out of print and into obscurity, and a major project of feminist scholarship continues to be the recovery of women's lost contributions. Feminism is a re-membering, a re-assembling of our lost past and lost parts of ourselves. We search for our mother's gardens, in Alice Walker's term; we search for our mothers—and this search (which is at times not easily distinguishable from nostalgia) figures prominently in contemporary women's fiction, as it does in feminist psychoanalytic theory, which pays new attention to the preoedipal stage of human development, excavating the mother buried by Freud's account.

In 1962, in *The Feminine Mystique,* Betty Friedan described the housewife's malaise as a loss of memory, of the ability to experience "the dimensions of both past and future." She compared housewives to men who had "portions of their brain shot away": "What they lost was . . . the ability . . . to order the chaos of concrete detail with an idea, to move according to a purpose . . . tied to the immediate situation in which they found themselves . . . they had lost their human freedom." Deprived of a "purpose stretching into the future [housewives] cannot grow [and so] lose the sense of who they are."[38] So essential is "forgetting" to what they do that Lee Sanders Comer termed it the housewife's "only contribution to the world."[39]

This explains why consciousness raising was—and is—crucial in feminist efforts. Consciousness raising is a re-membering, a bringing to mind of repressed parts of the self and experience. A recent project of "memory work" undertaken by the West German collective described in Frigga Haug's *Female Sexualization* makes clear the function of memory in change: "stepping back into the past, we embark upon a form of archaeology" that enables us to understand the processes that make us what we are and so to change what we are. By "memory work," the excavation of "ideologized" consciousness, we retrieve "elements of a new image of [self], on the basis of which [we] may possibly be able to construct

[37] Virginia Woolf, *A Room of One's Own* (New York: Harcourt, Brace & Co., 1957), 46–59, 86–98.

[38] Friedan, 312–13.

[39] Comer (n. 1 above).

alternatives for the future."[40] As Jane Flax suggests, " 'new' memory" is "a powerful impulse toward political action."[41]

* * *

Early feminist fiction offers critiques like Friedan's of the amnesia imposed by women's roles, associating forgetting with repetition, and repression with regression. Esther of Sylvia Plath's *The Bell Jar* (1963) can only explain a woman's consenting to motherhood in terms of amnesia, and recalls her fiance's saying "in a sinister knowing way that after I had children I . . . wouldn't want to write poems any more. So I began to think maybe it was true that when you were married and had children it was like being brainwashed and afterward you went about as numb as a slave in some private, totalitarian state."[42] Though Plath has her end "happily" adjusted to domesticity, this resolution is achieved by such willful blindness that one cannot help connecting Esther's repression with Plath's suicide a month after the novel was published. The protagonist of Fay Weldon's *Praxis* reads her mother's denial of an infidelity as repression: "At a time when women's instincts were so much at variance with the rules of society, such localized amnesias were only to be expected. But was this episode out of character; or was it that her whole life otherwise was out of character? Was my mother, from the age of thirty to the age of seventy, living out a part that did not suit her at all? I believe the latter."[43] Norma Jean of Sheila Ballantyne's *Norma Jean the Termite Queen* (1975) laments that her adjustment to the housewife role has been "a homicide against the first and original self," though she also realizes that if she accomplishes this "transformation" into "someone else" she will have "no means to remember . . . and so perceive no loss": "when this happens to wives, it is not regarded as tragic, but natural."[44] Norma Jean understands the difference between

---

[40] *Female Sexualization: A Collective Work of Memory,* ed. Frigga Haug and others, trans. Erica Carter (London: Verso, 1987), 48, 59, 49.

[41] Jane Flax, "Re-Membering the Selves: Is the Repressed Gendered?" *Michigan Quarterly Review* ("Women and Memory") 26, no. 1 (Winter 1987): 92–110, esp. 106. Other relevant essays in this collection are Mary Jacobus, "Freud's Mnemonic: Women, Screen Memories, and Feminist Nostalgia," 117–39; and Catharine R. Stimpson, "The Future of Memory: A Summary," 259–65.

[42] Sylvia Plath, *The Bell Jar* (New York: Bantam, 1981), 53, 69.

[43] Weldon (n. 12 above), 33.

[44] Sheila Ballantyne, *Norma Jean the Termite Queen* (New York: Doubleday, 1975), 194.

regression and more productive forms of return to the past; she knows that returning to her husband's idea of her would be "to die the death that has no resurrection" whereas her own therapeutic methods of "reaching back in time" enable her to "touch an old, original self," to "get back a part of some original self which lay buried, deep as any pharaoh, all those years," to make "gestures . . . associated with freedom."[45]

Lessing's *A Proper Marriage* (1952) powerfully describes the loss of self women undergo in pregnancy. Martha emerges at the end of each day "dazed. . . . Inside her stomach the human race had fought and raised its way through another million years of its history" (*PM*, 113). As she is giving birth, she is stunned into forgetfulness, incapable of connecting pain with painlessness: "there were two states of being, utterly disconnected . . . and Martha . . . could *not* remember" (*PM*, 144). When she emerges from her child's first few years to wonder what to do with the rest of her life, everyone—friends, family, husband, doctors—urges her to have a second child; and though her own amnesia conspires with their advice, "yet she did not altogether forget. And she did *not* choose to begin again" (*PM*, 252). Remembering is associated with choice.

Lessing is centrally concerned with memory because she is concerned with change—what enables it, what prevents it, what it accomplishes. Her critique of nostalgia in the early fifties, at a time when postwar British fiction was saturated in nostalgia, is remarkable indeed. Throughout *The Children of Violence*, Martha battles powerful nostalgic longings: "Nostalgia for what?" she wonders early in the series (*MQ*, 22); "Nostalgia for something doomed," comes the answer (*PM*, 81). Lessing's novels document the difficulty of learning—"a lot of time, a lot of pain, went into learning very little"[46]—and the disastrous consequences of *not* learning. Martha's mother Mrs. Quest represents the effects of a lifetime of repression and demonstrates that those who deny the past are doomed to repetition and incomprehension. When she consults her photograph album for the meaning of her life, "her mind went dark, it kept going dark," against "something concealed, something she could not meet, did not know how to meet" (*FGC*, 239), areas of "congealed pain" (*FGC*, 285) to which she has no access. Martha, having "blocked off the pain" of the past, had "blocked off half of her life with it. Her memory had gone" (*FGC*, 207); she is in danger of repeating this process; but in the final novels of the series, she

---

[45] Ibid., 128, 24, 128.

[46] Doris Lessing, *The Summer before the Dark* (New York: Bantam, 1973), 4 (hereafter cited as *SBD*).

sets about "resurrect[ing] her lost past" (*FGC*, 215), "digging it out" (*RS*, 85), excavating the past so that she can move into "something new" (*FGC*, 69, 176). At the end of this excavation, she has transformed the past into "a landscape she could move into and out again," a place "she could visit, test—as one might dip a hand into water to see if it is too hot to bear"; "she could live again through this time, that time . . . so that, if she wanted, the past enveloped, seeped through, the present" (*FGC*, 285). She has revitalized her past and made a connection with it that leads "her so much further than she had expected," opening "doors she had not known existed" (*FGC*, 285–86).

Martha's "work"—undertaken, appropriately, in "the basement"— has implications for her entire culture, accomplishing no less than "a future for our race" (*FGC*, 607). What is at stake in her quest for "something new" is more than individual freedom or fulfillment; it is the creation of a better world, an alternative to a death-bound society, a "four-gated city." Other feminist protagonists also find their personal survival linked to the collective life, though not usually so dramatically: Morag in Laurence's *The Diviners* finds her past intertwined with the history of Canada's earliest settlers; Frances in Drabble's *The Realms of Gold* (1975) discovers a kinship network that is surprisingly extensive; and individuals' lives in Drabble's *The Ice Age* (1979), *The Middle Ground,* and *The Radiant Way* (1987) are bound up with the collective life of England. Paule Marshall's *The Chosen Place, the Timeless People* (1969) and Maxine Hong Kingston's *The Woman Warrior* (1975) are similarly epic works that tell the stories of their cultures.

The protagonist's search for the past often takes the form of a journey home, a return to the family to confront mothers, fathers, grandparents, siblings, and cousins. In Atwood's *Surfacing* (1972) and *Lady Oracle,* in Drabble's *Jerusalem the Golden* (1967), *The Realms of Gold,* and *The Radiant Way,* and in Laurence's *The Diviners,* the protagonist looks in photograph albums—which are always kept by the mother—for clues about her past. Yet, as Carol P. Christ points out, women's quests tend to be vertical rather than horizontal: women dive, surface, fly.[47] Besides this, they "divine," "excavate," dig in, dig out, and engage in various sorts of archeological projects. Toni Morrison describes *Beloved* as "a project of 'literary archeology.' "[48] The speaker in Adrienne Rich's "Diving

[47] Carol P. Christ, *Diving Deep and Surfacing: Women Writers on Spiritual Quest* (Boston: Beacon, 1980). See also Jean E. Kennard, "Convention Coverage or How to Read Your Own Life," *New Literary History* 13, no. 1 (1981): 68–88, esp. 82.

[48] Quoted in Colin Walter's review of *Beloved,* "A Ghostly, Terrifying Tale of Lives in Slavery," *Insight* (October 12, 1987).

into the Wreck" embarks on an underwater archeological expedition, seeking in the "book of myths in which / our names do not appear" "the thing itself and not the myth."[49] Woolf's *Orlando* "dislodges" memories that are "cumbered with other matter like the lump of glass which, after a year at the bottom of the sea, is grown about with bones and dragon-flies coins and the tresses of drowned women."[50] Frances in Drabble's *The Realms of Gold* is an archaeologist by profession; Lesje in Atwood's *Life before Man* (1979) is a paleontologist; the protagonist of Rebecca Hill's *Among Birches* (1986) describes herself as "such a good archaeologist . . . poking among the ruins, trying to restore from fragments all that had been lost. Men didn't do this; they dropped socks. Territory mattered, not history."[51] Laurence's diviner-artist "undertakes the undertaker" in excavating the story of the undertaker as well as other buried lives.[52] The protagonist of *The Middle Ground* is inspired to remember by the smell of sewage wafting up from subterranean passages, a smell she compares wryly to that of Proust's *madeleine*.[53]

Most of Atwood's protagonists undertake projects of excavation. In *Surfacing*, the protagonist's search for her missing father takes her on a kind of underwater archaeological expedition; diving beneath the "surface" of the lake in search of his body, she makes discoveries that allow repressed memories to "surface" and she "surfaces" too, in possession of more than she knew she had lost—her past and herself. In *Bodily Harm* (1982), the central image is "digging" it out (or up): Rennie describes her background as "less like a background . . . than a subground, something that can't be seen but is nevertheless there, full of gritty old rocks and buried stumps . . . nothing you'd want to go into. Those who'd lately been clamoring for roots had never seen a root up close, Rennie used to say."[54] Though Rennie tries to stay on the "surfaces," her mastectomy forces her to "go into" harsh truths both personal and political, to confront "malevolence" that is more than "bodily" and become a "subversive" in the end.[55]

* * *

[49] Adrienne Rich, *Diving into the Wreck: Poems, Selected and New, 1950–1974* (New York: Norton, 1975), 197–98.

[50] Woolf, *Orlando* (n. 26 above), 101.

[51] Rebecca Hill, *Among Birches* (New York: Viking Penguin, 1987), 130.

[52] Laurence, *The Diviners* (n. 10 above), 399.

[53] Drabble, *The Middle Ground* (n. 13 above), 109.

[54] Margaret Atwood, *Bodily Harm* (New York: Simon & Schuster, 1982), 22–23.

[55] Ibid., 265.

Doane and Hodges define nostalgia as "not just a sentiment but also a rhetorical practice." Their definition makes clear the relation of nostalgia to textual practice: the past that is longed for is a place within discourse where the referent referred to something "real," "a past in which women 'naturally' function in the home to provide a haven of stability that is linguistic as well as psychic."[56] In a nostalgic mode—and Christopher Lasch's *The Culture of Narcissism* is exemplary—the referent is seen "as an authentic origin or center from which to disparage the degenerate present," a present in which literary texts no longer represent "the real world": "the battleground is representation itself."[57] Doane and Hodges urge feminists to "undermine nostalgic rhetoric" by "leaving cultural definitions of masculinity and femininity in play, rather than in place."[58]

Textual feminists subvert "nostalgic rhetoric" by mining the past to discover play rather than place. They suggest a view of the past not as fixed and finished but as so vitally connected to the present that it takes on new meaning in response to present questions and needs. As Laurence's Morag says, "a popular misconception is that we can't change the past—everyone is constantly changing their own past, recalling it, revising it."[59] As Maxine Hong Kingston suggests, "the reason we remember the past moment at all is that our present-day life is still a working-out of a similar situation"; "understanding the past changes the present. And the ever-evolving present changes the significance of the past."[60] Such questions have also been raised by contemporary philosophy of history, which is similarly concerned with understanding how the present determines our view of the past—with what Michael S. Roth calls "the presentist aspects of . . . historical inquiry."[61]

In novels by Lessing, Drabble, Laurence, Atwood, and Morrison, protagonists begin with a longing for "the true story," something real to which referents attach, which they relinquish for a view of the past as ever-changing and open to revision—a view they

[56] Doane and Hodges (n. 22 above), 14.

[57] Ibid., 8, 9–10, 3.

[58] Ibid., 142.

[59] Laurence, *The Diviners*, 60.

[60] Paula Rabinowitz, "Eccentric Memories: A Conversation with Maxine Hong Kingston," *Michigan Quarterly Review* ("Women and Memory") 26, no. 1 (Winter 1987): 177–87, esp. 179.

[61] Roth (n. 4 above), 123, cites literature on the role of the present in the writing of the past: e.g., R. G. Collingwood, *The Idea of History* (Oxford: Oxford University Press, 1946); and Hayden V. White, *Metahistory: The Historical Imagination in Nineteenth Century Europe* (Baltimore: Johns Hopkins University Press, 1978). See also Lowenthal (n. 11 above), 210–24, 324–64.

find enormously liberating, for if the past is a construct, it can be reconstructed. Laurence's Morag tries to remember "what really happened," contemplates the meanings of the family photographs ("I am remembering myself composing this interpretation"; "I don't even know how much of that memory really happened and how much of it I embroidered later on") and comes to realize that "what really happened" is not only not knowable but also not important—"a meaningless question. But one I keep trying to answer, knowing there is no answer." When she can acknowledge that what matters is the process of remembering, "the necessary doing of the thing—that mattered," she can assume the "authority" of "authorship" and "set down her title," the "title" of the novel we have just read—*The Diviners*.[62]

The sense of the past as evolving in confrontation with the present is mirrored in the narrative strategies of feminist fiction. Even in the most straightforward of these novels, chronology is disrupted, as it is in much contemporary and Modernist fiction. But one structure—the pattern of circular return—recurs with such frequency as to be practically a defining characteristic.[63] In novels as diverse as Atwood's *Lady Oracle*, Drabble's *The Waterfall* (1969), Fay Weldon's *Praxis*, Gail Godwin's *The Odd Woman* (1974), Erica Jong's *Fear of Flying* (1973), Lisa Alther's *Kinflicks* (1975), Ursula K. Le Guin's *The Dispossessed* (1974), and Anne Tyler's *Earthly Possessions* (1977), episodes set in the past alternate with episodes set in the present until, in the end, past becomes present; variations of this occur in Anne Richardson Roiphe's *Up the Sandbox* (1970), Marge Piercy's *Woman on the Edge of Time* (1976), Atwood's *Handmaid's Tale* (1986), and in "self-begetting novels"[64] that end with the protagonist ready to write the novel we

[62] Laurence, *The Diviners*, 8, 17–18, 60, 452–53.

[63] Antilinearity is by no means unique to women's fiction, as Patricia Drechsel Tobin's discussion of assaults on linearity in modern fiction suggests (*Time and the Novel: The Genealogical Imperative* [Princeton, N.J.: Princeton University Press, 1978], 27). For associations of the female and the cyclic, see Julia Kristeva, "Women's Time," trans. Alice Jardine and Harry Blake, *Signs: Journal of Women in Culture and Society* 7, no. 1 (Autumn 1981): 13–35; Robbie Pfeufer Kahn, "Women and Time in Childbirth and during Lactation," *Taking Our Time: Feminist Perspectives on Temporality*, ed. Frieda Johles Forman with Caoran Sowton (Elmsford, N.Y.: Pergamon, 1988), 20–36, esp. 25; and Susan Gubar, "The Representation of Women in Fiction," in *Selected Papers from the English Institute*, ed. and intro. Carolyn G. Heilbrun and Margaret R. Higonnet, N.S., no. 7 (Baltimore: Johns Hopkins University Press, 1981), 19–59, esp. 31. I discuss circular structures in women's novels in my forthcoming book on feminist fiction, *Breaking the Circle: Feminist Fiction and the Tradition* (Bloomington: Indiana University Press, 1991).

[64] So termed by Steven G. Kellmann, "The Fiction of Self-begetting," *Modern Language Notes* 91 (December 1976): 1234–56, esp. 1245.

have just read—*The Diviners* and *The Golden Notebook*. The alternation of past and present episodes draws attention to the vital interaction of past and present and allows a circling back over material that enables repetition with revision; final scene returns to first scene, with the difference between them providing measure of change, of a present transformed by remembering. The simultaneous backward and forward movement permits us "to read time backward" (in Paul Ricoeur's phrase) insofar as is possible on one reading; for though the linear sequence of language commits us to reading forward, understanding requires rereadings and depends on knowledge of the end. Ricoeur describes the experience of narrative in these terms: "By reading the end into the beginning and the beginning into the end, we learn to read time backward. . . . In this way, the plot does not merely establish human action 'in' time, it also establishes it in memory. And memory in turn repeats—re-collects—the course of events."[65]

In a sense, women's fictions have always been circular. In traditional fictions by and about women, women exchange "one domestic space for another" (in Elizabeth Abel's phrase), an exchange which reflects "the creative cul-de-sac of the romantic mode" (in Helene Moglen's term) where "marriage leads back to Victorian patriarchy rather than forward to a mature female identity" (in Karen Rowe's term).[66] When—as in Lessing's *The Grass Is Singing* (1950) and *A Proper Marriage* (1952)—the repetition of the mother's life is a "nightmare," the return to the beginning is a vicious circle representing the triumph of the past; but in Lessing's later fiction and in fiction by Drabble, Atwood, and Laurence, the circular structure represents a return that leads not back but forward, becoming means to a transformed present and future, allowing repetition in order for there to be escape from repetition, in order for there to be change. In *The Four-Gated City* (1969), Martha's circular return enables her to relearn what she has forgotten and to assimilate knowledge on deeper levels: "That is what learning is. You suddenly understand something you've understood all your life, but in a new way" (*FGC*, 97). This novel transforms the closed circle of repetition into cyclic returns that allow memory work or "re-collection": "Yes, forgetting, forgetting again and again, life brings one back to points in oneself . . . over

[65] Paul Ricoeur, "Narrative Time," in Mitchell, ed. (n. 4 above), 165–86, 179.

[66] Elizabeth Abel, Marianne Hirsch, and Elizabeth Langland, eds., *The Voyage In: Fictions of Female Development* (Hanover, N.H.: University Press of New England, 1983), 8. Helene Moglen, as quoted in Karen E. Rowe, " 'Fairy-born and Human Bred': Jane Eyre's Education in Romance," in Abel, Hirsch, and Langland, eds., 69–89, esp. 84.

and over again in different ways, saying without words: This is a place where you could learn if you wanted to. Are you going to learn this time or not? No? Very well then, I'll . . . find ways of bringing you back to it again. When you are ready, then" (*FGC*, 472).

In feminist *Kunstlerromane*, the protagonist's writing is her means to liberation. In *Lady Oracle*, Atwood contrasts a fictional form that entraps, the Gothics Joan writes for a living, to a mode that liberates, represented by Atwood's novel as a whole. Joan's Gothics promise escape, but they actually recycle the past in a dead end of repetition that leaves her trapped; like the junk food she is also addicted to, they provide a momentary high in exchange for a long-term letdown: "You can't change the past, oh, but I wanted to. . . . That was the one thing I really wanted to do." But as she begins to unravel the snarl of past, and her strategies of containment—psychological and literary—begin to break down, the Gothic formula ceases to function even as temporary relief. At the end she is left contemplating more future-oriented modes—"I won't write any more Costume Gothics . . . I think they were bad for me. But maybe I'll try some science fiction. The future doesn't appeal to me as much as the past, but I'm sure it's better for you."[67] Whether Joan does go on to more progressive forms, Atwood herself has forged a form which, by delving into the past, explodes conventional containments and breaks the hold of repetition.

Lessing's *The Golden Notebook* is, of all these texts, the most extensive exploration of questions of memory, narrative, and liberation. Anna has vowed never to write fiction again, she is so appalled by the "lying nostalgia" (*GN*, 63) of her best-selling first novel, *The Frontiers of War*. All her efforts "to write the truth" leave her "realising it's not true" (*GN*, 274): "How do I know that what I 'remember' was what was important? What I remember was chosen by Anna, of twenty years ago. I don't know what this Anna of now would choose" (*GN*, 137). She longs for a concrete, knowable "truth," but her every attempt at a "straight, simple, formless account" (*GN*, 63, 229) throws her back on memory. She imagines that visual images will provide greater certainty—"the absolute assurance of a smile, a look, a gesture, in a painting or a film" (*GN*, 110); "probably better as a film. Yes, the physical quality of life . . . not the analysis afterwards" (*GN*, 228)—but comes to realize that the visual image is as dependent upon memory as the verbal is: "What makes you think that the emphasis you have put on it is the correct emphasis?" (*GN*, 619). All representation throws her back

[67] Margaret Atwood, *Lady Oracle* (New York: Avon, 1976), 6, 379.

on the shaping, ordering, selecting faculty of the mind and, ulti-
mately, on memory.

However, Anna comes to understand memory as the means to
change. The reworking of material in the four notebooks and two
novels she is writing allows her to go over her life again and again
until she can get it right—to repeat, re-vise, to "name in a different
way" (GN, 616).[68] Every important event, issue, question, quality,
action, attitude, gets redefined in the course of the novel; every-
thing essential comes up for re-naming as, in the visionary and
re-visionary episodes of the fifth notebook—the golden notebook—
the value of "boulder pushing," of "taking a stand," of "the forms,"
of "making patterns," irony, and "naming" itself—all are re-named
as Anna wrests "out of the chaos, a new kind of strength" (GN, 467).
"Preserving the forms" and "just making patterns," for example, are
first viewed as cowardly limitations, but then are re-envisioned as
acts of the creative imagination (GN, 26, 275, 634); "naming" itself
is first seen as a fatal "fixing," "a 'naming' to save . . . from pain"
(GN, 489), but it too becomes identified with the creative, transfor-
mative imagination.

When Anna can accept that there is no reality apart from the
mind that perceives it and the language that expresses it, she can
accept that none of her versions is "true"—or all are "true," or
"truth" itself is a fiction, invented rather than discovered. Not that
there is "no reality," as in extreme versions of poststructuralist
thought, but that "truth" is a process, in the patterning rather than
the "patterns."[69] Having accepted that "the story of my life" can

---

[68] Judith Kegan Gardiner, "Female Identity and Writing by Women," Critical
Inquiry ("Writing and Sexual Difference," ed. Elizabeth Abel) 8, no. 2 (Winter
1981): 347–61, esp. 359, suggests that "the repetitive, overlapping style of the novel
imitates [the] process of remembering, as the narrator writes and reads herself,
creating and discarding partial and alternative selves." Noting that "Anna's effort to
retain her memories . . . keeps her personality intact and saves her from madness,"
Gardiner speculates that "male memory operates differently from female mem-
ory. . . . Men maintain a coherent sense of themselves by repression" (358–59). I
discuss various forms of male repression in the novel in "Women and Men in The
Golden Notebook: Divided Selves," in The [M]other Tongue: Essays in Feminist
Psychoanalytic Literary Interpretation, ed. Shirley Nelson Garner, Madelon
Sprengnether, and Claire Kahane (Ithaca, N.Y.: Cornell University Press, 1985),
280–305.

[69] Roberta Rubenstein, The Novelistic Vision of Doris Lessing: Breaking the
Forms of Consciousness (Urbana: University of Illinois Press, 1979), 102, 74, notes
that Lessing provides "no single authoritative view of events" and suggests that
"objectivity is an aesthetic and epistemological convention." Betsy Draine notes that
when Anna is "no longer bound to find the truth [she] is free to present her truth,
with renewed conviction" ("Nostalgia and Irony: The Postmodern Order of The
Golden Notebook," Modern Fiction Studies 26, no. 1 [Spring 1980]: 31–48, esp. 46).

never be more than "a record of how I saw myself at a certain point" (*GN*, 473), Anna is free to re-member and to re-vise. When she can relinquish her longing for "the true story," she can accept that she has written the novel we have just read, allowing her various versions, however "crude, unfinished, raw, tentative" (*GN*, 236), to come together into "something new." *The Golden Notebook* is a writerly text that (in Roland Barthes's terms) admits to its own uncertainties and contradictions, to its processes of production, and by involving the reader in those processes, allows "something new."[70] Like *The Children of Violence, The Golden Notebook* is concerned with the consequences of repressing, but here it is the male characters who block off, "stay cool," and are frozen in postures that make them incapable of change, whereas Anna's ability to stay open and enter experiences beyond her own enables her to break through to "something new." Though Lessing's early fiction gave us the word "matrophobia,"[71] *The Golden Notebook* finds value in female boundary confusion and relatedness, anticipating feminist revisionists Nancy Chodorow, Dorothy Dinnerstein, Jane Flax, Carol Gilligan, and Jean Baker Miller, who reinterpret female identity positively.[72]

Similarly, protagonists of Lessing's and Drabble's midlife identity crisis novels, *The Summer before the Dark* and *The Middle Ground*, discover that there is no one right "pattern." Lessing's Kate Brown seeks "the truth, whatever that was," "what she really felt" beneath the "worn" and "stereotyped" attitudes "custom allots" (*SBD*, 1–2), for she has come to realize that her image of herself and her marriage is "out of date"—that rather than being "the warm centre of the family," she has been "starved" by her

[70] Barthes contrasts the "readerly" mode of realism which is "product" and "can only be read" and, inscribed within ideology, is incapable of accommodating change, with the "writerly text" which, as process and capable of being "written" or "produced," is open to "play" and capable of accommodating change (*S/Z* [New York: Hill & Wang, 1974], 4–5).

[71] The term was coined by Lyn Sukenick in "Feeling and Reason in Doris Lessing's Fiction," in *Doris Lessing: Critical Studies*, ed. Annis Pratt and L. S. Dembo (Madison: University of Wisconsin Press, 1974), 98–118, esp. 102—as noted by Judith Kegan Gardiner, "A Wake for Mother: The Maternal Deathbed in Women's Fiction," *Feminist Studies* 4, no. 2 (June 1978): 146–65, esp. 164.

[72] Nancy Chodorow, *The Reproduction of Mothering: Psychoanalysis and the Sociology of Gender* (Berkeley: University of California Press, 1978); Dorothy Dinnerstein, *The Mermaid and the Minotaur* (New York: Harper & Row, 1976); Jane Flax, "The Conflict between Nurturance and Autonomy in Mother-Daughter Relationships and within Feminism," *Feminist Studies* 4, no. 2 (June 1978): 171–89; Carol Gilligan, *In a Different Voice: Psychological Theory and Women's Development* (Cambridge, Mass.: Harvard University Press, 1982); Jean Baker Miller, *Toward a New Psychology of Women* (Boston: Beacon, 1976).

children's indifference and her husband's infidelities (*SBD*, 52). Her quest leads her to repudiate the conventions that have governed her behavior as a woman: her conditioning as a sexual object now strikes her as "rubbish," "nonsense," "a con job," "a bloody waste of time" (*SBD*, 196), "a load of shit" (*SBD*, 200); and motherhood itself seems a "long, grinding process" which has turned "an unafraid young creature" into "an obsessed maniac" and then cast her off "like an old nurse" (*SBD*, 94).

The way back from these bleak insights is through "rememory" elicited in response to another person. By forming a friendship with a younger woman, a stranger, entering into a surrogate mother-daughter relationship of the sort that Lessing often shows as more liberating than family ties are, Kate re-remembers. Confronted by Maureen's matrophobia, she can defend Maureen's mother for "bringing you up, and making not a bad job of it" (*SBD*, 205); and in response to Maureen's "tell me a story," she finds memories that allow her to modify her view of her marriage "as a web of nasty self-deceptions" (*SBD*, 232): "It almost seemed as if the things she remembered were because of Maureen's interest—Maureen's need?" (*SBD*, 222)—a suggestion developed by Morrison in *Beloved*, of the therapeutic value of memory recalled in response to the needs of others. But Kate's realization that "what she really feels" is inconclusive and provisional—that "in a year or so's time" her experience of the summer "would not seem anything like it did now" (*SBD*, 232)—enables her to relinquish her quest for "the truth." Such discoveries turn out not to be particularly liberating, however, since she is unable to conceive of alternatives to the situation from which she began, and her most important lesson is to say "no": "her experiences of the last months, her discoveries, her self-definition; what she hoped were now strengths, were concentrated here . . . she was saying *no:* no, no, no, NO" (*SBD*, 144). Lessing envisions female "boundary confusions" as mere liabilities in this novel, and Kate ends by returning to the domestic situation that has been the source of the problem, in a closed circular return consistent with the bleak view of motherhood.

Drabble's *The Middle Ground* revises Lessing's midlife crisis novel, turning the "shit" which seemed to Kate Brown the essence of life, to "gold"—which is Kate Armstrong's term for her uncanny knack of transforming the raw materials of life to empowering art forms (*MG*, 19). Drabble's Kate begins where Lessing's Kate began, in a spirit of self-repudiation, only her disgust extends to women generally: "I'm . . . bloody sick of bloody women, I wish I'd never invented them" (*MG*, 2). Kate has "invented women" in that her journalism has helped make the women's movement, but now, having attained the goal of "women's liberation" and become a "free woman" (*MG*, 49, 59, 65, 66), she finds her "freedom" turned to "a narrow tunnel" and herself "trapped in stale repetition" (*MG*, 52), "locked in a bad circle" (*MG*, 66), "come to a dead end" (*MG*, 52–53). Kate's loss of a version of the past which makes sense of the present and a version of the present which makes sense of the past causes her to question the future: "If it is a mid-life crisis . . . what on earth is on the other side of it?" (*MG*, 10). She no longer believes in "freedom" or "progress," for herself or anyone else: "her implacable progress has been halted, a link has been broken" (*MG*, 10), and she now feels that freedom is "bad for people" (*MG*, 5). She is, moreover, overwhelmed by confusion—"when one was younger, one saw patterns everywhere, for the process of selection was so simple" (*MG*, 172), but now her self, her past, present, future, even the environment, seem to require "re-interpretation" (*MG*, 44).

"Re-interpretation" is enabled by a trip home. One of the things Kate is feeling as she sets out for Romley is that there is no connection between her past and present selves, "no blood flowed from one to the other, the cord was cut, she withered and grew dry" (*MG*, 109)—an image suggesting that such severance is death. "Connection" is enabled by the "strange distracting smell" of the sewage, which, rising from "the mysterious network of drains and pipes and tubes and gulleys and sewers"—a network associated with the "underworld," "the underground"—releases memories: "no revelations . . . just memories" (*MG*, 107–8). As in Woolf's fiction, "the great revelation" never comes;[73] rather, small "illuminations" occur in the form of Kate's seemingly random reflections about her past, her brother, her parents: "For she had loved these two terrible people, in the dawn of time, in the dark before dawn, in the underground she had loved them. And nothing in her conscious self, in her daylight self, had been able to love. Was this the problem, was this the fault?" (*MG*, 108–9). She fears that it is this which has distorted her relations with everyone ever after, leaving her damaged like her brother Peter who, for all his heroic will to change, remains twisted in his depths, locked into "some other darker pattern" which is incomprehensible, uncontrollable, unchangeable (*MG*, 121): "there was no denying it, the idea of Peter was inextricably linked in her mind with whatever it was that had gone wrong with her own life"; "there he was, standing in her mind like a dam in a river" (*MG*, 116).

[73] In pt. 3 of *To the Lighthouse*, Lily, pondering "the meaning of life," speculates that "the great revelation perhaps never did come. Instead there were little daily miracles, illuminations, matches struck unexpectedly in the dark" (New York: Harcourt Brace & Co., 1955), 240.

But Kate must go further, to confront the possibility that it was she who damaged him. Contrary to what she initially asserted, that "every single bad thing that's happened to me happened to me because I'm a woman" (*MG*, 5), "some other . . . pattern" emerges that suggests that it was being a woman that enabled her to survive. Peter was "the real victim" of her parents, "being the only boy." Her father "had nagged at Peter to better himself. . . . And Peter had been terrorised. . . . A sacrifice to progress" (*MG*, 110–11). She now senses that her refusal to compete, her "backhanded," "sinister female game" (*MG*, 122), made her complicit with what destroyed him, which suggests that she will need to forgive herself for being female before she can regain equanimity about women generally— and though this realization never quite surfaces, Drabble suggests the workings of subterranean processes too deep to articulate, rendering them imagistically: "The dirty, tangled roots of child- hood twisted back forever and ever, beyond all knowing. Impacted, interwoven, scrubby, interlocked, fibrous, cankerous, tuberous, ancient, matted" (*MG*, 122). Though the damage cannot be undone, to Kate or to Peter, and though the imagery suggests that beneath this pattern may be another and another, extending back infinitely, unknowable, unfathomable, for now, for the present, currents are set flowing that establish a revitalizing link between past and present.

Though nothing has changed in the end except Kate's perspec- tive, Kate has come through her crisis and ends at "the centre of a circle" of family and friends, a circle she has created by taking in and including all sorts of people of various classes, countries, and races: "Looking around her family circle, feeling as she sat there a sense of immense calm, strength, centrality, as though she were indeed the centre of a circle . . . but imagine a circle . . . a circle and a moving sphere, for this is her house and there she sits, she has everything and nothing, I give her everything and nothing" (*MG*, 255). This is not a vicious circle of determined behavior, but an image of harmony and inclusiveness that accommodates change— "Anything is possible, it is all undecided. . . . Nothing binds her, nothing holds her" (*MG*, 257). Whereas Lessing consigns her protagonist to the situation from which she began, Drabble leaves her Kate "confronted by choice." Whereas Kate Brown protects herself by saying no, for Kate Armstrong "saying yes is my special technique for preserving myself. . . . I don't know *why* it works, but it does" (*MG*, 8); and her female boundary confusions and connec- tions with others are affirmed as sources of strength and salvation.

The narrative structure of this novel is itself affirmation that the self is created through relationship: Drabble's use of a narrator who pieces the story together from the interpretations of Kate and Kate's friends invites the reader to participate in the creation of meaning and, in imaginative collaboration with the reader, confers value—"gives"—is confirmation of the value of community and communication. Like *The Golden Notebook, The Middle Ground* is a writerly text that might also be termed a "feminine text" in that the "female" qualities that enable the protagonist to change are also qualities of writerly narrative: openness, sympathetic participation, and process are not only central values that are represented by the protagonist but also they are affirmed by narrative form.

* * *

Though Morrison's *Beloved* is concerned with the liberation of the black community rather than the white, middle-class woman, this writerly text which depicts memory and narrative as means to liberation has affinities with feminist metafiction by Lessing, Laurence, Drabble, and Atwood.

The past that lies behind the action of *Beloved* is a "nightmare" which is by no means past: the "sixty million and more" victims of the diaspora to whom the novel is dedicated, "the black and angry dead" (*B*, 198), seize the present and possess it in the form of the murdered baby's ghost—"what a roaring" (*B*, 181). This is a world in which "anybody [you] knew, let alone loved, who hadn't run off or been hanged, got rented out, loaned out, bought up, brought back, stored up, mortgaged, won, stolen or seized" (*B*, 23); "so you protected yourself and loved small" (*B*, 162). "Reconstruction" is more than the period in which the novel is set: it is the task the characters face as they set about rebuilding the culture that has been decimated by slavery, learning how to love and trust and make the connections with others that will enable them to go on.

Silenced, isolated, loving small, they are at first determined to forget. Sethe "worked hard to remember as close to nothing as was safe" (*B*, 5–6) and not to "go inside" (*B*, 46); Paul D has "shut down a generous portion of his head" (*B*, 41). But the refusal to confront the pain of the past keeps the past continually alive, as Sethe's "talking about time" suggests: "I mean, even if I don't think it, even if I die, the picture of what I did, or knew, or saw is still out there. Right in the place where it happened . . . someday you be walking down the road and you hear something or see something going on. . . . And you think it's you thinking it up. . . . But no. It's when you bump into a rememory that belongs to somebody else. . . . It's never going away. . . . The picture is still there and what's more, if you go there—you who never was there—if you go and stand in the place where it was, it will happen again; it will be there for you, waiting for you. . . . Because even though it's all over—and done with—it's going to be always there waiting for you" (*B*, 35–36). Her daughter Denver gets the point: " 'If it's still there, waiting, that must mean that nothing ever dies.' Sethe looked right in Denver's face. 'Nothing ever does,' she said" (*B*, 36).

The idea that everything that's ever happened is still somewhere out there is truly terrifying: it clogs the world with the past, with our own and everyone else's, and allows the past to possess the future as well as the present. But this is an expression of Sethe's cathected imagination, a mind "loaded with the past" and "no room to imagine, let alone plan for, the next day" (*B*, 70), as Sethe herself says.

However, Morrison shows that even a past as horrific as this is not fixed but is open to revision by "rememory."[74] *Beloved* is about bringing what's dead to life, which "hurts," as Denver knows (*B*, 35); and dead parts come back to life in response to other people. When at the beginning of the novel Paul D meets Sethe after many years, "the closed portion of his head opened like a greased lock" (*B*, 41); and his arrival prompts her to think about "plans" ("Would there be a little space . . . a little time . . . to . . . trust things and remember things" [*B*, 18]), to give into "the temptation to trust and remember . . . to go ahead and feel. . . . Go ahead and *count on something*" (*B*, 38). Memory is linked to trust—for the third time—when she expresses her desire "to have him in her life": "Trust and rememory, yes. . . . The mind of him that knew her own. Her story was bearable because it was his as well—to tell, to refine and tell again. The things neither knew about the other—the things neither had word-shapes for—well, it would come in time" (*B*, 99). The association of trust and rememory suggests a connection between going inside and reaching outside, between risking the pain and confusion of going within and having the confidence that someone will be there: Sethe can risk remembering because she can trust that Paul D will (as he says) "hold [her] ankles" while she "goes inside" (*B*, 46).

Beloved is another "dead thing" that "comes to life," and though her return is sinister, it also allows an exorcism. One of the good things she inspires is "telling": hungry for stories, Beloved gets

---

[74] Morrison describes her interest in "ways in which the past influences today and tomorrow" (*Los Angeles Times* [October 14, 1987]) and refers to her writing generally as a way of "sorting out the past," of identifying "those things in the past that are useful and those things that are not" (Thomas Le Clair, " 'The Language Must Not Sweat': A Conversation with Toni Morrison," *New Republic* [March 21, 1981], 75–78, esp. 75–76).

Sethe to "feed her" with stories, and Sethe (like Lessing's Kate) is astonished to find "pleasure" in remembering: "It amazed Sethe . . . because every mention of her past life hurt. Everything in it was painful or lost . . . unspeakable. . . . But, as she began telling . . . she found herself wanting to, liking it . . . in any case it was an unexpected pleasure" (*B*, 58).

Beloved is also the story of Denver, a strange, lonely girl who learns early her mother's lesson of repression, going "deaf" rather than hear the truth which Nelson Lord tries to tell her (*B*, 104). When the ghost returns in the form of Beloved, she initially welcomes its companionship, but when the haunting gets out of control, she realizes that she will have to go out into the world and "ask somebody for help" (*B*, 243). At first she is paralyzed by memory and stands frozen on the porch, immobilized by her mother's and grandmother's warnings: "Out there were places in which things so bad had happened that when you went near them it would happen again. Like Sweet Home where time didn't pass and where, like her mother said, the bad was waiting for her as well . . . Grandma Baby said there was no defense" (*B*, 243–44). But at this point another kind of rememory comes to her rescue: "And then Baby Suggs laughed, clear as anything"—"You mean I never told you nothing about Carolina? About your daddy? You don't remember nothing about how come I walk the way I do and about your mother's feet, not to speak of her back? I never told you all that? Is that why you can't walk down the steps? My Jesus my." "But you said there was no defense." "There ain't." "Then what do I do?" "Know it, and go on out the yard. Go on" (*B*, 244). Denver gets herself out of the yard, but soon realizes that nobody is going to help her unless she "told it—told all of it" (*B*, 253).

The community responds to her pleas, reversing its former hostility with acts of caring. The final part of the novel offers several such reversals, repetitions of earlier events or situations with revisions. Though "the last time [Nelson Lord] spoke to [Denver] his words blocked up her ears," when he speaks to her again, telling her to "take care of herself," "she heard it as though it were what language was made for" (*B*, 252). Sethe's attempt to kill Edward Bodwin, when she imagines he is coming for her child, reiterates the central act of violence, her murder of her child, only this time she turns her rage against the white man instead of her own (*B*, 262). Similarly, when Denver tells Paul D that Miss Bodwin is teaching her things, " 'experimenting on me' . . . he didn't say, 'Watch out. Watch out. Nothing in the world more dangerous than a white schoolteacher' "—though there were few things worse in their pasts than a white schoolteacher "experimenting" on them,

Paul D does not perpetuate that pain, but instead turns his attention to the future and asks "Your mother all right?" (*B*, 266).

As a matter of fact, Sethe is not "all right"; she is so low that she has "no plans. No plans at all" (*B*, 272). But she is not so low that she is incapable of responding to Paul D's special quality, a quality of evoking "feeling" and the desire to "tell" which Morrison terms "blessedness"—"The thing in him, the blessedness that has made him the kind of man who can walk in a house and make the women cry. Because with him, in his presence, they could. Cry and tell him things they only told each other" (*B*, 272). Again, it is memory that enables Paul D to sort out his feelings: "Suddenly he remembers Sixo trying to describe what he felt about the Thirty-Mile Woman. She is a friend of my mind. She gather me, man. The pieces I am, she gather them and give them back to me in all the right order"; and he realizes that "he wants to put his story next to [Sethe's]." He tells her, "me and you, we got more yesterday than anybody. We need some kind of tomorrow." Their relationship is described in terms of the restoration of Sethe to herself ("You your best thing, Sethe" [*B*, 272–73]) and of the right working of time—of time that "stays put" and allows "plans."

Yet "this is not a story to pass on" (*B*, 275), and the ambiguity of this refrain—which is repeated three times—tantalizes. Its meaning depends on the meaning of "pass on": does it mean "to communicate" or "to die"? Does the line mean that this is not a story to let live—that is, that it is a story to forget; or that it is not a story to let die—that is, that it is a story to remember and tell? The ambiguity suggests a difficult balance in relation to the past: the past must be remembered, but not entirely; it must be forgotten, but not entirely; it can kill though it can also heal, and it is most healing when remembered in response to another and when "told." Sethe remembers in response to Beloved's need and her story becomes bearable because it is Paul D's as well; she envisions a future in which they find "word-shapes" with which to communicate, as he imagines putting his story next to hers. Morrison has chosen to tell this tale—to pass it on rather than let it pass on—in response to *our* need, and in a way that emphasizes the remembering and telling as means of reconstruction.

The receptive reader or listener is part of the community restored by the telling, and the story is the means of the restoration. In a remarkable passage, Morrison describes remembering and telling in terms of loving, feeding, nurturing, creating. Denver is mining the past in order to feed Beloved's "craving to know": "Denver was seeing it now and feeling it—through Beloved. Feeling how it must have felt to her mother. Seeing how it must have looked. And the more fine points she made, the more detail she provided, the more Beloved liked it. So she anticipated the questions by giving blood to the scraps her mother and grand-mother had told her—and a heartbeat. The monologue became, in fact, a duet as they lay down together, Denver's nursing Beloved's interest like a lover whose pleasure was to overfeed the loved . . . Denver spoke, Beloved listened, and the two did the best they could to create what really happened, how it really was" (*B*, 78). Remembering and telling are generative and restorative acts that endow the past with flesh, blood, and a heartbeat. By "going inside," then reaching outside and telling—by memory and narration—the characters rebuild their world.

Morrison has spoken of *Beloved* as a writerly text and of her fiction generally as demanding participatory reading.[75] *Beloved* enlists the reader's imagination by disrupting chronology and point of view. Past and present are interwoven and time varies according to point of view; point of view is—like time—fluid, shifting from first to third persons, and from one first person to another, in a way that suggests that all are involved with all, that the story is everybody's. This quality may be seen as expressing the connect-edness, affiliation, and boundary confusions associated with female identity, but Morrison relates voice in her novels specifically to oral tradition in the black community: "No author tells these stories. They are just told—meanderingly—as though they are going in several different directions at the same time. . . . I am simply trying to recreate something out of an old art form in my books—that something that defines what makes a book 'black.' "[76] Events move generally backward, as in an archaeological dig that unearths deeper and deeper layers, moving back to the originating events, the escape and the infanticide. The ending is open and ambiguous—in fact, it was not actually intended as an ending; Morrison says that she intended it as a transition to another part of the book, when the editors declared the book finished.[77]

[75] Personal communication, Claremont, Calif., October 1987. See also Evans (n. 3 above), 341: "Because it is the affective and participatory relationship between the artist or the speaker and the audience that is of primary importance. . . . To make the story appear oral, meandering, effortless, spoken—to have the reader *feel* the narrator without *identifying* that narrator, or hearing him or her knock about, and to have the reader work *with* the author in the construction of the book—is what's important. What is left out is as important as what is there."

[76] Nellie McKay, "An Interview with Toni Morrison," *Contemporary Literature* 24, no. 4 (1983): 413–29, esp. 420.

[77] Personal communication, Claremont, Calif., October 1987. Morrison says "there is always something more interesting at stake than a clear resolution in a novel" (McKay, 420).

Throughout the novel the characters have been made to realize that power lay "in the naming done by a whiteman" (*B*, 125), that "they were only Sweet Home men at Sweet Home. One step off that ground and they were trespassers among the human race . . . gelded workhorses whose neigh and whinny could not be translated into a language responsible humans spoke" (*B*, 125). Morrison's plural and multivocal text wrests the word from the white man and gives it not to the individual author Toni Morrison but to the black community as a whole. Morrison's writerly text is thus also a political text, a work that empowers the disenfranchised and gives speech to the silenced.

* * *

Some of the characteristics I attribute to feminist metafiction are qualities that have been associated with "women's writing" and female boundary fluidity—open-endedness, refusal of linearity, processiveness, inclusiveness.[78] However, I am less concerned with "women's writing" than with feminist fiction, and more specifically, with feminist metafiction, a highly self-conscious, self-reflexive mode that I associate with female identity only when the writer herself does—as Drabble and Lessing do. My description of feminist form has affinities with Rachel Blau DuPlessis's and Joanne Frye's,[79] though it more resembles descriptions offered by

[78] Christine Makward refers to the "key words" that appear in discussions of women's writing as "open, nonlinear, unfinished, fluid, exploded, fragmented, polysemic, attempting to 'speak the body,' " in her "To Be or Not to Be . . . a Feminist Speaker," in *The Future of Difference*, ed. Hester Eisenstein and Alice Jardine (New Brunswick, N.J.: Rutgers University Press, 1985), 95–105, esp. 96. See also Rachel Blau DuPlessis and Members of Workshop 9, "For the Etruscans: Sexual Difference and Artistic Production—the Debate over a Female Aesthetic," in Eisenstein and Jardine, eds., 128–56; and Josephine Donovan's description of a women's aesthetic rooted in "a woman-centered epistemology" in her article, "Toward a Women's Poetics," *Tulsa Studies in Women's Literature* 3, nos. 1/2 (Spring/Fall 1984): 99–110. Judith Kegan Gardiner suggests that "the processual nature of female identity illuminates diverse traits of writing by women": "female identity is a process" and "writing by women engages us in this process" ("Female Identity and Writing by Women" [n. 68 above], 349, 361).

[79] DuPlessis analyzes twentieth-century women's fiction as "writing beyond the ending," beyond the *telos* of romance and its "regimen of resolutions" (*Writing beyond the Ending: Narrative Strategies of Twentieth-Century Women Writers* [Bloomington: Indiana University Press, 1985], 21). Joanne S. Frye attributes to first-person narrative powers of subversion like those I attribute to metafiction, arguing that first-person narrative allows the protagonist "agency" and "engages the narrative process in rejecting fixed plot or teleological structure" (*Living Stories, Telling Lives: Women and the Novel in Contemporary Experience* [Ann Arbor:

Mary Jacobus, Margaret Homans, and Annette Kuhn, who attribute radical potential to self-conscious modes.[80] Feminist metafiction has affinities with the "polyphonic novel," which Julia Kristeva describes as engaging in a " 'transgression' of linguistic, logical, and social codes," and with Hélène Cixous's "*l'écriture féminine*," a "new insurgent writing" that subverts hierarchies and "wreck[s] partitions, classes, rhetorics, regulations and codes," thereby "chang[ing] the rules of the old game."[81]

Unfortunately, feminist fiction of the sort I have described has passed with the seventies, as white women's fiction has participated in postfeminist retrenchments of the eighties. Lessing, Drabble, and Atwood continue to be concerned with many of these same issues, but they no longer envision the possibility of change. In Drabble's 1987 *The Radiant Way,* Elizabeth concludes her search for the past with the questions, "What did it matter who her father was? . . . *What does it matter who I am?*"; and Alix, who has been politically committed all her life, withdraws from political action.[82] Atwood's *Cat's Eye* (1988) is a feminist quest gone awry, a search

---

University of Michigan Press, 1986], 71, 9). Frye refers to women's plots as "based on process rather than product" (40–41) and notes their writerly qualities: "the female experiences characterized in the novels extend beyond the novels' boundaries to the extraliterary world of the reader. These novels, therefore, call upon . . . the involvement that Roland Barthes calls 'writerly' " (201).

[80] Jacobus, "The Difference of View" (n. 9 above). Margaret Homans grounds some of Jacobus's generalizations in specific analyses of Anglo-American women writers, describing women writers as "simultaneously appropriating and rejecting the dominant discourse" (Margaret Homans, " 'Her Very Own Howl': The Ambiguities of Representation in Recent Women's Fiction," *Signs* 9, no. 2 [Winter 1983]: 186–205, esp. 205). Annette Kuhn, *Women's Pictures: Feminism and Cinema* (London: Routledge & Kegan Paul, 1982), distinguishes between two types of "cultural practice, one which tends to take processes of signification for granted and one which argues that the meaning production is itself the site of struggle" (17): "meaning production" is not "taken for granted, exactly because the ideological character of the signification process is regarded as itself something to be challenged" (18). She defines a "radical signifying practice" as "a mode of representation which . . . makes the moment of reading one in which meanings are set in play rather than consolidated or fixed" (12).

[81] Julia Kristeva, "Word, Dialogue, and Novel," in *Desire in Language: A Semiotic Approach to Literature and Art,* ed. Leon S. Roudiez (New York: Columbia University Press, 1980), 64–91, esp. 71, 86. Hélène Cixous, "The Laugh of the Medusa," trans. Keith Cohen and Paula Cohen, *Signs* 1, no. 4 (Summer 1976): 875–93, reprinted in *New French Feminisms: An Anthology,* ed. Elaine Marks and Isabelle de Courtivron (Amherst: University of Massachusetts Press, 1980), 245–64, esp. 250, 256. Again, Cixous's and Kristeva's generalizations make no reference to specific writers.

[82] Margaret Drabble, *The Radiant Way* (London: Weidenfeld & Nicolson, 1987), 385.

for the past yielding little illumination and ending in repetition of the word "nothing"; and the novel's self-conscious "post-feminism" is underscored by repetition of the word.[83] Lessing tends to sentimentality concerning women in the Jane Somers novels and to a chilling cynicism in *The Good Terrorist* (1985) and *The Fifth Child* (1988), but nowhere in her recent fiction do we find the political edge of *The Golden Notebook*.[84] In this climate *Beloved* stands out the more strikingly for its collective and liberatory vision, for a delving of the past that allows a transformed future.

Department of English
Scripps College

[83] Margaret Atwood, *Cat's Eye* (New York: Doubleday, 1989), 90, 238, 242.

[84] As I argue in *"The Diaries of Jane Somers:* Doris Lessing, Feminism, and the Mother," to be published in *Narrating Mothers*, ed. Brenda O. Daly and Maureen Reddy (Knoxville: University of Tennessee Press, 1991), in press.

Gender as a Personal and Cultural Construction

Nancy J. Chodorow

I WRITE THIS ARTICLE motivated by my concern (with Ma-
honey and Yngvesson 1992) that recent academic feminist theory
seems to have moved away from psychology. I believe that two
directions in contemporary feminist thought underlie this move.
My article tries to accommodate one of these directions; it takes issue
with the other. For despite the recent disenchantment with psychology,
the ongoing development of psychoanalytic feminism as an academic
enterprise suggests that some feminists continue to think that the psy-
chology of gender is important. We turned to the psychology of gender in
the first place because it seemed directly, experientially important to our
lives as women and because we thought that there was something in
psychology that helped account for the tenacity of gender relations.

First, contemporary feminism has been rightfully wary of universaliz-
ing claims about gender and of accounts that seem to reduce gender to a
single defining or characterizing feature. Psychological claims of all sorts
have been a special focus of this criticism. Psychoanalytic feminism, femi-
nist psychologies, and feminist psychoanalysis and therapy (the last of
these not so much noticed by academic feminists) have not paid sufficient
attention to differences and variation among women and to the variety,
instability, multiplicity, and contested nature of gender meanings. Psy-
choanalytic feminism and other feminist psychologies also often claim a
single factor or aspect of psychology as most important in defining
women or femininity. I offer in this article a more clinically and less
theoretically or developmentally based way of thinking about psycho-
logical gender in order to respond to these feminist criticisms of psychol-
ogy and psychoanalysis while at the same time retaining insights from
psychology that feminism has found useful. Such an approach also pro-

I am grateful to Janet Adelman, Barbara Laslett, Barrie Thorne, five anonymous
Signs reviewers, and several anonymous members of the *Signs* editorial board for careful
reading and valuable suggestions.

[*Signs: Journal of Women in Culture and Society* 1995, vol. 20, no. 3]

vides a corrective to this psychological theorizing itself by more fully describing psychological reality.

Second, the clinically based approach I here develop entails a claim that, I believe, runs counter to many feminists' assumptions. I suggest, that is, that gender cannot be seen as entirely culturally, linguistically, or politically constructed.[1] Rather, there are individual psychological processes in addition to, and in a different register from, culture, language, and power relations that construct gender for the individual. Meaning— at least about any linguistic or cultural categories that matter to us—is always psychologically particular to the individual. I draw upon psychoanalysis to give an account of how these processes operate in the capacity to create what I am calling personal meaning. By personal meaning, I refer to psychological experience as it is constituted by the psychodynamic processes described by psychoanalysis and in particular by emotion or affect and by unconscious fantasy.[2] I suggest that each person's sense of gender—her gender identity or gendered subjectivity—is an inextricable fusion or melding of personally created (emotionally and through unconscious fantasy) and cultural meaning.

When I claim that gender is inevitably personal as well as cultural, I do not mean only that people create individualized cultural or linguistic versions of meaning by drawing upon cultural or linguistic categories at hand. Rather, perception and meaning are psychologically created. As psychoanalysis documents, people use available cultural meanings and images, but they experience them emotionally and through fantasy, as well as in particular interpersonal contexts. Individuals thereby create new meanings in terms of their own unique biographies and histories of intrapsychic strategies and practices.

Neither emotion nor unconscious fantasy is originally linguistic or organized. Unconscious fantasy globally images aspects of self and other in immediate, emotionally cast terms. Unconscious fantasies can then become more or less elaborated in their articulation of story, characters, and affect, and they can become more or less expressed in conscious or preconscious fantasies. Emotional meaning, affective tone, and unconscious fantasies that arise from within and are not experienced linguistically interact with and give individual animation and interpretation to

---

[1] In much contemporary feminist theory, the cultural-linguistic and political are fused so that the cultural is seen always to embed the political. For a critique of this tendency, see Bloch 1993.

[2] On unconscious fantasy, see Arlow 1969 and Klein 1975d, 1975e. As this summary of psychoanalysis indicates, and as readers of my previous writing know, my interpretation of psychoanalysis is object-relational and Kleinian; it is not Lacanian. As I note elsewhere (1989, chap. 9), a Lacanian approach cannot really be argued: many of its claims are not subject to clinical or empirical evaluation, and this is the domain of argument in which other psychoanalysts put forth claims.

(i.e., make subjectively meaningful) cultural categories, stories, and language. Unconscious fantasies that are not ostensibly about gender at all also help articulate psychologically aspects of gender experience. At the same time, it is certainly the case that aspects of gender identity and unconscious gender fantasy draw upon language, cultural stories, and interpersonally transmitted emotional responses themselves conveyed by people (in the first instance parents and other caretakers) with their own personal-cultural sense of gender.

My account here makes a universal claim about human subjectivity and its constituent psychodynamic processes, just as a cultural theorist might universalize the claim that subjectivity is linguistically or discursively constituted. For those who draw upon psychoanalysis, the capacity to endow experience with nonverbal emotional and unconscious fantasy meaning—to create personal meaning—is an innate human capacity or potentiality and continues throughout life. Subjectivity here creates and re-creates, merges and separates fantasy and reality, inner and outer, unconscious and conscious, felt past and felt present, each element in the pair helping to constitute and to give meaning and resonance to the other. These capacities create meaning and individuality for the subject. Both in the psychoanalytic and in the cultural case, we hold in abeyance any universal claim about the content of what is thought or felt.

My approach aligns itself with other theories that claim the potential autonomy and creativity of consciousness. Among feminists, Patricia Hill Collins (1990) seems most willing to assert this independence and individuality, though she certainly does not minimize the centrality of relations of domination. She emphasizes that consciousness is created and not determined and stresses the importance for feminists of keeping constant attention to both the social-cultural-political and the individual creativities of consciousness. She points in particular to two traditional foci of psychoanalytic interest and of psychoanalytic feminist critique—heterosexuality and motherhood—and argues that the experience of these is created individually as much as it is imposed as domination: "There is always choice, and power to act, no matter how bleak the situation may be" (1990, 237).

That each person creates her own personal-cultural gender has implications for feminist theory. Feminist theory is right that gender cannot be seen apart from culture. Racial-ethnic, international feminist, discursive, linguistic, deconstructionist, and Foucauldian micropolitical and performative accounts of gender persuasively document the centrality of cultural and political meanings in constructions of gender as well as problems in generalizing, universalizing, and seeing gender as a single identity. But these theoretical approaches, because they do not consider individual personal emotional and fantasy meaning, do not fully capture the meaning of gender for the subject. They miss an important component of experienced gendered meaning and of gendered subjectivity.

I take the position that gendered meanings are certainly indeterminate and contested, but they are indeterminate and contested not only culturally and politically but also as they are shaped and reshaped by an emotional self. Like other processes of psychological meaning creation, gender identity, gender fantasy, the sense of gender, and the sexual identifications and fantasies that are part of this identity are formed and reformed throughout the life cycle. Individual feeling tone, senses of self, and unconscious emotionally imbued fantasies are as constitutive of subjective gender as language or culture.[3]

My individually based approach also has implications for psychologies of gender. Psychoanalysts and other psychological theorists need to recognize fully the inextricable cultural and linguistic contribution to constructions and fantasies of gender. Even with feminist input that challenges the differential valuation of male and female anatomy or psyche, many psychoanalysts and those who draw upon psychoanalysis continue to imply that there is a precultural or noncultural core of femininity and masculinity. Alternately, if they are cognizant of the cultural determinations of gender, they imply that these are superimposed upon a precultural essence, either a genitally determined subjective identity or some observed universal gender differences in psychic operation that we can "find" if we factor out culture. Yet, as I will argue, the clinical evidence does not suggest, as many psychoanalytically inspired theories imply, that we can differentiate between something fixed (a basic universal core of psychological gender meaning) and that which varies among individuals (e.g., varieties of fantasy, emotional tonality, or identifications built upon this more primary something). I disagree, then, with those who believe we can discover or have discovered universal developmental patterns of "the girl" and "the boy" or psychological patterns of "the woman" and "the man."[4]

We can elicit a reading of psychoanalysis as a theory of personal meaning by turning to more clinically based accounts and to those de-

---

[3] Dimen 1991 and Harris 1991 give clinically based accounts compatible with this claim. Dimen describes the intertwining of gender not only with cultural representations but with aspects of self-experience. Harris argues for the complexity, the contextual and variable salience, and the multiple figuration of gender and sexuality in anyone's psyche. These articles (see also Goldner 1991) bring the insights of feminist deconstructionism to the clinical community. Here I extend their arguments and return them to feminism.

[4] In writings and presentations addressed to psychoanalysts and therapists, I stress the cultural input to and political underpinnings of psychological gender as well as the tendency for psychoanalysis to make universalizing and essentializing claims about gender (see, e.g., Chodorow 1989, chap. 9; 1994). Though I mention these points here, they are not points that need to be emphasized for feminists. See n. 9 below for references to contemporary psychoanalytic and psychological theories of gender.

velopmental accounts that pay attention to emotional meaning creation and the rapid intrapsychic and intersubjective fluctuation of emotional meanings of selves and objects.[5] These theories and accounts describe how we personally animate and tint, emotionally and through conscious and unconscious fantasy, the anatomic, cultural, interpersonal, and cognitive world we experience and the meanings we create. The processes of personal animation that they describe—processes in which we use experiences and feelings from the past to give partial meaning to the present— were termed *transference* by Freud. As we act in terms of this incorporated past, we also transferentially shape the present. Contemporary psychoanalysts also emphasize that transference includes the way in which unconscious feelings and fantasies shape and give partial meaning to conscious feeling and experience.

The two major processes of transference are projection and introjection.[6] In projection or projective identification, we accord an emotional and fantasy meaning to others, objects, or concepts because of intrapsychic processes or we project fantasied or experienced aspects of ourselves into aspects of these others, objects, or concepts. Alternately, we take in (introject) aspects of the perceived world and give these a fantasy meaning and emotional casting (Klein 1975d, 1975e). When an object, experience, thought, or category of meaning is particularly important to us, we may experience it as a transitional phenomenon, as both personally created and presented from without (Winnicott 1958, 1965, 1971, 1989). All the traditionally described defensive processes can be employed in projection and introjection: we split experiences of self and other into good and bad, isolate or deny feelings or thoughts, repress or repudiate wishes and ideas, break connections between connected feelings or fantasies, or, alternately, we undifferentiate, confuse, and run together thoughts and perceptions that are separate.

These transferential processes—projective and introjective recastings of perceptions, interpersonal experiences, and identifications—are found whenever fantasy and emotional meanings are accorded to people and situations. They are an active and ongoing fact of life, both within and outside of analysis. They come not only from early relations and early people; they may also come from a person's current intrapsychic situation

---

[5] All psychoanalysts work at least partially from a clinical or transferential theory, though they may adhere to different metapsychologies; therefore, citation is not relevant here. My own personal favorite among descriptions of psychoanalytic process and the meanings and import of transference, fantasy, and psychological reality is that of Loewald 1980. On these matters, as well as on development as a process of emotional meaning and fantasy creation, see Winnicott 1958, 1965, 1971, 1989; Klein 1975d, 1975e; Spillius 1988; and Anderson 1992. On infantile affective development, see Stern 1985.

[6] Some analysts refer to these processes as externalization and internalization (see, e.g., Loewald 1980).

within and among people in her life, or from any important relationship or experience. They both constitute and contribute to personal psychological uniqueness.

According to infant researchers, the emotional or psychological infusing of perception and experience—whether seen as projective identification, transitional process, affective attunement and misattunement, or fantasy—is found from the earliest moments of perception and meaning creation (Stern 1985). Well before language develops, people, interactions—even things—are emotionally and fantasy toned, as caretakers accord them emotional and fantasy meaning and, with or without conscious intention, direct affect about them to infants. At the same time, infants themselves accord fantasy and emotional meaning to aspects of self and feeling, to things, meanings, others, and relationships. These fantasies develop reciprocally in the context of interpersonal experience and also from within, as the infant creates self-experience.

To consider our experience of personal meaning, as these approaches suggest, in terms of any individual's history of emotion, fantasy, and feeling can revise and expand our understanding of cultural and linguistic meaning. The demonstration that we create personal emotional meaning from birth and throughout life suggests that there is only a limited and particular historical sense in which cultural meaning "precedes" individual meaning. Insofar as we are talking about individual subjectivity, it does not do so. From earliest infancy, meaning is emotional as well as cognitive. Personal meaning, unconscious fantasy, and the potential for emotionally resonant experience begin to be created well before we acquire language. Cognitions, like knowing one's gender and having thoughts or experiences of gender, are infused with emotions, fantasies, tonalities. Both an individual, intrapsychic animation and a putting together of cultural categories (themselves emotionally laden and embedded) create the meaning of gender and gender identity for any individual.

That each person's gendered subjectivity is an individual creation addresses an aspect of the question of difference. Each person personally inflects and creates her "own" gender, and there are many individual masculinities and femininities. I see this discovery as a complement to, rather than a criticism or dismissal of, generalizations about gender psychology. We can probably generalize usefully about aspects of many women's and men's subjective senses of gender, prevalent variations in subjective senses of gender, and observed aspects of gender personality (which may or may not be related to their subjective sense of gender).[7]

[7] The distinction I draw between subjective sense of gender and observed differences in gender personality derives from Irene Fast's distinction between subjective and objective gender (1984, 77). Psychologists have tended to look more at objective gender—characteristics that typically differentiate the sexes or that do not. Subjective gender re-

We can also generalize usefully about gender within particular cultural, racial-ethnic, and class groups and during different historical periods. In all such generalizations, however, we need to be careful that our claims do not go beyond our data base, or that we specify the basis of our speculations that they can. We need to remember that generalization, certainly about features of personality or psychology, is implicitly statistical, rarely universal.[8]

In my own earlier work, for example, I attended to commonalities that from my research and observation seemed to characterize the mother-daughter relationship and mother-son relationship and prevalent patterns in female and male constructions of self and gender. I summarized a number of individual processes of self-construction and reconstruction, abstracting particular aspects of complex subjectivities and finding these aspects in common. My initial questions concerned the psychological effects on daughters (sons had been better studied by previous investigators) of being cared for primarily by mothers (women). My account, consonant with my account here, described how developing girls and boys constructed their unconscious, inner self–object world, their unconscious sense of self-boundaries (of connection or difference from others), and their sense of gender. I also suggested that, typically, mothers unconsciously as well as consciously experienced sons and daughters differently, because of their gender similarity or otherness. As many infant researchers have shown (see, among others, Stern 1985 and Winnicott 1958, 1965, 1971, 1989), unconscious fantasies and feelings are often communicated to the child, but the child herself creates, perhaps in typical ways, the meaning of these communications.

My discovery was that these processes contributed to the reproduction of mothering and to other aspects of the ideology and organization of gender (heterosexual asymmetries, ideologies of male superiority and

---

fers to personal constructions of masculinity and femininity, which have been the focus of both feminist and nonfeminist psychological and psychoanalytic investigations as well as of nonpsychological feminist interest in subjectivity. My own previous writings on gender (1978, 1989) are about both objective gender (I generalize about gender differences in constructions of self and internal self-object constellations) and subjective gender (the sense of one's femininity or masculinity). In this article, my focus is on subjective gender (though I note that many nonsubjectively gendered elements, like feeling-tone and fantasies, go into this subjective gender).

[8] Martin 1994 provides a careful discussion of the uses of generalization, the problem of false universalism (when commonalities are assumed, for spurious reasons and without evidence, to occur), and the problem of false difference (in which commonalities are assumed, for spurious reasons and equally without evidence, not to occur). On the usefulness of patterns, see also Frye 1990, 180. Within feminism, I think there has been a problem of translation as well as of empirical overgeneralization. What has often been assumed to be generalization or observation of prevalent patterns and noted as such for the clinician or social scientist has been translated as essentialism or universalism for the more humanistic theorist.

devaluation of women, and so forth). But this is not the same thing as claiming that gender ideologies are directly internalized, that society and culture precede individual psychological creativity. Indeed, *The Reproduction of Mothering* can be read as an account of how psyches produce social and cultural forms as much as vice versa. In either direction, the account was of empirically discovered, not theoretically deduced, connections. It was an account that I claimed had some generalizable features of personal gender and self-construction in a particular familial arrangement, not an account of the social determinants or construction of the psyche.

Thus I did not seek to define femininity as opposed to masculinity, or feminine gender identity as opposed to masculine gender identity, as absolute cultural or psychological essences. Nor did I imply that the object-relational constellations and preoccupations, psychic structure, processes, fantasies, and identifications that I described differentiated all men from all women. I generalized, I believe usefully, about the ways that many women and men operate psychologically and experience and define their selves. Such generalizations are useful to the extent that they speak to any particular individual's experience, to the extent that they help clinicians, or to the extent that they serve as guides for interpreting literature and biographies, and my previous work seems to have done all these things. To the extent that my claims do not fit individuals or particular groups of people, they are modifiable empirically to specify as much.[9]

This article, then, does not reject generalizations. My observation, however, is that over the years, many feminist psychoanalysts and psychologists (like psychoanalysts and psychologists in general) have tended to cast their claims in more universalized and essentialized terms. Contemporary as well as classical theories tend to make universalistic claims about women as opposed to men and to imply that they describe the core experience or essence of femininity or masculinity.[10] Such claims come up

---

[9] Elizabeth Abel 1990 provides a stunning example of this possibility as she shows how writers about race and class themselves draw from and modify psychoanalytic claims and as she herself uses psychoanalytic interpretive approaches (derived from both Lacanian psychoanalysis and from object-relations theory) to create race- and class-specific oedipal and pre-oedipal readings of mothers, fathers, sons, and daughters in their various relationships.

[10] I have in mind here American "primary femininity" theorists (e.g., Kestenberg 1968, 1980; Mayer 1985), as well as those American psychoanalysts who hold an asymmetrical castration model (e.g., Roiphe and Galenson 1981), as well as Lacanian (Lacan 1982), anti-Lacanian (e.g., Irigaray 1985), and mainstream (e.g., Chasseguet-Smirgel 1985, 1986; McDougall 1986) French psychoanalytic theorists. All these writers discuss seemingly inevitable stages of development, developmental tasks, innate femininity, or "the" psychology of women. My impression is that self-in-relation theorists (Jordan et al. 1991), women's ways of knowing theorists (Belenky et al. 1986), and theories about

against feminist recognition of diversity among women as well as against clinical observations of individuality. Part of the tenacity of gender is its personal individuality: to understand and address fully any individual's gender identity requires investigation of a unique confluence of personal and cultural meaning. In treatment, and hence in change, neither cultural-political gender, patients' understandings of themselves as participants in or as victims of gender inequality, nor generalizations about relationality are enough.

Another way to say this for psychoanalysts, for other clinicians, and, I believe, for psychological researchers is to note that there is a great gap between, on the one hand, what we experience and observe transferentially, clinically, and empirically of gender identity and sexual and gender fantasies and, on the other hand, what most theoretical and developmental accounts claim about inevitable stages of development, "the" psychology of women, or "the" role of gender in the transference. The claim that there are many masculinities and femininities, that gender is constructed in contextual, contradictory, and contingent ways, and that gender is a cultural or discursive product comes to us from contemporary feminist theory. Sources of empirical documentation for such claims come from paying attention clinically, ethnographically, and historically.

Different empirical sites make different contributions: we learn of the individuality and personal emotional meaning of gender, as well as of the individualized projective animations of cultural meanings, especially in the clinical consulting room. This is, of course, not the only site of such learning. Psychoanalytic literary critics elicit such learning from readings of texts, while sociologists of emotions find it in interviews (see, e.g., Hochschild 1989). Autobiographers also express the intertwining of the social, historical, and emotional.[11] But for those of us particularly interested in unconscious meaning, fantasy, and psychodynamic self-creation, psychoanalysis is the theory and practice that most exclusively and in most detail focuses on such processes.

My own psychoanalytic training, following upon my writing as a psychoanalytic scholar, came in response to my sense that psychoanalytic knowledge comes in the first instance from the psychoanalytic encounter,

---

women's voice or morality (e.g., Gilligan 1982; Gilligan, Rogers, and Tolman 1991; Brown and Gilligan 1992) also increasingly cast their theories not just as empirically (clinically, observationally, or experimentally) based findings but as universal and even normative claims about how women and men are, and even, by implication, should be. I review contemporary psychoanalytic writings in Chodorow 1989, chap. 9, and argue for diversity in Chodorow 1994.

[11] Pratt 1984 provides a particularly notable account in which each partially positioning memory or experience, each description of cultural, historical, or social location, is infused with grief, pain, joy, anger, uncertainty, fear, and other emotions that particularize that location, memory, and experience for her.

from investigation of the fine-tuned, ever-shifting interactions of self and other and intrapsychic constructions of each in that encounter. Psychoanalytic scholars, including psychoanalytic feminists (and I was no exception here), have always been in an ambiguous position, drawing upon a theory whose data emerge in a clinical consulting room to which they typically have little access (except in the case of their own analysis or therapy), inheritors of an applied psychoanalytic tradition that may bear little relation to the everyday practice and thinking of psychoanalysts themselves.[12]

In what follows, I give a few condensed clinical examples of personal sense of gender. I put forth these examples mainly to illuminate the emotional and fantasy animation of personal gender and to show how people recreate and charge recognizable cultural meanings in ways that emotionally, often conflictually, through unconscious and conscious fantasy, construct their own sense of personal gender. The meanings I describe are, finally, articulated in language but, as anyone who has been in therapy or analysis knows, this language often only approximates what feels like inner psychic reality. It is a product of interaction between therapist and patient as they work to create a consensual account of what is initially (and throughout) emotional, partially unconscious, fragmentary, indicated by disconnected thoughts—as they struggle, that is, to render experience that is not necessarily conscious or linguistic into language.

My examples also provide some evidence of the various axes of definition and emotional castings that different individuals may bring to their own gender construction. Even these few examples give some sense of the individuality and variability of people's constructions of gender. They thus both support and challenge contemporary feminism. They document clearly the instability, multiplicity, layering, contradiction, and contestation in constructions of gender but they also document that this unstable, multiple, layered, fragmented, and contested contradictoriness exists in emotional and intrapsychic as well as in cultural, linguistic, or discursive meaning.

My examples are not remarkable or notable: I do not particularly attract or choose patients who experience unusual gender conflict. They do not make a point through their extraordinary uniqueness, beyond the fact that all of our individual psyches, fantasies, fears, and conflicts are extraordinary. In some cases, the preoccupations these women express are central to what we have been working on throughout treatment; in others, they are constructions that are simply noted in passing. Other issues, in which gender is not so salient, are more central for them. My

---

[12] Psychoanalytic feminists besides myself who have sought clinical training include Jessica Benjamin, Muriel Dimen, Jane Flax, Juliet Mitchell, and Elizabeth Young-Bruehl. Psychoanalytic scholars in other fields also increasingly seek out psychoanalytic training.

more extended examples are of contemporary, middle-class, Euro-American women. I also discuss briefly a few women from non-Euro-American cultures. These women are all behaviorally and in terms of conscious identity heterosexual. (Of course, once we explore—especially in the clinical setting, where attention is directed to such matters—any person's unconscious fantasy life and multiple sexual and other identifications, nobody has a single sexual orientation.)[13]

I believe we can see, from just these few examples, how idiosyncratically constructed and emotionally shaped a sense of gendered self is, and how gender can be intertwined with other issues of selfhood and feeling. My restriction of my examples to women who share sociocultural positional attributes makes the case for individual emotional and fantasy construction stronger. My Euro-American patients share, presumably, a Euro-American cultural gender and social organization of gender: they were primarily taken care of by mothers; they saw fathers as dominant and attractive in recognizable Euro-American cultural ways (as exciting, seductive, cuddly, or domineering); they were not explicitly taught that women were inferior and men superior; they could be said developmentally to have followed the Lacanian path from the imaginary mother-child semiotic realm to the phallic-symbolic world of the father. These brief examples are only meant to suggest variation and individuality, and I will not follow the details of change or variation in any one person.[14]

---

[13] I do not have as much clinical experience with lesbian as with heterosexual women, or with non-Euro-American as with Euro-American women. The clinical experience I have had, as well as my reading in the autobiographical and fictional literature and in feminist and gay-lesbian research and theory, leads me to conclude that the processes (though not, I emphasize again, the content) of emotional, fantasy, and self-construction I describe characterize non-Euro-American, nonheterosexual subjectivities as well. My work with heterosexual women always includes investigation of multiple levels of conscious and unconscious sexuality and sense of sexual orientation. My work with Euro-American women has not in the same way problematized their whiteness and its contribution to their sense of gender and sexuality, though aspects of ethnicity do arise (always with the same personal casting that I describe for gendered subjectivity)— e.g., being of Jewish, German, Italian, or New England origin. I do not set the terms of our discussions, and as many writers note, whiteness is for many Americans an unmarked and unnoticed aspect of identity (see Frankenberg 1993). Moraga 1986 provides one of the single best exemplars of an account of a particularized, emotional, fantasy-imbued construction of a sexual, gendered, and racial-ethnic subjectivity that is also constituted culturally. See also Pratt 1984. Erik Erikson is the psychoanalyst who has written most brilliantly and extensively about working clinically with patients' multiplex, partial, and conflicting ethnic, racial, historical, and cultural identities (Erikson 1959; 1964, chap. 3).

[14] My brevity is mainly for reasons of confidentiality. I have also chosen not to give details of family background or particular biographical facts or events for the same reason. Reviewers have wished for more such detail, and as a case reader myself, I can only sympathize with such a desire. The writing of case vignettes is a complicated business, which I cannot sufficiently go into here. Most personalized cases in any event involve fictive constructions of background, family pattern, and profession. Since my point is to

For Ms. A, male-female difference is central to the meaning of gender, and an emotion, anger, is one key to gender construction. In the first part of her analysis, she strives constantly to image me as a father with whom she struggles and to get me to engage in such struggle. She wants to experience a dismissive, condemnatory, accusatory anger toward me that she identifies with her father and with men. Our interaction is experienced in terms of emotional power struggles, struggles that take on gendered undertones. Alternately, they are between man and woman and between man and man.

Ms. A is terrified of her own anger, and she is also fearful of mine. Women's anger, as Ms. A tells it, destroys absolutely. There is no surviving it. Mothers can destroy children, and children can destroy mothers. Ms. A worries that her own rage destroyed her mother and that she might destroy me. If she does so, I will not be there for her. By contrast, men's anger is sudden, violent, and explosive, but when it is all over, you are still there. If Ms. A could be a man, she would not have to fear destroying with anger, and she could still express her considerable rage.

For Ms. A, then, invulnerable anger is one of the main meanings of masculinity. Gender struggles, victory, and defeat animate images of gender difference, and her fantasy particularizes an adolescent daughter's angry struggle with her father. I emphasize the subjective centrality of adolescence here: when we look at individual constructions and animations of gender, different periods may be more or less salient for different people. Stage theories of different varieties draw our attention to potentially important processes for numbers of people, but they do not adequately predict what will be criterial periods in an individual case.[15]

Ms. A also constructs gender around a different male-female polarity and desire to have masculine attributes. Her preoccupations and fantasies

---

show the contribution of emotional tonality and unconscious fantasy to constructions of gender and the individuality of these constructions, I do not think that the absence of biographical specificity is central. I call my patients (I suppose somewhat formally) by their last names, reciprocally, as I am called Dr. Chodorow. I also use the term *patient* rather than *client,* mainly because that is the standard practice of analysts (although I also personally like the significations of care and cure in such a term). Quotations in my case examples have in most cases been taken during an analytic session. When patients are on the couch, I often take notes during a session; when they are sitting up and facing me, I take notes after the session.

[15] I have in mind, for instance, Freudian stage theory and Lacanian theory, which place gender as an oedipal achievement, and currently competing second-year genital phase or rapprochement theories, which argue that feelings about gender and genitals first become significant in the second year (e.g., Roiphe and Galenson 1981; Fast 1984; Benjamin 1988). As far as I am aware, the empirical evidence still suggests that "core gender identity"—the early self-labeling sense that almost everyone develops of being female or male—is an achievement of the second and third year. See Stoller 1968; Money and Ehrhardt 1972. For a recent empirical study that queries the relation between the development of genital self-recognition and gender self-definition, see de Marneffe 1993.

here have origins in latency, and I have found that gender fantasies and feelings are often consolidated during this period. The object-relational origins of these sorts of latency gender fantasies are likely to be in relation to a brother or to (fantasied or perceived) maternal or paternal expectations about a brother in comparison to oneself. In her analysis, we discover a previously unconscious fantasy of being forever young, in fact, a young boy. As friends got married and had children, Ms. A did not compare herself. She realizes that this is because she experiences herself as not grown up and not female. Like Peter Pan, she contemptuously dismissed such practices. Having a child would have destroyed the fantasy of being forever young and a boy (heterosexual intercourse also challenges it).

Being a boy has other advantages: you are in a much less vulnerable position than if you are a grown woman or a little girl. "Part of the secret is being a boy: that changes everything. I'm childless and can't decide to settle down with G because I've chosen not to. It makes it okay to be angry and on edge; that's how boys are. Not only is it okay, but you can't be hurt. A sense that part of myself is male, and powerful. That makes it okay, and there's pride in that, part of my strength. I don't have to be afraid because of that. I'm secretly strong." She remembers exuberant images of power, playing king of the mountain and football with the neighborhood boys. She says, "Boys and men are free; they have more room; they take up more physical space. They don't have to care how they look or dress." Such fantasies serve as a defense against Ms. A's notion (a notion recognized at different times by different women but often prepubertally) that a woman or girl should grow up and fulfill a powerless, dependent feminine role. Not wanting to grow up, imagining not growing up and time not moving on, also connect for Ms. A to specific cultural images that have resonated psychologically, especially Peter Pan but also Tom Sawyer. Ms. A also recalls childhood fantasy identifications with heroic knights who swashbuckled their way to success, rescuing damsels in distress (which she emphatically was not), and she is intrigued with the-boy-dressed-as-a-girl-playing-a-boy parts in plays like *As You Like It* and *Twelfth Night*.

At one time, then, Ms. A's fantasy about gender and power concerns the fantasy of male anger and interpersonal aggression; at another, it concerns comparative strength and the ability to defend oneself. Gender difference also expresses itself in what she sees as boys' and men's ability to not care. In all these cases, central to Ms. A's gender construction is the sense that femininity is vulnerable in a way that masculinity is not. If she is accosted or threatened sexually or physically, she feels, as a female, that she provoked it because of the badness of female anger. But in the fantasy of being a boy or young man, she has no such feelings.

Ms. B often arrives late for her analytic hours, coming straight from meetings with her male employer. She herself has set up these work meetings to occur just before her hours, and she finds them very hard to leave. Despite consciously and intentionally having sought out analysis, she experiences her sessions as an obligation and an unwanted pull away from the excitement of her relationship with her employer. She compares the obligation to her childhood experience, in which she found the weekly good-byes with her father, divorced from her mother, painful and difficult. Many of her hours are preoccupied with issues with her employer. By contrast, I am unnoticed, sometimes dismissed with a perfunctory "Sorry I'm late," but usually just ignored. I feel like—and she confirms that I am—taken for granted background, a maternal nag who can be kept waiting, who wants only to talk about boring, petty issues like lateness, schedules, and phone numbers. Most of the time, Ms. B feels strongly that what she needs is a powerful man, a perfect, idealized man who will rescue her and make her feel wonderful rather than rejecting her as she feels her father did. As she puts it (in unacknowledged identification with and tribute to Patsy Cline), she "falls to pieces" whenever she thinks of an old boyfriend who has rejected her overtures to get back together.

In contrast to her idealized images of her father and of men, her images of her mother and maternal femininity are almost sordid. Her mother, she feels, was weak, unable to care for herself or her children, unable to find good love relationships, unable to keep a nice house. Here Ms. B compares her father with her mother and, alternately, me with her mother. At these moments, I am not petty, a drag, or a doormat, in implicit or explicit contrast to an exciting man. Rather, in contrast to Ms. B's sordid mother, I am seen as good and pure.

The psychological defense Ms. B employs in constructing these conscious and unconscious fantasies of self, other, and gender is splitting. All the good parts of the other go to one person—good father/men versus bad mother/women/me; pure me versus impure mother. Splitting also occurs within the self. Ms. B has, as she tells it, good secret wishes that have to be kept secret, because then they will come true. She has to protect these good wishes both from the bad parts of herself, parts that she identifies with her mother, and from me, because I am a woman and women make things difficult for her. She says, "Recently, my main experiences with women, with my mother, my close friends, are difficult. From childhood, a man could make it all better. Women, my mother, can't give me what I need or long for, to feel desirable."

Yet Ms. B also feels shame and conflict about her dominant gender fantasies. She idealizes masculine rescue or (occasionally) idealizes me; she worries, as she puts it, "that all my positive secrets revolve around men." Putting all the good into men and all the bad into women, when she herself is a woman, leaves her identified with her shameful, sordid mother. Moreover, she has political objections to her fantasies: they are not the kinds of unconscious fantasies or thoughts that women today wish to discover. They are therefore quite hard to recognize and acknowledge. She says, "I resist that idea—how *could* I think that way?" But she then immediately wonders, "Have I ever admired a woman I worked with?"

Ms. B's construction of gender has a unique emotional configuration that differs in emphases from those of Ms. A. Ms. B does not want to be, and she does not fantasize herself as, a man. Rather, she emphatically wants to have a man. Emotionally, cognitively, and in conscious fantasy she emphasizes heterosexual femininity. Ms. B's idealization of men involves how they can rescue her; for Ms. A, men's and boys' seeming self-sufficiency and ability not to care are central. For Ms. B, shame and excitement are emotionally central to gender feelings; for Ms. A, anger becomes a defining criterion of gender. In some particulars, these two cases resemble two of three typical patterns of female development described by Freud (1931). Ms. B resembles the girl who rejects her mother and women and develops heterosexual femininity. She desires men sexually, to give her something the mother did not and could not give. Ms. A resembles the girl who eschews femininity and develops a masculine identification (for Freud, identification with the father). Such an identification may or may not include behavioral lesbian object choice.[16]

For Ms. C, the most salient aspects of gender are even less organized around the male-female polarity. Unlike Ms. A or Ms. B, Ms. C is preoccupied neither with wanting to have the privileges or attributes of a man nor with wanting to have a man sexually. As Freud's classic theory would have it, Ms. C organizes her gender bodily, though not in terms of maleness and femaleness but in terms of the little girl–mother polarity. Ms. C feels herself an inadequate girl with inadequate little genitals, inadequate not in comparison with males who possess a penis but in comparison with grown women with adult genitals and reproductive capacities. Memories of this inadequacy come from both early latency and from early and middle adolescence.

The dominant feeling-tone of shame in Ms. C's experience of her female body extends to and undermines her comparative fantasy, so that this fantasy entails its own negation. In Ms. C's view, grown women's bodies have their own problems. Pregnancy and menstruation, for example, give women cramps; make them weak, sluggish, and heavy; and remind women that they are tied to uncontrollable bodies. Heterosexual relation-

---

[16] Freud describes a third pattern, in which the girl gives up sexuality in general as well as the masculine identifications that might lead to achievement in nonsexual spheres. She becomes generally inhibited in gender, sexuality, and sublimations. For discussion of the multiplicity of women in Freud's writings, see Chodorow 1994.

ships pose a conflictual solution to this shame, one that generates a further quandary. Strong, masculine men can help Ms. C appreciate her feminine body and make her feel successfully feminine, but they also by their presence serve as a reminder of her weakness and the general shamefulness and weakness of femininity. However, if she chooses men whom she perceives as not so masculine, so that she is not so reminded of her own weakness, Ms. C feels inadequate as a heterosexual feminine woman—in its own way shameful. A further quandary comes with her being a feminist. As Ms. C puts it, "I hate to think that women are weak."

For Ms. C, gender as a male-female polarity and feminine inadequacy vis-à-vis men are not as intensely experienced as the little girl–grown woman dichotomy. When these do enter into her fantasy and feelings, they center more on work than on body or sexuality. Being a woman gets tied up with being unable to compete in the work world: "You're too weak, not tough enough to be in that world. Dependent." Work functions, covertly, as a locus for overcoming femininity. Ms. C wants to be "king of the hill," "top man on the totem pole," receiving acknowledgment and recognition as a man, from men, or as a nongendered person (implicitly male) from other nongendered people. But this in turn becomes tricky because wanting recognition is a kind of dependence, and hence feminine, weak, and gendered.

Because of the fantasy and fear that grown women, tied to their female bodies, are weak and that work success is masculine, competent women are somewhat of an oxymoron. She describes a business meeting with a group of women and how impressed she was with their competence: "It wasn't a kill-or-be-killed model of interaction, but I'm not committed to it. I'm stuck in the kill-or-be-killed model. I didn't know how to behave in that setting. I'm more comfortable in the other—what I gloss as men, but it's not only men. I know how to handle myself in situations with lots of direct challenges to ideas. It doesn't make me happy, but it's involving. I feel prevented from fitting into a more flattened landscape, one without hierarchy. If it's not up or down, on the way up or on the way down, struggling against being put down, I'll disappear."

There is no emotional or cognitive space in Ms. C's view for being competent, nonhierarchical, and a woman. Her own professional aspirations and ways of thinking and preferring to interact are, in her view, masculine. She does not know how to act otherwise, but such aspirations still create conflicts. She experiences, and gets pleasure in experiencing, work in the kill-or-be-killed model, but she also does not like it, morally or politically. Moreover, the pleasure is conflictual and shameful. And there is always the fear that she will be found out. She will be found to be not a man but a woman—even worse, not a woman but a little girl, an inadequate woman.

Ms. D expresses still another construction of gender, another feeling-tone and object of desire. She wants mother, not father; breast, not penis; nurturance, not protective rescue or autonomy. For Ms. D, being a woman and being with women elicit thoughts of her mother and feelings of being left out. She experiences a kind of sad neediness thinking of women's relationships with men. She feels that men have a special ability to bind women to them that women do not have, or that she does not have. With women friends, she feels a pervasive sense of wanting more and being angry and sad at not getting it. The problem of being a woman is that, to women, you are not unique. Ms. D imagines that for me, my women patients are all alike. They all get arbitrary, inconsistent attention, whereas my men patients are unique and prized. She feels excluded and hopeless. So there is jealousy of men because women favor them and of other women, who she assumes get the same indifferent attention and nonattention from mother/women that she does.

I do not believe that the tonality of this "left-outness" and jealousy is usefully considered oedipal (or "negative-oedipal"—for a girl, wanting mother and wanting to get rid of father) or pre-oedipal (presuming a two-person relationship). The fantasy is triadic, involving mother and father and images of sexuality, but it fuses breast wishes, greed, neediness, feeling empty, feeling interchangeable with other women (interchangeable for women, not for men, whose desires are not relevant here), and a sense that feeding and filling are what women give to men. In this construction of gender, male-female differences are emotionally intertwined with and imaged in terms of sibling concerns. Feelings of empty, needy sadness range across Ms. D's life and are central to her personal animations and evocations of gender. Clearly, a Kleinian understanding, organized around the breast rather than the penis as central to gender difference and the projected and introjected goodness/plenitude and badness/destructiveness of the breast and self, makes much more sense of Ms. D's psychology in general and her sense of gender in particular than a classically Freudian understanding.[17]

We can see many contributing factors in the sense of personal gender in these four examples. For all four of these women, part of the meaning of gender involves feelings and fantasies about the parent of either gender and their relationship to him or her. Feelings about and relationships with other family members may also figure here. These meanings go beyond explicit and implicit gender messages and the labeled gender of the par-

[17] Klein's suggestive writings on gender have, unfortunately, not been elaborated upon by her followers (see Klein [1928] 1975a, [1945] 1975b, [1957] 1975c). Modern Kleinians have taken investigation of the oedipus complex in directions that do not attend to or problematize gender but instead look at the generalized child in relation to the (heterosexual) parental couple (see, e.g., Britton 1992).

ent. They center on immediate feelings and the particular way these feelings animate the sense of relationship to the parent. If a mother seems depressed or ineffectual, this tonality lends partial meaning to femininity (in its many aspects—sexuality, maternality, sense of self, competence, and so forth) and to conscious and unconscious senses of and fantasies about womanliness. If a father is experienced as domineering, warm and cuddly, exciting but absent, gender meanings develop accordingly. I do not mean to imply here that the sense of gender comes directly from the parent who has that gender label. My emphasis is on the fact that any label (man, woman, mother, father, sister, brother, feminine, masculine) gains meaning not just from language, once learned, but from personally experienced emotion and fantasy in association with that person.[18]

Emotions contribute to personal gender. Global affects like anxiety or depression may invest gender, as may more defined emotions like envy, rage, anger, shame, or disgust. Feelings about anatomy and body adequacy may or may not link to these feelings. As I note earlier, for Ms. A, anger and her father's anger describe gender: neither shame, guilt, nor sexual anatomy seem salient. Another patient notes that her anger at her mother and preference for her father, while they may have helped her achieve professional success, weakened and destroyed her mother. Another observes and resents her mother's flirtatiousness: her mother even flirts with this woman's own boyfriends, making her feel dumpy, inadequate, and furious.

Shame and guilt, in my experience, often seem central to women's feelings and fantasies about mother, self, and gender. For Ms. C, shame about her inadequate female body in comparison to that of her mother affects gendered subjectivity. Ms. B finds shame about her mother's rundown house, inability to hold down a job, and unattractive boyfriends much more accessible than guilt toward her mother. For her, female sexuality—especially maternal sexuality—is desperate and shameful. Ms. B does not fantasize, as do some other women, that she can protect her mother and does not express a perception of her mother's entrapment (whether of her own psychological making or the making of a sexist

[18] As with the question of behavioral and self-identified sexual orientation in relation to the psychodynamics of sexual desire, the question of "cross-gender" labels is tricky. We can certainly claim that some daughters and sons experience their father's femininity or their mother's masculinity. But this experiencing can take many forms. It can involve the affective communication of unconscious parental cross-identifications or fantasies or, alternatively, of unconscious parental cross-labeling of, experiencing of, or fantasies about the child. It can involve a more conscious or preconscious filial sense that some parental behavior crosses gender—say, a marine sergeant mother, a cross-dressing father, a father who does infant care, two lesbian mothers who follow a traditional gender pattern of homemaker and breadwinner. Children may also infer that others—teachers, neighbors, grandparents, clinicians, journalists—believe that a particular parent's personality, behavior, role in the family, or sense of self crosses gender.

culture). She expresses only repudiation and horror. By contrast, other patients, of both divorced and married parents, feel guilt more than shame toward their mothers—guilt for leaving home, for being professionally successful, for surviving their mothers, for having, in their view, harmed them.

My impression is that we can see this form of guilt particularly clearly in some non-Euro-American women who have grown up in classically patriarchal families, in a behavior I think of as "weeping for the mother." I borrow the term *classic patriarchy* from Denise Kandiyoti (1988), who uses it to describe societies like those of North Africa, the Muslim Middle East, China, and India that have explicit, ideologically valued, religiously underpinned, father-dominant kinship systems, usually accompanied by female purdah, veiling, or other forms of exclusion and restriction of females. If we refer in particular to a culturally and religiously transmitted belief that marriage as an institution should be totally husband-controlled and to the explicit teaching and modeling of female subservience, my own classification of classic patriarchies might include other Mediterranean peasant societies and Latino cultures as well. From the psychodynamic point of view of the daughter, this situation contrasts with the Euro-American cases I have discussed earlier, in which daughters do not make central to their family accounts an explicitly differential valuation of men and women or an observation of maternal subservience.[19]

Ms. R cannot stop crying when she thinks of her mother. Her mother was always sad and seemingly helpless, dependent on a patriarchal, angry husband who ordered her around. She images her mother at home alone, dutifully cooking meals, waiting for her husband, crying. Ms. R's physical pleasures and independent activities, like walking at night, seeing movies on her own, cooking treats and desserts just for herself, and having lovers, always remind her that her mother could not go out alone, had to cook regular meals, had no lovers before or since her marriage, and probably has had at most a marginally satisfying sex life with her husband. Ms. R herself feels sad and helpless that she cannot help her sad and helpless mother.

Ms. R's conscious construction of gender includes a strong feminism and anger at male privilege and societal sexism. She understands her feminism to be a result of growing up in an ideologically male-dominant family that explicitly valued her brothers over herself and her sisters. She wanted a feminist analyst who recognized male dominance in society and

---

[19] On Latino cultures, see Espín 1984; Alarcón 1985; and Moraga 1986. Oliva Espín and Cherrié Moraga describe the direct teaching of male superiority and female inferiority and the psychological effects of this on daughters in Latino and Chicano culture. Norma Alarcón and Moraga also describe a kind of sadness that I would relate to what I am calling weeping for the mother, though Moraga's sadness, like that of Ms. S whom I describe below, is more mitigated by anger than the sadness described by Alarcón.

culture and who would see that Ms. R's problems were caused by this male dominance. This shared belief was meant to be exempt from psychological exploration. More particularly, Ms. R expected that a feminist analyst would not blame her mother for being passive and subservient but would understand her mother's inescapable helplessness in the face of a marital role and relationship she hated. A feminist would not pathologize Ms. R's mother's own weeping.

But weeping for her mother and feeling sad and guilty about her interferes with Ms. R's own freedom. Accordingly, Ms. R also finds herself worrying that having chosen an analyst who (in her view) would be sympathetic to her mother might mean that this analyst might not fully accept Ms. R's own want and needs. "I go back and forth," she says. "Children have intense needs, but it isn't my mother's fault." She is caught in a conflictual personal dilemma: how can she not feel guilty and sad toward her mother, free herself from her mother and have her own life, while not blaming but understanding her mother, who was the agent (through maternal teaching and through modeling) of so much of her daughter-self's sense of female inferiority?

Ms. S, from a similar family and different classically patriarchal culture, feels sad for her mother's entrapment in a marriage with a dominating husband who controls everything. Like Ms. R, Ms. S mitigates her feelings somewhat by strong anger at her mother's situation. Unlike Ms. R, she also mitigates her feelings of sadness and anger by identifying, albeit at the cost of conflict and guilt, with the men in her family who dominate. Her substantial achievements are part of this flight to masculine identifications, but she hopes at the same time that her accomplishments will rebound back on her mother and give her mother as well as herself strength. She weeps for herself as well as for her mother, recognizing her own dependence upon and search for confirmation from men.

Ms. T, another daughter from a classically patriarchal family, cries like her mother cried, is miserable like her mother was miserable. She does not know why her mother cried or why she herself has to. Ms. T's mother and grandmother told sad, sad stories of their lives. Ms. T's grandmother was sent away to school at a young age; her life, as she told her granddaughter, was very sad. According to Ms. T, this sadness was passed on to her daughter, and this daughter, Ms. T's mother, in turn wept at everything. She wept for her mother and for her father, the latter who died when Ms. T was three. Thirty years later, Ms. T cannot stop crying about her grandmother's life and her grandfather's death. Ms. T's mother wanted her daughter to listen to her sad feelings all the time; in turn, Ms. T wants her husband and me to listen all the time to her own sad feelings.

By contrast, as she sees it, Ms. T's father was always cheerful, the life of the party. She eventually acknowledges what she has denied, that if things did not go the way he wanted, her father got controlling and furious. He did not want to hear personal problems. She also reluctantly acknowledges that her mother was always busy managing a house, household help, several children, and taking care of her own mother. But these acknowledgments are easily reburied, as Ms. T returns to the image of her exciting father planning excursions and playing with her in the water, being the energy of the family, and of her mother, crying about her unhappy life and the unhappy life of her mother.

The intrapsychic experience of the relationship to the mother, observation of her, comparison of her to father or to other women or mother figures, seems an important ingredient in cultural and personal gender. I focus more (but not exclusively) on this relationship in this article because it is one I have thought much about, not because, as I reiterate above, it has universal or exclusive preeminence in animating gendered subjectivity. Even these few case examples show the contribution emotion and fantasy make to gender meaning and document difference and multiplicity in how such meaning is constructed. Mother-daughter relationships and the unconscious fantasy and emotional constructions and symbolizations of the self and mother are not all alike, interpersonally or intrapsychically. As I note elsewhere (1994, 85), the relation to the mother can come to symbolize nurturance or its rejection, intimacy or fear of intimacy, guilt at independence or resentment at dependence, passivity or activity, aggression or submission, attraction to or fear of female genitality or anatomy, and many other issues. These emotional animations can link to cultural gender in many ways, through images of wifehood or motherhood, through fantasies about giving and the breast, through images of domination and submission or of purity and impurity. These are some aspects of the relationship that tend to be psychologically symbolized, accorded emotional meaning, entered into self-construction, fantasy, and the sense of gender, but there is no single way in which they are worked out for all or most women in contrast to all or most men, or for the women or men of a particular racial-ethnic or class group, or for women or men of particular sexual identities.

Nor does *oedipal* or *pre-oedipal* do justice to the overwhelming power of and individual variation within different daughters' (and sons') guilts, rages, feelings of loyalty and disloyalty, wishes to protect and repair, or sexual desires for their mother or father or to their relation to these parents and the way these relationships affect their sense of gendered self. Several of my patients, for instance, fear that if they have their own lives, make their own choices, or act on their own desires, they will destroy their mothers, but this is one element in an otherwise individually constructed psyche and its fantasy content as well as dominant feeling-tone—anxiety, depression, anger, guilt, shame, sadness, loss, fear of falling apart—varies.

I could make the same case about the contingent cultural and personal meaning of the father and the relation to him and about men's constructions of gender, as well. For all the women I have worked with (I offer here an empirical observation, not a universal claim), perceived paternal power and paternal appreciation were important contributions to sense of self and gender, but the nature of this contribution varied. For Ms. B and Ms. T, a feminine idealization of men seems to grow directly out of fantasies about their fathers; men's reported domineering behavior pales before their excitement and seductiveness (both felt and hoped for). Ms. A and Ms. R instead rage at men's self-absorption, self-righteousness, and sexism. They are quite comfortable excoriating their fathers' claims to masculinity, aggression, and overcontrol, whereas it is a pain more than they can bear to acknowledge any sense of maternal failure or limitation. By contrast, Ms. B, Ms. C, and even Ms. T find it easy to criticize mothers, whom they seem to feel certain have the strength to survive their onslaught, whereas they protect and ignore paternal inadequacy and weakness. We find women who image furious, rejecting fathers, whirlwinds of power and anger, and others who see fathers as rejecting their efforts to become strong and powerful. Some fathers seem to ignore their daughters' existence; others seduce and excite. There are fathers who disappoint, fathers whose enthusiasm for a latency-age stamp collector or doll player fades as a daughter becomes pubescent, and fathers who become overattentive as womanly curves develop.

The meanings I have focused on differentiate individual women and characterize each woman's prevalent animation of gender. For some women (Ms. A, Ms. C in her work identity, Ms. R, and Ms. S), being female contrasts with being male—a man or boy. For others (Ms. B and Ms. T), it evokes a desperate, driven hunger for men. For some (Ms. D, Ms. R, Ms. S, and Ms. T), it signifies a mother who weeps or a mother who is yearningly longed for; for others (Ms. C) it contrasts being an adult woman with being a little girl. But gendered meanings can also be differently animated at different times, involved with different conscious and unconscious fantasies, tinged by varying moods, and affected alternately by guilt, fear, desire, and rage. A single identification or relationship, a particular sexual imaging (mother-daughter, father-daughter, penis, breasts, femaleness, maleness) can thus carry a variety of relational themes, a number of fantasized, evoked, memorialized experiences. One day breasts (one's own or one's mother's) are the topic of discussion; the next day fantasies about pregnancy surface; the day after that, thoughts and feelings about vaginas emerge; the fourth day, fantasies about a brother's penis come to mind. Emotional, fantasy, and projective animation affect anatomical perceptions as well, generating a variety of symbolizations and fantasy constructions. Within, say, fantasies about anatomical male in relation to female, at one moment father versus mother may be significant, at another penis versus vagina, at another penis versus no penis, at another breasts versus no breasts. But sometimes in imaging anatomy, small versus big are the criterial differences: young girl versus woman, or young boy versus man; no breasts versus big breasts, little penis versus big penis, hairless pubic area versus pubis covered with hair, young boy with small penis versus large mother with breasts. These gendered meanings do not necessarily oppose masculine and feminine: the differences that can go into gendered meaning creation are u. ending and can themselves shift for any individual moment by moment.

The fluidity and changeability of emotionally cast transferences in clinical experience make clear the specificity of any person's gendered subjectivity. Gender transferences, fantasies, and preoccupations and the emotional tonalities that accompany these vary for people over the life cycle, day by day and (as clinicians will know) in the course of treatment or even within any particular clinical hour. At one moment in an hour, an early experience of incest may be prominent, at another attachment to the mother, at another idealization of the father. The clinical encounter demonstrates the moment-to-moment shifting and developing of gender and its varying salience, complexity, and multiplicity as different elements in the gendered sense of self become important (and as gender itself is more or less salient in a current moment or period of transference). Now the controlling, intrusive mother is central in the creation of gender, now the dominant father, now the excited little girl, now the one humiliated by her excitement. Now the swaggering little boy expresses himself, now the fearful one, now the boy excited by his triumphant possession of mother, now the boy afraid of engulfment or longing for his father. Clinical work demonstrates how all elements of existence—anatomy, cultural meanings, individual family, economic and political conditions, class, race, socialization practices, the impact of parental personality—are refracted and constructed through the projections and introjections and fantasy creations that give them psychological meaning.

One theme that intersects with all these clinical examples and has been central to the feminist appropriation and critique of psychology is that all the women I discuss reflect some psychological preoccupation with some aspect of gender inequality within the gendered subjectivity that they animate and construct. A person's personally animating masculinity and femininity, developing an emotionally and fantasy-imbued gender identity, includes, among other elements, animating not just difference but differential value and power. Often but not always, these contrasts note male dominance, privilege, or superiority.[20] As these meanings are con-

---

[20] See Stein 1995 for a particularly interesting case discussion of a man who emphatically experienced his mother and women as dominant, privileged, and superior.

structed and reconstructed in personal gender, however, they are en-
tangled with the specifics of individual emotion and fantasy, with aspects
of self, with imaging of particular families, and in particular cultural
contexts. The prevalent psychological intertwining of sexuality, gender,
inequality, and power, all saturated with introjective and projective
meaning, demonstrates why a cultural as well as a clinical stance are
necessities for psychoanalysts. Likewise, the personal resonance of these
intertwinings explains why a cultural stance alone is not enough.

All of the gender identifications and fantasies I describe are both cul-
tural and personal. A social or cultural critic could claim (and would be
partially right) that you do not need a psychology to explain many of
these images, fantasies, and gender constructions. It is well documented
that men have more power, can express anger, take up more space, and
are catered to by women. It is culturally mandated that women be pas-
sive. Women are expected to give in to and give up to men and do not give
to their daughters as they give to their sons and husbands. The views
about these matters expressed by my patients come from their particular
families and from culture in general, and we should not minimize this
culturally instigated inflection of the meanings of masculinity and femi-
ninity. It is "realistic" to have these beliefs and thoughts; they are a good
analysis of a sexist society. We are less likely to find them gender-reversed
either in reconstructions or in transferences (but see Stein 1995). Assess-
ment of the cultural and social setting is also part of my patients' ap-
praisals of and feelings about their situations.[21]

In these accounts we recognize familiar social as well as cultural
patterns—for example, a divorce, an elusive father, and a rejected little
girl who thinks everything will be all right if Daddy rescues her. We could
consider her, as she considers herself, a victim determined by family
circumstances and gender inequality. Some observers or critics might ask,
as she does, how you can have an image of a rich, vibrant, fertile mother
when mother has been a victim of the feminization of poverty. Similarly,
in a culture that valorizes exciting masculinity—not with stories like
Peter Pan and *As You Like It* but with *Cinderella, Sleeping Beauty,* and
gothic romances—it might be expected that girls and women would
idealize men and devalue women.

But an explanation in terms of cultural values or meanings is not the
whole, and this is why we are always walking a fine line in combining
cultural and personal understanding. The existence of cultural and social
gender inequality does not explain the range of fantasy interpretations
and varieties of emotional castings women bring to this inequality. We
have only to look at the number of accounts by daughters of vibrant,

---

[21] For an especially powerful account of the impact of differential valuation on girls'
emotional and fantasied sense of gendered self and sexuality, see Benjamin 1988, 1991.

creative mothers who were extremely poor and oppressed to understand that the feminization of poverty is not an adequate explanation for a sense of powerless and female neediness.[22] My patients feel miserable, anxious, and conflicted about their thoughts about gender and gender inequality, one about her hidden fantasy of being a powerful male and coveting what she sees as male powers, another about her sad desires for maternal nurturance, another about her scorn of noncompetitive women, another about her desperate need for men, another about rage at paternal dominance and sadness about her mother, another about sadness at paternal absence. Their warding off and protection of these unconscious fantasies has kept them from living as they wish—from having fulfilling relationships and from moving ahead professionally when such professional achievements interfere with a fantasy of being a boy, with feeling needy and dependent, with a sense that professional participation threatens sexual shame. A belief that men can be angry, temperamental, or demanding and that women or mothers are powerless is both a social analysis and a powerful motivator of guilt and inhibition, of a need to repair and not to move ahead of mother. Guilt and sadness about mother are particularly prevalent female preoccupations and as likely to limit female autonomy, pleasure, and achievement as any cultural mandate. This is so even if the conditions under which female autonomy, pleasure, and achievement tend to involve surpassing mother are a product of unequal gender arrangements and beliefs. Similarly, women's shame vis-à-vis men, whether of dependence or of discovery in masculine pursuits, is certainly situated in a cultural context in which such pursuits are coded as masculine in the first place. But this shame is also experienced in itself, inflected with many unconscious fantasies that often stem from a time in development well before such coding could be known. It is a conflict in itself, and it inflects the general sense of self and gender as well as interacting with specific cultural expectations and meanings.

I suggest, then, that gender is an ongoing emotional creation and intrapsychic interpretation, of cultural meanings and of bodily, emotional, and self-other experience, all mediated by conscious and uncon-

[22] I note Collins's claim above: "The existence of Afrocentric feminist thought suggests that there is always choice, and power to act, no matter how bleak the situation may be" (1990, 237). As Collins puts it, "Human ties can be freeing and empowering, as is the case with Black women's heterosexual love relationships or in the power of motherhood in African-American families and communities. Human ties can also be confining and oppressive. . . . The same situation can look quite different depending on the consciousness one brings to interpret it" (227). As a black feminist and black woman, Collins represents (and describes, in her chapters on sexual politics, on African-American motherhood as experience, and on the cultural and political images derived from African-American mothers) some of the most powerful accounts we can find of female strength, power, and vibrant fertility in the face of sexual exploitation, racism, poverty, single motherhood, and heterosexual domination. See also Walker 1977.

scious fantasy. We cannot capture this emotional, unconscious fantasy meaning either in terms of cultural gender meanings, as feminists have tended to do, or in terms of monolithic claims about genital structure or function or pre-oedipal and oedipal developmental patterns, which has been the characteristic psychoanalytic pattern. (I myself have done both.) The focus of the psychoanalyst or psychologist on intrapsychic or psychological elements, as if these can be contrasted with or considered apart from the external world and culture, and the feminist theorist's focus on discursive or cultural processes and patterns both miss a large part of what goes to constitute gender.

Anyone's emotionally and linguistically constructed gender, the personally animated gendered self and world she inhabits, is a continuously invoked and reshaped project involving self, identity, body imagery, sexual fantasy, images and fantasies about parents, cultural stories, and unconscious and conscious fantasies about intimacy, dependency, and nurturance. The particular sense of self and relationship and the particular relation to and fantasies about the body, arising in the individual family in which someone grows up and giving any individual's gender a unique feeling and fantasy animation, are especially discoverable in clinical work. Such fantasies and emotions are also familiar to us from biography, autobiography, and fiction. My examples reflect, indicate, and build upon historically situated, cultural, discursive constructions of gender. But none of the women I discuss simply entered the realm of the symbolic or placed herself within a cultural discourse or unequal society or polity. From birth to the present, all have intensely imbued or constructed their gender with individual feelings—of anger, envy, guilt, resentment, shame, wistful desire, rageful entitlement, sadness, jealousy, horror, disgust—and with characteristic defensive patterns—of denial, splitting, projection, repression. This personal casting and emotional tonality pervade any person's sense of gender. All aspects of a particular person's psychological makeup—prevalent defenses, unconscious fantasies—give a unique feeling animation to gendered subjectivity.

As feminists, we have fine-tuned theories of discursive, cultural, and political gender that are sensitive to historical, class, racial, or ethnic specificity or positionality and cognizant of the contingent, contradictory, fragmentary, or ambiguous character of enactments and constructions of gender. But these cannot, finally, reveal to us how gender is constructed—what culturally situated discursive meanings are for a particular person who experiences or constructs gendered meanings or a gender identity. The complex, contradictory, specific, changing construction of personal gender through unconscious fantasy and emotional shaping—which we can see particularly clearly under the light of clinical illumination in the transference process—constitutes gender for any individual.

My argument, then, is an empirically derived one. Based on my reading of psychoanalytic theory and my clinical experience, I argue that feminist theory should once again fully take psychology seriously. The capacities and processes for the creation of personal meaning that psychoanalysis describes contribute to gendered subjectivity as do cultural categories and the enactment or creation of social or cultural roles. But both psychoanalysis and feminism are also projects directed toward transformative change. An understanding of the contribution of personal meaning to gendered subjectivity, I believe, better fosters goals of transformations in subjectivity and consciousness that psychoanalysis and feminism share.

Department of Sociology
University of California, Berkeley

References

Abel, Elizabeth. 1990. "Race, Class, and Psychoanalysis? Opening Questions." In *Conflicts in Feminism,* ed. Marianne Hirsch and Evelyn Fox Keller, 184–204. London and New York: Routledge.

Alarcón, Norma. 1985. "What Kind of a Lover Have You Made Me, Mother: Towards a Theory of Chicanas' Feminism and Cultural Identity through Poetry." In *Perspectives on Feminism and Identity in Women of Color,* ed. Audrey T. McCluskey, 85–110. Bloomington: Indiana University Press.

Anderson, Robin, ed. 1992. *Clinical Lectures on Klein and Bion.* London and New York: Tavistock/Routledge.

Arlow, Jacob A. 1969. "Unconscious Fantasy and Disturbances of Conscious Experience." *Psychoanalytic Quarterly* 38:1–27.

Belenky, Mary Field, Blythe McVicker Clinchy, Nancy Rule Goldberger, and Jill Mattuck Tarule. 1986. *Women's Ways of Knowing: The Development of Self, Voice, and Mind.* New York: Basic.

Benjamin, Jessica. 1988. *The Bonds of Love: Psychoanalysis, Feminism, and the Problem of Domination.* New York: Pantheon.

———. 1991. "Father and Daughter: Identification with Difference—a Contribution to Gender Heterodoxy." *Psychoanalytic Dialogues* 1:277–99.

Bloch, Ruth H. 1993. "A Culturalist Critique of Trends in Feminist Theory." *Contention* 2:79–106.

Britton, Ronald. 1992. "The Oedipus Situation and the Depressive Position." In Anderson 1992, 34–45.

Brown, Lyn Mikel, and Carol Gilligan. 1992. *Meeting at the Crossroads: Women's Psychology and Girls' Development.* Cambridge, Mass.: Harvard University Press.

Chasseguet-Smirgel, Janine. 1985. *Creativity and Perversion.* London: Free Association Books.

———. 1986. *Sexuality and Mind.* New York: New York University Press.

Chodorow, Nancy J. 1978. *The Reproduction of Mothering: Psychoanalysis and the Sociology of Gender.* Berkeley: University of California Press.

———. 1989. *Feminism and Psychoanalytic Theory.* New Haven, Conn.: Yale University Press; Cambridge: Polity.

———. 1994. *Femininities, Masculinities, Sexualities: Freud and Beyond.* Lexington: University Press of Kentucky; London: Free Association Books.

Collins, Patricia Hill. 1990. *Black Feminist Thought: Knowledge, Consciousness, and the Politics of Empowerment.* New York and London: Routledge.

de Marneffe, Daphne. 1993. "Toddlers' Understandings of Gender." Ph.D. dissertation, University of California, Berkeley.

Dimen, Muriel. 1991. "Deconstructing Difference: Gender, Splitting and 'Transitional Space.' " *Psychoanalytic Dialogues* 1:335–52.

Erikson, Erik. 1959. *Identity and the Life Cycle.* New York: International Universities Press.

———. 1964. *Insight and Responsibility.* New York: Norton.

Espín, Oliva. 1984. "Cultural and Historical Influences on Sexuality in Hispanic/ Latin Women: Implications for Psychotherapy." In *Pleasure and Danger: Exploring Female Sexuality,* ed. Carol Vance, 149–64. New York: Monthly Review Press.

Fast, Irene. 1984. *Gender Identity: A Differentiation Model.* Hillsdale, N.J.: Lawrence Erlbaum.

Frankenberg, Ruth. 1993. *White Women, Race Matters: The Social Construction of Whiteness.* Minneapolis: University of Minnesota Press.

Freud, Sigmund. 1931. "Female Sexuality." In *The Standard Edition of the Complete Psychological Works,* 21:225–43. London: Hogarth.

Frye, Marilyn. 1990. "The Possibility of Feminist Theory." In *Theoretical Perspectives on Sexual Difference,* ed. Deborah Rhode, 174–84. New Haven, Conn.: Yale University Press.

Gilligan, Carol. 1982. *In a Different Voice: Psychological Theory and Women's Development.* Cambridge, Mass.: Harvard University Press.

Gilligan, Carol, Annie Rogers, and Deborah Tolman. 1991. *Women, Girls, and Psychotherapy: Reframing Resistance.* Binghamton, N.Y.: Haworth.

Goldner, Virginia. 1991. "Toward a Critical Relational Theory of Gender." *Psychoanalytic Dialogues* 1:249–72.

Harris, Adrienne. 1991. "Gender as Contradiction." *Psychoanalytic Dialogues* 1:197–224.

Hochschild, Arlie. 1989. *The Second Shift.* New York: Viking.

Irigaray, Luce. 1985. *This Sex Which Is Not One.* Ithaca, N.Y.: Cornell University Press.

Jordan, Judith, Alexandra Kaplan, Jean Baker Miller, Irene Stiver, and Janet Surrey. 1991. *Women's Growth in Relation.* New York: Guilford.

Kandiyoti, Denise. 1988. "Bargaining with Patriarchy." *Gender and Society* 2:274–90.

Kestenberg, Judith. 1968. "Outside and Inside, Male and Female." *Journal of the American Psychoanalytic Association* 16:457–520.

———. 1980. "The Inner-Genital Phase." In *Early Feminine Development: Contemporary Psychoanalytic Views,* ed. David Mendel. New York: Spectrum.

Klein, Melanie. (1928) 1975a. "Early Stages of the Oedipus Conflict." In Klein 1975b, 186–98.

——— . (1945) 1975b. "The Oedipus Complex in the Light of Early Anxieties." In Klein 1975b, 370–419.

——— . (1957) 1975c. "Envy and Gratitude." In Klein 1975a, 176–235.

——— . 1975d. *Envy and Gratitude and Other Works, 1946–1963.* New York: Delta.

——— . 1975e. *Love, Guilt and Reparation and Other Works, 1921–1945.* New York: Delta.

Lacan, Jacques. 1982. *Feminine Sexuality,* ed. Juliet Mitchell and Jacqueline Rose. New York: Norton.

Loewald, Hans. 1980. *Papers on Psychoanalysis.* New Haven, Conn.: Yale University Press.

Mahoney, Maureen, and Barbara Yngvesson. 1992. "The Construction of Subjectivity and the Paradox of Resistance: Reintegrating Feminist Anthropology and Psychology." *Signs: Journal of Women in Culture and Society* 18:44–73.

Martin, Jane Roland. 1994. "Methodological Essentialism, False Difference, and Other Dangerous Traps." *Signs* 19:630–57.

Mayer, Elizabeth Lloyd. 1985. " 'Everybody Must Be Just Like Me': Observations on Female Castration Anxiety." *International Journal of Psycho-Analysis* 66:331–47.

Mc Dougall, Joyce. 1986. *Theatres of the Mind: Illusion and Truth on the Psychoanalytic Stage.* London: Free Association Books.

Money, John, and Anke A. Ehrhardt. 1972. *Man and Woman, Boy and Girl.* Baltimore: Johns Hopkins University Press.

Moraga, Cherrié. 1986. "From a Long Line of Vendidas: Chicanas and Feminism." In *Feminist Studies/Critical Studies,* ed. Teresa de Lauretis, 173–90. Madison: University of Wisconsin Press.

Pratt, Minnie Bruce. 1984. "Identity: Skin, Blood, Heart." In *Yours in Struggle: Three Feminist Perspectives on Anti-Semitism and Racism,* ed. Elly Bulkin, Minnie Bruce Pratt, and Barbara Smith, 9–63. Brooklyn, N.Y.: Long Haul.

Roiphe, Herman, and Eleanor Galenson. 1981. *Infantile Origins of Sexual Identity.* New York: International Universities Press.

Spillius, Elizabeth Bott, ed. 1988. *Melanie Klein Today: Developments in Theory and Practice,* vols. 1, 2. London and New York: Routledge.

Stein, Ruth. 1995. "Analysis of a Case of Transsexualism." *Psychoanalytic Dialogues,* vol. 5.

Stern, Daniel N. 1985. *The Interpersonal World of the Infant.* New York: Basic.

Stoller, Robert. 1968. *Sex and Gender,* vol. 1. New York: Science House.

Walker, Alice. 1977. "In Search of Our Mothers' Gardens." In *Working It Out,* ed. Sara Ruddick and Pamela Daniels, 93–102. New York: Pantheon.

Winnicott, D. W. 1958. *Collected Papers: Through Paediatrics to Psycho-Analysis.* London: Tavistock.

——— . 1965. *The Maturational Processes and the Facilitating Environment.* New York: International Universities Press.

——— . 1971. *Playing and Reality.* New York: Basic.

——— . 1989. *Psycho-Analytic Explorations.* Cambridge, Mass.: Harvard University Press.

The Construction of Subjectivity and the Paradox of Resistance: Reintegrating Feminist Anthropology and Psychology

Maureen A. Mahoney and Barbara Yngvesson

F EMINIST THEORY and women's history have long grappled with the problem of documenting women's position as victims of their culturally constructed subordinate status while also celebrating women's strength and creativity in resisting that subordination. Indeed, accounts of the history of any subordinated group raise the same dual issue; a case in point is Herbert Gutman's account (1977) of black historiography as a history first of what was done for slaves, then to slaves, and ultimately by slaves.[1] That subordinates have resisted relations of domination is clear. Explanations of such resistance are unsatisfying, however, because they emphasize the force of political economy and dominant cultural discourses and shy away from theorizing about the way relationships of power (whether based on class, gender, or legal entitlement) are constructed psychologically and reproduced through everyday practice. Without an account of how subjects experience these relationships of power, we cannot explain what impels them to

This article is the result of many years of collaboration and would not have been possible without the interest and support of many colleagues. The idea for it emerged from a jointly taught course that combined theory in anthropology and psychology to address problems in the construction of gender. Subsequently, a faculty development grant from Hampshire College allowed us to carry out the research and initial drafting of a paper that was circulated to faculty in the feminist studies program at the college and then presented at a faculty seminar. A later version of the paper was presented in May 1991, at the biannual meeting of the Western Association of Women Historians. We especially want to thank Jessica Benjamin, Margaret Cerullo, Jane Collier, Betty Farrell, Penina Glazer, Dirk Hartog, Nina Payne, Miriam Slater, Steve Weisler, and Alice Wexler, as well as the reviewers of the manuscript for *Signs,* for their helpful comments on earlier drafts. Jeanne Barker-Nunn, our editor at *Signs,* made extremely helpful suggestions for our preparation of the final manuscript.
    [1] See also Willis 1981; Craton 1982; Comaroff 1985; Scott 1985; Gordon 1988.

[*Signs: Journal of Women in Culture and Society* 1992, vol. 18, no. 1]

resist domination and to make change. For this we require an under-
standing of motivation and the processes by which subjects come to want
to conform or resist.

This article focuses upon the issue of motivation and presents a theory
of active subjects who participate in the construction of the wants and
needs that culture enjoins them to desire or to resist.[2] In developing this
account, we suggest that current Lacanian-derived psychological expla-
nations of subjectivity constituted by contradictory identities, although
promising, are inadequate to explain resistance because they describe a
fundamentally asocial subject and thus miss the crucial relational ground
for the subject's experience of such contradictions. By contrast, anthro-
pological theory's emphasis upon the social production of meaning and
subjective interests misses a complete account of motivation, as the subject
of these accounts is either a kind of loose cannon in a life that "consists
of retellings" and performances that are "always in flux" (Bruner 1986,
12) or she is viewed as a product of intersecting systems of power and
knowledge (Abu-Lughod 1990). These systems' points of intersection are
rightly seen as sites of struggle for the subject, but there is no explanation
of how this struggle constructs her desires, thus enabling her active par-
ticipation in either supporting or resisting relations of power.[3]

---

[2] Our focus on motivation is developed through attention to what psychoanalysts
term "desire" and what anthropologists and sociologists refer to as "agency." Agency
describes the subject's capacity to make meanings in her interaction with others, while
desire describes the "wants" that compel action. Only by connecting desire with agency
can we explain the reproduction and transformation of social meanings as other than an
"unintended consequence" of action (Giddens 1979) and provide a theory of an agentic
subject who is neither intentional nor driven by "need deficits" (see below, p. 8). By
"subjectivity" we mean the experience of self as a subject who acts, who has wants, and
who must sometimes act "against the grain" in the face of contradictory desires. Where
it has been necessary to use pronouns for individual subjects, children, or parents, we
have referred to them as "she" to avoid awkward phrasing. Of course, all these catego-
ries are clearly made up of both males and females.

[3] The concept of self-authorship, particularly developed in Barbara Myerhoff's work, is
described in Bruner (1986). Anthropological research on the creativity of power builds on
Michel Foucault (1982) as well as on Pierre Bourdieu's practice theory (1977). Bourdieu,
who emphasizes the indeterminacy of practice and the inventiveness of the agent, nonethe-
less describes a subject whose actions are guided by mental dispositions "embedded in the
agents' very bodies" (1977, 15). Michel de Certeau argues that Bourdieu's emphasis on
learned dispositions transforms his agent into an "immobile stone figure [who] makes the
circular movement of the theory possible" (1984, 58). In an effort to move away from deter-
minism and self-authorship, Faye Ginsburg's discussion (1989, 137–45) of the ways abor-
tion activists construct their histories in procreation narratives avoids the extreme fluidity of
processes such as those described by Bruner by connecting narrative to life history on the
one hand and to political economy (feminism and social movements of the 1960s and
1970s; white, Western, middle-class expectations and conventions) on the other. Similarly,
Lila Abu-Lughod's discussion (1986, 171–259) of the performance of *ghinnawas*, "little
songs," by Bedouin women moves between the creativity of specific performances and the
constraints of dominant discursive forms. Both of these accounts presuppose a subject who
is constrained by discourse but also creative. Our aim in this article is to provide a theoreti-
cal explanation of this capacity.

To develop a theory of the subject that does attend both to dominant cultural discourses and to the relational contexts in which meanings are produced, we turn to object relations theory and recent research in developmental psychology that suggests how an active infant constructs wants and needs. We find D. W. Winnicott's model (1982a) particularly helpful in moving beyond the dichotomy of a determined or a determining subject by suggesting the psychological process through which cultural meanings are simultaneously discovered and created. This paradox, reminiscent of Bourdieu's observation that cultural meanings are experienced as "the simple unearthing, at once accidental and irresistible, of a buried possibility" (1977, 79), explains how meanings emerge in relations of power where "even the most autonomous agent is in some degree dependent, and the most dependent actor . . . retains some autonomy" (Giddens 1979, 93).

Thinking of not only power but meanings as being relational entails a theory of a subject who makes meanings in and through these relations rather than one who is made as an effect of language. This requires a new conception of the infant as an active participant in the construction of her own subjectivity and has implications for our understanding of identities as neither arbitrarily set within existing systems of meaning nor freely chosen. It also provides a theoretical basis for an understanding of actors as agents capable of producing their own domination as well as of resisting it.

We begin with a brief discussion of Lacanian-derived feminist explanations of resistance, as these have received so much attention in recent literature, then turn to an account of the active infant and to object-relations theory to build an analysis of the social construction of desire (the psychoanalytic bedrock of motivation). We finally examine cross-cultural examples of how desire has been constructed and transformed by particular, historically situated female subjects.

Feminist Lacanian analyses of the subject: Split subjectivity as an explanation of change

Feminist theorists attempting to explain gender relations and female identity have arrived at the problem of subjectivity from a number of different directions, all asking how selves are defined and redefined in the context of historical change and how particular actors or subjects participate in these changes.[4] Those who seek accounts of the construction of subjectivity have increasingly used Lacan's formulations as a point of

[4] See, e.g., Mitchell and Rose (1982); Henriques et al. (1984); Hollway (1984); Davis (1986); de Lauretis (1987); Butler (1990); Flax (1990); Hartog (1990); Coombe (1991).

departure, some more critically than others.[5] These theorists share several assumptions about subjectivity: (1) it is constructed by language; (2) language offers discourses of identity within which subjects may position themselves; (3) subjects are simultaneously positioned in multiple but intersecting discourses, so that identities are not unitary but rather contradictory and shifting; (4) there is no "true" self to which these identifications or subject positions correspond.

Central to the project for social change in these accounts is the rejection of the concept of the true self. Rather, individuals are described as agents who playfully manipulate the identities provided by discourse, moving between them, satirizing, and having fun in ways that are disruptive of conventional notions of fixed gender identity. Judith Butler, for example, argues that women can mobilize contradictory discourses of identity to make "gender trouble" through what she calls "the subversive play of gendered meanings" (1990, 33). Her work describes a strategy of change based on playful performance that subverts the notion of a fixed gender identity by switching terms, trappings, and language.

The metaphor of theater lends itself particularly well to this notion of resistance and change. An illustrative example is *Belle Reprieve,* a recent collaborative production based on *Streetcar Named Desire* by the lesbian theater company Split Britches and the gay theater company Bloolips in which Bette Bourne (a man in drag) plays (at) the part of Blanche Dubois. Another example is the playful deployment of images and characters from mass culture texts such as the "Star Trek" television series by heterosexual women in "fanzine" clubs. Rosemary Coombe (1991, 22) writes that "fanziners . . . construct communities and articulate new gender identities by literally rewriting their favorite television series characters . . . to explore their own subordinate status, voice frustrations and anger with existing social conditions, envision and construct alternatives, share new understandings, and express utopian aspirations." In these rewritings, "the links between anatomy, gender, desire and sexual practice are sundered" (22) in stories that depict love relationships between Kirk and Spock and that endow "male" characters with combinations of gender traits, inscribing their bodies "with ranges of sensitivity, expanded zones of erogeneity and heightened receptivity to tactile pleasure and physical comfort" (23).

Although we agree that this kind of playful exposure of the tensions of fixed gender identities may well be a route to social change, we suggest that given identities are not dislodged so easily. Most theorists working in this tradition, however, imply that they are. Theresa de Lauretis, for

---

[5] Mitchell and Rose (1982) present themselves as his interpreters from a feminist perspective, while Butler (1990) offers a more critical view.

example, describes a feminist subject whose awareness of the contradictions of gender identity becomes "a critical vantage point" for her that can provide the creative potential for resistance (1990, 136). Indeed, de Lauretis's feminist subject actively chooses dislocation and the experience of marginalization. But this does not explain how it is that some actors are able to manipulate their location in the landscape of marginal identities whereas others cling tenaciously to the security of those that are given (what de Lauretis terms staying "home"[135]), with all of the repression of contradiction that that position entails.

Is self-dislocation indeed self-determined? Butler avoids this problem by positing a subject whose agency is simply "enabled by the tool lying there" (1990, 145). That is, agency is a function of discourse for Butler, who denies the relevance of self-conscious experience. Subversion is the result of inevitable "necessary failures," occasional incoherent performances of what Butler describes as the "injunction to be a given gender" (145). We suggest that this approach, however, while explaining possible reconfigurations of identity, is unsatisfying either as a theory or a politics of change as it sees the subject as essentially a marionette, a "fembot" who performs a particular subject position "in the mode of belief" (141). Although Butler avoids the problem of self-determined awareness by looking to discourse as the source of agency, her only extended example of subversion, a description of the construction of lesbian butch and femme identities, ironically suggests a more complex process of invention, one in which the resignification of "masculine" and "feminine" identities is produced in a powerful emotional context that impels actors who "like [their] boys to be girls" or, by contrast, "prefer that their girls be boys" (123). The dissonant "female body" in these exchanges becomes the object of lesbian femme desire, acted out by subjects who have preferences, likes, and wants rather than discursively dictated "compulsions to repeat" and whose preferences are shaped in (and produce) emotionally laden exchanges with others.

To explain both the playful process of cultural invention that Butler describes and the more routine processes of repetition that reproduce conventional forms of gendered identity, we require a theory that explains how preferences, likes, and wants are shaped, and why it is that some people are moved to make gender trouble while others are not. This requires us to move beyond the Lacanian notion of the entry into language as the key moment in the construction of subjectivity and to attend to the relevance of personal history in real relationships—especially the parent-child relationship—to show how the infant's struggle with issues of power in the unequal relation of parent and child shapes her experience of desire and provides the ground for resistance and change both preverbally and after the entry into language. Parent-child relations are the earliest embodiment of power for the developing child, and it is in struggles at this site of power that the capacity for accommodation and resistance to other forms of culturally shaped inequality is produced. This recalls Michel Foucault's insight that all social relations are power relations and that power is not "imposed from above" but is "rooted in the social nexus" (1982, 222). Although our analysis emphasizes the relational aspect of the construction of subjectivity, we locate these relations of interdependence in the complex and overlapping structures of power (including language) through which they take shape.

The active infant and the development of subjectivity

Our relational analysis of the emergence of subjectivity departs from the Lacanian view in three ways: first, we see the infant as an active participant in the construction of her own subjectivity; second, we argue that desire and motivation are constructed in ongoing social relationships suffused by power relations (not just in language); and third, the negotiation of meaning in these relationships allows the ground for creativity as well as conformity, for accepting the traditional and for breaking away from it.

The concept of the infant as an active meaning-maker in a world constituted through intersubjective experience as well as language is most persuasively put forth by Daniel Stern (1985). Influenced by Jean Piaget, who conceptualized the infant as motivated not by "need-deficits" (the classical psychoanalytic view) but by curiosity, Stern broadens Piaget's focus upon the cognitive development of infants to incorporate affective experience as well. In addition to challenging drive theory, Stern also rejects the dominant theory of infant development that postulates an infant who begins life in a state of fusion with the mother and whose key problematic is separation and individuation.

Classical (Freudian) psychoanalytic theory posits an infant initially in a state of fusion with the mother. Psychological differentiation—the attainment of an ego marked by a sense of self distinct from the caregiving other—is a developmental accomplishment in this view. The subjectivity of the infant emerges through the dual pressures of instinctual needs on the one hand and the vicissitudes of mothering behavior or societal demands on the other. This model assumes that tension reduction is the basis for motivation (needs build up causing anxiety, a caregiving other intervenes to satisfy needs, the infant returns to its preferred state of quiescence) and that the central developmental task is separation and individuation accompanied by loss of union. (Margaret Mahler is currently the most prominent proponent of this view in contemporary psychoanalytic theory [Mahler, Pine, and Bergman 1975].) According to this model, separation is necessary and inevitable but accomplished through frustration or anxiety, resulting in a longing for return to the earlier time of passive fusion.[6] These assumptions inform psychoanalytic approaches as diverse as Winnicott's and Lacan's, and are fundamental to Freudian explanations of the origin of desire.[7]

By contrast, Stern argues that infants are far more integrated (aware of their physical cohesion) and neurologically more sophisticated than assumed by most psychoanalytic theorists. Based on his review of research on early development, Stern makes the case that the infant is stimulus seeking and motivated to make sense of the world both affectively and cognitively from the earliest stages of infancy. His empirical studies suggest that one of the most problematic tasks for infants is to become engaged in relationship, rather than to separate, and that this process begins in the earliest stages of caregiver-infant interaction, long predating the entry into language relations.[8]

Because our approach to agency takes from Lacanian theory the insight that notions of difference and identity are culturally constituted but also includes an understanding of subjectivity that allows for creativity not entirely contained within an existing cultural order, it is worth elaborating on the distinctions between Stern's and Lacan's infant. Lacan's theory, unlike Stern's, assumes an initial psychological fusion between infant and mother. According to Lacan, the entry into language (the

[6] Nancy Chodorow's ground-breaking work in feminist psychology (1978) also bases a developmental account on the assumption of the infant's initial fusion with the mother. Her explanation of the origin of gender identification challenges the inevitability of differentiation as the key (and desirable) developmental accomplishment. She argues instead that the differentiation process is a defensive one, thrust on boys because their mothers do not identify with them and therefore force them to seek (gender) identification elsewhere. Girls remain in a relatively fused, or relational, position, based upon mutual identification between mother and daughter. This results in the capacity and desire for nurturing and therefore the reproduction of motherhood. Stern's assumption of an already differentiated infant places engagement in relationship as the central problem of development, for girls as well as boys. It also undercuts the idea of a wish to return to an early state of fusion as a motivator in human development.

[7] Lacan's theory postulates that the relationships that characterize "the imaginary" are constituted by the subject's entry into the symbolic order, and thus he explicitly denies the biological grounds of development and a definition of drives that implies that sexuality is in any way pre-given in "nature." Rather, the interpretation of nature itself is a cultural representation, according to Lacan (Mitchell and Rose 1982, esp. 5–6, 33–37).

[8] Stern's persuasive analysis of the affective context in which agency develops is marred by his inclination to essentialize the active infant. Thus, e.g., his position that very young infants "have intentions in mind" and that the capacity for agency is somehow built in seems to reflect an Anglo-American cultural bias (see the section "Inequality and the Cultural Construction of Desire" below) that infants, like the adults they will become, are intentional creatures. The argument for the relational development of agency does not need an intentional infant, simply one who is engaged in relationships that are themselves the foundation for the development of a culturally grounded agency.

symbolic) shatters this unity but does not produce a differentiated, autonomous subject. Rather, language offers only the illusion of wholeness and control, covering over the fact of fragmentation and split subjectivity. This illusion begins to emerge in the mirroring phase, the first stage in the child's incorporation of the symbolic order of language, when the infant sees its image reflected by others as a consolidated, whole subject over which she seems to have control (Lacan 1977). Yet the "I" is passively constituted through its positioning in discursive relations; for Lacan, according to Juliet Mitchell, "language does not arise from within the individual, it is always out there in the world outside, lying in wait for the neonate." Mirroring conceals from the conscious subject a fragmented and uncertain identity, "a being created in the fissure of a radical split" in its relationship to its mother in infancy: "the identity that seems to be that of the subject is in fact a mirage arising when the subject forms an image of itself by identifying with others' perceptions of it. When the human baby learns to say 'me' and 'I' it is only acquiring these designations from someone and somewhere else, from the world which perceives and names it" (Mitchell 1982, 5).

For Lacan, the entry into language forecloses access to what he terms "the real," that is, the experience of self-completion through unity with the mother. The preverbal experience is forever cast into the realm of the imaginary, where relationships reside as identifications of the ego (i.e., they are imagined) and where the quest for wholeness is desired in fantasy born out of the lost relationship. The implication of this loss of real relationship for the construction of subjectivity is that the meaning of "I" for Lacan's subject "is purely a function of the moment of utterance. The 'I' can shift and change places, because it only ever refers to whoever happens to be using it at the time" (Rose 1982, 31). This is the theoretical basis of feminist notions of split subjectivity discussed above. By stressing the power of language and discourse in the emergence of subjectivity, this analysis seems to deny the possibility of agency. The subject, in her quest for control over the anxiety produced by the experience of loss, becomes the passive construction of her position in discourses of identity lying in wait for her rather than an active participant in their creation.

This view of a child whose main developmental task is to seek an integrated sense of herself as a separate being but whose mirrored self shifts with her shifting positions vis-à-vis others has influenced a range of feminists interested in the construction of agency and desire.[9] Our earlier discussion of the work of Butler and de Lauretis suggests some of the

[9] See, e.g., Mitchell and Rose (1982); also Hollway (1984); Urwin (1984); Kaplan (1986); de Lauretis (1987).

problems in attempting to make a place for a self-constructing subject in this framework; an explanation of how specific actors come to take on individual identities requires some attention to them as engaged in relationship, not simply "positioned" as performers or spectators. Left unexplored by Lacanian feminists is what it means for any individual to grasp a contradiction implied by simultaneous positioning in multiple but intersecting discourses, much less to act on its implications.

Stern's approach is helpful here in developing a culturally grounded theory of agency in that it focuses on the emotional or affective texture of caregiver-infant interaction and of the relationship that develops from it. Indeed, Stern argues that even as late as nine to twelve months of age when infants have begun to engage in prelinguistic behavior, "affective exchange is still the predominant mode and substance of communications with the mother. . . . The two go on simultaneously" (1985, 133). In this model, children depend on the caregiving other to bring them into experiences of interaffectivity and intersubjective relatedness (see 128–37). At the same time, Stern demonstrates, the infant takes an active role in initiating and pursuing specific forms of exchange with the caregiving others, arguing that ultimately, "as the infant is able, the framework of meanings becomes mutually created" (134).

Stern's child is engaged in relationship, not merely mirrored. The initial dependence of the child on a caregiver who "provides the semantic element, all by herself at first, and continues to bring the infant's behavior into her framework of created meanings" (134) gives way to a more mutual process in which the infant "creates the caregiver" as the caregiver creates the infant. This process of mutual meaning-making is both embedded in and influenced by the prelinguistic patterns of affective communication that have been set in motion from the beginning by both child and caregiver. This child is not simply a passive recipient of cultural meanings nor driven by "need-deficits" but becomes engaged in a particular system of cultural meanings because of an active proclivity to make sense of the world and because she is dependent in this quest on caregiving other(s) who are affectively engaged both with the child and with the cultural meaning system in which they live.

An important consequence of this view is that, in contrast to Lacan's theory, it presents no radical break with early experience at the moment language enters in; that is, it does not see the real as foreclosed by the symbolic but, rather, views linguistic experience as laid upon the earlier affective foundation. The centrality of affect in this model provides a developmental account of how the meanings of cultural symbols become embodied at multiple levels of consciousness. As Robert Levine notes in a brief but provocative discussion, the acquisition of culture is analogous to the child's changing emotional and cognitive relationship to the house in which she or he grows up; "earlier meanings are not lost but form the intuitive bases for emotional responsiveness to symbols even after the latter have been understood at a reflective level" (1984, 86). This model suggests both why meaning systems are difficult to change at the level of rational argument and why change is possible in moments of social experience that call forth deeply embedded affective structures that move subjects emotionally and help to "change their minds and actions" (Abu-Lughod 1986, 177).

Inequality and the cultural construction of desire: Anglo-American and Ilongot developmental stories

Unlike Lacanian-derived models, Stern's work focuses less on the implications of inequality in the caretaker/child relationship than on the mutual construction of affectivity and meaning. Other researchers, such as Carol Gilligan and Grant Wiggins (1988), have attended to the tension between affectivity and inequality in the relations of parent and child and to the implications of this for the development of subjectivity and of agency. Infants in all cultural settings are born into a situation of dependence on others who are more powerful; they are dependent on adult caretakers as providers of both physical and emotional support and as skilled interpreters of what the infant needs (i.e., of what, culturally speaking, this support consists). Gilligan and Wiggins argue that this dependence creates in infants and young children "feelings of helplessness and powerlessness in relation to others" (1988, 114). At the same time, however, children also require emotional connection to survive and "the dynamics of attachment relationships create a very different awareness of self—as capable of having an effect on others, as able to move others and be moved by them" (114). Aware that "although the nature of the attachment between child and parent varies across individual and cultural settings and although inequality can be heightened or muted by familial or societal arrangements," Gilligan and Wiggins argue that "all people are born into a situation of inequality and no child survives in the absence of adult connection" (115).

The social construction of agency thus takes place in the context of parent-child relations through the interactions of caretakers with children. These interactions both reflect and reproduce culturally shaped relations of difference (differences that might be constructed, e.g., in gendered, class, or ethnic terms) as these intersect with and infuse the unequal relations of parent and child.[10]

[10] Of course it is women who in all cultures take the role of nurturers of young infants. We have not emphasized the gender of the caregiver because we want to move away from the tendency of theories such as Nancy Chodorow's (1978) to suggest that

As we will see below in several ethnographic studies, children produce parents in these interactions even as parents produce the child in a dynamic process that shapes cultural interpretations of what infants need and of what makes a good mother. These studies suggest that the relational environments through which a child becomes engaged in the production of cultural meanings, and thus in fashioning herself as a cultural subject, differ along a number of dimensions. Cultures vary in the construction of mothering, childhood, and the developmental process as well as in the interpretation of the child's activity in this process; there is broad cultural variation in how the dependence of child on caregiver is understood; and material and political conditions affect both the "knowledges" and practices of parenting.[11] We are most interested in the ways in which needs as culturally defined become mutually created in the interaction between caregiver and child. This cultural construction of needs, mediated through caregiver-infant interaction, is a crucial link in the process of the emergence of desire—of the capacity to want and to make things happen.

For westerners, the most familiar paradigm of development is what Eleanor Ochs and Bambi S. Schieffelin have termed the "Anglo-American white middle-class developmental story" (1984, 276). This model recognizes newborns as communicative partners and social beings and mothers as engaging in conversation with preverbal infants and facilitating dyadic interaction by attempting to take the perspective of the baby. A second characteristic of this model (particularly among the middle class) is a tendency to be uncomfortable with competence differentials between baby and adult, and therefore (a) to simplify behavior to match what are perceived to be the competence levels of the child and (b) to "richly interpret what the young child is expressing" and therefore "act as if the child is more competent than his behavior would more strictly indicate"

---

there are universal psychological implications of women's mothering based on the fact of same-sex identification. We take from the Lacanian perspective the view that identifications, even gender identifications, are multiple, and from Benjamin (1987, 1991) the idea that girls wish to identify with their fathers as well as their mothers. In addition, as the following discussion demonstrates, we emphasize the complexity of constraints embodied by language and stories of development that are particular to cultures and are crucial to the social construction of psychological needs and desires. From this perspective, the implications of the gender of the caregiver and infant cannot be disconnected from the cultural context, and an analysis would lead to an account of the diversity of the experiences of women and girls. Nevertheless, in cultures where women are constructed as dependent and men as independent, we would expect psychological outcomes similar to the ones Benjamin suggests in her account of the psychological origins of dominance and submission.

[11] Nancy Scheper-Hughes (1985) suggests that culture shapes the interpretation of whether infants need or want even the most fundamental forms of physical support (such as food, milk). Her argument emphasizes material conditions of poverty, hunger, and disease as the key variables that affect cultural interpretations in this area.

(Ochs and Schieffelin 1984, 287). While Ochs and Schieffelin focus on the development of language in this process, their analysis provides a broader cultural model of discomfort with inequality (defined as incompetence) that necessitates dependence. The insistence on competence thus reveals the broader cultural goal of independence.

What is missing in their account, however, is a recognition of the power dynamics that result from this Western model of development. A 1984 British study by Cathy Urwin of parent-child relations involving very young preverbal children as well as children beginning the entry into language focuses on the active participation of young children and the collaboration of caregiving adults in interactions through which they take up subject positions of power vis-à-vis parents. Thus dependence is transformed into independence through the intersubjective matrix of parent-child exchanges. By examining these parent-child interactions in play situations, in caretaking, around the dinner table, and other everyday settings, Urwin shows how the mother's response to cues given by the child permits the child to assume increasingly more assertive and controlling positions in these interactions.

Urwin argues that the parent's willingness to cede control to the baby— the mother's recognition of the baby's social potency—contributes to the infant's own engagement in power relations. For example, Urwin describes a baby whose spontaneous cough becomes intentional in an effort to gain a response from the mother, distancing him from the particular situation that produced the cough and providing him with a sense of his own incipient power to elicit a response. She argues that "in this disjunction [between intentional use of the act of coughing to elicit a specific response from the mother and the situation that initially prompted the coughing] we are already seeing the contribution of power relations to the formation of unconscious [preverbal, non-self-reflective] processes" (297). The baby is an active participant in the production of the relations, but the baby's sense of control over the mother depends equally on the mother's collaboration, her willingness to recognize the baby's intention in using the cough to elicit a response. The net effect, according to Urwin, is that "in fantasy, [babies] are actually controlling the regularities of the event and producing its truth themselves" (283).

The strength of Urwin's analysis is that it emphasizes the effect on the baby of the mother's culturally shaped assumptions about what is appropriate as a response to an infant (283). The baby is afforded the experience of power in this interaction because of the mother's participation in a discourse of mothering that dictates that mothers respond to their infant's signals, try to figure out what they need, and bolster them in their quest for the illusion of autonomy and control in their social interactions. This interactional dynamic emerges over time as the mother and baby accommodate to each other, and it becomes (to use Urwin's words) "underpinned" with "emotional investment" (300). Thus, Urwin argues, the adult's sense of what the child needs and the child's developing sense of her own wants are the product of a "specific and extensive relational history" (300).

While Urwin's study reveals the interactional dynamic in which mother and child are engaged and how this is shaped by a specific discourse of mothering, it leaves unexamined a number of white middle-class cultural assumptions that frame the questions she asks and her interpretation of parent-child interaction. The treatment by mothers of their young infants as communicative partners is assumed as a "given" by Urwin, who does not explore the implications of this stance for the construction of the subjectivity of the infant. Similarly, while she underscores the dependence of the infant on adult response to interpret its wants and the implications of this dependence for the infant's growing efforts at control, Urwin does not consider the more general implications of a cultural pattern that assumes that accommodation to the child is an appropriate adult response and that it is necessary for adults to interpret the needs of young children.

The consequence of these cultural practices is that while children are treated as social agents from the beginning, their sense of control is founded on the willingness of a powerful adult to cede that control to the baby. Adults assume that children are intentional beings and need the adult to interpret their wants; this assumption leads to practices in which children come to know not only what interpretations are possible, but who can make them as well. This analysis suggests that Urwin's emphasis on development as a struggle for autonomy and her interpretation of the parent as "playing with power and control" (293) is itself shaped by the discursive framework she describes. These frameworks construct development as the natural consequence of an infant who is understood to be a particular kind of social being (communicative from the beginning), in need of a particular kind of caregiving (attentive to interpreting needs and willing to cede control) to bring it into a particular kind of adulthood (autonomous and in control). Thus the Western ideal of individuality is embodied and reproduced.

A further consequence of Urwin's emphasis on development as a struggle for autonomy is that her interpretation of caregiver-infant exchange stresses the culturally dictated positioning of subjects vis-à-vis one another while downplaying their emotional engagement with one another. Urwin's account suggests (although she does not seem aware of it) that parent-infant interaction is similar to Lacan's analysis of mirroring for both parent and child, both of whom are "subordinated to the image" that provides them with an illusion of control (276). Thus Urwin misses the extent to which control is held in the affective context of the relationship, in the ongoing experience of interaffectivity that develops prior to and along with the emergence of language (see our discussion of Stern on this issue, above). Attention to the affective engagement of caregiver and child, in contrast to the exclusive emphasis on the development of language, would suggest how an understanding of mothering (of appropriate response to an infant) is embodied in the same range of cognitive and affective, conscious and unconscious ways as infants begin to experience their needs.[12]

A study by Michelle Rosaldo of the Ilongot, a society of hunters and horticulturalists in Northern Luzon, the Philippines, presents another example of how the acts of infants and young children precipitate responses that both reflect and produce understandings of what children need (1980, 63–76). Here infants are constructed as weak, unknowing, uncommunicative, lacking sociability, and isolated from the strengthening world of adult interdependence. What they need, then, is to be protected from spirits until they can be coaxed into the adult world of knowledge.

Describing an event in which an infant of three or four months of age fell from a low-hung cradle, Rosaldo notes that the mother, without pausing to feel the child's head for injury, "took the infant to her chest, spat at her forehead and chestbone, and in a soft, steady voice, called over its whimpers, 'Come, little girl; come, come back here.' The baby's heart, she explained to me later, did not 'know' what had happened, and so needed her voice to prevent it from starting and jumping or fleeing in fright" (63). Ilongot babies are viewed as lacking understanding and awareness. Like sick people, weak and spiritually vulnerable, babies are susceptible to disruption and shock and must be continually soothed and attended: "Never leaving their babies alone or far from the touch of another, Ilongots speak with some horror of what they know of American missionary custom, with its bottles and isolating cribs. Whether tied in a sling on the back or swung in a cradle, the Ilongot baby wants sound, motion, and usually, feeding. Its cries are upsetting to adults and, if

---

[12] Contrast, e.g., Urwin's description of a calm and amused mother who reflects on the way her baby "uses" coughing as a signal to her with the following account of a new mother's sense of desperation in failing to get her newborn to go to sleep: "When I came home I was just thrilled the first day and then I really think [the depression] started that first night when I got up with her and she wouldn't go back to sleep. She would wake up around 4:30 and stay up until 6:30 or 7:30 in the morning. She just didn't go back to sleep. . . . It was almost as though it was going to go on forever so I felt completely . . . almost like it was hopeless, I felt like there was no hope. I felt despair" (Mahoney, in progress). This mother's experience was precisely that she was not in control. Mirroring, and the illusion of control that a caregiver gives the infant (as in Urwin's bemused mother), cannot explain this moment, nor can it suggest the implications of such a moment for the emergence of the infant's sense of subjectivity.

unattended, conducive to disruption, heart loss, and illness in both parent and the child itself" (63–64).

The development of the Ilongot self is perceived as a growth of awareness in response to life experiences. Children are viewed as beginning to develop knowledge by the time they are three or four and only at this point, when they come to know their needs, are children given a name. Their lack of adult awareness is acknowledged in the Ilongot belief that children must be regulated by adult words or threats. Thus the child's growing awareness develops in the context of multiple caretakers, who fondle it, carry it, and quiet its cries with lullabies. As the child grows older, it is regulated by commands from the parent, who is described as "the very 'essence' (*pu'un*) of 'fear' " (71).

Rosaldo's analysis of Ilongot constructions of infants as fearful, unknowing, and wanting to be soothed contrasts with the Anglo-American understanding of infants as intentional and as needing adults to interpret what they have in mind. Each kind of knowledge interprets infant activity in a different way, and this in turn results in different understandings of the developmental process: among the Ilongot, the gradual acquisition of knowledge (and thus of increased autonomy) through an extending network of interactions (experience) with others; among the Anglo-American middle class, a struggle for autonomy envisioned as breaking away from a confining dependence on others. In both, the good mother can be understood only in terms of a particular kind of wanting infant; and the power of each (the capacity for control) is produced in the interdependence of good mothering practices with cultural understandings of what infants need. These understandings and practices emerge in particular kinds of relational contexts: a world of multiple caretakers for the Ilongot child, a setting in which one adult facilitates the infant's growing interpretive skill among the Anglo-American middle class.

Power and recognition: The paradox of agency

Conceptualizing the child as an active participant seeking to make sense of the world with the support of the social surround gives us a basis for explaining agency in the taking on of cultural form; it does not explain, however, the connection of agency to resistance. How does the concept of agency allow for movement beyond familiar understandings of self and relationship to the creation of new ones?

For this we turn to the work of D. W. Winnicott, which provides a model of the development of the self that locates the potential for creativity in the maintenance of a tension between being with and being apart. Winnicott's account of the construction of subjectivity, taken up more recently by Jessica Benjamin, departs sharply from other psychoanalytic formulations (even other object relations theorists with whom both are identified) in insisting on the importance of creativity as a dimension of agency and in showing how this emerges from the intersubjective exploration of territory that derives neither from subject nor object but is at the same time "me" and "not me." In Winnicott's words, "here is a part of the ego that is not a body-ego." It is not based on the satisfaction of physiological needs but, rather, on the infant's experiences of relating to the other. For Winnicott, these experiences do not necessarily serve to consolidate a sense of self as separate and ego-bounded; rather, in the blurring and shifting of boundaries emerges the potential for creativity. Thus one of his favorite metaphors for object relations is the seashore, simultaneously a distinct and ever-changing border. Winnicott's mystification of motherhood, his notion that women are instinctively attuned to their own biological offspring, has been properly criticized by feminists as essentialist, reducing the problem of the social construction of motherhood to a biologically based behavior.[13] The focus on this aspect of his theory, however, has obscured the importance of his insight into the nature of psychological development in which the self is constituted as simultaneously separate and connected.

This process is fraught with tension, however. Winnicott describes a power struggle in which the infant, at the stage of dawning awareness of the possibility of being both connected and autonomous, experiments with the extent to which she has control over the caregiver.[14] In so doing, the infant metaphorically destroys the mother as part of the developmental process in which she learns to use the mother. Use of the mother, for Winnicott, signifies the ability to engage in a nonfused, nonsymbiotic relationship with her and does not imply instrumentality (Winnicott 1982d, 89).[15] The mother's response to this move for control is critical in this account, since her survival of the destruction (by refusing either to give in to the infant's demands or to retaliate) establishes her as outside of the infant's omnipotent control (90). That is, the failed attempt to destroy the mother convinces the infant that the mother is real, not a projection of the infant's fantasies. This places the mother out in the

---

[13] For a clear articulation of his position, see Winnicott (1965).

[14] Winnicott, following traditional psychoanalytic theory, sees this struggle as part of a process of differentiation from a state of fusion with the mother. As we have seen, Daniel Stern reverses the differentiation paradigm by proposing that the infant begins in a state of relative coherence and separation and moves toward relationship. We suggest that the newborn infant is neither completely fused nor differentiated and awaits the complex cultural constructions of dependence and inequality that will shape its subjectivity and render relationship or autonomy as psychologically and culturally problematic.

[15] We agree with Jessica Benjamin (1987, 37) that Winnicott's language here is problematic and obscures his meaning.

world, which is the only condition under which she can continue, paradoxically, to recognize the infant's subjectivity.

Benjamin enriches this analysis by emphasizing that the infant's dawning sense of autonomy and thus of agency is dependent upon recognition by an other that the infant is a subject who acts (Benjamin 1987, 38–39). It is in this recognition of agency by an other who is powerful (cannot be destroyed) that the intrapsychic experience of potency and desire is constituted: "The paradox of recognition, the need for acknowledgment that turns us back to dependence on the other, brings about a struggle for control. This struggle can result in the realization that if we fully negate the other, that is if we assume complete control over him and destroy his identity and will, then we have negated ourselves as well. For there is no one there to recognize us, no one there for us to desire" (Benjamin 1987, 39). This paradox of recognition, in which agency and potency are inextricable from a recognizing other, locates power at the heart of an explanation of agency. For Benjamin, as for Winnicott, the dependence-independence dialectic can be overcome with the acceptance of the paradox that each is possible only in the presence of the other. Benjamin's project is to show how the experience of this paradox can be "painful, or even intolerable" (50) and lead to a defensive posture in which the psyche fails to hold in tension the polarity but rather splits them, in favor of either dependence or independence. Such defensive splitting "also sets the stage for domination. Opposites can no longer be integrated; one side is devalued, the other idealized. . . . [The] inability to sustain the tension of paradox manifests itself in all forms of domination" (50). For Benjamin, this psychic maneuver explains the grip of gender domination in the unconscious, as girls settle for their status as object of desire, dependent on the male, who represents independence and agency. The split between autonomy and dependence is represented culturally in Western ideologies of gender and in the psychology of male independence and domination and of female dependence and submission (12 and passim).[16]

Although Benjamin explores the psychic basis for domination, she also suggests the possibility of a relationship characterized by equality, or what she terms mutuality. The difficulty with this account is that Benjamin does not address fully the broader context of structural inequality in which interpersonal interactions inevitably take place. Thus the expe-

---

[16] Nancy Chodorow (1978, 1989) also poses the question of the origins of gender differentiation and inequality and locates the problem as both a cultural and a psychological one. Benjamin's work departs from Chodorow's in showing how girls, as well as boys, are motivated by a desire for autonomy as well as relationship. Thus her analysis addresses a criticism that is made of Chodorow's work (as well as of Carol Gilligan's and Jean Baker Miller's)—that she elevates relational capacities of girls and women but loses sight of their parallel struggle for agency and autonomy (although her more recent writing [1989, 1–19] acknowledges this issue).

rience of a relationship as mutual in the intersubjective sphere may obscure the extent to which it is suffused with culturally defined power relations. In our view, such experiences simultaneously embody broader patterns of social inequality (a newborn, after all, is not equal to a mother) and at the same time provide the psychological ground for the experience of empowerment, thereby allowing for action, resistance, and social change.

According to this intersubjective view, a sense of empowerment or agency emerges from a paradox similar to the one that produces the experience of autonomy and can similarly be thwarted by a failure to sustain the tension. The clearest exposition of this idea is in Winnicott's concept of the transitional object (1982b). Winnicott sees the use of a transitional object as important in the infant's discovery and negotiation of phenomena that are me or not me. He suggests that a soft object (or tune or mannerism) may become vitally important to the infant, for example, at bedtime. It is essential for Winnicott that this object does not simply stand for or symbolize the absent mother or breast. Rather "its not being the breast (or the mother), although real is as important as the fact that it stands for the breast (or mother)" (1982b, 6). That is, it represents the space between the mother and child. Winnicott underscores in his discussion of transitional objects the possibility of a continuum between self and other by sustaining the paradox that the transitional object "comes from without from our point of view, but not so from the point of view of the baby. Neither does it come from within; it is not a hallucination" (1982b, 5). Thus it is simultaneously and paradoxically invented and found; the baby both creates the object and the object is "there waiting to be created" (1982d, 89).[17] In this way the problem of whether agency is located in the self or in society dissolves in favor of a paradox: it is simultaneously in both.

As noted, feminist critics of object-relations theory recognize the potential for mystification in Winnicott's account of the relation of the mother and infant in that he assumes a universal, instinctive maternal response. In part, this is linked to his assumption (following classical psychoanalytic theory) that the baby initially experiences herself as fused with the mother and that the mother somehow reciprocally senses what the baby needs. This apparently biologically based empathy with one's infant need not be the basis of the transitional experiences Winnicott described, however, even though the caregiver's response to the infant is a vital piece of the story. Rather, a relationally based theory in which the infant is seen as both integrated and differentiated at birth provides a

---

[17] See Phillips (1988, 98–126 and passim) for a useful account of Winnicott's theory and his departure from Melanie Klein's position on infant development.

more satisfactory grounding for an analysis of the central challenge of the development of self in which being with is as central an issue as being apart and in which power relations are inescapable from the beginning.

It is this developmental account of power relations that links Winnicott's position with Foucault's analysis, more commonly associated with a Lacanian framework (see Henriques et al. 1984). According to Foucault, struggles in power relations "underline everything which makes individuals truly individual" on the one hand, while on the other they "attack everything which separates the individual, breaks his links with others, splits up community life, forces the individual back on himself and ties him to his own identity in a constraining way" (1982, 211–12). Power, for Foucault, can only be exercised over a free subject, a subject "thoroughly recognized and maintained . . . as a person who acts" (220). By contrast, where "determining factors saturate the whole there is no relationship of power" (221). The fine balance between determination and resistance is central to Foucault's analysis and resembles Winnicott's description of the subtle play of creativity and constraint in what he terms the "continuity-contiguity moment," a "third area . . . contrasted with inner or personal psychic reality and with the actual world in which the individual lives" (1982c, 103), an "intermediate area of experience, unchallenged in respect of its belonging to inner or external (shared) reality" (1982b, 14). It is in this potential space between self and other, first experienced by the infant with the transitional object, that play, creativity, and agency (understood as the invention of new meanings) are made possible.[18] This understanding of playfulness as the ground for resistance helps explain how the strategies of "parodic proliferation" of gendered meanings described in Butler's work (1990) are possible.

This model of the potential inherent in the blurring of boundaries experienced in the developmental struggle with inequality and dependence stands in contrast to Lacan's account of the foreclosing of the real experience of preverbal life by the entry into language. What for Lacanians is a gap—the unbridgeable space between the symbolic, in which selves and relationships are constituted, and the presymbolic—becomes a creative moment based on dependence and resistance, a moment that for Winnicott is productive of meanings and values. The ambiguity of this moment, constituted by the tension between discovering meanings that are already there and shaping new meanings, is what allows for a sense of empowerment in subjects whose agency is reproducing existing hierarchies even as they are creating the spaces for new forms of rela-

[18] In a parallel analysis, Foucault argues that it is in the tension between constraint and resistance that relations of power open up "a whole field of responses, reactions, results, and possible inventions" (1982, 220).

tionship.[19] In Winnicott's words, "in any cultural field *it is not possible to be* original except on a basis of tradition . . . The interplay between originality and the acceptance of tradition as the basis for inventiveness [is] one example . . . of the interplay between separateness and union" (1982c, 99).

To summarize, then, we have argued for a theory of agency in which dependence is a condition of independence and inequality is a condition of resistance. We have suggested that conditions for creativity emerge out of the subject's struggles with her or his status as unequal and dependent. The child's initial encounters with the dynamics of power and dependence as described by Winnicott are experienced, according to Benjamin, as paradox or contradiction that, we suggest, has the potential to produce either change or conformity. We now move to examine relational settings characteristic of adult life that produce a potential for creativity out of similar structural positions of inequality and dependence, focusing on the contradictions inherent in gender and race as key sites where struggles with power and dependence take place. In these struggles, the invention of new forms is shown to be shaped by and dependent on old meanings, and the interplay of resistance and determination produces practices and understandings that are simultaneously of an existing order and a reimagining of it.

Agency in everyday practice

We begin with an essay by Patricia Williams in which she describes her effort to "pin herself down in history" (1988, 5). Williams's account takes up many of the themes on which we have focused, providing a compelling portrayal of the ways a national history of racial oppression is embodied, and of how struggle with what is at the same time me and not me and the blurring of boundaries this implies becomes a source both of refusal and of revelation. The account begins with Williams's entry into law school and her mother's observation, just before her first day of class, that "the Millers were lawyers, so you have it in your blood" (6). The reference is to Austin Miller, a white Tennessee lawyer who purchased Williams's great-great-grandmother Sophie in 1850, when she was twelve, and immediately impregnated her. When Sophie's daughter, Mary, was born, she was taken from her mother to be raised as a house servant. The essay in which this event is described, "On Being the Object of Property," is an extended exploration of what Williams terms the "profoundly troubling paradox" that "self-possession in the full sense of

[19] This approach provides a psychological theorization of the "indeterminacy" central to Bourdieu's theory of practice (1977) and the unintended consequences in Giddens's practical consciousness (1979).

that expression" requires "claiming for myself a heritage the weft of whose genesis is my own disinheritance" (6–7). She suggests through her comment that her mother was "devaluing that part of herself that was not Harvard and refocusing my vision to that part of herself that was hard-edged, proficient, Western. She hid the lonely, black, defiled-female part of herself and pushed me forward as the projection of a competent self, a cool rather than despairing self, a masculine rather than a feminine self" (6).

Much of the essay recounts Williams's struggle with this contradiction and, specifically, with the tension evoked by the embodiment of a sense of self in which what was "in her blood" (an imagery of connection and belonging that cuts across race, class, and gender in American society) was that which set her apart from a "me" that (to use Bourdieu's phrase) history had "turned into nature" (Bourdieu 1977, 78). That is, as Williams writes, "I must assume, *not just as history but as an ongoing psychological force,* that, in the eyes of white culture, irrationality, lack of control, and ugliness signify not just the whole slave personality, not just the whole black personality, but me" (Williams 1988, 11, emphasis added).

Williams argues that this splintering of the self, represented by the alienation of black children from their white fathers or from their almost-white mothers, is a function of an ideological system in which market relations and slave law came together to produce a polarized world of black irrationality, lack of control, and ugliness on one hand and of "pure will," aesthetic beauty, and control on the other. This worldview became an "ongoing psychological force" for her, Williams implies, through countless mundane interactions: the repeated experience of white people's "looking through" her, what she terms their "ignore-ance" (11, 23), the retelling of tales, such as the story of Williams's great-great-grandmother Sophie's sale and the removal of her daughter or the giving away of her godmother Marjorie at age six to be raised "among her darker-skinned cousins" when her light-skinned mother left the family to marry a white man (12).

These events suggest both the invisibility of the black person and her construction (by the law and in everyday "common sense") as one who should be acted upon, an object, and active only in disobedience (13). Williams compares the situation of the black person to Mary Beth White-head, whose capacity for autonomy was "locked away in word vaults" by virtue of having signed a contract. By contrast, Williams's great-great-grandmother was made powerless by a contract that she did not sign but of which she was the object (14–15). In this liberal legal world, the world of burgermeister and slavemaster, it is the contract that "does," not the parties to it, who are "in a passive relationship to a document" (13).

Williams describes her own "raging" against this invisibility and the passivity it implied, specifically in her encounter with an all-white, all-male summer basketball camp at Dartmouth College. Her response to being jostled, smacked, and pushed into the gutter by "about a hundred of these adolescents, fresh from the courts" was to "snatch . . . off my brown silk headrag, my flag of African femininity and propriety, my sign of meek and supplicatory place and presentation" and to hiss: " 'Don't I exist for you?! See Me! And deflect, godammit!' " Their response, however, indicated that they "had no idea . . . that I was talking to them or about them," and she was "manumitted back into silence" (23).

By contrast to the passive relationship in which the contract does and blacks are invisible, Williams describes her relationship with her god-mother Marjorie, the woman who was "given away by her light-skinned mother when she was only six" (12). Marjorie fed her, with tales and with "canned fruit and heavy roasts, mashed potatoes, pickles and vanilla pudding, cocoa, Sprite, or tea" (17); and when Marjorie lay dying in the hospital, Patricia Williams fed her, in "a complex ritual of mirroring and self-assembly": "The physical act of holding the spoon to her lips was not only a rite of nurture and of sacrifice, it was the return of a gift. It was a quiet bowing to the passage of time and the doubling back of all things. The quiet woman who listened to my woes about work and school required now that I bend my head down close to her and listen for mouthed word fragments, sentence crumbs. I bent down to give meaning to her silence, her wandering search for words" (17).

This passage, together with others in which Williams describes exchanges "whose currency was a relational ethic" rather than value determined by "the material things I could offer" (18), suggests the relational contexts that shaped her capacity to reconcile the "disenfranchised little black girl of myself that felt powerless, vulnerable" with the "doer," "hard-edged and proficient" (6). Marjorie provided for her a mirror in which she could "remember myself, draw an internal picture that is smooth and whole . . . stare myself down until the features reassemble themselves like lost sheep" (17). It was in these relationships that she could become a person who could "look straight at people, particularly white people" and "insist on the right to my presence no matter what" (11).

Williams suggests that while the law fragments, dividing person from person and splintering the self, relationships make whole. And she returns throughout the essay to the theme of like/not like, and of how the boundaries constructed by law become a source of struggle for a divided self. For Williams, like the creative lesbians described by Butler, these boundaries are destabilized in the dynamics of exchange where transgressions of conventional categories of difference can constitute "a highly complex and structured position of desire" (Butler 1990, 123). The capacity for this is not simply in the construction of difference, however, and the contradictions this implies. It is in the interplay of likeness and difference, as what is like and what is not like shift places in the context of specific histories, lives, and relationships: with godmothers, law school teachers, Dartmouth students, and neighbors; in hospitals, families, schools, and workplaces. It is in these mundane interactions that both black and white, male and female identities are destabilized, even as the oppositions that constitute these identities are reproduced.

The tension between reproduction and resistance that runs through Williams's essay is also central to Carolyn Steedman's story about Amarjit, a nine-year-old Punjabi girl whom she met while teaching remedial English in an industrial town of north England in the early 1980s (1985). Like Williams's narrative, Steedman's too tells of the invention of new meanings that emerge within the spaces created by hierarchies of difference, in this case intersecting differences of race, gender, and class in the transitional context of an unfamiliar and dominant culture.

About half the children in Amarjit's school spoke English as a second or third language, and a small group of these students came to Steedman each day for extra help in reading and writing. Amarjit took home a reading primer, *The Green Man and the Golden Bird,* and returned the next day to tell Steedman, "I like this book. I really like this book. . . . I love this book. I don't read my reading book. I sing it in bed at night" (139). Amarjit focused on a particular passage in the story in which a mother buys a caged golden bird for her two children and the daughter begs her to let it go: "The song is so sad I can't bear to listen to it. The bird wants to get out and fly away" (139). The mother refuses, saying that the bird cost her a lot of money. Amarjit set these words to music of her own, "incorporating the irregular rhythms of prose in regular melody" (139).

Steedman argues that Amarjit "read herself" in the lines about the yearning of the bird to fly, suggesting that this reading expressed in metaphorical form her emotional relationship to an economic system which was "a dominant feature of [Punjabi] girls' understanding of themselves" (148). Contemplation of this text—in what Steedman refers to as "a hallowed place of safety for [Amarjit's] enterprise," her bed—allowed Amarjit to think both about "the difficult linguistic relationship of the present and the conditional" and about social and emotional issues relating to "her own position between what is, and what might be" (139–40).

Drawing on literature about the position of women in Punjabi Sikh society, Steedman notes the "dangerous emotional territory that the young Punjabi bride must traverse" in a society where women are put "at the service of men" and where, "having no economic or social alternative, women are inexorably drawn into marriage [in an] enforced flight from a loving and protecting mother to a mother-in-law" (150–51). Steedman suggests that the imagery Amarjit drew on in developing her song, and her manipulation of this imagery

> allowed her to dwell on both economic value and economic restriction. The metaphors she was able to use allowed her not only the idea of "the wings of liberty," but also, by permitting direct comparison between the expensive bird and herself, allowed her to move beyond the traditional European usage of this image . . . and to see the flight to freedom overshadowed by restriction.
>
> It seems likely that the *cost* of the bird in the story was the feature that Amarjit most wanted to dwell on, for its price expressed most clearly the contradictions of the adult role she was trying to confront. By dealing with the bird's price she drew on another set of [Punjabi Sikh] cultural referents . . . and saw herself as both valued and resented, the costly item that would inevitably disappear from the home, its flight sought out and seen as inevitable, its resting place fragile and insecure. [150]

Steedman's analysis places Amarjit in a social disjuncture and sees the song as an act of play "that allows her both to know this disjuncture and to work out its implications for her future" (138). Like Williams's interpretation of the "profoundly troubling paradox" of a heritage in which disinheritance (her great-grandmother's removal to be raised as a house servant) derives from the same act that imbues her with value (her "blood likeness" to the white lawyer who impregnated her great-great-grandmother), Amarjit, too, struggles with the contradictions of being both a daughter and a "guest in her parents' home," a "thing that has to be given away" (151). It is from this struggle that Amarjit comes to know her value in Punjabi Sikh society as well as to imagine "getting out and flying away."

A key feature of Steedman's analysis, as in Williams's, is the account of "invisibility" for Amarjit in a white society that (in Williams's words) "treated me as though I were transparent" (11). Similarly, Steedman argues that working-class children like Amarjit are "invisible children" (152) and that this shapes the indifference with which their productions are met by teachers, peers, and others with whom they deal on a daily basis. This, in turn, shapes the potential for refusal and resistance, a theme that emerges strongly in Williams's essay but is only hinted at in the story of nine-year-old Amarjit. Steedman, while recognizing that her own relationship to Amarjit was that of "a white woman teacher and a black child in racist, late-twentieth-century Britain" (152) nonetheless sought to recognize the child's creativity and, moved by the song, played it for children and teachers at the daily school assembly. Yet "there was no way of imagining, on their part or their teachers', what could have been a good and acceptable piece of work from Amarjit," (158) and the children began to laugh. Thus "the sense of power, the intellectual pleasure of knowing that something has been worked out, was . . . denied to all the children in that cold hall" (158).

Steedman's account of this denial of agency, juxtaposed with Williams's narrative of the "complex ritual of mirroring and self-assembly" in her relationship with her godmother Marjorie, are illustrative of what Benjamin calls "the paradox of recognition, the need for acknowledgment that turns us back to dependence on the other" (1987, 39). The children's laughter at the assembly meant that they were all denied "the sense of power . . . of knowing that something has been worked out" (Steedman 1985, 158); in Williams's relationship with Marjorie, by contrast, her acknowledgment of Marjorie's need for nurture was the "return of a gift," it was "the doubling back of all things," a reversed asymmetry in which her feeding Marjorie, now dependent, was a reenactment of Marjorie's "gifts" to the child Patricia, whose entreaties for tales about "roots" were answered with a parable about a polar bear universe in which humans "were ideally designed to provide polar bears with meat" (16–17).

The emergence of agency at a point of disjuncture or contradiction that moves an "invisible" subject to activity is at the center of our final example, taken from Hendrik Hartog's analysis of the memoirs of Abigail Bailey, an eighteenth-century American housewife (1990). Hartog's analysis traces Abigail Bailey's struggle for what he terms "self-ownership" (4) within a legal and religious culture in which her identity was dependent on that of her husband. This theme is familiar from Natalie Davis's work depicting the connection of autonomy to relationship in the lives of sixteenth-century French women, where embeddedness in a patriarchal family structure prompted rather than precluded self-discovery (1986, 53; see also Davis 1983). Bailey's memoirs are particularly helpful in examining the process of self-discovery because she is so articulate in framing the terms in which it takes place. In a diary that represents "an intense and unswerving reflection on her marital relations," Bailey "constantly monitors the changing discourse of her marriage," reconstructing "arguments, prayers, and invocations of religious authority" (6).

The normative structures that shape Bailey's manuscript are eighteenth-century evangelical Christianity and the legal theory of coverture. According to this theory, a married woman's legal identity was "covered" by that of her husband, and for women of this period, marriage simply meant "exchanging one dependence for another" (13). In the words of an eighteenth-century legal text, " 'all Women, in the Eye of the Law, are either married or to be married; and their Desires are Subject to their Husbands' " (14). Bailey's submission to this construction of womanhood is affirmed in her own words: "As, while I lived with my parents, I esteemed it my happiness to be in subjection to them: so now I thought it must be a still greater benefit to be under the aid of a judicious companion, who would rule his own house" (13).

At the same time that Abigail Bailey was "under the legal control" of her husband, she saw her primary relationship as being to God, and Hartog argues that it was through her relationship to her husband that she affirmed her identity as a religious subject. In this sense, "coverture was hard work for the self" (15–16). The narrative that begins with Abigail Bailey's wedding in 1767 and ends with her divorce in 1792 tells of this hard work and of the way it was shaped by her interpretation of legal rights and of religious duties as she sought to remain a good wife even as she claimed her right to separate from her husband.

A key piece of this narrative of work involves the process of breaking what Hartog terms the "habit of submission mandated both by coverture and by the religious mandates of marital unity" (45). According to these mandates, marriage involved not simply a civil contract but "the permanent union of two souls" (35). When her husband Asa's conduct (his violent and abusive behavior, his adultery, and most serious, his incestuous relationship with their daughter) threatened to implicate her in his sinful behavior, Abigail Bailey "had to separate from him or risk . . . her own eternal damnation" (35). The struggle for Abigail Bailey centered on the tension between duty and submission, and on the paradox that to fulfill her duty as a good wife she must not submit. It was in her long struggle over this issue (her fasting, praying, and numerous efforts at separation) that the sense of what being a good wife meant gradually emerged as the product of what Urwin calls "a specific and extensive relational history" (1984, 300). In the course of this history, her daughter Phoebe's incest became an opportunity and not only a disaster. "In 'allowing' her father to succumb to his passion, Phoebe ironically gave her mother the legal and moral right to seek a separation. . . . Because she, Phoebe, was nearly destroyed as a result of her 'habit of obedience,' Abigail could imagine breaking up her marriage" (49–50).

In documenting the course of Abigail Bailey's marriage and divorce, Hartog notes that her capacity eventually to challenge her husband's authority "rested on the same normative assumptions that underlay his conventional assertions of authority" (52). In this sense, her self-assertion reaffirmed the religious and legal structures that shaped her self-understanding as submissive and dutiful and consolidated the relational networks within which she lived her life, even as she constructed a space for self-assertion. As in Davis's portrayal of self-discovery in the lives of sixteenth-century women in France, the self always emerges in relationship to others—to family, patrons, lovers, God—and the person only takes shape "as part of a field of relations" (63). It is the inextricability of autonomy from connection, and the paradox this implies in explaining self-construction as contingent on who one is known (and knows oneself) to be, that locates these historical subjects within our narrative of agency and the construction of desire. They suggest the contingency of empowerment on relational engagement and of agency, the capacity to "make things happen," on the involuntary reproduction of familiar forms.

Conclusion

We have argued that an explanation of resistance must account for how the motivation to resist—the desire to act "against the grain"—is constructed psychologically. While acknowledging the importance of anthropological theory that emphasizes the production of selves and meanings at the intersection of overlapping structures of power, we suggest that an explanation of resistance requires a theory of the subject as not being simply produced in relations of power but as making meanings in her relationships with others.

Our analysis thus emphasizes the relational context of both creativity and conformity. That subjects want to resist must be understood in the context not only of an acting or speaking subject but of a reacting or listening subject as well. The interplay of the two—what we have termed "recognition," following Benjamin and Winnicott, is what affords the potential for resistance and creativity as well as for conformity. Likewise, misrecognition or failure of recognition by others may set the ground for disempowerment. Steedman's account of the failed interpretation of Amarjit's song by the audience of schoolchildren and Williams's description of how she sought to "give meaning to [Marjorie's] silence" as she lay dying just as Marjorie had once been for her a mirror in which she could "remember herself" suggest the different ways in which listening may empower or disempower, provide moments of awakening or of repression, and may be complicitous with or subversive of official speech. Listening is at the heart of emotional engagement, shaping the capacity of the other to speak. Whether the listener may be experienced as friend or enemy,[20] it is in this dialogue that the disjunctures and conjunctures of culture are reshaped into the subjective forms of desire, empowering

[20] Bourdieu (1987, 225) complicates this idea with his notion of "false friend," one who presents her or himself as supportive but in fact represents other interests. See also Ginsburg (1989) on the construction of abortion activists "in dialogue with the enemy" (196).

subjects who are not only complicit but capable as well of resisting relations of domination.

School of Social Science
Hampshire College

References

Abu-Lughod, Lila. 1986. *Veiled Sentiments: Honor and Poetry in a Bedouin Society*. Berkeley and Los Angeles: University of California Press.
_____ . 1990. "The Romance of Resistance: Tracing Transformations of Power through Bedouin Women." *American Anthropologist* 17(1):41–55.
Benjamin, Jessica. 1987. *The Bonds of Love: Psychoanalysis, Feminism and the Problem of Domination*. New York: Pantheon.
_____ . 1991. "Father and Daughter: Identification with Difference—a Contribution to Gender Heterodoxy." *Psychoanalytic Dialogues* 1(3):277–99.
Bourdieu, Pierre. 1977. *Outline of a Theory of Practice*. Cambridge: Cambridge University Press.
_____ . 1987. "The Force of Law: Toward a Sociology of the Juridical Field." *Hastings Law Journal* 38(5):805–53.
Bruner, Edward M. 1986. "Experience and Its Expressions." In *The Anthropology of Experience*, ed. Victor W. Turner and Edward M. Bruner. Urbana: University of Illinois Press.
Butler, Judith. 1990. *Gender Trouble: Feminism and the Subversion of Identity*. New York: Routledge.
Chodorow, Nancy. 1978. *The Reproduction of Mothering: Psychoanalysis and the Sociology of Gender*. Berkeley: University of California Press.
_____ . 1989. *Feminism and Psychoanalytic Theory*. New Haven, Conn., and London: Yale University Press.
Comaroff, Jean. 1985. *Body of Power, Spirit of Resistance*. Chicago: University of Chicago Press.
Coombe, Rosemary. 1991. "The Celebrity Image and Cultural Identity: Publicity Rights and the Subaltern Politics of Gender." Unpublished manuscript, University of Toronto, Faculty of Law.
Craton, Michael. 1982. *Testing the Chains: Resistance to Slavery in the British West Indies*. Ithaca, N.Y.: Cornell University Press.
Davis, Natalie Zemon. 1983. *The Return of Martin Guerre*. Cambridge, Mass.: Harvard University Press.
_____ . 1986. "Boundaries and the Sense of Self in Sixteenth Century France." In *Reconstructing Individualism: Autonomy, Individuality and the Self in Western Thought*, ed. Thomas Heller, Morton Sosna, and David Wellbery, 53–63. Stanford, Calif.: Stanford University Press.
de Certeau, Michel. 1984. *The Practice of Everyday Life*. Berkeley and Los Angeles: University of California Press.
de Lauretis, Theresa. 1987. *Technologies of Gender: Essays in Theory, Film, and Fiction*. Bloomington: Indiana University Press.

————. 1990. "Eccentric Subjects: Feminist Theory and Historical Consciousness." *Feminist Studies* 16(1):115–50.

Flax, Jane. 1990. *Thinking Fragments: Psychoanalysis, Feminism and Postmodernism in the Contemporary West.* Berkeley and Los Angeles: University of California Press.

Foucault, Michel. 1982. "The Subject and Power." In *Michel Foucault: Beyond Structuralism and Hermeneutics*, ed. Herbert L. Dreyfus and Paul Rabinow. Chicago: University of Chicago Press.

Giddens, Anthony. 1979. *Central Problems in Social Theory: Action, Structure and Contradiction in Social Analysis.* Berkeley and Los Angeles: University of California Press.

Gilligan, Carol, and Grant Wiggins. 1988. "The Origins of Morality in Early Childhood Relationships." In *Mapping the Moral Domain*, ed. Carol Gilligan, Jamie Victoria Ward, and Jill McLean Taylor, 111–38. Cambridge, Mass.: Harvard University Press.

Ginsburg, Faye. 1989. *Contested Lives: The Abortion Debate in an American Community.* Berkeley and Los Angeles: University of California Press.

Gordon, Linda. 1988. *Heroes of Their Own Lives: The Politics and History of Family Violence.* New York: Viking.

Gutman, Herbert. 1977. *The Black Family in Slavery and Freedom: 1750–1925.* New York: Pantheon.

Hartog, Hendrik. 1990. "Abigail Bailey's Coverture: Law in a Married Woman's Consciousness." Unpublished manuscript, University of Wisconsin—Madison, Institute for Legal Research.

Henriques, Julian, et al. 1984. *Changing the Subject.* New York: Methuen.

Hollway, Wendy. 1984. "Gender Difference and the Production of Subjectivity." In Henriques et al. 1984, 227–63.

Kaplan, Cora. 1986. "The Thorn Birds: Fiction, Fantasy, Femininity." In *Formations of Fantasy*, ed. Victor Burgin, James Donald, and Cora Kaplan, 142–66. London and New York: Methuen.

Lacan, Jacques. 1977. "The Mirror Stage as Formative of the Function of the I as Revealed in Psychoanalytic Experience." In *Ecrits: A Selection*, 1–7. New York and London: Norton.

Levine, Robert. 1984. "Properties of Culture: An Ethnographic View." In *Culture Theory*, ed. Richard A. Shweder and Robert A. Levine, 67–87. London and New York: Cambridge University Press.

Mahler, Margaret, Fred Pine, and Anni Bergman. 1975. *The Psychological Birth of the Human Infant: Symbiosis and Individuation.* New York: Basic.

Mitchell, Juliet. 1982. "Introduction I." In Mitchell and Rose 1982, 1–26.

Mitchell, Juliet, and Jacqueline Rose, eds. 1982. *Feminine Sexuality: Jacques Lacan and the Ecole Freudienne.* New York and London: Norton.

Ochs, Eleanor, and Bambi B. Schieffelin. 1984. "Language Acquisition and Socialization." In *Culture Theory*, ed. Richard A. Shweder and Robert A. LeVine, 276–320. New York and London: Cambridge University Press.

Phillips, Adam. 1988. *Winnicott.* Cambridge, Mass.: Harvard University Press.

Rosaldo, Michelle. 1980. *Knowledge and Passion: Ilongot Notions of Self and Social Life.* New York: Cambridge University Press.

Rose, Jacqueline. 1982. "Introduction II." In Mitchell and Rose 1982, 27–57.

Scheper-Hughes, Nancy. 1985. "Culture, Scarcity, and Maternal Thinking." *Ethos* 13(4):291–317.

Scott, James. 1985. *Weapons of the Weak: Everyday Forms of Peasant Resistance.* New Haven, Conn.: Yale University Press.

Steedman, Carolyn. 1985. " 'Listen, How the Caged Bird Sings': Amarjit's Song." In *Language, Gender, and Childhood,* ed. Carolyn Steedman, Cathy Urwin, and Valerie Walkerdine, 137–63. London and Boston: Routledge & Kegan Paul.

Stern, Daniel. 1985. *The Interpersonal World of the Infant.* New York: Basic.

Urwin, Cathy. 1984. "Power Relations and the Emergence of Language." In Henriques et al. 1984, 264–322.

Williams, Patricia. 1988. "On Being the Object of Property." *Signs: Journal of Women in Culture and Society* 14(1):5–24.

Willis, Paul. 1981. *Learning to Labour: How Working Class Kids Get Working Class Jobs.* New York: Columbia University Press.

Winnicott, D. W. (1960) 1965. "The Theory of the Parent-Infant Relationship." In *The Maturational Process and the Facilitating Environment.* New York: International University Press.

———. 1982a. *Playing and Reality.* New York: Tavistock.

———. (1951) 1982b. "Transitional Objects and Transitional Phenomena." In Winnicott 1982a, 1–25.

———. (1967) 1982c. "The Location of Cultural Experience." In Winnicott 1982a, 95–103.

———. (1969) 1982d. "The Use of an Object and Relating through Identifications." In Winnicott 1982a, 86–94.

Purity, Impurity, and Separation

María Lugones

> *Note to the reader: This writing is done from within a hybrid imagination, within a recently articulate tradition of latina writers who emphasize mestizaje and multiplicity as tied to resistant and liberatory possibilities. All resemblance between this tradition and postmodern literature and philosophy is coincidental, though the conditions that underlie both may well be significantly tied. The implications of each are very different from one another.*

VOY A EMPEZAR en español y en la cocina. Two uses of the verb *separar*. El primer sentido. Voy a separar la yema de la clara, separar un huevo. I will *separate* the white from the yolk. I will *separate* an egg. I crack the egg and I now slide the white onto one half of the shell and I place the egg white in a bowl. I repeat the operation till I have separated all of the egg white from the yolk. Si la operación no ha sido exitosa, entonces queda un poquito de yema en la clara. If the operation has not been successful, a bit of the yolk stains the white. I wish I could begin again with another egg, but that is a waste, as I was taught. So I must try to lift all the yolk from the white with a spoon, a process that is tedious and hardly ever entirely successful. The intention is to separate, first cleanly and then, in case of failure, a bit messily, the white from the yolk, to split the egg into two parts as cleanly as one can. This is an exercise in purity.

It is part of my interest in this article to ask whether separation is always or necessarily an exercise in purity. I want to investigate the politics of purity and how they bear on the politics of separation. In the process I will take neither the dominant nor the "standard" tongue as my anchor in playing with "separation," as those who separate may do so not in allegiance to but in defiance of the dominant intention. As I uncover a connection between impurity and resistance, my Latina imagination moves from resistance to mestizaje. I think of mestizaje as an example

[*Signs: Journal of Women in Culture and Society* 1994, vol. 19, no. 2]

of and a metaphor for both impurity and resistance. I hold on to the metaphor and adopt *mestizaje* as a central name for impure resistance to interlocked, intermeshed oppressions.[1] Much of the time, my very use of the word *separate* exhibits a form of cultural mestizaje.[2]

If something or someone is neither/nor, but kind of both, not quite either,

if something is in the middle of either/or,

if it is ambiguous, given the available classification of things,

if it is mestiza,

if it threatens by its very ambiguity the orderliness of the system, of schematized reality,

if given its ambiguity in the univocal ordering it is anomalous, deviant,

can it be tamed through separation? Should it separate so as to avoid taming? Should it resist separation? Should it resist through separation? Separate as in the separation of the white from the yolk?

Segundo sentido. Estoy haciendo mayonesa. I am making mayonnaise. I place the yolk in a bowl, add a few drops of water, stir, and then add oil drop by drop, very slowly, as I continue stirring. If I add too much oil at once, the mixture se separa, it separates. I can remember doing the operation as an impatient child, stopping and saying to my mother "Mamá, la mayonesa se separó." In English, one might say that the mayonnaise curdled. Mayonnaise is an oil-in-water emulsion. As all emulsions, it is unstable. When an emulsion curdles, the ingredients become separate from each other. But that is not altogether an accurate description: rather, they coalesce toward oil or toward water, most of the water becomes separate from most of the oil—it is instead, a matter of different degrees of coalescence.[3] The same with mayonnaise; when it separates, you are left with yolky oil and oily yolk.

Going back to mestizaje, in the middle of either/or, ambiguity, and thinking of acts that belong in lives lived in mestizo ways,

thinking of all forms of mestizaje,

thinking of breaching and abandoning dichotomies,

thinking of being anomalous willfully or unwillfully in a world of precise, hard-edged schema,

thinking of resistance,

---

[1] I thank Marilyn Frye for her criticism of the choice of *interlocking* in *interlocking oppressions*. I agree with her claim to me that the image of interlocking is of two entirely discrete things, like two pieces of a jigsaw puzzle, that articulate with each other. I am not ready to give up the term because it is used by other women of color theorists who write in a liberatory vein about enmeshed oppressions. I think *interwoven* or *intermeshed* or *enmeshed* may provide better images.

[2] This is the same form found in my use of *operation, apparatus,* and *individual*. Providing linguistic puzzles is part of the art of curdling.

[3] For this use of *emulsion,* see *Pharmaceutica Acta Helvetiae* 1991.

resistance to a world of purity, of domination, of control over our possibilities,

is separation not at the crux of mestizaje, ambiguity, resistance? Is it not at the crux both of its necessity and its possibility? Separation as in the separation of the white from the yolk or separation as curdling?

When I think of mestizaje, I think both of separation as curdling, an exercise in impurity, and of separation as splitting, an exercise in purity. I think of the attempt at control exercised by those who possess both power and the categorical eye and who attempt to split everything impure, breaking it down into pure elements (as in egg white and egg yolk) for the purposes of control. Control over creativity. And I think of something in the middle of either/or, something impure, something or someone mestizo, as both separated, curdled, and resisting in its curdled state. Mestizaje defies control through simultaneously asserting the impure, curdled multiple state and rejecting fragmentation into pure parts. In this play of assertion and rejection, the mestiza is unclassifiable, unmanageable. She has no pure parts to be "had," controlled.

Inside the world of the impure

There was a muchacha who lived near my house. La gente del pueblo talked about her being una de las otras, "of the Others." They said that for six months she was a woman who had a vagina that bled once a month, and that for the other six months she was a man, had a penis and she peed standing up. They called her half and half, mita'y mita, neither one nor the other but a strange doubling, a deviation of nature that horrified, a work of nature inverted. [Anzaldúa 1987, 19]

and Louie would come through—
melodramatic music, like in the
mono—tan tan taran!—Cruz
Diablo, El Charro Negro! Bogart smile (his smile as deadly as his vaisas!) He dug roles, man,
and names—like "Blackie," "Little Louie ..."
Ese, Louie ...
Chale, man, call me "Diamonds!"

[Montoya 1972, 173]

Now my mother, she doesn't go for cleanliness, orderliness, static have-come-from-nowhere objects for use. She shows you the production, her production. She is always in the middle of it and you will never see

*the end. You'll have to follow her through her path in the chaotic pro-
duction, you'll have to know her comings and goings, her fluidity
through the production. You'll have to, that is, if you want to use any of
it. Because she points to what you need in her own way, her person is the
"here" that ensures her subjectivity, she is the point of reference, and if
you don't know her movements, her location, you can't get to the end of
the puzzle. Unless she wants you to, and sometimes, she'll do that for
you, because she hasn't stored that much resistance. She doesn't have
names for things (oh, she has them somewhere, but uses them very little),
as if she always saw them in the making, in process, in connection, not
quite separable from the rest. She says "it," "under that," "next to me."
"These go in the thing for things." And if you follow her movements up
to the very present, you know just what she means, just what her hand
is needing to hold and just where she left it and her words are very helpful
in finding it. Now, clean, what you call clean, you will not see clean
either. You'll see half way. Kind of. In the middle of either/or. She doesn't
see things as broken, finished, either. It's rather a very long process of
deterioration. Not a now you see it, now you don't, gone forever. Just
because it fell on the floor and broke in half and you glued it and you
have to fill it half way, so stuff doesn't drip from the side, it doesn't stop
being a tureen (or a flower pot for "centros de mesa," or maybe it'll be good
as one of those thingamajigs to put things in). It's still good. And it hasn't
changed its "nature" either. She has always had multiple functions for it,
many possibilities. Its multiplicity has always been obvious to her.*

*Getting real close, like a confidence, you tell me, "Because certain
individuals can get too accustomed to being helped." That snatch of
mestizaje—"certain individuals"—the Southamerican use of "indi-
viduos" chiseled into your English. Makes me feel good, in the know. I
know what you mean mujer, Southamerican style. Just like my "opera-
tion." Claro que se dice real close, it's not just for everyone's ears. You
make me feel special. I know, I know about "certain individuals." Like
the "apparatus" you borrow from me or I borrow from you.*

*"Culture is what happens to other people." I've heard something like
that. I'm one of the other people, so I know there is something funny
there. Renato Rosaldo helps me articulate what is peculiar, paradoxical.
As he is critiquing classic norms in anthropology marking off those who
are visible from those who are invisible in a culture, Rosaldo articulates
the politics underlying them: "Full citizens lack culture, and those most
culturally endowed lack full citizenship" (1989, 198). Part of what is
funny here is that people with culture are people with a culture unknown
by full citizens, not worth knowing. Only the culture of people who are*

culturally transparent is worth knowing, but it does not count as a culture. The people whose culture it is are postcultural. Their culture is invisible to them and thus nonexistent as such. But postcultural full citizens mandate that people with a culture give up theirs in favor of the nonexistent invisible culture. So, it's a peculiar status: I have "culture" because what I have exists in the eyes of those who declare what I have to be "culture." But they declare it "culture" only to the extent which they know they don't know it except as an absence that they don't want to learn as a presence and they have the power not to know. Furthermore they have the power to order me to cease to know. So, as I resist and know, I am both visible and invisible. Visible as other and invisible as myself, but these aren't separable bits. And I walk around as both other and myselves, resisting classification.

Rosaldo criticizes the "broad rule of thumb under classic anthropological norms . . . that if it's moving it isn't cultural" (1989, 209). "The blurred zones within a culture and the zones between cultures are endowed by the norms with a curious kind of hybrid invisibility" (1989, 209). Paradoxically "culture" needs to be both static, fixed and separate, different from the "postcultural" (1989, 199) to be seen. So, if it's different but not static, it isn't "culture." But if it's different, if it's what "other people do," it's cultural. If the people who do it are other but what they do is not static, it is and it isn't culture. It's in the middle, anomalous, deviant, ambiguous, impure. It lacks the mark of separation as purity. If it's hybrid, it's in the middle of either/or twice.

The play between feminine and masculine elements that we contain in heterosexist eyes;
   the parody of masculine/feminine, the play with illusion that transgresses gender boundaries, the "now you see 'it' now you don't" magic tricks aimed at destroying the univocal character of the "it" that we disdain with playful intention;
   the rejection of masculine/feminine in our self-understanding that some of us make our mark;
   all contain a rejection of purity.

In every one of these examples there is curdling, mestizaje, lack of homogeneity. There is tension. The intentions are curdled, the language, the behavior, the people are mestizo.

I. Control, unity, and separation

Guide to the reader: I will presuppose that as I investigate the conceptual world of purity, you will keep the world of mestizaje, of curdled beings, constantly superimposed onto it, even when that is made difficult by the writing's focus on the logic of purity. Sometimes the logic of purity dominates the text, sometimes the logic of curdling does. But at other points both worlds become vivid as coexisting and the logic of what I say depends on the coexistence. The reader needs to see ambiguity, see that the split-separated are also and simultaneously curdled-separated. Otherwise one is only seeing the success of oppression, seeing with the lover of purity's eyes. The reader also needs to, as it were, grant the assumptions of the lover of purity to understand his world. The fundamental assumption is that there is unity underlying multiplicity. The assumption is granted for the sake of entering the point of view and for the purposes of contestation. The questioning is done from within la realidad mestiza and the intent of the questioning is to clarify, intensify, aid the contestation between the two realities. As I enter the world of purity, I am interested in a cluster of concepts as clustered: control, purity, unity, categorizing. Control or categorizing in isolation from this network are not my concern.

My aim is to distinguish between multiplicity (mestizaje) and fragmentation and to explain connections that I see between the terms of this distinction and the logics of curdling (impurity) and of splitting (purity). Fragmentation follows the logic of purity. Multiplicity follows the logic of curdling. The distinction between fragmentation and multiplicity is central to this essay. I will exhibit it within individuals and within the social world.[4]

According to the logic of curdling, the social world is complex and heterogenous and each person is multiple, nonfragmented, embodied. Fragmented: in fragments, pieces, parts that do not fit well together, parts taken for wholes, composite, composed of the parts of other beings, composed of imagined parts, composed of parts produced by a splitting imagination, composed of parts produced by subordinates enacting their dominators' fantasies. According to the logic of purity, the social world is both unified and fragmented, homogenous, hierarchically ordered. Each person is either fragmented, composite, or abstract and unified— not exclusive alternatives. Unification and homogeneity are related principles of ordering the social world. Unification requires a fragmented and hierarchical ordering. Fragmentation is another quise of unity, both in the collectivity and the individual. I will connect mestizaje in individuals to mestizaje in groups and thus in the social world, and I will connect fragmentation within individuals to the training of the multiple toward a homogenous social world.

I do not claim ontological originality for multiplicity here. Rather both the multiple-mestizo and the unified-fragmented coexist, each have

---

[4] It is important to problematize the singularity of "social world" and the distinction between social world and individual.

their histories, are in contestation and in significant logical tension. I reveal the logics underlying the contestation. Sometimes my use of language strongly suggests a claim of originality for the multiple. I speak of the multiple as trained into unity and of its being conceived as internally separable. I could say that to split-separate the multiple is to exercise a split imagination. But if what is imagined is to gain a powerful degree of reality, unity must be more than a reading or interpretation. It must order people's lives and psyches. The becoming of the order is a historical process of domination in which power and ideology are at all times changing into each other.

Monophilia and purity are cut from the same cloth. The urge to control the multiplicity of people and things attains satisfaction through exercises in split separation. The urge to control multiplicity is expressed in modern political theory and ethics in an understanding of reason as reducing multiplicity to unity through abstraction, categorization, from a particular vantage point.[5] I consider this reduction expressive of the urge to control because of the logical fit between it and the creation of the fragmented individual. I understand fragmentation to be a form of domination.

I see this reduction of multiplicity to unity as being completed through a complex series of fictions. Once the assumption of unity underlying multiplicity is made, further fictions rationalize it as a discovery. The assumption makes these fictions possible, and they, in turn, transform it from a simple assumption into a fiction.

The assumption of unity is an act of split separation; as in conceiving of what is multiple as unified, what is multiple is understood as internally separable, divisible into what makes it one and the remainder. Or, to put it another way: to conceive of fragmentation rather than multiplicity is to exercise a split-separation imagination. This assumption generates and presupposes others. It generates the fictional construction of a vantage point from which unified wholes, totalities, can be captured. It generates the construction of a subject who can occupy such a vantage point. Both the vantage point and the subject are outside historicity and concreteness. They are both affected by and effect the reduction of multiplicity. The vantage point is privileged, simple, one-dimensional. The subject is fragmented, abstract, without particularity. The series of fictions hides the training of the multiple into unity as well as the survival of the multiple. It is only from a historical enmeshing in the concrete that the training of

---

[5] I have based this description of the connection between the urge to control and modern political theory and ethics on Iris Marion Young's "Impartiality and the Civic Public" (in Young 1990b). Much of what I say in Sec. I is a restatement and elaboration on secs. 1 and 2 of Young's article. I have also benefited from Mangabeira Unger 1975 and Pateman 1988 in coming to this understanding.

the multiple into fragmented unities can be seen; that is, it can be seen from a different logic, one that rejects the assumption of unity. The ahistoricity of the logic of purity hides the construction of unity.

In understanding the fictitious character of the vantage point it is important that we recognize that its conception is itself derivative from the conception of reality as unified. If we assume that the world of people and things is unified, then we can conceive of a vantage point from which its unity can be grasped. The conception of the vantage point follows the urge to control; it is not antecedent to it, because unity is assumed. The vantage point is then itself beyond description, except as an absence: "outside of" is its central characteristic. The vantage point is not of this world, it is otherworldly, as ideal as its occupant, the ideal observer. It exists only as that from which unity can be perceived.

The subject who can occupy such a vantage point, the ideal observer, must himself be pure, unified, and simple so as to occupy the vantage point and perceive unity amid multiplicity.[6] He must not himself be pulled in all or several perceptual directions; he must not perceive richly. Reason, including its normative aspect, is the unified subject. It is what characterizes the subject as a unity. A subject who in its multiplicity perceives, understands, grasps its worlds as multiple sensuously, passionately as well as rationally without the splitting separation between sense/emotion/reason lacks the unidimensionality and the simplicity required to occupy the privileged vantage point. Such a subject occupies the vantage point of reason in a pragmatic contradiction, standing in a place where all of the subject's abilities cannot be exercised and where the exercise of its abilities invalidates the standpoint. So a passionate, needy, sensuous, and rational subject must be conceived as internally separable, as discretely divided into what makes it one—rationality—and into the confused, worthless remainder—passion, sensuality. Rationality is understood as this ability of a unified subject to abstract, categorize, train the multiple to the systematicity of norms, of rules that highlight, capture, and train its unity from the privileged vantage point.

The conception of this subject is derivative from the assumption of unity and separability. The very "construction" of the subject presupposes that assumption. So, though we are supposed to understand unity in multiplicity as that which is perceived by the rational subject occupying the vantage point of reason, we can see that the logic of the matter goes the other way around. Control cannot be rationally justified in this manner, as the urge to control antecedes this conception of reason. Part of my claim here is that the urge for control and the passion for purity are conceptually related.

---

[6] The ideal observer, unified subject is male. This fictitious subject is not marked in terms of gender for reasons explained below.

If the modern subject is to go beyond conceptualizing the reduction to actually exercising control over people and things, then these fictions must be given some degree of reality. The modern subject must be dressed, costumed, masked so as to appear able to exercise this reduction of heterogeneity to homogeneity, of multiplicity to unity. The modern subject must be masked as standing separate from his own multiplicity and what commits him to multiplicity. So, his own purification into someone who can step squarely onto the vantage point of unity requires that his remainder become of no consequence to his own sense of himself as someone who justifiably exercises control over multiplicity. So his needs must be taken care of by others hidden in spaces relegated outside of public view, where he parades himself as pure. And it is important to his own sense of things and of himself that he pay little attention to the satisfaction of the requirements of his sensuality, affectivity, embodiment.

Satisfying the modern subject's needs requires beings enmeshed in the multiple as the production of discrete units occurs amid multiplicity. Such production is importantly constrained by its invisibility and worthlessness in the eyes of those who attempt to control multiplicity. To the extent that the modern subject succeeds in this attempt to control mutiplicity, the production is impelled by his needs. Those who produce it become producers of the structuring "perceived" by the lover of purity from the rational vantage point as well as its products. So in the logic of the lover of purity they exhibit a peculiar lack of agency, autonomy, self-regulating ability.[7]

As the lover of purity, the impartial reasoner is outside history, outside culture. He occupies the privileged vantage point with others like him, all characterized by the "possession" of reason. All occupants of this vantage point are homogeneous in their ability to comprehend and communicate. So "culture," which marks radical differences in conceptions of people and things, cannot be something they have. They are instead "postcultural" or "culturally transparent."[8]

Since his embodiment is irrelevant to his unity, he cannot have symbolic and institutionalized inscriptions in his body that mark him as someone who is "outside" his own production as the rational subject. To the extent that mastering institutional inscriptions is part of the program of unification, there cannot be such markings of his body. His difference cannot be thought of as "inscriptions" but only as coincidental, nonsymbolic marks. As his race and gender do not identify him in his own eyes, he is also race and gender transparent.

[7] See Smith 1974 and Hartsock 1988 for arguments backing this account.

[8] See Rosaldo 1989, 200 and 203, for his use of *postcultural* and *culturally transparent*. I am using *postcultural* as he does. His use of *culturally transparent* was suggestive to me in reaching my own account.

Paradoxically, the lover of purity is also constituted as incoherent, as contradictory in his attitude toward his own and others' gender, race, culture. He must at once emphasize them and ignore them. He must be radically self-deceiving in this respect. His production as pure, as the impartial reasoner, requires that others produce him. He is a fiction of his own imagination, but his imagination is mediated by the labor of others. He controls those who produce him, who to his eyes require his control because they are enmeshed in multiplicity and thus unable to occupy the vantage point of control. They are marked as other than himself, as lacking the relevant unity. But the lack is not discovered, it couldn't be, since the unity is itself assumed. The lack is symbolically produced by marking the producers as gendered, racialized, and "cultured." The marking signifies that they are enmeshed in multiplicity and thus are different from the lover of purity. But he must deny the importance of the markings that separate them.

If women, the poor, the colored, the queer, the ones with cultures (whose cultures are denied and rendered invisible as they are seen as our mark) are deemed unfit for the public, it is because we are tainted by need, emotion, the body. This tainting is relative to the modern subject's urge for control through unity and the production and maintenance of himself as unified. To the extent that he is fictional, the tainting is fictional: seeing us as tainted depends on a need for purity that requires that we become "parts," "addenda" of the bodies of modern subjects—Christian white bourgeois men—and make their purity possible. We become sides of fictitious dichotomies. To the extent that we are ambiguous—non-dichotomous—we threaten the fiction and can be rendered unfit only by decrying ambiguity as nonexistent—that is, by halving us, splitting us. Thus we exist only as incomplete, unfit beings, and they exist as complete only to the extent that what we are, and what is absolutely necessary for them, is declared worthless.

The lover of purity is shot through and through with this paradoxical incoherence. When confronted with the sheer overabundance of the multiple, he ignores it by placing it outside value when it is his own substance and provides his sustenance. So, he is committed both to an overevaluation and to a devaluation of himself, a torturing of himself, a disciplining or training of himself that puts him at the mercy of his own control. The incoherence is dispelled through separation, his own from himself. As he covets, possesses, destroys, pleases himself, he disowns his own urges and deeds. So he is always rescued from his own incoherence by self-deception, weakness of the will, aggressive ignorance. After he ignores the fundamental and unfounded presupposition of unity, all further ignoring becomes easier. He shuns impurity, ambiguity, multiplicity as they threaten his own fiction. The enormity of the threat keeps him from understanding it. So, the lover of purity remains ignorant of his own impurity, and thus the threat of all impurity remains significantly uncontained. The lover of purity cannot see, understand, and attempt to control the resistance contained in the impure. He can only attempt control indirectly, through the complex incoherence of affirming and denying impurity, training the impure into its "parts" and at the same time separating from it, erecting sturdy barriers both around himself and between the fictional "parts" of impure beings.

In *Purity and Danger,* Mary Douglas (1989) sees the impulse toward unity as characteristic of social structures, and she understands pollution behavior—behavior to control pollution, impurity—as a guarding of structure from the threat of impurity. According to Douglas, impurity, dirt, is what is "out of place" relative to some order. What is impure is anomalous and ambiguous because it is out of place. It threatens order because it is not definable, so separation from it is a manner of containing it. She also sees power in impurity. But it is not her purpose to distinguish between oppressive and nonoppressive structuring. My purpose here is precisely to understand the particular oppressive character of the modern construction of social life and the power of impurity in resisting and threatening this oppressive structuring.

Part of what is interesting in Douglas is that she understands that what is impure is impure relative to some order and that the order is itself conventional. What is impure is anomalous. Douglas describes several ways of dealing with anomalies, but she does not emphasize that rendering something impure is a way of dealing with it. The ordering renders something out of place. Its complexity is altered by the ordering. The alteration is not only conceptual since its "life" develops in relation to this order. So, for example, the multiplicitous beings required for the production of the unified subject are anomalous as multiple. Unity renders them anomalous. So they are altered to fit within the logic of unification. They are split over and over in accordance with the relevant dichotomies of the logic of unity. As anomalous, they remain complex, defying the logic of unity. That which is multiplicitous metamorphoses over and over in its history of resisting alteration and as the result of alteration. Both the logic of control and unity and the logic of resistance and complexity are at work in what is impure. That is why I have and will continue to use *impure* ambiguously both for something complex that is in process and thus cannot really be split-separated and for that which is fragmented.

When seen as split, the impure/multiplicitous are seen from the logic of unity, and thus their multiplicity can neither be seen nor understood. But splitting can itself be understood from the logic of resistance and countered through curdling separation, a power of the impure. When seen from the logic of curdling, the alteration of the impure to unity is seen as fictitious and as an exercise in domination: the impure are rendered uncreative, ascetic, static, realizers of the contents of the modern subject's imagination. Curdling, in contrast, realizes their against-the-grain creativity, articulates their within-structure-inarticulate powers.[9] As we come to understand curdling as resisting domination, we also need to recognize its potential to germinate a nonoppressive pattern, a mestiza consciousness, una conciencia mestiza.[10]

Interrupción

Oh, I would entertain the thought of separation as really clean, the two components untouched by each other, unmixed as they would be if I could go away with my own people to our land to engage in acts that were cleanly ours! But then I ask myself who my own people are. When I think of my own people, the only people I can think of as my own are transitionals, liminals, border-dwellers, "world"-travelers, beings in the middle of either/or. They are all people whose acts and thoughts curdle-separate. So as soon as I entertain the thought, I realize that separation into clean, tidy things and beings is not possible for me because it would be the death of myself as multiplicitous and a death of community with my own. I understand my split or fragmented possibilities in horror. I understand then that whenever I desire separation, I risk survival by confusing split separation with separation from domination, that is, separation among curdled beings who curdle away their fragmentation, their subordination. I can appreciate then that the logic of split-separation and the logic of curdle-separation repel each other, that the curdled do not germinate in split separation.

II. Split selves

Dual personality

What Frank Chin calls a "dual personality" is the production of a being who is simultaneously different and the same as postcultural subjects, a split and contradictory being who is a product of the ethnocentric racist imagination (1991). It is one way of dealing with the anomaly of being cultured and culturally multiplicitous. The case I know best is rural

---

[9] See Douglas 1966: "In other words, where the social system is well-articulated, I look for articulate powers vested in the points of authority; where the social system is ill-articulated, I look for inarticulate powers vested in those who are a source of disorder" (99).

[10] See Anzaldúa 1987, esp. 41–51, on the Coatlicue State, and 77–91 on la Conciencia de la Mestiza.

Chicanos. *Chicano* is the name for the curdled or mestizo person. I will name the dual personality *mexican/american,* with no hyphen in the name, to signify that if the split were successful there would be no possibility of dwelling or living on the hyphen.[11]

The rural mexican/american is a product of the anglo imagination, sometimes enacted by persons who are the targets of ethnocentric racism in an unwillful parody of themselves. The anglo imagines each rural mexican/american as having a dual personality: the authentic mexican cultural self and the american self. In this notion, there is no hybrid self. The selves are conceptually different, apparently contradictory but complementary; one cannot be found without the other. The anglo philosophy is that mexican/americans should both keep their culture (so as to be different and not full citizens) and assimilate (so as to be exploitable), a position whose contradictoriness is obvious. But as a split dual personality, the authentic mexican can assimilate without ceasing to be "cultured," the two selves complementary, the ornamental nature of the mexican self resolving the contradiction.

The mexican/american can assimilate because the *mexican* in *mexican/american* is understood to be a member of a superfluous culture, the culture an ornament rather than shaping or affecting american reality. A simple but stoic figure who will defend the land no matter what, the mexican/american will never quite enter the twentieth century and will not make it in the twenty-first, given that in this scheme for the next century the land will no longer be used for farming but for the recreation of the anglo upper class. The authentic mexican is a romantic figure, an anglo myth, alive in the pages of John Nichols's *Milagro Beanfield War* (1976): fiercely conservative and superexploitable.

As americans, rural mexican/americans are not first-class citizens because the two sides of the split cannot be found without each other. The complementarity of the sides becomes clearer: the assimilated mexican cannot lose culture as ornamental and as a mark of difference. So a mexican/american is not a postcultural american. The promise of postculturalism is part of what makes assimilation appealing, since the mexican/american knows that only postculturals are full citizens. But assimilation does not make the mexican/american postcultural. So making the anglo ideals of progress and efficiency one's own serves one only to become exploitable but not to achieve full participation in anglo life. Anglos declare mexican/americans unfit for control and portray them as men and women of simple minds given to violence, drink, and hard work, accustomed to hardship and poverty, in particular.

[11] Sonia Saldivar-Hull used the expression "living on the hyphen" in the panel discussion "Cultural Identity and the Academy," tenth annual Interdisciplinary Forum of the Western Humanities Conference on Cultures and Nationalisms, University of California, Los Angeles.

The dual personality is part of the mythical portrait of the colonized (Memmi 1967). The split renders the self into someone unable to be culturally creative in a live culture. Thus "authentic" mexican craft shops exhibit santos, trasteros, colchas, reredos. Mexican artists cannot depart from the formulaic; they are supposed to be producing relics for the anglo consumer of the picturesque. The mythical portrait therefore has acquired a degree of reality that both justifies and obscures anglo dominance. The portrait does not lack in appeal. It makes one feel proud to be raza because the portrait is heroic. It also makes one stilted, stiff, a cultural personage not quite sure of oneself, a pose, pure style, not quite at ease in one's own cultural skin, as if one did not quite know one's own culture, precisely because it is not one's own but a stereotype and because this authentic culture is not quite a live culture: it is conceived by the anglo as both static and dying. As Rosaldo says, part of the myth is that "if it moves, it is not cultural" (1989, 212). This authentic mexican culture bears a relation to traditional culture. It is tradition filtered through anglo eyes for the purposes of ornamentation. What is anglo, authentically american, is also appealing: it represents progress, the future, efficiency, material well being. As american, one moves; as mexican, one is static. As american, one is beyond culture; as mexican, one is culture personified. The culturally split self is a character for the theatrics of racism.

The dual personality concept is a death-loving attempt to turn raza into beautiful zombies: an attempt to eradicate the possibility of a mestizo/a consciousness, of our infusing every one of our possibilities with this consciousness and of our moving from traditional to hybrid ways of creation, including the production of material life.

As split, mexican/americans cannot participate in public life because of their difference, except ornamentally in the dramatization of equality. If we retreat and accept the "between raza" nonpublic status of our concerns, to be resolved in the privacy of our communities, we participate in the logic of the split. Our communities are rendered private space in the public/private distinction. Crossing to the anglo domain only in their terms is not an option either, as it follows the logic of the split without the terms ever becoming our own, that is the nature of this—if not of all—assimilation. So, the resistance and rejection of the culturally split self requires that we declare our communities public space and break the conceptual tie between public space and monoculturally conceived anglo-only concerns: it requires that the language and conceptual framework of the public become hybrid.

Fragmentation

In *Justice and the Politics of Difference* (1990a) and "Polity and Difference" (in 1990b), Iris Young highlights the concept of a group as central to her understanding of the heterogenous public, a conception of the civic public that does not ignore heterogeneity through reducing it to a fictitious unity. Instead of a unified public realm "in which citizens leave behind their particular group affiliations, histories, and needs to discuss a general interest or common good," she argues for "a group differentiated citizenship and a heterogenous public" (1990b, 121).

She understands a social group as "a collective of persons differentiated from at least one other group by cultural forms, practices, or way of life" (1990a, 43). Groups become differentiated through the encounter and interaction between social collectivities that experience some differences in their way of life and forms of association as well as through social processes such as the sexual division of labor. Group members have "an affinity with other persons by which they identify with one another and by which other people identify them" (1990b, 122). Group identity partly constitutes "a person's particular sense of history, understanding of social relations and personal possibilities, her or his mode of reasoning, values and expressive styles" (1990b, 122). Their similar way of life or experience prompts group members "to associate with each other more than with those not identified with the group, or in a different way" (1990a, 43). A social group is not something one joins but, rather, "one finds oneself as a member of a group whose existence and relations one experiences as always already having been" (1990b, 122). But groups are fluid, "they come into being and may fade away" (1990b, 123). Though there is a lack of clarity in how Young identifies particular groups, as I understand her, Black Americans, lesbians, differently abled women, Latinas, and Navajo are examples of social groups.

Young thinks that the "inclusion and participation of everyone in public discussion and decision making requires mechanisms of group representation" (1990a, 115). The "ideal of the public realm of citizenship as expressing a general will, a point of view and interest that citizens have in common and that transcends their differences . . . , leads to pressures for a homogeneous citizenry" (1990a, 116–17). In arguing for group representation as the key to safeguarding the inclusion and participation of everyone without falling into an egoistic, self-regarding view of the political process, Young tells us that "it is possible for persons to maintain their group identity and to be influenced by their perceptions of social events derived from their group specific experience and at the same time to be public spirited, in the sense of being open to listening to the claims of others and not being concerned for their own gain alone" (1990a, 120). She sees group representation as necessary because she thinks differences are irreducible: "People from one perspective can never completely understand and adopt the point of view of those with other group-based perspectives and histories" (1990a, 121). Though differences are irreducible, group representation affords a solution to the homogeneization of the public because "commitment to the need and desire to decide together the society's policies fosters communication across those differences" (1990a, 121).

In her conception of the heterogenous public, "each of the constituent groups affirms the presence of the others and affirms the specificity of its experience and perspective on social issues," arriving at "a political program not by voicing some 'principles of unity' that hide differences but rather by allowing each constituency to analyze economic and social issues from the perspective of its experience" (1990a, 123).

Young sees that each person has multiple group identifications and that groups are not homogenous but rather that each group has group differences cutting across it (1990a, 123; 1990b, 48). Social groups "mirror in their own differentiations many of the other groups in the wider society" (1990a, 48). There are important implications of group differences within social groups. Significantly, "individual persons, as constituted partly by their group affinities and relations, cannot be unified, themselves are heterogenous and not necessarily coherent" (1990a, 48). Young sees a revolution in subjectivity as necessary. "Rather than seeking a wholeness of the self, we who are the subjects of this plural and complex society should affirm the otherness within ourselves, acknowledging that as subjects we are heterogenous and multiple in our affiliations and desires" (1990a, 124). Young thinks the women's movement offers some beginning models for the development of a heterogenous public and for revolutionizing the subject through the practices it has instituted to deal with issues arising from group differences within social groups. From the discussion of racial and ethnic blindness and the importance of attending to group differences among women "emerged principled efforts to provide autonomously organized forums [for women] who see reason for claiming that they have as a group a distinctive voice that might be silenced in a general feminist discourse" (1990a, 162). Those discussions have been joined by structured discussion among differently identifying groups of women" (1990a, 162–63).

Young's complex account suggests the problem but not the solution to what I understand as the fragmentation of the subject, a consequence of group oppression where group oppression follows the logic of unity, of purity. I think we need a solution to the problem of walking from one of one's groups to another, being mistreated, misunderstood, engaging in self-abuse and self-betrayal for the sake of the group that only distorts our needs because they erase our complexity. Young lacks a conceptual basis for a solution because she lacks a conception of a multiple subject who is not fragmented. I think she does not see the need for such a conception because she fails to address the problem of the interlocking of oppressions. Fragmentation is conceptually at odds with seeing oppressions as interlocked.

I am not disagreeing with Young's rejection of the individualism that follows from thinking of social groups as "invidious fictions, essentializing arbitrary attributes" (1990a, 46), nor with her rejection of an ideal of interests as common, of the universal, homogeneous subject, and of assimilation. I do not disagree with her account of social groups either nor with her account of the problematic nature of one's subjectivity when formed in affiliation with a multiplicity of groups. But her account leaves us with a self that is not just multiplicitous but fragmented, its multiplicity lying in its fragmentation. In order to explain this claim I need to introduce the concepts of thickness and transparency.

Thickness and transparency are group relative. Individuals are transparent with respect to their group if they perceive their needs, interests, ways, as those of the group and if this perception becomes dominant or hegemonical in the group. Individuals are thick if they are aware of their otherness in the group, of their needs, interests, ways, being relegated to the margins in the politics of intragroup contestation. So, as transparent, one becomes unaware of one's own difference from other members of the group.

Fragmentation occurs because one's interests, needs, ways of seeing and valuing things, persons, and relations are understood not as tied simply to group membership, but as the needs, interests, and ways of transparent members of the group. Thick members are erased. Thick members of several oppressed groups become composites of the transparent members of those groups. As thick, they are marginalized through erasure, their voices nonsensical. The interlocking of memberships in oppressed groups is not seen as changing one's needs, interests, and ways qualitatively in any group but, rather, one's needs, interests, and ways are understood as the addition of those of the transparent members. They are understood with a "pop-bead logic," to put it as Elizabeth Spelman does in *Inessential Woman* (1988). The title *All the Women Are White, All the Blacks Are Men, But Some of Us Are Brave* (Hull, Scott, and Smith 1982) captures and rejects this logic. White women are transparent as women; black men are transparent as black. Black women are erased and fighting against erasure. Black women are fighting for their understanding of social relations, their personal possibilities, their particular sense of history, their mode of reasoning and values and expressive styles being understood as neither reducible to anything else nor as outside the meaning of being black and of being Women. Black and women are thus conceived as plural, multiplicitous, without fragmentation.

The politics of marginalization in oppressed groups is part of the politics of oppression, and the disconnection of oppressions is part of these politics. Avoiding recognition of the interlocking of oppressions serves many people well, but no one is served so well by it as the pure, rational, full-fledged citizen. So I see a cross fertilization between the logic of purity used to exclude members of oppressed groups from the civic public and the separation and disconnection of oppressions. Liberatory work that makes vivid that oppressions must be fought as interlocked is consistently blocked in oppressed groups through the marginalization of thick members.

So unless one understands groups as explicitly rejecting the logic of fragmentation and embracing a nonfragmented multiplicity that requires an understanding of oppressions as interlocked, group representation does most group members little good. It indeed fails at safeguarding the "inclusion and participation of everyone" in the shaping of public life. The logic of impurity, of mestizaje, provides us with a better understanding of multiplicity, one that fits the conception of oppressions as interlocked. I mean to offer a statement of the politics of heterogeneity that is not necessarily at odds with Young's, but its logic is different. Hers, though formulated in rejection of the logic of purity, is oddly consistent with though not necessarily tied to it. Mine is inconsistent with it. Communication across differences in her model may well fail to recognize that one is listening to voices representative only of transparents, voices that embody the marginalization of thick members and contain their fragmentation.

Social homogeneity, domination through unification, and hierarchical ordering of split social groups are connected tightly to fragmentation in the person. If the person is fragmented, it is because the society is itself fragmented into groups that are pure, homogenous. Each group's structure of affiliation to and through transparent members produces a society of persons who are fragmented as they are affiliated to separate groups. As the parts of individuals are separate, the groups are separate, in an insidious dialectic.

Heterogeneity in the society is consistent with and may require the presence of groups. But groups in a genuinely heterogenous society have complex, nonfragmented persons as members, that is, they are heterogenous themselves. The affiliative histories include the formation of voices in contestation that reveal the enmeshing of race, gender, culture, class, and other differences that affect and constitute the identity of the group's members. This is a very significant difference in direction from the one suggested by the postmodern literature, which goes against a politics of identity and toward minimizing the political significance of groups.[12] The position presented in this article, a position that I also see in the literature on mestizaje, affirms a complex version of identity politics and a complex conception of groups.

[12] Two examples that come vividly to mind are the positions suggested in Butler 1990 and Haraway 1990.

Interrupción: Lesbian separation

When I think of lesbian separation I think of curdle separation. In this understanding of separation I am a lesbian separatist. We contain in our own and in the heterosexist construction of ourselves all sorts of ambiguities and tensions that are threatening to purity, to the construction of women as for use, for exploitation. We are outside the lover of purity's pale, outside his conceptual framework. Even the attempt to split our selves into half man/half woman recognizes our impurity. In our own conception we defy splitting separation by mocking the purity of the man/woman dichotomy or rejecting it.

But "Watchale esa!" doesn't resonate in its impurity implicitly in all lesbian ears, and not all lesbian hips move inspired by a latin beat.
Lesbians are not the only transitionals, impure, ambiguous beings. And if we are to struggle against "our" oppression, Latina Lesbian cannot be the name for a fragmented being. Our style cannot be outside the meaning of Latina and cannot be outside the meaning of Lesbian. So, our struggle, the struggle of lesbians, goes beyond lesbians as a group. If we understand our separation as curdle-separation, then we can rethink our relation to other curdled beings. Separation from domination is not split-separation.

III. Impurity and resistance

People who curdle-separate are themselves people from whom others split-separate, dissociate, withdraw. Lovers of purity, controllers through split-separation not only attempt to split-separate us but also split-separate from us in ways I have discussed, such as ghettoization and conceptual exclusion. They also attempt to split-separate us from others who are themselves curdled through the logic of marginalization, of transparency. The logic of transparency shines in the constructed lover of purity himself, the modern subject, the impartial reasoner. He is the measure of all things. He is transparent relative to his position in the hetero-relational patriarchy, to his culture, his race, his class, his gender. His sense is the only sense. So curdled thoughts are nonsensical. To the extent that his sense is the instrument of our communication, we become susceptible to the logic of transparency and see split-separation from other curdled beings as sensical in our resistance to oppression. We also become susceptible to being agents of the lover of purity in carrying out the oppression of other curdled beings, in constructing his made-to-order orderly world. Thus curdle-separation is blocked, barred, made into a hard to reach resistant and liberatory possibility. It is also dangerous because curdled beings may adopt the logic of transparency in self-contradiction and act as agents of the lover of purity in coercing us into fragmentation and oppression. I think this is a risk that we can minimize only by speaking the language of curdling among curdled beings in separation and living its logic and by listening for, responding to, evoking, sometimes demanding, such language and logic. I think this is a risk we must take because the logic of split-separation does not contain resistance but co-optation. So we have to constantly consider and reconsider the question: Who are our own people?

I don't think we can consider "our own" only those who reject the same dichotomies we do. It is the impulse to reject dichotomies and to live and embody that rejection that gives us some hope of standing together as people who recognize each other in our complexity. The hope is based on the possibilities that the unsettling quality of being a stranger in our society reveals to us, the possibilities that purification by ordeal reveals to us. I think this is Anzaldúa's point in thinking of a borderland: "It is a constant state of transition. The prohibited and forbidden are its inhabitants . . . those who cross over, pass over, or go through the confines of the 'normal.' . . . Ambivalence and unrest reside there and death is no stranger" (1987, 3–4). For her, "To live in the Borderlands means you are neither hispana india negra espanola ni gabacha, eres mestiza, mulata, half-breed . . . [you're] half and half—both woman and man, neither—a new gender. . . . In the Borderlands you are the battleground where enemies are kin to each other" (1987, 194).

But, of course, that is thin ground for thinking of others as "our own": that we might be revealed to each other as possible through the tramplings and denials and torturings of our ambiguity. A more solid ground because it is a more positive ground is the one that affirms the lack of constraint of our creativity that is at the center of curdling; that holds on to our own lack of script, to our being beings in the making; that might contain each other in the creative path, who don't discount but look forward to that possibility.

Ambiguous, neither this nor that, unrestrained by the logic of this and the logic of that, and thus its course not mapped, traced already in movements, words, relations, structures, institutions; not rehearsed over and over into submission, containment, subordination, asceticism—we can affirm the positive side of our being threatening as ambiguous. If it is ambiguous it is threatening because it is creative, changing, defiant of norms meant to subdue it. So we find our people as we make the threat good, day to day, attentive to our company in our groups, across groups. The model of curdling as a model for separation is a model for worldly separation—the separation of border-dwellers, of people who live in a crossroads, people who deny purity and are looking for each other for the possibility of going beyond resistance.

IV. The art of curdling

Curdle-separation is not something that happens to us but something we do. As I have argued, it is something we do in resistance to the logic of control, to the logic of purity. Though transparents fail to see its sense, and thereby keep its sense from structuring our social life, that we curdle testifies to our being active subjects, not consumed by the logic of control. Curdling may be a haphazard technique of survival as an active subject, or it can become an art of resistance, metamorphosis, transformation.

I recommend the cultivation of this art as a practice of resistance into transformation from oppressions as interlocked. It is a practice of festive resistance:

Bi- and multilingual experimentation;
code-switching;
categorial blurring and confusion;
caricaturing the selves we are in the worlds of our oppressors, infusing them with ambiguity;
practicing trickstery and foolery;
elaborate and explicitly marked gender transgression;
withdrawing our services from the pure or their agents whenever possible and with panache;
drag;
announcing the impurity of the pure by ridiculing his inability at self-maintanance;
playful reinvention of our names for things and people, multiple naming;
caricaturing of the fragmented selves we are in our groups;
revealing the chaotic in production;
revealing the process of producing order if we cannot help producing it;
undermining the orderliness of the social ordering;
marking our cultural mixtures as we move;
emphasizing cultural mestizaje;
crossing cultures;
etc.

We not only create ourselves and each other through curdling but also announce ourselves to each other through this art, our curdled expression. Thus curdled behavior is not only creative but also constitutes itself as a social commentary. All curdled behavior, thought, and expression contain and express this second level of meaning, one of social commentary. When curdling becomes an art of resistance, the curdled presentation is highlighted. There is the distance of metacomment, autoreflection, looking at oneself in someone else's mirror and back in one's own, of self-aware experimentation. Our commentary is not straightforward: the commentary underlines the curdling and constitutes it as an act of social creative defiance. We often intend and cultivate with style this social commentary, this meta meaning of our curdling. When confronted with our curdling or curdled expression or behavior, people often withdraw. Their withdrawal reveals the devaluation of ambiguity *as threatening* and is thus also a metacomment. It announces that, though we will not be acknowledged, we have been seen as threatening the univocity of life lived in a state of purity, their management of us, their power over us.

Latin American and Caribbean Area Studies Program
State University of New York at Binghamton

References

Anzaldúa, Gloria. 1987. *Boarderlands/La Frontera: The New Mestiza.* San Francisco: Spinsters/Aunt Lute.

Butler, Judith. 1990. *Gender Trouble.* New York: Routledge.

Chin, Frank. 1991. "Come All Ye Asian American Writers of the Real and the Fake." In *The Big Aiiieeeee!* ed. Jeffery Paul Chan, Frank Chin, Lawson Fusao Inada, and Shawn Wong. New York: Meridian.

Douglas, Mary. 1989. *Purity and Danger.* London: Ark Paperbacks.

Haraway, Donna. 1990. "A Manifesto for Cyborgs." In Feminism/Post modernism, ed. Linda J. Nicholson. New York: Routledge.

Hartsock, Nancy C. M. 1988 "The Feminist Standpoint: Developing the Ground for a Specifically Feminist Historical Materialism." In *Discovering Reality: Feminist Perspectives on Epistomology, Metaphysics, Methodology, and Philosophy of Science,* ed. Sandra Harding and Merrill Hintikka. Boston: Reidel.

Hull, Gloria T., Patricia Bell Scott, and Barbara Smith, eds. 1982. *All the Women Are White, All the Blacks Are Men, But Some of Us Are Brave.* New York: Feminist Press.

Mangabeira Unger, Roberto. 1975. *Knowledge and Politics.* New York: Free Press.

Memmi, Albert. 1967. *The Colonizer and the Colonized.* Boston: Beacon.

Montoya, José. "El Louie." In *Literatura Chicana, Texto y Contexto,* ed. Antonio Castaneda Shular, 173–76. Englewood Cliffs, N.J.: Prentice- Hall.

Nichols, John. 1976. *Milagro Beanfield War.* New York: Ballantine.

Pateman, Carole. 1988. *The Sexual Contract.* Stanford, Calif.: Stanford University Press.

Pharmaceutica Acta Helvetiae. 1991. "Physical Parameters and Release Behaviors of W/O/W Multiple Emulsions Containing Cosurfactants and Different Specific Gravity of Oils." *Pharmaceutica Acta Helvetiae,* vol. 66, no. 12 (1991). (Vogt-Schild A.G., Druck and Verlag Zuchwilerstrasse 21, Postfach 748 CH-4501 Solothurn.)

Rosaldo, Renato. 1989. *Culture and Truth.* Boston: Beacon.

Smith, Dorothy. 1974. "Women's Perspective as a Radical Critique of Sociology." Sociological Enquiry 44(1): 7–14.

Spelman, Elizabeth. 1988. *Inessential Woman.* Boston: Beacon.

Young, Iris Marion. 1990a. *Justice and the Politics of Difference.* Princeton, N.J.: Princeton University Press.

———. 1990b. *Throwing Like a Girl and Other Essays in Feminist Philosophy and Social Theory.* Bloomington: Indiana University Press.

Differences and Identities: Feminism and the Albuquerque Lesbian Community

Trisha Franzen

THIS ARTICLE is about the politicization of the Albuquerque, New Mexico, lesbian community. It is also very much about race, class, sexuality, and difference. It traces how three subcommunities of lesbians in this southwestern city defined themselves and each other during the period 1965–80, the years when feminism became a significant influence among them.

I came out in Buffalo, New York, in a lesbian community where I perceived continuity between members of the older lesbian community, gay liberation activists, and lesbians active in the women's movement. In that environment, many of us "new" lesbians learned the social and political lessons of lesbian culture from our "elders," that is, from those women who had lived as lesbians before the emergence of contemporary feminism and the articulation of lesbian theory. Among our core lessons was to listen to women's life stories and not to privilege the written word over the lived experience. Feminist and lesbian theory were accepted only if validated by lesbians' own lives. Issues of race and class were raised and debated as they connected with our lives. The process was, to use Cherríe Moraga and Gloria Anzaldúa's term, "theory in the flesh" (1981, 23).

When I moved to Albuquerque in 1980, I did not find analogous connections within its lesbian community. I soon became part of a feminist lesbian network, the core of which was overwhelmingly Anglo in a

I wish to thank those women who contributed to this research: the women of the Albuquerque lesbian community who shared their histories with me; Liz Lapovsky Kennedy, whose work with Madeline Davis inspired and guided my work and who supported this project in many ways; Jane Slaughter, who read this article in its early stages, offered constructive criticism, and always encouraged my efforts; Louise Lamphere, who made important suggestions for clarifying my argument; Chris Ruggiero, whose enthusiasm sustained me through numerous revisions; and Kristine Long, whose suggestions in the final stages of editing strengthened the article.

[*Signs: Journal of Women in Culture and Society* 1993, vol. 18, no. 4]

city where Anglos are barely the majority. Most of the women I met had moved to New Mexico as adults and had come to their lesbian identities within the women's movement. There did not seem to be much connection between this part of the Albuquerque lesbian community and an indigenous pre–women's movement one. There were no elders within the feminist lesbian circles, no women who had been active in the public bar community and were now involved in the feminist lesbian activities.

I found the absence of women of color and lesbian elders startling. The stratification I found between newly out feminist lesbians and native-born Albuquerque lesbians challenged my personal experience and my understanding of the emerging works in lesbian and gay history that suggested that politicization follows a sense of shared identity and community consciousness (see, e.g., D'Emilio 1983). The lack of racial integration was disturbing in light of the increasingly strong challenges being made to feminist theory and activism by poor and working-class women and women of color.[1] Within lesbian studies, the invisibility of less-privileged lesbians was being countered by writers, activists, and scholars who were demanding that lesbians too examine the assumption that "all women's issues are the same" (Gibbs and Bennett 1980, 49).

Concurrent with these discussions were the feminist sexuality debates that asked, among other questions, who rightfully could claim lesbian and feminist identities and whether there are politically correct and incorrect sexual behaviors.[2] The relevance of this last controversy to issues of diversity and interconnections within the lesbian community was not immediately clear. What was clear was that it was not easy to talk about sex within feminist lesbian circles in Albuquerque. Even discussions concerning sexual behavior, roles, and S/M were suspect and were often met with silencing sarcasm and ridicule. An attempt to hold a public forum at the feminist bookstore on what was termed at the time "the sexual fringe" deteriorated into a battle between two hostile camps and a years-long public silence on these issues.

All these issues made me want to know why the Albuquerque lesbian community had split the way it had. This curiosity led to a formal research project based on interviews with lesbians who were involved with this community between 1965 and 1980. The interviews were open-ended and semistructured, focusing on each woman's experience as a lesbian in this southwestern city. Throughout this project I attempted to balance my sample on the factors of race/ethnicity and class as well as

---

[1] Some of the early works include Bethel and Smith 1979; Davis 1981; Moraga and Anzaldúa 1981.

[2] See, e.g., Cook 1977, 42–61; Rich 1980, 62–91; Faderman 1981; Samois 1981; Ferguson, Zita, and Addelson 1982, 147–88; Linden et al. 1982; Snitow, Stansell, and Thompson 1983; and Vance 1984.

between lesbians who were born and raised in New Mexico and those who settled there as adults. Therefore, when I refer to native New Mexicans I am talking not about Native Americans but women of all races from New Mexico. The result provided diversity though it does not completely match the racial/ethnic composition of the city. I supplemented this data with newspaper articles, findings from a 1981 community survey, and records from the National Lesbian Feminist Organization and Siren, an early women's music production and education group.

While the questions for this research originated in my personal experiences in this community, I myself did not move to Albuquerque until 1980 and was not a participant in the community during the period I studied. I was, by the time I was doing this research, part of what I am terming the feminist lesbian network. I was publicly out, working for a lesbian-owned business, active in lesbian and gay organizations, and associated with a lesbian softball team. I was also involved in other feminist institutions and organizations and through that work built connections with lesbians who had played important roles in this community in other than the feminist lesbian network. When my research became more systematic, these women were key, sharing their stories with me in interviews and acting as brokers by contacting old friends and convincing women who did not know me that I could be trusted. Nevertheless, throughout this project it was easier to find feminist lesbians willing to be interviewed, as working-class and older lesbians and lesbians of color were far more reluctant to talk with me. During the years I worked on this project I presented various drafts of this article at public forums in Albuquerque.

For the purpose of this article I have had to impose a static framework on what were dynamic divisions within a complex community. The three groups I compare are defined only on the basis of their public lesbian activities: women who were socially and politically active as lesbians within feminism; women who were socially active as lesbians, usually through the bars, but were not politically active or were not politically active as lesbians; and closeted women who were not socially or politically active as lesbians. What is important to remember is that there were active feminists in all three groups. The differentiating identifications for women in this article are not their feminist identities but, again, their public lesbian activities or "outness." Some women from all three groups, for example, were associated with the Women's Center at the University of New Mexico, but many more of the women from the first group than from the second or third. I did not ask any of the feminists in my sample to define themselves by any particular theoretical position—radical feminist, liberal feminist, socialist feminist, etc.—nor did I delve into the sexual attitudes or behaviors of any of the women in this study.

As background, some sense of New Mexican history is helpful. The state's history is one of repeated colonizations, military, civil, and cultural. It is also a history of resistance. This resistance, along with the state's geographical position, has resulted in the survival of various Native American cultures and the evolution of a uniquely New Mexican Hispanic tradition. Anglos arrived in significant numbers only in the second half of the nineteenth century, along with a small number of African Americans. New Mexico was a territory of the United States after the Treaty of Guadalupe-Hidalgo in 1846 but did not become a state until 1912.

Since World War II, Albuquerque has seen a tremendous growth in population as part of the general migration to Sunbelt regions and the increase in U.S. Department of Defense bases and laboratories. Between 1960 and 1980, this city's population increased 65 percent. Most of these new Albuquerqueans are Anglo (U.S. Census 1960, 1980). Given New Mexican history, this population growth has produced concerns about outsiders and the preservation of what is special about New Mexico generally.

Politically, during the 1960s New Mexico was the site of a civil rights struggle that was regionally focused while also influenced by and part of the national civil rights movement. As with the larger movement, demands for civil rights were followed by the eruption of racial and cultural tensions that heightened the political consciousness of people of color throughout the region and underscored the gaps between those not privileged in this society and those who are.

The long and complex history of racial/cultural conflict and assimilation contrasts with what little we know of lesbians and gay men in Albuquerque. This is the first systematic research done on the Albuquerque lesbian and gay community, although lesbian and gay historians have begun to document the growth of sexuality-based communities on other urban areas (see, e.g., Kennedy and Davis 1993). These histories have begun to identify the factors contributing to the development of such communities that led to gay liberation and the emergence of lesbian activism within feminism. Relevant to this time period and region are two World War II–related phenomena: the urban growth fostered by wartime mobilization and job opportunities and the relatively laissez-faire attitude toward sexuality of the military during the war (Berube 1989). While the subsequent repression of the McCarthy era certainly scarred these young communities, such crackdowns did not break them. In fact, this period may have broadened gay self-consciousness of oppression. In spite of the vagaries of public opinion and policy during these years, lesbian and gay communities continued to grow. In Albuquerque this growth is documented by the increase in public spaces where gay men and lesbians could gather in relative safety during the 1960s and 1970s. The earliest gay bar remembered by my narrators was the Newsroom, which later became Duke's Cave. According to Paula: "It was pretty awful looking. Very small, very smoky. It was down under [a straight bar]. The bathroom leaked into the . . . I mean I don't know what was leaking exactly, but the bathroom was above and it never worked right. It wasn't scary, but a horrible dump. But I had a lot of fun there." The Newsroom fits the stereotype of early gay bars: smoky, dark, and a little sleazy. The police came regularly, sometimes stopping action throughout the bar to check IDs. To add to the risk and excitement, there were occasional fights. According to my informants, however, the limits of this bar were far over-shadowed by the relief patrons felt in finding a lesbian/gay community.

During this period, gay men also gathered at the coffee houses that served the Albuquerque "beat" crowd; although comfortable and ac-cepted in these public places, they made up only a small percentage of the clientele. For their part, Albuquerque lesbians frequented a jazz bar in Santa Fe, sixty miles to the north. This establishment was owned and managed by a French woman named Claude, who set the tone for non-conforming gender behavior by appearing some evenings in a flamboyant evening gown and full makeup and other nights in a tuxedo and slicked-back hair. This bar attracted a mature, mixed crowd—women and men, gay and straight—and was a favorite of middle-class lesbians.[3]

These gathering places were followed by what came to be called the Old Heights, the first of several bars run by a gay couple, Bill and Larry. One woman remembered it as opening in 1958. While their first bar was not a great improvement over the Newsroom, the New Heights, which opened several years later, was. It was attached to one of the most elegant restaurants in the city, which employed a number of gay men. Bill and Larry are remembered with great fondness as being, according to Bar-bara, "extremely gracious": "I felt real safe in the New Heights. With them I always felt safe. If people got tossed in jail, they'd go and do your bail."

The number of bars continued to grow. By the mid-1960s, lesbians could choose from the Wellington, a relatively fancy bar and restaurant; the Limelight, a large, rustic establishment located in the mountains east of the city; Mildred's, an in-town bar; the Upstairs Lounge, an after-hours club; and Crickets, a women's private club. Part of a family bar in the town north of Albuquerque also served as a gay bar for a short period of time.

Except for Crickets, these were all mixed bars (i.e., serving lesbians and gay men) with full liquor licenses. Crickets, owned by a Native

---

[3] Many of the women I interviewed spoke of knowing of a separate Santa Fe lesbian network of older wealthy women who had settled in Santa Fe or Taos and participated in the artistic circles of those cities.

American woman, operated under a private club liquor license, as does a lesbian bar that opened later. There was no agreement among my interviewees about the reasons for this difference in liquor licenses. One bar owner stated that the private club license was the only legal means to have an all-women's bar. But those who patronized these "clubs" argued that such licenses were cheaper and easier to obtain. There was speculation that family connections had helped the bar owners obtain their licenses.

Many of the bars were located along a section of Central Avenue, the old U.S. Route 66, about two miles east of downtown Albuquerque and just east of the University of New Mexico. This area is currently undergoing gentrification, but historically it has been dominated by small commercial operations, stores, motels, and a few shopping centers. The surrounding residential areas are predominantly Anglo middle-class neighborhoods and are considered nice places to live. While there is no "gay ghetto" in Albuquerque, many lesbians and gay men do live in these neighborhoods. The Metropolitan Community Church and Common Bond, the city's largest gay organization, are housed in this relatively uptown section.

For the lesbians of this earlier era, finding the bars was often synonymous with finding a named identity and a community. Robin, an Anglo born and raised in Albuquerque, had always had a sense of herself as different and had always been attracted to women. She was introduced to her first gay bar when she was in college in Albuquerque and became part of a circle of women who were also attracted to other women.

> We would all go to the Caravan (a straight bar) for happy hour. But we [Robin and her girlfriend] kept being left behind. They'd say, "Well, we're going home now," or make up something. We'd sit there . . . and it's eight o'clock, thinking what's wrong with these people. So one time I got pissed at Sue in the parking lot. I said, "Goddamn it, what's going on here? You ride with me and we're supposed to spend the evening doing something and then you take off with those folks." She got out of the car, went over to those others, talked to them and came back. And she just said, I'll never forget it, "Get in." On the way . . . she said, "Remember when I said there was a place I would never take you?" I said, "Yeah?" She said, "We're going there now." And I said, "Damn. Alright. It's about time."

Albuquerque lesbians remember the late sixties and early seventies as good times. While the bars ranged from plush to sleazy, lesbians felt they had choices about where to socialize, and they recall harassment as minimal. Public lesbian culture in Albuquerque, according to the women who frequented the bars, shared many of the features identified by other lesbian historians (Nestle 1987; Kennedy and Davis 1993). One's social and sexual lives involved butch-femme roles with the accompanying dating etiquette and dress codes. Private parties supplemented nights at the bars. At these parties, the lesbians who did go to the bars socialized with their more closeted friends. Softball was a very important lesbian activity and teams drew women of all races and classes from across the city. This sport provided another opportunity for closeted women to interact with more public lesbians and for lesbians in general to meet and socialize with each other outside of the bars. Among the memorable teams were the Dukettes (Albuquerque is the Duke City, named for the Duke of Albuquerque, Spain), also known as the "Dykettes," a team of older butches. One woman recalled, "You could hardly tell their gender."

Across the board, lesbians active in the bars and the closeted networks in the 1960s emphasize the solidarity they felt among themselves and between lesbians and gay men. The lesbians not only shared the public bar space with gay men but also considered them their friends. For some lesbians these men provided compatible dates for those occasions that called for a heterosexual cover.

While the bars were the centers of gay life in Albuquerque as elsewhere, many lesbians who frequented the bars were also in contact with closeted lesbians. As my research progressed, I became increasingly conscious of the interconnections and overlappings among the various lesbian social networks through friendships, school, softball, and parties, convincing me that the closeted lesbians were important players in the history of the public community and the growth of feminism.

My research suggests that in this community during this period, the bar-going lesbians and the lesbians who did not socialize at the bars defined themselves in part against each other, but in an opposition free of hostility. They saw in each other two ways to be lesbian, one based on safety and passing and one based on risk and an identity that was articulated and affirmed by a community. While one group's identity was centered at the bars, the closeted women kept theirs private within their homes and the homes of their closest friends.

To understand how these two subgroups related to each other, it is important to recognize that within each were individuals who had known each other often from childhood on. They had gone to school together, played sports with each other, and worked with each other. From these shared histories they could identify with each other. It also was not unusual for women to move back and forth between these two groups. Robin frequented the bars far less when she became involved with Alice, who was completely closeted. Conversely, Gloria had never gone to the bars and was part of a closeted circle until she gained more job security, when she celebrated by going to the bar for the first time. In these ways these two groups were in flux.

When asked, most closeted women gave concerns about their jobs as their reason for avoiding public lesbian spaces. They felt they had to struggle hard enough as women to achieve economic self-sufficiency and accepted remaining in the closet as the price they had to pay for it. Only a few of the women mentioned that they did not like the bars or could not identify with the women in them.

It appears therefore that the decisions of the closeted women served as constant reminders to the public/bar lesbians of the dangers involved in participating in public gay life as well as demonstrating another, less risky way to be gay. Nevertheless, the lesbians I interviewed who were part of these social networks before the reemergence of the women's movement did not convey any sense of resentment or judgment toward each others' choices about the bars. In several cases, younger lesbians mentioned older, closeted lesbians who had served as on-the-job mentors, passing on survival strategies and warnings about the dangers of not being discreet. Although the lessons were not always appreciated immediately, they were respected in retrospect. Several quite out lesbians strongly stated their support for the decisions of closeted women, especially those in education. As one Chicana stated, there was a "live and let live attitude" within the community.

The respectful acceptance of different choices and different ways to be lesbian was strongest among women who had grown up and gone to school together, regardless of differences in race and class. On the other hand, the closeted networks of women who were not native Albuquerqueans conveyed a sense of distance from bar lesbians. Nor did the "natives' " sense of solidarity extend to the feminists who became part of the Albuquerque lesbian scene in the late sixties and early seventies. The bar lesbians were confused and put off by their actions and ideas. The extent to which the bar lesbians viewed feminism as foreign is best captured by the name given the women most frequently credited with introducing feminist lesbianism to Albuquerque. Consistently this group is referred to as the "Boston crazies." What was clear about these feminists, according to one bar lesbian, was that they were "not us."

If one group of lesbians discussed in this article centered their lesbian identities at the bars and the other in their homes, this third group built their identities around the Women's Center at the University of New Mexico. While straight women and lesbians from the other categories were important in the development of the center, according to my informants, feminist lesbianism was centered there. The women in this third network connected with each other on the basis of their feminism and lesbianism. Many of them were students at the University of New Mexico as undergraduates, graduate students, and law students. Joan, for example, an Anglo from a middle-class family, was introduced to feminism and lesbianism at the university. She became involved in consciousness-raising groups and came out as a lesbian about the same time she became one of the first staff members at the Rape Crisis Center and a founder of a women's concert production company.

Although feminist lesbianism was centered at the university, tensions between feminist lesbians and other lesbians were clearest at the bars. Several of the feminist lesbians remember the arrangements in the early 1970s as "old gays on one side, new gays on the other." When asked if there was much interaction, one feminist stated, "Very little between old gay and new gay. Very little. Only old gays we saw were those at the bar. And I think they viewed us as interlopers into their space. That we were dilettantes and eating pussy just to see what it tasted like and would go home to our hubbies. I mean they felt their area was being invaded." This informant also discussed what had happened when she had attended a "jock" party several years earlier with women who were part of Robin's circle. She saw women disappearing two-by-two into the bedrooms but found that no one was willing to discuss the fact that they were lesbians. She concluded, "Seeing lesbians dealing with each other in such a dishonest way sent me back into the closet, though a different closet from the one I had known when I was thirteen." This woman did not claim her lesbian identity until lesbian feminism was an option.

The split between these two sectors of the community can also be seen around specific issues. As I mentioned earlier, bar lesbians had often socialized with gay men and felt a sense of solidarity with them. Barbara, for example, stated that she preferred mixed bars. When her friends started going to the lesbian bar in the 1970s, she went with them but missed the guys. In contrast, Joan, a feminist lesbian, does not recall knowing any gay men. "We hated all men. Just hated them because the political rhetoric was that gays got together with other men because they hated women."

This difference may have more complex roots than separatist rhetoric. The differing histories of the individuals in these groups suggest that the extent of their earlier relationships with men influenced their acceptance of and interaction with gay men. Few of the bar or closeted lesbians I interviewed had ever been seriously involved with men in romantic or sexual ways. The males in their lives, besides family and work colleagues, had been these gay men with whom they shared public gay spaces and a sense of refuge from straight society. In contrast, many of the feminist lesbians had been married or recently involved in heterosexual relationships. For example, one feminist recalls that at its inception all of the women in her consciousness-raising group identified themselves as heterosexual and several were married. Looking back, she realizes that all these women eventually came out. In short, while the older lesbians tended to confront sexism and their lack of heterosexual privilege in the public sphere—in school, on the job, when trying to get a mortgage—the feminist lesbians had struggled over gender issues in intimate relationships with husbands and boyfriends.

Feminist lesbians also had a disdain for butch/femme roles and the dress and etiquette codes associated with them. On the other side, bar lesbians saw the feminist uniform of Levis, flannel shirts, work boots, and short hair as unattractive, even sloppy. Interestingly, while the feminist lesbians were reacting strongly against such roles, among the bar lesbians there was some sense that the importance and rigidity of these roles had diminished by this time. One woman told this story to illustrate that point:

> I think when our age group came out I think it was that we saw this whole butch/femme thing as a game. Like some people really took this seriously. The fem would never touch the butch in bed. The butch would always make love to the fem. I think we saw it as more of a game, and if you needed to play the game you did, depending on who you went out with. I remember this scene in my apartment with this woman. And it was the first time we were going to give a hug. I went here [around the waist] and she went here [around the waist]. And we had a collision. And she said, "Ah we're going to have to work something out here. This isn't going to work." I said, "Okay." And I went up here [around the shoulders].

After 1978 the divisions within the lesbian community became even more pronounced with the opening of a second lesbian bar. While the first exclusively lesbian bar originally had been downtown, it soon moved and remained for the rest of its existence on the predominantly Hispanic, working-class west side. In the late 1970s a native New Mexican Chicana who had worked in the first lesbian bar opened a new bar in the predominantly Anglo Northeast Heights. The owner of this new bar stated that she opened her establishment to "provide women with a nicer place." What resulted was a self-segregation based on class and race, with middle-class and Anglo women going to the new bar and the older bar's clientele becoming increasingly working-class or poor women and women of color.

Not surprisingly, the feminist lesbians generally abandoned the older bar and patronized the newer one. But this arrangement did not have a long honeymoon. As stated earlier, both of these "women's" bars were run under private club licenses that made the clubs nonprofit organizations in which individuals bought memberships. These "members" theoretically had some say in the management of "their club." This situation appears to have produced higher expectations for these clubs than for gay bars generally, and even higher ones for the new bar and its owner. The feminists assumed that the owner of the new bar would run it more democratically and expected what was to the owner's mind a private business to be run according to feminist principles. Not long after the bar opened, a group of feminist lesbians asked for a meeting with the owner and confronted the owner about certain of her management decisions, claiming that they were frustrated by the owner's lack of support for their activities and their politics. On her part, the owner claims that "they wanted a share of the profits." Whatever happened, whatever the motives, these differences were not resolved amicably, and to this day the owner identifies the feminists as "trouble-making radicals."

Another example of the difficulties between these groups can be seen in a story I first heard as part of the oral history of the feminist lesbian community. I had been told about a great party that had been held, the highlight of which was two popular women appearing dressed only in cowboy boots, hats, and guns and holsters. This story was passed on as hilarious, a celebration of the outrageous behavior that was part of the early days of feminist lesbianism. I had no reason to doubt this analysis until I heard a very different version from the woman whose home was the site of the party. This Anglo, native New Mexican lesbian had only recently discovered feminism and had become part of a central feminist lesbian circle. She ran her business, which involved giving lessons mostly to children, out of her home. Her feminist friends had wanted to have a party at her house but she resisted because she was afraid it would hurt her business. They held the party anyway when she was away on a business trip. She only found out about the party when women she barely knew came up to her at the bar and said how much they liked her house. When she finally figured out the connection between the drop in her business and the people who claimed to have been in her home, she tried to confront her feminist friends about the party. They refused to hear her and shunned her afterward as being too bourgeois and closeted.

But these particular instances of suspicion and overt hostility needed to be contextualized within a greater sense of separation between the two networks sharing the public lesbian space. Although the feminist lesbians frequented the bars, they did so with other feminists, straight, gay, and undecided. This group was very much caught up in the excitement of the women's liberation movement. Their activism centered around the University of New Mexico, and they were instrumental in founding and maintaining the U.N.M. Women's Center and Women Studies Program, the Albuquerque Rape Crisis Center, and the Shelter for Victims of Domestic Violence. As lesbians, they had to struggle for recognition of their lives and lesbian issues within these organizations as well as in others such as the National Organization for Women and the New Mexico chapter of the National Women's Political Caucus. They were an important presence at a left-feminist sit-in at the campus newspaper in the early 1970s and at the state hearings for the Equal Rights Amendment. In 1976 an out lesbian was elected homecoming queen at the University of New Mexico (although the governor refused to crown her).

It was often in the political arena that the third category of lesbians, the women in the closeted networks, came into contact with the feminist lesbians. A significant number of closeted lesbians became leaders in women's political organizations and worked alongside the out feminist lesbians, though they themselves remained closeted. In spite of this shared work, women from each group had suspicions about the other. The closeted lesbians did not feel that the open lesbians understood and respected their decisions to remain closeted. They also felt that the feminist lesbians were interested only in the sexuality issue, the lesbian perspective, and would not support them in their struggles around less specifically lesbian concerns, especially those based on class and race. On their part, the feminist lesbians felt betrayed by the closeted lesbians' less-than-wholehearted support of their position, support that frequently would have necessitated abandoning their closets. The feminist lesbians interpreted the closeted lesbians' personal and political decisions as internalized oppression.

Significantly, no specifically lesbian formal organization was founded in Albuquerque until a chapter of the National Lesbian Feminist Organization was begun in 1978. The gay student organization at the University of New Mexico, founded in 1970, has been and remains a predominantly male group.

*   *   *

As far as the indigenous lesbian community was concerned, feminist lesbianism as political theory and practice might just as well have dropped from a spaceship. That is how alien these new lesbians, these new ways of being lesbians were to the women who made up the early public community and closeted networks. The more important question, however, is why this combination of political philosophy and personal identification was greeted with suspicion and resistance and perceived of as imposed and invasive in Albuquerque. When there appeared a group of lesbians articulating an analysis of lesbian oppression, why was this group rejected by the native community? And what does this history of the lesbian community in Albuquerque have to contribute to lesbian history and theory?

In Albuquerque, neither shared lesbian identities nor shared feminist identities were sufficient bases for solidarity across the lesbian community. Why? This research suggests that sexuality is at the core of all the issues involved and that sexuality is a problematic basis for political solidarity among women. The feminist sexuality debates made this point clear. Among other complications, women have been divided into good and bad, esteemed or despised, protected or exploited, all on the basis of sexuality. And in the dominant culture's portrayals of female sexuality, that very sexual Other that all women should fear becoming has often been the poor woman, the woman of color, and the lesbian.

Did lesbian theory and practice take these issues into account when lesbians were confronting each other in Albuquerque? In a limited way, yes. Feminists knew how calling women lesbians was a threat used to divide women and keep women in their places, but there was no recognition of how sexuality interacted with racism and classism to separate women from each other within lesbian communities. Albuquerque feminist lesbians could not talk about sex, but without talking about sex they could not really talk about being lesbians. Only now is the diversity of lesbian voices being heard, and it has taken time for lesbians to research and reveal the history needed to build theory and examine how race and class differences are entwined with sexuality and issues of trust and power. Now lesbians are asking if we feared identifying with each other because in that identity would be claiming a sexuality that was threatening.

What does it mean that for lesbians claiming one's sexuality makes us sexual outlaws? Joan Nestle (1987) describes the struggle against this labeling and speaks of how feminism appeared to offer a comforting respectability to lesbians. Lesbians could be the best feminists, but only if we discarded all in lesbianism that might be seen as tainted by heterosexuality. In Albuquerque there was certainly that sense that feminist lesbians wanted other lesbians to "clean up their acts." This included, for example, discarding both the behavior and appearances associated with butch/femme roles. Feminist lesbians in Albuquerque interpreted these roles as pseudo-heterosexuality rather than what Elizabeth Lapovsky Kennedy and Madeline Davis, from their study of the Buffalo lesbian community, see as an authentically lesbian-developed set of sexual norms (1993). Feminist lesbians in Albuquerque also wanted to rid lesbianism of its overt sexuality, of sexual desire based on difference seen clearly in roles but also associated with working-class lesbians and lesbians of color.

On the other side of this hostility were the bar lesbians' views of feminist lesbians. In a state where civil rights struggles had produced a heightened awareness of race and class privilege and where longtime New Mexicans felt their material and cultural lives threatened by a rapid influx of newcomers, having a group of newly out, newly New Mexican, middle-class, educated, Anglo women start telling them how to be lesbians understandably might antagonize the women who had made up the public lesbian community in Albuquerque, many of whom were lesbians of color and from poor and working-class backgrounds.

In mutual suspicion, these groups confronted each other over who defined "real" lesbians. The feminist lesbians came informed, and in their eyes validated, by feminist and lesbian-feminist theory that viewed lesbians as superior feminists. Yet few of them had much experience living as lesbians, negotiating the realities of being self-supporting women while finding a positive sexual identity in a society that condemned lesbians. The public and the closeted lesbians had that practice, had "theory in the flesh," but little articulated analysis of their lives and their oppression. There were few links between these two groups to foster a dialogue.

Such a dialogue might have been possible if there had been any other organized group within the gay/lesbian community. The lack of any community-based homophile or Gay Liberation activities is important here. There was no gay civil rights activism in Albuquerque up to the emergence of feminism: no Mattachine chapter, no Daughters of Bilitis, or any other group that might have provided a base for a shared political consciousness or even a sense of an organized political community. This absence of a grass-roots, sexuality-based movement kept Albuquerque from following the pattern of politicization historians have identified in cities in which there was greater continuity between the public gay/lesbian communities and gay/lesbian political activism. The consequence was the splits I saw when I entered this community.

But such tensions were not all that existed in the Albuquerque lesbian community. It seems equally important that differences based on race and class had always existed, and yet solidarity within the sexuality-based community had been possible before lesbian feminism was introduced. This appears to be due to the long history lesbians in Albuquerque had had with each other before feminism. The women who had grown up, gone to school, and played ball together knew each other well enough across class and racial lines that even when they made different choices on how to live as lesbians, those choices could be understood and respected without denying each others' subjectivity. To me, what existed between these two groups is an example of what Marilyn Frye (1983) and Maria Lugones (1990) termed "loving perception," as opposed to the "arrogant perception" that existed between them and the feminist lesbians.

Although this brief history of the Albuquerque lesbian community demonstrates how race, class, and other power issues interconnect with sexuality in our lives, it also warns of the limitations of theory. Trying to be both activists and theorists, the feminist lesbians of Albuquerque proceeded in the best way they knew how, given both their reliance on theory and the state of lesbian and feminist theory at that point in time. Today, unfortunately, those roles are becoming increasingly separate, and, if anything, academically based feminists are even more dependent upon theory as the means to gain status within their professional lives. All feminists need to heed the critiques of our dependence on theory and to keep our theory connected with the realities of women's lives. (See, e.g., Christian 1990 and Rebolledo 1990.)

In Albuquerque, many of the early feminist lesbian leaders left, a couple became important theorists, one helped found Olivia Records (a lesbian-owned recording company), another headed a national gay organization, a few are again living straight lives. The lesbians who remained in Albuquerque found that the city is too small and the need for one another too great for lesbians to ignore each other. Additionally, the Albuquerque lesbian community has been too dynamic a scene for these earlier divisions to solidify. With new leaders and the time for trust to grow through continuing interaction and dialogue, lesbians in Albuquerque are perhaps in the vanguard in building a multicultural feminist lesbian community.

Anna Howard Shaw Women's Center
Albion College

References

Bérubé, Allan. 1989. *Coming Out under Fire: Lesbian and Gay Americans and the Military during World War II.* New York: Free Press.

Bethel, Lorraine, and Barbara Smith, eds. 1979. *Conditions: five,* the black women's issue.

Christian, Barbara. 1990. "The Race for Theory." In *Making Faces, Making Soul—Haciendo* Caras: *Creative and Critical Perspectives by Women of Color,* ed. Gloria Anzaldúa, 335–45. San Francisco: Aunt Lute.

Cook, Blanche Weisen. 1977. "Female Support Networks and Political Activism: Lillian Wald, Crystal Eastman, and Emma Goldman." *Chrysalis* 3:43–61.

Davis, Angela Y. 1981. *Women, Race and Class.* New York: Vintage.

D'Emilio, John. 1983. *Sexual Politics, Sexual Communities: The Making of a Homosexual Minority in the United States.* Chicago: University of Chicago Press.

Faderman, Lillian. 1981. *Surpassing the Love of Men.* New York: Morrow.

Ferguson, Ann, Jacquelyn Zita, and Kathryn Pyne Addelson. 1982. "On 'Compulsory Heterosexuality and Lesbian Existence': Defining Terms." In *Feminist Theory: A Critique of Ideology,* ed. Nannerl O. Keohane, Michelle Z. Rosaldo, and Barbara C. Gelpi, 147–88. Chicago: University of Chicago Press.

Frye, Marilyn. 1983. *The Politics of Reality: Essays in Feminist Theory.* Trumansburg, N.Y.: Crossing.

Gibbs, Joan, and Sara Bennett, eds. 1980. *Top Ranking: A Collection of Articles on Racism and Classism in the Lesbian Community.* Brooklyn, N.Y.: February Third Press.

Kennedy, Elizabeth Lapovsky, and Madeline Davis. 1993. *Boots of Leather, Slippers of Gold: The History of a Lesbian Community.* New York: Routledge & Kegan Paul.

Linden, Robin Ruth, Darlene R. Pagano, Diana E. H. Russell, and Susan Leigh Star, eds. 1982. *Against Sadomasochism: A Radical Feminist Analysis.* East Palo Alto, Calif.: Frog in the Well.

Lugones, Maria. 1990. "Playfulness, 'World'-Travelling and Loving Perception." In *Making Faces, Making Soul/Haciendo Caras,* ed. Gloria Anzaldúa. San Francisco: Aunt Lute.

Moraga, Cherríe, and Gloria Anzaldúa, eds. 1981. *This Bridge Called My Back: Writings by Radical Women of Color.* Watertown, Mass.: Persephone.

Nestle, Joan. 1987. *A Restricted Country.* Ithaca, N.Y.: Firebrand.

Rebolledo, Tey Diana. 1990. "The Politics of Poetics: Or, What Am I, a Critic, Doing in This Text Anyhow?" In *Making Faces, Making Soul—Haciendo Caras: Creative and Critical Perspectives by Women of Color,* ed. Gloria Anzaldúa, 346–55. San Francisco: Aunt Lute.

Rich, Adrienne. 1980. "Compulsory Heterosexuality and Lesbian Existence." *Signs* 5(4):631–60.

Samois, ed. 1981. *Coming to Power: Writings and Graphics on Lesbian S-M.* Boston: Alyson.

Snitow, Ann, Christine Stansell, and Sharon Thompson, eds. 1983. *Powers of Desire: The Politics of Sexuality.* New York: Monthly Review.

U.S. Census of Population: 1960, Final Report. PHC(1)-4, 1–54. Washington, D.C.: Government Printing Office.

U.S. Census of Population and Housing: 1980. PHC 80-2-62, Census Tracts. Washington, D.C.: Government Printing Office.

Vance, Carole, ed. 1984. *Pleasure and Danger: Exploring Female Sexuality.* Boston: Routledge & Kegan Paul.

Getting It Right

Marilyn Frye

ONCE UPON A TIME it was possible to use the terms *politically correct* and *politically incorrect* nonironically, the former as a term of positive evaluation, the latter as a term of negative evaluation. This is not to say that those who used these terms nonironically always used them simply to express an honest judgment: the terms also were used rhetorically as instruments of embrace and repudiation or inclusion and exclusion, to mark boundaries of affiliation, engage in dominance displays, and so on. And they were sometimes used ironically, with reversed valences. But in the recent national tempest about "diversity" and the canonical curriculum, the ironic reversal of values on these terms has been made so ubiquitous as to have actually changed their meanings, so that in common parlance *politically correct* is a term of negative valuation signifying a "praxis" of righteous bullying combined with superficial and faddish political thought or programs, a term generally employed as a deliberate insult, and *politically incorrect* is a term of positive valuation generally used to express a snotty sort of pride in resistance or immunity to what is claimed to be the banal moralizing of the politically correct.[1] When people object to racism, sexism, and so on, and recommend changes in behavior, they are accused of accusing others of being politically incorrect; but whether they are acting with integrity or not, they do not actually use the term *politically incorrect* to characterize the things they object to—it is simply no longer available as a piece of nonironic critical vocabulary.[2]

[1] This reversal of meanings is reminiscent of Nietzsche's analysis of morality and his eagerness to be "immoral" or amoral—to be free of a morality that is designed and promoted specifically to weaken the oppressed. At least since Nietzsche's time, any moral argument for change and any political strategy of taking the moral high ground is liable to this kind of backlash, either earnestly or cynically deployed.

[2] The disappearance of items of critical vocabulary should not go unremarked, for it tends to suppress criticism. It interests me that some of the folks who happily ironize this vocabulary to flatness are themselves most upset with postmodernists who, they suppose, would ironize the meaning out of their own favorite critical vocabulary (*truth, knowledge, individual, objective, real, man, necessary*, etc.).

[*Signs: Journal of Women in Culture and Society* 1992, vol. 17, no. 4]

But perversely I persist in being able to hear the phrase *politically correct* nonironically and as a positive term. It sounds like a phrase I might have coined to name something I want to be—I want to "be political" and to get things right and not get them wrong. This seems to be the route both to my own narrow happiness and to my fullest possible positive engagement in the welfare and happiness of many others both near and distant. But to say I aspire to be politically correct must sound absurd or absurdly naive—or worse, merely cranky—unless some positive, nonironic meaning can be pumped back into that term. I will not actually try to restore the term *politically correct* to its (perhaps imaginary) former luster and usefulness, but I do want to ruminate about politics and "getting it right" in ways that at least suggest what the term *politically correct* might mean if it were not just a curse. Then I will offer some views on the right (vs. wrong, not vs. left) politics of culture and curriculum.

Politics

It is useful for some purposes to think of the politics of a situation as like climate and weather, topology and soil: a multidimensional, multileveled, temporally extended, constantly changing, moving medium, a highly structured and fluid play of powers, which both sustains and threatens all the vital processes of human community existence; a sum of forces and pressures, currents, turbulences and calms, variations of density. The conditions of and in this medium at any particular time and place determine what can be done and by whom. That is, they determine and delimit the potential significance and effect of the actions and communications of agents who are variously located within and defined by it. Like the weather or climate, these conditions encourage or promote some social life processes and individual actions as they suppress or prohibit others, sometimes very generally over a wide spatiotemporal region, sometimes specifically or fleetingly. Conditions within this "sociosphere" (conceived on analogy with the ecologist's "biosphere") also tend to generate, promote, suppress, or disperse other conditions within it. All states and processes in it and of it are interdependent.

No metaphor perfectly renders its entire field. This elemental metaphor suggests that the structures and flows of power are, like the weather, something that humans do not create and cannot control or alter beyond the fabrication of barriers and shelters. But the jet streams, thunderstorms, and sunshine of the sociosphere are in fact products of human action, interaction, and interpretation, and can be altered by human action, interaction, and interpretation.[3] Nevertheless, it is a benefit of this

---

[3] I do not mean they are pure products of human construction. I am not a neo-idealist sort of constructionist. For instance, I think that although nowadays famines are

metaphor that it may attune the poet/philosopher/theorist to the fact that the whole unfathomably complex and fluid product of species-historic social construction, the planetary human life in which all human individuals are immersed, is not a "construct" like an artifact—like an automobile, for example—that can be tinkered with, dismantled, or demolished by an individual or a small work crew. It is not even like a very big artifact like the Sears Tower that can be demolished or structurally revised by concerted socially organized marshaling of resources and labor. It is also not "beyond us" like a massive computer no one person understands, but whose plug we might pull. Considered in relation to our individual and collective grasps and our semantic and material technologies, the systems and plays of power that constitute us as collectives are much more like the weather than like these other socially created constructions. Projects of changing them have to be more like organic gardening than like factory retooling.

Given this metaphoric image of what politics is, I understand a person's politics to be in significant part a matter of alignment and affiliation. Likewise, the politics of any policy, practice, project, or way of doing things, or the politics of a group, organization, or institution, is in large part a matter of how it works to align and affiliate people. Acts and habits, policies and practices, ways of doing things—those of individuals and of all kinds of collectivities—direct and regulate the flow of people's energies and the other resources the people command. They join our energies to some of the currents of power in our situations, adding to the effect of both; they set our energies against some currents, generating friction that may strengthen or deplete either or both. Each person is aligned with and against and at various angles to various forces and currents, and in this each is with others—and not with other others. By virtue of one's own acts and one's places in collectives and their processes, one is a fellow traveler with some and "part of the problem" to others; to some, one is both. Every aspect of one's life, no matter how trivial or local to oneself, is in some way (in many ways, simultaneously and not necessarily consistently) located in the currents and landscapes of politics and tends to reinforce or to alter some aspects of one's alignment and affiliation within that fluid structure. (Obvious examples of the sorts of alignments and oppositions in question are such things as where one shops—national chains or locally owned businesses, minority-owned businesses, and so on—and how and where one disposes of one's trash. Perhaps less obvious are such things as whom one greets and does not greet on the street, whether one is or is not engaged in grading and

---

socially constructed, the fact that plants capable of providing human nutrition do not generally grow abundantly in deserts is not. The construction and politics of famine would be different if they did.

certifying students, to whom and at what provocation one donates money, how one uses humor in intragroup bonding rituals. But giving examples, here, can be misleading, since I am claiming that in fact everything one does and thinks, every attitude one strikes, everything one says aligns one's energies and resources with and against various currents of power at various levels of social organization.)

People's politics—those of individuals and of groups—also have to do with their practical understanding of politics at all its levels and in all its complexity. The point and purpose of political understanding (I do not refer only to explicit or theoretical understanding but also to common sense, street smarts, taste, and other modes of being savvy) is to generate maps and instruments and good intuitions that guide individuals' and groups' negotiation and navigation in the currents of the sociosphere so that the net effect is to engage wills and resources in movement that enhances and furthers the well-beings of individuals, of groups, and of social-historic processes that it is good to enhance and further. The politics of anything is about will and value: aligning, allying, and engaging individual and collective will with that which is of value, which includes engaging will in the making of value.[4] Political understanding should contribute to getting this connection of will and value right. (If a person or group or process is getting it right in part by virtue of a sound working understanding of the politics of a situation, we could say—but we cannot, of course—that she/he/it is politically correct.)

But political understanding and the right alignments and affiliations are difficult to achieve. I suppose that virtually everyone lives constantly, almost from birth, with some understanding, more or less adequate or accurate, of the local politics of their situations. As Bob Dylan observed, it doesn't take a weatherman to know which way the wind blows.[5] We are attuned to what powers we command and what powers will be directed by others for us and against us, and we negotiate the currents both intuitively and deliberately like a white-water canoeist or a sailor in high and shifting winds. A great deal of this multilayered and context-

---

[4] Sarah Hoagland's *Lesbian Ethics* (Palo Alto, Calif.: Institute of Lesbian Studies, 1988) presents lesbian community as a partly deliberate project of creating value, as opposed to just aligning ourselves with or against values in a preexisting scheme of value.

[5] To give some examples from my own culture and time: A black male suspected of shoplifting in a suburban mall has little chance of avoiding being perceived and treated as an incorrigible criminal; a white male, even one whose age and class status put him somewhat at risk, has a better chance. And virtually all black males and all white males know this from a very young age, whether or not they have thought it through at an articulate level. Children know whom they can get in trouble by saying certain things about them to certain people. Women know how to get what they want by convincing men it is what the men want (a strategy that has its limits, as the history of reformist feminism shows). I take such things to be examples of people's knowledge of the politics of their situations.

sensitive knowledge seems to be with us like the perceptions we have of our physical environments by way of peripheral vision. In both cases, a constant flow of invaluable and highly interpreted information is readily available to us, and we rely on it spontaneously and faithfully, while very rarely taking explicit cognizance of it.

People everywhere know "by the seat of their pants" a great deal of the intricacy of local politics. We operate intelligently and quite effectively with and within that system of powers even when its main tendency is to disempower and disable us, even to disable us as perceivers and interpreters of our circumstances. But the many layers and structures on larger scales are not as readily perceived, interpreted, negotiated. Relative to the locus of a single awareness keyed to the specificities of a single life, such politics generally are diffuse, obscure, and remote. For one thing, they operate in ways that are causally complex and diffuse and they constitute blocks and channels that are not encountered experientially either as barriers or as externally engineered. (I refer, e.g., to the many and intricately related remote causes of the needs and fears at play in the politics of the average academic department office and to the many forces that construct appetites a person experiences as elementally and personally one's own or as just natural to human beings, e.g., who one finds congenial, whose love or alliance one needs, what one's material desires and needs are. Also, I am thinking of such things as barriers to social intercourse across ages, races, ethnic communities, religions, and so on, which often influence people very decisively without ever being recognized as barriers.) In addition, the regional, continental, and global prevailing winds, currents, fronts, storms, and seasons of power—macroscopic phenomena—are obscure because they are obscured: they are veiled and disguised by those in the most powerful groups through the services of their willing or unwitting propagandists (among which should be counted most professors, members of the clergy, professionals, and participants in the production of mass media). Active promotion of various kinds of error and false consciousness about political structures, processes, and forces is integral to some of the operations of power.[6] And what makes the task of political understanding even more difficult is that we (at least U.S. persons within my own ken) are accustomed to locating larger-scale causes by observing uniformities of effect: where something particular and local happens repeatedly in the same way, we postulate a common, more general cause. But in the case of politics (as, indeed, in the case of material weather), the currents of power do not have the same consequences for all the individuals and groups they affect, not even for all those similarly situated with respect to various institutions and cate-

---

[6] At the local level people also take advantage of opportunities to manipulate others' perceptions of what is going on and they often enough succeed magnificently, but at that level and scale it is easier to detect and correct for deceit.

gories. To intuit the politics of a situation one has to sense and think quite differently than one does in diagnosing, for instance, the causes of the repeated occurrence of a certain ailment in a certain population of schoolchildren.[7]

For these and other reasons, patient and skillful observation and acute intuition are required to recognize and understand the politics of a situation, even though some aspects of it, especially aspects that operate at a local, microscopic level, are quite obvious and familiar. It is often not at all obvious which acts and policies of individuals or collectives will in fact align and ally them as they would—or should—want to be aligned and allied.

In the academy

Suppose you are a person seriously interested in minimizing your contribution to situations in which sentient beings suffer and maximizing your contribution to the existence of sustainable situations of living that systematically promote their individual and collective thriving.[8] Or suppose you are more modest or more parochial in your aspirations, and you commit yourself only to sustainable good circumstances for a group or category of folk with whom you identify; imagine that it is a group that has for some long time been subject to oppression, exploitation, ethnic or racial hatred, destruction of culture, or similar evils. Suppose you are a particular person situated in some particular time, place, and station. With what people, what trends and forces, what currents, what institutions should you align and ally yourself, and how could you accomplish such alignment and alliance?

I am someone with such aspirations, with both global and parochial reference, and I am situated just so. Almost everyone on my campus who knows me or knows of me would categorize me as some sort of radical who could be counted upon to be on the "politically correct" side of every issue and, for example, to be in favor of affirmative action, curriculum integration, and multiculturalism, and to align and ally myself with others who favor these things.[9] Some think my support of and identifi-

---

[7] For another discussion of this point, see Marilyn Frye, *The Politics of Reality: Essays in Feminist Theory* (Freedom, Calif.: Crossing Press, 1983), "Introduction," xi–xiii.

[8] There is no difficulty in your affirming that thriving may consist of different things for different people, and you need not assume you can know just what will conduce to whose welfare. You need not be arrogant or patronizing.

[9] *Curriculum integration,* in my neck of the woods, refers to syllabus-revision projects aimed at incorporating into courses materials by and about people other than elite, racially privileged males. It has been used most, in my hearing, in reference more specifically to including (integrating, not merely adding) materials by and about women in the syllabi of courses that hitherto contained only material by men and generated from men's perspectives.

cation with such causes is dependable only because it is automatic, un-reflective, "knee-jerk." But I cannot be counted on. In fact I am, very reflectively indeed, very uncertain about the projects and policies being pursued under these rubrics. Though I am well aware of some good outcomes for some people, such projects and policies are also risky and harmful in ways their supporters (among which I can at least some of the time be counted) have not adequately assessed, and I suspect that the long-term political drift of these projects and policies may be regressive rather than progressive.

Let me rehearse some of these difficulties, which I am by no means the first to note. Consider affirmative action in higher education student admissions and faculty hiring. Affirmative action hiring practices certainly have interrupted or prevented some cases of unjust or unfair closure to or elimination of job candidates. But it is most successful as a quite selective strategy of assimilation, co-optation, and tokenism. It tends to induct into the "mainstream" the most assimilable individuals, those whose already-acquired skills, manners, accents, and values are most like or complementary to those of the people who are already securely ensconced in the academy.[10] Those who are not thus socialized become the multiple proofs that "qualified women and minorities" cannot be found. Hence, predictably, affirmative action has worked better to assimilate white middle- and upper-middle-class women into white-male-dominated education domains and professions than it has to assimilate African American, Asian, Latino, or Native American people; in many academic settings, the numbers of members of ethnic or racialized minorities have actually been decreasing in the last few years.

Furthermore, in the United States, beginning with the era of the civil rights movement, educated and politicized women and men who are African American, Latina/Latino, or Native American, and educated and politicized white women of all classes, have constituted relatively active and resourceful populations of malcontents well situated to assume leadership in movements for radical, transforming change that would drastically alter the distribution and flow of power. The opportunity for more education and an academic or professional career may draw members of these groups (and has drawn many) into activities, intellectual milieus, and lives that alienate them from those with whom they might have worked revolutionary change. This has worked especially well, in my

[10.] For instance, my own life and career have been directly and decisively affected by institutional affirmative action; without it, I almost surely would not have been in the academy for so many years. But I am so highly assimilable that it is shocking that a corrective such as affirmative action was even necessary. Though I am a woman (which is the misfortune that affirmative action was needed to neutralize) and a lesbian, I am Anglo-Saxon, Christian-cultured, born-and-bred middle class, silver-spoon educated, and generally pass as "normal" in appearance and manner, at least in academic settings.

opinion, for (or, more accurately, against) middle- and upper-middle-class white women, as well as educationally advantaged white working-class women.

And the most stunning success of affirmative action has been as a strategy of tokenism: nearly every academic setting and activity includes one "woman" and/or one "minority," often enough in the body of one and the same person, which signals deceptively to all and sundry that if you behave well and "achieve," you can succeed, no matter what your race, sex, or national origin, and that the institution is indeed an "equal opportunity employer."

For those who cherish the status quo, such workings of affirmative action should be counted as goods. But in many cases they do not perceive this and they resist affirmative action. Their narrow perspectives and bigotry, and for some the self-serving belief that the traditional initiation processes have all along been democratic and merit based, make them think of affirmative action as upsetting, rather than protectively adapting, the status quo. Because of this resistance, affirmative action policies and processes have to operate to a great extent by bureaucratic coercion, generating multistep procedures, wasteful and irritating paper trails of documentation, and administrative policing (some of which is, itself, cynically permissive). They thus encourage and promote a climate of cynical manipulation of rules and of people, and they promote resentment and suspicion of those supposed to have benefited from the process.[11]

Affirmative action institutionally affirms and thus ever more deeply entrenches a liberal bureaucratic politics according to which (1) assimilating (some of) those who are marginalized into the "mainstream" is the way to resolve social problems of race, class, and gender; (2) formal justice (e.g., publicly advertised job openings constituting formal equality of access to the job market) is all the justice that is needed; and (3) formal justice can be achieved by coercive and bureaucratic regulation of social processes. This is not a politics with which I willingly align myself. Currents in the sociosphere that promote co-optation of potential change agents, tokenism, cynicism, and manipulation are not currents to which I happily join my energies.

Curriculum integration is the curricular version of affirmative action. The by-now-familiar idea is that the standard college and university curriculum covers a very narrow range of the cultural product of humans on this planet while presenting that slim product as identical with culture itself, and that it is desirable to introduce into that curriculum content that refers to a much wider range of cultural product and culture pro-

---

[11] I do not think you can make significant changes without occasioning some resentment and suspicion, not to say hostility, but I do think one should anticipate this cost and attempt to ensure that one is getting something for it.

ducers, that is, material by and about "women and minorities" and other marginalized or erased folk. It is thought, or hoped, that the integration (not mere addition) of that material will not leave the previous content intact, but will transform it.

Some people have critically noticed that in the process of curriculum integration scholars have quickly canonized (tokenized) a few cultural products and their producers through making them the standard representatives of the "other" that is to be integrated. Two other things seem less often attended to: the matter of how this process of integration will transform the "new" material, and the matter of the continued production of "new" material in cultural loci outside the arena of this transforming marriage of the traditional canon and the "other" knowledge. I fear a replication of colonialism. European colonial cultures were profoundly affected and altered by their integration of the cultures of the peoples they conquered, but this "transformation," one of whose rather interesting products is contemporary U.S. culture, was not markedly beneficial to the cultural groups whose cultures were being integrated. Integration of their cultural product into the "curriculum" of the colonizing culture was not a mechanism of emancipation for them. In fact, many "integrated" cultures did not survive to the day when their members might benefit from seeing themselves reflected in the media and the arts of the transformed dominant culture (nor would those hapless individuals have recognized their reflection). I am concerned that women's studies, African-American studies, and other ethnic or area studies—academic cultures that are providing the dominant academic culture with its "new" subjects, materials, and methods—might likewise not survive the transformation of the traditional curriculum.[12]

"Multiculturalism" has a sweeter sound to me than "affirmative action" or "curriculum integration."[13] It seems to affirm plurality instead of unification/co-optation by integration or assimilation. Most of the students and faculty members in U.S. universities in the present era need to be vastly more informed and appreciative of multiplicity, plurality, and diversity, both among and within cultures. Most of us lack and need deep and subtle understandings of the complexities of interaction and influence among cultures. Many of us need some profound encounters with some particular cultures beyond our own. These understandings and

---

[12] It does not comfort me that substantial private and government funding is available for curriculum integration projects.

[13] But I am sobered by the news that in the university at which I work, the term *affirmative action* has become *lingua non grata* among those who are institutionally responsible for promoting "diversity" and that the term *multiculturalism* is now preferred. If it is just a new name for the old policies, this linguistic shift is not good. Only time will tell whether this marks, rather, a real shift in those people's vision and understanding of what they want to be promoting.

encounters seem to be the likely antidotes to racism, ethnosolipsism, and other destructive rigidities of thought and practice that lock us into alignment with currents of oppression, exploitation, imperialism, and many forms of habitual cruelty and abusiveness among ourselves. It seems to me highly desirable for students, faculty, and administrators to find and to create ways to turn the resources of colleges and universities to the encouragement of such learning. One significant historical/structural barrier to this is that most of the people in whose hands these resources and this project would be (or is) have themselves been socialized as cultural thieves and exoticists. They may not be able to figure out (and will not be able to seek and accept suitable help in figuring out) how to promote appreciation of cultural plurality without promoting just more annihilative assimilation. These people, one should bear in mind, benefit continuously and in multiple ways from privileges they have and maintain at the expense of others, including precisely those others whose culture and work they might want to "integrate" or even to be transformed by. These people (we, they, you), one should not forget, grew up on the *National Geographic* and read the Nature Company and Banana Republic catalogs in the bathroom and in bed; they (we, you) are the direct descendants of the folks who conceived and created the African Hall in the American Museum of Natural History in New York City that communicates "abundantly about 20th century United States" but is "reticent, even mute, about Africa."[14]

To promote multiculturalism and not cultural colonialism requires that we promote a world in which there are multiple, thriving, relatively autonomous, mutually respectful and appreciative cultures (or other kinds of loci of social living and culture-making for which the term *culture* might not be quite apt). In the microcosm of the U.S. academy, this translates into the necessity of cultivating and nurturing multiple nuclei of study, research, and creative activity that are not primarily "integrative" but rather are constructive projects of generating knowledge and generating culture at and beyond the boundaries of traditional and dominant disciplines, methods, and subject matters. Instead of allocating yet more resources to traditional disciplines presumably to reform them, resources should be channeled to programs of African-American studies, many programs of ethnic and area studies, women's studies, lesbian and gay studies, and special focus programs in the disciplines and the arts, where the resources will support people and work that create, express, and articulate knowledges rooted in many different kinds of lives and circumstances.

[14] Donna J. Haraway, *Primate Visions: Gender, Race and Nature in the World of Modern Science* (New York: Routledge, 1989), 27.

The notion of multiculturalism is suggestive of novelty and change both for multiple programs and projects other than traditional disciplines and studies, and for those traditional activities as well. The creative powers of nontraditional projects will be released when they are recognized as having integrity of their own and are free not to refer constantly to mainstreams of Anglo-European culture, disciplinary canons, and standards of value that are already deeply engraved in the traditional curriculum, not even for the purpose of reforming or transforming them. And, on the other hand, if people doing the research and scholarship that have been traditional in U.S. universities for a century or so were to recognize their subject matter as the products of quite specific cultures and situations—were to embrace their enterprise as one "area study" among others—they might well begin to understand and amplify the complex oppressive and liberatory, conservative and transgressive, currents in the materials and circumstances they already study, the culture they already participate in constructing. The traditional curriculum might be rediscovered, or re-construed, in ways that preserve it from being an exercise in cultural chauvinism and/or cultural imperialism, and the culture it expresses and helps to construct might be both invigorated and made nontoxic to other cultures. Participants in these enterprises then could with integrity claim the same respect that is being claimed by the people and works they formerly erased, marginalized, and/or colonized. Those who perceive that their own power is preserved by the traditional way of doing the traditional curriculum will want to resist such a reconception of their work, of course.

The notion of multiculturalism also suggests a changed understanding of the campus. It cannot continue to be conceived as a relatively closed and self-contained place where scholars, researchers, and artists are cloistered. There still are many habits and policies in universities that serve to restrict the mobility of members of university communities, to restrict primary physical locales of our work to college campuses, requiring us to be "in residence" a great deal of the time and imposing barriers to our taking "leaves." An interest in multiculturalism would suggest allocating more resources to travel and enacting generous practices regarding leaves of absence for scholars (both faculty and students) whose projects require physical removal from campuses and physical presence in other sites of human living. (I am thinking not so much of scholars visiting "other's" cultures as of scholars working in the various locales of their own cultures.) It would also suggest much more various and generous definitions of "research" and "scholarship."

To sum up, the notion of multiculturalism seems to me to imply a very different picture of the university or college than that implied by the notion of curriculum integration (or even transformation). Integration suggests a flow to already-existing centers and an evolution of a single all-purpose complex that "reflects" everyone approximately equally and meets the educational needs of all different sorts of people. Multiculturalism suggests a flow that is governed by a plurality of centers of gravity and the evolution of a system with no center. And it suggests a picture of universities as things not run hierarchically by business-management principles. These are things most administrators and faculty members— even the "tenured radicals"—neither envisage nor want.

Getting it right

The reflections that make me ambivalent about support of the apparently progressive initiatives in academia do lead me to revise my relatively jolly suggestion that "correct" is what I want my politics—those alignments and alliances—to be.

"Correcting" a situation seems to be precisely what is attempted by means such as affirmative action and curriculum integration projects. To correct is to bring something into conformance with preestablished rule; it pertains to regimentation; it has to do with the perception of something as deviant or deviating from some rule or norm and manipulations of some sort to bring it into line. The power struggle in the academy has to do with who is going to determine what the "rule" is; practices within the institutions will proceed by the same logic of correction, whoever gets to set the rule. Thinking of a sound, loving, pluralistic politics as "correct" may not help one divorce oneself from thinking by such a logic.

For those of us who would like to contribute to the end of the world regime of oppression, I think it is counterproductive to try directly to control (correct) the actions and processes (such as practices and curricula in the academy) that contribute to constituting and maintaining the present climate. The metaphor of politics as weather and climate suggests that coercion, regulation, seduction, even persuasion (which it is difficult to distinguish from coercion)[15] are too narrow, too mechanical, and too specifically adapted to the inner workings of a specific local system to be ways of directing energies and wills to profound and structural change. The politics of knowledge and culture I favor is a practice that minimizes adversarial, coercive, and/or reformist engagement (struggle) with established institutions and disciplines and frees one's energy for maintaining, strengthening, and creating other knowledges. The politics of the university I favor is one which frees students, scholars, researchers, and artists for such preservation and creativity.

[15] See Joyce Trebilcot, "Dyke Methods," in *Lesbian Philosophies and Cultures,* ed. Jeffner Allen (Albany: State University of New York Press, 1990), 15–29.

A person situated roughly as I am (like many if not most other academics in the United States), with aspirations such as I have owned here, is not well advised to try to reform the "traditional curriculum" of universities or of Western culture. She is better advised to join others in committing herself to practices of new construction. As for the question of whether I am getting it right when I promote such a politics of separation, creation, and autonomy, I cannot, of course, be certain. But I am quite sure such a politics at least does not get it wrong in the same old way.

Department of Philosophy
Michigan State University

When a Looker Is Really a Bitch: Lisa Olson, Sport, and the Heterosexual Matrix

Lisa Disch and Mary Jo Kane

Introduction

I N SEPTEMBER 1990, Lisa Olson, a sports reporter for the *Boston Herald,* was sexually harassed in the locker room of the New England Patriots football team. The incident was initiated by one player who walked over to Olson and thrust his penis toward her, asking " 'Do you want to take a bite out of this?' " It escalated quickly as several more players paraded past her, "modeling" their genitals in a mock strip tease while various others shouted: " 'Did she look, did she look?' 'Get her to look'; 'That's what she wants'; 'Is she looking?' 'Make her look' " (Heymann 1990, 15–17). Olson resisted the players' accusations by reporting the incident to her editor. Although she wanted the matter to be handled privately, she refused to dismiss it as insignificant and demanded that the instigators identify themselves and apologize to her. Against her wishes, the story broke four days later in the *Globe,* the more prestigious of the two Boston-area papers. The publicity incited Patriots owner Victor Kiam to call Olson a "classic bitch," adding, "No wonder the players can't stand her" (Mannix 1990, 74).

The incident and Kiam's response to it prompted National Football League Commissioner Paul Tagliabue to call for an independent investigation to be conducted by prominent Harvard Law School professor

Earlier versions of this article were presented by Lisa Disch at the Midwest Society for Women in Philosophy in October 1993 and by Mary Jo Kane at the North American Society for Sport Sociology in November 1993. We thank anonymous *Signs* reviewers for their comments. Diana Saco, Jacqueline Zita, and Jonathan Sweet offered suggestions on this work in its early stages, as did Naomi Scheman, who gave it an exceptionally close and generous reading. Special thanks go to Lisa Bower and Jennifer Pierce for helping us to differentiate penises from phalluses, to Steven Gerencser for his analysis of the marathon, and to Jeanne Barker-Nunn for contributing her expertise in interdisciplinary writing to the final revisions of this article.

[*Signs: Journal of Women in Culture and Society* 1996, vol. 21, no. 2]

Philip Heymann.[1] It also sparked hundreds of reports and editorials, touching off a national debate over what some characterized as the propriety of having women sports reporters in men's locker rooms and what others defined as a violation of a reporter's gender-neutral right of access to the players. For many commentators, issues of gender difference and sexual tension took precedence over Olson's rights as a professional; they argued that assigning women reporters to cover the locker room "courts disaster" (Hart 1990, 17) and that Olson and the *Herald* had been "asking for trouble" (Mannix 1990, 74). In contrast, others denied the relevance of sex and gender altogether, asserting that women reporters have an equal "right to talk to an athlete, to look for stories, to be treated no worse and no better than men are treated" (Madden 1990b, 49). Strangely, Olson remained a figure in this controversy long after she had been forced to stop covering sports in the Boston area and even left the United States for Australia where she covers sports for another Rupert Murdoch newspaper.[2] In June 1992, the *Boston Globe* resurrected the controversy by publishing a five-page attack on Olson's character and professional reputation.[3] Her name made the Boston papers again six months later when, after a game between the Patriots and the Miami Dolphins, Dolphins wide receiver Mark Clayton invoked her presence for no apparent reason, shouting to a locker room full of male reporters: "Close the door and keep Lisa Olson outside! Keep that dick-watching bitch outside" (Henkel 1993, 1).[4]

Why this explosion of hostility against a sports reporter engaged in the performance of so routine a part of her job as interviewing a source? It

---

[1] By November, the Heymann Commission had compiled a sixty-page report confirming that Olson had in fact been harassed and suggesting that the incident may even have been premeditated. Tagliabue then fined three players $2,500 each (approximately one day's pay) and fined the team $50,000, sums that were never collected. When questioned about why the fines were never paid, Tagliabue responded, "At some point, enough is enough," evidently meaning that the players had been adequately chastised (Nelson 1994, 240).

[2] Area fans threatened Olson with phone calls, letters containing sexual references and obscene drawings, and even death warnings. Easily recognizable by her long red hair, Olson could not cover a game in Boston without fans shouting at her and even showering her with beer. In hope of defusing the situation, the *Herald* reassigned her to cover basketball and hockey instead of football, but to no avail (Montville 1991).

[3] At a panel discussion at the annual meeting of the Association for Women in Sports Media, held in Minneapolis in May 1993, it emerged that the putative exposé was based primarily on leaked documents of pretrial depositions from the civil suit Olson initiated against the Patriots. Because of a family illness, Olson settled before these proceedings were completed, although only her opponents had given evidence. The depositions and, consequently, the *Globe* article, told the story of the incident from only one perspective.

[4] In contrast to Olson's original harassment, three male sportswriters immediately reported Clayton's remarks, which prompted Clayton to respond by attempting to organize a team boycott against them. Dolphins management countered immediately by forcing Clayton to issue a public apology for the remark (Henkel 1993).

is well known that players spout obscenities in the locker room as a matter of course and pay tribute to women reporters' presence there with hurled offerings of jockstraps, dirty socks, and wads of athletic tape (Huckshorn 1990, 1E). As journalist Mariah Burton Nelson puts it, "Sexual harassment is as familiar to female [sports] journalists as the scent of sweat" (1994, 228). Olson herself was not the first woman reporter to cover sports in Boston. And she was neither the first woman assigned to cover the Patriots nor the first to be harassed by them (Heymann 1990, 6). But by most accounts, what happened to Olson was an unprecedentedly intense, protracted, and collective display of hostility.

The players explained their actions by claiming that Olson was a "looker," a term that one male sports columnist explained as designating a woman "who tended to peek excessively" (Durslag 1991, C3). This term was not unique to the incident between Olson and the Patriots but, according to several women sports reporters, is a common point of contention between them and the players (Heymann 1990, 6). In fact, in the culture of the locker room, this term has the status of a "charge" that the players understand to designate a "crime" that is unique to women reporters.

From a purely legal standpoint, this charge is illegitimate, as a Federal Court ruling in 1978 established women sports reporters' constitutional right of equal access to interviews with the players—even when its exercise would mean entering men's locker rooms.[5] Women currently make up only eight hundred out of ten thousand sports journalists, and most of these are reporters. Only one dozen write regular columns and only four major newspapers have women sports editors (Nelson 1994, 229). In the context of this struggle for gender equity, former sports reporter Melissa Ludtke warns that taking the players' charge seriously would be a step backward, arguing that it deflects attention from the "central question of fairness" to resurrect the specter of "women . . . who only wanted to gaze at naked men" (Ludtke 1990b, 5). Although we concur with Ludtke that the charge is illegitimate and that looking cannot be taken literally as a crime, a feminist critical analysis cannot afford to dismiss such claims as a mere rhetorical smoke screen for more central questions of fairness defined as equality before the law. As Olson herself explained two years later, what was at issue in the incident was not rights but power: "We are taught to think we must have done something wrong and it took me a

---

[5] Melissa Ludtke, then a sports reporter for *Sports Illustrated,* was refused access to the New York Yankees locker room during the 1977 World Series. She joined suit with Time, Inc. (the parent company of *Sports Illustrated*), claiming a violation of the equal protection clause of the Fourteenth Amendment. In 1978, the Federal District Court ruled that all reporters, regardless of sex, must have equal access to the players (Boutilier and SanGiovanni 1983).

while to realize I hadn't done anything wrong. They resented a woman in their domain and it all became a power issue" (Brown 1993, 1C).

Lisa Olson gauged the stakes in this conflict more shrewdly than did many of her defenders, who tended to position her as a victim of the players' disrespect, bad taste, or "outrageous harassment" (*Boston Herald* 1990, B14). Olson's antagonists also knew precisely what was at stake in the locker room. By the charge of "looking," by their repeated references to Olson as a "classic bitch," and by Clayton's later emendation of that remark to "dick-watching bitch," they designated Olson as a threat. Further, by his gloss on looking as "peeking excessively," sports columnist Melvin Durslag named Olson's alleged crime in a way that unwittingly disclosed her agency.

What can it mean to peek excessively? Literally an oxymoron, this charge points beyond the conventions that govern relations between women sports reporters and players in the locker room to those that govern gender relations more broadly. Drawing on the work of Teresa de Lauretis, we understand *excess* as feminist agency that is made possible by "a *disidentification* with femininity that does not necessarily revert or result in an identification with masculinity" (1990, 126). To put it simply, it is a resistance that goes beyond refusing a particular social role to destablize the very construction of gender as a binary opposition. We contend that a woman sports reporter confounds gender oppositions. In her professional capacity, she is an authoritative critic of athletic performance who enjoys backstage access to cultural heroes and a public forum in which to speak about what she sees. Thus, her profession affords her prerogatives over male athletes that exceed those that can be permitted to her as a woman. Looking, then, is a charge that is deployed by players, management, owners, and—in Olson's case—fans to impute lascivious interest to a woman sports reporter's gaze. An attempt to contain the excess of her professional position, the charge confers a stereotype of envy and desire that reinforces oppositional gender norms. Olson's excess was her refusal to accede to the charge of looking despite months of publicity that would have embarrassed a more conventional woman; in effect, she publicly contested its status as a crime.

What if the problem with a "dick-watching bitch" is not that she is a *dick-watcher* but that she is a *bitch*? *Bitch* is, as Lillian Robinson has observed in a different context, an appellation that a woman earns by her "intrusion into male certainties" (1993, 10). Robinson's observation directs us to re-read this incident not simply as an assault on Olson and on legal principles of equality but as a defensive reaction against a woman in a position of power. As one feminist analyst noted at the time of the controversy, assertions by Kiam and the players that Olson was asking for trouble by entering the locker room deny that power, stereotyping

Olson as the victim of a justified attack (Matchan 1990). In contrast, we suggest that it was not Olson's vulnerability as a woman that prompted this confrontation but rather that Olson—as a bitch—had the players at a disadvantage: hers was an intrusion not just into the locker room but into certainties about gender relations and sex differences that sport serves to guarantee.

It is a commonplace among sport sociologists that professional athletics participates in the construction of gender as an asymmetrical relation between two mutually exclusive but complementary categories and establishes that social construction as a fact of nature. We take up this commonplace to argue that sport serves as an affirmation of what Judith Butler calls the heterosexual matrix (1990, chap. 2). We mean by this that sport constructs not only the gender order but binary sexual difference as well; in turn, the certainties it affirms go beyond gender complementarity to the more precarious fiction of oppositional sexual orientation. Consequently, we modify Robinson's assessment of what it means to be termed a bitch by viewing the position of the woman sports reporter as an intrusion not just into male certainties but into gender certainties more generally.

Our argument, which rests on Butler's work, will seem counterintuitive to feminists who take for granted that gender is to sex as culture is to nature. Indeed, Butler refutes precisely this assumption that gender is the cultural reflection of a natural sexual binary. Instead she argues that gender designates the social practices by which that binary is made to seem inherent in nature. Butler introduces the concept of the heterosexual matrix in order to disclose what she calls the "compulsory order of sex/gender/desire," the cultural logic that makes binary sex difference seem to be the cause of the social effects by which it is constructed, that stabilizes masculine and feminine gender identification, and that regulates the orientation of desire in such a way as to establish heterosexuality as the natural and inevitable outcome of normal psychological development (1990, 6–7). We argue that by calling her a dick-watching bitch, Olson's antagonists disclose the woman sports reporter's potential to break up this logic: by her intrusion into the locker room, she destabilizes the opposition between masculinity as that which is both penetrating and impenetrable and femininity as that which is receptive and deferential in the face of male power.

Taking the players at their word, this article offers a feminist deconstruction of looking, which we analyze as an excess rather than a crime. We take as our starting point the words of Jacqueline Rose, who directs a "feminism concerned with the question of looking" to "stress the particular and limiting opposition of male and female which any image seen to be flawless is serving to hold in place" (1986, 232). We argue that sport i̶ ̶ ̶technology for the production of flawless images of gender difference that serve to regulate heterosexual desire and that looking is a technology by which athletic performance organizes ambiguous relations of difference into oppositional gender certainties. The presence in the locker room of a woman sports reporter is an intrusion into these certainties because the access and critical voice that she enjoys as a professional are in excess of that which she ought to enjoy as a woman. The charge of looking is deployed to contain this excess by turning her look of appraisal and her authoritative critical voice into a crime.

Sport and the construction of white civility

We have discussed the incident thus far as if gender certainties were the only thing at stake in the Olson-Patriots incident. This is misleading insofar as it leaves unstated the fact that Olson is a white woman, that the players who harassed her were black, and that the men who supported them—the owners, management, players, sports columnists, and probably many Boston area fans—were white. We argue that race, although unmentioned in the coverage and in most of the commentaries, is one key to understanding how this incident played out in public. The controversy exemplified one way that sport, race, and gender work together to the benefit of white masculinity. Analyses of the incident at the time it occurred, which tended to focus either on Olson's perspective or on that of the players, were alike in overlooking this complex of relations. These analyses missed an opportunity to effect a realignment of forces that could destabilize white masculinity, a fragile identity whose articulation is achieved, in part, through sport. Thus, although gender will be our primary lens of analysis, we argue that a feminist deconstruction of this incident must be "race-cognizant" as well (Frankenberg 1993, chap. 6).

It is not often that a sexual assault on a well-educated white woman meets with public congratulations, especially when it is orchestrated by a group of black men. And how often do the media fail to mention race in such a story, especially when the victim is white and her attackers are black? For the sake of comparison, recall the newspaper coverage of the 1989 rape and beating of a woman investment banker in Central Park that conformed to the far more typical pattern of demonizing the attackers and canonizing the victim. In this instance, racial themes were at first invoked implicitly, with the twelve youths involved identified cautiously as part of a "loosely organized gang" from "Upper Manhattan" (Pitt 1989b, A1). Subsequently, race was raised to the central explanatory variable of the incident as the *New York Times* undertook a virtual sociological study of "wilding," which it characterized as a "pastime" by which "packs" of teenagers from "housing projects" "rampage" against "joggers and bikers" in the park.[6] One need not even read beneath the surface of these accounts to get the story they tell of untamed black youths preying on fitness-conscious whites.[7]

Given the way such stories are typically narrated, it is worth asking why a group of black men who exposed themselves to a white professional woman on the job and then boasted—in their own words—of giving her what she "wanted" were not castigated as attackers but celebrated as avengers. Five months after the confrontation, Patriots owner Victor Kiam was still saluting his players when, at an awards banquet for an Old-Timers Athletic Association, he quipped: "Do you know what Lisa Olson has in common with the Iraqis? They've both seen Patriot missiles up close" (Times News Services 1991, C2). Beyond Kiam's predictable support for his team, male sports reporters and fans attacked Olson in numerous columns, letters to the editor, and calls that "deluged" Boston area radio shows (Matchan 1990, 29). What dynamics would be at work to make Kiam, the Patriots management, several white male sports columnists, and scores of fans resist a typical race narrative and side with the players?

In the first place, these are highly paid professional athletes in the employ of a white corporate executive. Further, they are symbols of an ideal of masculinity in which a good deal of cultural capital (literal and figurative) is invested.[8] Historically, professional sport has worked to forge male solidarity around an anachronistic ideal of sovereign masculinity. Sociologist Michael Kimmel has argued that its emergence in the late nineteenth-century United States was prompted by a "perceived crisis

---

[6] These stories quoted experts who theorized "wilding" as a practice engaged in by marginalized youth as a protest against people who "seem to personify unattainable affluence" and as an acting out of a more general aimlessness that comes from having an unsupervised and unstructured lifestyle (Pitt 1989a, 1989c).

[7] Such narratives are especially irresponsible given that they perpetrate a kind of "rhetorical wilding" against the demographics of such crimes. As the *Times* itself reported during this same period, the crimes are neither exclusively perpetrated by blacks nor exclusively directed against middle-class whites. And in this particular instance, again as reported by the *Times,* the youths involved, though of color, were not all black. Neither were they gang members nor habitual delinquents. Contrary to the lurid metaphors and the speculative sociology of "wilding," some of the assailants were "A-students" and children of parents whom the paper approvingly characterized as "disciplinarians" (Kaufman 1989, A1).

[8] Sport as big business has become so ingrained in our society that teams do not have to play a game or sell a ticket to generate revenue. Billions of dollars are spent annually on licensed sports products (e.g., baseball hats and trading cards). In 1992, e.g., retail sales of all licensed sports merchandise totaled $12.2 billion (Gorman and Calhoun 1994). Media rights are another major source of income. In 1994, Rupert Murdoch, the publisher of the *Herald,* purchased the broadcasting rights to cover the National Football League for his Fox Television Network at a cost of $1.6 billion (*Media Week* 1994). These serve as but two examples of the connections among sport, capitalism, and masculinity.

of masculinity" among white middle-class males whose autonomy was compromised by political and economic transformations (1990, 57). This presumed crisis was precipitated by the domestication of the frontier, by the mechanization and routinization of labor that eroded economic autonomy, by the rise of the women's movement, and by the influx of immigrants into industrial centers. Similarly, Michael Messner has argued that, in the face of the increasing bureaucratization of this society, the professional athlete was an exemplar of irrefutable physical sexual difference and superiority; in the face of social and cultural plurality, athletic performance served as a rallying point for male identity. In football, the most militarist of the sports with which Americans are identified, male athleticism serves, "in the face of women's challenges to male dominance, to symbolically link men of diverse ages and socioeconomic backgrounds" (Messner 1988, 202). To be an exemplar of masculinity puts the black male athlete in an ambiguous position with respect to race by affording him an experience that, in this racist society, is unique: he will be seen first as a man and second as a black man.

This privileged status that the black male athlete enjoys against other black men does not erase his racial identity, however. Sport works paradoxically to forge solidarity in that while it unites men around an anachronistic ideal of masculinity, it also manages to differentiate them by race and class. Messner quotes one white male professional who invoked a black male athlete in just this paradoxical fashion, declaring: "A woman can do the same job as I can do—maybe even be my boss. But I'll be *damned* if she can go out on the football field and take a hit from Ronnie Lott," a black NFL player celebrated for making aggressive tackles (1990, 103). To this man, Lott reaffirms the self-evident natural foundation of male superiority. Thus, he expresses solidarity with Lott as one of the bottom-line guarantors of white professional masculinity in a time of feminist incursions into middle-class occupations. Yet to celebrate Lott as a fearsome hitter is also to denigrate him, as Lott is made to "play the role of the primitive other, against whom higher status men define themselves as modern and civilized" (Messner 1990, 103).

In a different context, labor historian David Roediger has identified such claims to civility as intrinsic to the "pleasures of whiteness" (1991, 13). These pleasures constituted a positive race identity that was addressed to the emerging working class. Over the course of the nineteenth century, whiteness served to reconcile the republican ideal of the independent citizen suited to the elite citizen body of a primarily agricultural nation with the political and economic transformations wrought by industrial capitalism. This pleasure worked both to offset white workers' "fear of dependency on wage labor" and to fortify their dignity against the "necessities of capitalist work discipline" (Roediger 1991, 13). In turn, Roediger argues, blackness was not simply regarded as the other of white racial identity but simultaneously denigrated and admired as a symbol of spirituality and physicality, sources of resistance against the industrial discipline to which white workers had submitted. Insofar as black athletes today are simultaneously celebrated and denigrated as emblems of male potency and explosive physicality, they help to pay middle- and working-class white men what Roediger calls the "wages of whiteness" (1991).

A further paradox for the black male athletes themselves is that they are the least empowered by the idealized masculinity for which they are the standard-bearers. Though sport may appear to be a way to break out of typical patterns of race and class oppression, it actually reproduces them. To begin with, the odds of a black male youth making a living playing professional sports are two to 100,000 (Messner 1990). Harry Edwards puts it starkly: "Statistically, you have a better chance of getting hit by a meteorite in the next 10 years than getting work as an athlete" (Oates 1979, A32). Despite these odds, college talent scouts continue to recruit black teenagers "to out-of-state colleges with dreams not of a degree but of the NBA in their heads. . . . The failure of these players following years of work at (and exploitation by) schools let folks back home know these men were just pawns in a game" (George 1992, 201). For those few black men who achieve professional careers in sport, racially patterned employment discrimination assigns them to the least powerful, least secure, most expendable, and most exploited positions (Edwards 1984). One of the most overt patterns of racial oppression in sport is the distribution of power through control over material resources. In professional sports, black male athletes are disproportionately represented in lower-status occupational positions. In the National Football League, for example, there are no black owners or general managers although 68 percent of all players are black (Lapchick and Benedict 1993). In addition, in 1995 only two out of thirty NFL teams had a black head coach. Sport is so inextricably bound up with the ideology and structure of white male privilege that although it may appear to advantage blacks, in fact it only confirms that privilege. In Edwards's words, "America has progressed from a 'Jim Crow' pre–Jackie Robinson era to a post-Robinson era characterized by . . . 'Mr. James Crow, Esquire' " (Edwards 1982, 20).

White men's responses to the confrontation between Olson and the Patriots conform to the pattern Messner has identified with sport more generally, constructing the black male athlete simultaneously as a rallying point for heterosexual masculinity and as a marker of implicit race and class difference. For example, there was Victor Kiam's remark that the *Herald* was "asking for trouble" by sending Olson into the locker room. Similarly, there was the warning of one male sports reporter that, "traditionally, vulgarity is a part of the locker room scene. It isn't to be recommended, but if one isn't tough enough to brace oneself for the crudeness one is apt to encounter there, one should cover tea dances" (Durslag 1991, C3). Finally, there was the frequently stated suspicion summed up by Patriots running back John Stephens, who demanded: "What kind of woman wants to be in a [men's] locker room?" (Madden 1990a, 66). Such remarks suggested that the locker room is a realm of brute physicality in which women are particularly at risk. In so doing, they implicitly sexualize Olson and the players. She becomes not a professional whose job brings her into the locker room and into contact with other professionals but an adventure-seeker in a domain of unchecked physical and sexual energy.

In sum, we argue that owners, fans, and media professionals sided with the players in celebrating them as avengers of an affront to what Robinson would call male certainties. But this was no simple affirmation of interracial solidarity. Even while rallying in their defense, these on-lookers constructed the players' actions as an uncontrolled physical and sexual response. This construction worked simultaneously to confirm the biological basis of male supremacy and to specify elite white males' privileged position over the black men they mark as violent and the white women they mark as inherently vulnerable.

Reconsidering looking

When the Patriots and their sympathizers charged Lisa Olson with looking, they were defending the certainties that she challenged by entering the locker room. The centrality of looking to the construction of white middle-class gender certainties is something that feminist theorists have long appreciated. As Virginia Woolf has argued, the power of the "patriarch who has to conquer" depends on the "looking-glass vision" of feminine adoration, that magnifying glance "possessing the magic and delicious power of reflecting the figure of man at twice its natural size" ([1919] 1957, 35–36). This is what Naomi Scheman terms the "specular economy of patriarchy," in which woman serves not only as the feminine spectacle who poses as an object of vision but also as the adoring audience who mirrors man's performance in such a way as to exaggerate his potency and overlook his inadequacies (1993, 152). As feminine spectacle, woman defers desire, signaling that she does not desire directly but desires to be desired by man; as adoring audience she defers her own agency, paying him a rapt attention that constitutes "phallocratic reality," that realm in which men's actions, emotions, and values command center stage (Frye 1983, 167). Peeking excessively would violate this specular economy.

Yet Olson's looking was not a simple violation, for most of the men at whom she would have looked, as a sports reporter assigned to cover an NFL team, were black. As bell hooks has argued, in the "phallocentric politics of spectatorship" described by feminist theorists and film theorists both the adoring woman and the man whose image she magnifies are white (1992, 118). Historically speaking, hooks points out, looking was central to the politics of "racialized power relations" because "slaves were denied their right to gaze" (1992, 115). This proscription of blacks' gaze was imposed most violently on black men, whose looking at white women (real or imagined) was understood by whites to be the ultimate race crime and punished by the ultimate race retribution. Is it possible that in the Patriots locker room this historical relation was reversed? Not exactly. Whereas it is the case that the charge of looking was deployed against a white woman by black men, it makes a difference that the men in this case were athletes and the woman a sports reporter. We shall argue that just as the black male athlete is in an ambiguous position as the standard-bearer of an ideal of masculine supremacy that both celebrates and denigrates his physicality, so is the white woman sports reporter in an ambiguous position with respect to the privileges and prohibitions typically accorded white femininity.[9]

On one hand, then, feminist analyses of the gaze vindicate men's widespread anxieties about looking; on the other, they suggest an interpretation of looking that differs from that of the players in an important way. The players define looking as a sex crime, which constructs Olson as a voyeur and their behavior toward her as a justifiable expression of modesty. Hence the clarion call of defensive player Ronnie Lippett who, upon seeing Olson in the locker room just before the incident, began handing towels to his teammates and shouting: "Cover your boys, there is a lady in the locker room!" (Heymann 1990, 16). Similarly, Kiam complained (erroneously) that Olson was "sitting on the floor" during the interview, where she "could look at their privates" (Eskenazi 1990, B15). Taken at face value, it appears that the players deployed the charge of looking merely to protect their penises from the untoward curiosity of the female voyeur.

---

[9] Where are black women in the specular economy of the locker room? They are as absent from it as they are from feminist theories that, as hooks has argued, "in no way acknowledge black female spectatorship" (1992, 123). The dozen or so black women covering sports in this country account for approximately 1.5 percent of women sports reporters and for less than one-tenth of 1 percent of sports reporters overall (Nelson 1994, 251). If, as hooks suggests, black female spectators learn to look with an "oppositional gaze" precisely because they are excluded by the specular economy of middle-class whites, then it might be easier for black women sports reporters to laugh off the charge of looking or to refute it in their relations with black male athletes. With so few black women covering sports, however, it is hard to know whether this would be borne out in the locker room.

The problem with the players' insistence that looking is a sexual transgression is that this construction is unilaterally contested by the women they accuse of doing it. As sports reporter Christine Brennan put it, "[we] go into locker rooms not because we want to, but because we have to. The locker room is the place where writers interview athletes. It's not exciting or sexy or tantalizing. It's cramped and steamy and messy" (1990, D1). Although they resist being charged with voyeurism, women sports reporters nonetheless understand that the players have a legitimate concern for privacy. Viewed in this light, looking can be interpreted as a kind of occupational hazard for players and women sports reporters alike. The problem, then, is to reconcile the concern over privacy with the sports reporters' equally reasonable expectation of equal access to the players, a legally won right that they must exercise if they are to do their jobs competitively with their male counterparts. Sports reporter Michele Himmelberg put it this way: "The issue for managers, reporters, and athletes is mutual respect. How do you protect the athletes' privacy while respecting a reporter's professional duties?" (1991, 65).

Whereas women reporters contest the construction of looking as voyeurism, the players in turn contest its construction as an occupational hazard shared by athletes and writers who work in locker rooms. They routinely bait women reporters by going out of their way to expose themselves. Mariah Burton Nelson comments: "Talk to women who cover men's sports on a daily basis and you hear about players who walk past, deliberately brushing their genitals against their arm" (1994, 228–29). It appears that what occurred between Olson and the Patriots was not an unusual display but an exaggeration of a normal routine. Moreover, we suggest that neither the women sports reporters nor the players quite get what is at stake in the charge of looking. We counter that looking is neither a perversion to which women sports reporters are particularly susceptible nor a concern that they share with the players but a charge that players use to discipline a woman sports reporter, that is, to render her docile by displacing her from her authoritative position as a reporter who looks critically at players and reassigning her to a sexualized position of wanton femininity (Foucault 1979). The term *looker* is ambiguous in this regard. Where the players use it to suggest that a female reporter is a sex-hungry voyeur, to most it would suggest that she is a feminine spectacle, an exceptionally attractive woman who advertises herself as an object of male desire. Either way, the term sexualizes her and, as such, constitutes a discourse: an ideological construct that delineates the practice of a social relationship in such a way as to anchor and reproduce normal certainties by containing potential transgressions against them (Althusser 1971).

Taken straightforwardly, then, the charge of looking is as misleading as Ludtke suggested. Glossed as peeking excessively, however, the term evinces a profound ambivalence: the players want her to peek but not to look. Where peeking is expected in the specular economy of patriarchy, looking exceeds it. The players' ambivalence directs our analysis beyond their actual privates and the legalistic concern for privacy to something less tangible: cultural anxiety over the precarious relationship of the penis to the phallus, which Joan Scott deems a "veiled and evasive signifier . . . which gains its power through the promise it holds out but never entirely fulfills" (1991, 779). What is the promise of the phallus to which Scott alludes? It is fulfillment of the desire for certainty. This promise can never be made good except in the intangible patterns of linguistic devices and cultural habits that organize ambiguous relations of difference into tidy oppositions.

Scott's conception of the phallus is distinct from that underlying the popular expression "phallic symbol," which is playfully invoked whenever a feature of the physical or built environment appears to pay tribute to male potency—such as a mountain peak or skyscraper, a geyser or rocket launching. In contrast, Scott conceives of the phallus as the paradigmatic instance of meaning-in-opposition; that is to say, it exemplifies the principle of negation whereby any term is defined not by what it is but by its difference from what it is not. Scott calls the phallus evasive, because while it holds out the promise of certainty, it ultimately refers only to otherness and lack, the negations by which meanings are secured in an oppositional system. This means, as Jacqueline Rose observes, that the "status of the phallus is a fraud"; it is not a symbol of potency but instead a contradiction that calls attention to the "precariousness of any identity assumed" on the principle of otherness. This precariousness is due to the fact that sexual difference, the putatively natural binary on which the phallic principle is supposedly based, is merely a "legislative divide" that follows from that principle and therefore cannot serve to ground it. If sexual difference is itself the product of the phallic order rather than its origin, then the promise of the phallus is false: it stands on an opposition of its own making, not on a certainty that is given by nature. Thus, as Rose puts it with undisguised irony, the concept of the phallus is an "impossibility writ large" (1986, 64–65).

We link this argument to sport through the performance of the male athlete, which signifies athletic excellence in the same evasive way that the phallus signifies potency. As sport sociologists have argued, male athletic performance is constructed as commonsense evidence of the superiority of the male body and its absolute difference from that of the female. Like the status of the phallus, however, this superiority is a fraud. Its seemingly irrefutable evidence of male potency is not grounded in the certainties of biology but is, rather, produced by athletic performances that construct excellence in terms of attributes such as muscle mass, strength, and speed in which men typically have an advantage over women (Birrell and Cole 1990; Bryson 1990). Thus, masculine athletic superiority is, like any identity assumed on the phallic principle, precarious.

This precariousness helps to explain the antagonism between players and women sports reporters that prompts the charge of looking. What makes Olson or any other woman sports reporter a potential looker is the fact that she is authorized as a reporter to ask hard questions and as a sports reporter to do so in the locker room. Christine Brennan explained: "When Joe Montana does well, or makes a mistake, the fans . . . want to know why. They can't ask Montana themselves, but I can ask on their behalf" (1990, D2). This means, as one male reporter explained, that the sports "reporter's presence is adversarial," an unwanted intrusion that often comes at the worst possible time: "The players' manliness gets compromised by losing, there's a natural need for a scapegoat, and then to have that intrusion of little people with notebooks?" (Globetti, 1990, 92).[10] When the person with the notebook—and, of course, the pen—is female, this combination of privileged access, critical gaze, and public voice is potentially explosive: she is in a position to demystify the phallic promise of unfailing potency not so much by what she sees but by where she sees and how.

If the performance of the male athlete is, like the phallus, understood to be an evasive signifier rather than an unquestionable symbol of potency, it is not difficult to understand why peeking is welcomed in the culture of the locker room and looking—or peeking excessively—is a threat. Peeking is an allowance that players both grant to women sports reporters and expect from them because it stabilizes their precarious identities. It flatters them that their manhood is so overwhelming a curiosity to women that they cannot keep themselves—as one player put it—from "sneaking a peek," but so imposing a force that they dare not look too directly or too long (Nelson 1994, 247). In other words, peeking is not an offense but a ceremonial tribute that confirms the oppositional fiction that the phallus is something possessed by man and lacking from but desired by woman. As a gesture of desire that is appropriately deferential, peeking underwrites the fiction of phallic opposition without threatening to disclose its instability. Thus, the promise of the phallus does not require the proscription of the female gaze but rather "the subtle directing of the allowable lines of [women's] sight" (Scheman 1993, 152).

This care to foster peeking but to prohibit peeking excessively is not unique to relations between players and women sports reporters; to the

---

[10] One irony of the Olson-Patriots incident is that Olson's presence could not be deemed an intrusion at a bad time. The interview took place the day after a victory, following a light workout, and she was interviewing a player who had been instrumental in that victory.

contrary, it is commonly practiced by filmmakers and the ratings decisions of the Motion Picture Association of America (MPAA). A *New York Times* analysis reported that there is an understood double standard in Hollywood whereby ratings decisions exhibit a pattern of treating male nudity with greater deference than it does female nudity (Andrews 1992, H13–14). The attitude of the MPAA "seems to be that male nudity is fine as long as it is obscured"—that is, a naked penis can be presented publicly as long as the audience's view of it is masked by night, distance, or some other prop (Andrews 1992, H13). If a penis is directly exposed to the camera for more than a fleeting "peek," the film usually earns the more restrictive NC-17 rating; in contrast, it can linger on an unobstructed female frontal nude and still earn an R rating. Richard Dyer's (1992) study of male pin-ups suggests one further way the camera can commit the crime of looking. Dyer observed that male pin-ups take care to avoid any suggestion that the male body is vulnerable to invasion. In contrast to the inviting and usually passive pose of the female pin-up, the male will be displayed in action or ready for action. If in repose, the backdrop will be one that suggests masculine activity.

The examples of both sport and cinema suggest that the mystique of the phallus requires that public presentations of the male body be carefully orchestrated to produce a flawless image of phallic masculinity. On the movie screen as in the locker room, the presentation of the penis is subtly managed within the parameters of deference. A woman sports reporter is in a rare position to transgress those parameters by virtue of the intersection of her occupation with her gender. Whereas most women who gain access to strongholds of patriarchal power in this society do so at the cost of being able to criticize what goes on there, and certainly at the cost of going public with that criticism, the woman sports reporter is uniquely privileged by a potent combination of insider access, critical vision, and public voice (Kane and Disch 1993). She is a publicly recognized critic of male performance whose profession authorizes her to question athletes in the locker room immediately after a contest in the hope that she will catch them off guard. As an authorized transgression of typical parameters of deference, her looking unsettles the certainties of binary sex, gender complementarity, and oppositional sexual orientation on which phallic potency is grounded. It is an excess that must be contained by constructing it as a crime.

By calling Olson a looker, the players put a hold on her that enables them to perform what Mary Daly has called a patriarchal reversal (Daly 1978, 79). To carry Daly's felicitous phrase into a sport context, a reversal in wrestling is an oppositional maneuver that is performed from a subordinate position on an opponent who has achieved a position of dominance. It is a defensive strategy to offset the power of the opposition and seize the advantage. As much as it offers a literal picture of power as a physical capacity, this metaphor is also a graphic reminder that power is never the property of an individual but that it is dynamic and shifting, the effect of instabilities in relationships. The patriarchal reversal does not take place whenever a woman challenges the typical gender hierarchy by taking a position in a traditionally male profession; rather, it occurs only when such a challenge to traditional gender roles also destabilizes the certainties on which the conception of gender as a social construction based on a natural binary depends.

The ingenuity of the patriarchal reversal is that the players disciplined Olson by taking the very thing they claimed not to want her to see and—in their words—making her look. By strutting naked in her line of sight, the players asserted their prerogative to orchestrate the way Olson looked at them (cf. Silverman 1983, 231). It is evident from the Heymann report, which reconstructed the confrontation on the basis of interviews with Olson and the players, that this was a contest over looking. Zeke Mowatt made the opening bid in a struggle to catch Olson's eye: "Look at her. She's just watching. I'm going to tell her about herself." The report recounts that Olson "looked up and saw Mowatt walking across the room looking at her [with] what she interpreted as a purposeful look in his eyes." She responded by averting her gaze, "turn[ing] to face Hurst [the player whom she was interviewing] more directly." Mowatt continued across the locker room, narrowing his sights on Olson while other players began shouting: " 'Make her look, make her look,' 'Is she looking? Is she looking?' " When Mowatt reached the area of Hurst's locker, Olson "lifted her head." At this, Mowatt "smiled and purposely displayed himself to her in a suggestive way." Laughter erupted and shouts from other players continued, especially "Is she looking? Is she looking at it?" (Heymann 1990, 16–18).

By getting Olson to look up at him, Mowatt had established a foothold for the patriarchal reversal. Olson's sight lines were precisely described so that if she looked to either side she could be accused of "peeking excessively." There was nothing for her to do but counter with an appropriate gesture: "Embarrassed by Mowatt's action, Olson quickly lowered her head . . . [and] kept her eyes down" (Heymann 1990, 19). This was the moment of reversal and the players celebrated it. They had literally stared her down, displacing her from a position of authority to a posture of deference. Olson was finally a confirmed dick-watcher, but no longer a bitch.

If the gaze of the woman sports reporter unsettles the heterosexual matrix whereby gender and sexual certainties are secured, then the patriarchal reversal reinstates those certainties by turning her prerogative of insider access into an intimidating proximity. When it is read in this way, not as another instance of harassment but in the terms of the patriarchal reversal, this confrontation between Olson and the Patriots magnifies the subtle relations by which the heterosexual matrix is secured, shows how a woman who looks with authority exceeds that matrix, and dramatizes how her agency will be contained. In sum, against the players' protestations about privacy, we contend that this was a performance designed not to teach Olson *not* to look but to teach her *how* to look.

Exposing the sport continuum

To understand why looking is so deeply threatening that it would provoke such a dramatic response by the players and inspire such anger in fans, it is necessary to appreciate the relationship between sport and the apparently compulsory logic of oppositions that Butler calls the heterosexual matrix. We have already noted how professional sport participated in the elaboration of the particular middle-class construction of gender that assigned men and women to oppositional and complementary roles. In 1972, the federal government set the stage for a transformation of the social meaning of sport by enacting Title IX, the statute that prohibits sex discrimination in educational settings. With its passage, which fostered a tremendous increase in women's athletic participation, sport would no longer be a secured stronghold of masculinity but, as Messner put it, "a crucial arena of struggle over basic social conceptions of masculinity and femininity" (1988, 199).

One way that sport is made to hold out against this challenge is, as we have mentioned, by the construction of athleticism in terms of activities and skills that celebrate anachronistic masculinity; such a construction ensures that male performance will serve, like the phallus, as the definitive standard against which all else is compared and fails to measure up. For example, sports that require muscle mass, strength, and speed are more prestigious than those that emphasize beauty and flexibility. Similarly, as athletic accomplishments, physical skills such as hitting or hurling an object are considered vastly superior over tumbling gracefully through space. In sum, sport is the most important public arena for the performance of gender as an asymmetrical, oppositional relation based on natural sexual differences; as such, it helps to reaffirm the belief that a gender order that accords primacy to males is not a mere social construction but a reflection of men's natural physical superiority.

But the practice of sport does more to establish gender certainties than simply providing apparent validation of the physical superiority and social supremacy of males. It also has the far more insidious effect of recasting sexual differences that range along a continuum (Epstein 1990) into a dichotomy. By denying the manifest evidence that physical differences vary along a continuum and thereby perpetuating the assumption that binary opposition is inherent in nature, sport both confirms the logic of the heterosexual matrix and translates it into everyday experience. It is larger-than-life proof that sex differences are dichotomous by nature, confirmation that oppositional gender identities mimic this natural binary, and a commonsense affirmation that heterosexual orientation is normative because it is natural.

Consider that in the world of sport a contestant is never simply an athlete but must be categorized as either a female athlete or a male athlete. In tennis, for example, athletes do not just play tennis, they play men's tennis and women's tennis. Although tennis players compete in mixed doubles, there is no competition for mixed singles. And why not? Because the purpose of these distinctions is to take the continuum of variation among individual characteristics such as strength, speed, and height and construct it as an oppositional sexual binary.

By teaching us how to read athletic performance as incontrovertible proof of binary sexual difference, sport suppresses evidence of a sexual continuum (Kane 1995). As such, it is consistent with the work of feminist theorists who argue that the reproduction of phallic power requires ongoing efforts to organize ambiguous relations of difference into oppositional gender certainties. For sport to admit evidence of a continuum would be tantamount to exposing as precarious the binary sexual difference that gives oppositional gender identity its apparent foundation in nature. Building on the work of Eleanor Metheny, we argue that the suppression of this continuum is accomplished by a variant of sport typing, the concept Metheny introduced to argue that individual athletes are socialized to participate in sports that are consistent with prevailing gender stereotypes (1965).[11] We argue that sport typing is only one of several interrelated devices by which ambiguous relations of difference that are or could be disclosed by athletic performances are organized into oppositional gender certainties. In addition to sport typing, these devices include erasure, regendering, and selective gender comparison.

Whereas Metheny understood sport typing as reflecting gender stereotypes, we argue somewhat differently that it works to suppress evidence of a continuum. As Metheny noted, this happens in part by typing some sports as exclusively masculine and differentiating them against others that are typed as exclusively feminine (e.g., football vs. synchronized

[11] Of course, sports can also be typed with respect to social class. Participation patterns indicate that members of the upper and upper-middle social strata are more likely to engage in individualized sports such as golf and tennis, which depend largely on access to private facilities and equipment. In contrast, blue-collar workers are more likely to participate in team sports, such as softball, which are typically played on public grounds and often sponsored by a labor union, business, or church (Eitzen and Sage 1984).

swimming). While it is not unheard of for women to play football, their participation is treated as an aberration, thereby constructing a potential contestation of binary sexual difference in such a way as to reaffirm it. In sports where both men and women participate, however, typing works instead to segregate their performance into oppositional categories. In the case of gymnastics, for example, women and men compete in entirely different events. Women's events, such as the balance beam and floor exercise, call for movement that emphasizes flexibility and grace, whereas men's events, such as rings and pommel horse, call for movement that emphasizes speed and explosive force.[12]

Erasure, the second device of binary enforcement, comes into play when athletes fail to conform to the prescriptions of sport typing. Erasure occurs through the media's silence about the existence of hundreds of sport clubs and leagues in which women participate in sports such as rugby or ice hockey that have traditionally been typed as masculine.[13] Although theoretically erasure could also be deployed against males who participate against type, there are few sports typed as exclusively feminine because definitions of athleticism have historically been equated with masculinity. Even when males do perform against type, they can usually be made to affirm typical gender certainties, as in figure skating, which provides a clearly delineated masculine role for the male skater. In contrast, women cannot participate in sports such as rugby or football without displaying an athleticism that is typed as masculine. Because their participation cannot be reinterpreted as feminine, it has to be erased.

The third device of binary enforcement, regendering, occurs when a woman athlete displays superior athleticism in a skill or activity traditionally typed as masculine. For example, when a woman hits a baseball exceptionally far, she is typically congratulated for hitting "just like a man." This device both reinforces the equation of superior athleticism with maleness and suppresses evidence of a continuum on which the performances of women and men would be interspersed. Regendering is particularly insidious because it creates the impression that female athleticism is both accepted and enthusiastically supported; in order to receive that support, however, the female athlete must be regendered as male, if only temporarily.

---

[12] Gymnastics is one of the more extreme examples of sport typing. In tennis, the typing is more subtle because men and women use the same equipment and are required to perform the same physical skills, the only difference being that a women's match is shorter (three sets as opposed to five). The rules of the sport reproduce a misleading sexual stereotype by suggesting that women's capacity for endurance is less than men's.

[13] For example, thousands of women play rugby and ice hockey throughout North America. Further, their participation is not merely recreational; it is highly structured competition organized into leagues and intercollegiate conferences (Olson 1994).

The marathon is a particularly good example of the work that sport does to suppress the continuum because it is a competition in which men and women run on the same course, at the same time, in the same event. With men and women runners interspersed for miles along the same road, the marathon graphically discloses a performance continuum that cannot be reorganized by any of the devices we have discussed so far. This is where selective gender comparison, the fourth device of binary enforcement, comes in. Deployed primarily though not exclusively through media coverage, selective gender comparison recasts this one race as two different contests.

Although it happens throughout the race, selective gender comparison is particularly evident at the end, where the coverage constructs two separate finishes. First, there is the men's finish. Even though typically the first ten runners will cross the line within six or seven minutes of each other, the media constructs a battle between the two or three front-runners. After telling the story of the lead men, the commentators shift their focus to the front-running women, literally editing out that portion of the continuum that lies between the leaders of the so-called men's race and the first women finishers. The first woman to cross the line, typically finishing somewhere in the top sixty runners, will be compared only to the other lead women and to the winner of the men's race. Gender-based comparisons with the remaining male contestants vanish from the media landscape: we will neither be directed to watch her compete against the men who finish with her nor will we hear that she has just beaten the several thousand men who will cross the finish line behind her.[14] This selective gender comparison ensures that we will never think of women competing against men and prevailing over them, despite the graphic evidence of the marathon where women run interspersed among men and cross the finish line ahead of them. Such coverage fits performance differences into approved gender relations by making one sort of gender comparison (the women's winner to the men's winner) and dismissing any other (the women's winner just beat the rest of the men). This articulation serves in turn to suppress evidence of a gender continuum and produce a gender binary.

By virtue of these various devices that serve to reorganize a continuum of difference as a binary opposition and to establish that opposition as natural, we learn from professional sport to see oppositional sexual difference when we look at bodies in motion. This means that professional sport is more than an arena for the display of athletic excellence, more

[14] These approximations are based on the 1994 Twin Cities (Minneapolis/St. Paul) Marathon, which is one of the top five marathons in the country. Out of 5,499 contestants who finished, 4,076 were men and 1,423 were women. The lead woman finished sixty-sixth overall, which means that 4,011 men finished behind her.

than a mechanism for the accumulation of corporate wealth, more even than an apparatus for the reproduction of race and gender ideology. It is also one of the most visible public institutions by which the cultural logic of Butler's heterosexual matrix becomes everyday experience. Our analysis of these devices, which discloses the precariousness of the gender differences that seem so certain on the playing field, helps to explain how something so apparently trivial as looking could ignite a national controversy. Looking poses a challenge not just to the players but to the cultural truths about sex, gender, and desire that sport makes seem self-evident.

Looking down: Apologetic women/phallic men

How the public performance of sport invests the male athlete with phallic power and affords a site for contesting that power has been the subject of a great deal of scholarship. There is much less in the way of critical analysis of the men's locker room, however, because it is difficult for scholars to observe it unobtrusively (Sabo and Panepinto 1990; Curry 1991). It is ironic that an NFL team's confrontation with a woman sports reporter over "looking" should facilitate such analysis, but it did. In effect, the controversy served to fling open the very door the Patriots players had so urgently wanted to close against Lisa Olson by generating multiple accounts of locker room culture from diverse perspectives. The players and their sympathizers defended a typical view of the locker room as one of the few men's clubs that ought to stand fast in an era of challenges to gender-based exclusion in other domains. In this hyper-masculine culture, even men sports reporters admitted feeling intimidated, as one put it, by having to conduct interviews among "forty-seven people of extraordinary size who question not only your right to question them, but to share the air that they breathe" (Globetti 1990, 92). Despite feeling ill at ease there, both men and women sports reporters contested the players' exclusive claim to the locker room. But as we shall demonstrate, these accounts were striking for the differences they revealed in the way that men and women sports reporters relate to players. These differences emphasized just how far women are from equality with their male counterparts in the locker room, their legal rights notwithstanding.

Patriots owner Victor Kiam reasserted the typical view of the locker room when he declared: "To the players, their locker room is their castle. Every man has a castle" (Freeman 1990b, 25). As Eve Kosofsky Sedgwick has argued, the castle metaphor is an "ideological construction" that "reaches *back* to an emptied-out image of mastery and integration under feudalism" to hold out a promise of sovereignty to men in a time when they no longer rule over the domestic realm (1985, 14). Former Washington Redskins player Dave Butz revealed precisely this desire to return to the gender mores of a more traditional generation when he remarked that Olson's "mother should have told her that if she stepped into a men's locker room, she would be entering a man's world" (Butz 1990, C5). By their use of the castle metaphor, Kiam and the players support our claim that there was more at stake in the locker room than the players' privacy; it signals that the woman sports reporter who enters this so-called castle will be seen as a traitor to its retrogressive image of masculinity. Further, any hostility toward her will be explained as a justifiable reaction to an attack on the battlements. As Kiam put it: "Why not stand in front of her [naked] if she is an intruder?" (Mannix 1990, 74).

But the Patriots' conception of the locker room as a last bastion of male sovereignty did not go uncontested. In a column worth quoting at length, *Washington Post* sports reporter Tony Kornheiser describes the locker room as a realm in which the players are as vulnerable as they are powerful. He begins with images of power: "It's there, directly after a game, when reactions are still raw and unvarnished, that an athlete reveals himself. His nakedness is in a way a metaphor for his honesty, and in another way a symbol of his narcissism; you'd be surprised how many athletes revel [in] being naked there, how many of them strut around in self-idealization of the ancient warrior god" (1990, D6). Although this vision of players naked and strutting is consonant with the ideological construction of the locker room as a domain of anachronistic privilege, Kornheiser reveals an aspect of their nakedness that is at odds with the castle metaphor—honesty.

In contrast to strutting nakedness, naked honesty suggests a lack of protection and a vulnerability to exposure that Kornheiser acknowledges when he writes: "This is the sacred place, the place where the secrets of being an athlete will become known to you. But you go inside and see behind the Wizard's curtain, and realize it's a wind machine and a projector. Disillusioned, staring at bodies puffed and purpled with bruises, you quickly ask yourself, 'What am I doing here?' " (1990, D6). Kornheiser's words are a reminder that the locker room is the place where male athletes prepare for their on-the-field performance and the place where they recuperate after the game. Far from being a castle in which players simply and unquestionably rule, the locker room is the place where their bodies are suited up to be invincible; consequently it is also a place where those bodies can be vulnerable. While Kornheiser's remarks confirm that the locker room culture celebrates male physicality, they also reveal that this culture is fragile. Its fragility consists of the fact that in the locker room, as on the playing field, male physical superiority is not a biological given but an ideological construct that must be produced by ritual performances that promote male narcissism and exclude male vulnerability.

How do the players sustain a culture of narcissism? By acting out the phallic principle of opposition and defining themselves against what they are not. Sport sociologists identify locker room talk, verbal exchanges whereby male athletes celebrate heterosexual aggression against women, as a common method of oppositional self-definition (Kidd 1987; Curry 1991). In a study of fragments of such verbal exchanges in the men's locker rooms of two Big Ten sport teams, Tim Curry found that players routinely engage in bragging about sexual conquests over women—real or imagined—and in "jokes and storytelling about homosexuals" to enhance their image of themselves as "practicing heterosexuals" (1991, 128, 130). Interestingly, Curry found that in addition to these narcissistic or demeaning types of talk, there was honest talk in which athletes spoke about "women as real people, persons with whom the athletes have ongoing social relationships" (128). Such talk was not broadcast to the entire group, however, but shared in private tones for fear that its public disclosure would be ridiculed as evidence of a vulnerability unbecoming to phallic masculinity.

We argue that a woman sports reporter, a professional who enters the locker room with a gaze of appraisal and publicly recognized critical authority, will be deemed a bitch because her occupation poses a challenge to the very matrix of negation and opposition that stabilizes not just male certainties but heterosexual identity. If this claim is correct, then we should find that intruding into the locker room is unsettling to women sports reporters as well as to players; consequently, we might expect that they might make accommodations to the culture of the locker room, reaffirming their identities as women even as they assert their rights as professionals. We find support for this seemingly paradoxical hypothesis in the accounts of the locker room published by women sports reporters in the aftermath of the confrontation between Olson and the Patriots. The accounts divulged what Ludtke called the "unwritten rules of the road," the code of conduct that women sports reporters routinely follow to brush off the " 'little' bothersome things that happen all the time" but about which they cannot complain for fear of being "dismissed as someone who can't do the job" (1990a, B21).

These rules spelled out the dictates of an apologetic: an overtly deferential posturing that works to reaffirm normal certainties in situations where they are threatened. This apologetic is the women reporters' response to a classic double bind. As reporters they have nothing to write about if they cannot blend in, but as women they cannot make themselves appear at home in the domain of the locker room without being perceived to invite sexual attentions. Their way out of this dilemma, as Huckshorn describes it, is to "strive for perfect comportment. A cross between Miss Manners and Mary Richards," two figures who exemplify desexualized, white middle-class femininity (1990, 1E). In other words, they put on a version of what Butler terms the "female masquerade," a compensatory performance whereby a woman who exceeds the boundaries of her socially sanctioned identity makes an exaggerated show of gender propriety to reassure potential antagonists.[15] Butler argues that such posturing "can be interpreted as an effort to renounce the 'having' of the Phallus in order to avert retribution by those from whom it must have been procured through castration" (1990, 51). In other words, it is the strategy whereby a dick-watcher reassures male athletes that she is not a bitch.

The first rule of this apologetic is to expect that you will be hazed and to accept it as the price of admission. As Ludtke puts it, "Tolerate the teasing, since you are after all working in the athlete's locker room" (Ludtke 1990a, B21). Christine Brennan adds that the point is not just to "tolerate" the climate of the locker room but to laugh in the face of harassment. She writes, "Let's face it, I'm an outsider in the players' domain. I have to learn to laugh when Dexter Manley shouts out, 'Hey, Chris, come here. I've got something to show you.' I can't take that seriously" (Brennan 1990, D2). Although looking can be a joke when the players facetiously invite it, the code quite specifically enjoins women reporters to take extraordinary precautions against being perceived as initiating it themselves. To that end, the third rule is to maintain eye-to-eye contact with the players at all times (Huckshorn 1990, 1E). Brennan underscores the importance of the measure, asserting: "I have never, ever been in the shower area of any team, and I avoid the pathway to the shower for obvious reasons. I keep eye contact at all times, and carry an 8-by-11 notebook, so when I look down, I look down at the notebook" (Brennan 1990, D2). Beyond avoiding any behavior that could be interpreted as looking, Brennan goes out of her way to show her respect for the players by the visible, elaborate care she takes against doing so.

The injunction governing eye contact is accompanied by a corollary: remember that you cannot act just like your male colleagues. Ludtke cautions, "A woman reporter never assumed that she could act exactly as male reporters do, which meant lingering around the locker room and conversing in a friendly fashion with the players. If she did that, chances are she would be accused of flirting" (Ludtke 1990a, B21). Sports reporter Leah Secondo is even more emphatic: "I go in there, do what I have to do and get the hell out. I make sure my eyes don't stay

---

[15] Apologetic posturing is not unique to women. Examples of a black apologetic are plentiful as, e.g., the stereotype of blacks' willingness to laugh that Toni Morrison calls a "metonym for racial accommodation" (1992, xiii). For lesbians and gays in the military, the Clinton Administration's "don't ask, don't tell, don't pursue" policy prescribes a homosexual apologetic.

anywhere too long so people don't get the wrong idea" (quoted in Cramer 1994).

Several men sports reporters, most of whom sympathized with Olson, gave accounts of how they conduct themselves in the locker room that confirmed that women must be more cautious than their male counterparts in their interactions with the players. Although these men also reported being harassed by players—being showered with buckets of water, punched, or teased about their physical inadequacies—most found the concept of looking incomprehensible and objected to its being leveled at Olson or any other women sports reporter. Kornheiser described looking as an integral part of any sports journalist's job: "You look at the naked bodies, of course you look—men and women" (1990, D6). Similarly, Madden argued that the idea that any reporter would peek excessively is ludicrous, precisely because a sports reporter sees players' bodies all the time: "The last thing any of us who have been to locker rooms care to look at is athletes' bodies; they are as common to us as a blackboard is to a teacher" (1990b, 49).

How can male reporters be so unapologetic about looking? Mariah Burton Nelson once pursued this question indirectly with Tim Brown, All-Pro wide receiver for the Los Angeles Raiders, whom she asked whether he "had ever seen a man sneaking a peek." Initially attempting to brush off the question, Brown then denied it: "If somebody saw something like that going on, you'd all know about it 'cause it'd probably be in all the papers." When Nelson pressed the issue, Brown became so agitated that he pushed her (1994, 248). Contrary to Tim Brown, who asserts that a male reporter's looking would cause such a stir as to be widely publicized, we argue that what he reveals by his response is that it is altogether inconceivable that the players would address this charge to another man. For a male athlete to accuse a male reporter of looking—of peeking excessively, that is—would be tantamount to admitting that players want male reporters to peek in the first place. Obviously, for male athletes to admit the possibility of such a desire would amount to a betrayal of the heterosexual matrix by the very standard-bearers who make its compulsory order seem so natural.

Whereas men sports reporters cannot be charged with looking, it seems that the women cannot escape it. If they act just like their male counterparts, they risk being deemed voyeurs who find the locker room a turn-on; yet if they follow its unwritten code, they in effect apologize for looking before they have even been accused of it, thereby legitimating the charge. Do all women sports reporters comply with this code? Given how it mimics others associated with white middle-class heterosexual femininity—the exaggerated propriety of Miss Manners or the flaky vulnerability of Mary Richards—there is good reason to question its generalizability. In turn, it is important to note that all of the women who gave accounts of the apologetic were white and college-educated. Despite this, we maintain that one should not be too quick to dismiss these accounts as purely anecdotal evidence of a phenomenon that is peculiar to white women sports journalists. As we noted earlier, the regulation of looking is not unique to the locker room; films and male pin-ups also model apologetic posturing by the deference that is accorded male nudity and the care that is taken to produce appropriately rugged images of masculinity. Even if such posturing were peculiar to white professional women, we think it unlikely that the codes that were divulged in the wake of Olson's confrontation with the Patriots are confined to the men's locker room, although they may be especially exaggerated there.

Looking up: How a bitch is a resister

Thanks to the Patriots, whose confrontation with Lisa Olson generated a virtual ethnography of the men's locker room, we can now answer the question we posed at the outset of this article: Why this protracted punishment of a sports reporter who had done no more than engage in the ordinary task of conducting an interview? Because Lisa Olson committed a simple but fundamental crime: she refused to perform the apologetic. Initially, she did not laugh off the attack by the players but demanded that they identify themselves to her and apologize, albeit privately. Once the story broke, she would not back down from this demand despite being harassed by fans. On the contrary, she took an even stronger stand, asserting, "Words are fine, but I want some action. . . . I want the people who did this to be identified and I want them severely punished" (Gee 1990, 62). In addition, she had the self-respect to decry what one sports columnist called Kiam's "backhanded" apology (Madden 1990a, 66), countering, "An apology is not accepted when he is telling blatant lies [about me] on television" (Freeman 1990a, 80).

Further, Olson refused to concede the men's locker room to the athletes, laying claim to it as her professional domain and contesting the players' insinuation that she was a voyeur. Against unwritten rules against lingering and looking, Olson insisted that both of these are part of the job she is expected to do there. In a column published only a few days after the story initially broke, Olson wrote: "I was naive enough to believe the Patriots understood what it meant to be a reporter. That they knew it was my business to look around the locker room. I am not a stenographer. There is much more to reporting than writing down quotes. It is my job to observe who is injured, to see who is throwing chairs, to capture the mood of the day" (Olson 1990, 74). What is striking about this statement is its anger, an obvious violation of the apologetic, and the opposition Olson draws between being a stenographer, typically a female service-sector job, and being a professional reporter. Her assertion that looking marks the difference between the two serves to implicitly (and unintendedly) indict every woman sports reporter who, for fear of being hit with this charge, keeps her eyes down and takes notes. Thus, besides having the obvious effect of challenging the man's castle ideology, this resistance contested the prescriptions of the apologetic.

Perhaps the most eloquent testimony to the force of Olson's disruption of the apologetic came from women sports reporters themselves. Although most of the columns they wrote in the wake of the confrontation expressed support for Olson, the very fact that these women were moved to spell out their previously unwritten code suggests that she inspired uneasiness by transgressing it. Only one woman sports reporter, Kristin Huckshorn, owned up to this uneasiness in a remarkably candid column that began: "Why doesn't Lisa Olson shut up? I admit it. That is what I have been thinking ever since Olson, a Boston sportswriter, began publicly explaining how she was sexually harassed by five New England Patriots in their locker room last month" (1990, 1E). Huckshorn rewrote the story of this confrontation to show that by going public with her story, Olson had not only challenged the players but also women sports journalists who play by the rules. Acknowledging that Olson's act called her to task for her own complicity with a demeaning code of silence, Huckshorn admitted, "I wish she would shut up because I was one of those women who kept quiet." Huckshorn ended the column by exhorting other women sports reporters to stand by Olson, not taking pity on her but joining her in resistance: "By speaking out, Lisa Olson is destroying the fragile status quo. She is bringing an old and dreaded issue back to the forefront. She is reminding us that the battle is not yet won. . . . She makes me wonder: If I had spoken up all along, would this still be happening now? I wish she would shut up. She makes me wish that I hadn't" (Huckshorn 1990, 1E).

As Huckshorn retold the story, Olson's speaking out was a resistance that confronted Huckshorn and others with the fact that winning access to the locker room was an empty victory if women sports reporters are required to engage in a parody of femininity once inside. The nationwide reaction to Olson made it clear that under the terms of this compromise women sports reporters were accorded neither professional respect nor legal equality. And by breaking the rules so publicly, Olson dramatized for these women that they bore some responsibility for accepting it. The broader significance of this analysis of looking, then, is that it not only shows how sport participates in producing the heterosexual matrix on the field and in the locker room, but also that it tells one story of resistance against the apologetic codes in which charges such as looking are embedded and by which they are sustained.

Department of Political Science (Disch)
University of Minnesota
Center for Research on Girls and Women and Sport (Kane)
University of Minnesota

References

Althusser, Louis. 1971. *Lenin and Philosophy,* trans. Ben Brewster. New York: Monthly Review.

Andrews, Suzanna. 1992. "She's Bare. He's Covered. Is There a Problem?" *New York Times,* November 1, H13–14.

Birrell, Susan, and Cheryl L. Cole. 1990. "Double Fault: Renee Richards and the Construction and Naturalization of Difference." *Sociology of Sport Journal* 7(1):1–21.

Boston Herald. 1990. "Editors Commend Olson." *Boston Herald,* October 7, B14.

Boutilier, Mary, and Lucinda SanGiovanni. 1983. *The Sporting Woman.* Champaign, Ill.: Human Kinetics.

Brennan, Christine. 1990. "Jocks, Gender, and Justice: A Woman Sports Reporter's View from the Men's Locker Room." *Washington Post,* September 30, D1–2.

Brown, Curt. 1993. "Reporter Still Feels Pain of Harassment." *Minneapolis Star and Tribune,* May 31, 1C.

Bryson, Lois. 1990. "Challenges to Male Hegemony in Sport." In *Sport, Men, and the Gender Order,* ed. Michael A. Messner and Don Sabo, 173–84. Champaign, Ill.: Human Kinetics.

Butler, Judith. 1990. *Gender Trouble.* New York: Routledge.

Butz, Dave. 1990. "Respect Should Keep Women out of Men's Locker Rooms." *Washington Post,* October 7, C5.

Cramer, Judith. 1994. "Conversations with Women Sport Journalists." In *Women, Media and Sport,* ed. Pamela J. Creedon, 159–80. Thousand Oaks, Calif.: Sage.

Curry, Tim. 1991. "Fraternal Bonding in the Locker Room: A Profeminist Analysis of Talk about Competition and Women." *Sociology of Sport Journal* 8(2):119–35.

Daly, Mary. 1978. *Gyn/Ecology: The Metaethics of Radical Feminism.* Boston: Beacon.

de Lauretis, Teresa. 1990. "Eccentric Subjects: Feminist Theory and Historical Consciousness." *Feminist Studies* 16(1):115–50.

Durslag, Melvin. 1991. "She Would Be Wiser to Forget the Lawsuit." *Los Angeles Times,* April 29, C3.

Dyer, Richard. 1992. "Don't Look Now: The Male Pin-Up." In *The Sexual Subject,* ed. Screen, 265–76. New York: Routledge.

Edwards, Harry. 1982. "Race in Contemporary American Sports." *National Forum* 62:19–22.

———. 1984. "The Collegiate Athletic Arms Race: Origin and Implications of the 'Rule 48' Controversy." *Journal of Sport Sociology International* 8(1):4–22.

Eitzen, Stan, and George Sage, eds. 1984. *Sociology of American Sport.* 2d ed. Dubuque, Iowa: Brown.

Epstein, Judith. 1990. "Either/Or–Neither/Both: Sexual Ambiguity and the Ideology of Gender." *Genders* 7:99–142.

Eskenazi, Gerald. 1990. "Harassment Charge Draws NFL's Attention." *New York Times,* September 27, B11, B15.

Foucault, Michel. 1979. *Discipline and Punish,* trans. Alan Sheridan. New York: Vintage.

Frankenberg, Ruth. 1993. *White Women, Race Matters: The Social Construction of Whiteness.* Minneapolis: University of Minnesota Press.

Freeman, Mike. 1990a. "Kiam Apologizes to Olson, Fans, Media." *Boston Globe,* September 26, 75, 80.

———. 1990b. "Patriots Fine Player for Sex Harassment." *Boston Globe,* September 25, 1, 25.

Frye, Marilyn. 1983. *The Politics of Reality.* Truman, N.Y.: Crossing.

Gee, M. 1990. "Kiam Says He's Sorry." *Boston Herald,* October 1, 1, 62.

George, Nelson. 1992. *Elevating the Game.* New York: HarperCollins.

Globetti, Michael. 1990. "Locker Rooms: Classless Ditches." *Boston Herald,* September 26, 92.

Gorman, Jerry, and Kirk Calhoun. 1994. *The Name of the Game: The Business of Sports.* New York: Wiley.

Hart, Jeffrey. 1990. "No Matter Athlete's Behavior, Women Out of Place." *Times Herald* (Norristown, N.J.), October 22, 17.

Henkel, Cathy. 1993. "Listen Carefully to Olson's Side." *Association for Women in Sports Media (AWSM) Newsletter,* February, 1–3.

Heymann, Philip B. 1990. *Report of Special Counsel to the Commissioner of the National Football League.* New York: National Football League.

Himmelberg, Michele. 1991. "Hot Showers, Cold Shoulder." *Women's Sports and Fitness* 13(2):65.

hooks, bell. 1992. *Black Looks: Race and Representation.* Boston: South End.

Huckshorn, Kristin. 1990. "Woman Reporter Rightfully Rocks the Boat." *San Jose Mercury News,* October 3, 1E.

Kane, Mary Jo. 1995. "Resistance/Transformation of the Oppositional Binary: Exposing Sport as a Continuum." *Journal of Sport and Social Issues* 19(2):213–40.

Kane, Mary Jo, and Lisa Disch. 1993. "Sexual Violence and the Reproduction of Male Violence in the Locker Room: The Lisa Olson Incident." *Sociology of Sport Journal* 10(4):331–52.

Kaufman, Michael T. 1989. "Park Suspects: Children of Discipline." *New York Times,* April 29, A1, B24.

Kidd, Bruce. 1987. "Sports and Masculinity." In *Beyond Patriarchy: Essays by Men on Pleasure, Power, and Change,* ed. Michael Kaufman, 250–65. Toronto: Oxford University Press.

Kimmel, Michael S. 1990. "Baseball and the Reconstitution of American Masculinity, 1880–1920." In *Sport, Men, and the Gender Order,* ed. Michael A. Messner and Don Sabo, 55–65. Champaign, Ill.: Human Kinetics.

Kornheiser, Tony. 1990. "A Woman's Place." *Washington Post,* October 9, D1, D6.

Lapchick, Richard E., and Jeffrey R. Benedict. 1993. "1993 Racial Report Cards." *Center for the Study of Sport in Society Digest* (Northeastern University), Summer, 4–8.

Ludtke, Melissa. 1990a. "Olson Harassment a Stark Reminder." *Boston Herald,* September 30, B21.

———. 1990b. "What Women Want: Equal Access for Interviews, Not Bad Jokes." *Los Angeles Times,* October 14, 5.

Madden, Michael. 1990a. "Even in His Backhanded Apology, Kiam Misses the Point." *Boston Globe,* September 30, 66.

———. 1990b. "Return to the Scene of the Grime." *Boston Globe,* September 24, 41, 49.

Mannix, Kevin. 1990. "Kiam: 'She's a Classic Bitch.' " *Boston Herald,* September 24, 74.

Matchan, Linda. 1990. "Further Abuse of Olson Is Called Typical." *Boston Globe,* October 3, 29, 36.

Media Week. 1994. *Media Week* 4(1):13.

Messner, Michael A. 1988. "Sports and Male Domination: The Female Athlete as Contested Ideological Terrain." *Sociology of Sport Journal* 5(3):197–211.

———. 1990. "Masculinities and Athletic Careers: Bonding and Status Differences." In *Sport, Men, and the Gender Order,* ed. Michael A. Messner and Don Sabo, 97–108. Champaign, Ill.: Human Kinetics.

Metheny, Eleanor. 1965. *Connotations of Movement in Sport and Dance.* Dubuque, Iowa: Brown.

Montville, Leigh. 1991. "A Season of Torment." *Sports Illustrated,* May 13, 60–65.

Morrison, Toni. 1992. "Introduction: Friday on the Potomac." In *Race-ing Justice, Engendering Power: Essays on Anita Hill, Clarence Thomas, and the Construction of Social Reality,* ed. Toni Morrison, vii–xxx. New York: Pantheon.

Nelson, Mariah Burton. 1994. *The Stronger Women Get the More Men Love Football.* New York: Harcourt Brace.

Oates, Bob. 1979. "The Great American Tease: Sport as a Way Out of the Ghetto." *New York Times.* June 8, A32.

Olson, Lisa. 1990. "A Lesson from 'The Chick.' " *Boston Herald,* September 24, 74.

Olson, Lynn. 1994. "Women's Sports Continue to Grow." *USA Hockey Girls and Women's Newsletter* (USA Hockey Association), October, 1.

Pitt, David E. 1989a. "Gang Attack: Unusual for Its Viciousness." *New York Times,* April 25, B5.

———. 1989b. "Jogger's Attackers Terrorized at Least 9 in 2 Hours." *New York Times,* April 22, A1, 30.

———. 1989c. "More Crimes Tied to Gang in Park Rape." *New York Times,* April 24, B1.

Robinson, Lillian S. 1993. "Roving Reporter." *Women's Review of Books* 10 (June): 9–10.

Roediger, David. 1991. *Wages of Whiteness.* New York: Verso.

Rose, Jacqueline. 1986. *Sexuality in the Field of Vision.* New York: Verso.

Sabo, Don, and Joe Panepinto. 1990. "Football Ritual and the Social Reproduction of Masculinity." In *Sport, Men, and the Gender Order,* ed. Michael A. Messner and Don Sabo, 115–26. Champaign, Ill.: Human Kinetics.

Scheman, Naomi. 1993. *Engenderings: Constructions of Knowledge, Authority, and Privilege.* New York: Routledge.

Scott, Joan. 1991. "The Evidence of Experience." *Critical Inquiry* 17 (Summer): 773–97.

Sedgwick, Eve Kosofsky. 1985. *Between Men: English Literature and Male Homosocial Desire.* New York: Columbia University Press.

Silverman, Kaja. 1983. *The Subject of Semiotics.* New York: Oxford.

Times News Services. 1991. "Kiam Apologizes for a Joke about Olson Told at Dinner." *Los Angeles Times,* February 7, C2.

Woolf, Virginia. [1919] 1957. *A Room of One's Own.* New York: Harcourt Brace.

"The Teachers, They All Had Their Pets": Concepts of Gender, Knowledge, and Power

Wendy Luttrell

Tell me what you remember about being in school.

What I remember most about school was that if you were poor you got no respect and no encouragement. I mean if you didn't have cute ringlets, an ironed new uniform, starched shirts, and a mother and father who gave money to the church, you weren't a teacher's pet and that meant you weren't encouraged.

What I didn't like about school, the teachers they had their own pet. If you were a pet you had it made, but if you weren't they didn't take up no attention with you. Everybody knew that the teachers treated the kids who were dressed nice and all better—the teachers all had their pets.

Introduction

THIS ARTICLE is about what two groups of women remember about being in school and what their stories tell us about the twisted relations of gender, knowledge, and power. It is part of a larger research project that illuminates the ways in which gender, race, and class together shape the knowledge that women define

I would like to acknowledge the women who shared their school memories with me, especially those who read and responded to portions of my manuscript. I am indebted to many others who have read versions of this paper; special thanks to Mary Hawkesworth, Nancy Hewitt, Dorothy Holland, Naomi Quinn, Robert Shreefter, Jean Stockard, and John Wilson for their insightful and critical comments. Finally, I would like to thank the *Signs* editors and anonymous reviewers for their help revising the manuscript.

[*Signs: Journal of Women in Culture and Society* 1993, vol. 18, no. 3]

and claim for themselves. My goal in the project is to draw new bound-
aries for the by-now familiar discussion of "women's ways of knowing"
that will allow us to move between more theoretical discussions about
women as knowers and more empirically grounded discussions about
how social differences make a difference in women's knowing and, in so
doing, to revitalize discussion about how to improve women's education.

Since the pathbreaking work of Nancy Chodorow (1978) and Carol
Gilligan (1982), many compelling yet incomplete claims have been made
about how women construct and value knowledge in ways that are re-
lational, oriented more toward sustaining connection than achieving au-
tonomy, and governed by interests to attend to others' needs.[1] Similarly,
some feminist accounts have invested women with distinctive intuitive
and/or emotional capabilities, citing women's exclusion from other ways
of acquiring knowledge under patriarchy and locating women's knowl-
edge in the "body," or female sexuality.[2] Still others have written about
women's epistemic advantage in viewing the world more wholistically
based on their particular "standpoint."[3] In contrast, men's ways of
knowing have been associated with instrumental reason and abstract
rules, oriented toward gaining mastery over nature, and governed by
interests in dominating others; by this account, men's social position
intrudes on their ability to see the world accurately.[4] The dangers of this
gender symbolism within feminist discussions of epistemology have been
noted by several scholars, one of whom warns against claims that un-
wittingly reproduce "patriarchal stereotypes of men and women—flirting
with essentialism, distorting the diverse dimensions of human knowing,
and falsifying the historical record of women's manifold uses of reasons
in daily life" (Hawkesworth 1989, 547).[5] These theoretical speculations
and debates notwithstanding, however, very little empirical work has
been done that either maps out women's diversity as knowers or describes
the varied and changing conditions under which different women claim
and construct knowledge.[6]

---

[1] There is an ongoing dialogue about how gender shapes what and how women
know. This debate has spanned the disciplines, including philosophy, psychology, sociol-
ogy, and education (Chodorow 1978; Gilligan 1982, 1988, 1990; McMillan 1982; Har-
ding and Hintikka 1983; Lloyd 1984; Martin 1985; Belenky et al. 1986; Smith 1987;
Levesque-Lopman 1988; Bordo and Jaggar 1989; Ruddick 1989; Collins 1990).
[2] See Daly 1973, 1978; Cixous 1976, 1981; Griffin 1980; Irigaray 1985; Trask
1986.
[3] O'Brien 1981; Jaggar 1983; Rose 1983; Hartsock 1985; Smith 1987; and Collins
1990 represent the range of feminist "standpoint" theorists.
[4] See Gilligan 1982; Keller 1984; Bordo 1986; Harding 1986; Tronto 1989.
[5] See also Harding and Hintikka 1983; Grant 1987; and Heckman 1987.
[6] *Women's Ways of Knowing* (Belenky et al. 1986) is a noteworthy example of re-
search that considers the different contexts within which women claim and/or deny
knowledge (as children in abusive relationships, as female students in school, as new

My research seeks to fill this gap in the scholarship by juxtaposing the views, values, and schooling experiences of two groups of women who have been underrepresented and misrepresented in the literature: learners in adult basic education classes. I was interested in exploring what skills and knowledge these women learners claimed, dismissed, denied, and minimized in themselves and what skills and knowledge they sought to acquire by returning to school. School was by no means the only site where these women defined, valued, and/or claimed knowledge.[7] Through their past and present schooling experiences, however, they had developed certain views about themselves and others as authoritative or deficient knowers that I sought to untangle.[8]

I was particularly concerned about how the women saw themselves as knowers, as the literature characterizes them as "dropouts" who had been damaged by or failed at school and as individuals seeking a "second chance" by participating in adult basic education. My experience as an educator of adults made me question this oversimplified characterization. Instead, I had heard adult basic education learners, particularly women, define their relationship to schooling in ambivalent, sometimes oppositional, and often contradictory ways. Moreover, I had heard adult learners talk about the gaps between "schoolwise" and "commonsense" knowledge and knowing, and I wondered about the consequences of these distinctions for adult literacy learning and teaching (Luttrell 1989). Through extensive classroom observation and in-depth interviews, I sought to provide a more complicated and rich account of women's paradoxical relationship to schooling, knowledge, and power.

Research process

My research can best be described as a comparative ethnography of two adult basic education programs: the first a community-based pro-

---

mothers raising children, e.g.). The conclusions they draw, however, have more to do with developmental stages of knowing than with the historical, political, or ideological conditions that shape women's knowing.

[7] I have been influenced by Mary Hawkesworth's suggestion that feminist theories of knowledge would be improved if we focused more on the process of knowing than on the knowers themselves. She defines knowledge or a way of knowing as a "convention rooted in the practical judgments of a community of fallible inquirers who struggle to resolve theory-dependent problems under specific historical conditions" (1989, 549). I am interested in how the women came to define themselves as a "community of fallible inquirers" with specific problems and in how these communities and problems are shaped by gender, race, and class.

[8] Indeed, as several black feminist scholars have noted, school may not be the best site for exploring African-American women's claims to knowledge. Instead, black churches and/or black community organizations serve as more informative contexts for how African-American women develop their authority and knowledge. See Grant 1982; Giddings 1984; Gilkes 1985, 1988; Collins 1990.

gram in Philadelphia and the second a workplace literacy program at a North Carolina state university. I interviewed three hundred women about their reasons for returning to school, observed several classes in each program, and selected fifteen women from each program to interview in depth about their school, family, and work lives.

In 1980 I began collecting data from the community-based program in Philadelphia that I had helped organize in 1976 as part of a larger program serving the needs of local women as they faced changes in the community. Once stable and vibrant, this historically white, ethnic (mostly Irish and Polish), and working-class neighborhood had lost its industrial base, suffering economic decline and rising unemployment. In addition, the community had long been ignored by public institutions. Local residents complained about poor health services, nonexistent child-care facilities, a lack of recreational facilities, increased rates of drug and alcohol abuse, environmental hazards, and a rising crime rate. In the face of city, state, and federal cutbacks, neighborhood women were taking on new or additional burdens to make ends meet. Some women were entering the labor force for the first time, while others were seeking more lucrative employment so they could support their families. For everyone, the integrity and quality of community life was being called into question. This questioning included a profound shift in what had traditionally been expected from women residents. In response to these changes, the Women's Program offered a wide range of educational opportunities, counseling services, on-site child care, vocational training, and a battered women's hotline.

In developing new adult education curriculum materials for the program, during 1980–83 I interviewed 180 women who had grown up in the neighborhood and had participated in the program. These interviews were loosely structured to elicit discussion about the women's views about community needs and why they had returned to school.[9] At the same time I observed several classes noting student-student and teacher-student interactions and student responses to the coursework and its demands. After a year of observation I conducted three in-depth interviews over a year's time with selected women in their homes. In the course of these interviews, I met family members and friends, observing the women in an environment outside of school that enabled me to better elicit and

---

[9] The purpose of these interviews was to develop a curriculum guide for adult basic learners that identified certain "generative" themes. The concept of generative theme is drawn from the work of Brazilian educator and political activist Paulo Freire 1970, 1973, 1987. The two most talked-about concerns that emerged in these interviews were parenting and unemployment. The curriculum guides that I wrote based on these generative themes are titled *Women in the Community: A Curriculum Guide for Students and Teachers* (Luttrell 1981) and *Building Multi-Cultural Awareness: A Teaching Approach for Learner-centered Education* (Luttrell 1982).

contextualize the women's educational experiences, views, and values. I tape-recorded and then transcribed each interview.[10]

My stratified, selective sample represented the basic demographic profile of women in the community, including marital status, occupation, income, educational level, religion, and race. The sample also reflected the basic profile of program participants in terms of age, family situation, past attendance and type of school, academic achievement, and level of participation in the classroom, program, or community. In addition to these sampling guidelines, all the women I interviewed were mothers with children still living at home. This decision was based on the results of the unstructured interviews with program participants and/or graduates in which the overwhelming response to the question, "why are you returning to school," was the general statement, "to better myself." Upon further probing about what it meant to "better" oneself, 80 percent of the women volunteered that they were returning to school to become "better mothers." Less than half of these same women explained that they were in school to secure "better jobs" and roughly a third mentioned that a high school diploma would increase their willingness and confidence to converse with family members, particularly husbands. I wanted to explore these findings more fully in the in-depth interviews.[11]

The Philadelphia interviewees were all white and had been raised in the neighborhood. Most still lived within blocks of where they had been born and where extended family members still resided. They had all attended neighborhood schools during the 1940s, 1950s, and early 1960s. One-third had gone to parochial school, and two-thirds had gone to public school.[12] Five of the fifteen women had graduated from high school, and the rest had dropped out either before or during their sophomore year of high school. They had all moved in and out of the work force as factory hands, clerical workers, waitresses, or hospital or teachers' aides. Two-thirds of the women were married at the time of the

[10] The focus of each in-depth interview was loosely defined and depended on how each woman responded to the opening question. In the first interview I asked the women to tell me what they remembered about being in school; in the second interview I asked them to describe themselves as learners; and in the third interview I asked about why they were returning to school. As we talked about their schooling experiences, the women offered detailed accounts of their work and family histories as well.

[11] I elaborate elsewhere on the range and thematic content of the reasons that the women gave for returning to school (Luttrell 1992). Briefly stated, my argument is that the women's shared reasons for attending adult basic education programs illuminate the hidden structure of schools that are organized around women's work as mothers and the ideology of maternal omnipotence.

[12] The Philadelphia women's school careers varied. While a third had at one point attended Catholic coeducational grammar school, only two of these had attended Catholic all-girl high schools. Of the women who had attended public coeducational grammar and high schools, two had attended the public girls' high school before it had become coed.

interviews, although over the course of the study half of these became divorced single mothers. (Of the unmarried women, only two had never been married.)

In 1985, I began the second case study in which I followed the same research protocol as in the first. Again I entered the field as a teacher, curriculum-development specialist, and researcher. The second program was considerably smaller than the first and offered only literacy and high school equivalency classes to selected members of the university's maintenance staff. This program had served approximately two hundred people over a ten-year period, including janitors, housekeepers, painters, electricians, landscapers, and members of the motor pool. The majority, however, were black female housekeepers. I interviewed fifty women participants, and a year later selected fifteen women to interview in depth.

The North Carolina women were all black and had been raised in southern rural communities, although they now resided in communities close to the university. Most had grown up on tenant farms, and all but two had tended tobacco and picked cotton in their youths. All had attended segregated rural grammar schools, often in one-room schoolhouses, and reported sporadic school attendance for reasons I will discuss later. All were employed as housekeepers at the university and shared similar work histories that included domestic work in white people's homes. Throughout the interviews they offered accounts of the tremendous social and political changes in the South that had fundamentally challenged their expectations and roles as black women.

In responding to the question about why they were returning to school, the North Carolina women also replied that school would help them to "better themselves." Upon further inquiry, 85 percent of them mentioned their desire to become "better mothers"; half explained that while it was unlikely, perhaps a high school diploma would translate into a better job; and slightly more than half said they had always meant to finish school but that extenuating circumstances had made this impossible. To elaborate on these findings, my sample included only women who were mothers with at least one child living at home.

There were significant differences in the two samples of women. While equal numbers had gotten pregnant as teenagers, a higher proportion of the Philadelphia women had gotten married as a result. Whereas two-thirds of the Philadelphia women were or had been married, two-thirds of the North Carolina women had been single heads of households for most of their lives. Because of life cycle differences, several of the North Carolina women but none of the Philadelphia women were grandmothers raising school-age grandchildren.

While the two groups of women attended school during the same historical period, their schooling experiences were quite different, as I will elaborate later in the article. While a third of the North Carolina women had changed grammar schools several times during their childhood, only one Philadelphia woman had experienced such transitions. Although most of the North Carolina women had attended rural high schools, there were three who had attended small city public high schools, with two of them graduating. One of these women had attended an all-black college for one year. None of the Philadelphia women had attended college. Worth noting is that the educational skills of both groups of women ranged from roughly third grade to ninth grade level.

Finally, whereas none of the North Carolina women had spent any time out of the labor force since becoming mothers, roughly half of the Philadelphia women had been out of the paid labor force when raising children under school age. The North Carolina women on average earned less than the Philadelphia women, but all the women's family incomes had fluctuated considerably over the past fifteen years.

Interpretive methodology

My intention in contrasting the accounts of both groups of women is to shed light on the problem of interpretation rather than to generalize about either group. I share Gilligan's interest in "the interaction of experience and thought, in different voices and the dialogues to which they give rise" rather than in the "origins of the differences described or their distribution in a wider population, across cultures, or through time" (1982, 2). Indeed, there are many layers of contrast in the life experiences of the women I interviewed, including race, region, ethnicity, religion, schooling, levels of economic deprivation, and political participation, to name just a few, and all of these variations give rise to the different voices and dialogues.

Documenting, describing, and analyzing these variations has demanded tedious and systematic coding procedures that treat each woman's interview as its own text while also looking for themes and patterns that emerge across all the women's interviews. The coding procedure I developed to address inter- and intragroup patterns was two-pronged. First I examined *what* the women said—specifically, what they identified as difficult or problematic in their schooling and how they had sought to resolve these problems. Second, I examined *how* they narrated their recollections of the past—specifically, whom they identified as primary actors and the events that defined for them the problems they encountered in school, how they ordered their stories, and what themes tied the stories together.

To interpret what I have come to call the women's schooling narratives, I have drawn on the traditions of cultural studies and narrative analysis.[13] My analytical task has been to discern both the meanings and the conditions that shaped the stories that the women told (Johnson 1986/87). I have tried to write about their stories in ways that the women would recognize, but also in ways that reveal underlying assumptions or structural relations that they may not recognize or agree with.[14]

Deciding how to label the two groups of women has been yet another problem of interpretation. Worth noting is that there was no single way that each group of women referred to themselves and their family backgrounds. For example, while the North Carolina women consistently referred to themselves and their family members as "black," the Philadelphia women never once referred to themselves as "white." The North Carolina women most often referred to their families as having been "poor" and/or having "country ways." Most of the Philadelphia women described their family background in religious (Catholic), ethnic (Irish or Polish), and/or class (such as "working class," "blue collar," or "union") terms, yet some simply referred to themselves as being "working" or "neighborhood" women.

Critics warn us that labels such as any of those mentioned above can fix our understandings of how gender, race, and class shape our identities, perspectives, and histories.[15] With this in mind, I have chosen to refer to the groups by locality, as the Philadelphia women and the North Carolina women, and to focus on the similarities and differences in how they made sense of and negotiated gender, race, and class relations. Having said all this, I also want to emphasize that these schooling narratives should not be understood as static. The women's stories are reconstructed and retrospective—a way that each woman has made sense of her past in light of the present. Also, what each woman wanted me to know about herself and her schooling influenced what she said and how she organized her narrative. Thus, the narratives are dependent on numerous personal, social, and political factors, not the least of these being

[13] By cultural studies I am referring to the work of the Birmingham Centre for Contemporary Cultural Studies such as that of Willis 1977, Hebdige 1979, and Hall 1986; historians Williams 1961, 1965, 1976 and Thompson 1963; Connell 1982, 1985 and the feminist critics of or contributors to cultural studies, including McRobbie 1978, 1984, 1991; McCabe 1981; Radway 1984; Long 1986; Roman 1987, 1988; and Holland and Eisenhart 1990, to name a few. The narrative analysts include Labov 1972; Mishler 1986; and Personal Narratives Group 1989.

[14] See Smith 1987 for a discussion of her collaborative research project with Alison Griffith on women's work as mothers in relation to schooling. She refers to her attempt to bridge between women's experiences and social organizations of power as "institutional ethnography" and warns feminists against establishing a feminist version of reality that supersedes those whose experiences are being investigated. I have tried to be sensitive to this warning by making it clear when I am presenting the women's experiences and interpretations and when I am presenting my own.

[15] Such critical works include, but are not limited to Hall 1986; Flax 1987; Steedman 1987; Alcoff 1988; hooks 1990; Williams 1991; and Higginbotham 1992.

how they viewed me as an educated, white, middle-class woman who had been their teacher.[16] Moreover, my request for a history of schooling and my underlying assumption that there must be a story as to why these women who had perceived themselves as school failures decided to pursue education as adults also shaped both the telling of the stories and my own interpretation.[17] This, coupled with the women's own desire to tell their life stories (made most evident by the frequent comment "I could write a book about my life"), converged to produce the schooling narratives on which this article is built.

In reviewing the literature I found very little research documenting how adult literacy learners reflected on their past schooling experiences, a curious gap given the conventional wisdom that says past schooling experiences are determining factors in current educational pursuits.[18] Most relevant for interpreting the schooling narratives was the work of sociolinguist Charlotte Linde in which she observes that people "seem to take enormous zest in discussing their experiences in school, however horrific the stories they tell about it" (n.d., chap. 2, p. 4). She attributes this to the fact that American culture places little emphasis on class as a legitimate explanation for why people end up in the particular social position that they do; instead, there seems to be an unspoken assumption that important life decisions are made in schools, decisions for which people feel compelled to account. Richard Sennett and Jonathan Cobb (1972) echo this viewpoint in their discussion of white working-class men's "defensive" accounts about school that the authors attribute to the hidden injury of class. Lillian Rubin (1976) refers to this phenomenon in

---

[16] I have been influenced by the work of several feminist scholars writing about the problems and possibilities of feminist research methods, including McRobbie 1982; Stanley and Wise 1983; Strathern 1987; Stacey 1988; and Devault 1990. For an excellent discussion of the theoretical and political underpinnings of this issue of self-reflexivity in ethnographic research and writing, see Mascia-Lees, Sharpe, and Cohen 1989.

[17] In her paper "Interpreting Women's Narratives: Towards an Alternative Methodology," Susan Chase makes a similar point about her interviews with women about their career histories. "The request for a career history is essentially this: in a world in which so few women have highly paid, prestigious, leadership positions, there must be a story about how you acquired one of those jobs. The nature of the interaction surrounding the request and the telling—the smoothness of both the asking and the response, the ease with which the career history is formulated and told—show that women shared this assumption with us" (1991, 17).

[18] There are no studies of how adult literacy learners view their skills, knowledge, or competencies except for the work of Arlene Fingeret 1983a, 1983b, which ignores the issue of how social differences affect these views. With the notable exception of Kathleen Rockhill's 1987 study of Hispanic women literacy learners, there are no ethnographies of adult basic education programs and/or classrooms. Nor are there any studies of school culture or student resistance like those of Ogbu 1974; Willis 1977; McRobbie 1978, 1991; Weis 1985, 1988; Holland and Eisenhart 1990; or Fine 1991 that examine adult basic education learners and their compliance and/or resistance to school.

her discussion of the "ambivalent" educational views and values of white working-class respondents. Although my research confirms such observations, I will suggest that class is not the only unspoken or unrecognized explanation as to why people end up in the social positions they do. Indeed, the women's stories reveal a much more complicated web of gender, race, and class relations for which they feel compelled to account.

One of the themes around which the women narrated their schooling experiences is that of teachers' pets. In the following sections I discuss the teacher's pet theme as an illustration of the women's shared view of schooling as a struggle over identities, values, and the acquisition of schoolwise knowledge. This struggle pits middle-class teachers against working-class students, "good" girls against "bad" girls, and light-skinned blacks against dark-skinned blacks as symbolic antagonists in the struggle for knowledge and power. I then examine how each group of women differently identified the problems and conditions of this struggle, leading to distinct versions of the teacher's pet theme. The Philadelphia women consistently framed their schooling struggles around issues of discipline and resistance; the North Carolina women framed theirs around issues of access and ability. In both cases, however, the women's understanding of teachers' pets ultimately served to undermine their claims to knowledge and power. The article concludes by considering the pedagogical implications of this embattled view of schooling.

Teachers' pets: How social differences make a difference in school

While each woman had her own unique story to tell, none of the women interviewed had felt comfortable in school. This shared discomfort, while expressed differently by the two groups of women, was attributed primarily to the fact that there were important differences between teachers and students and among certain students. Indeed, the women's feelings and thoughts about teachers' pets crystallized in story form how the women understood and acted on these social differences.[19] In these stories the women describe whom and how teachers chose certain students as pets; what the women thought about these "pets"; how they felt about having or not having been chosen as a pet; and how this had affected their success and failure in school.

For both groups of women the most frequent difference that characterized uncomfortable teacher-student relationships was class. Cora, one of the North Carolina women, began her schooling narrative with the following remark, which might be called the "abstract" of her experience

---

[19] The concept of teacher's pet parallels the concept of common sense that I discuss in Luttrell 1989.

in school:[20] "Back a long time ago when I was going to school, and I can remember just as good as elementary school—if your parents wasn't a doctor, a lawyer, or a teacher, or someone you know, high, then the teachers would look down on you. That's right. And they wouldn't, they just wouldn't, you know, well, they would class you as nobody." Being "classed as nobody," "looked down upon," treated with "no respect and no encouragement" because of class differences figured prominently in all the women's narratives. These class differences not only were related to what their parents did for a living but also served to distinguish students from each other and from their teachers in terms of knowledge and power. Mary's discussion was typical of the conversations I had with the Philadelphia women about their teachers (which sometimes included me and my difference as well):

The teachers were always different from us. They lived in different neighborhoods—they just weren't like the rest of us.

How would you describe how the teachers were different?

I don't know, as my superiors I guess. I always saw them as more intelligent. I never saw them as equal.

You said that they lived in different neighborhoods. Where did your teachers live?

They didn't live in our neighborhood, but then there were a couple who did in grade school. That surprised me when I found out.

Why?

Because I always thought of them (I guess I should say you) as being real rich. I just didn't think they were like us. They were from a higher class and must have been real smart to go to college in the first place. I just never felt very comfortable with them.

Regardless of whether the women liked or disliked a particular teacher, they viewed them as different from themselves, which (as Mary's words above illustrate) was often expressed in geographic terms. The Philadelphia women most often explained that teachers were not like students or parents because teachers came from other neighborhoods, most specifically from the suburbs.

The Philadelphia women believed that the suburbs fostered different kinds of relationships between people, particularly family members and neighbors. As Eileen remarked, the suburbs produced people who "just

[20] "Abstract" is Labov's term (1972, 363).

don't know about certain things. You know, when I grew up everybody in the neighborhood knew everything about me, who my mother was, what my father did, what we were doing on a Friday night. I had relatives everywhere and they kept me and my sisters in line; we couldn't do anything without everybody knowing about it. The teachers, they didn't know. I guess you could say I liked that about them, but then again, they didn't care to know much about us." The Philadelphia women viewed their teachers as outsiders to their communities. Moreover, teachers had different concerns, life-styles, activities, and opportunities, not all of which the women thought were beneficial to family or community life. Doris characterized teachers' concerns in the following way: "You know teachers are married to lawyers and doctors. They're worried about different things, things like nice clothes and what country club they're going to belong to. They have children, it isn't like they didn't know about children, but their children are different, like they assume their children are going to college, but they don't expect our kids are going to college. Then again, there's a lot that goes on in college that isn't so great for kids."[21]

While the Philadelphia women drew suburban-urban distinctions, the North Carolina women drew urban-rural distinctions to talk about class. Thirteen of the fifteen North Carolina women interviewed recalled that their teachers were different because they "came from the city." More than half told stories about how their parents were reluctant to deal with teachers or take part in school activities because of their own "country ways" or an inability to read or write. Cora gave the following account of a childhood incident that she continues to have strong feelings about as an adult:

> Cause I was going to say that my parents, they was well, decent people. But they couldn't read and write, you know what I mean. And they was clean peoples, they never got in no trouble. They never did nobody no harm or nothing. But they just couldn't read and write and they was honest and hard working. And when they would go to PTA meetings, well naturally I would have to go along to try to explain to them what's going on so they could, you know, and they tried their best to do whatever was right. And them teachers said things that, but just because they had no profession they looked down on them and they looked down on me too. You know and then back then wearing home-made dresses and things, I wasn't

[21] Rubin 1976 notes that the working-class parents she interviewed expressed concern that by attending college their children might be exposed not only to views that conflict with their family and community values but also to views that devalue and dismiss a working-class way of life that these parents have worked hard to achieve.

dirty or raggedy but I just wore home-made clothes that my mother would make for me because they only made but so much you know. And like if I want to participate in a play the teacher would pick all over me and get somebody else.

How did the teachers do that exactly?

Well, you see we would be sitting in the classroom in elementary school and the teacher would say, "We're going to have a play." And she would read out the parts. If you raised your hand and somebody else behind you or either on the other side of the classroom that's mother or father was in professional business, well they got the part that they raised their hand for. If you were the only person that raised your hand, in fact I was the only person to raise my hand for a part, then the teacher would probably give it to me. But then she would tell me after school, "Be sure you get that, learn this part, be sure to get the right costume." And you know, everything like that. She would tell me so much so that I would be hating that I raised my hand for the part. And I'd have to go home and talk to my momma and see if they can squeeze out enough money for the costume. And then one time my momma went to ask the teacher for if she could kind of describe a little bit the way that the costume she wanted me to have so she could make it. And the teacher was kind of rude to her, so much so that it kind of hurt my feelings. Then my momma told me, "If you really want to be in that play okay, but I wouldn't even bother." But I didn't really understand. I was only in the third or fourth grade. I didn't quite understand what my momma said, "If you really wants to be then I will go back to her again and get some understanding about it." It gave me sort of an inferiority complex cause I saw how the teacher was talking to my momma. I loved her and I just didn't want nobody to be hurting her feelings.

Cora's story captures how social differences between teachers, parents, and students were lived out, felt, and interpreted. Cora's perception that the teacher was anxious that she might not learn her lines or that her mother would not provide the right costume confirmed not only her sense of difference but also her sense of deficiency as a learner and performer. For Cora, school—but particularly the teacher—had actively undermined the efficacy, dignity, mastery, and cultural inheritance of her background.

It is notable that while the Philadelphia women most often described their teachers as outsiders with different concerns and values, the North Carolina women described themselves and their parents as being the outsiders. As outsiders, they had "come up with country ways" of living for which they were made to feel ashamed and rejected. I will return to this point and its significance later. At this point, my emphasis is on how the theme of teachers' pets illustrated the women's shared awareness of class divisions and struggles through which they learned to view their place in school and to project their futures. As Jeanne, a Philadelphia woman remembers, "I wasn't encouraged much in school, mostly the teachers didn't think much of me. They didn't think much of my background, I guess you could say. I wasn't the teacher's pet type, you know the kind that got picked to stand in front of the line or to pass out paper or pencils. I suppose the teachers didn't think I had promise or was going anywhere."

Being a "teacher's pet type" also referred to how different students understood and acted on their femininities. Both groups of women offered examples of how teachers favored girls over boys in school, yet through this preference the women noted that traditional constraints were being put on girls to be "pretty," "cute," and "good." Said one, "The teachers liked the girls better. But then I think it was easier for my brothers in school because nobody expected them to be quiet. But I couldn't keep my mouth shut, talking all the time and I was loud too, so the teacher, she didn't care too much for me." In the words of another, "I was Miss 'Tough Girl.' I was a real bully and a troublemaker. A lot of us played tough, but you couldn't be too tough or you would stand out in class. The teachers didn't treat the girls as rough as the boys—I guess because girls aren't supposed to be as bad as boys—but anyway I was pretty bad."

To be chosen as a female pet, girls had to comply to traditional, middle-class femininity, which for some women was either unrealistic or simply impossible: "Life was rough on the streets. You couldn't go around being Miss Priss and stay alive. So I got tough and the teachers didn't like me." "I didn't have no frilly dresses with lace and skirts and all. I was worried about soles on my shoes. There were lots of days I didn't go to school because I was just too ashamed of my clothes." Both groups of women believed that teachers preferred not only smart but *good* girls as well. As Sallie, a Philadelphia woman, explained, "I remember Miss Fulton and her sister. They lived in this really beautiful house and would invite all their goodies to their house. The goodies were smart kids—they liked smart girls. But you also had to behave and act like a lady if you were going to get invited to their place."

Considerable research documents teachers' differential behaviors toward boys and girls and its negative effect on girls' school achievement.[22]

---

[22] For examples, see Martin 1972; Serbin et al. 1973; Brophy and Goode 1974; Stacey, Bereaud, and Daniels 1974; Dweck et al. 1978; Best 1983; Stockard 1985; Sadker and Sadker 1986; Jones 1989.

While this research confirms the women's perceptions that teachers behaved differently toward boys and girls, it simplifies the social learning that goes on in the classroom. Despite the fact that most education theory and practice implicitly assumes that teachers direct gender socialization in the classroom, we know little about how teachers react to boys and girls who do not fit into expected gender roles. Moreover, we know little about how students interpret teachers' different attitudes and behaviors toward boys and girls or what students do to get teachers to respond to them in specific ways. More important in this case, we do not know how girls from different classes, races, or ethnic backgrounds interpret their interactions with teachers.

What we learn from these women's schooling narratives is that girls do not all have the same opportunities to look, act, and be treated as "feminine" or as "teachers' pets." Indeed, the women's stories illustrate the complexities of gender relations in the classroom—how female socialization is problematic rather than given. Most important, these narratives illustrate that the two groups of women differed in how they perceived these complexities and problems and as a result developed different views about the connection between gender, knowledge, and power.

There were striking similarities within each group of women as they recalled their roles in and responses to teachers' pets. The Philadelphia women described themselves as having made choices about whether they would pursue being a teacher's pet. As Debra explained, "I remember one girl used to act in a real cutsie way and the teacher would be so impressed. I didn't like the teacher and I didn't like the girls who acted like that. I just wouldn't be cutsic like that—not even if it did impress the teacher." Debra reasoned that if the teacher chose you to be a pet, you risked losing friends; other kids would be jealous. And even if you did choose to act "cutsie" and "sit like a lady," you knew it was an "act" rather than the real thing. Helen talked about this dilemma:

I was a teacher's pet so I got by pretty well. [Laughing.]

A couple of other women have laughed just like you when they describe themselves as teacher's pet, can you explain this?

Because you know you are and it's uncomfortable. I mean either they like you or they don't, but when I was a kid I guess I was a smooth talker. I was real cute and learned how to bat my eyes, look cute, sit like a lady, and boy the teachers really ate that stuff up. I guess I felt bad because I felt like I had conned them.

The choice to become a teacher's pet, to represent oneself falsely in order to win the teacher's approval, was not a happy one. Those Philadelphia

women who did get chosen as pets and were successful in school de-
scribed their achievements with guilt or discomfort. As Helen continued,
"I used to feel so bad for my sister. I mean, I didn't even have to study and
I got A's. The teachers liked me cause I knew how to win them over with
my smile. But my sister, she worked so hard and didn't get anywhere. I
couldn't feel too good about how I was doing when she was having such
a hard time." At the same time, others who did not get chosen or saw
themselves rejecting the opportunity to be teacher's pet also suffered
(eleven of the fifteen Philadelphia women interviewed).

The North Carolina women, however, did not talk about their choices
about being teacher's pets. These women, who were all dark-skinned,
saw themselves as noncontenders in the contest to win the teacher's
approval. They did, however, observe lighter-skinned students making
this choice. As Gloria explained, there were always some girls "putting
on the dog" in order to attract the teacher's attention. Integrally woven
into the North Carolina women's accounts of school was the persistent
memory that teachers favored light-skinned children over dark-skinned
children. Bessie recalled: "What I didn't like about school, the teachers
they had their own pets. Like if you were light skinned, you had it made.
But if you were *Black,* they didn't take up no attention with you." Not
just one, but all the North Carolina women referred to the role of skin
color, emphasizing that teachers' pets were cute, good, smart, higher
class, and "what we used to call 'yeller,' back then." They described how
teachers "passed right over," "looked straight through," or "looked over
the top of" darker-skinned children. As Gladys added, "I suspect it was
'cause them teachers were yeller too."

Mary Helen Washington (1982, 208–17) claims that this "intimida-
tion of color" surfaces as a recurring theme in the lives and literature of
black women. In the introduction to her anthology *Black-Eyed Susans*
she writes: "In almost every novel or autobiography written by a black
woman, there is at least one incident [of] the dark-skinned girl who
wishes to be either white or light-skinned with 'good hair' " (1975, xv).
One such example, *Lemon Swamp and Other Places,* the life history of
Mamie Garvin Fields (1983), highlights the complexities of the color line.
Her story suggests that distinctions made on the basis of color cannot be
explained simply as class differences. She describes how members of the
same family with lighter skin color were awarded greater recognition,
resources, and success in school. Growing up in a middle-class black
community in Charleston, South Carolina, in the early 1900s, she recalls:

> When I was a little girl, I recognized that there was a difference,
> because my brother Herbert used to tease me and call me black—
> "blakymo"—although he was as black as I was. It used to make me

so mad I would almost fight him. He would say, "Well, we are the black ones and they [their siblings] are the light ones. They can do this and that." We used to joke this way, but it wasn't all joke either. One reason why I didn't go to our private school for Negroes in Charleston was that, back then, honors were always given to mulatto children, light-skinned half-sisters and brothers, grands and great-grands of white people. It didn't matter what you did if you were dark. Used to leading my class up through elementary school, I hated this idea, so I began to say I wanted to go somewhere else. [Fields 1983, 47]

For the North Carolina women interviewed, lighter skin meant having more opportunities to learn because the teachers would "take up more attention with the lighter-skinned kids." Bessie remembered Dorothy, a light-skinned girl, whom Bessie resents to this day:

You know, if you come to school dressed real nice, you know with one of them ruffle dresses, little bows and stuff on your hair, looking real neat, the teacher would take up time with you. Something that she would tell her, she probably wouldn't tell me. Like this girl, her name was Dorothy. She was the teacher's pet. She had light skin, pretty black hair, she came from a wealthy family, you know.

What was it that made her the teacher's pet?

I believe it was her lighter skin. And then the clothes she would wear. And the teacher would have PTA meetings, and my mom she never went to no PTA meeting or nothing like that. I reckon that showed the teacher you wasn't interested in your child. So that was that and the teacher wouldn't take up no time. But she took up time with Dorothy with her light skin and pretty black hair.

These differences did not exist simply in the realm of attitudes within the black community or in the society at large, but got lived out daily in the lives of black students as part of acquiring school knowledge and basic skills. Embedded in the North Carolina women's perceptions of themselves as learners was a legacy of being ignored by their black teachers who reinforced the message of dominant white society—that black children need not be educated.[23]

Both groups of women organized their schooling narratives around the theme of teachers' pets as a cautionary tale about how social differ-

[23] It would be important, of course, to know how the "Dorothys" felt about their approval from the teacher in order to fill out the picture of black students' experiences and interpretations of power relations in the classroom.

ence makes a difference in school. The moral of their tale is that school divides students against each other and against themselves along the fault lines of gender, race, and class in the struggle for schoolwise knowledge. Yet the two groups of women negotiated these divisions differently, and thus each presented a distinct version of what was at stake.

Discipline, resistance, and the struggle to be heard

The Philadelphia women most often framed their struggles in school around the issue of discipline and resistance.[24] This emphasis emerged most clearly as they described school as "boring," "routine," or a "farce." They attributed their problems in school to teachers who were more interested in order and discipline than in teaching anything of interest: "Everything was just like routine. Everyday we did the same thing over and over. The teachers weren't interested in teaching us; they were there to keep order."

The Philadelphia women's version of school is linked to their view of authority relations, specifically their memories of the arbitrary rules and harsh disciplinary behavior of nuns and teachers. Without any prompting, all fifteen provided detailed examples of what they considered to be unfair or unnecessary restrictions on both their person and their learning. Their frustration was captured by the repeated phrase that teachers had "treated us like children, to be seen but not heard." They saw teachers being overattentive and/or restrictive in terms of student behavior and personal style (clothing, hairdo, makeup) while at the same time "ignoring" students' needs or concerns, as explained by the following two women:

> Well, I was used to making money, being on my own. But they treated me like a child. The rules were ridiculous. You had to read what they wanted you to read. Your dress couldn't be too short, you couldn't wear too much makeup, your bangs couldn't be too long—there were rules for everything. Things were very regimented and rigid—they treated us like children.

[24] This same observation is made by Lois Weis (1983, 235–61) in her comparative study of black community college students in a large northeastern U.S. city with students in two other accounts (Willis 1977; London 1978). These authors identified distinctly negative attitudes toward authority and school knowledge among white, working-class students, which they argue is based on a working-class rejection of mental labor. In contrast, I will argue that the women's attitude toward authority stems from what they perceive is the school's dismissal of working-class women's labor. Paralleling my findings, Weis observed that black students did not reject the authority of teachers or question the legitimacy of their knowledge. Instead, they resented teachers for what they perceived were racist motives in ignoring or dismissing black students (1983, 244).

I like going to school as an adult. In my classes you can talk person to person, not child to adult like in school. When I went to school you wouldn't have dreamed of telling a teacher how to do something or making a suggestion about anything. The teachers just didn't respect kids and their ideas. They bothered you about talking in class or being a problem in class, but they couldn't be bothered if you had a problem, like you didn't understand something or you couldn't concentrate.

The importance of order and discipline extended beyond the classroom, as Peggy and Doreen described:

What the nun said was rule. If a nun hit you, then you deserved it. In some families if you told your parents that a nun hit you, then you got hit at home because obviously the nuns were always right. But in my family if I told them a nun hit me they could understand why I was upset, but they would never challenge it.

I had an attitude towards authority even when I knew I would get in trouble in school and then again at home. In those days the teacher called your parents and you got it twice—once at school and then again at home. Parents didn't think to challenge the teachers. There was no discussion about why you were in trouble, if the teacher said it was so, it was so.

Teachers' authority and discipline was a backdrop against which the Philadelphia women either claimed a voice or were silenced. Indeed, the metaphor of voice persisted throughout their schooling narratives as they told stories about their struggles to "control my mouth," "speak my mind," and "tell the teacher off."[25] This struggle, or "attitude towards authority" as twelve of the fifteen Philadelphia women called it, was described as a character trait that had interfered with their school success. It explained why they were not chosen as or had rejected being teachers' pets and why they were not the "teacher's pet type" or "suited" for school. Those women who described themselves as good students dealt with what they considered arbitrary or unnecessary discipline through silence: "I learned at a young age to button my lip. You couldn't win with the teachers; they hated fresh mouthed kids, so . . . [long pause].

[25] I also found that in response to the question about why they were returning to school, two-thirds of the Philadelphia women surveyed gave examples that drew on their desire to be able to "speak up" and "voice" their opinions and be heard by family members, social service agents, and school or city officials. See also Belenky et al. 1986 for their observations about women's silence and voice in the educational process.

My sister couldn't put up with it and she didn't do well, I guess you could say it was more my style to take it, so I did real well in school."

There are several ways to interpret the Philadelphia women's discussion of teacher's authority and discipline. On one level, it could be argued that their preoccupation with discipline and resistance was based on unresolved childhood images and expectations of what power and authority should be. Perhaps their resentment about being "treated like children" and about others being teachers' pets is a projection of their feelings about parent-child and sibling relations onto teacher-student relations in the classroom.[26] But on another level, their complaints about "being treated like children" and their quest for a voice reveal their implicit critique of schooling. Sounding much like the low-income high school girls (white, black, and Hispanic) in Michelle Fine's study (1991), the Philadelphia women felt at best muted and at worst silenced by schooling practices that ignored the exigencies of poor and working-class families and communities, particularly for young women in their roles as caretakers. Teachers' middle-class conceptions of childhood simply did not correspond to the demands placed on working-class girls, as the following quotations illuminate:

> I had a lot of responsibility for my younger brothers and sisters. I accepted it at the time. I used to babysit at the age of ten, but now that I think of it, I was really young to be doing all that. In the first grade I had to wake my mother up to let her know I was ready to go to school. Everyone I knew came from big families—we were all used to a lot of responsibility.

> I remember going shopping for clothes for my brother and sister when I was twelve. My mother just didn't have the time 'cause she was working hard to support all of us by herself.

The Philadelphia women had worked hard to keep themselves and often their families together, taking care of siblings, preparing meals, shopping, cleaning, and often managing a job after school as well. Yet, despite its centrality and importance in their everyday lives, school undermined the knowledge, value, and authority invested in caretaking. Joanne explained that she never expected school to encourage or validate her, but had her own views about the value of caretaking when she dropped out of school at sixteen: "My mother worked as a waitress for sixty-five cents an hour and raised three children without any assistance.

---

[26] This kind of interpretation follows from the Frankfurt school, specifically Adorno et. al's 1950 study of the authoritarian personality. See Waller 1932 and Sennett 1980 for discussion of the fear and illusion of authority.

She just really didn't have any time to encourage us much. But I also worked since I was fifteen—I was very independent and I didn't expect to get any encouragement, especially from the teachers. I had to be very responsible, not like a child in school. When my mother died my sister was only thirteen and I took care of her. I'm very proud that she made it through school and graduated, even if I didn't." Joanne's story was not uncommon in that she took pride in and valued her mother's and her own ability to independently support themselves and others. Yet she didn't expect to get validated for her caretaking skills or knowledge in school. Instead, school penalized working-class girls for their commitments and responsibilities at home and rewarded "good girl" behavior and traditional middle-class femininity, an image of women as domestic, tranquil, attractive, and dependent on others for economic support.[27] School denied the reality and legitimacy of working-class femininity, an image of women as hardworking, responsible caregivers.

There was much at stake in the Philadelphia women's view of their schooling as embattled, especially in light of the school "choices" for which they felt compelled to account. Debra described herself weighing the following choices:

> I didn't really want to be a smart kid in school. I don't know—maybe it was the friends I hung with. If I did something too good, they would look at me funny. They thought why are you doing that? You don't have to do that to get through.
>
> *So you didn't want to look like you were trying?*
>
> Mostly I didn't want to try too hard for the teachers.[28]

Debra's distinguishing between the demands of "the girls she hung with" and the demands of teachers or school is similar to Ann's distinguishing between school and work in her account of why she chose the "commercial" rather than the "academic" track:

> I wasn't interested in the academic track. I didn't know why I needed to study history and all. I was interested in learning what I

---

[27] This dominant image of femininity or the "cult of true womanhood," a term coined by Welter 1978, emerged during the mid-nineteenth century as part of the consolidation of the American middle class. Polite and proper middle-class manners, styles, and values were associated with "feminized" traits and were important for class mobility.

[28] Debra's reference to "the friends I hung with" emerges in contrast to the "teacher's pet" types. The contrast between these two groups of girls is notable throughout the Philadelphia women's narratives as a set of embattled relationships that characterized school.

needed for a job like typing, bookkeeping, and the commercial courses. I couldn't wait to get out of school where I could be on my own, where I could be myself and do what I wanted to do. Some of it was to have my own money so I could buy what I wanted for myself, but we all, all the girls I hung with, all of us were in commercial and we knew what we wanted. We knew what we needed to do to, you know, about life, we knew about life even if we didn't know what they were teaching us about in school.

These accounts are reminiscent of Helen's pondering the pros and cons of being the "teacher's pet" and Peggy's concerns about the costs and benefits of her "mouthing off" toward teachers. Such inner dialogues about "choice" persisted throughout the Philadelphia women's narratives as they accounted for not only their school decisions but also their claims to "schoolwise" knowledge that they posed in opposition to their own "streetwise" or "commonsense" knowledge.[29] As Debra explained:

It was crazy the way they treated us as if we were children. We did everything adults do and we had a lot of experience under our belts. It was as if we were supposed to pretend like we had nothing to do except come to school everyday and be good little girls. I guess we also thought we knew more than they did so we didn't have to do the school work. The girls I hung with, we all thought we had one up on the teachers.

What did you know more about?

Getting by in life. We knew how to get over on the teachers. We all thought we were so smart. Now that I look back at it, we were all wrong.

Tina's account of having dropped out of school serves as a good example of the Philadelphia women's antagonistic and paradoxical relationship to school:

I didn't even consider going back to school when I found out I was pregnant. All those restrictions and all those hang-ups, I thought I'm having a baby and I'm going to not go to school and be a kid anymore. It was like my adult statement.

So you wanted the baby?

Well, the baby wasn't planned. But I wasn't going back to school. No way. I took the books and dumped them in a corner some place.

[29] See Luttrell 1989 for elaboration of this point.

Tina resisted the discipline of school and asserted her autonomy and independence by making what she calls her "adult statement." While she admits that her pregnancy was not intended, her decision to drop out of school was, and thus served as a way for Tina simultaneously to oppose school authorities and to stake a claim to her own values, interests, and knowledge. From Tina's perspective, her pregnancy was not the problem; school was. Pregnancy and motherhood offered her an opportunity to escape the disciplining force of school (as does Ann's view of work as a way to escape from the disciplinary force of school). Nevertheless, Tina's resistance to school had its own cost in that it drew on dominant gender ideologies, including the familiar but false dichotomy between "good" and "bad" girls that characterizes female sexuality and power. On the one hand, Tina's "problem with authority," her "mouth," and ultimately her sexual activity defined her as a "bad" girl. Yet, at the same time, her impending marriage and motherhood defined her not only as a "good" girl but also as the envy of the "girls she hung with":[30] "I remember in the beginning that my friends used to come visit after school and talk about how much fun it must be, taking care of the baby, buying cute clothes and all. We lived with his mother then and it wasn't so easy, but they didn't know about that part of it. Still, it was better than being in school."

Ironically, Tina's decision to drop out of school was a "statement" (again the metaphor of voice) in which she resisted one "regime" of discipline and authority (school and teachers) only to accept a different "regime" (family, husband, mother-in-law).[31] It is not that Tina would have made a different choice if she were to do it again but, rather, as she explains regarding her current participation in school, that "I don't want my daughters making the same mistake I did. Part of why I'm in school now is to show them that they have options and that they need to finish school before they decide to get married and have kids."

In the end, the Philadelphia women's view of schooling kept them from acknowledging the full range of their abilities. The false yet clear division of what they "knew" from what school wanted them to know ultimately served to limit their claims to knowledge and power. Regrettably, in order to resist the discipline of school and class-based ideologies

[30] McRobbie 1978 argues that fashion, beauty, and female sexuality all contribute to working-class feminine antischool culture, which paradoxically pushes girls into compliance with stereotypical female roles. McRobbie observed that working-class girls asserted their sexualities within the classroom as part of their counterschool culture. The girls' corollary fascination with marriage (partly because it was the only legitimate means through which their sexualities could be expressed) was also part of their counterschool culture that ultimately worked to insure their complicity in dominant gender and class relations.

[31] This notion of regimes of discipline and authority is borrowed from Foucault 1977, 1979.

about knowledge and the value of upward mobility, the Philadelphia women were forced to borrow on gender-based ideologies that located their source of knowledge, power, and resistance in traditionally defined female domains and concerns such as marriage, motherhood, and female sexuality. Thus, as part of a "choice" to assert their female working-class interests, concerns, and knowledge, the Philadelphia women's abilities and desires for intellectual or academic mastery were minimized, denied, or repressed.

Access, ability, and the struggle to be seen

The North Carolina women framed their struggles in school around the issues of access and ability. This emphasis emerged most clearly through their stories about difficulties attending school, inequities in school resources, and their anxieties about "falling behind" that persisted throughout their narratives. In contrast to the Philadelphia women's characterization of school as routine or boring, the North Carolina women most often described it as a luxury, something they enjoyed when able to attend. As Ola explained, "We loved going to school. We enjoyed it, it was all we had to enjoy sometimes." Or as Lois emphasized, school was reserved for rainy days when they were not needed on the farm: "Most times we were working on the farm and we wouldn't go to school nothing but rainy days, no way. Sometimes daddy would let my younger brothers and sisters go, but not me, I was the oldest."

The North Carolina women's narratives focused on the problems encountered by both teachers and children in rural segregated schools. Their stories highlighted the difficulties black teachers faced in one-room schoolhouses with little or no heat or supplies where they were expected to manage forty to fifty children ranging in age and grade level. Similarly, the North Carolina women offered accounts of long and sometimes dangerous walks to school, bad weather, and irregular attendance that made it hard to keep up with the demands of school. For example, Ella started school at nine years of age when her younger brother was old enough to walk the five miles to school with her. Louise explained that she didn't attend school until she was eight years old when her teacher offered to pick her up in the mornings. And Jackie remembered that by the time she and her siblings got to school their hands were so cold that it took them half the morning to warm up. Lilly explained that she and her sister were required to help their mother with the wash in the morning and most days "we just never made it."

Unlike the Philadelphia women, these women never mentioned being "treated like children." If anything, they saw school as a welcomed opportunity to get out of adult responsibilities at home, such as taking care of siblings, farming, or washing. Moreover, they did not focus on the discipline or demands of school but rather on the demands of rural poverty. Louise illuminates this recurring concern among the North Carolina women: "What I remember most was being tired. By the time we got to school, there was no bus long and then for black childrens, the morning was half over. We be missing how the teacher told us to do the work, or were just too tired to think."

Teacher-student relationships were profoundly affected by rural poverty as well. Perhaps most striking were the North Carolina women's descriptions of teachers that focused more on their caretaking rather than on their disciplining characteristics. They recalled with great fondness the "good" teachers who "took special care," fixed hot food, bought them clothes, and acknowledged their particular family/work responsibilities and demands. Not surprisingly, these descriptions echo the writings of black teachers of the time who found ways to pass on schoolwise knowledge despite untenable conditions.[32] School practices could not so easily separate out the daily survival needs of black children from their intellectual needs. Teachers who showed concern about poverty, lack of transportation, and the harshness of farm work inspired students to persist despite overwhelming odds.[33]

Linked to the issue of poverty was the all-pervasive reality of racism that shaped schooling practices. Throughout their narratives, the North Carolina women drew on metaphors of vision rather than voice to narrate their experiences in school.[34] Their narratives were charged with memories of painful events that had made them feel invisible both within the classroom as darker-skinned children and outside the classroom as

---

[32] See Fields 1983; Giddings 1984; Stuckey 1988; and Collins 1990.

[33] I learned firsthand about what was at stake for the North Carolina women when they placed themselves into a teacher's "care" and immersed themselves in the traditions of schooling. It has always been my practice to call students at home if they miss several classes. During the first month of teaching in the workplace literacy program I called one student who had been absent to find out what was keeping her out of class and to offer my assistance if needed. As it happened, she was waiting until payday so that she could buy a new pair of glasses. She was getting headaches from reading and had not yet been able to afford the new prescription. I offered to loan her the money so that she would not miss two more weeks of class. She did not take me up on the offer, but she returned to class the next day. Later, during the end-of-the-year evaluation meeting, she commented on her motivation for continuing in the program: "I figured if you cared enough to call me at home then you must really think that I can do the work. Then too if you cared enough to call me and to loan me the money, then I should care enough about myself to be in class everyday and not give up on myself. I just never had a teacher to call me like that."

[34] See Williams 1988, where the author starts out her essay "on being invisible" as a way to narrate her own place in history.

blacks attending segregated schools. Ola's story is but one example of being "passed by" by white society in both literal and symbolic terms:

> When we were little there was no bus for black children. Everyday we be walking to school and watch that big yellow bus drive by. It would stop right up in front of us to pick up the white childrens. And when we were little, this is the truth. A white person, if you were riding on the road, you know down the highway, and you was in front of them, that white person would run you off of that road to get in front of you. They didn't care. And then one time daddy had all his little childrens in the car, I don't know where we was going. Anyway, a white man come up, and daddy had to pull over and if he hadn't a went like that, the white man probably a killed us all. My daddy just pulled over to the side and let him go right on by. I remember we used to stand over on the side and watch all the white childrens pass right on by to school.

Lilly described how the teachers "looked over the top" of dark-skinned children:

> We really had a hard time in school cause if we know something, like if I go home and do my homework and really learn something and really get into it, we go back to school the next day. Then the teacher start asking about the lesson, getting us to go to the board and asking questions, we sitting and raising our hands and they would just look over the top of us. Now, all the little dark-skinned childrens, the teachers didn't take up no time with them. All the little light-skinned kids, teachers would take up time with them. And I got, [pause] I had went so far I just got tired. I had got to the place where I didn't care if I learned anything or not.

And Geraldine talked about black students' invisibility within the entire system of education: "Long and then nobody cared if black children went to school. There were no officers coming around to see if you was in school." Struggling to make themselves "seen" was draining and left the North Carolina women with little if any energy for their own creative, intellectual, and emotional development in schools.

Coupled with their sense of having been rejected was a sense of humiliation and shame. Repeatedly, the North Carolina women said they had felt "ashamed" because of their clothes or appearance, their size in relation to the other children, their inability to keep up in class, or their parents who had "country ways." (All fifteen of the women interviewed described an event in which they had been shamed in school.) Most often, they recounted that children "picked" on them and that teachers added flame to the fires.[35]

> The kids picked at us so much about our clothes, they picked about me carrying a brown bag and eating biscuits for lunch. I got to where I would go behind the gym or go behind the building or go to a classroom where nobody else was around and eat my lunch. It would never have gotten out except for my biology teacher. He happened to see me one day going into a classroom. I thought I was in there by myself and I pulled out the jelly biscuit. He was standing at the door looking at me and I didn't know he was cause he was looking through the glass on the door. And getting back to biology class, we was dissecting a frog and I couldn't quite get it cause I was so fat. I was fat and my fingers were clumsy. He spoke up right there in front of the class, everybody was listening to him and he says, "Doyle, you could dissect that frog if you would leave off eating all those biscuits. And you wouldn't be so big and fat." And everybody in class laughed and I tell you, I hated to go into class after that. And sometimes I would tell my mother that I had forgot my lunch, but I wouldn't forget, I was just too ashamed to carry it, the brown bag. If he had never told them about me carrying biscuits, but they [the teachers] looked down on me.

Fond memories of teachers who had taken "special care" paralleled with equal frequency such memories of teachers calling attention to students' deficiencies, both social and intellectual. Whereas the Philadelphia women provided stories in which they were angry with or shamed by teachers' extreme punishment (tying students to chairs, locking students in closets, hitting students with rulers, etc.), the North Carolina women shared stories in which they had been shamed by a teachers' cruel or arbitrary verbal abuse, as this one of Geraldine's: "In the classroom I got along most of the time, I knew the lesson and stuff like that. But she [her teacher] would always be saying that was I dumb or something like that. Maybe that come from me having kind of a stutter, and she said from that. In front of the whole class she would talk about me." In such stories, some women recalled being shamed by their teachers for things related to being poor (having inadequate clothes or no shoes), having "country ways" (bringing brown bags with biscuits), or not being able to attend school regularly. Indeed, Beverly explains that she dropped out of school

---

[35] Like the Philadelphia women, some of the North Carolina women referred to the girls they hung with, their "friend girls" in contrast to the "teacher's pet" types, but more often they talked about children who "picked" on them. These were the embattled relationships that organized their schooling narratives.

to insure that her new baby could one day attend school without shame: "And when I had my son I said, I don't want him to come up poor, go to school half ragged and everything. And then at that time white people liked for you to work in their houses so I told momma I ain't going back to school cause I want my son to wear nice clothes, you know and all to school too."

Others, like Geraldine, recalled having suffered public humiliation for what was most often referred to as being a "slow learner." Most telling was the finding that all the North Carolina women chronicled their school narratives according to whether they were passed onto the next grade or were kept behind. In light of the fact that they attended one-room schoolhouses or schools with only a few rooms, I asked how they knew what "grade" level they were in. Even without age-graded class-rooms, standardized tests, or formalized report cards, the North Carolina women perceived that they had been judged by some set of rational, performance-based set of standards that did not correspond with their abilities or opportunities to perform. Nevertheless, they internalized these standards and explained the moral behind their failure: they had been "slow learners." Gloria sums up what more than half the North Carolina women said about their problem in school: "My problem was that I was a slow learner. I didn't catch on the way the other childrens did. I was always behind trying to catch up; the teachers didn't take up no time with me. Except in third grade with Miss Johnson. She was a good teacher and she made sure that I stayed up with the class."

Despite images of themselves as invisible and as slow learners, the North Carolina women also agreed that school held little promise for them. It did not offer upward mobility and, as Ola explains, schoolwise knowledge was not perceived as necessary for their work as women in their families: "Long back at that time we didn't have nothing to go to school for. All of us, like a bunch of girls would get together, they'd say, 'What good is going to school? We's out here on the farm so we ain't going to do nothing but stay out here on the farm and have babies, farm, and keep house.' You can do that, you can learn that from momma and daddy. You don't need to go to school for that, to stay out on the farm or to babysit and clean house for white peoples." Or as Beverly further explained why she had dropped out of school, "I decided I'm just going to give up my education so [my son] could get his. Cause education didn't mean nothing to me back them, it didn't lead to nothing. Now I see that we both should probably have went on to school, but I just made sure that he went to school and graduated."

Whether they attributed their problem in school to one of limited access, ability, or promise, the North Carolina women did not view school as posing a set of conflicting choices for them. Ironically, despite the fact that school held no promise for them, the North Carolina women were more free to immerse themselves in school values, styles, and authority. They were not concerned over who knew more, teachers or students, but rather who was allowed to know or who was capable of knowing, who was encouraged and who was passed over. It was not the authority or legitimacy of schoolwise knowledge that was at stake in the North Carolina women's school struggles but, rather, their own legitimacy as school students.

Effects of school organization and mission

How do we account for the women's different versions of school and what do these versions tell us about the twisted relations of gender, knowledge, and power? In this section I will consider the effects of school organization and mission on the women's different versions of school. My argument is that the two school contexts—one rural-community and the other urban-comprehensive—organized the relationship between gender, knowledge, and power differently and thus generated different views among the women about these twisted relations.

Writing about how gender relations operate differently according to school organization, Elisabeth Hansot and David Tyack (1988) characterize the rural-community and the urban-comprehensive school in the following ways. In the rural-community school, age and cognitive proficiency organized instruction, whereas in the urban-comprehensive school, gender organized the curriculum. In the 1920s, "progressive" school reform sought to design the curriculum to address the so-called different needs of boys and girls. Educational reformers worried about the way high schools were differentiating students by class, yet these same reformers tended to see differentiation by gender as natural and desirable. Whereas the explicit goal of the urban comprehensive school was to prepare students for adult occupations, fashioned primarily around the needs of industry, the implicit effect was to replicate in the school the same sexual division of labor that students would be expected to accommodate as adults. Thus, according to Hansot and Tyack, gender gained greater "institutional salience" in the urban public schools, even as school practices worked to obscure this salience. Moreover, gender gained greater, if not hidden, salience in the urban public school because of the rigid institutional boundaries that separated family, work, and school. In rural communities, these boundaries were more fluid, viewed by students as "part of a seamless web of community contexts, each interwoven with and legitimating the other" (1988, 752). In contrast, the urban school system was large and bureaucratic, no longer analogous in either structure or operation to families, churches, or community life.

Thus, school was viewed by students as set apart from, rather than integral to, other institutions that prepared them for their future roles and responsibilities. Furthermore, because gender relations varied from one institution to the other, students in urban-comprehensive schools were forced to negotiate different gender expectations. For example, a young girl might find that in school she did the same work as boys and was rewarded in the same way for her efforts. But when she entered the work force and found that her opportunities were limited and that she was not rewarded in the same way as her male counterparts, she was forced to somehow make sense of the discrepancy. How she made sense of and negotiated changing gender practices and meanings was not simply the result of personal insight but was also governed by historical, cultural, ideological, and institutional forces.

In this light, let us consider how each school context generated a different set of gender practices and problems for the women to negotiate. Consider the Philadelphia women's view of school as both stemming from and answering to the urban-comprehensive school's organization and mission.[36] Organized around the requirements of industry, the urban-comprehensive school emphasized the obedience and discipline required in working-class jobs as it prepared students to enter a sex-segregated labor force (Bowles and Gintis 1976). The "commercial track" and the "kitchen practice" (the latter referred to by one Philadelphia woman as "where they put the real low life in the school") were part of this preparation where girls learned clerical or waitressing skills while boys learned a skilled trade in "shop" classes. I would argue that the Philadelphia women made sense of this school organization in class rather than gender terms. For example, to explain why they chose the commercial track, the women drew on class-based antagonisms between teachers and students and between schoolwise and streetwise knowledge to account for their "choices." Their explanations pit their middle-class teachers, for whom they did not want to "work too hard" and with whom they did not share the same life concerns or values, against their peers, with whom they shared common interests, knowledge, and authority about how to "get by in life."[37] Similarly, the Philadelphia women

---

[36] There were in fact three school contexts, including Catholic school. I discuss the particular effects of Catholic School on the women's aspirations in Luttrell 1992. However, in terms of framing their school "problems," there was no difference between those Philadelphia women who attended public and those who attended parochial school. This may be due to the small number of women who attended Catholic school in the sample. Future research might yield important contrasts.

[37] Such antagonistic relationships are reminiscent of how Thompson 1963 accounts for the development of class consciousness, as a process that happens when people articulate and identify their interests, capabilities, or concerns as being common to others like themselves and against those whose interests are different from (and usually opposed to) theirs.

made sense of the separation between schools, families, and workplaces and of the discrepant gender expectations of each in class terms. Recall how the women resented their middle-class teachers for refusing to acknowledge the multiple responsibilities of working-class girlhood and thus rejected schools as a way to claim a voice (i.e., knowledge and authority) about family life and its demands. Yet regrettably, these class-based understandings of school worked against the Philadelphia women's abilities to see the implicit gender inequalities organizing school, families, and workplaces, as in the case of Tina who opted for marriage and motherhood, which she viewed as natural and desirable, over school.

Then, in contrast, consider the North Carolina women's views of school as both stemming from and answering to the organization and mission of the rural-community school. Organized as part of a seamless web of family, work, church, and community contexts, each woven with and legitimating the other, the rural segregated school context produced a different set of gender practices and problems for the women to negotiate. The rural school did not track students according to gender, nor were the gender practices in school so different from those on the farm, in families, or in church. Through their daily caretaking efforts, black teachers in rural schools promoted the value of what is traditionally defined as "women's work" to sustain family life. In this seamless web of caretaking institutions (school, families, church), black female teachers implicitly, if not explicitly, promoted the knowledge and authority of black women in their efforts to preserve black communities. In contrast to the female teachers in urban-comprehensive schools who were supervised by male principals, these black teachers in rural schools also exercised more autonomous authority, especially in isolated one-room schools. Thus through their affiliation with black female teachers, the North Carolina women were encouraged to claim rather than to deny their knowledge as women as part of their schooling.

Regrettably, however, the affiliation was made problematic by the "racial uplift" mission of the black rural-community school. At the time when the North Carolina women attended school, black middle-class female teachers who had been assigned to rural schools were committed to racial uplift that "equated normality with conformity to white, middle-class models of gender roles and sexuality" (Higginbotham 1992, 271). Exposed to the domestic science movement as a way to promote the moral uplifting of rural blacks, these teachers sought to correct black country ways, including speech, appearance, behavior, dress, and etiquette, that were viewed as impediments to social mobility not only within black communities but also within white society.[38] This model

---

[38] Fields 1983, 88–90, refers to this influence in her teacher training.

contrasted sharply with the vocational model and thus generated different relationships between female teachers and students. We can recall that the North Carolina women spoke about the school's mission to correct country ways with shame and humiliation. Moreover, they interpreted the school's mission in race and class-based terms, citing in anger all the ways in which teachers invoked the "intimidation of color" as they "passed over" groups of darker-skinned students or neglected to encourage students whose parents were not professionals. Less recognized was the way in which teachers invoked traditional, middle-class styles of femininity as part of their uplift mission. Instead, the North Carolina women remembered with fondness those teachers who had made them "feel special" by attending to their daily needs. Yet by buying bows and dresses for those girls who because of poverty could not attain a traditionally feminine image, these teachers unwittingly promoted split images of femininity.

Yet, whatever their goals, the efforts of black, middle-class teachers were undermined by the racism and segregation that signaled to rural black children living in poverty that they were worth less than white children. Whatever schoolwise knowledge black students might claim would not be recognized by the larger white society, nor would it provide them occupational mobility, regardless of gender. Organizing instruction around age and cognitive proficiency, when regular school attendance was sporadic if not impossible for girls as well as boys, also served to promote the view that individual ability more than anything else accounted for school success. Admittedly, such organization was not intended to undermine black students' beliefs in their academic abilities. Yet the North Carolina women's narratives speak to the unintended consequences of institutional practices that, when joined with racist ideologies about blacks' inferior intelligence, converged to support their perceptions of themselves as slow learners.

Thus each group of women understood and negotiated the twisted relations of gender, knowledge, and power differently according to school organization and mission. I do not offer this explanation as a complete account but, rather, as a corrective to essentialist accounts that ignore the varied and changing contexts within and against which women construct and claim knowledge. In the next section I want to broaden the scope of our understanding of these contexts and obstacles by considering the ideological dimensions of the women's view of school as a battleground, and particularly of the teacher's pet theme.

Another version of the teacher's pet theme

While both groups of women viewed teachers' pets as having knowledge and power, on closer scrutiny we can see that this is a distortion, if not an illusion. Despite their distinct versions of school and teachers' pets, both groups of women shared contradictory insights about the process of schoolwise knowing. On the one hand, the women believed that the acquisition of schoolwise knowledge was not haphazard, random, or idiosyncratic. It was not Dorothy as an individual, that is, but Dorothy as a light-skinned, middle-class, traditionally feminine black girl that made her the teacher's pet and enabled her success in school. It was not Helen as an individual, but feminine, cute, and obedient Helen as a "type" that accounted for her school achievements. Whether defined in race, class, or gender terms, both groups of women believed that teachers chose pets and passed on schoolwise knowledge according to interests that were in conflict with the students' own. The women's experience of teachers' pets served to corroborate what they already knew about social divisions. Moreover, these relationships served as a way to express their affiliation with and opposition to certain collective identities, interests, values, and knowledge. Yet at the same time, the women also shared the belief that teachers acted on personal prejudices and preferences rather than on structural imperatives of either the educational system or the society at large when they chose their pets. Put another way, the theme of teachers' pets offered the women an individual and psychologized explanation of knowledge and power for what is in fact a structural and political relationship.

The women's shared view of school was based on gender ideologies that pitted good girls against bad girls in the struggle for schoolwise knowledge. This good girl/bad girl dichotomy falsified gender relations in the classroom. Likewise, the light skin/dark skin dichotomy falsified race relations, making it appear as if it was a teacher's individual prejudice rather than institutional racism that undermined black students' success. Lighter-skinned blacks were sanctioned as smart and as successful learners at the expense of darker-skinned blacks, thereby dividing black students against each other and undermining their collective knowledge and power. At the same time, the light skin/dark skin dichotomy also falsified gender relations, making it appear that it was only the color line rather than patriarchal impositions that colluded in dividing the black rural female students against each other.

Furthermore, the women understood the relationship between teachers and their pets as a form of patronage whereby teachers chose individual students to be theirs or to "own." The pet's ability to succeed thus was dependent on her patron, the teacher. According to the terms of this relationship, the patron promised support, encouragement, and praise in exchange for the pet's productivity and achievement. Additionally, this relationship was understood as a unique, one-to-one relationship between a particular teacher and a particular student (your pet cannot also be my pet). As a result, the women learned to view the nature of knowledge and power as personalized and individual rather than collective or social. Moreover, this personalized image of the teacher's pet connoted an affective bond. Being someone's pet suggested an emotional or even erotically tinged relationship between pets and their owners (as in the common expression, "petting"). In this individual, personal, emotional, and perhaps erotically tinged relationship between teachers and pets, a process of deception and objectification took place. Girls who participated in such relationships were seen or saw themselves as presenting a false self to attract the teacher's attention. Because the pet's achievements and school knowledge was gained through such deception, it was at once false and suspect. Thus the women came simultaneously to long for and to distrust the pet's recognition, attention, and power. Last but not least, the concept of teacher's pet implied that a student was less than a teacher, the human pet being an infantilized person. Thus the pet's power was based on diminution and was ultimately self-negating.[39]

In all these cases, the pet and her power could never be autonomous from the realm of the teacher. Ironically, then, the concept of teacher's pet makes it appear that those who are not teachers' pets have no knowledge or power. The view of teachers' pets or good girls as powerful based on their ability to get approval of those in power masked the real threat to patriarchal power: those who chose not to be or are not chosen to be pets, the bad girls.

I would argue that the women's shared views about teachers' pets exposes the force of patriarchal impositions, particularly how split images of femininity undermine women's knowing. These split images, invoked by the women as symbolic antagonists in the teacher's pet theme, served to locate the source of their power in female attractiveness, desirability, and submission rather than in intellectual capabilities or in collective identities and interests.

Implications for feminist education research and reform

The varied contexts within and against which women construct, value, and claim knowledge and power have profound implications for how we think about improving women's education. The contextualized account of women's ways of knowing that I have developed here suggests that we must acknowledge the politics of being female when we consider how schools shortchange girls, moving beyond analyses based simply on female socialization or gender identity development.

---

[39] I am indebted to John Wilson for starting me thinking about the ideological nature of the pet's power.

There is still much to know about the politics of women's knowing—how different women understand and negotiate gender, race, and class relations across institutional contexts and within different schools—before we can develop pedagogical practices that address the multivaried ways that women claim and deny knowledge. I believe that comparative ethnographic research holds the most promise toward this end. The task for feminist educators, as I see it, is to become ethnographers, in the broadest and best sense of the word, actively and systematically observing what students are doing, listening to what they are saying, and probing what they are feeling despite school practices that conspire to distort, mute, or silence what they know and have to say about themselves and the world around them.[40]

When we listen and take seriously what the women in this study have to say about school, especially in their shared theme of teacher's pet, we gain critical insight into how schools shortchange girls and what is to be done. I will briefly sketch two implications about how to improve women's education that I draw from their accounts.

Revising school mission and organization

The teacher's pet theme reminds us that what is most memorable about schooling is not what is learned, but how we learn. By viewing school in terms of embattled relationships, the women held teachers and students accountable for what school organization and mission ignores or dismisses: the knowledge and ethics of care.

Educational philosopher Jane Roland Martin (1985) has argued that the explicit mission of schooling in this century has been to prepare students for what she calls "productive" processes that focus primarily on the workplace and the public/political spheres of life, spheres that until recent history have been associated with men. Missing from such models are discussions about society's "reproductive" processes, including all those activities that define and maintain communities, families, and private life, spheres that continue to be associated with women. As a result, schools promote a narrow view of citizenship, one that privileges the ethics of work and public life over the ethic of care. Whereas schools introduce students to such values as property, justice, freedom, and equality that support political and economic development, what goes unacknowledged are values such as empathy, nurturance, and sensitivity that support personal growth and development. Evaded in the curriculum are the skills, knowledge, and values that have to do with "taking care": everything from knowing about and caring for human bodies, to

---

[40] Gilligan 1990 and Fine 1991 both write about how schools actively silence what girls already know about the world. This silencing drives girls' knowledge "underground" or causes them to develop a split consciousness.

knowing about and attending to human feelings and relationships.[41] Moreover, these skills and knowledge, passed down within families and communities, are not viewed with the same reverence or value as those skills and knowledge that are passed down in schools. While we may pay lip service to the values and ethics of caretaking, we have yet to incorporate them into our educational practices and policies. Thus, schools fail to prepare students for citizenship in the broadest sense, as agents of social justice infused with an ethic of care.

The women's schooling narratives highlight the shortcomings of this narrow mission and separation of productive from reproductive skills and knowledge. While being careful not to reify these separate spheres, it is important to note that school policies and practices that enforce rigid boundaries between these two spheres of activity have particularly damaging effects on poor and working-class girls who may be major contributors to family survival. The failure of schools to broaden their mission and organization not only compromises poor and working-class girls' success in school but also, more fundamentally, threatens to disenfranchise them as citizens lacking either visibility or a voice.

Rethinking school success

The women's stories about teachers' pets speaks to the fact that attending to the ethics and politics of relationships is what makes a difference in women's (and, for that matter, men's) education. Their charged memories about being or not being a pet force us to consider what Frederick Erikson (1987) calls the "politics of legitimacy, trust and assent" as key factors that affect school success. The women's distinct version of teachers' pets illustrates the varied ways in which schools can betray girls' trust and legitimacy as they are played out in school mission, organization, curriculum, pedagogical practice, and student-teacher relationships (including but not limited to the teacher's pet phenomenon). For when school practices and policies acknowledge and validate some students over others, certain students will experience school as a no-win situation where they risk feeling unconnected and unknown, either betrayed by school or feeling as if they have betrayed themselves and others. Indeed, that was what had bothered the women about teachers' pets—that these relationships had allowed some students to "feel special" at the expense of others. Thus from their vantage point, school had violated the rules and ethics of relationships. Teachers' pets had enhanced the hold of teachers and certain students on the privilege of their social

---

[41] See the American Association of University Women's report *How Schools Shortchange Girls* (Wellesley College for Research on Women 1992) for an excellent discussion of the formal, hidden, and evaded curriculum and its effects on the education of girls.

difference (whether gender-, race-, or class-based), and thus served as a ritual celebration of social injustice.

Perhaps the women's view of school as a set of embattled relationships of power and care helps to resolve the seeming paradox about why women who did not see themselves as successful students nevertheless sought education as adults. Ironically, what had propelled the women out of school as girls is also what had propelled them back to school as adult women: their desire to be viewed as legitimate, to connect and be known, and to remake their relationship to self and others through adult basic education. As feminist educators we should take heed of women's paradoxical relationship to schooling by working to transform the material and ideological conditions under which students and teachers enter into relationships of knowledge, power, and care.

Department of Sociology
Duke University

References

Adorno, Theodor, et al. 1950. *The Authoritarian Personality.* New York: Harper & Brothers.

Alcoff, Linda. 1988. "Cultural Feminism versus Post-Structuralism: The Identity Crisis in Feminist Theory." *Signs: Journal of Women in Culture and Society* 13(3):405–36.

Belenky, Mary Field, Blythe McVicker Clinchy, Nancy Rule Goldberger, and Jill Mattuck Tarule. 1986. *Women's Ways of Knowing: The Development of Self, Voice, and Mind.* New York: Basic.

Best, Raphaela. 1983. *We've All Got Scars: What Boys and Girls Learn in Elementary School.* Bloomington: Indiana University Press.

Bordo, Susan. 1986. "The Cartesian Masculinization of Thought." *Signs* 11(3):439–56.

Bordo, Susan, and Alison Jaggar, eds. 1989. *Gender, Body, Knowledge: Feminist Reconstructions of Being and Knowing.* New Brunswick, N.J.: Rutgers University Press.

Bowles, Samuel, and Herbert Gintis. 1976. *Schooling in Capitalist America.* New York: Basic.

Brophy, Jere, and Thomas Goode. 1974. *Teacher-Student Relationships: Causes and Consequences.* New York: Holt, Rinehart, & Winston.

Chase, Susan. 1991. "Interpreting Women's Narratives: Towards an Alternative Methodology." Paper presented at the Southern Sociological Society Meetings, Atlanta, Georgia, April 6.

Chodorow, Nancy. 1978. *The Reproduction of Mothering: Psychoanalysis and the Sociology of Gender.* Berkeley and Los Angeles: University of California Press.

Cixous, Hélène. 1976. "The Laugh of the Medusa." *Signs* 1(4):875–93.

———. 1981. "Castration or Decapitation?" *Signs* 7(1):41–55.

Collins, Patricia Hill. 1990. *Black Feminist Thought: Knowledge, Consciousness, and the Politics of Empowerment.* London: HarperCollins Academic.

Connell, R. W. 1985. *Teachers' Work.* Sydney: George Allen & Unwin.

Connell, R. W., et al. 1982. *Making the Difference: Schools, Families and Social Division.* Sydney: George Allen & Unwin.

Daly, Mary. 1973. *Beyond God the Father.* Boston: Beacon.

———. 1978. *Gyn/Ecology: The Metaethics of Radical Feminism.* Boston: Beacon.

Devault, Marjorie. 1990. "Talking and Listening from Women's Standpoint: Feminist Strategies for Interviewing and Analysis." *Social Problems* 37(1):96–116.

Dweck, Carol S., William Davidson, Sharon Nelson, and Bradley Enna. 1978. "Sex Differences in Learned Helplessness: II. The Contingencies of Evaluation Feedback in the Classroom. III. An Experimental Analysis." *Developmental Psychology* 14:268–76.

Erickson, Frederick. 1987. "Transformation and School Success: The Politics and Culture of Educational Achievement." *Anthropology and Education Quarterly,* 18(4):335–56.

Fields, Mamie Garvin, with Karen Fields. 1983. *Lemon Swamp and Other Places.* New York: Free Press.

Fine, Michelle. 1991. *Framing Dropouts: Notes on the Politics of an Urban Public High School.* Albany: State University of New York Press.

Fingeret, Arlene. 1983a. "Social Network: A New Perspective on Independence and Illiterate Adults." *Adult Education Quarterly* 33(3):133–46.

———. 1983b. "Common Sense and Book Learning: Culture Clash?" *Lifelong Learning* 6(8):22–24.

Flax, Jane. 1987. "Postmodernism and Gender Relations in Feminist Theory." *Signs* 12(4):621–43.

Foucault, Michel. 1977. *Discipline and Punish: The Birth of the Prison.* New York: Pantheon.

———. 1979. *The History of Sexuality,* vol. 1: *An Introduction,* trans. Robert Hurley. London: Allen Lane.

Freire, Paulo. 1970. *Pedagogy of the Oppressed.* New York: Seabury.

———. 1973. *Education for Critical Consciousness.* New York: Continuum.

———. 1987. *Literacy: Reading the Word and the World.* South Hadley, Mass.: Bergin & Garvey.

Giddings, Paula. 1984. *When and Where I Enter: The Impact of Black Women on Race and Sex in America.* New York: Bantam.

Gilkes, Cheryl Townsend. 1985. " 'Together and in Harness': Women's Traditions in the Sanctified Church." *Signs* 10(4):678–99.

———. 1988. "Building in Many Places: Multiple Commitments and Ideologies in Black Women's Community Work." In *Women and the Politics of Empowerment,* ed. Ann Bookman and Sandra Morgen, 53–76. Philadelphia: Temple University Press.

Gilligan, Carol. 1982. *In a Different Voice: Psychological Theory and Women's Development.* Cambridge, Mass.: Harvard University Press.

————. 1988. *Mapping the Moral Domain: A Contribution of Women's Thinking to Psychological Theory and Education.* Cambridge, Mass.: Harvard University Press.

————. 1990. *Making Connections: The Relational Worlds of Adolescent Girls at Emma Willard School.* Cambridge, Mass.: Harvard University Press.

Grant, Jacquelyn. 1982. "Black Women and the Church." In *But Some of Us Are Brave,* ed. Gloria T. Hull, Patricia Bell Scott, and Barbara Smith, 141–52. Old Westbury, N.Y.: Feminist Press.

Grant, Judith. 1987. "I Feel Therefore I Am: A Critique of Female Experience as a Basis for Feminist Epistemology." *Women and Politics* 7(3):99–114.

Griffin, Susan. 1980. *Woman and Nature: The Roaring Inside Her.* New York: Harper Colophon.

Hall, Stuart. 1986. "Gramsci's Relevance to the Analysis of Racism and Ethnicity." *Communication Inquiry* 10:5–27.

Hansot, Elisabeth, and David Tyack. 1988. "Gender in American Public Schools: Thinking Institutionally." *Signs* 13(4):741–60.

Harding, Sandra. 1986. *The Science Question in Feminism.* Ithaca, N.Y.: Cornell University Press.

Harding, Sandra, and Merrill Hintikka, eds. 1983. *Discovering Reality: Feminist Perspectives on Epistemology, Metaphysics, and Philosophy of Science* Dordrecht: Reidel.

Hartsock, Nancy. 1985. *Money, Sex and Power: Towards a Feminist Historical Materialism.* Boston: Northeastern University Press.

Hawkesworth, Mary E. 1989. "Knowers, Knowing, Known: Feminist Theory and Claims of Truth." *Signs* 14(3):533–57.

Hebdige, Dick. 1979. *Subculture: The Meaning of Style.* New York: Methuen.

Heckman, Susan. 1987. "The Feminization of Epistemology: Gender and the Social Sciences." *Women and Politics* 7(3):65–83.

Higginbotham, Evelyn Brooks. 1992. "African-American Women's History and the Metalanguage of Race." *Signs* 17(2):251–74.

Holland, Dorothy, and Margaret Eisenhart. 1990. *Educated in Romance: Women, Achievement and College Culture.* Chicago: University of Chicago Press.

hooks, bell. 1990. *Yearning: Race, Gender, and Cultural Politics.* Boston: South End Press.

Irigaray, Luce. 1985. *Speculum of the Other Woman,* trans. Gillian Gill. Ithaca, N.Y.: Cornell University Press.

Jaggar, Alison. 1983. *Feminist Politics and Human Nature.* Totowa, N.J.: Rowman & Allanheld.

Johnson, Richard. 1986/87. "What Is Cultural Studies Anyway?" *Social Text: Theory, Culture, Ideology* 16:38–40.

Jones, M. Gail. 1989. "Gender Bias in Classroom Interactions." *Contemporary Education* 60(4):218–22.

Keller, Evelyn Fox. 1984. *Reflections on Gender and Science.* New Haven, Conn.: Yale University Press.

Labov, William. 1972. *Language in the Inner City: Studies in the Black English Vernacular.* Philadelphia: University of Pennsylvania Press.

Levesque-Lopman, Louise. 1988. *Claiming Reality: Phenomenology and Women's Experience.* Totowa, N.J.: Rowman & Littlefield.

Linde, Charlotte. n.d. "Life Stories: The Creation of Coherency." Institute for Research on Learning, Palo Alto, Calif.

Lloyd, Genevieve. 1984. *The Man of Reason: Male and Female in Western Philosophy.* London: Methuen.

London, Howard B. 1978. *The Culture of a Community College.* New York: Praeger.

Long, Elizabeth. 1986. "Women, Reading, and Cultural Authority: Some Implications of the Audience Perspective in Cultural Studies." *American Quarterly* 38(4):591–612.

Luttrell, Wendy. 1981. *Women in the Community: A Curriculum Guide for Students and Teachers.* Harrisburg: Pennsylvania State Department of Education.

———. 1982. *Building Multi-Cultural Awareness: A Teaching Approach for Learner-centered Education.* Harrisburg: Pennsylvania State Department of Education.

———. 1989. "Working-Class Women's Ways of Knowing: Effects of Gender, Race, and Class." *Sociology of Education* 62:33–46.

———. 1992. "Claiming Authority, Claiming Self Worth: Women's Narratives of 'Schoolwise' Knowledge and Power." Unpublished manuscript, Duke University.

McCabe, Toni. 1981. "Schools and Careers: For Girls Who Do Want to Wear the Trousers." In *Feminism for Girls: An Adventure Story,* ed. Angela McRobbie and Toni McCabe, 57–79. London: Routledge & Kegan Paul.

McMillan, Carol. 1982. *Women, Reason and Nature.* Oxford: Basic Blackwell.

McRobbie, Angela. 1978. "Working Class Girls and the Culture of Femininity." In *Women Take Issue: Aspects of Women's Subordination,* ed. Women Studies Group CCCS, 96–108. London: Hutchinson.

———. 1982. "The Politics of Feminist Research: Between Talk, Text and Action." *Feminist Review,* no. 12, 46–57.

———. 1984. *Gender and Generation.* London: Macmillan.

———. 1991. *Feminism and Youth Culture: From "Jackie" to "Just Seventeen."* Boston: Unwin Hyman.

Martin, Jane Roland. 1985. *Reclaiming a Conversation.* New Haven, Conn.: Yale University Press.

Martin, Roy. 1972. "Student Sex and Behavior as Determinants of the Type and Frequency of Teacher-Student Contact." *Journal of School Psychology* 10(4):339–44.

Mascia-Lees, Frances, Patricia Sharpe, and Colleen Ballerino Cohen. 1989. "The Postmodern Turn in Anthropology: Cautions from a Feminist Perspective." *Signs* 15(1):7–33.

Mishler, Elliot. 1986. *Research Interviewing: Context and Narrative.* Cambridge, Mass.: Harvard University Press.

O'Brien, Mary. 1981. *The Politics of Reproduction.* London: Routledge & Kegan Paul.

Ogbu, John. 1974. *The Next Generation: An Ethnography of Education in an Urban Neighborhood.* New York and London: Academic Press.

Personal Narratives Group. 1989. *Interpreting Women's Lives: Feminist Theory and Personal Narratives*. Bloomington: Indiana University Press.

Radway, Janice. 1984. *Reading the Romance: Women, Patriarchy and Popular Culture*. Chapel Hill: University of North Carolina Press.

Rockhill, Kathleen. 1987. "Literacy as Threat/Desire: Longing to Be Somebody." In *Women and Education: A Canadian Perspective*, ed. Jane Gaskell and A. T. McLaren, 315–33. Calgary: Detselig Enterprises.

Roman, Leslie. 1987. "Punk Femininity: The Formation of Young Women's Gender Identities and Class Relations in the Extramural Curriculum within a Contemporary Subculture." Ph.D. dissertation, University of Wisconsin Madison.

———. 1988. "Intimacy, Labor, and Class: Ideologies of Feminine Sexuality in the Punk Slam Dance." In *Becoming Feminine: The Politics of Popular Culture*, ed. Leslie Roman, Linda Christian-Smith, and Elizabeth Ellsworth, 143–84. London: Falmer.

Rose, Hilary. 1983. "Hand, Brain and Heart: A Feminist Epistemology for the Natural Sciences." *Signs* 9(10):73–90.

Rubin, Lillian. 1976. *Worlds of Pain: Life in the Working-Class Family*. New York: Basic.

Ruddick, Sara. 1989. *Maternal Thinking: Toward a Politics of Peace*. Boston: Beacon.

Sadker, Myra, and David Sadker. 1986. "Sexism in the Classroom: From Grade School to Graduate School." *Phi Delta Kappan* 68:512.

Sennett, Richard. 1980. *Authority*. New York: Vintage.

Sennett, Richard, and Jonathan Cobb. 1972. *The Hidden Injuries of Class*. New York: Knopf.

Serbin, Lisa, K. Daniel O'Leary, Ronald Kent, and Illene Tonick. 1973. "A Comparison of Teacher Response to the Preacademic and Problem Behavior of Boys and Girls." **Child Development** 44(4):796–804.

Smith, Dorothy. 1987. *The Everyday World as Problematic: A Feminist Sociology*. Boston: Northeastern University Press.

Stacey, Judith. 1988. "Can There Be a Feminist Ethnography?" *Women's Studies International Forum* 11(1):21–27.

Stacey, Judith, Susan Bereaud, and Joan Daniels, eds. 1974. *And Jill Came Tumbling After: Sexism in American Education*. New York: Dell.

Stanley, Liz, and Sue Wise. 1983. *Breaking Out: Feminist Consciousness and Feminist Research*. London: Routledge & Kegan Paul.

Steedman, Carolyn. 1987. *Landscape for a Good Woman*. New Brunswick, N.J.: Rutgers University Press.

Stockard, Jean. 1985. "Education and Gender Equality: A Critical View." In *Research in Sociology of Education and Socialization*, ed. Alan C. Kerckhoff, 5:293–321. Greenwich, Conn.: JAI.

Strathern, Marilyn. 1987. "An Awkward Relationship: The Case of Feminism and Anthropology." *Signs* 12(2):276–92.

Stuckey, Elspeth. 1988. "Invisible Women: The Black Female Educator in the Segregated South." Paper presented at the Southeastern Women Studies Association Annual Meeting, University of North Carolina, Chapel Hill.

Thompson, Edward P. 1963. *The Making of the English Working-Class.* New York: Vintage.

Trask, Haunani-Kay 1986. *Eros and Power: The Promise of Feminist Theory.* Philadelphia: University of Pennsylvania Press.

Tronto, Joan. 1989. "Women and Caring: What Can Feminists Learn about Morality from Caring?" In Bordo and Jaggar, eds.

Waller, Willard. 1932. *Sociology of Teaching.* New York: Wiley.

Washington, Mary Helen. 1982. "Teaching Black-Eyed Susans: An Approach to the Study of Black Women Writers." In *All the Women Are White and All the Blacks Are Men, But Some of Us Are Brave,* ed. G. Hull, P. B. Scott, and B. Smith, 208–17. Old Westbury, N.Y.: Feminist Press.

Washington, Mary Helen, ed. 1975. *Black-Eyed Susans.* New York: Anchor/ Doubleday.

Weis, Lois. 1983. "Schooling and Cultural Production: A Comparison of Black and White Lived Culture." In *Ideology and Practice in Schooling,* ed. Michael Apple and Lois Weis. Philadelphia: Temple University Press.

———. 1985. *Between Two Worlds: Black Students in an Urban Community College.* Boston: Routledge & Kegan Paul.

———. 1988. *Class, Race, and Gender in American Education.* Albany: State University of New York Press.

Wellesley College Center for Research on Women. 1992. *How Schools Shortchange Girls: A Study of Major Findings on Girls and Education.* Washington, D.C.: American Association of University Women.

Welter, Barbara. 1978. "The Cult of True Womanhood: 1820–1860." In *The American Family in Social-Historical Perspective,* ed. Michael Gordon, 313–33. New York: St. Martin's Press.

Williams, Patricia. 1988. "On the Object of Property." *Signs* 14(1):5–24.

———. 1991. *The Alchemy of Race and Rights: Diary of a Law Professor.* Cambridge, Mass.: Harvard University Press.

Williams, Raymond. 1961. *Culture and Society.* New York: Penguin.

———. 1965. *The Long Revolution.* New York: Penguin.

———. 1976. *Keywords: A Vocabulary of Culture and Society.* New York: Oxford University Press.

Willis, Paul. 1977. *Learning to Labour: How Working-Class Kids Get Working-Class Jobs.* Westmead: Saxon House, Teakfield.

About the Contributors

NANCY J. CHODOROW is professor of sociology at the University of California, Berkeley, as well as a faculty member of the San Francisco Psychoanalytic Institute and a psychoanalyst in private practice. She is the author of *The Reproduction of Mothering* (Berkeley and Los Angeles: University of California Press, 1978), *Feminism and Psychoanalytic Theory* (New Haven, Conn.: Yale University Press; Cambridge: Polity, 1979), and *Femininities, Masculinities, Sexualities: Freud and Beyond* (Lexington: University Press of Kentucky; London: Free Association Books, 1994). She is working on a book currently titled "The Power of Feelings: Personal Meaning and the Psychoanalytic Encounter."

LISA DISCH is associate professor of political science at the University of Minnesota at Minneapolis St. Paul. She is the author of *Hannah Arendt and the Limits of Philosophy* (Ithaca, N.Y.: Cornell University Press, 1994), "Publicity-Stunt Participation and Soundbite Polemics: The Health Care Debate, 1994," *Journal of Health Politics, Policy and Law* 21, no. 1 (Spring 1996): 3–33, "Claire Loves Julie: Reading the Story of Women's Friendship in *La Nouvelle Héloïse*," *Hypatia* 9 (Summer 1994): 19–45, and "More Truth Than Fact: Storytelling as Critical Understanding in the Political Writings of Hannah Arendt," *Political Theory* 21 (November 1993): 665–94.

ANN DuCILLE is professor of American and African American literature at the University of California, San Diego. She is the author of *The Coupling Convention: Sex, Text, and Tradition in Black Women's Fiction* (New York: Oxford University Press, 1993) and *Skin Trade* (Cambridge, Mass.: Harvard University Press, 1966). A Guggenheim fellow in 1994–95, she is working on two other book projects: "Inconspicuous Consumption," a study of the development of the black middle class in literature, and "The Black Feminist Reader," an edited volume of black feminist criticism.

TRISHA FRANZEN is director of the Anna Howard Shaw Center for Women's Studies and Programs at Albion College, Albion, Michigan. She received her Ph.D. in American studies from the University of New Mexico and has taught women's studies there and at the State University of New York at Buffalo. Her book *Spinsters and Lesbians: Independent Womanhood in the United States* was published in 1996 (New York

University Press). She lives in Albion, where she also serves on the Board of Education.

SUSAN STANFORD FRIEDMAN   is Virginia Woolf Professor of English and women's studies at the University of Wisconsin—Madison. She is the author of *Psyche Reborn: The Emergence of H.D.* (1981; reprint, Bloomington: Indiana University Press, 1987) and *Penelope's Web: Gender, Modernity, H.D.'s Fiction* (Cambridge: Cambridge University Press, 1990) and the coauthor of *A Woman's Guide to Therapy* (Englewood Cliffs, N.J.: Prentice Hall, 1979). She is the editor of *Joyce: The Return of the Repressed* (Ithaca, N.Y.: Cornell University Press, 1993) and the coeditor of *Signets: Reading H.D.* (Madison: University of Wisconsin Press, 1991). She has published many articles on feminist theory and pedagogy, narrative theory, women's poetry, modernism, and psychoanalysis. She currently is at work on the book-length manuscripts "H.D. and Freud: Diary and Analysis of Letters, 1932–1935" and "Mules and Modernism: Poetics, Politics, and Narrative." Her commitment to multicultural education goes back to early teaching and learning experiences in Upward Bound and at Brooklyn College.

MARILYN FRYE   is professor of philosophy at Michigan State University, where she also teaches feminist theory in the women's studies program. She is the author of *The Politics of Reality: Essays in Feminist Theory* (Trumansburg, N.Y.: Crossing, 1983) and of *Willful Virgin: Essays in Feminism, 1976–1992* (Freedom, Calif.: Crossing, 1992). She is working on a book on categories and kinds.

EVELYN NAKANO GLENN   is professor of women's studies and ethnic studies at the University of California, Berkeley. She has written extensively on work and technology issues, racial ethnic women, and the political economy of family and household. She is author of *Issei, Nisei, Warbride: Three Generations of Japanese American Women in Domestic Service* (Philadelphia: Temple University Press, 1986) and coeditor (with Grace Chang and Linda Forcey) of *Mothering: Ideology, Experience, and Agency* (New York: Routledge, 1994). Her current research centers on the race-gender construction of labor and citizenship.

GAYLE GREENE   is professor of English and women's studies at Scripps College, Claremont, California. She has coedited *The Woman's Part: Feminist Criticism of Shakespeare* (Bloomington: Indiana University Press, 1980), *Making a Difference: Feminist Literary Criticism* (London: Methuen, 1985), and *Changing Subjects: The Making of Feminist Criti-*

cism (New York: Routledge, 1993). She has written two books on contemporary women's fiction—*Changing the Story: Feminist Fiction and Tradition* (Bloomington: Indiana University Press, 1992) and *Doris Lessing: The Poetics of Change* (Ann Arbor: University of Michigan Press, 1994)—and writes regularly for *The Nation*. She currently is working on a book on cancer and the environment and on a biography of Alice Stewart, a pioneer radiation epidemiologist.

EVELYN BROOKS HIGGINBOTHAM is professor of African-American studies and of African-American religious history at Harvard University. She is the author of *Race, History, and Feminist Theory* (Chapel Hill: University of North Carolina Press, in press) and *Righteous Discontent: The Women's Movement in the Black Baptist Church, 1880–1920* (Cambridge, Mass.: Harvard University Press, 1993) and is general editor of the *Guide to Afro-American History* (Cambridge, Mass.: Harvard University Press, in press).

RUTH-ELLEN BOETCHER JOERES is professor of German at the University of Minnesota at Minneapolis St. Paul, where she works in the social and literary history of German women in the eighteenth to twentieth centuries and in comparative feminist theories. She is (with Barbara Laslett) a former editor of *Signs* and author or editor of several books, including *German Women in the Eighteenth and Nineteenth Centuries: A Social and Literary History* with Mary Jo Maynes (1986), *Interpreting Women's Lives: Feminist Theory and Personal Narratives* as part of the Personal Narratives Group (1989), and *The Politics of the Essay: Feminist Perspectives* with Elizabeth Mittman (1993), all from Indiana University Press (Bloomington).

MARY JO KANE is a sports sociologist and associate professor in the School of Kinesiology at the University of Minnesota at Minneapolis St. Paul. She also is the director of the Center for Research on Girls and Women in Sport. She has written numerous articles on sport and gender, with an emphasis on media portrayals of female athletes. Her current research focuses on the institutionalization of violence against women in men's athletics.

BARBARA LASLETT is professor of sociology at the University of Minnesota at Minneapolis St. Paul and the former editor (with Ruth-Ellen Boetcher Joeres) of *Signs*. She is the former editor of *Contemporary Sociology* and president of the Social Science History Association. Her scholarly work has focused on the historical sociology of gender relations, social change and the family, and social reproduction and on bringing a feminist perspective to the history of American sociology.

MARÍA LUGONES   teaches at the State University of New York at Binghamton and at the Escuela Popular Nortena. She is a philosopher and popular educator. Her works include *Pilgrimages/Perigrinajes: Essays in Pluralist Feminism* (Albany: State University of New York Press, in press) and *Intimate Interdependencies: Essays in Collectivism* (Boulder, Colo.: Westview, in press).

WENDY LUTTRELL   is an assistant professor in the departments of cultural anthropology and sociology at Duke University, where she also serves as assistant director of the Center for Teaching and Learning. She writes about how gender, race, class, and sexual identities are formed and transformed as part of the schooling process. She has published articles in several anthologies, including *Women and the Politics of Empowerment* (Philadelphia: Temple University Press, 1988), *Education and Gender Equality* (London: Falmer, 1992), and *Color, Class and Country: Experiences of Gender* (London and Atlantic Highlands, N.J.: Zed, 1994). She is author of the forthcoming *Schoolsmart and Motherwise: An Ethnography of Women's Learning* (New York: Routledge) and has translated her research findings into adult basic education materials. Currently, she is conducting ethnographic research into the views about parenthood, sexuality, and schooling held by pregnant teens and teen mothers.

MAUREEN A. MAHONEY   is professor of psychology and dean of the School of Social Science at Hampshire College, Amherst, Mass., where she also teaches in the feminist studies program. She has conducted research on the history of cultural concepts of childhood in the United States and in the influence of employment and social support systems on how women experience their transition to motherhood. Her current work, forthcoming in *Feminist Studies,* examines the problem of silence in feminist psychology. She is coeditor (with Urie Bronfenbrenner) of *Influences in Human Development* (Hinsdale, Ill.: Dryden, 1976).

BARBARA YNGVESSON   is professor of anthropology at Hampshire College, Amherst, Mass., where she also teaches in the feminist studies program. Her research has centered on how culturally constructed systems of difference, especially class and race, are resisted and reproduced through law. She is the author of *Virtuous Citizens, Disruptive Subjects: Order and Complaint in a New England Court* (New York: Routledge,

1993) and coauthor (with Carol Greenhouse and David Engel) of *Law and Community in Three American Towns* (Ithaca, N.Y.: Cornell University Press, 1994). Her current research examines the negotiation of motherhood and the construction of family in "open" adoptions in the United States.

IRIS MARION YOUNG teaches ethics and political philosophy at the University of Pittsburgh, where she is affiliated with the women's studies program and the philosophy department. She is the author of *Throwing Like a Girl and Other Essays in Feminist Philosophy and Social Theory* (Bloomington: Indiana University Press, 1990) and *Justice and the Politics of Difference* (Princeton, N.J.: Princeton University Press, 1990). Her recent work centers on communicative democracy and draws on feminist discussions of politics and storytelling and the problems that speaking for others entails.

Index

Abel, Elizabeth, 80, 223

"Abigail Bailey's Coverture" (Hartog), 296–71

Abu-Lughod, Lila, 246n3

Academic feminism: and Albuquerque lesbian community, 307–8; and black women's studies, 70–108; and dilemma of thinking about women as a group, 158–59; insularity of, 12; need for more complex ways of thinking about race and ethnicity, 111–16; and need for theory that combines social and personal meaning making, 216–18, 245–47; and political correctness, 318–25

Academy: affirmative action in, 319–20; curriculum integration in, 320–21; multiculturalism in, 321–24

Affirmative action: in academy, 319–20

African-American Grain, In the (Callahan), 94–95, 98

African Americans: and racial tensions in Los Angeles, 109–10

African American women. *See* black women

African American women's history, 3–26; need for examination of class and gender within 5–8; need for theory about race, 3–5. *See also* Black women's studies

African American women's studies. *See* Black women's studies

Agency: connection to resistance, 259–64; creativity as dimension of, 263; and desire, 246n2; Winnicott on, 263

AIDS: and race, 24–25

Alarcón, Norma, 234n19

Albrecht, Lisa, and Rose Brewer: *Bridges of Power,* 148

Albuquerque's lesbian community, 297–312; butch/femme roles in, 303, 306, 309; conflict between theory and practice in, 310–11; history of, 300–330; and lesbian feminism, 299, 304–8, 310; role of gay bars in formation of, 301–4, 306–7; segregation within, 297–98; solidarity with gay men, 305–6; subgroups within, 299; and women's movement, 298

Allen, Paula Gunn, 125

Alther, Lisa, *Kinflicks,* 200

Amirthanayagam, Indran, 133

Ammons, Elizabeth: *Conflicting Stories,* 82

Among Birches (Hill), 198

Andrews, William, 81

Angelou, Maya, 74

Anglo-American white middle-class developmental story, 255–58; contrasted with that of Ilongot, 258–59

251, 256–58; psychoanalytic theories of, 250; role of cultural discourses in, 247–48, 252; of self as simultaneously separate and connected, 260; and splintering of self, 264–65; tension between affectivity and inequality in, 254; transference in, 220–21; role of cultural discourses in, 247–48, 252

Psychology: of power relations, 245; movement of feminist theory away from, 216, 242. *See also* Object relations theory; Psychoanalysis; Psychological development

Purity and Danger (Douglas), 285

Purity, logic of: as ahistorical, 282; and rationality, 282–84; relation to logic of curdling, 279–81; relation to separation, 275; and the subject, 282

Race: binary categories of, 111; and class and gender, 159–60, 364–66; and conflict world-wide, 131–35; and construction of gender, 14–15; and construction of sexuality, 14–15; as cultural identity, 19–23; defined, 5–9, 111n4; and division of labor, 29; as double-voiced discourse, 18–25; and education of black girls, 357–98; and feminism, 112; and gender construction of domestic service, 37–45; and gender as interlocking systems, 6, 9–10, 27, 59–60; and gender as relational constructs, 60–61; as justification for dual labor system, 58; and lady/woman distinction, 13–14; as linked to welfare and drug use, 6; as metalanguage, 7–8; as myth, 6–7; and nationalism, 20–22; and reproductive labor, 28–29; and sexually transmitted disease, 17–18; and slavery, 8; as social construction, 5–8; and sport, 331–35; and womanhood, 9–10. *See also* Feminist narratives of race and ethnicity; Narratives about race and ethnicity; Racism

"Race," Writing and Difference (Gates), 5

Racial-ethnic women: bitterness as being limited to domestic work, 41–43; defined, 28n4; and reproductive labor, 27–69; and tracking into domestic work, 37–40

Racial uplift: paradoxical effect on girls' schooling, 387–88; as example of problems with generalizing about black women, 23–24

Racism: and justification for tracking into domestic service, 40–41; and exclusion from nursing schools, 51–52; role in conflict between racial and ethnic groups, 110; role of cultural narratives in, 114; and schooling practices, 381, 388

Radhakrishnan, R., 126, 128, 146–48

Radiant Way, The (Drabble), 197, 214

Railroads: as sites of racial contestation, 12–14

Rationality: and purity, 282

Razack, Sherene, 128

Razack, Sherene, and Mary Lou Fellows, 123n19

Scheper-Hughes, Nancy, 255n11
Schools: effects of organization and mission of on women's learning, 385–90; effects of structure on gender relations, 386–87; ethical dimensions of relationships within, 392–93; and lack of attention to reproductive processes, 391–92; as sites of political conflict and social action, 432–73; and tracking of racial-ethnic women into domestic service, 37–38. *See also* women's schooling
Scott, James C., 26n67
Scott, Joan, 338
Scott, Patricia Bell, 75
Secondo, Leah, 349
Sedgwick, Eve Kosofsky, 346
Sennett, Richard, and Jonathan Cobb, 365
Serial collectivity: as constraint, 171; and practio-inert reality, 170–71; and relation between series and groups, 168–69, 180; and serialized action, 171. *See also* seriality
Seriality: as constraint and experience of otherness, 170, 176; defined, 173; gender as, 173–76, 178–81; as level of social existence, 173; as milieu of action, 171; and race or nationality, 176–78; as structural relation to material objects, 173
Sexual division of labor: effect on school organization, 385–87; and service work, 27–69; and seriality, 175
Sexuality: debates, feminist, 298; as problematic basis for political solidarity among women, 309; and race and class differences, 309; as social construction, 15–18; violence and racialized construction of, 15–17
Shange, Ntozake, 98
Showalter, Elaine, 192
Shulman, Alix Kates, 194; *Burning Questions,* 192
Silko, Leslie Marmon, 114, 125
Singer, Linda, 168
Sisterhood Is Powerful (Morgan), 116
Sister Outsider (Lorde), 117–18
Slave experience: gendering of, 10
Smith, Barbara, 73–75, 86, 98; "Toward a Black Feminist Criticism," 117
Smith, Beverly, 75
Smith, Valerie, 75
Specular economy, 335–42; and male criticism, 99–101; Scheman on, 335; Woolf on, 335. *See also* looking
Spelman, Elizabeth, 86, 105, 120, 159–60, 164, 179, 197; *Inessential Woman,* 7
Spillers, Hortense, 75